300 Best Jobs® Without a Four-Year Degree

Third Edition

Part of JIST's Best Jobs® Series

Michael Farr and Laurence Shatkin, Ph.D.

Also in JIST's *Best Jobs* Series

- ❋ *Best Jobs for the 21st Century*
- ❋ *200 Best Jobs for College Graduates*
- ❋ *250 Best Jobs Through Apprenticeships*
- ❋ *50 Best Jobs for Your Personality*
- ❋ *40 Best Fields for Your Career*
- ❋ *225 Best Jobs for Baby Boomers*
- ❋ *250 Best-Paying Jobs*
- ❋ *10 Best College Majors for Your Personality*

- ❋ *150 Best Jobs for Your Skills*
- ❋ *175 Best Jobs Not Behind a Desk*
- ❋ *150 Best Jobs Through Military Training*
- ❋ *150 Best Jobs for a Better World*
- ❋ *200 Best Jobs for Introverts*
- ❋ *150 Best Low-Stress Jobs*
- ❋ *150 Best Recession-Proof Jobs*

JIST Works
America's Career Publisher®

300 Best Jobs Without a Four-Year Degree, Third Edition

© 2009 by JIST Publishing

Published by JIST Works, an imprint of JIST Publishing
7321 Shadeland Station, Suite 200
Indianapolis, IN 46256-3923

Phone: 800-648-JIST   Fax: 877-454-7839
E-mail: info@jist.com   Web site: www.jist.com

Some Other Books by the Authors

Michael Farr

The Quick Resume & Cover Letter Book

Same-Day Resume

Overnight Career Choice

Top 100 Careers Without a Four-Year Degree

100 Fastest-Growing Careers

Laurence Shatkin

Quick Guide to College Majors and Careers

90-Minute College Major Matcher

Your $100,000 Career Plan

New Guide for Occupational Exploration

150 Best Recession-Proof Jobs

Quantity discounts are available for JIST products. Please call 800-648-JIST or visit www.jist.com for a free catalog and more information.

Visit www.jist.com for information on JIST, free job search information, tables of contents and sample pages, and ordering information on our many products.

Acquisitions Editor: Susan Pines
Development Editor: Stephanie Koutek
Cover and Interior Designer: Aleata Halbig
Cover Image: Claudio Baba, iStock Photography

Interior Layout: Aleata Halbig
Proofreaders: Jovanna San Nicolas-Shirley, Paula Lowell
Indexer: Cheryl Lenser

Printed in the United States of America

13 12 11 10   9 8 7 6 5 4 3 2

Library of Congress Cataloging-in-Publication Data

Farr, Michael.
   300 best jobs without a four-year degree / Michael Farr and Laurence
   Shatkin. -- 3rd ed.
        p. cm. -- (JIST's best jobs series)
   Includes index.
   ISBN 978-1-59357-658-5 (alk. paper)
1. Vocational guidance. 2. Employment forecasting. 3. Job hunting. I. Shatkin, Laurence. II. Title. III. Title: Three hundred best
jobs without a four-year degree.
   HF5381.F4562 2009
   331.702'33--dc22

                           2008051123

ISBN 978-1-59357-658-5

This Is a Big Book, But It Is Very Easy to Use

This book is designed for people who want to move ahead in their careers and have or are considering getting on-the-job training, vocational training, or a two-year degree.

It helps you explore your career options in a variety of interesting ways. The nice thing about this book is that you don't have to read it all. Instead, we designed it to allow you to browse and find information that most interests you.

The Table of Contents will give you a good idea of what's inside and how to use the book, so we suggest you start there. The first part is made up of interesting lists that will help you explore jobs based on pay, interests, education or training level, personality type, and many other criteria. The second part provides descriptions for the 300 jobs that met our criteria for this book (high pay, fast growth, and large number of openings). Just find a job that interests you in one of the lists in Part I and look up its description in Part II. Simple.

How We Selected the Best Jobs Without a Four-Year Degree

Deciding on the "best" job is a choice that only you can make, but objective criteria can help you identify jobs that are, for example, better paying than other jobs with similar duties. Here is an explanation of the process we used to determine which jobs to include in this book.

We identified 484 major jobs that require less education or training than a bachelor's degree and sorted them from highest to lowest in terms of earnings, growth rate through 2016, and number of annual openings. We then assigned a number to their relative position on each list. The job position numbers on the three lists were then summed, and jobs with the best total scores were put on top, followed by jobs in order of their total scores on down the list. We included the 300 jobs with the best total scores in the book. The first list in Part I is called "The 300 Best Jobs That Don't Require a Four-Year Degree," and it contains the 300 jobs with the best combined scores on all three measures (earnings, growth rate, and openings). You can find descriptions for all 300 best jobs in Part II.

We are not suggesting that the 300 jobs with the best overall scores for earnings, growth, and number of openings are all good ones for you to consider—some will not be. But the 300 jobs that met our criteria present such a wide range of jobs that you are likely to find one or more that will interest you. The jobs that met our "best jobs" criteria are also more likely than average to have higher pay, faster projected growth, and a larger number of openings than other jobs at similar levels of education and training.

(continued)

(continued)

Some Things You Can Do with This Book

- ⊛ Identify more-interesting or better-paying jobs that don't require additional training or education.
- ⊛ Develop long-term plans that may require additional training, education, or experience.
- ⊛ Explore and select a training or educational program that relates to a career objective.
- ⊛ Find reliable earnings information to negotiate pay.
- ⊛ Prepare for interviews and the job search.

These are a few of the many ways you can use this book. We hope you find it as interesting to browse as we did to put together. We have tried to make it easy to use and as interesting as occupational information can be.

When you are done with this book, pass it along or tell someone else about it. We wish you well in your career and in your life.

Credits and Acknowledgments: While the authors created this book, it is based on the work of many others. The occupational information is based on data obtained from the U.S. Department of Labor and the U.S. Census Bureau. These sources provide the most authoritative occupational information available. The noneconomic job-related information is from the O*NET database, which was developed by researchers and developers under the direction of the U.S. Department of Labor. They, in turn, were assisted by thousands of employers who provided details on the nature of work in the many thousands of job samplings used in the database's development. We used the most recent version of the O*NET database, release 13. We appreciate and thank the staff of the U.S. Department of Labor for their efforts and expertise in providing such a rich source of data. The taxonomy of college majors (the Classification of Instructional Programs) is from the U.S. Department of Education.

Table of Contents

Table of Contents

Table of Contents

Introduction

We kept this Introduction short to encourage you to actually read it. For this reason, we don't provide many details on the technical issues involved in creating the job lists or descriptions. Instead, we give you short explanations to help you understand and use the information the book provides for career exploration or planning. We think this brief and user-oriented approach makes sense for most people who will use this book.

Why We Created This Book

Several years ago we wrote a book titled *Best Jobs for the 21st Century*. It was very well received and has since been revised several times. It covers all major jobs at all levels of education and training and includes only those with the best combined rankings for earnings, projected growth rate, and number of job openings. It is a very good book for those who want to consider jobs at all levels of education and training, but over one-third of the jobs included require a four-year college degree or higher.

So we decided that the world needs a good book for the many people who want to get ahead or change jobs, but who do not have a four-year college degree and are not planning to obtain one in the next few years.

This is that book.

Where the Information Comes From

The information we used in creating this book comes from three major government sources:

* **The U.S. Department of Labor:** We used several data sources to construct the information we put into this book. We started with the jobs included in the U.S. Department of Labor's O*NET database. The O*NET includes information on about 950 occupations and is now the primary source of detailed information on occupations. The Labor Department updates the O*NET on a regular basis, and we used the most recent one available, version 13. Because we also wanted to include earnings, growth, and number of openings—information not included in the O*NET—we used sources at the U.S. Department of Labor's Bureau of Labor Statistics (BLS). The Occupational Employment Statistics survey provided the most reliable figures on earnings we could

obtain, and the Employment Projections program provided the nation's best figures on job growth and openings. These two BLS programs use a slightly different system of job titles than the O*NET does, but we were able to link the BLS data to all of the O*NET job titles we used to develop this book.

❋ **The U.S. Census Bureau:** Data on the demographic characteristics of workers came from the Current Population Survey (CPS), conducted by the U.S. Census Bureau. This includes our information about the proportion of workers in each job who are men and women, are self-employed, or work part time. As with the BLS data, we had to match slightly different sets of job titles, but we were able to identify CPS data for almost all the O*NET jobs.

❋ **The U.S. Department of Education:** We used the Classification of Instructional Programs, a system developed by the U.S. Department of Education, to cross-reference the education or training programs related to each job.

Of course, information in a database format can be boring and even confusing, so we did many things to help make the data useful and present it to you in a form that is easy to understand.

How the 300 Best Jobs Were Selected

The "This Is a Big Book, But It Is Very Easy to Use" section at the beginning of this book gives a brief description of how we selected the jobs we include in this book. Here are a few more details:

1. We began by creating our own database of information from the O*NET, the Census Bureau, and other sources to include the information we wanted. This database covers about 950 job titles at all levels of education and training. Of these, 638 require up to but not more than a two-year associate degree—including those requiring short-term to long-term on-the-job training, work experience in a related field, or postsecondary vocational training.

2. We eliminated 86 O*NET jobs for which we lacked useful information, plus an additional 14 jobs that are expected to employ fewer than 500 workers per year and to shrink rather than grow in workforce size. We also removed 54 jobs because they have annual earnings of less than $20,920, which means that 75% of workers earn more than the workers in these jobs.

3. We ranked the remaining 484 jobs three times, based on these major criteria: median annual earnings, projected growth through 2016, and number of job openings projected per year.

4. We then added the three numerical rankings for each job to calculate its overall score.

5. To emphasize jobs that tend to pay more, are likely to grow more rapidly, and have more job openings, we selected the 300 job titles with the best total overall scores.

For example, the job with the best combined score for earnings, growth, and number of job openings is Registered Nurses, so this job is listed first even though it is not the best-paying job (which is Air Traffic Controllers), the fastest-growing job (which is Veterinary Technologists and Technicians), or the job with the most openings (which is Office Clerks, General).

Understand the Limits of the Data in This Book

In this book, we use the most reliable and up-to-date information available on earnings, projected growth, number of openings, and other topics. The earnings data came from the U.S. Department of Labor's Bureau of Labor Statistics. As you look at the figures, keep in mind that they are estimates. They give you a general idea about the number of workers employed, annual earnings, rate of job growth, and annual job openings.

Understand that a problem with such data is that it describes an average. Just as there is no precisely average person, there is no such thing as a statistically average example of a particular job. We say this because data, while helpful, can also be misleading.

Take, for example, the yearly earnings information in this book. This is highly reliable data obtained from a very large U.S. working population sample by the Bureau of Labor Statistics. It tells us the average annual pay received as of May 2007 by people in various job titles (actually, it is the median annual pay, which means that half earned more and half less).

This sounds great, except that half of all people in that occupation earned less than that amount. For example, people who are new to the occupation or with only a few years of work experience often earn much less than the median amount. People who live in rural areas or who work for smaller employers typically earn less than those who do similar work in cities (where the cost of living is higher) or for bigger employers. People in certain areas of the country earn less than those in others. Other factors also influence how much you are likely to earn in a given job in your area. For example, Aircraft Mechanics and Service Technicians in the Detroit-Livonia-Dearborn, Michigan, metropolitan division have median earnings of $56,740, probably because Northwest Airlines has a hub in Detroit and its mechanics are unionized. By comparison, the Allentown-Bethlehem-Easton, Pennsylvania, metropolitan area has no major airline hub and only a small aircraft service facility with nonunionized workers. Aircraft Mechanics and Service Technicians there earn a median of only $31,540.

Beginning wages vary greatly, too, depending not only on location and size of employer, but also on what skills and educational credentials a new hire brings to the job.

Also keep in mind that the figures for job growth and number of openings are projections by labor economists—their best guesses about what we can expect between now and 2016. Those projections are not guarantees. A catastrophic economic downturn, war, or technological breakthrough could change the actual outcome.

Finally, don't forget that the job market consists of both job openings and job *seekers*. The figures on job growth and openings don't tell you how many people will be competing with you to be hired. The Department of Labor does not publish figures on the supply of job candidates, so we are unable to tell you about the level of competition you can expect. Competition is an important issue that you should research for any tentative career goal. The *Occupational Outlook Handbook* provides informative statements for many occupations. You should speak to people who educate or train tomorrow's workers; they probably have a good idea of how many graduates and trainees find rewarding employment and how quickly. People in the workforce can provide insights into this issue as well. Use your critical thinking skills to evaluate what people tell you. For example, educators or trainers may be trying to recruit you, whereas people in the workforce may be trying to discourage you from competing. Get a variety of opinions to balance out possible biases.

So, in reviewing the information in this book, please understand the limitations of the data. You need to use common sense in career decision making as in most other things in life. We hope that, by using that approach, you find the information helpful and interesting.

Data Complexities

For those of you who like details, we present some of the complexities inherent in our sources of information and what we did to make sense of them here. You don't need to know these things to use the book, so jump to the next section of the Introduction if details bore you.

We selected the jobs on the basis of economic data, and we include information on earnings, projected growth, and number of job openings for each job throughout this book. We think this information is important to most people, but getting it for each job is not a simple task.

Education or Training Required

The 300 jobs selected for this book were chosen partly on the basis of the amount of education or training that they typically require for entry: All 300 jobs require some minimum amount of education or training, but for all the jobs, this minimum requirement is never as much as four years of college. We base the educational requirement on ratings supplied by the Bureau of Labor Statistics.

You should keep in mind that some people working in these jobs may have credentials that differ considerably from the level listed here. For example, although Air Traffic Controllers need to have completed only long-term on-the-job training, almost one-third of these workers have a bachelor's degree. More than half of Registered Nurses have a bachelor's, and although it is possible to enter this occupation with an associate degree or a diploma from an approved nursing program, career opportunities without the bachelor's are considerably more limited.

Some workers who have more than the minimum required education for their job have earned a bachelor's degree *after* being hired, but others entered the job with this educational credential, and the more advanced degree may have given them an advantage over other job seekers with less education. Some workers with *less* than the normal minimum requirement may have been hired on the basis of their work experience in a similar job. So don't assume that the one-line statement of "Education Required" in the Part II job descriptions gives a complete picture of how best to prepare for the job. If you're considering the job seriously, you need to investigate this topic in greater detail. Informative sources are listed in the last section of this introduction.

Earnings

The employment security agency of each state gathers information on earnings for various jobs and forwards it to the U.S. Bureau of Labor Statistics (BLS). This information is organized in standardized ways by a BLS program called Occupational Employment Statistics, or OES. To keep the earnings for the various jobs and regions comparable, the OES screens out certain types of earnings and includes others, so the OES earnings we use in this book represent straight-time gross pay exclusive of premium pay. More specifically, the OES earnings include each job's base rate; cost-of-living allowances; guaranteed pay; hazardous-duty pay; incentive pay, including commissions and production bonuses; on-call pay; and tips. The OES earnings do not include back pay, jury duty pay, overtime pay, severance pay, shift differentials, nonproduction bonuses, or tuition reimbursements. Also, self-employed workers are not included in the estimates, and they can be a significant segment in certain occupations. When data on annual earnings for an occupation is highly unreliable, the OES does not report a figure, which meant that we reluctantly had to exclude from this book a few occupations such as Hunters and Trappers.

For each job, we report three figures related to earnings:

* The Annual Earnings figure shows the median earnings (half earn more, half earn less).
* The Beginning Wage figure shows the 10th percentile earnings (the figure that exceeds the earnings of the lowest 10% of the workers). This is a rough approximation of what a beginning worker may be offered.
* The Earnings Growth Potential figure represents the ratio between the 10th percentile and the median. In a job for which this figure is high, you have great potential for increasing your earnings as you gain experience and skills. When the figure is low, it means you will probably need to move on to another occupation to improve your earnings substantially. For the 300 jobs in this book, the earnings growth potential ranges from a high of 60.4% for Athletes and Sports Competitors to a low of 10.5% for Postal Service Clerks. Because the percentage figures would be hard to interpret, we use verbal tags to indicate the level of Earnings Growth Potential: "very low" when the percentage is less than 25%, "low" for 25%–35%, "medium" for 35%–40%, "high" for 40%–50%, and

"very high" for any figure higher than 50%. For the highest-paying jobs, those for which BLS reports the median earnings as "more than $145,600," we are unable to calculate a figure for Earnings Growth Potential.

The median earnings for all workers in all occupations were $31,410 in May 2007. The 300 jobs in this book were chosen partly on the basis of good earnings, so their average is higher: $35,038. (This is a weighted average, which means that jobs with larger workforces are given greater weight in the computation.)

The beginning (that is, 10th percentile) wage for all occupations in May 2007 was $16,060. For the 300 jobs in this book, the weighted average is a respectable $22,318. The earnings growth potential for these jobs is rated very high for 15 jobs, high for 79 jobs, medium for 110 jobs, low for 92 jobs, and very low for 4 jobs.

The earnings data from the OES survey is reported under a system of job titles called the Standard Occupational Classification system, or SOC. Most of these jobs have an exact counterpart in the O*NET system of job titles that we use in this book, so it is easy for us to attach earnings information to most of our job titles. But a small number of the O*NET jobs simply do not have earnings data available for them from the sources we used and, therefore, were not included. In some other cases, an SOC title cross-references to more than one O*NET job title. For example, the O*NET has separate information for Automotive Master Mechanics and for Automotive Specialty Technicians, but the BLS reports earnings for a single SOC occupation called Automotive Service Technicians and Mechanics. Therefore you may notice that the salary we report for Automotive Master Mechanics ($34,170) is identical to the salary we report for Automotive Specialty Technicians. In reality, there probably is a difference, but this is the best information available.

Projected Growth and Number of Job Openings

This information comes from the Office of Occupational Statistics and Employment Projections, a program within the Bureau of Labor Statistics (BLS) that develops information about projected trends in the nation's labor market for the next ten years. The most recent projections available cover the years from 2006 to 2016. The projections are based on information about people moving into and out of occupations. The BLS uses data from various sources in projecting the growth and number of openings for each job title—some data comes from the Census Bureau's Current Population Survey and some comes from an Occupational Employment Statistics (OES) survey. The BLS economists assumed a steady economy with a major war, depression, or other upheaval. They also assumed that recessions may occur during the decade covered by these projections, as would be consistent with the business cycles we have experienced for several decades. However, because the projections cover 10 years, the figures for job growth and openings are intended to provide an average of both the good times and the bad times.

Like the earnings figures, the figures on projected growth and job openings are reported according to the Standard Occupational Classification (SOC) classification. So, again, we had to exclude a few jobs from this book because this information is not available for them. As with earnings, some of the SOC jobs crosswalk to more than one O*NET job. To continue the example we used earlier, the Department of Labor reports growth (14.3%) and openings (97,350) for one SOC occupation called Automotive Service Technicians and Mechanics, but in this book we report these figures separately for the O*NET occupation Automotive Master Mechanics and for the O*NET occupation Automotive Specialty Technicians. When you see that Automotive Master Mechanics has a 14.3% projected growth rate and 97,350 projected job openings and Automotive Specialty Technicians has the same two numbers, you should realize that the 14.3% rate of projected growth represents the *average* of these two occupations—one may actually experience higher growth than the other—and that these two occupations will *share* the 97,350 projected openings.

We had to do some special calculations to derive the figures for projected growth and annual job openings for Vocational Education Teachers, Postsecondary. The only figures available from the Department of Labor apply to a combination of 38 postsecondary teaching jobs. (The 37 other jobs require too much education to be considered for this book.) We looked at the trends of the last several years and discovered that none of these jobs grew or took on workers at a significantly faster rate than the other 37. Therefore, in preparing the Part I lists and the Part II descriptions, we assumed that Vocational Education Teachers, Postsecondary, will share the same rate of projected job growth as the other 37 jobs, 22.9%. To compute this job's share of the 237,478 projected job openings for the 38 jobs, we used the ratio of its workforce size (97,550 workers) to the workforce size of the combined job (1,380,870).

Job-growth figures may not be as easy to interpret as salary figures. For example, is projected growth of 15% good or bad? Keep in mind that the average (mean) growth projected for all occupations by the BLS is 10.4%. One-quarter of the SOC occupations have a growth projection of 3.2% or lower. Growth of 11.6% is the median, meaning that half of the occupations have more, half less. Only one-quarter of the occupations have growth projected at more than 17.4%.

Although the jobs in this book were selected as "best" partly on the basis of job growth, their mean growth—10.7%—is only slightly higher than the mean for all jobs. Among these 300 jobs, the job ranked 75th by projected growth has a figure of 16.4%, the job ranked 150th (the median) has a projected growth of 11.3%, and the job ranked 225th has a projected growth of 8.4%.

On the other hand, the number of job openings for the 300 best jobs is higher than the national average for all occupations. The BLS projects an average of about 35,000 job openings per year for the 750 occupations that it studies, but for the 300 occupations included in this book, the average is about 43,200 openings. The job ranked 75th for job openings has a figure of about 42,200 annual openings, the job ranked 150th (the median) has about 15,800 openings projected, and the job ranked 225th has about 7,900 openings projected.

However, keep in mind that figures for job openings depend on how BLS defines an occupation. For example, consider the college teaching jobs. The Office of Occupational

Statistics and Employment Projections recognizes one occupation called Teachers, Postsecondary, and projects 237,478 annual job openings for this occupation. As explained earlier in this introduction, we divided this huge occupation into 38 separate occupations, following the practice of O*NET and of the OES program. The "average" number of openings for all occupations changes substantially, depending on whether you deal with college teachers as one or 38 occupations. So it follows that because the way BLS defines occupations is somewhat arbitrary, any "average" figure for job openings is also somewhat arbitrary.

Perhaps you're wondering why we present figures for both job growth *and* number of openings. Aren't these two ways of saying the same thing? Actually, you need to know both. Consider the occupation Makeup Artists, Theatrical and Performance, which is projected to grow at the astounding rate of 39.8%. There should be lots of opportunities in such a fast-growing job, right? Not exactly. This is a tiny occupation, with only about 2,100 people currently employed. So, even though it is growing rapidly, it will not create many new jobs (about 400 per year). Now consider Team Assemblers. Because of the decline of domestic manufacturing, this occupation is hardly growing at all—it's growing at the glacial rate of 0.1%. Nevertheless, this is a huge occupation that employs over 1.25 million workers. So, even though its growth rate is unimpressive, it is expected to take on over 260,000 new workers each year as existing workers retire, die, or move on to other jobs. That's why we base our selection of the best jobs on both of these economic indicators and why you should pay attention to both when you scan our lists of best jobs.

Other Job Characteristics

Like the figures for earnings, some of the other figures used to create the lists of jobs in this book are shared by more than one job title. Usually this is the case for occupations that are so small that the Bureau of Labor Statistics (BLS) does not release separate statistics for them. For example, the occupation Cardiovascular Technologists and Technicians has a total workforce of only about 45,000 workers, so BLS does not report a specific figure for the percentage of women workers. In this case, we had to use the figure that BLS reports for a group of occupations it calls Diagnostic Related Technologists and Technicians. We relied on this same figure for four other jobs: Diagnostic Medical Sonographers, Nuclear Medicine Technologists, Radiologic Technicians, and Radiologic Technologists. You may notice similar figure-sharing among related jobs where we list the percentages of workers in specific age brackets.

Information in the Job Descriptions

We used a variety of government and other sources to compile the job descriptions we provide in Part II. Details on these various sources are mentioned later in this Introduction in the section "Part II: The Job Descriptions."

Part I: The Best Jobs Lists

There are 66 separate lists in Part I of this book—look in the Table of Contents for a complete list of the lists. The lists are not difficult to understand because they have clear titles and are organized into groupings of related lists.

Depending on your situation, some of the job lists in Part I will interest you more than others. For example, if you are young, you may be interested to learn the highest-paying jobs that employ high percentages of workers age 16–24. Other lists show jobs within interest groupings, by personality type, by level of education, and in other ways that you might find helpful in exploring your career options.

Whatever your situation, we suggest that you use the lists that make sense for you to help explore career options. Following are the names of each group of lists along with short comments on each group. You will find additional information in a brief introduction provided at the beginning of each group of lists in Part I.

Here is an overview of each major group of lists you will find in Part I.

Best Jobs Overall: Lists of Jobs with the Highest Pay, Fastest Growth, and Most Openings

Four lists are in this group, and they are the ones that most people want to see first. The first list presents all 300 job titles in order of their combined scores for earnings, growth, and number of job openings. Three more lists in this group present the 100 jobs with the highest earnings, the 100 jobs projected to grow most rapidly, and the 100 jobs with the most openings.

Best Jobs Lists by Demographic

This group of lists presents interesting information for a variety of types of people based on data from the U.S. Census Bureau. The lists are arranged into groups for workers age 16–24, workers age 55 and older, part-time workers, self-employed workers, women, and men. We created five lists for each group, basing the last four on the information in the first list:

* The jobs having the highest percentage of people of each type
* The 25 jobs with the best combined scores for earnings, growth, and number of openings
* The 25 jobs with the highest earnings
* The 25 jobs with the highest growth rates
* The 25 jobs with the largest number of openings

Best Jobs Lists Based on Levels of Education and Experience

We created separate lists for each level of education and training as defined by the U.S. Department of Labor. We put each of the 300 job titles into one of the lists based on the education and training required for entry. Jobs within these lists are presented in order of their total combined scores for earnings, growth, and number of openings. The lists include jobs in these groupings:

* Short-term on-the-job training
* Moderate-term on-the-job training
* Long-term on-the-job training
* Work experience in a related job
* Postsecondary vocational training
* Associate degree

Best Jobs Lists Based on Interests

These lists organize the 300 jobs into groups based on interests. Within each list, jobs are presented in order of their total scores for earnings, growth, and number of openings. Here are the 16 interest areas used in these lists: Agriculture and Natural Resources; Architecture and Construction; Arts and Communication; Business and Administration; Education and Training; Finance and Insurance; Government and Public Administration; Health Science; Hospitality, Tourism, and Recreation; Human Service; Information Technology; Law and Public Safety; Manufacturing; Retail and Wholesale Sales and Service; Scientific Research, Engineering, and Mathematics; Transportation, Distribution, and Logistics.

Best Jobs Lists Based on Personality Types

These lists organize the 300 jobs into six personality types, which are described in the introduction to the lists: Realistic, Investigative, Artistic, Social, Enterprising, and Conventional. The jobs within each list are presented in order of their total scores for earnings, growth, and number of openings.

Best Jobs Through Apprenticeship Training

This list presents 50 best jobs for which a federally registered apprenticeship is an available entry route. Apprenticeship programs combine worksite training with night classes. Apprentices earn while they learn, and they receive a credential known as journey worker status. The jobs are sorted by their total scores for earnings, growth, and openings.

Best Jobs Through Military Training

This list contains 50 best jobs for which military training is an available entry route. The jobs are presented in order of their total scores for earnings, growth, and number of openings.

Bonus Lists: Jobs Employing a High Percentage of People Without a Four-Year Degree

These two lists show jobs in which very few workers hold a bachelor's degree. The first list includes all the jobs from the 300 in which more than 90% of the workers have not finished four years of college. The second list shows the best 50 jobs from this set, sorted by their total scores for earnings, growth, and number of openings.

Bonus Lists: Jobs with the Greatest Changes in Outlook Since the Previous Edition

These two lists show the jobs that have had the greatest revisions to their job-growth projections since the previous edition of this book. One lists the 25 jobs with the greatest increase in job-growth projection, and the other lists the 25 jobs with the greatest decrease.

Part II: The Job Descriptions

This part of the book provides a brief but information-packed description for each of the 300 jobs that met our criteria for this book. The descriptions in Part II are presented in alphabetical order by job title. This makes it easy to look up any job you find in Part I that you want to learn more about.

Job Title →

Avionics Technicians

Data Elements →

- ❋ Education/Training Required: Postsecondary vocational training
- ❋ Annual Earnings: $48,100
- ❋ Beginning Wage: $33,050
- ❋ Earnings Growth Potential: Low
- ❋ Growth: 8.1%
- ❋ Annual Job Openings: 1,193
- ❋ Self-Employed: 0.0%
- ❋ Part-Time: 0.0%

Summary Description and Tasks →

Install, inspect, test, adjust, or repair avionics equipment, such as radar, radio, navigation, and missile control systems in aircraft or space vehicles. Set up and operate ground support and test equipment to perform functional flight tests of electrical and electronic systems. Test and troubleshoot instruments, components, and assemblies, using circuit testers, oscilloscopes, and voltmeters. Keep records of maintenance and repair work. Coordinate work with that of engineers, technicians, and other aircraft maintenance personnel. Interpret flight test data to diagnose malfunctions and systemic performance problems. Install electrical and electronic components, assemblies, and systems in aircraft, using hand tools, power tools, and soldering irons. Adjust, repair, or replace malfunctioning components or assemblies, using hand tools and soldering irons. Connect components to assemblies such as radio systems, instruments, magnetos, inverters, and in-flight refueling systems, using hand tools and soldering irons. Assemble components such as switches, electrical controls, and junction boxes, using hand tools and soldering irons. Fabricate parts and test aids as required. Lay out installation of aircraft assemblies and systems, following documentation such as blueprints, manuals, and wiring diagrams. Assemble prototypes or models of circuits, instruments, and systems so that they can be used for testing. Operate computer-aided drafting and design applications to design avionics system modifications.

Personality Type →

Personality Type: Realistic. These occupations frequently involve work activities that include practical, hands-on problems and solutions. They often deal with plants; animals; and real-world materials such as wood, tools, and machinery. Many of the occupations require working outside and don't involve a lot of paperwork or working closely with others.

GOE Information →

GOE—Interest Area/Cluster: 13. Manufacturing. **Work Group:** 13.12. Electrical and Electronic Repair. **Other Jobs in This Work Group:** Electric Motor, Power Tool, and Related Repairers; Electrical and Electronics Installers and Repairers, Transportation Equipment; Electrical and Electronics Repairers, Commercial and Industrial Equipment; Electronic Equipment Installers and Repairers, Motor Vehicles; Electronic Home Entertainment Equipment Installers and Repairers; Radio Mechanics.

Skills →

Skills—Installation: Installing equipment, machines, wiring, or programs to meet specifications. **Repairing:** Repairing machines or systems, using the needed tools. **Equipment Maintenance:** Performing routine maintenance and determining when and what kind of maintenance is needed. **Troubleshooting:** Determining what is causing an operating error and deciding what to do about it. **Operation and Control:** Controlling operations of equipment or systems. **Operation Monitoring:** Watching gauges, dials, or other indicators to make sure a machine is working properly. **Quality Control Analysis:** Evaluating the quality or performance of products, services, or processes. **Science:** Using scientific methods to solve problems.

Education/Training Program(s) →

Education and Training Programs: Airframe Mechanics and Aircraft Maintenance Technology/Technician Training; Avionics Maintenance Technology/Technician Training.

Related Knowledge/Courses →

Related Knowledge/Courses—Engineering and Technology: Equipment, tools, and mechanical devices and their uses to produce motion, light, power, technology, and other applications. **Mechanical Devices:** Machines and tools, including their designs, uses, benefits, repair, and maintenance. **Computers and Electronics:** Electric circuit boards, processors, chips, and computer hardware and software, including applications and programming. **Telecommunications:** Transmission, broadcasting, switching, control, and operation of telecommunications systems. **Production and Processing:** Inputs, outputs, raw materials, waste, quality control, costs, and techniques for maximizing the manufacture and distribution of goods. **Design:** Design techniques, principles, tools, and instruments involved in the production and use of precision technical plans, blueprints, drawings, and models.

Work Environment →

Work Environment: Indoors; noisy; contaminants; hazardous conditions; sitting; using hands on objects, tools, or controls.

We used the most current information from a variety of government sources to create the descriptions. We designed the descriptions to be easy to understand, and the sample that follows—with an explanation of each of its component parts—will help you better understand and use the descriptions.

⁕ **Job Title:** This is the job title for the job as defined by the U.S. Department of Labor and used in its O*NET database.

⁕ **Data Elements:** The information on education, earnings, growth, annual openings, percentage of self-employed workers, and percentage of part-time workers comes from various government databases, as we explained earlier in this Introduction.

⁕ **Summary Description and Tasks:** The first part of each job description provides a summary of the occupation in bold type. It is followed by a listing of tasks that are generally performed by people who work in the job. This information comes from the O*NET database; where necessary, we edited the tasks to keep them from exceeding 2,200 characters.

⁕ **Personality Type:** The O*NET database assigns each job to its most closely related personality type. Our job descriptions include the name of the related personality type. You can find more information on the personality types as well as a brief definition of each type in the introduction to the lists of jobs based on personality types in Part I.

⁕ **GOE Information:** This information cross-references the Guide for Occupational Exploration (or the GOE), a system developed by the U.S. Department of Labor that organizes jobs based on interests. We use the groups from the *New Guide for Occupational Exploration*, Fourth Edition, as published by JIST. That book uses a set of interest areas based on the 16 career clusters developed by the U.S. Department of Education and used in a variety of career information systems. Here we include the major interest area the job fits into, its more-specific work group, and a list of O*NET job titles that are in this same GOE work group. Note that **all titles listed here require less than a four-year degree.** This information will help you identify other job titles that have similar interests or require similar skills. You can find more information on the GOE and its interest areas in the introduction to the lists of jobs based on interests in Part I.

⁕ **Skills:** The O*NET database provides data on 35 skills, so we decided to list only those that were most important for each job rather than list pages of unhelpful details. For each job, we identified any skill with a rating for level of mastery that was higher than the average rating for this skill for all jobs and a rating for importance that was higher than very low. We order the skills by the amount by which their ratings exceed the average rating for all occupations, from highest to lowest. If there are more than eight such skills, we include only those eight with the highest ratings. If no skill has a rating higher than the average for all jobs, we say "None met the criteria." Each skill name is followed by a brief definition.

⁂ **Education/Training Program(s):** This part of the job description provides the name of the educational or training program or programs for the job. It will help you identify sources of formal or informal training for a job that interests you. To get this information, we used a crosswalk created by the National Crosswalk Service Center to connect information in the Classification of Instructional Programs (CIP) to the O*NET job titles we use in this book. We made various changes to connect the O*NET job titles to the education or training programs related to them and also modified the names of some education and training programs so they would be more easily understood. In 22 cases, we abbreviated the listing of related programs for the sake of space; such entries end with "others."

⁂ **Related Knowledge/Courses:** This entry can help you understand the most important knowledge areas that are required for a job and the types of courses or programs you will likely need to take to prepare for it. For each job, we identified the highest-rated knowledge area in the O*NET database, so every job has at least one listed. We identified any additional knowledge area with a rating that was higher than the average rating for that knowledge area for all jobs. We listed as many as six knowledge areas, with definitions, in descending order.

⁂ **Work Environment:** We included any work condition with a rating that exceeded the midpoint of the rating scale. The order does not indicate any condition's frequency on the job. Consider whether you like these conditions and whether any of these conditions would make you uncomfortable. Keep in mind that when hazards are present (for example, contaminants), protective equipment and procedures are provided to keep you safe.

Getting all the information we used in the job descriptions was not a simple process, and it is not always perfect. Even so, we used the best and most recent sources of data we could find, and we think that our efforts will be helpful to many people.

Sources of Additional Information

Hundreds of sources of career information exist, so here are a few we consider most helpful in getting additional information on the jobs listed in this book.

Print References

⁂ *O*NET Dictionary of Occupational Titles:* Revised on a regular basis, this book provides good descriptions for all jobs listed in the U.S. Department of Labor's O*NET database. There are almost 950 job descriptions at all levels of education and training, plus lists of related job titles in other major career information sources, educational programs, and other information. Published by JIST.

❋ *New Guide for Occupational Exploration,* **Fourth Edition:** The new edition of the GOE is cross-referenced in the descriptions in Part II. The *New GOE* provides helpful information to consider about each of the interest areas and work groups, descriptions of all O*NET jobs within each GOE group, and many other features useful for exploring career options. This most recent edition is published by JIST.

❋ *Enhanced Occupational Outlook Handbook:* Updated regularly, this book provides thorough descriptions for 270 major jobs in the current *Occupational Outlook Handbook,* brief descriptions for the O*NET jobs that are related to each, brief descriptions of thousands of more-specialized jobs from the *Dictionary of Occupational Titles,* and other information. Published by JIST.

Internet Resources

❋ **The U.S. Department of Labor Bureau of Labor Statistics Web site:** The Department of Labor Bureau of Labor Statistics Web site (www.bls.gov) provides a lot of career information, including links to other Web pages that provide information on the jobs covered in this book. This Web site is a bit formal and, well, confusing, but it will take you to the major sources of government career information if you explore its options.

❋ **O*NET site:** Go to http://online.onetcenter.org for a variety of information on the O*NET database, including links to sites that provide detailed information on the O*NET job titles presented in Part II of this book.

❋ **CareerOneStop:** This site (www.careeronestop.org) is operated by the Minnesota Department of Labor on behalf of the U.S. Department of Labor and provides access to state and local information about occupations. It also can identify a one-stop career center near you that can help you find local job openings and providers of education and training.

Thanks

Thanks for reading this Introduction. You are surely a more thorough person than those who jumped into the book without reading it, and you will probably get more out of the book as a result. We wish you a satisfying career and, more important, a good life.

PART I

The Best Jobs Lists: Jobs That Don't Require a Four-Year Degree

This part contains a lot of interesting lists, and it's a good place for you to start using the book. Here are some suggestions for using the lists to explore career options:

❋ The Table of Contents at the beginning of this book presents a complete listing of the list titles in this section. You can browse the lists or use the table of contents to find those that interest you most.

❋ We gave the lists clear titles, so most require little explanation. We provide comments for each group of lists.

❋ As you review the lists of jobs, one or more of the jobs may appeal to you enough that you want to seek additional information. As this happens, mark that job (or, if someone else will be using this book, write it on a separate sheet of paper) so that you can look up the description of the job in Part II.

❋ Keep in mind that all jobs in these lists meet our basic criteria for being included in this book, as explained in the Introduction. All lists, therefore, contain jobs that require less than a four-year degree and that have high pay, high growth, or large numbers of openings. The economic measures are easily quantified and are often presented in lists of best jobs in the newspapers and other media. Although required education or training, earnings, growth, and openings are important, you also should consider other factors in your career planning, such as location, liking the people you work with, and having opportunities to be creative. Many other factors that may help define the ideal job for you are difficult or impossible to quantify and thus aren't used in this book, so you will need to weigh the importance of these issues yourself. Consider using some of the career exploration resources listed in the last part of the Introduction.

⧉ All data used to create these lists comes from the U.S. Department of Labor and the Census Bureau. The earnings figures are based on the average annual pay received by full-time workers. Because the earnings represent the national averages, actual pay rates can vary greatly by location, amount of previous work experience, and other factors.

Some Details on the Lists

The sources of the information we used in constructing these lists are presented in this book's Introduction. Here are some additional details on how we created the lists:

⧉ Some jobs have the same scores for one or more data elements. For example, in the category of fastest-growing, two jobs (Court Reporters and Surgical Technologists) are expected to grow at the same rate, 24.5 percent. Therefore, we ordered these two jobs alphabetically, and their order has no other significance. Avoiding these ties was impossible, so understand that the difference of several positions on a list may not mean as much as it seems.

⧉ Likewise, it is unwise to place too much emphasis on small differences in outlook information: projections for job growth and job openings. For example, Refuse and Recyclable Material Collectors are projected to have 37,785 job openings per year, whereas 37,731 openings are projected for Helpers—Carpenters. This is a difference of only 54 jobs spread over the entire United States, and of course it is only a projection. Before 2007, the Bureau of Labor Statistics rounded these projections to the nearest 1,000 and would have assigned these two occupations the same figure (38,000), which would have given Helpers—Carpenters the higher rank on the basis of alphabetical ordering. So, again, keep in mind that small differences of position on a list aren't very significant.

Best Jobs Overall: Lists of Jobs with the Highest Pay, Fastest Growth, and Most Openings

The four lists that follow are this book's premier lists. They are the lists that are most often mentioned in the media and the ones that most readers want to see.

To create these lists, we ranked 484 major jobs according to a combination of their earnings, growth, and openings. We then selected the 300 jobs with the best total scores for use in this book. (The process for ranking the jobs is explained in more detail in the Introduction.)

The first list presents all 300 best jobs according to these combined rankings for pay, growth, and number of openings. Three additional lists present the 100 jobs with the top scores in each of three measures: annual earnings, projected percentage growth through 2016, and number of annual openings. Descriptions for all the jobs in these lists are included in Part II.

The 300 Best Jobs That Don't Require a Four-Year Degree

This list arranges all 300 jobs that were selected for this book in order of their overall scores for pay, growth, and number of openings, as explained in the Introduction. The job with the best overall score was Registered Nurses. Other jobs follow in order of their total scores for pay, growth, and openings. These 300 jobs are the ones we use throughout this book: in the other lists in Part I and in the descriptions found in Part II.

A wide variety of jobs are on the list. Among the top 20 are jobs in health care, sales, education, and law enforcement. The top 100 also include several management and supervisory jobs, proving that these kinds of jobs do exist for people without a college degree.

As you look over the list, remember that jobs near the top of the list are not necessarily "good" jobs—nor are jobs towards the end of the list necessarily "bad" ones for you to consider. Their position in the list is simply a result of their total scores based on pay, growth, and number of openings. This means, for example, that some jobs with low pay and modest growth but a high number of openings appear higher on the list, while some jobs with higher pay and modest growth but a low number of openings appear towards the end of the list. A "right" job for you could be anywhere on this list.

The 300 Best Jobs That Don't Require a Four-Year Degree

Job	Annual Earnings	Percent Growth	Annual Openings
1. Registered Nurses	$60,010	23.5%	233,499
2. Sales Representatives, Wholesale and Manufacturing, Technical and Scientific Products	$68,270	12.4%	43,469
3. Dental Hygienists	$64,740	30.1%	10,433
4. Criminal Investigators and Special Agents	$59,930	17.3%	14,746
5. Immigration and Customs Inspectors	$59,930	17.3%	14,746
6. Police Detectives	$59,930	17.3%	14,746
7. Police Identification and Records Officers	$59,930	17.3%	14,746
8. Vocational Education Teachers, Postsecondary	$45,850	22.9%	19,313
9. Paralegals and Legal Assistants	$44,990	22.2%	22,756
10. Executive Secretaries and Administrative Assistants	$38,640	14.8%	235,314
11. Advertising Sales Agents	$42,820	20.3%	29,233
12. Computer Support Specialists	$42,400	12.9%	97,334
13. First-Line Supervisors/Managers of Construction Trades and Extraction Workers	$55,950	9.1%	82,923
14. Self-Enrichment Education Teachers	$34,580	23.1%	64,449
15. Sales Representatives, Wholesale and Manufacturing, Except Technical and Scientific Products	$50,750	8.4%	156,215

(continued)

(continued)

The 300 Best Jobs That Don't Require a Four-Year Degree

Job	Annual Earnings	Percent Growth	Annual Openings
16. Construction and Building Inspectors	$48,330	18.2%	12,606
17. Real Estate Brokers	$58,860	11.1%	18,689
18. Police Patrol Officers	$49,630	10.8%	37,842
19. Sheriffs and Deputy Sheriffs	$49,630	10.8%	37,842
20. Correctional Officers and Jailers	$36,970	16.9%	56,579
21. Radiologic Technicians	$50,260	15.1%	12,836
22. Radiologic Technologists	$50,260	15.1%	12,836
23. Licensed Practical and Licensed Vocational Nurses	$37,940	14.0%	70,610
24. Pipe Fitters and Steamfitters	$44,090	10.6%	68,643
25. Plumbers	$44,090	10.6%	68,643
26. Automotive Master Mechanics	$34,170	14.3%	97,350
27. Automotive Specialty Technicians	$34,170	14.3%	97,350
28. First-Line Supervisors/Managers of Landscaping, Lawn Service, and Groundskeeping Workers	$38,720	17.6%	18,956
29. Customer Service Representatives	$29,040	24.8%	600,937
30. Surgical Technologists	$37,540	24.5%	15,365
31. Real Estate Sales Agents	$40,600	10.6%	61,232
32. Claims Examiners, Property and Casualty Insurance	$53,560	8.9%	22,024
33. Insurance Adjusters, Examiners, and Investigators	$53,560	8.9%	22,024
34. First-Line Supervisors/Managers of Non-Retail Sales Workers	$67,020	3.7%	48,883
35. Respiratory Therapists	$50,070	22.6%	5,563
36. Bill and Account Collectors	$29,990	22.9%	118,709
37. Construction Carpenters	$37,660	10.3%	223,225
38. Rough Carpenters	$37,660	10.3%	223,225
39. Interior Designers	$43,970	19.5%	8,434
40. Talent Directors	$61,090	11.1%	8,992
41. Technical Directors/Managers	$61,090	11.1%	8,992
42. Flight Attendants	$61,120	10.6%	10,773
43. Legal Secretaries	$38,810	11.7%	38,682
44. Environmental Science and Protection Technicians, Including Health	$39,370	28.0%	8,404
45. Forest Fire Fighters	$43,170	12.1%	18,887
46. Municipal Fire Fighters	$43,170	12.1%	18,887
47. Physical Therapist Assistants	$44,130	32.4%	5,957
48. Truck Drivers, Heavy and Tractor-Trailer	$36,220	10.4%	279,032
49. Electricians	$44,780	7.4%	79,083

The 300 Best Jobs That Don't Require a Four-Year Degree

Job	Annual Earnings	Percent Growth	Annual Openings
50. First-Line Supervisors/Managers of Mechanics, Installers, and Repairers	$55,380	7.3%	24,361
51. First-Line Supervisors/Managers of Transportation and Material-Moving Machine and Vehicle Operators	$49,850	10.2%	16,580
52. Dental Assistants	$31,550	29.2%	29,482
53. First-Line Supervisors/Managers of Office and Administrative Support Workers	$44,650	5.8%	138,420
54. First-Line Supervisors/Managers of Personal Service Workers	$33,900	15.5%	37,555
55. Bookkeeping, Accounting, and Auditing Clerks	$31,560	12.5%	286,854
56. First-Line Supervisors/Managers of Police and Detectives	$72,620	9.2%	9,373
57. Medical Assistants	$27,430	35.4%	92,977
58. Bus and Truck Mechanics and Diesel Engine Specialists	$38,640	11.5%	25,428
59. Brokerage Clerks	$37,360	20.0%	10,826
60. Diagnostic Medical Sonographers	$59,860	19.1%	3,211
61. Roofers	$33,240	14.3%	38,398
62. First-Line Supervisors/Managers of Helpers, Laborers, and Material Movers, Hand	$40,640	12.5%	13,877
63. Social and Human Service Assistants	$26,630	33.6%	80,142
64. Automotive Body and Related Repairers	$35,690	11.6%	37,469
65. Food Service Managers	$44,570	5.0%	59,302
66. Painters, Construction and Maintenance	$32,080	11.8%	101,140
67. Aircraft Mechanics and Service Technicians	$49,010	10.6%	9,708
68. Fitness Trainers and Aerobics Instructors	$27,680	26.8%	51,235
69. Gaming Supervisors	$42,980	23.4%	4,602
70. Radiation Therapists	$70,010	24.8%	1,461
71. Tile and Marble Setters	$38,720	15.4%	9,066
72. Cardiovascular Technologists and Technicians	$44,940	25.5%	3,550
73. Pharmacy Technicians	$26,720	32.0%	54,453
74. Mates—Ship, Boat, and Barge	$57,210	17.9%	2,665
75. Pilots, Ship	$57,210	17.9%	2,665
76. Ship and Boat Captains	$57,210	17.9%	2,665
77. Brickmasons and Blockmasons	$44,070	9.7%	17,569
78. Industrial Machinery Mechanics	$42,350	9.0%	23,361
79. Mobile Heavy Equipment Mechanics, Except Engines	$41,450	12.3%	11,037
80. First-Line Supervisors/Managers of Correctional Officers	$55,720	12.5%	4,180
81. Interpreters and Translators	$37,490	23.6%	6,630

(continued)

(continued)

The 300 Best Jobs That Don't Require a Four-Year Degree

Job	Annual Earnings	Percent Growth	Annual Openings
82. Cargo and Freight Agents	$37,060	16.5%	9,967
83. Operating Engineers and Other Construction Equipment Operators	$38,130	8.4%	55,468
84. Aircraft Structure, Surfaces, Rigging, and Systems Assemblers	$45,420	12.8%	6,550
85. First-Line Supervisors/Managers of Housekeeping and Janitorial Workers	$32,850	12.7%	30,613
86. Massage Therapists	$34,870	20.3%	9,193
87. Medical Secretaries	$28,950	16.7%	60,659
88. Bus Drivers, Transit and Intercity	$33,160	12.5%	27,100
89. Maintenance and Repair Workers, General	$32,570	10.1%	165,502
90. Private Detectives and Investigators	$37,640	18.2%	7,329
91. Storage and Distribution Managers	$76,310	8.3%	6,994
92. Transportation Managers	$76,310	8.3%	6,994
93. Forest Fire Fighting and Prevention Supervisors	$65,040	11.5%	3,771
94. Municipal Fire Fighting and Prevention Supervisors	$65,040	11.5%	3,771
95. Cement Masons and Concrete Finishers	$33,840	11.4%	34,625
96. Medical Records and Health Information Technicians	$29,290	17.8%	39,048
97. Occupational Therapist Assistants	$45,050	25.4%	2,634
98. Court Reporters	$45,330	24.5%	2,620
99. Heating and Air Conditioning Mechanics and Installers	$38,360	8.7%	29,719
100. Refrigeration Mechanics and Installers	$38,360	8.7%	29,719
101. Water and Liquid Waste Treatment Plant and System Operators	$37,090	13.8%	9,575
102. Funeral Directors	$50,370	12.5%	3,939
103. Sheet Metal Workers	$39,210	6.7%	31,677
104. Police, Fire, and Ambulance Dispatchers	$32,660	13.6%	17,628
105. Coroners	$48,400	4.9%	15,841
106. Environmental Compliance Inspectors	$48,400	4.9%	15,841
107. Equal Opportunity Representatives and Officers	$48,400	4.9%	15,841
108. Government Property Inspectors and Investigators	$48,400	4.9%	15,841
109. Licensing Examiners and Inspectors	$48,400	4.9%	15,841
110. Human Resources Assistants, Except Payroll and Timekeeping	$34,970	11.3%	18,647
111. Medical and Clinical Laboratory Technicians	$34,270	15.0%	10,866
112. Gaming Managers	$64,410	24.4%	549
113. Nursing Aides, Orderlies, and Attendants	$23,160	18.2%	321,036

The 300 Best Jobs That Don't Require a Four-Year Degree

Job	Annual Earnings	Percent Growth	Annual Openings
114. Preschool Teachers, Except Special Education	$23,130	26.3%	78,172
115. Mapping Technicians	$33,640	19.4%	8,299
116. Surveying Technicians	$33,640	19.4%	8,299
117. Production, Planning, and Expediting Clerks	$39,690	4.2%	52,735
118. Purchasing Agents, Except Wholesale, Retail, and Farm Products	$52,460	0.1%	22,349
119. Receptionists and Information Clerks	$23,710	17.2%	334,124
120. Aviation Inspectors	$51,440	16.4%	2,122
121. Freight and Cargo Inspectors	$51,440	16.4%	2,122
122. Transportation Vehicle, Equipment and Systems Inspectors, Except Aviation	$51,440	16.4%	2,122
123. Audio and Video Equipment Technicians	$36,050	24.2%	4,681
124. Lodging Managers	$44,240	12.2%	5,529
125. Athletes and Sports Competitors	$38,440	19.2%	4,293
126. Coaches and Scouts	$27,840	14.6%	51,100
127. Emergency Medical Technicians and Paramedics	$28,400	19.2%	19,513
128. Electrical Engineering Technicians	$52,140	3.6%	12,583
129. Electronics Engineering Technicians	$52,140	3.6%	12,583
130. Landscaping and Groundskeeping Workers	$22,240	18.1%	307,138
131. Security and Fire Alarm Systems Installers	$35,390	20.2%	5,729
132. Architectural Drafters	$43,310	6.1%	16,238
133. Civil Drafters	$43,310	6.1%	16,238
134. Telecommunications Equipment Installers and Repairers, Except Line Installers	$54,070	2.5%	13,541
135. Veterinary Technologists and Technicians	$27,970	41.0%	14,674
136. First-Line Supervisors/Managers of Food Preparation and Serving Workers	$28,040	11.3%	154,175
137. Drywall and Ceiling Tile Installers	$36,520	7.3%	30,945
138. First-Line Supervisors/Managers of Production and Operating Workers	$48,670	–4.8%	46,144
139. First-Line Supervisors/Managers of Retail Sales Workers	$34,470	4.2%	221,241
140. Telecommunications Line Installers and Repairers	$47,220	4.6%	14,719
141. Nuclear Medicine Technologists	$64,670	14.8%	1,290
142. Office Clerks, General	$24,460	12.6%	765,803
143. Medical Transcriptionists	$31,250	13.5%	18,080
144. Boilermakers	$50,700	14.0%	2,333
145. Industrial Engineering Technicians	$47,490	9.9%	6,172

(continued)

(continued)

The 300 Best Jobs That Don't Require a Four-Year Degree

Job	Annual Earnings	Percent Growth	Annual Openings
146. Security Guards	$22,570	16.9%	222,085
147. Environmental Engineering Technicians	$40,690	24.8%	2,162
148. Civil Engineering Technicians	$42,580	10.2%	7,499
149. Construction Laborers	$27,310	10.9%	257,407
150. Electrical Power-Line Installers and Repairers	$52,570	7.2%	6,401
151. Commercial Pilots	$61,640	13.2%	1,425
152. Sailors and Marine Oilers	$32,570	15.7%	8,600
153. Wholesale and Retail Buyers, Except Farm Products	$46,960	–0.1%	19,847
154. Industrial Production Managers	$80,560	–5.9%	14,889
155. Medical Equipment Repairers	$40,320	21.7%	2,351
156. Mechanical Drafters	$44,740	5.2%	10,902
157. Elevator Installers and Repairers	$68,000	8.8%	2,850
158. Railroad Conductors and Yardmasters	$58,650	9.1%	3,235
159. Ship Engineers	$56,090	14.1%	1,102
160. Highway Maintenance Workers	$32,600	8.9%	24,774
161. Motorboat Mechanics	$34,210	19.0%	4,326
162. Tellers	$22,920	13.5%	146,077
163. Electrical and Electronics Repairers, Commercial and Industrial Equipment	$47,110	6.8%	6,607
164. Postal Service Mail Carriers	$44,500	1.0%	16,710
165. Tapers	$42,050	7.1%	9,026
166. Solderers and Brazers	$32,270	5.1%	61,125
167. Welders, Cutters, and Welder Fitters	$32,270	5.1%	61,125
168. Demonstrators and Product Promoters	$22,570	18.0%	32,779
169. Glaziers	$35,230	11.9%	6,416
170. Computer, Automated Teller, and Office Machine Repairers	$37,100	3.0%	22,330
171. Insurance Appraisers, Auto Damage	$51,500	12.5%	1,030
172. Reinforcing Iron and Rebar Workers	$37,890	11.5%	4,502
173. Camera Operators, Television, Video, and Motion Picture	$41,850	11.5%	3,496
174. Locksmiths and Safe Repairers	$33,230	22.1%	3,545
175. Air Traffic Controllers	$112,930	10.2%	1,213
176. Chefs and Head Cooks	$37,160	7.6%	9,401
177. Court Clerks	$32,330	8.8%	16,163
178. License Clerks	$32,330	8.8%	16,163
179. Municipal Clerks	$32,330	8.8%	16,163
180. Emergency Management Specialists	$48,380	12.3%	1,538

The 300 Best Jobs That Don't Require a Four-Year Degree

Job	Annual Earnings	Percent Growth	Annual Openings
181. Cooks, Restaurant	$21,220	11.5%	238,542
182. Skin Care Specialists	$27,190	34.3%	6,643
183. Hairdressers, Hairstylists, and Cosmetologists	$22,210	12.4%	73,030
184. Interviewers, Except Eligibility and Loan	$27,320	9.5%	54,060
185. Structural Iron and Steel Workers	$42,130	6.0%	6,969
186. Tire Repairers and Changers	$21,880	20.2%	18,829
187. Billing, Cost, and Rate Clerks	$29,970	4.4%	81,885
188. Billing, Posting, and Calculating Machine Operators	$29,970	4.4%	81,885
189. Statement Clerks	$29,970	4.4%	81,885
190. Truck Drivers, Light or Delivery Services	$26,380	8.4%	154,330
191. Eligibility Interviewers, Government Programs	$39,110	3.1%	11,337
192. Fine Artists, Including Painters, Sculptors, and Illustrators	$42,070	9.9%	3,830
193. Electrical Drafters	$49,250	4.1%	4,786
194. Electronic Drafters	$49,250	4.1%	4,786
195. Helpers—Pipelayers, Plumbers, Pipefitters, and Steamfitters	$25,350	11.9%	29,332
196. Millwrights	$46,090	5.8%	4,758
197. Helpers—Carpenters	$24,340	11.7%	37,731
198. Helpers—Installation, Maintenance, and Repair Workers	$22,920	11.8%	52,058
199. City and Regional Planning Aides	$35,870	12.4%	3,571
200. Social Science Research Assistants	$35,870	12.4%	3,571
201. Nuclear Power Reactor Operators	$70,410	10.6%	233
202. Refuse and Recyclable Material Collectors	$29,420	7.4%	37,785
203. Subway and Streetcar Operators	$50,520	12.1%	587
204. Bus Drivers, School	$25,860	9.3%	59,809
205. Tour Guides and Escorts	$22,110	21.2%	15,027
206. Mechanical Engineering Technicians	$47,280	6.4%	3,710
207. Locomotive Engineers	$57,520	2.9%	3,548
208. Machinists	$35,230	−3.1%	39,505
209. Teacher Assistants	$21,580	10.4%	193,986
210. Cooks, Institution and Cafeteria	$21,340	10.8%	111,898
211. Dispatchers, Except Police, Fire, and Ambulance	$33,140	1.5%	29,793
212. Geological Sample Test Technicians	$50,950	8.6%	1,895
213. Geophysical Data Technicians	$50,950	8.6%	1,895
214. Aerospace Engineering and Operations Technicians	$54,930	10.4%	707
215. Aircraft Cargo Handling Supervisors	$37,760	23.3%	523
216. Helpers—Brickmasons, Blockmasons, Stonemasons, and Tile and Marble Setters	$26,260	11.0%	22,500

(continued)

(continued)

The 300 Best Jobs That Don't Require a Four-Year Degree

Job	Annual Earnings	Percent Growth	Annual Openings
217. Payroll and Timekeeping Clerks	$33,810	3.1%	18,544
218. Pesticide Handlers, Sprayers, and Applicators, Vegetation	$28,560	14.0%	7,443
219. Fire Inspectors	$50,830	11.0%	644
220. Fire Investigators	$50,830	11.0%	644
221. Tree Trimmers and Pruners	$29,800	11.1%	9,621
222. Commercial Divers	$41,610	17.7%	248
223. Animal Trainers	$26,190	22.7%	6,713
224. Automotive Glass Installers and Repairers	$31,470	18.7%	3,457
225. Pest Control Workers	$29,030	15.5%	6,006
226. Fashion Designers	$62,810	5.0%	1,968
227. Insulation Workers, Mechanical	$36,570	8.6%	5,787
228. Makeup Artists, Theatrical and Performance	$35,250	39.8%	392
229. Farmers and Ranchers	$33,360	−8.5%	129,552
230. Medical Equipment Preparers	$27,040	14.2%	8,363
231. Secretaries, Except Legal, Medical, and Executive	$28,220	1.2%	239,630
232. Library Technicians	$27,680	8.5%	29,075
233. Embalmers	$36,800	14.3%	1,660
234. Photographers	$27,720	10.3%	16,100
235. First-Line Supervisors/Managers of Agricultural Crop and Horticultural Workers	$38,510	−0.4%	11,898
236. First-Line Supervisors/Managers of Animal Husbandry and Animal Care Workers	$38,510	−0.4%	11,898
237. First-Line Supervisors/Managers of Aquacultural Workers	$38,510	−0.4%	11,898
238. Shipping, Receiving, and Traffic Clerks	$26,990	3.7%	138,967
239. Nuclear Equipment Operation Technicians	$66,140	6.7%	1,021
240. Nuclear Monitoring Technicians	$66,140	6.7%	1,021
241. Recreational Vehicle Service Technicians	$31,760	18.2%	2,442
242. Insurance Claims Clerks	$32,040	−1.3%	42,246
243. Insurance Policy Processing Clerks	$32,040	−1.3%	42,246
244. Excavating and Loading Machine and Dragline Operators	$34,050	8.3%	6,562
245. Loan Interviewers and Clerks	$31,680	−0.9%	40,217
246. Pipelayers	$31,280	8.7%	8,902
247. Chemical Technicians	$40,740	5.8%	4,010
248. Residential Advisors	$23,050	18.5%	8,053
249. Plasterers and Stucco Masons	$36,430	8.1%	4,509
250. Slaughterers and Meat Packers	$22,500	12.7%	15,511
251. Bailiffs	$36,900	11.2%	2,223

The 300 Best Jobs That Don't Require a Four-Year Degree

Job	Annual Earnings	Percent Growth	Annual Openings
252. Maintenance Workers, Machinery	$35,590	−1.1%	15,055
253. Sound Engineering Technicians	$46,550	9.1%	1,194
254. Bakers	$22,590	10.0%	31,442
255. Locomotive Firers	$45,310	2.9%	3,548
256. Hazardous Materials Removal Workers	$36,330	11.2%	1,933
257. Tank Car, Truck, and Ship Loaders	$33,140	9.2%	4,519
258. Stonemasons	$36,950	10.0%	2,657
259. Control and Valve Installers and Repairers, Except Mechanical Door	$46,140	0.3%	3,855
260. Broadcast Technicians	$32,230	12.1%	2,955
261. Helpers—Electricians	$24,880	6.8%	35,109
262. Food Batchmakers	$23,730	10.9%	15,704
263. Power Plant Operators	$56,640	2.7%	1,796
264. Avionics Technicians	$48,100	8.1%	1,193
265. Reservation and Transportation Ticket Agents and Travel Clerks	$29,820	1.1%	30,754
266. Motorcycle Mechanics	$30,300	12.5%	3,564
267. Postal Service Clerks	$45,050	1.2%	3,703
268. Inspectors, Testers, Sorters, Samplers, and Weighers	$30,310	−7.0%	75,361
269. Correspondence Clerks	$29,500	12.0%	4,334
270. Industrial Truck and Tractor Operators	$28,010	−2.0%	89,547
271. Gaming Surveillance Officers and Gaming Investigators	$27,440	33.6%	2,124
272. Rail Car Repairers	$44,970	5.1%	1,989
273. Painters, Transportation Equipment	$36,000	8.4%	3,268
274. Structural Metal Fabricators and Fitters	$31,030	−0.2%	20,746
275. Insulation Workers, Floor, Ceiling, and Wall	$31,280	8.4%	6,580
276. Pile-Driver Operators	$47,550	8.3%	701
277. Mechanical Door Repairers	$31,880	14.9%	1,706
278. Team Assemblers	$24,630	0.1%	264,135
279. Postal Service Mail Sorters, Processors, and Processing Machine Operators	$43,700	−8.4%	6,855
280. Meat, Poultry, and Fish Cutters and Trimmers	$21,050	10.9%	17,920
281. Physical Therapist Aides	$22,990	24.4%	4,092
282. Chemical Plant and System Operators	$50,860	−15.3%	5,620
283. Septic Tank Servicers and Sewer Pipe Cleaners	$32,740	10.2%	3,156
284. Stationary Engineers and Boiler Operators	$47,640	3.4%	1,892
285. Airfield Operations Specialists	$38,320	11.8%	245

(continued)

(continued)

The 300 Best Jobs That Don't Require a Four-Year Degree

Job	Annual Earnings	Percent Growth	Annual Openings
286. Animal Control Workers	$29,320	12.5%	3,377
287. Parts Salespersons	$28,130	−2.2%	52,414
288. Laborers and Freight, Stock, and Material Movers, Hand	$21,900	2.1%	630,487
289. Statistical Assistants	$32,540	7.6%	4,836
290. Petroleum Pump System Operators, Refinery Operators, and Gaugers	$53,010	−13.4%	4,477
291. Title Examiners, Abstractors, and Searchers	$37,200	−1.2%	6,880
292. Concierges	$25,540	14.1%	4,893
293. Merchandise Displayers and Window Trimmers	$24,830	10.7%	9,103
294. Umpires, Referees, and Other Sports Officials	$24,770	16.0%	4,461
295. Rail Yard Engineers, Dinkey Operators, and Hostlers	$39,020	2.9%	3,548
296. Postmasters and Mail Superintendents	$57,900	−0.8%	1,627
297. Desktop Publishers	$35,510	1.0%	6,420
298. Multiple Machine Tool Setters, Operators, and Tenders, Metal and Plastic	$30,390	0.3%	15,709
299. Agricultural Technicians	$33,630	6.6%	4,049
300. Food Science Technicians	$33,630	6.6%	4,049

Jobs 4, 5, 6, and 7 share 14,746 openings. Jobs 18 and 19 share 37,842 openings. Jobs 21 and 22 share 12,836 openings. Jobs 24 and 25 share 68,643 openings. Jobs 26 and 27 share 97,350 openings. Jobs 32 and 33 share 22,024 openings. Jobs 37 and 38 share 223,225 openings. Jobs 40 and 41 share 8,992 openings with each other and with three other jobs not included in this list. Jobs 45 and 46 share 18,887 openings. Jobs 74, 75, and 76 share 2,665 openings. Jobs 91 and 92 share 6,994 openings. Jobs 93 and 94 share 3,771 openings. Jobs 99 and 100 share 29,719 openings. Jobs 105, 106, 107, 108, and 109 share 15,841 openings. Jobs 115 and 116 share 8,299 openings. Jobs 120, 121, and 122 share 2,122 openings. Jobs 128 and 129 share 12,583 openings. Jobs 132 and 133 share 16,238 openings. Jobs 166 and 167 share 61,125 openings. Jobs 177, 178, and 179 share 16,163 openings. Jobs 187, 188, and 189 share 81,885 openings. Jobs 193 and 194 share 4,786 openings. Jobs 199 and 200 share 3,571 openings. Jobs 207, 255, and 295 share 3,548 openings. Jobs 212 and 213 share 1,895 openings. Jobs 219 and 220 share 644 openings. Job 235, 236, and 237 share 11,898 openings with each other and with two other jobs not included in this list. Jobs 239 and 240 share 1,021 openings. Jobs 242 and 243 share 42,246 openings. Jobs 299 and 300 share 4,049 openings.

The 100 Best-Paying Jobs That Don't Require a Four-Year Degree

We sorted all 300 jobs based on their annual median earnings from highest to lowest. *Median earnings* means that half of all workers in these jobs earn more than that amount and half earn less. We then selected the 100 jobs with the highest earnings to create the list that follows.

This is a very popular list for obvious reasons. It includes jobs at all levels of training, although many of the better-paying jobs do require technical training and/or work experience.

For example, the highest-paying job on the list is Air Traffic Controllers, a job that requires considerable training and on-the-job experience. Among the top 25, several require management, supervision, or technical skills.

Keep in mind that the earnings reflect the national average for all workers in the occupation. This is an important consideration, because starting pay in the job is usually much less than the pay that workers can earn with several years of experience. (You can see figures for starting pay in the Part II job descriptions.) Earnings also vary significantly by region of the country, so actual pay in your area could be substantially different.

The 100 Best-Paying Jobs That Don't Require a Four-Year Degree

Job	Annual Earnings
1. Air Traffic Controllers	$112,930
2. Industrial Production Managers	$80,560
3. Storage and Distribution Managers	$76,310
4. Transportation Managers	$76,310
5. First-Line Supervisors/Managers of Police and Detectives	$72,620
6. Nuclear Power Reactor Operators	$70,410
7. Radiation Therapists	$70,010
8. Sales Representatives, Wholesale and Manufacturing, Technical and Scientific Products	$68,270
9. Elevator Installers and Repairers	$68,000
10. First-Line Supervisors/Managers of Non-Retail Sales Workers	$67,020
11. Nuclear Equipment Operation Technicians	$66,140
12. Nuclear Monitoring Technicians	$66,140
13. Forest Fire Fighting and Prevention Supervisors	$65,040
14. Municipal Fire Fighting and Prevention Supervisors	$65,040
15. Dental Hygienists	$64,740
16. Nuclear Medicine Technologists	$64,670
17. Gaming Managers	$64,410
18. Fashion Designers	$62,810
19. Commercial Pilots	$61,640
20. Flight Attendants	$61,120
21. Talent Directors	$61,090
22. Technical Directors/Managers	$61,090
23. Registered Nurses	$60,010

(continued)

(continued)

The 100 Best-Paying Jobs That Don't Require a Four-Year Degree

Job	Annual Earnings
24. Criminal Investigators and Special Agents	$59,930
25. Immigration and Customs Inspectors	$59,930
26. Police Detectives	$59,930
27. Police Identification and Records Officers	$59,930
28. Diagnostic Medical Sonographers	$59,860
29. Real Estate Brokers	$58,860
30. Railroad Conductors and Yardmasters	$58,650
31. Postmasters and Mail Superintendents	$57,900
32. Locomotive Engineers	$57,520
33. Mates—Ship, Boat, and Barge	$57,210
34. Pilots, Ship	$57,210
35. Ship and Boat Captains	$57,210
36. Power Plant Operators	$56,640
37. Ship Engineers	$56,090
38. First-Line Supervisors/Managers of Construction Trades and Extraction Workers	$55,950
39. First-Line Supervisors/Managers of Correctional Officers	$55,720
40. First-Line Supervisors/Managers of Mechanics, Installers, and Repairers	$55,380
41. Aerospace Engineering and Operations Technicians	$54,930
42. Telecommunications Equipment Installers and Repairers, Except Line Installers	$54,070
43. Claims Examiners, Property and Casualty Insurance	$53,560
44. Insurance Adjusters, Examiners, and Investigators	$53,560
45. Petroleum Pump System Operators, Refinery Operators, and Gaugers	$53,010
46. Electrical Power-Line Installers and Repairers	$52,570
47. Purchasing Agents, Except Wholesale, Retail, and Farm Products	$52,460
48. Electrical Engineering Technicians	$52,140
49. Electronics Engineering Technicians	$52,140
50. Insurance Appraisers, Auto Damage	$51,500
51. Aviation Inspectors	$51,440
52. Freight and Cargo Inspectors	$51,440
53. Transportation Vehicle, Equipment and Systems Inspectors, Except Aviation	$51,440
54. Geological Sample Test Technicians	$50,950
55. Geophysical Data Technicians	$50,950
56. Chemical Plant and System Operators	$50,860
57. Fire Inspectors	$50,830
58. Fire Investigators	$50,830

The 100 Best-Paying Jobs That Don't Require a Four-Year Degree

Job	Annual Earnings
59. Sales Representatives, Wholesale and Manufacturing, Except Technical and Scientific Products	$50,750
60. Boilermakers	$50,700
61. Subway and Streetcar Operators	$50,520
62. Funeral Directors	$50,370
63. Radiologic Technicians	$50,260
64. Radiologic Technologists	$50,260
65. Respiratory Therapists	$50,070
66. First-Line Supervisors/Managers of Transportation and Material-Moving Machine and Vehicle Operators	$49,850
67. Police Patrol Officers	$49,630
68. Sheriffs and Deputy Sheriffs	$49,630
69. Electrical Drafters	$49,250
70. Electronic Drafters	$49,250
71. Aircraft Mechanics and Service Technicians	$49,010
72. First-Line Supervisors/Managers of Production and Operating Workers	$48,670
73. Coroners	$48,400
74. Environmental Compliance Inspectors	$48,400
75. Equal Opportunity Representatives and Officers	$48,400
76. Government Property Inspectors and Investigators	$48,400
77. Licensing Examiners and Inspectors	$48,400
78. Emergency Management Specialists	$48,380
79. Construction and Building Inspectors	$48,330
80. Avionics Technicians	$48,100
81. Stationary Engineers and Boiler Operators	$47,640
82. Pile-Driver Operators	$47,550
83. Industrial Engineering Technicians	$47,490
84. Mechanical Engineering Technicians	$47,280
85. Telecommunications Line Installers and Repairers	$47,220
86. Electrical and Electronics Repairers, Commercial and Industrial Equipment	$47,110
87. Wholesale and Retail Buyers, Except Farm Products	$46,960
88. Sound Engineering Technicians	$46,550
89. Control and Valve Installers and Repairers, Except Mechanical Door	$46,140
90. Millwrights	$46,090
91. Vocational Education Teachers, Postsecondary	$45,850
92. Aircraft Structure, Surfaces, Rigging, and Systems Assemblers	$45,420
93. Court Reporters	$45,330

(continued)

(continued)

The 100 Best-Paying Jobs That Don't Require a Four-Year Degree

Job	Annual Earnings
94. Locomotive Firers	$45,310
95. Occupational Therapist Assistants	$45,050
96. Postal Service Clerks	$45,050
97. Paralegals and Legal Assistants	$44,990
98. Rail Car Repairers	$44,970
99. Cardiovascular Technologists and Technicians	$44,940
100. Electricians	$44,780

The 100 Fastest-Growing Jobs That Don't Require a Four-Year Degree

We created this list by sorting all 300 best jobs by their projected growth over the ten-year period from 2006 to 2016. Growth rates are one measure to consider in exploring career options, as jobs with higher growth rates tend to provide more job opportunities.

Jobs in the health care and personal care dominate the 20 fastest-growing jobs. Veterinary Technologists and Technicians is the job with the highest growth rate—the number employed is projected to grow by almost half from 2006 to 2016. You can find a wide range of rapidly growing jobs in a variety of fields and at different levels of training and education among the jobs in this list.

The 100 Fastest-Growing Jobs That Don't Require a Four-Year Degree

Job	Percent Growth
1. Veterinary Technologists and Technicians	41.0%
2. Makeup Artists, Theatrical and Performance	39.8%
3. Medical Assistants	35.4%
4. Skin Care Specialists	34.3%
5. Gaming Surveillance Officers and Gaming Investigators	33.6%
6. Social and Human Service Assistants	33.6%
7. Physical Therapist Assistants	32.4%
8. Pharmacy Technicians	32.0%
9. Dental Hygienists	30.1%
10. Dental Assistants	29.2%
11. Environmental Science and Protection Technicians, Including Health	28.0%

The 100 Fastest-Growing Jobs That Don't Require a Four-Year Degree

Job	Percent Growth
12. Fitness Trainers and Aerobics Instructors	26.8%
13. Preschool Teachers, Except Special Education	26.3%
14. Cardiovascular Technologists and Technicians	25.5%
15. Occupational Therapist Assistants	25.4%
16. Customer Service Representatives	24.8%
17. Environmental Engineering Technicians	24.8%
18. Radiation Therapists	24.8%
19. Court Reporters	24.5%
20. Surgical Technologists	24.5%
21. Gaming Managers	24.4%
22. Physical Therapist Aides	24.4%
23. Audio and Video Equipment Technicians	24.2%
24. Interpreters and Translators	23.6%
25. Registered Nurses	23.5%
26. Gaming Supervisors	23.4%
27. Aircraft Cargo Handling Supervisors	23.3%
28. Self-Enrichment Education Teachers	23.1%
29. Bill and Account Collectors	22.9%
30. Vocational Education Teachers, Postsecondary	22.9%
31. Animal Trainers	22.7%
32. Respiratory Therapists	22.6%
33. Paralegals and Legal Assistants	22.2%
34. Locksmiths and Safe Repairers	22.1%
35. Medical Equipment Repairers	21.7%
36. Tour Guides and Escorts	21.2%
37. Advertising Sales Agents	20.3%
38. Massage Therapists	20.3%
39. Security and Fire Alarm Systems Installers	20.2%
40. Tire Repairers and Changers	20.2%
41. Brokerage Clerks	20.0%
42. Interior Designers	19.5%
43. Mapping Technicians	19.4%
44. Surveying Technicians	19.4%
45. Athletes and Sports Competitors	19.2%
46. Emergency Medical Technicians and Paramedics	19.2%
47. Diagnostic Medical Sonographers	19.1%
48. Motorboat Mechanics	19.0%

(continued)

(continued)

The 100 Fastest-Growing Jobs That Don't Require a Four-Year Degree

Job	Percent Growth
49. Automotive Glass Installers and Repairers	18.7%
50. Residential Advisors	18.5%
51. Construction and Building Inspectors	18.2%
52. Nursing Aides, Orderlies, and Attendants	18.2%
53. Private Detectives and Investigators	18.2%
54. Recreational Vehicle Service Technicians	18.2%
55. Landscaping and Groundskeeping Workers	18.1%
56. Demonstrators and Product Promoters	18.0%
57. Mates—Ship, Boat, and Barge	17.9%
58. Pilots, Ship	17.9%
59. Ship and Boat Captains	17.9%
60. Medical Records and Health Information Technicians	17.8%
61. Commercial Divers	17.7%
62. First-Line Supervisors/Managers of Landscaping, Lawn Service, and Groundskeeping Workers	17.6%
63. Criminal Investigators and Special Agents	17.3%
64. Immigration and Customs Inspectors	17.3%
65. Police Detectives	17.3%
66. Police Identification and Records Officers	17.3%
67. Receptionists and Information Clerks	17.2%
68. Correctional Officers and Jailers	16.9%
69. Security Guards	16.9%
70. Medical Secretaries	16.7%
71. Cargo and Freight Agents	16.5%
72. Aviation Inspectors	16.4%
73. Freight and Cargo Inspectors	16.4%
74. Transportation Vehicle, Equipment and Systems Inspectors, Except Aviation	16.4%
75. Umpires, Referees, and Other Sports Officials	16.0%
76. Sailors and Marine Oilers	15.7%
77. First-Line Supervisors/Managers of Personal Service Workers	15.5%
78. Pest Control Workers	15.5%
79. Tile and Marble Setters	15.4%
80. Radiologic Technicians	15.1%
81. Radiologic Technologists	15.1%
82. Medical and Clinical Laboratory Technicians	15.0%
83. Mechanical Door Repairers	14.9%

The 100 Fastest-Growing Jobs That Don't Require a Four-Year Degree

Job	Percent Growth
84. Executive Secretaries and Administrative Assistants	14.8%
85. Nuclear Medicine Technologists	14.8%
86. Coaches and Scouts	14.6%
87. Automotive Master Mechanics	14.3%
88. Automotive Specialty Technicians	14.3%
89. Embalmers	14.3%
90. Roofers	14.3%
91. Medical Equipment Preparers	14.2%
92. Concierges	14.1%
93. Ship Engineers	14.1%
94. Boilermakers	14.0%
95. Licensed Practical and Licensed Vocational Nurses	14.0%
96. Pesticide Handlers, Sprayers, and Applicators, Vegetation	14.0%
97. Water and Liquid Waste Treatment Plant and System Operators	13.8%
98. Police, Fire, and Ambulance Dispatchers	13.6%
99. Medical Transcriptionists	13.5%
100. Tellers	13.5%

The 100 Jobs with the Most Openings That Don't Require a Four-Year Degree

We created this list by sorting all 300 best jobs by the number of job openings that each is expected to have per year. Jobs that employ lots of people are also likely to have more job openings in a given year. Many of these occupations, such as Construction Laborers, are not among the highest-paying jobs. But jobs with large numbers of openings often provide easier entry for new workers, make it easier to move from one position to another, or are attractive for other reasons. Some of these jobs may also appeal to people re-entering the labor market, part-time workers, and workers who want to move from one employer to another. And some of these jobs pay quite well, offer good benefits, or have other advantages.

The 100 Jobs with the Most Openings
That Don't Require a Four-Year Degree

Job	Annual Openings
1. Office Clerks, General	765,803
2. Laborers and Freight, Stock, and Material Movers, Hand	630,487
3. Customer Service Representatives	600,937
4. Receptionists and Information Clerks	334,124
5. Nursing Aides, Orderlies, and Attendants	321,036
6. Landscaping and Groundskeeping Workers	307,138
7. Bookkeeping, Accounting, and Auditing Clerks	286,854
8. Truck Drivers, Heavy and Tractor-Trailer	279,032
9. Team Assemblers	264,135
10. Construction Laborers	257,407
11. Secretaries, Except Legal, Medical, and Executive	239,630
12. Cooks, Restaurant	238,542
13. Executive Secretaries and Administrative Assistants	235,314
14. Registered Nurses	233,499
15. Construction Carpenters	223,225
16. Rough Carpenters	223,225
17. Security Guards	222,085
18. First-Line Supervisors/Managers of Retail Sales Workers	221,241
19. Teacher Assistants	193,986
20. Maintenance and Repair Workers, General	165,502
21. Sales Representatives, Wholesale and Manufacturing, Except Technical and Scientific Products	156,215
22. Truck Drivers, Light or Delivery Services	154,330
23. First-Line Supervisors/Managers of Food Preparation and Serving Workers	154,175
24. Tellers	146,077
25. Shipping, Receiving, and Traffic Clerks	138,967
26. First-Line Supervisors/Managers of Office and Administrative Support Workers	138,420
27. Farmers and Ranchers	129,552
28. Bill and Account Collectors	118,709
29. Cooks, Institution and Cafeteria	111,898
30. Painters, Construction and Maintenance	101,140
31. Automotive Master Mechanics	97,350
32. Automotive Specialty Technicians	97,350
33. Computer Support Specialists	97,334
34. Medical Assistants	92,977

The 100 Jobs with the Most Openings That Don't Require a Four-Year Degree

Job	Annual Openings
35. Industrial Truck and Tractor Operators	89,547
36. First-Line Supervisors/Managers of Construction Trades and Extraction Workers	82,923
37. Billing, Cost, and Rate Clerks	81,885
38. Billing, Posting, and Calculating Machine Operators	81,885
39. Statement Clerks	81,885
40. Social and Human Service Assistants	80,142
41. Electricians	79,083
42. Preschool Teachers, Except Special Education	78,172
43. Inspectors, Testers, Sorters, Samplers, and Weighers	75,361
44. Hairdressers, Hairstylists, and Cosmetologists	73,030
45. Licensed Practical and Licensed Vocational Nurses	70,610
46. Pipe Fitters and Steamfitters	68,643
47. Plumbers	68,643
48. Self-Enrichment Education Teachers	64,449
49. Real Estate Sales Agents	61,232
50. Solderers and Brazers	61,125
51. Welders, Cutters, and Welder Fitters	61,125
52. Medical Secretaries	60,659
53. Bus Drivers, School	59,809
54. Food Service Managers	59,302
55. Correctional Officers and Jailers	56,579
56. Operating Engineers and Other Construction Equipment Operators	55,468
57. Pharmacy Technicians	54,453
58. Interviewers, Except Eligibility and Loan	54,060
59. Production, Planning, and Expediting Clerks	52,735
60. Parts Salespersons	52,414
61. Helpers—Installation, Maintenance, and Repair Workers	52,058
62. Fitness Trainers and Aerobics Instructors	51,235
63. Coaches and Scouts	51,100
64. First-Line Supervisors/Managers of Non-Retail Sales Workers	48,883
65. First-Line Supervisors/Managers of Production and Operating Workers	46,144
66. Sales Representatives, Wholesale and Manufacturing, Technical and Scientific Products	43,469
67. Insurance Claims Clerks	42,246
68. Insurance Policy Processing Clerks	42,246

(continued)

(continued)

The 100 Jobs with the Most Openings That Don't Require a Four-Year Degree

Job	Annual Openings
69. Loan Interviewers and Clerks	40,217
70. Machinists	39,505
71. Medical Records and Health Information Technicians	39,048
72. Legal Secretaries	38,682
73. Roofers	38,398
74. Police Patrol Officers	37,842
75. Sheriffs and Deputy Sheriffs	37,842
76. Refuse and Recyclable Material Collectors	37,785
77. Helpers—Carpenters	37,731
78. First-Line Supervisors/Managers of Personal Service Workers	37,555
79. Automotive Body and Related Repairers	37,469
80. Helpers—Electricians	35,109
81. Cement Masons and Concrete Finishers	34,625
82. Demonstrators and Product Promoters	32,779
83. Sheet Metal Workers	31,677
84. Bakers	31,442
85. Drywall and Ceiling Tile Installers	30,945
86. Reservation and Transportation Ticket Agents and Travel Clerks	30,754
87. First-Line Supervisors/Managers of Housekeeping and Janitorial Workers	30,613
88. Dispatchers, Except Police, Fire, and Ambulance	29,793
89. Heating and Air Conditioning Mechanics and Installers	29,719
90. Refrigeration Mechanics and Installers	29,719
91. Dental Assistants	29,482
92. Helpers—Pipelayers, Plumbers, Pipefitters, and Steamfitters	29,332
93. Advertising Sales Agents	29,233
94. Library Technicians	29,075
95. Bus Drivers, Transit and Intercity	27,100
96. Bus and Truck Mechanics and Diesel Engine Specialists	25,428
97. Highway Maintenance Workers	24,774
98. First-Line Supervisors/Managers of Mechanics, Installers, and Repairers	24,361
99. Industrial Machinery Mechanics	23,361
100. Paralegals and Legal Assistants	22,756

Jobs 15 and 16 share 223,225 openings. Jobs 31 and 32 share 97,350 openings. Jobs 37, 38, and 39 share 81,885 openings. Jobs 46 and 47 share 68,643 openings. Jobs 50 and 51 share 61,125 openings. Jobs 67 and 68 share 42,246 openings. Jobs 74 and 75 share 37,842 openings. Jobs 89 and 90 share 29,719 openings.

Best Jobs Lists by Demographic

We decided that it would be interesting to include lists in this section that show what sorts of jobs different types of people are most likely to have. For example, what jobs have the highest percentages of men or young workers? We're not saying that men or young people should consider these jobs over others, but it is interesting information to know.

In some cases, the lists can give you ideas for jobs to consider that you might otherwise overlook. For example, perhaps women should consider some jobs that traditionally have high percentages of men in them. Or older workers might consider some jobs typically held by young people. Although these aren't obvious ways of using these lists, the lists may give you some good ideas of jobs to consider. The lists may also help you identify jobs that work well for others in your situation—for example, jobs with plentiful opportunities for part-time work, if that's something you want to do.

All lists in this section were created through a similar process. We began with the 300 best jobs that don't require a four-year degree and sorted those jobs in order of the primary criterion for each set of lists. For example, we sorted the 300 jobs based on the percentage of workers age 16 to 24 from highest to lowest percentage and then selected the jobs with a high percentage (46 jobs with a percentage greater than 20). From this initial list of jobs with a high percentage of each type of worker, we created four more-specialized lists:

* 25 Best Jobs Overall (the subset of jobs that have the highest combined scores for earnings, growth rate, and number of openings)
* 25 Best-Paying Jobs
* 25 Fastest-Growing Jobs
* 25 Jobs with the Most Openings

Again, each of these four lists includes only jobs that have high percentages of the specific type of worker. The same basic process was used to create all the lists in this section. The lists are very interesting, and we hope you find them helpful.

Best Jobs with the Highest Percentages of Workers Age 16–24

From our list of 300 jobs used in this book (or, to be precise, the 290 for which we had information about the age of workers), this list contains jobs with the highest percentages (more than 20 percent) of workers age 16 to 24, presented in order of the percentage of these young workers in each job. Younger workers are found in all jobs, but jobs with higher percentages of younger workers may present more opportunities for initial entry or upward mobility. Many jobs with the highest percentages of younger workers are those that don't require extensive training or education, but there is a wide variety of jobs in different fields among these jobs.

Best Jobs with the Highest Percentages of Workers Age 16–24

Job	Percent Age 16–24
1. Helpers—Brickmasons, Blockmasons, Stonemasons, and Tile and Marble Setters	41.2%
2. Helpers—Carpenters	41.2%
3. Helpers—Electricians	41.2%
4. Helpers—Pipelayers, Plumbers, Pipefitters, and Steamfitters	41.2%
5. Recreational Vehicle Service Technicians	39.9%
6. Tire Repairers and Changers	39.9%
7. Athletes and Sports Competitors	34.5%
8. Coaches and Scouts	34.5%
9. Umpires, Referees, and Other Sports Officials	34.5%
10. Residential Advisors	34.0%
11. Tellers	33.8%
12. Helpers—Installation, Maintenance, and Repair Workers	33.6%
13. Cooks, Institution and Cafeteria	33.1%
14. Cooks, Restaurant	33.1%
15. Library Technicians	32.5%
16. Laborers and Freight, Stock, and Material Movers, Hand	30.3%
17. Fitness Trainers and Aerobics Instructors	30.2%
18. City and Regional Planning Aides	28.0%
19. Environmental Science and Protection Technicians, Including Health	28.0%
20. Social Science Research Assistants	28.0%
21. Tour Guides and Escorts	27.4%
22. Embalmers	26.6%
23. Plasterers and Stucco Masons	25.9%
24. Landscaping and Groundskeeping Workers	25.5%
25. Pesticide Handlers, Sprayers, and Applicators, Vegetation	25.5%
26. Tree Trimmers and Pruners	25.5%
27. Pharmacy Technicians	24.7%
28. Surgical Technologists	24.7%
29. Veterinary Technologists and Technicians	24.7%
30. Receptionists and Information Clerks	24.5%
31. Animal Trainers	23.8%
32. Construction Laborers	23.7%
33. Customer Service Representatives	22.8%
34. Hazardous Materials Removal Workers	22.6%
35. Roofers	22.4%
36. First-Line Supervisors/Managers of Food Preparation and Serving Workers	21.4%

Best Jobs with the Highest Percentages of Workers Age 16–24

Job	Percent Age 16–24
37. Interviewers, Except Eligibility and Loan	20.9%
38. Sailors and Marine Oilers	20.8%
39. Concierges	20.2%

The jobs in the following four lists are derived from the preceding list of the jobs with the highest percentages of workers age 16–24.

25 Best Jobs Overall with High Percentages of Workers Age 16–24

Job	Percent Age 16–24	Annual Earnings	Percent Growth	Annual Openings
1. Customer Service Representatives	22.8%	$29,040	24.8%	600,937
2. Environmental Science and Protection Technicians, Including Health	28.0%	$39,370	28.0%	8,404
3. Surgical Technologists	24.7%	$37,540	24.5%	15,365
4. Pharmacy Technicians	24.7%	$26,720	32.0%	54,453
5. Fitness Trainers and Aerobics Instructors	30.2%	$27,680	26.8%	51,235
6. Veterinary Technologists and Technicians	24.7%	$27,970	41.0%	14,674
7. Roofers	22.4%	$33,240	14.3%	38,398
8. Athletes and Sports Competitors	34.5%	$38,440	19.2%	4,293
9. Receptionists and Information Clerks	24.5%	$23,710	17.2%	334,124
10. Coaches and Scouts	34.5%	$27,840	14.6%	51,100
11. First-Line Supervisors/Managers of Food Preparation and Serving Workers	21.4%	$28,040	11.3%	154,175
12. Landscaping and Groundskeeping Workers	25.5%	$22,240	18.1%	307,138
13. Sailors and Marine Oilers	20.8%	$32,570	15.7%	8,600
14. Construction Laborers	23.7%	$27,310	10.9%	257,407
15. Recreational Vehicle Service Technicians	39.9%	$31,760	18.2%	2,442
16. Animal Trainers	23.8%	$26,190	22.7%	6,713
17. Embalmers	26.6%	$36,800	14.3%	1,660
18. Tellers	33.8%	$22,920	13.5%	146,077
19. Pesticide Handlers, Sprayers, and Applicators, Vegetation	25.5%	$28,560	14.0%	7,443
20. City and Regional Planning Aides	28.0%	$35,870	12.4%	3,571
21. Social Science Research Assistants	28.0%	$35,870	12.4%	3,571
22. Interviewers, Except Eligibility and Loan	20.9%	$27,320	9.5%	54,060

(continued)

(continued)

25 Best Jobs Overall with High Percentages of Workers Age 16–24

Job	Percent Age 16–24	Annual Earnings	Percent Growth	Annual Openings
23. Tour Guides and Escorts	27.4%	$22,110	21.2%	15,027
24. Tire Repairers and Changers	39.9%	$21,880	20.2%	18,829
25. Tree Trimmers and Pruners	25.5%	$29,800	11.1%	9,621

25 Best-Paying Jobs with High Percentages of Workers Age 16–24

Job	Percent Age 16–24	Annual Earnings
1. Environmental Science and Protection Technicians, Including Health	28.0%	$39,370
2. Athletes and Sports Competitors	34.5%	$38,440
3. Surgical Technologists	24.7%	$37,540
4. Embalmers	26.6%	$36,800
5. Plasterers and Stucco Masons	25.9%	$36,430
6. Hazardous Materials Removal Workers	22.6%	$36,330
7. City and Regional Planning Aides	28.0%	$35,870
8. Social Science Research Assistants	28.0%	$35,870
9. Roofers	22.4%	$33,240
10. Sailors and Marine Oilers	20.8%	$32,570
11. Recreational Vehicle Service Technicians	39.9%	$31,760
12. Tree Trimmers and Pruners	25.5%	$29,800
13. Customer Service Representatives	22.8%	$29,040
14. Pesticide Handlers, Sprayers, and Applicators, Vegetation	25.5%	$28,560
15. First-Line Supervisors/Managers of Food Preparation and Serving Workers	21.4%	$28,040
16. Veterinary Technologists and Technicians	24.7%	$27,970
17. Coaches and Scouts	34.5%	$27,840
18. Fitness Trainers and Aerobics Instructors	30.2%	$27,680
19. Library Technicians	32.5%	$27,680
20. Interviewers, Except Eligibility and Loan	20.9%	$27,320
21. Construction Laborers	23.7%	$27,310
22. Pharmacy Technicians	24.7%	$26,720
23. Helpers—Brickmasons, Blockmasons, Stonemasons, and Tile and Marble Setters	41.2%	$26,260
24. Animal Trainers	23.8%	$26,190
25. Concierges	20.2%	$25,540

25 Fastest-Growing Jobs with High Percentages of Workers Age 16–24

Job	Percent Age 16-24	Percent Growth
1. Veterinary Technologists and Technicians	24.7%	41.0%
2. Pharmacy Technicians	24.7%	32.0%
3. Environmental Science and Protection Technicians, Including Health	28.0%	28.0%
4. Fitness Trainers and Aerobics Instructors	30.2%	26.8%
5. Customer Service Representatives	22.8%	24.8%
6. Surgical Technologists	24.7%	24.5%
7. Animal Trainers	23.8%	22.7%
8. Tour Guides and Escorts	27.4%	21.2%
9. Tire Repairers and Changers	39.9%	20.2%
10. Athletes and Sports Competitors	34.5%	19.2%
11. Residential Advisors	34.0%	18.5%
12. Recreational Vehicle Service Technicians	39.9%	18.2%
13. Landscaping and Groundskeeping Workers	25.5%	18.1%
14. Receptionists and Information Clerks	24.5%	17.2%
15. Umpires, Referees, and Other Sports Officials	34.5%	16.0%
16. Sailors and Marine Oilers	20.8%	15.7%
17. Coaches and Scouts	34.5%	14.6%
18. Embalmers	26.6%	14.3%
19. Roofers	22.4%	14.3%
20. Concierges	20.2%	14.1%
21. Pesticide Handlers, Sprayers, and Applicators, Vegetation	25.5%	14.0%
22. Tellers	33.8%	13.5%
23. City and Regional Planning Aides	28.0%	12.4%
24. Social Science Research Assistants	28.0%	12.4%
25. Helpers—Pipelayers, Plumbers, Pipefitters, and Steamfitters	41.2%	11.9%

25 Jobs with the Most Openings with High Percentages of Workers Age 16–24

Job	Percent Age 16–24	Annual Openings
1. Laborers and Freight, Stock, and Material Movers, Hand	30.3%	630,487
2. Customer Service Representatives	22.8%	600,937
3. Receptionists and Information Clerks	24.5%	334,124
4. Landscaping and Groundskeeping Workers	25.5%	307,138

(continued)

(continued)

25 Jobs with the Most Openings with High Percentages of Workers Age 16–24

Job	Percent Age 16–24	Annual Openings
5. Construction Laborers	23.7%	257,407
6. Cooks, Restaurant	33.1%	238,542
7. First-Line Supervisors/Managers of Food Preparation and Serving Workers	21.4%	154,175
8. Tellers	33.8%	146,077
9. Cooks, Institution and Cafeteria	33.1%	111,898
10. Pharmacy Technicians	24.7%	54,453
11. Interviewers, Except Eligibility and Loan	20.9%	54,060
12. Helpers—Installation, Maintenance, and Repair Workers	33.6%	52,058
13. Fitness Trainers and Aerobics Instructors	30.2%	51,235
14. Coaches and Scouts	34.5%	51,100
15. Roofers	22.4%	38,398
16. Helpers—Carpenters	41.2%	37,731
17. Helpers—Electricians	41.2%	35,109
18. Helpers—Pipelayers, Plumbers, Pipefitters, and Steamfitters	41.2%	29,332
19. Library Technicians	32.5%	29,075
20. Helpers—Brickmasons, Blockmasons, Stonemasons, and Tile and Marble Setters	41.2%	22,500
21. Tire Repairers and Changers	39.9%	18,829
22. Surgical Technologists	24.7%	15,365
23. Tour Guides and Escorts	27.4%	15,027
24. Veterinary Technologists and Technicians	24.7%	14,674
25. Tree Trimmers and Pruners	25.5%	9,621

Best Jobs with High Percentages of Workers Age 55 and Over

Older workers don't change careers as often as younger ones do, and on the average, they tend to have been in their jobs for quite some time. Many of the jobs with the highest percentages of workers age 55 and over—and those with the highest earnings—require considerable preparation, either through experience or through education and training. These are not the sort of jobs most younger workers could easily get. That should not come as a big surprise, as many of these folks have been in the workforce for a long time and therefore have lots of experience.

But go down the list of the jobs with the highest percentages (more than 20 percent) of older workers and you will find a variety of jobs that many older workers could more easily enter if they were changing careers. Some would make good "retirement" jobs, particularly if they allowed for part-time work or self-employment.

Best Jobs with the Highest Percentages of Workers Age 55 and Over

Job	Percent Age 55 and Over
1. Farmers and Ranchers	52.3%
2. Multiple Machine Tool Setters, Operators, and Tenders, Metal and Plastic	40.0%
3. Bus Drivers, School	38.2%
4. Bus Drivers, Transit and Intercity	38.2%
5. Demonstrators and Product Promoters	38.2%
6. Tank Car, Truck, and Ship Loaders	34.6%
7. Real Estate Brokers	34.5%
8. Real Estate Sales Agents	34.5%
9. Fine Artists, Including Painters, Sculptors, and Illustrators	33.9%
10. Lodging Managers	31.6%
11. Funeral Directors	31.0%
12. Private Detectives and Investigators	30.4%
13. Court Clerks	30.4%
14. License Clerks	30.4%
15. Municipal Clerks	30.4%
16. Postal Service Clerks	29.8%
17. Control and Valve Installers and Repairers, Except Mechanical Door	28.8%
18. Mechanical Door Repairers	28.8%
19. Medical Equipment Repairers	28.3%
20. Bookkeeping, Accounting, and Auditing Clerks	28.2%
21. Aviation Inspectors	28.1%
22. Freight and Cargo Inspectors	28.1%
23. Transportation Vehicle, Equipment and Systems Inspectors, Except Aviation	28.1%
24. Tour Guides and Escorts	27.7%
25. Coroners	27.0%
26. Environmental Compliance Inspectors	27.0%
27. Equal Opportunity Representatives and Officers	27.0%
28. Government Property Inspectors and Investigators	27.0%
29. Licensing Examiners and Inspectors	27.0%
30. Gaming Supervisors	26.9%

(continued)

(continued)

Best Jobs with the Highest Percentages of Workers Age 55 and Over

Job	Percent Age 55 and Over
31. Construction and Building Inspectors	26.8%
32. Medical Records and Health Information Technicians	26.1%
33. Electrical and Electronics Repairers, Commercial and Industrial Equipment	26.0%
34. First-Line Supervisors/Managers of Housekeeping and Janitorial Workers	25.7%
35. Executive Secretaries and Administrative Assistants	25.5%
36. Legal Secretaries	25.5%
37. Medical Secretaries	25.5%
38. Secretaries, Except Legal, Medical, and Executive	25.5%
39. Maintenance and Repair Workers, General	25.3%
40. Millwrights	25.2%
41. Ship Engineers	25.0%
42. Gaming Surveillance Officers and Gaming Investigators	24.9%
43. Security Guards	24.9%
44. Postal Service Mail Sorters, Processors, and Processing Machine Operators	24.8%
45. Postal Service Mail Carriers	24.2%
46. Purchasing Agents, Except Wholesale, Retail, and Farm Products	23.8%
47. Correspondence Clerks	23.7%
48. Nuclear Equipment Operation Technicians	23.5%
49. Nuclear Monitoring Technicians	23.5%
50. Flight Attendants	23.2%
51. Payroll and Timekeeping Clerks	22.9%
52. Desktop Publishers	22.9%
53. Structural Metal Fabricators and Fitters	22.7%
54. Geological Sample Test Technicians	22.6%
55. Geophysical Data Technicians	22.6%
56. Truck Drivers, Heavy and Tractor-Trailer	22.5%
57. Truck Drivers, Light or Delivery Services	22.5%
58. Stationary Engineers and Boiler Operators	22.5%
59. Emergency Management Specialists	22.5%
60. Commercial Pilots	22.4%
61. Animal Trainers	22.2%
62. Self-Enrichment Education Teachers	22.1%
63. Licensed Practical and Licensed Vocational Nurses	22.0%
64. Interviewers, Except Eligibility and Loan	22.0%

Best Jobs with the Highest Percentages of Workers Age 55 and Over

Job	Percent Age 55 and Over
65. First-Line Supervisors/Managers of Mechanics, Installers, and Repairers	22.0%
66. Gaming Managers	22.0%
67. Human Resources Assistants, Except Payroll and Timekeeping	21.9%
68. Maintenance Workers, Machinery	21.7%
69. Fire Inspectors	21.6%
70. Fire Investigators	21.6%
71. Industrial Machinery Mechanics	21.6%
72. First-Line Supervisors/Managers of Personal Service Workers	21.4%
73. Machinists	21.4%
74. Embalmers	21.4%
75. Concierges	21.3%
76. Eligibility Interviewers, Government Programs	21.1%
77. First-Line Supervisors/Managers of Non-Retail Sales Workers	21.0%
78. Sales Representatives, Wholesale and Manufacturing, Except Technical and Scientific Products	21.0%
79. Sales Representatives, Wholesale and Manufacturing, Technical and Scientific Products	21.0%
80. Registered Nurses	21.0%
81. Railroad Conductors and Yardmasters	21.0%
82. Photographers	20.8%
83. Industrial Production Managers	20.6%
84. First-Line Supervisors/Managers of Office and Administrative Support Workers	20.5%
85. Locomotive Engineers	20.4%
86. Locomotive Firers	20.4%
87. Rail Yard Engineers, Dinkey Operators, and Hostlers	20.4%
88. Billing, Cost, and Rate Clerks	20.3%
89. Billing, Posting, and Calculating Machine Operators	20.3%
90. Statement Clerks	20.3%
91. First-Line Supervisors/Managers of Retail Sales Workers	20.1%

The jobs in the following four lists are derived from the preceding list of the jobs with the highest percentages of workers age 55 and over.

25 Best Jobs Overall with High Percentages of Workers Age 55 and Over

Job	Percent Age 55 and Over	Annual Earnings	Percent Growth	Annual Openings
1. Registered Nurses	21.0%	$60,010	23.5%	233,499
2. Sales Representatives, Wholesale and Manufacturing, Technical and Scientific Products	21.0%	$68,270	12.4%	43,469
3. Executive Secretaries and Administrative Assistants	25.5%	$38,640	14.8%	235,314
4. Real Estate Brokers	34.5%	$58,860	11.1%	18,689
5. Self-Enrichment Education Teachers	22.1%	$34,580	23.1%	64,449
6. Sales Representatives, Wholesale and Manufacturing, Except Technical and Scientific Products	21.0%	$50,750	8.4%	156,215
7. Licensed Practical and Licensed Vocational Nurses	22.0%	$37,940	14.0%	70,610
8. Construction and Building Inspectors	26.8%	$48,330	18.2%	12,606
9. First-Line Supervisors/Managers of Non-Retail Sales Workers	21.0%	$67,020	3.7%	48,883
10. Truck Drivers, Heavy and Tractor-Trailer	22.5%	$36,220	10.4%	279,032
11. Gaming Managers	22.0%	$64,410	24.4%	549
12. Bookkeeping, Accounting, and Auditing Clerks	28.2%	$31,560	12.5%	286,854
13. Flight Attendants	23.2%	$61,120	10.6%	10,773
14. First-Line Supervisors/Managers of Mechanics, Installers, and Repairers	22.0%	$55,380	7.3%	24,361
15. Real Estate Sales Agents	34.5%	$40,600	10.6%	61,232
16. First-Line Supervisors/Managers of Personal Service Workers	21.4%	$33,900	15.5%	37,555
17. Aviation Inspectors	28.1%	$51,440	16.4%	2,122
18. Freight and Cargo Inspectors	28.1%	$51,440	16.4%	2,122
19. Transportation Vehicle, Equipment and Systems Inspectors, Except Aviation	28.1%	$51,440	16.4%	2,122
20. Security Guards	24.9%	$22,570	16.9%	222,085
21. Gaming Supervisors	26.9%	$42,980	23.4%	4,602
22. Legal Secretaries	25.5%	$38,810	11.7%	38,682
23. First-Line Supervisors/Managers of Office and Administrative Support Workers	20.5%	$44,650	5.8%	138,420
24. Medical Secretaries	25.5%	$28,950	16.7%	60,659
25. Medical Records and Health Information Technicians	26.1%	$29,290	17.8%	39,048

Jobs 17, 18, and 19 share 2,122 openings.

25 Best-Paying Jobs with High Percentages of Workers Age 55 and Over

Job	Percent Age 55 and Over	Annual Earnings
1. Industrial Production Managers	20.6%	$80,560
2. Sales Representatives, Wholesale and Manufacturing, Technical and Scientific Products	21.0%	$68,270
3. First-Line Supervisors/Managers of Non-Retail Sales Workers	21.0%	$67,020
4. Nuclear Equipment Operation Technicians	23.5%	$66,140
5. Nuclear Monitoring Technicians	23.5%	$66,140
6. Gaming Managers	22.0%	$64,410
7. Commercial Pilots	22.4%	$61,640
8. Flight Attendants	23.2%	$61,120
9. Registered Nurses	21.0%	$60,010
10. Real Estate Brokers	34.5%	$58,860
11. Railroad Conductors and Yardmasters	21.0%	$58,650
12. Locomotive Engineers	20.4%	$57,520
13. Ship Engineers	25.0%	$56,090
14. First-Line Supervisors/Managers of Mechanics, Installers, and Repairers	22.0%	$55,380
15. Purchasing Agents, Except Wholesale, Retail, and Farm Products	23.8%	$52,460
16. Aviation Inspectors	28.1%	$51,440
17. Freight and Cargo Inspectors	28.1%	$51,440
18. Transportation Vehicle, Equipment and Systems Inspectors, Except Aviation	28.1%	$51,440
19. Geological Sample Test Technicians	22.6%	$50,950
20. Geophysical Data Technicians	22.6%	$50,950
21. Fire Inspectors	21.6%	$50,830
22. Fire Investigators	21.6%	$50,830
23. Sales Representatives, Wholesale and Manufacturing, Except Technical and Scientific Products	21.0%	$50,750
24. Funeral Directors	31.0%	$50,370
25. Coroners	27.0%	$48,400

25 Fastest-Growing Jobs with High Percentages of Workers Age 55 and Over

Job	Percent Age 55 and Over	Percent Growth
1. Gaming Surveillance Officers and Gaming Investigators	24.9%	33.6%
2. Gaming Managers	22.0%	24.4%
3. Registered Nurses	21.0%	23.5%
4. Gaming Supervisors	26.9%	23.4%
5. Self-Enrichment Education Teachers	22.1%	23.1%
6. Animal Trainers	22.2%	22.7%
7. Medical Equipment Repairers	28.3%	21.7%
8. Tour Guides and Escorts	27.7%	21.2%
9. Construction and Building Inspectors	26.8%	18.2%
10. Private Detectives and Investigators	30.4%	18.2%
11. Demonstrators and Product Promoters	38.2%	18.0%
12. Medical Records and Health Information Technicians	26.1%	17.8%
13. Security Guards	24.9%	16.9%
14. Medical Secretaries	25.5%	16.7%
15. Aviation Inspectors	28.1%	16.4%
16. Freight and Cargo Inspectors	28.1%	16.4%
17. Transportation Vehicle, Equipment and Systems Inspectors, Except Aviation	28.1%	16.4%
18. First-Line Supervisors/Managers of Personal Service Workers	21.4%	15.5%
19. Mechanical Door Repairers	28.8%	14.9%
20. Executive Secretaries and Administrative Assistants	25.5%	14.8%
21. Embalmers	21.4%	14.3%
22. Concierges	21.3%	14.1%
23. Ship Engineers	25.0%	14.1%
24. Licensed Practical and Licensed Vocational Nurses	22.0%	14.0%
25. Commercial Pilots	22.4%	13.2%

25 Jobs with the Most Openings with High Percentages of Workers Age 55 and Over

Job	Percent Age 55 and Over	Annual Openings
1. Bookkeeping, Accounting, and Auditing Clerks	28.2%	286,854
2. Truck Drivers, Heavy and Tractor-Trailer	22.5%	279,032

25 Jobs with the Most Openings with High Percentages of Workers Age 55 and Over

Job	Percent Age 55 and Over	Annual Openings
3. Secretaries, Except Legal, Medical, and Executive	25.5%	239,630
4. Executive Secretaries and Administrative Assistants	25.5%	235,314
5. Registered Nurses	21.0%	233,499
6. Security Guards	24.9%	222,085
7. First-Line Supervisors/Managers of Retail Sales Workers	20.1%	221,241
8. Maintenance and Repair Workers, General	25.3%	165,502
9. Sales Representatives, Wholesale and Manufacturing, Except Technical and Scientific Products	21.0%	156,215
10. Truck Drivers, Light or Delivery Services	22.5%	154,330
11. First-Line Supervisors/Managers of Office and Administrative Support Workers	20.5%	138,420
12. Farmers and Ranchers	52.3%	129,552
13. Billing, Cost, and Rate Clerks	20.3%	81,885
14. Billing, Posting, and Calculating Machine Operators	20.3%	81,885
15. Statement Clerks	20.3%	81,885
16. Licensed Practical and Licensed Vocational Nurses	22.0%	70,610
17. Self-Enrichment Education Teachers	22.1%	64,449
18. Real Estate Sales Agents	34.5%	61,232
19. Medical Secretaries	25.5%	60,659
20. Bus Drivers, School	38.2%	59,809
21. Interviewers, Except Eligibility and Loan	22.0%	54,060
22. First-Line Supervisors/Managers of Non-Retail Sales Workers	21.0%	48,883
23. Sales Representatives, Wholesale and Manufacturing, Technical and Scientific Products	21.0%	43,469
24. Machinists	21.4%	39,505
25. Medical Records and Health Information Technicians	26.1%	39,048

Jobs 13, 14, and 15 share 81,885 openings.

Best Jobs with High Percentages of Part-Time Workers

Look over the list of the jobs with high percentages (more than 25 percent) of part-time workers and you will find some interesting things. For example, many of the jobs on the list involve providing services at times when most other people are not working. Some are in the field of health care.

Some part-time workers may want the freedom of time that this work arrangement can provide, but others may work part time because they can't find full-time employment in these areas. These folks may work in other full- or part-time jobs to make ends meet. If you want to work part time now or in the future, these lists will help you identify jobs that are more likely to provide that opportunity. If you want full-time work, the lists may also help you identify jobs for which such opportunities are more difficult to find. In either case, it's good information to know in advance.

Note: The earnings estimates in the following lists are based on a survey of both part-time and full-time workers. On average, part-time workers earn about 10 percent less per hour than full-time workers.

Best Jobs with the Highest Percentages of Part-Time Workers

Job	Percent Part-Time Workers
1. Library Technicians	65.0%
2. Dental Hygienists	58.7%
3. Demonstrators and Product Promoters	56.1%
4. Massage Therapists	42.9%
5. Self-Enrichment Education Teachers	41.3%
6. Athletes and Sports Competitors	39.1%
7. Coaches and Scouts	39.1%
8. Umpires, Referees, and Other Sports Officials	39.1%
9. Fitness Trainers and Aerobics Instructors	38.2%
10. Teacher Assistants	38.0%
11. Dental Assistants	35.7%
12. Bus Drivers, School	34.1%
13. Bus Drivers, Transit and Intercity	34.1%
14. Receptionists and Information Clerks	31.7%
15. Hairdressers, Hairstylists, and Cosmetologists	31.1%
16. Cooks, Institution and Cafeteria	29.9%
17. Cooks, Restaurant	29.9%
18. Tour Guides and Escorts	29.0%
19. Interpreters and Translators	28.5%
20. Vocational Education Teachers, Postsecondary	27.8%
21. Physical Therapist Aides	27.1%
22. Physical Therapist Assistants	27.1%
23. Tellers	27.1%
24. Makeup Artists, Theatrical and Performance	26.3%
25. Skin Care Specialists	26.3%

Best Jobs with the Highest Percentages of Part-Time Workers

Job	Percent Part-Time Workers
26. Office Clerks, General	26.0%
27. Preschool Teachers, Except Special Education	25.1%

The jobs in the following four lists are derived from the preceding list of the jobs with the highest percentages of part-time workers.

25 Best Jobs Overall with High Percentages of Part-Time Workers

Job	Percent Part-Time Workers	Annual Earnings	Percent Growth	Annual Openings
1. Dental Hygienists	58.7%	$64,740	30.1%	10,433
2. Self-Enrichment Education Teachers	41.3%	$34,580	23.1%	64,449
3. Dental Assistants	35.7%	$31,550	29.2%	29,482
4. Fitness Trainers and Aerobics Instructors	38.2%	$27,680	26.8%	51,235
5. Physical Therapist Assistants	27.1%	$44,130	32.4%	5,957
6. Vocational Education Teachers, Postsecondary	27.8%	$45,850	22.9%	19,313
7. Preschool Teachers, Except Special Education	25.1%	$23,130	26.3%	78,172
8. Makeup Artists, Theatrical and Performance	26.3%	$35,250	39.8%	392
9. Interpreters and Translators	28.5%	$37,490	23.6%	6,630
10. Receptionists and Information Clerks	31.7%	$23,710	17.2%	334,124
11. Skin Care Specialists	26.3%	$27,190	34.3%	6,643
12. Office Clerks, General	26.0%	$24,460	12.6%	765,803
13. Massage Therapists	42.9%	$34,870	20.3%	9,193
14. Coaches and Scouts	39.1%	$27,840	14.6%	51,100
15. Athletes and Sports Competitors	39.1%	$38,440	19.2%	4,293
16. Tellers	27.1%	$22,920	13.5%	146,077
17. Bus Drivers, Transit and Intercity	34.1%	$33,160	12.5%	27,100
18. Demonstrators and Product Promoters	56.1%	$22,570	18.0%	32,779
19. Bus Drivers, School	34.1%	$25,860	9.3%	59,809
20. Cooks, Restaurant	29.9%	$21,220	11.5%	238,542
21. Hairdressers, Hairstylists, and Cosmetologists	31.1%	$22,210	12.4%	73,030
22. Library Technicians	65.0%	$27,680	8.5%	29,075
23. Physical Therapist Aides	27.1%	$22,990	24.4%	4,092
24. Teacher Assistants	38.0%	$21,580	10.4%	193,986
25. Tour Guides and Escorts	29.0%	$22,110	21.2%	15,027

25 Best-Paying Jobs with High Percentages of Part-Time Workers

Job	Percent Part-Time Workers	Annual Earnings
1. Dental Hygienists	58.7%	$64,740
2. Vocational Education Teachers, Postsecondary	27.8%	$45,850
3. Physical Therapist Assistants	27.1%	$44,130
4. Athletes and Sports Competitors	39.1%	$38,440
5. Interpreters and Translators	28.5%	$37,490
6. Makeup Artists, Theatrical and Performance	26.3%	$35,250
7. Massage Therapists	42.9%	$34,870
8. Self-Enrichment Education Teachers	41.3%	$34,580
9. Bus Drivers, Transit and Intercity	34.1%	$33,160
10. Dental Assistants	35.7%	$31,550
11. Coaches and Scouts	39.1%	$27,840
12. Fitness Trainers and Aerobics Instructors	38.2%	$27,680
13. Library Technicians	65.0%	$27,680
14. Skin Care Specialists	26.3%	$27,190
15. Bus Drivers, School	34.1%	$25,860
16. Umpires, Referees, and Other Sports Officials	39.1%	$24,770
17. Office Clerks, General	26.0%	$24,460
18. Receptionists and Information Clerks	31.7%	$23,710
19. Preschool Teachers, Except Special Education	25.1%	$23,130
20. Physical Therapist Aides	27.1%	$22,990
21. Tellers	27.1%	$22,920
22. Demonstrators and Product Promoters	56.1%	$22,570
23. Hairdressers, Hairstylists, and Cosmetologists	31.1%	$22,210
24. Tour Guides and Escorts	29.0%	$22,110
25. Teacher Assistants	38.0%	$21,580

25 Fastest-Growing Jobs with High Percentages of Part-Time Workers

Job	Percent Part-Time Workers	Percent Growth
1. Makeup Artists, Theatrical and Performance	26.3%	39.8%
2. Skin Care Specialists	26.3%	34.3%
3. Physical Therapist Assistants	27.1%	32.4%
4. Dental Hygienists	58.7%	30.1%

25 Fastest-Growing Jobs with High Percentages of Part-Time Workers

Job	Percent Part-Time Workers	Percent Growth
5. Dental Assistants	35.7%	29.2%
6. Fitness Trainers and Aerobics Instructors	38.2%	26.8%
7. Preschool Teachers, Except Special Education	25.1%	26.3%
8. Physical Therapist Aides	27.1%	24.4%
9. Interpreters and Translators	28.5%	23.6%
10. Self-Enrichment Education Teachers	41.3%	23.1%
11. Vocational Education Teachers, Postsecondary	27.8%	22.9%
12. Tour Guides and Escorts	29.0%	21.2%
13. Massage Therapists	42.9%	20.3%
14. Athletes and Sports Competitors	39.1%	19.2%
15. Demonstrators and Product Promoters	56.1%	18.0%
16. Receptionists and Information Clerks	31.7%	17.2%
17. Umpires, Referees, and Other Sports Officials	39.1%	16.0%
18. Coaches and Scouts	39.1%	14.6%
19. Tellers	27.1%	13.5%
20. Office Clerks, General	26.0%	12.6%
21. Bus Drivers, Transit and Intercity	34.1%	12.5%
22. Hairdressers, Hairstylists, and Cosmetologists	31.1%	12.4%
23. Cooks, Restaurant	29.9%	11.5%
24. Cooks, Institution and Cafeteria	29.9%	10.8%
25. Teacher Assistants	38.0%	10.4%

25 Jobs with the Most Openings with High Percentages of Part-Time Workers

Job	Percent Part-Time Workers	Annual Openings
1. Office Clerks, General	26.0%	765,803
2. Receptionists and Information Clerks	31.7%	334,124
3. Cooks, Restaurant	29.9%	238,542
4. Teacher Assistants	38.0%	193,986
5. Tellers	27.1%	146,077
6. Cooks, Institution and Cafeteria	29.9%	111,898

(continued)

(continued)

25 Jobs with the Most Openings with High Percentages of Part-Time Workers		
Job	Percent Part-Time Workers	Annual Openings
7. Preschool Teachers, Except Special Education	25.1%	78,172
8. Hairdressers, Hairstylists, and Cosmetologists	31.1%	73,030
9. Self-Enrichment Education Teachers	41.3%	64,449
10. Bus Drivers, School	34.1%	59,809
11. Fitness Trainers and Aerobics Instructors	38.2%	51,235
12. Coaches and Scouts	39.1%	51,100
13. Demonstrators and Product Promoters	56.1%	32,779
14. Dental Assistants	35.7%	29,482
15. Library Technicians	65.0%	29,075
16. Bus Drivers, Transit and Intercity	34.1%	27,100
17. Vocational Education Teachers, Postsecondary	27.8%	19,313
18. Tour Guides and Escorts	29.0%	15,027
19. Dental Hygienists	58.7%	10,433
20. Massage Therapists	42.9%	9,193
21. Skin Care Specialists	26.3%	6,643
22. Interpreters and Translators	28.5%	6,630
23. Physical Therapist Assistants	27.1%	5,957
24. Umpires, Referees, and Other Sports Officials	39.1%	4,461
25. Athletes and Sports Competitors	39.1%	4,293

Best Jobs with High Percentages of Self-Employed Workers

About 8 percent of all working people are self-employed. Although you may think of the self-employed as having similar jobs, they actually work in an enormous range of situations, fields, and work environments that you may not have considered.

Among the self-employed are people who own small or large businesses, as many real estate brokers and funeral directors do; professionals who own their own practices, as many lawyers, psychologists, and medical doctors do; people working on a contract basis for one or more employers, as many interior designers do; people running home consulting or other businesses; and people in many other situations. They may go to the same worksite every day, as most attorneys do; visit multiple employers during the course of a week, as many models do; or do most of their work from home, as many craft artists do. Some work part time, others full time, some as a way to have fun, some so they can spend time with their kids or go to school.

The point is that there is an enormous range of situations, and one of them could make sense for you now or in the future.

The following list contains jobs in which more than 20 percent of the workers are self-employed.

Best Jobs with the Highest Percentages of Self-Employed Workers

Job	Percent Self-Employed Workers
1. Farmers and Ranchers	100.0%
2. Massage Therapists	64.0%
3. Real Estate Brokers	63.5%
4. Fine Artists, Including Painters, Sculptors, and Illustrators	62.6%
5. Real Estate Sales Agents	60.2%
6. Animal Trainers	56.9%
7. Photographers	54.3%
8. Lodging Managers	53.0%
9. First-Line Supervisors/Managers of Non-Retail Sales Workers	45.4%
10. Food Service Managers	44.8%
11. Hairdressers, Hairstylists, and Cosmetologists	44.5%
12. First-Line Supervisors/Managers of Landscaping, Lawn Service, and Groundskeeping Workers	44.1%
13. Painters, Construction and Maintenance	42.2%
14. Makeup Artists, Theatrical and Performance	39.7%
15. Skin Care Specialists	38.9%
16. First-Line Supervisors/Managers of Personal Service Workers	38.6%
17. First-Line Supervisors/Managers of Retail Sales Workers	34.2%
18. Tile and Marble Setters	33.8%
19. Construction Carpenters	31.8%
20. Rough Carpenters	31.8%
21. First-Line Supervisors/Managers of Housekeeping and Janitorial Workers	30.7%
22. Private Detectives and Investigators	29.7%
23. Talent Directors	29.5%
24. Technical Directors/Managers	29.5%
25. Gaming Supervisors	29.2%
26. Tree Trimmers and Pruners	28.9%

(continued)

(continued)

Best Jobs with the Highest Percentages of Self-Employed Workers

Job	Percent Self-Employed Workers
27. Merchandise Displayers and Window Trimmers	28.6%
28. Locksmiths and Safe Repairers	28.3%
29. Athletes and Sports Competitors	27.0%
30. Interior Designers	26.3%
31. Tapers	24.9%
32. First-Line Supervisors/Managers of Agricultural Crop and Horticultural Workers	24.8%
33. First-Line Supervisors/Managers of Animal Husbandry and Animal Care Workers	24.8%
34. First-Line Supervisors/Managers of Aquacultural Workers	24.8%
35. Brickmasons and Blockmasons	24.5%
36. First-Line Supervisors/Managers of Construction Trades and Extraction Workers	24.4%
37. Umpires, Referees, and Other Sports Officials	24.0%
38. Fashion Designers	23.6%
39. Drywall and Ceiling Tile Installers	23.0%
40. Stonemasons	22.8%
41. Coaches and Scouts	22.7%
42. Motorboat Mechanics	22.6%
43. Motorcycle Mechanics	21.9%
44. Interpreters and Translators	21.6%
45. Self-Enrichment Education Teachers	21.5%
46. Demonstrators and Product Promoters	20.8%
47. Automotive Glass Installers and Repairers	20.7%
48. Landscaping and Groundskeeping Workers	20.5%
49. Pesticide Handlers, Sprayers, and Applicators, Vegetation	20.5%
50. Roofers	20.1%
51. Tour Guides and Escorts	20.1%

The jobs in the following four lists are derived from the preceding list of jobs with the highest percentages of self-employed workers. Where the following lists give earnings estimates, keep in mind that these figures are based on a survey that *doesn't include self-employed workers*. The median earnings for self-employed workers in these occupations may be significantly higher or lower.

25 Best Jobs Overall with High Percentages of Self-Employed Workers

Job	Percent Self-Employed Workers	Annual Earnings	Percent Growth	Annual Openings
1. Self-Enrichment Education Teachers	21.5%	$34,580	23.1%	64,449
2. First-Line Supervisors/Managers of Landscaping, Lawn Service, and Groundskeeping Workers	44.1%	$38,720	17.6%	18,956
3. First-Line Supervisors/Managers of Construction Trades and Extraction Workers	24.4%	$55,950	9.1%	82,923
4. Interior Designers	26.3%	$43,970	19.5%	8,434
5. Real Estate Brokers	63.5%	$58,860	11.1%	18,689
6. Gaming Supervisors	29.2%	$42,980	23.4%	4,602
7. Construction Carpenters	31.8%	$37,660	10.3%	223,225
8. Real Estate Sales Agents	60.2%	$40,600	10.6%	61,232
9. Rough Carpenters	31.8%	$37,660	10.3%	223,225
10. First-Line Supervisors/Managers of Non-Retail Sales Workers	45.4%	$67,020	3.7%	48,883
11. Food Service Managers	44.8%	$44,570	5.0%	59,302
12. Talent Directors	29.5%	$61,090	11.1%	8,992
13. Technical Directors/Managers	29.5%	$61,090	11.1%	8,992
14. Landscaping and Groundskeeping Workers	20.5%	$22,240	18.1%	307,138
15. Massage Therapists	64.0%	$34,870	20.3%	9,193
16. Tile and Marble Setters	33.8%	$38,720	15.4%	9,066
17. First-Line Supervisors/Managers of Personal Service Workers	38.6%	$33,900	15.5%	37,555
18. Interpreters and Translators	21.6%	$37,490	23.6%	6,630
19. Brickmasons and Blockmasons	24.5%	$44,070	9.7%	17,569
20. Roofers	20.1%	$33,240	14.3%	38,398
21. Painters, Construction and Maintenance	42.2%	$32,080	11.8%	101,140
22. Private Detectives and Investigators	29.7%	$37,640	18.2%	7,329
23. Athletes and Sports Competitors	27.0%	$38,440	19.2%	4,293
24. Coaches and Scouts	22.7%	$27,840	14.6%	51,100
25. Lodging Managers	53.0%	$44,240	12.2%	5,529

Jobs 7 and 9 share 223,225 openings. Jobs 12 and 13 share 8,992 openings.

25 Best-Paying Jobs with High Percentages of Self-Employed Workers

Job	Percent Self-Employed Workers	Annual Earnings
1. First-Line Supervisors/Managers of Non-Retail Sales Workers	45.4%	$67,020
2. Fashion Designers	23.6%	$62,810
3. Talent Directors	29.5%	$61,090
4. Technical Directors/Managers	29.5%	$61,090
5. Real Estate Brokers	63.5%	$58,860
6. First-Line Supervisors/Managers of Construction Trades and Extraction Workers	24.4%	$55,950
7. Food Service Managers	44.8%	$44,570
8. Lodging Managers	53.0%	$44,240
9. Brickmasons and Blockmasons	24.5%	$44,070
10. Interior Designers	26.3%	$43,970
11. Gaming Supervisors	29.2%	$42,980
12. Fine Artists, Including Painters, Sculptors, and Illustrators	62.6%	$42,070
13. Tapers	24.9%	$42,050
14. Real Estate Sales Agents	60.2%	$40,600
15. First-Line Supervisors/Managers of Landscaping, Lawn Service, and Groundskeeping Workers	44.1%	$38,720
16. Tile and Marble Setters	33.8%	$38,720
17. First-Line Supervisors/Managers of Agricultural Crop and Horticultural Workers	24.8%	$38,510
18. First-Line Supervisors/Managers of Animal Husbandry and Animal Care Workers	24.8%	$38,510
19. First-Line Supervisors/Managers of Aquacultural Workers	24.8%	$38,510
20. Athletes and Sports Competitors	27.0%	$38,440
21. Construction Carpenters	31.8%	$37,660
22. Rough Carpenters	31.8%	$37,660
23. Private Detectives and Investigators	29.7%	$37,640
24. Interpreters and Translators	21.6%	$37,490
25. Stonemasons	22.8%	$36,950

25 Fastest-Growing Jobs with High Percentages of Self-Employed Workers

Job	Percent Self-Employed Workers	Percent Growth
1. Makeup Artists, Theatrical and Performance	39.7%	39.8%
2. Skin Care Specialists	38.9%	34.3%
3. Interpreters and Translators	21.6%	23.6%
4. Gaming Supervisors	29.2%	23.4%
5. Self-Enrichment Education Teachers	21.5%	23.1%
6. Animal Trainers	56.9%	22.7%
7. Locksmiths and Safe Repairers	28.3%	22.1%
8. Tour Guides and Escorts	20.1%	21.2%
9. Massage Therapists	64.0%	20.3%
10. Interior Designers	26.3%	19.5%
11. Athletes and Sports Competitors	27.0%	19.2%
12. Motorboat Mechanics	22.6%	19.0%
13. Automotive Glass Installers and Repairers	20.7%	18.7%
14. Private Detectives and Investigators	29.7%	18.2%
15. Landscaping and Groundskeeping Workers	20.5%	18.1%
16. Demonstrators and Product Promoters	20.8%	18.0%
17. First-Line Supervisors/Managers of Landscaping, Lawn Service, and Groundskeeping Workers	44.1%	17.6%
18. Umpires, Referees, and Other Sports Officials	24.0%	16.0%
19. First-Line Supervisors/Managers of Personal Service Workers	38.6%	15.5%
20. Tile and Marble Setters	33.8%	15.4%
21. Coaches and Scouts	22.7%	14.6%
22. Roofers	20.1%	14.3%
23. Pesticide Handlers, Sprayers, and Applicators, Vegetation	20.5%	14.0%
24. First-Line Supervisors/Managers of Housekeeping and Janitorial Workers	30.7%	12.7%
25. Motorcycle Mechanics	21.9%	12.5%

25 Jobs with the Most Openings with High Percentages of Self-Employed Workers

Job	Percent Self-Employed Workers	Annual Openings
1. Landscaping and Groundskeeping Workers	20.5%	307,138
2. Construction Carpenters	31.8%	223,225
3. Rough Carpenters	31.8%	223,225
4. First-Line Supervisors/Managers of Retail Sales Workers	34.2%	221,241
5. Farmers and Ranchers	100.0%	129,552
6. Painters, Construction and Maintenance	42.2%	101,140
7. First-Line Supervisors/Managers of Construction Trades and Extraction Workers	24.4%	82,923
8. Hairdressers, Hairstylists, and Cosmetologists	44.5%	73,030
9. Self-Enrichment Education Teachers	21.5%	64,449
10. Real Estate Sales Agents	60.2%	61,232
11. Food Service Managers	44.8%	59,302
12. Coaches and Scouts	22.7%	51,100
13. First-Line Supervisors/Managers of Non-Retail Sales Workers	45.4%	48,883
14. Roofers	20.1%	38,398
15. First-Line Supervisors/Managers of Personal Service Workers	38.6%	37,555
16. Demonstrators and Product Promoters	20.8%	32,779
17. Drywall and Ceiling Tile Installers	23.0%	30,945
18. First-Line Supervisors/Managers of Housekeeping and Janitorial Workers	30.7%	30,613
19. First-Line Supervisors/Managers of Landscaping, Lawn Service, and Groundskeeping Workers	44.1%	18,956
20. Real Estate Brokers	63.5%	18,689
21. Brickmasons and Blockmasons	24.5%	17,569
22. Photographers	54.3%	16,100
23. Tour Guides and Escorts	20.1%	15,027
24. First-Line Supervisors/Managers of Agricultural Crop and Horticultural Workers	24.8%	11,898
25. First-Line Supervisors/Managers of Animal Husbandry and Animal Care Workers	24.8%	11,898

Jobs 2 and 3 share 223,225 openings. Jobs 24 and 25 share 11,898 openings.

Best Jobs Employing High Percentages of Women

To create the eight lists that follow, we sorted the 300 best jobs according to the percentages of women and men in the workforce. We knew we would create some controversy when we first included the best jobs lists with high percentages (more than 70 percent) of men and women in earlier editions. But these lists aren't meant to restrict women or men from considering job options; our reason for including these lists is exactly the opposite. We hope the lists help people see possibilities that they might not otherwise have considered.

The fact is that jobs with high percentages of women or high percentages of men offer good opportunities for both men and women if they want to do one of these jobs. So we suggest that women browse the lists of jobs that employ high percentages of men and that men browse the lists of jobs with high percentages of women. There are jobs in both sets of lists that pay well, and women or men who are interested in them and who have or can obtain the necessary education and training should consider them.

An interesting and unfortunate tidbit to bring up at your next party is that the average earnings for the jobs with the highest percentages of women is $32,966, compared to average earnings of $38,378 for the jobs with the highest percentages of men. But earnings don't tell the whole story. We computed the average growth and job openings of the jobs with the highest percentages of women and found statistics of 14.6 percent growth and 78,950 openings, compared to 8.7 percent growth and 33,972 openings for the jobs with the highest percentages of men. This discrepancy reinforces the idea that men have had more problems than women in adapting to an economy dominated by service and information-based jobs. Many women may simply be better prepared for these jobs, possessing more appropriate skills for the jobs that are now growing rapidly and have more job openings.

Best Jobs Employing the Highest Percentages of Women

Job	Percent Women
1. Dental Hygienists	98.6%
2. Preschool Teachers, Except Special Education	97.7%
3. Executive Secretaries and Administrative Assistants	96.9%
4. Legal Secretaries	96.9%
5. Medical Secretaries	96.9%
6. Secretaries, Except Legal, Medical, and Executive	96.9%
7. Dental Assistants	95.4%
8. Licensed Practical and Licensed Vocational Nurses	94.2%
9. Hairdressers, Hairstylists, and Cosmetologists	93.4%
10. Makeup Artists, Theatrical and Performance	93.4%
11. Receptionists and Information Clerks	92.7%

(continued)

(continued)

Best Jobs Employing the Highest Percentages of Women

Job	Percent Women
12. Payroll and Timekeeping Clerks	92.4%
13. Teacher Assistants	92.3%
14. Medical Records and Health Information Technicians	92.0%
15. Human Resources Assistants, Except Payroll and Timekeeping	91.9%
16. Registered Nurses	91.3%
17. Desktop Publishers	91.2%
18. Medical Assistants	90.4%
19. Medical Equipment Preparers	90.4%
20. Medical Transcriptionists	90.4%
21. Bookkeeping, Accounting, and Auditing Clerks	90.3%
22. Occupational Therapist Assistants	89.4%
23. Paralegals and Legal Assistants	89.1%
24. Nursing Aides, Orderlies, and Attendants	88.9%
25. Statement Clerks	88.1%
26. Billing, Cost, and Rate Clerks	88.1%
27. Billing, Posting, and Calculating Machine Operators	88.1%
28. Insurance Claims Clerks	87.6%
29. Insurance Policy Processing Clerks	87.6%
30. Eligibility Interviewers, Government Programs	86.3%
31. Tellers	84.8%
32. Massage Therapists	84.1%
33. Skin Care Specialists	83.0%
34. Interviewers, Except Eligibility and Loan	82.1%
35. Office Clerks, General	81.9%
36. Court Clerks	80.7%
37. Municipal Clerks	80.7%
38. License Clerks	80.7%
39. Pharmacy Technicians	80.1%
40. Surgical Technologists	80.1%
41. Veterinary Technologists and Technicians	80.1%
42. Physical Therapist Assistants	78.4%
43. Physical Therapist Aides	78.4%
44. Medical and Clinical Laboratory Technicians	78.1%
45. Court Reporters	76.8%
46. Title Examiners, Abstractors, and Searchers	76.8%
47. Loan Interviewers and Clerks	76.7%

Best Jobs Employing the Highest Percentages of Women

Job	Percent Women
48. Brokerage Clerks	75.4%
49. Correspondence Clerks	75.4%
50. Cargo and Freight Agents	75.4%
51. Tour Guides and Escorts	74.2%
52. Flight Attendants	74.2%
53. Radiation Therapists	74.1%
54. Cardiovascular Technologists and Technicians	72.9%
55. Diagnostic Medical Sonographers	72.9%
56. Nuclear Medicine Technologists	72.9%
57. Radiologic Technologists	72.9%
58. Radiologic Technicians	72.9%
59. Library Technicians	72.4%
60. First-Line Supervisors/Managers of Office and Administrative Support Workers	72.2%
61. Social and Human Service Assistants	70.5%
62. Customer Service Representatives	70.4%

The jobs in the following four lists are derived from the preceding list of the jobs employing the highest percentages of women. Keep in mind that the earnings estimates in the following lists are based on a survey of *all* workers, not just women. On average, women earn about 75 percent of the earnings of men in the same occupation. The earnings differences for the occupations in the following lists may be significantly higher or lower.

25 Best Jobs Overall Employing High Percentages of Women

Job	Percent Women	Annual Earnings	Percent Growth	Annual Openings
1. Registered Nurses	91.3%	$60,010	23.5%	233,499
2. Dental Hygienists	98.6%	$64,740	30.1%	10,433
3. Executive Secretaries and Administrative Assistants	96.9%	$38,640	14.8%	235,314
4. Customer Service Representatives	70.4%	$29,040	24.8%	600,937
5. Paralegals and Legal Assistants	89.1%	$44,990	22.2%	22,756
6. Medical Assistants	90.4%	$27,430	35.4%	92,977
7. Surgical Technologists	80.1%	$37,540	24.5%	15,365
8. Licensed Practical and Licensed Vocational Nurses	94.2%	$37,940	14.0%	70,610

(continued)

(continued)

25 Best Jobs Overall Employing High Percentages of Women

Job	Percent Women	Annual Earnings	Percent Growth	Annual Openings
9. Dental Assistants	95.4%	$31,550	29.2%	29,482
10. Physical Therapist Assistants	78.4%	$44,130	32.4%	5,957
11. Radiation Therapists	74.1%	$70,010	24.8%	1,461
12. Social and Human Service Assistants	70.5%	$26,630	33.6%	80,142
13. First-Line Supervisors/Managers of Office and Administrative Support Workers	72.2%	$44,650	5.8%	138,420
14. Radiologic Technicians	72.9%	$50,260	15.1%	12,836
15. Radiologic Technologists	72.9%	$50,260	15.1%	12,836
16. Bookkeeping, Accounting, and Auditing Clerks	90.3%	$31,560	12.5%	286,854
17. Cardiovascular Technologists and Technicians	72.9%	$44,940	25.5%	3,550
18. Occupational Therapist Assistants	89.4%	$45,050	25.4%	2,634
19. Pharmacy Technicians	80.1%	$26,720	32.0%	54,453
20. Court Reporters	76.8%	$45,330	24.5%	2,620
21. Nursing Aides, Orderlies, and Attendants	88.9%	$23,160	18.2%	321,036
22. Preschool Teachers, Except Special Education	97.7%	$23,130	26.3%	78,172
23. Receptionists and Information Clerks	92.7%	$23,710	17.2%	334,124
24. Legal Secretaries	96.9%	$38,810	11.7%	38,682
25. Brokerage Clerks	75.4%	$37,360	20.0%	10,826

Jobs 14 and 15 share 12,836 openings.

25 Best-Paying Jobs Employing High Percentages of Women

Job	Percent Women	Annual Earnings
1. Radiation Therapists	74.1%	$70,010
2. Dental Hygienists	98.6%	$64,740
3. Nuclear Medicine Technologists	72.9%	$64,670
4. Flight Attendants	74.2%	$61,120
5. Registered Nurses	91.3%	$60,010
6. Diagnostic Medical Sonographers	72.9%	$59,860
7. Radiologic Technicians	72.9%	$50,260
8. Radiologic Technologists	72.9%	$50,260
9. Court Reporters	76.8%	$45,330
10. Occupational Therapist Assistants	89.4%	$45,050

25 Best-Paying Jobs Employing High Percentages of Women

Job	Percent Women	Annual Earnings
11. Paralegals and Legal Assistants	89.1%	$44,990
12. Cardiovascular Technologists and Technicians	72.9%	$44,940
13. First-Line Supervisors/Managers of Office and Administrative Support Workers	72.2%	$44,650
14. Physical Therapist Assistants	78.4%	$44,130
15. Eligibility Interviewers, Government Programs	86.3%	$39,110
16. Legal Secretaries	96.9%	$38,810
17. Executive Secretaries and Administrative Assistants	96.9%	$38,640
18. Licensed Practical and Licensed Vocational Nurses	94.2%	$37,940
19. Surgical Technologists	80.1%	$37,540
20. Brokerage Clerks	75.4%	$37,360
21. Title Examiners, Abstractors, and Searchers	76.8%	$37,200
22. Cargo and Freight Agents	75.4%	$37,060
23. Desktop Publishers	91.2%	$35,510
24. Makeup Artists, Theatrical and Performance	93.4%	$35,250
25. Human Resources Assistants, Except Payroll and Timekeeping	91.9%	$34,970

25 Fastest-Growing Jobs Employing High Percentages of Women

Job	Percent Women	Percent Growth
1. Veterinary Technologists and Technicians	80.1%	41.0%
2. Makeup Artists, Theatrical and Performance	93.4%	39.8%
3. Medical Assistants	90.4%	35.4%
4. Skin Care Specialists	83.0%	34.3%
5. Social and Human Service Assistants	70.5%	33.6%
6. Physical Therapist Assistants	78.4%	32.4%
7. Pharmacy Technicians	80.1%	32.0%
8. Dental Hygienists	98.6%	30.1%
9. Dental Assistants	95.4%	29.2%
10. Preschool Teachers, Except Special Education	97.7%	26.3%
11. Cardiovascular Technologists and Technicians	72.9%	25.5%
12. Occupational Therapist Assistants	89.4%	25.4%
13. Customer Service Representatives	70.4%	24.8%
14. Radiation Therapists	74.1%	24.8%

(continued)

(continued)

25 Fastest-Growing Jobs Employing High Percentages of Women

Job	Percent Women	Percent Growth
15. Court Reporters	76.8%	24.5%
16. Surgical Technologists	80.1%	24.5%
17. Physical Therapist Aides	78.4%	24.4%
18. Registered Nurses	91.3%	23.5%
19. Paralegals and Legal Assistants	89.1%	22.2%
20. Tour Guides and Escorts	74.2%	21.2%
21. Massage Therapists	84.1%	20.3%
22. Brokerage Clerks	75.4%	20.0%
23. Diagnostic Medical Sonographers	72.9%	19.1%
24. Nursing Aides, Orderlies, and Attendants	88.9%	18.2%
25. Medical Records and Health Information Technicians	92.0%	17.8%

25 Jobs with the Most Openings Employing High Percentages of Women

Job	Percent Women	Annual Openings
1. Office Clerks, General	81.9%	765,803
2. Customer Service Representatives	70.4%	600,937
3. Receptionists and Information Clerks	92.7%	334,124
4. Nursing Aides, Orderlies, and Attendants	88.9%	321,036
5. Bookkeeping, Accounting, and Auditing Clerks	90.3%	286,854
6. Secretaries, Except Legal, Medical, and Executive	96.9%	239,630
7. Executive Secretaries and Administrative Assistants	96.9%	235,314
8. Registered Nurses	91.3%	233,499
9. Teacher Assistants	92.3%	193,986
10. Tellers	84.8%	146,077
11. First-Line Supervisors/Managers of Office and Administrative Support Workers	72.2%	138,420
12. Medical Assistants	90.4%	92,977
13. Billing, Cost, and Rate Clerks	88.1%	81,885
14. Billing, Posting, and Calculating Machine Operators	88.1%	81,885
15. Statement Clerks	88.1%	81,885
16. Social and Human Service Assistants	70.5%	80,142
17. Preschool Teachers, Except Special Education	97.7%	78,172
18. Hairdressers, Hairstylists, and Cosmetologists	93.4%	73,030

25 Jobs with the Most Openings Employing High Percentages of Women

Job	Percent Women	Annual Openings
19. Licensed Practical and Licensed Vocational Nurses	94.2%	70,610
20. Medical Secretaries	96.9%	60,659
21. Pharmacy Technicians	80.1%	54,453
22. Interviewers, Except Eligibility and Loan	82.1%	54,060
23. Insurance Claims Clerks	87.6%	42,246
24. Insurance Policy Processing Clerks	87.6%	42,246
25. Loan Interviewers and Clerks	76.7%	40,217

Jobs 13, 14, and 15 share 81,885 openings. Jobs 23 and 24 share 42,246 openings.

Best Jobs Employing High Percentages of Men

If you haven't already read the intro to the previous group of lists, jobs with high percentages of women, consider doing so. Much of the content there applies to these lists as well.

We didn't include these groups of lists with the assumption that men should consider only jobs with high percentages of men or that women should consider only jobs with high percentages of women. Instead, these lists are here because we think they are interesting and perhaps helpful in considering nontraditional career options. For example, some men would do very well in and enjoy some of the jobs with high percentages of women but may not have considered them seriously. Similarly, some women would very much enjoy and do well in some jobs that traditionally have been held by high percentages of men. We hope that these lists help you consider options that you simply didn't seriously consider because of gender stereotypes.

In the jobs on the following lists, more than 70 percent of the workers are men, but increasing numbers of women are entering many of these jobs.

Best Jobs Employing the Highest Percentages of Men

Job	Percent Men
1. Automotive Body and Related Repairers	99.4%
2. Automotive Glass Installers and Repairers	99.4%
3. Cement Masons and Concrete Finishers	99.3%
4. Bus and Truck Mechanics and Diesel Engine Specialists	99.1%
5. Electrical Power-Line Installers and Repairers	99.1%

(continued)

(continued)

Best Jobs Employing the Highest Percentages of Men

Job	Percent Men
6. Roofers	98.9%
7. Mobile Heavy Equipment Mechanics, Except Engines	98.6%
8. Rail Car Repairers	98.6%
9. Excavating and Loading Machine and Dragline Operators	98.5%
10. Automotive Master Mechanics	98.4%
11. Automotive Specialty Technicians	98.4%
12. Brickmasons and Blockmasons	98.4%
13. Stonemasons	98.4%
14. Operating Engineers and Other Construction Equipment Operators	98.3%
15. Pile-Driver Operators	98.3%
16. Pipe Fitters and Steamfitters	98.2%
17. Pipelayers	98.2%
18. Plumbers	98.2%
19. Electricians	98.1%
20. Commercial Pilots	97.8%
21. Pest Control Workers	97.8%
22. Reinforcing Iron and Rebar Workers	97.8%
23. Structural Iron and Steel Workers	97.8%
24. Nuclear Power Reactor Operators	97.7%
25. Power Plant Operators	97.7%
26. Stationary Engineers and Boiler Operators	97.7%
27. Construction Carpenters	97.6%
28. Rough Carpenters	97.6%
29. Security and Fire Alarm Systems Installers	97.6%
30. Tile and Marble Setters	97.6%
31. First-Line Supervisors/Managers of Construction Trades and Extraction Workers	97.4%
32. Heating and Air Conditioning Mechanics and Installers	97.3%
33. Refrigeration Mechanics and Installers	97.3%
34. Drywall and Ceiling Tile Installers	97.1%
35. Millwrights	97.1%
36. Tapers	97.1%
37. Sheet Metal Workers	96.9%
38. Boilermakers	96.9%
39. Elevator Installers and Repairers	96.9%
40. Glaziers	96.9%
41. Hazardous Materials Removal Workers	96.9%

Best Jobs Employing the Highest Percentages of Men

Job	Percent Men
42. Insulation Workers, Floor, Ceiling, and Wall	96.9%
43. Insulation Workers, Mechanical	96.9%
44. Plasterers and Stucco Masons	96.9%
45. Septic Tank Servicers and Sewer Pipe Cleaners	96.9%
46. Motorboat Mechanics	96.6%
47. Motorcycle Mechanics	96.6%
48. Forest Fire Fighters	96.5%
49. Municipal Fire Fighters	96.5%
50. Construction Laborers	96.3%
51. Highway Maintenance Workers	96.2%
52. Industrial Machinery Mechanics	96.2%
53. Maintenance Workers, Machinery	96.2%
54. Maintenance and Repair Workers, General	96.0%
55. Water and Liquid Waste Treatment Plant and System Operators	96.0%
56. Commercial Divers	95.4%
57. Control and Valve Installers and Repairers, Except Mechanical Door	95.4%
58. Helpers—Installation, Maintenance, and Repair Workers	95.4%
59. Mechanical Door Repairers	95.4%
60. Recreational Vehicle Service Technicians	95.4%
61. Tire Repairers and Changers	95.4%
62. Truck Drivers, Heavy and Tractor-Trailer	94.8%
63. Truck Drivers, Light or Delivery Services	94.8%
64. Aircraft Mechanics and Service Technicians	94.7%
65. Solderers and Brazers	94.1%
66. Welders, Cutters, and Welder Fitters	94.1%
67. Refuse and Recyclable Material Collectors	93.9%
68. Helpers—Brickmasons, Blockmasons, Stonemasons, and Tile and Marble Setters	93.8%
69. Helpers—Carpenters	93.8%
70. Helpers—Electricians	93.8%
71. Helpers—Pipelayers, Plumbers, Pipefitters, and Steamfitters	93.8%
72. Landscaping and Groundskeeping Workers	93.8%
73. Pesticide Handlers, Sprayers, and Applicators, Vegetation	93.8%
74. Tree Trimmers and Pruners	93.8%
75. Locomotive Engineers	93.5%
76. Locomotive Firers	93.5%

(continued)

(continued)

Best Jobs Employing the Highest Percentages of Men

Job	Percent Men
77. Rail Yard Engineers, Dinkey Operators, and Hostlers	93.5%
78. Railroad Conductors and Yardmasters	93.5%
79. Subway and Streetcar Operators	93.5%
80. Machinists	93.3%
81. Industrial Truck and Tractor Operators	92.8%
82. Forest Fire Fighting and Prevention Supervisors	92.8%
83. Municipal Fire Fighting and Prevention Supervisors	92.8%
84. Painters, Construction and Maintenance	92.3%
85. First-Line Supervisors/Managers of Landscaping, Lawn Service, and Groundskeeping Workers	92.0%
86. First-Line Supervisors/Managers of Mechanics, Installers, and Repairers	91.5%
87. Telecommunications Line Installers and Repairers	91.4%
88. Construction and Building Inspectors	91.2%
89. Computer, Automated Teller, and Office Machine Repairers	90.3%
90. Environmental Engineering Technicians	90.1%
91. Mapping Technicians	90.1%
92. Surveying Technicians	90.1%
93. Police Patrol Officers	87.2%
94. Sheriffs and Deputy Sheriffs	87.2%
95. Air Traffic Controllers	87.0%
96. Locksmiths and Safe Repairers	86.1%
97. Medical Equipment Repairers	86.1%
98. Storage and Distribution Managers	85.4%
99. Transportation Managers	85.4%
100. Airfield Operations Specialists	85.2%
101. Aviation Inspectors	85.2%
102. Freight and Cargo Inspectors	85.2%
103. Mates—Ship, Boat, and Barge	85.2%
104. Pilots, Ship	85.2%
105. Sailors and Marine Oilers	85.2%
106. Ship and Boat Captains	85.2%
107. Ship Engineers	85.2%
108. Transportation Vehicle, Equipment and Systems Inspectors, Except Aviation	85.2%
109. Avionics Technicians	84.8%
110. Electrical and Electronics Repairers, Commercial and Industrial Equipment	84.8%
111. Telecommunications Equipment Installers and Repairers, Except Line Installers	84.8%

Best Jobs Employing the Highest Percentages of Men

Job	Percent Men
112. First-Line Supervisors/Managers of Police and Detectives	84.5%
113. Audio and Video Equipment Technicians	84.4%
114. Broadcast Technicians	84.4%
115. Camera Operators, Television, Video, and Motion Picture	84.4%
116. Sound Engineering Technicians	84.4%
117. Parts Salespersons	83.7%
118. Industrial Production Managers	83.6%
119. Painters, Transportation Equipment	83.4%
120. Aircraft Cargo Handling Supervisors	83.3%
121. First-Line Supervisors/Managers of Helpers, Laborers, and Material Movers, Hand	83.3%
122. First-Line Supervisors/Managers of Transportation and Material-Moving Machine and Vehicle Operators	83.3%
123. Laborers and Freight, Stock, and Material Movers, Hand	83.1%
124. Tank Car, Truck, and Ship Loaders	83.1%
125. First-Line Supervisors/Managers of Production and Operating Workers	80.6%
126. Aerospace Engineering and Operations Technicians	79.4%
127. Civil Engineering Technicians	79.4%
128. Concierges	79.4%
129. Electrical Engineering Technicians	79.4%
130. Electronics Engineering Technicians	79.4%
131. Industrial Engineering Technicians	79.4%
132. Mechanical Engineering Technicians	79.4%
133. Architectural Drafters	78.2%
134. Civil Drafters	78.2%
135. Electrical Drafters	78.2%
136. Electronic Drafters	78.2%
137. First-Line Supervisors/Managers of Agricultural Crop and Horticultural Workers	78.2%
138. First-Line Supervisors/Managers of Animal Husbandry and Animal Care Workers	78.2%
139. First-Line Supervisors/Managers of Aquacultural Workers	78.2%
140. Mechanical Drafters	78.2%
141. Animal Control Workers	77.7%
142. Fire Inspectors	77.7%
143. Fire Investigators	77.7%
144. Gaming Surveillance Officers and Gaming Investigators	77.0%

(continued)

(continued)

Best Jobs Employing the Highest Percentages of Men

Job	Percent Men
145. Security Guards	77.0%
146. Chefs and Head Cooks	76.1%
147. Farmers and Ranchers	75.0%
148. Criminal Investigators and Special Agents	74.0%
149. Immigration and Customs Inspectors	74.0%
150. Police Detectives	74.0%
151. Police Identification and Records Officers	74.0%
152. First-Line Supervisors/Managers of Non-Retail Sales Workers	72.8%
153. Sales Representatives, Wholesale and Manufacturing, Except Technical and Scientific Products	72.8%
154. Sales Representatives, Wholesale and Manufacturing, Technical and Scientific Products	72.8%
155. Bailiffs	71.8%
156. Correctional Officers and Jailers	71.8%
157. Computer Support Specialists	71.1%
158. Meat, Poultry, and Fish Cutters and Trimmers	70.1%

The jobs in the following four lists are derived from the preceding list of the jobs employing the highest percentages of men. Keep in mind that the earnings estimates in the following lists are based on a survey of *all* workers, not just men. On average, men earn about 133 percent of the earnings of women in the same occupation. The earnings differences for the occupations in the following lists may be significantly higher or lower.

25 Best Jobs Overall Employing High Percentages of Men

Job	Percent Men	Annual Earnings	Percent Growth	Annual Openings
1. Sales Representatives, Wholesale and Manufacturing, Technical and Scientific Products	72.8%	$68,270	12.4%	43,469
2. Criminal Investigators and Special Agents	74.0%	$59,930	17.3%	14,746
3. Immigration and Customs Inspectors	74.0%	$59,930	17.3%	14,746
4. Police Detectives	74.0%	$59,930	17.3%	14,746
5. Police Identification and Records Officers	74.0%	$59,930	17.3%	14,746
6. Computer Support Specialists	71.1%	$42,400	12.9%	97,334
7. Construction and Building Inspectors	91.2%	$48,330	18.2%	12,606

25 Best Jobs Overall Employing High Percentages of Men

Job	Percent Men	Annual Earnings	Percent Growth	Annual Openings
8. First-Line Supervisors/Managers of Construction Trades and Extraction Workers	97.4%	$55,950	9.1%	82,923
9. Correctional Officers and Jailers	71.8%	$36,970	16.9%	56,579
10. Police Patrol Officers	87.2%	$49,630	10.8%	37,842
11. Sheriffs and Deputy Sheriffs	87.2%	$49,630	10.8%	37,842
12. Sales Representatives, Wholesale and Manufacturing, Except Technical and Scientific Products	72.8%	$50,750	8.4%	156,215
13. First-Line Supervisors/Managers of Landscaping, Lawn Service, and Groundskeeping Workers	92.0%	$38,720	17.6%	18,956
14. Pipe Fitters and Steamfitters	98.2%	$44,090	10.6%	68,643
15. Plumbers	98.2%	$44,090	10.6%	68,643
16. Automotive Master Mechanics	98.4%	$34,170	14.3%	97,350
17. Automotive Specialty Technicians	98.4%	$34,170	14.3%	97,350
18. Mates—Ship, Boat, and Barge	85.2%	$57,210	17.9%	2,665
19. Pilots, Ship	85.2%	$57,210	17.9%	2,665
20. Ship and Boat Captains	85.2%	$57,210	17.9%	2,665
21. Forest Fire Fighters	96.5%	$43,170	12.1%	18,887
22. Municipal Fire Fighters	96.5%	$43,170	12.1%	18,887
23. Landscaping and Groundskeeping Workers	93.8%	$22,240	18.1%	307,138
24. First-Line Supervisors/Managers of Non-Retail Sales Workers	72.8%	$67,020	3.7%	48,883
25. First-Line Supervisors/Managers of Police and Detectives	84.5%	$72,620	9.2%	9,373

Jobs 2, 3, 4, and 5 share 14,746 openings. Jobs 10 and 11 share 37,842 openings. Jobs 14 and 15 share 68,643 openings. Jobs 16 and 17 share 97,350 openings. Jobs 18, 19, and 20 share 2,665 openings. Jobs 21 and 22 share 18,887 openings.

25 Best-Paying Jobs Employing High Percentages of Men

Job	Percent Men	Annual Earnings
1. Air Traffic Controllers	87.0%	$112,930
2. Industrial Production Managers	83.6%	$80,560
3. Storage and Distribution Managers	85.4%	$76,310
4. Transportation Managers	85.4%	$76,310

(continued)

(continued)

25 Best-Paying Jobs Employing High Percentages of Men

Job	Percent Men	Annual Earnings
5. First-Line Supervisors/Managers of Police and Detectives	84.5%	$72,620
6. Nuclear Power Reactor Operators	97.7%	$70,410
7. Sales Representatives, Wholesale and Manufacturing, Technical and Scientific Products	72.8%	$68,270
8. Elevator Installers and Repairers	96.9%	$68,000
9. First-Line Supervisors/Managers of Non-Retail Sales Workers	72.8%	$67,020
10. Forest Fire Fighting and Prevention Supervisors	92.8%	$65,040
11. Municipal Fire Fighting and Prevention Supervisors	92.8%	$65,040
12. Commercial Pilots	97.8%	$61,640
13. Criminal Investigators and Special Agents	74.0%	$59,930
14. Immigration and Customs Inspectors	74.0%	$59,930
15. Police Detectives	74.0%	$59,930
16. Police Identification and Records Officers	74.0%	$59,930
17. Railroad Conductors and Yardmasters	93.5%	$58,650
18. Locomotive Engineers	93.5%	$57,520
19. Mates—Ship, Boat, and Barge	85.2%	$57,210
20. Pilots, Ship	85.2%	$57,210
21. Ship and Boat Captains	85.2%	$57,210
22. Power Plant Operators	97.7%	$56,640
23. Ship Engineers	85.2%	$56,090
24. First-Line Supervisors/Managers of Construction Trades and Extraction Workers	97.4%	$55,950
25. First-Line Supervisors/Managers of Mechanics, Installers, and Repairers	91.5%	$55,380

25 Fastest-Growing Jobs Employing High Percentages of Men

Job	Percent Men	Percent Growth
1. Gaming Surveillance Officers and Gaming Investigators	77.0%	33.6%
2. Environmental Engineering Technicians	90.1%	24.8%
3. Audio and Video Equipment Technicians	84.4%	24.2%
4. Aircraft Cargo Handling Supervisors	83.3%	23.3%
5. Locksmiths and Safe Repairers	86.1%	22.1%
6. Medical Equipment Repairers	86.1%	21.7%
7. Security and Fire Alarm Systems Installers	97.6%	20.2%

25 Fastest-Growing Jobs Employing High Percentages of Men

Job	Percent Men	Percent Growth
8. Tire Repairers and Changers	95.4%	20.2%
9. Mapping Technicians	90.1%	19.4%
10. Surveying Technicians	90.1%	19.4%
11. Motorboat Mechanics	96.6%	19.0%
12. Automotive Glass Installers and Repairers	99.4%	18.7%
13. Construction and Building Inspectors	91.2%	18.2%
14. Recreational Vehicle Service Technicians	95.4%	18.2%
15. Landscaping and Groundskeeping Workers	93.8%	18.1%
16. Mates—Ship, Boat, and Barge	85.2%	17.9%
17. Pilots, Ship	85.2%	17.9%
18. Ship and Boat Captains	85.2%	17.9%
19. Commercial Divers	95.4%	17.7%
20. First-Line Supervisors/Managers of Landscaping, Lawn Service, and Groundskeeping Workers	92.0%	17.6%
21. Criminal Investigators and Special Agents	74.0%	17.3%
22. Immigration and Customs Inspectors	74.0%	17.3%
23. Police Detectives	74.0%	17.3%
24. Police Identification and Records Officers	74.0%	17.3%
25. Correctional Officers and Jailers	71.8%	16.9%

25 Jobs with the Most Openings Employing High Percentages of Men

Job	Percent Men	Annual Openings
1. Laborers and Freight, Stock, and Material Movers, Hand	83.1%	630,487
2. Landscaping and Groundskeeping Workers	93.8%	307,138
3. Truck Drivers, Heavy and Tractor-Trailer	94.8%	279,032
4. Construction Laborers	96.3%	257,407
5. Construction Carpenters	97.6%	223,225
6. Rough Carpenters	97.6%	223,225
7. Security Guards	77.0%	222,085
8. Maintenance and Repair Workers, General	96.0%	165,502
9. Sales Representatives, Wholesale and Manufacturing, Except Technical and Scientific Products	72.8%	156,215
10. Truck Drivers, Light or Delivery Services	94.8%	154,330
11. Farmers and Ranchers	75.0%	129,552

(continued)

(continued)

25 Jobs with the Most Openings Employing High Percentages of Men

Job	Percent Men	Annual Openings
12. Painters, Construction and Maintenance	92.3%	101,140
13. Automotive Master Mechanics	98.4%	97,350
14. Automotive Specialty Technicians	98.4%	97,350
15. Computer Support Specialists	71.1%	97,334
16. Industrial Truck and Tractor Operators	92.8%	89,547
17. First-Line Supervisors/Managers of Construction Trades and Extraction Workers	97.4%	82,923
18. Electricians	98.1%	79,083
19. Pipe Fitters and Steamfitters	98.2%	68,643
20. Plumbers	98.2%	68,643
21. Solderers and Brazers	94.1%	61,125
22. Welders, Cutters, and Welder Fitters	94.1%	61,125
23. Correctional Officers and Jailers	71.8%	56,579
24. Operating Engineers and Other Construction Equipment Operators	98.3%	55,468
25. Parts Salespersons	83.7%	52,414

Jobs 5 and 6 share 223,225 openings. Jobs 13 and 14 share 97,350 openings. Jobs 19 and 20 share 68,643 openings. Jobs 21 and 22 share 61,125 openings.

Best Jobs Lists Based on Levels of Education and Experience

The lists in this section organize the 300 best jobs into groups based on the education or training typically required for entry. Unlike in the previous section, here we don't include separate lists for highest pay, growth, or number of openings. Instead, we provide one list that includes all the occupations in our database that fit into each of the education levels and that ranks them by their total combined score for earnings, growth, and number of openings.

These lists can help you identify a job with higher earnings or upward mobility but with a similar level of education to the job you now hold. For example, you will find jobs within the same level of education that require similar skills, yet one pays significantly better than the other, is projected to grow more rapidly, or has significantly more job openings per year. This information can help you leverage your present skills and experience into jobs that might provide better long-term career opportunities.

You can also use these lists to explore possible job options if you were to get additional training, education, or work experience. For example, you can use these lists to identify occupations that offer high potential and then look into the education or training required to get the jobs that interest you most.

The lists can also help you when you plan your education. For example, you might be thinking about a construction job but you aren't sure what kind of work you want to do. The lists show that Drywall and Ceiling Tile Installers need moderate-term on-the-job training and earn $36,520, while Automotive Glass Installers and Repairers need long-term on-the-job training but earn an average of $31,470. If you want higher earnings without lengthy training, this information might make a difference in your choice.

The Education Levels

A clear relationship exists between education and earnings—the more education or training you have, the more you are likely to earn. The lists that follow arrange all the jobs that met our criteria for inclusion in this book (see the Introduction) by level of education, training, and work experience. These are the levels typically required for a new entrant to begin work in the occupation.

We included on each list all the occupations in our database that fit into each of the education levels. We then arranged these occupations based on their total scores for earnings, growth, and number of openings.

The following definitions are used by the federal government to classify jobs based on the minimum level of education or training typically required for entry into a job. We use these definitions to construct the lists in this section. Use the training and education level descriptions as guidelines that can help you understand what is generally required, but understand that you will need to learn more about specific requirements before you make a decision on one career over another.

- **Short-term on-the-job training:** It is possible to work in these occupations and achieve an average level of performance within a few days or weeks through on-the-job training.

- **Moderate-term on-the-job training:** Occupations requiring this type of training can be performed adequately after a one- to 12-month period of combined on-the-job and informal training. Typically, untrained workers observe experienced workers performing tasks and are gradually moved into progressively more difficult assignments.

- **Long-term on-the-job training:** This training requires more than 12 months of on-the-job training or combined work experience and formal classroom instruction. This includes occupations that use formal apprenticeships for training workers that may take up to four years. It also includes intensive occupation-specific, employer-sponsored training, such as police academies. Furthermore, it includes occupations that require natural talent that must be developed over many years.

- **Work experience in a related occupation:** This type of job requires experience in a related occupation. For example, police detectives are selected based on their experience as police patrol officers.

* **Postsecondary vocational training:** This requirement can vary from training that involves a few months to usually less than one year. In a few instances, as many as four years of training may be required.
* **Associate degree:** This degree usually requires two years of full-time academic work beyond high school.

Another Warning About the Data

We warned you in the Introduction to use caution in interpreting the data we use, and we want to do it again here. The occupational data we use is the most accurate available anywhere, but it has its limitations.

For example, in the Introduction we noted that for each job in this book we identify the *minimum* amount of education or training that normally is required for entry. In some cases, additional education or training may be helpful, especially if you are competing for limited job openings.

Similarly, you need to be cautious about assuming that more education or training always leads to higher income. It is true that people with jobs that require long-term on-the-job training typically earn more than people with jobs that require short-term on-the-job training. (For the jobs in this book, the difference is an average of $40,493 versus an average of $25,180.) However, some people with short-term on-the-job training do earn more than the average for the highest-paying occupations listed in this book; furthermore, some people with long-term on-the-job training earn much less than the average shown in this book—this is particularly true early in a person's career.

So as you browse the following lists, please use them as a way to be encouraged rather than discouraged. Education and training are very important for success in the labor market of the future, but so are ability, drive, initiative, and—yes—luck.

Having said this, we encourage you to get as much education and training as you can. You used to be able to get your schooling and then close the schoolbooks forever, but this isn't a good attitude to have now. You will probably need to continue learning new things throughout your working life. This can be done by going to school, which is a good thing for many people to do. But further schooling is not necessary for many of the jobs in this book. (In fact, later in Part I you can see bonus lists of the jobs in which very few workers hold a bachelor's degree.) Many workers continue their learning through workshops, adult education programs, certification programs, employer training, professional conferences, Internet training, or reading related books and magazines. Upgrading your computer skills—and other technical skills—is particularly important in our rapidly changing workplace, and you avoid doing so at your peril.

Best Jobs Requiring Short-Term On-the-Job Training

Job	Annual Earnings	Percent Growth	Annual Openings
1. Bill and Account Collectors	$29,990	22.9%	118,709
2. Office Clerks, General	$24,460	12.6%	765,803
3. Receptionists and Information Clerks	$23,710	17.2%	334,124
4. Landscaping and Groundskeeping Workers	$22,240	18.1%	307,138
5. Human Resources Assistants, Except Payroll and Timekeeping	$34,970	11.3%	18,647
6. Sailors and Marine Oilers	$32,570	15.7%	8,600
7. Security Guards	$22,570	16.9%	222,085
8. Tellers	$22,920	13.5%	146,077
9. Interviewers, Except Eligibility and Loan	$27,320	9.5%	54,060
10. Truck Drivers, Light or Delivery Services	$26,380	8.4%	154,330
11. Helpers—Pipelayers, Plumbers, Pipefitters, and Steamfitters	$25,350	11.9%	29,332
12. Court Clerks	$32,330	8.8%	16,163
13. License Clerks	$32,330	8.8%	16,163
14. Municipal Clerks	$32,330	8.8%	16,163
15. Helpers—Carpenters	$24,340	11.7%	37,731
16. Helpers—Installation, Maintenance, and Repair Workers	$22,920	11.8%	52,058
17. Refuse and Recyclable Material Collectors	$29,420	7.4%	37,785
18. Shipping, Receiving, and Traffic Clerks	$26,990	3.7%	138,967
19. Loan Interviewers and Clerks	$31,680	–0.9%	40,217
20. Medical Equipment Preparers	$27,040	14.2%	8,363
21. Helpers—Brickmasons, Blockmasons, Stonemasons, and Tile and Marble Setters	$26,260	11.0%	22,500
22. Tire Repairers and Changers	$21,880	20.2%	18,829
23. Tree Trimmers and Pruners	$29,800	11.1%	9,621
24. Correspondence Clerks	$29,500	12.0%	4,334
25. Postal Service Mail Carriers	$44,500	1.0%	16,710
26. Industrial Truck and Tractor Operators	$28,010	–2.0%	89,547
27. Reservation and Transportation Ticket Agents and Travel Clerks	$29,820	1.1%	30,754
28. Teacher Assistants	$21,580	10.4%	193,986
29. Residential Advisors	$23,050	18.5%	8,053
30. Physical Therapist Aides	$22,990	24.4%	4,092
31. Laborers and Freight, Stock, and Material Movers, Hand	$21,900	2.1%	630,487
32. Helpers—Electricians	$24,880	6.8%	35,109
33. Postal Service Clerks	$45,050	1.2%	3,703

(continued)

(continued)

Best Jobs Requiring Short-Term On-the-Job Training

Job	Annual Earnings	Percent Growth	Annual Openings
34. Food Batchmakers	$23,730	10.9%	15,704
35. Postal Service Mail Sorters, Processors, and Processing Machine Operators	$43,700	−8.4%	6,855
36. Meat, Poultry, and Fish Cutters and Trimmers	$21,050	10.9%	17,920

Jobs 12, 13, and 14 share 16,163 openings.

Best Jobs Requiring Moderate-Term On-the-Job Training

Job	Annual Earnings	Percent Growth	Annual Openings
1. Advertising Sales Agents	$42,820	20.3%	29,233
2. Correctional Officers and Jailers	$36,970	16.9%	56,579
3. Customer Service Representatives	$29,040	24.8%	600,937
4. Truck Drivers, Heavy and Tractor-Trailer	$36,220	10.4%	279,032
5. Brokerage Clerks	$37,360	20.0%	10,826
6. Bookkeeping, Accounting, and Auditing Clerks	$31,560	12.5%	286,854
7. Medical Assistants	$27,430	35.4%	92,977
8. Roofers	$33,240	14.3%	38,398
9. Cargo and Freight Agents	$37,060	16.5%	9,967
10. Operating Engineers and Other Construction Equipment Operators	$38,130	8.4%	55,468
11. Painters, Construction and Maintenance	$32,080	11.8%	101,140
12. Dental Assistants	$31,550	29.2%	29,482
13. Social and Human Service Assistants	$26,630	33.6%	80,142
14. Cement Masons and Concrete Finishers	$33,840	11.4%	34,625
15. Aircraft Structure, Surfaces, Rigging, and Systems Assemblers	$45,420	12.8%	6,550
16. Maintenance and Repair Workers, General	$32,570	10.1%	165,502
17. Mapping Technicians	$33,640	19.4%	8,299
18. Surveying Technicians	$33,640	19.4%	8,299
19. Pharmacy Technicians	$26,720	32.0%	54,453
20. Production, Planning, and Expediting Clerks	$39,690	4.2%	52,735
21. Medical Secretaries	$28,950	16.7%	60,659
22. Bus Drivers, Transit and Intercity	$33,160	12.5%	27,100
23. Police, Fire, and Ambulance Dispatchers	$32,660	13.6%	17,628

Best Jobs Requiring Moderate-Term On-the-Job Training

Job	Annual Earnings	Percent Growth	Annual Openings
24. Drywall and Ceiling Tile Installers	$36,520	7.3%	30,945
25. Construction Laborers	$27,310	10.9%	257,407
26. Locksmiths and Safe Repairers	$33,230	22.1%	3,545
27. Subway and Streetcar Operators	$50,520	12.1%	587
28. Tapers	$42,050	7.1%	9,026
29. Eligibility Interviewers, Government Programs	$39,110	3.1%	11,337
30. Railroad Conductors and Yardmasters	$58,650	9.1%	3,235
31. Demonstrators and Product Promoters	$22,570	18.0%	32,779
32. Highway Maintenance Workers	$32,600	8.9%	24,774
33. Billing, Cost, and Rate Clerks	$29,970	4.4%	81,885
34. Billing, Posting, and Calculating Machine Operators	$29,970	4.4%	81,885
35. Statement Clerks	$29,970	4.4%	81,885
36. Cooks, Institution and Cafeteria	$21,340	10.8%	111,898
37. Bailiffs	$36,900	11.2%	2,223
38. Insulation Workers, Mechanical	$36,570	8.6%	5,787
39. Payroll and Timekeeping Clerks	$33,810	3.1%	18,544
40. Tour Guides and Escorts	$22,110	21.2%	15,027
41. Locomotive Engineers	$57,520	2.9%	3,548
42. Animal Trainers	$26,190	22.7%	6,713
43. Bus Drivers, School	$25,860	9.3%	59,809
44. Hazardous Materials Removal Workers	$36,330	11.2%	1,933
45. Dispatchers, Except Police, Fire, and Ambulance	$33,140	1.5%	29,793
46. Pile-Driver Operators	$47,550	8.3%	701
47. Excavating and Loading Machine and Dragline Operators	$34,050	8.3%	6,562
48. Locomotive Firers	$45,310	2.9%	3,548
49. Pest Control Workers	$29,030	15.5%	6,006
50. Pesticide Handlers, Sprayers, and Applicators, Vegetation	$28,560	14.0%	7,443
51. Secretaries, Except Legal, Medical, and Executive	$28,220	1.2%	239,630
52. Control and Valve Installers and Repairers, Except Mechanical Door	$46,140	0.3%	3,855
53. Maintenance Workers, Machinery	$35,590	–1.1%	15,055
54. Gaming Surveillance Officers and Gaming Investigators	$27,440	33.6%	2,124
55. Rail Yard Engineers, Dinkey Operators, and Hostlers	$39,020	2.9%	3,548
56. Tank Car, Truck, and Ship Loaders	$33,140	9.2%	4,519
57. Mechanical Door Repairers	$31,880	14.9%	1,706
58. Insurance Claims Clerks	$32,040	–1.3%	42,246

(continued)

(continued)

Best Jobs Requiring Moderate-Term On-the-Job Training

Job	Annual Earnings	Percent Growth	Annual Openings
59. Insurance Policy Processing Clerks	$32,040	−1.3%	42,246
60. Painters, Transportation Equipment	$36,000	8.4%	3,268
61. Slaughterers and Meat Packers	$22,500	12.7%	15,511
62. Title Examiners, Abstractors, and Searchers	$37,200	−1.2%	6,880
63. Pipelayers	$31,280	8.7%	8,902
64. Inspectors, Testers, Sorters, Samplers, and Weighers	$30,310	−7.0%	75,361
65. Septic Tank Servicers and Sewer Pipe Cleaners	$32,740	10.2%	3,156
66. Team Assemblers	$24,630	0.1%	264,135
67. Insulation Workers, Floor, Ceiling, and Wall	$31,280	8.4%	6,580
68. Animal Control Workers	$29,320	12.5%	3,377
69. Concierges	$25,540	14.1%	4,893
70. Statistical Assistants	$32,540	7.6%	4,836
71. Merchandise Displayers and Window Trimmers	$24,830	10.7%	9,103
72. Structural Metal Fabricators and Fitters	$31,030	−0.2%	20,746
73. Multiple Machine Tool Setters, Operators, and Tenders, Metal and Plastic	$30,390	0.3%	15,709
74. Parts Salespersons	$28,130	−2.2%	52,414

Jobs 17 and 18 share 8,299 openings. Jobs 33, 34, and 35 share 81,885 openings. Jobs 41, 48, and 55 share 3,548 openings. Jobs 58 and 59 share 42,246 openings.

Best Jobs Requiring Long-Term On-the-Job Training

Job	Annual Earnings	Percent Growth	Annual Openings
1. Police Patrol Officers	$49,630	10.8%	37,842
2. Sheriffs and Deputy Sheriffs	$49,630	10.8%	37,842
3. Pipe Fitters and Steamfitters	$44,090	10.6%	68,643
4. Plumbers	$44,090	10.6%	68,643
5. Flight Attendants	$61,120	10.6%	10,773
6. Talent Directors	$61,090	11.1%	8,992
7. Technical Directors/Managers	$61,090	11.1%	8,992
8. Claims Examiners, Property and Casualty Insurance	$53,560	8.9%	22,024
9. Insurance Adjusters, Examiners, and Investigators	$53,560	8.9%	22,024
10. Forest Fire Fighters	$43,170	12.1%	18,887
11. Municipal Fire Fighters	$43,170	12.1%	18,887

Best Jobs Requiring Long-Term On-the-Job Training

Job	Annual Earnings	Percent Growth	Annual Openings
12. Construction Carpenters	$37,660	10.3%	223,225
13. Rough Carpenters	$37,660	10.3%	223,225
14. Coaches and Scouts	$27,840	14.6%	51,100
15. Electricians	$44,780	7.4%	79,083
16. Mobile Heavy Equipment Mechanics, Except Engines	$41,450	12.3%	11,037
17. Tile and Marble Setters	$38,720	15.4%	9,066
18. Automotive Body and Related Repairers	$35,690	11.6%	37,469
19. Boilermakers	$50,700	14.0%	2,333
20. Cooks, Restaurant	$21,220	11.5%	238,542
21. Interpreters and Translators	$37,490	23.6%	6,630
22. Industrial Machinery Mechanics	$42,350	9.0%	23,361
23. Purchasing Agents, Except Wholesale, Retail, and Farm Products	$52,460	0.1%	22,349
24. Brickmasons and Blockmasons	$44,070	9.7%	17,569
25. Nuclear Power Reactor Operators	$70,410	10.6%	233
26. Athletes and Sports Competitors	$38,440	19.2%	4,293
27. Water and Liquid Waste Treatment Plant and System Operators	$37,090	13.8%	9,575
28. Air Traffic Controllers	$112,930	10.2%	1,213
29. Audio and Video Equipment Technicians	$36,050	24.2%	4,681
30. Environmental Compliance Inspectors	$48,400	4.9%	15,841
31. Equal Opportunity Representatives and Officers	$48,400	4.9%	15,841
32. Government Property Inspectors and Investigators	$48,400	4.9%	15,841
33. Licensing Examiners and Inspectors	$48,400	4.9%	15,841
34. Heating and Air Conditioning Mechanics and Installers	$38,360	8.7%	29,719
35. Refrigeration Mechanics and Installers	$38,360	8.7%	29,719
36. Sheet Metal Workers	$39,210	6.7%	31,677
37. Electrical Power-Line Installers and Repairers	$52,570	7.2%	6,401
38. Elevator Installers and Repairers	$68,000	8.8%	2,850
39. Wholesale and Retail Buyers, Except Farm Products	$46,960	–0.1%	19,847
40. Motorboat Mechanics	$34,210	19.0%	4,326
41. Glaziers	$35,230	11.9%	6,416
42. Reinforcing Iron and Rebar Workers	$37,890	11.5%	4,502
43. Telecommunications Line Installers and Repairers	$47,220	4.6%	14,719
44. Bakers	$22,590	10.0%	31,442
45. Automotive Glass Installers and Repairers	$31,470	18.7%	3,457
46. Photographers	$27,720	10.3%	16,100

(continued)

(continued)

Best Jobs Requiring Long-Term On-the-Job Training

Job	Annual Earnings	Percent Growth	Annual Openings
47. Millwrights	$46,090	5.8%	4,758
48. Umpires, Referees, and Other Sports Officials	$24,770	16.0%	4,461
49. Chemical Plant and System Operators	$50,860	−15.3%	5,620
50. Recreational Vehicle Service Technicians	$31,760	18.2%	2,442
51. Petroleum Pump System Operators, Refinery Operators, and Gaugers	$53,010	−13.4%	4,477
52. Structural Iron and Steel Workers	$42,130	6.0%	6,969
53. Farmers and Ranchers	$33,360	−8.5%	129,552
54. Airfield Operations Specialists	$38,320	11.8%	245
55. Fine Artists, Including Painters, Sculptors, and Illustrators	$42,070	9.9%	3,830
56. Machinists	$35,230	−3.1%	39,505
57. Motorcycle Mechanics	$30,300	12.5%	3,564
58. Power Plant Operators	$56,640	2.7%	1,796
59. Rail Car Repairers	$44,970	5.1%	1,989
60. Stationary Engineers and Boiler Operators	$47,640	3.4%	1,892
61. Stonemasons	$36,950	10.0%	2,657
62. Plasterers and Stucco Masons	$36,430	8.1%	4,509

Jobs 1 and 2 share 37,842 openings. Jobs 3 and 4 share 68,643 openings. Jobs 6 and 7 share 8,992 openings with each other and with three other jobs not included in this list. Jobs 8 and 9 share 22,024 openings. Jobs 10 and 11 share 18,887 openings. Jobs 12 and 13 share 223,225 openings. Jobs 30, 31, 32, and 33 share 15,841 openings with each other and with another job not included in this list. Jobs 34 and 35 share 29,719 openings.

Best Jobs Requiring Work Experience in a Related Job

Job	Annual Earnings	Percent Growth	Annual Openings
1. Sales Representatives, Wholesale and Manufacturing, Technical and Scientific Products	$68,270	12.4%	43,469
2. Criminal Investigators and Special Agents	$59,930	17.3%	14,746
3. Immigration and Customs Inspectors	$59,930	17.3%	14,746
4. Police Detectives	$59,930	17.3%	14,746
5. Police Identification and Records Officers	$59,930	17.3%	14,746
6. Vocational Education Teachers, Postsecondary	$45,850	22.9%	19,313
7. Self-Enrichment Education Teachers	$34,580	23.1%	64,449
8. Gaming Managers	$64,410	24.4%	549

Best Jobs Requiring Work Experience in a Related Job

Job	Annual Earnings	Percent Growth	Annual Openings
9. First-Line Supervisors/Managers of Non-Retail Sales Workers	$67,020	3.7%	48,883
10. Mates—Ship, Boat, and Barge	$57,210	17.9%	2,665
11. Pilots, Ship	$57,210	17.9%	2,665
12. Ship and Boat Captains	$57,210	17.9%	2,665
13. Executive Secretaries and Administrative Assistants	$38,640	14.8%	235,314
14. First-Line Supervisors/Managers of Construction Trades and Extraction Workers	$55,950	9.1%	82,923
15. Real Estate Brokers	$58,860	11.1%	18,689
16. Construction and Building Inspectors	$48,330	18.2%	12,606
17. First-Line Supervisors/Managers of Landscaping, Lawn Service, and Groundskeeping Workers	$38,720	17.6%	18,956
18. First-Line Supervisors/Managers of Police and Detectives	$72,620	9.2%	9,373
19. Sales Representatives, Wholesale and Manufacturing, Except Technical and Scientific Products	$50,750	8.4%	156,215
20. Forest Fire Fighting and Prevention Supervisors	$65,040	11.5%	3,771
21. Industrial Production Managers	$80,560	−5.9%	14,889
22. Municipal Fire Fighting and Prevention Supervisors	$65,040	11.5%	3,771
23. Storage and Distribution Managers	$76,310	8.3%	6,994
24. Transportation Managers	$76,310	8.3%	6,994
25. Gaming Supervisors	$42,980	23.4%	4,602
26. First-Line Supervisors/Managers of Mechanics, Installers, and Repairers	$55,380	7.3%	24,361
27. First-Line Supervisors/Managers of Correctional Officers	$55,720	12.5%	4,180
28. First-Line Supervisors/Managers of Personal Service Workers	$33,900	15.5%	37,555
29. Private Detectives and Investigators	$37,640	18.2%	7,329
30. Aviation Inspectors	$51,440	16.4%	2,122
31. Freight and Cargo Inspectors	$51,440	16.4%	2,122
32. Transportation Vehicle, Equipment and Systems Inspectors, Except Aviation	$51,440	16.4%	2,122
33. First-Line Supervisors/Managers of Transportation and Material-Moving Machine and Vehicle Operators	$49,850	10.2%	16,580
34. First-Line Supervisors/Managers of Office and Administrative Support Workers	$44,650	5.8%	138,420
35. First-Line Supervisors/Managers of Food Preparation and Serving Workers	$28,040	11.3%	154,175
36. First-Line Supervisors/Managers of Housekeeping and Janitorial Workers	$32,850	12.7%	30,613

(continued)

Best Jobs Requiring Work Experience in a Related Job

Job	Annual Earnings	Percent Growth	Annual Openings
37. Ship Engineers	$56,090	14.1%	1,102
38. First-Line Supervisors/Managers of Helpers, Laborers, and Material Movers, Hand	$40,640	12.5%	13,877
39. Food Service Managers	$44,570	5.0%	59,302
40. First-Line Supervisors/Managers of Production and Operating Workers	$48,670	–4.8%	46,144
41. First-Line Supervisors/Managers of Retail Sales Workers	$34,470	4.2%	221,241
42. Aircraft Cargo Handling Supervisors	$37,760	23.3%	523
43. Coroners	$48,400	4.9%	15,841
44. Lodging Managers	$44,240	12.2%	5,529
45. Emergency Management Specialists	$48,380	12.3%	1,538
46. Fire Inspectors	$50,830	11.0%	644
47. Fire Investigators	$50,830	11.0%	644
48. Postmasters and Mail Superintendents	$57,900	–0.8%	1,627
49. Chefs and Head Cooks	$37,160	7.6%	9,401

Jobs 2, 3, 4, and 5 share 14,746 openings. Jobs 10, 11, and 12 share 2,665 openings. Jobs 20 and 21 share 3,771 openings. Jobs 23 and 24 share 6,994 openings. Jobs 30, 31, and 32 share 2,122 openings. Job 43 shares 15,841 openings with four other jobs not included in this list. Jobs 46 and 47 share 644 openings.

Best Jobs Requiring Postsecondary Vocational Training

Job	Annual Earnings	Percent Growth	Annual Openings
1. Licensed Practical and Licensed Vocational Nurses	$37,940	14.0%	70,610
2. Automotive Master Mechanics	$34,170	14.3%	97,350
3. Automotive Specialty Technicians	$34,170	14.3%	97,350
4. Surgical Technologists	$37,540	24.5%	15,365
5. Preschool Teachers, Except Special Education	$23,130	26.3%	78,172
6. Court Reporters	$45,330	24.5%	2,620
7. Fitness Trainers and Aerobics Instructors	$27,680	26.8%	51,235
8. Real Estate Sales Agents	$40,600	10.6%	61,232
9. Nursing Aides, Orderlies, and Attendants	$23,160	18.2%	321,036
10. Aircraft Mechanics and Service Technicians	$49,010	10.6%	9,708
11. Bus and Truck Mechanics and Diesel Engine Specialists	$38,640	11.5%	25,428
12. Commercial Pilots	$61,640	13.2%	1,425
13. Emergency Medical Technicians and Paramedics	$28,400	19.2%	19,513

Best Jobs Requiring Postsecondary Vocational Training

Job	Annual Earnings	Percent Growth	Annual Openings
14. Massage Therapists	$34,870	20.3%	9,193
15. Architectural Drafters	$43,310	6.1%	16,238
16. Civil Drafters	$43,310	6.1%	16,238
17. Insurance Appraisers, Auto Damage	$51,500	12.5%	1,030
18. Security and Fire Alarm Systems Installers	$35,390	20.2%	5,729
19. Telecommunications Equipment Installers and Repairers, Except Line Installers	$54,070	2.5%	13,541
20. Electrical and Electronics Repairers, Commercial and Industrial Equipment	$47,110	6.8%	6,607
21. Skin Care Specialists	$27,190	34.3%	6,643
22. Hairdressers, Hairstylists, and Cosmetologists	$22,210	12.4%	73,030
23. Makeup Artists, Theatrical and Performance	$35,250	39.8%	392
24. Mechanical Drafters	$44,740	5.2%	10,902
25. Medical Transcriptionists	$31,250	13.5%	18,080
26. Camera Operators, Television, Video, and Motion Picture	$41,850	11.5%	3,496
27. Commercial Divers	$41,610	17.7%	248
28. Electrical Drafters	$49,250	4.1%	4,786
29. Electronic Drafters	$49,250	4.1%	4,786
30. Embalmers	$36,800	14.3%	1,660
31. Sound Engineering Technicians	$46,550	9.1%	1,194
32. Avionics Technicians	$48,100	8.1%	1,193
33. Solderers and Brazers	$32,270	5.1%	61,125
34. Welders, Cutters, and Welder Fitters	$32,270	5.1%	61,125
35. Computer, Automated Teller, and Office Machine Repairers	$37,100	3.0%	22,330
36. Library Technicians	$27,680	8.5%	29,075
37. Desktop Publishers	$35,510	1.0%	6,420

Jobs 2 and 3 share 97,350 openings. Jobs 15 and 16 share 16,238 openings. Jobs 28 and 29 share 4,786 openings. Jobs 33 and 34 share 61,125 openings.

Best Jobs Requiring an Associate Degree

Job	Annual Earnings	Percent Growth	Annual Openings
1. Registered Nurses	$60,010	23.5%	233,499
2. Dental Hygienists	$64,740	30.1%	10,433
3. Paralegals and Legal Assistants	$44,990	22.2%	22,756

(continued)

(continued)

Best Jobs Requiring an Associate Degree

Job	Annual Earnings	Percent Growth	Annual Openings
4. Radiologic Technicians	$50,260	15.1%	12,836
5. Radiologic Technologists	$50,260	15.1%	12,836
6. Physical Therapist Assistants	$44,130	32.4%	5,957
7. Radiation Therapists	$70,010	24.8%	1,461
8. Computer Support Specialists	$42,400	12.9%	97,334
9. Respiratory Therapists	$50,070	22.6%	5,563
10. Veterinary Technologists and Technicians	$27,970	41.0%	14,674
11. Environmental Science and Protection Technicians, Including Health	$39,370	28.0%	8,404
12. Diagnostic Medical Sonographers	$59,860	19.1%	3,211
13. Interior Designers	$43,970	19.5%	8,434
14. Cardiovascular Technologists and Technicians	$44,940	25.5%	3,550
15. Electrical Engineering Technicians	$52,140	3.6%	12,583
16. Electronics Engineering Technicians	$52,140	3.6%	12,583
17. Occupational Therapist Assistants	$45,050	25.4%	2,634
18. Medical Records and Health Information Technicians	$29,290	17.8%	39,048
19. Funeral Directors	$50,370	12.5%	3,939
20. Legal Secretaries	$38,810	11.7%	38,682
21. Nuclear Medicine Technologists	$64,670	14.8%	1,290
22. Industrial Engineering Technicians	$47,490	9.9%	6,172
23. Environmental Engineering Technicians	$40,690	24.8%	2,162
24. Medical and Clinical Laboratory Technicians	$34,270	15.0%	10,866
25. Civil Engineering Technicians	$42,580	10.2%	7,499
26. Nuclear Equipment Operation Technicians	$66,140	6.7%	1,021
27. Nuclear Monitoring Technicians	$66,140	6.7%	1,021
28. Medical Equipment Repairers	$40,320	21.7%	2,351
29. Aerospace Engineering and Operations Technicians	$54,930	10.4%	707
30. Geological Sample Test Technicians	$50,950	8.6%	1,895
31. Geophysical Data Technicians	$50,950	8.6%	1,895
32. Fashion Designers	$62,810	5.0%	1,968
33. Mechanical Engineering Technicians	$47,280	6.4%	3,710
34. First-Line Supervisors/Managers of Agricultural Crop and Horticultural Workers	$38,510	–0.4%	11,898
35. First-Line Supervisors/Managers of Animal Husbandry and Animal Care Workers	$38,510	–0.4%	11,898
36. First-Line Supervisors/Managers of Aquacultural Workers	$38,510	–0.4%	11,898
37. City and Regional Planning Aides	$35,870	12.4%	3,571

Best Jobs Requiring an Associate Degree			
Job	Annual Earnings	Percent Growth	Annual Openings
38. Social Science Research Assistants	$35,870	12.4%	3,571
39. Chemical Technicians	$40,740	5.8%	4,010
40. Agricultural Technicians	$33,630	6.6%	4,049
41. Food Science Technicians	$33,630	6.6%	4,049
42. Broadcast Technicians	$32,230	12.1%	2,955

Jobs 4 and 5 share 12,836 openings. Jobs 15 and 16 share 12,583 openings. Jobs 26 and 27 share 1,021 openings. Jobs 30 and 31 share 1,895 openings. Jobs 34, 35, and 36 share 11,898 openings. Jobs 37 and 38 share 3,571 openings. Jobs 40 and 41 share 4,049 openings.

Best Jobs Lists Based on Interests

This group of lists organizes the 300 best jobs into 16 interest areas. You can use these lists to identify jobs quickly based on your interests. Within each interest area, jobs are listed in order of their combined score on earnings, job growth, and job openings.

Find the interest area or areas that appeal to you most and review the jobs in those areas. When you find jobs you want to explore in more detail, look up their descriptions in Part II. You can also review interest areas in which you've had past experience, education, or training to see whether other jobs in those areas would meet your current requirements.

Note: The 16 interest areas used in these lists are those used in the *New Guide for Occupational Exploration,* Fourth Edition, published by JIST. The original Guide for Occupational Exploration (GOE) was developed by the U.S. Department of Labor as an intuitive way to assist in career exploration. The 16 interest areas used in the *New GOE* are based on the 16 career clusters that the U.S. Department of Education's Office of Vocational and Adult Education developed around 1999 and that many states now use to organize their career-oriented programs and career information.

Descriptions for the 16 Interest Areas

Brief descriptions follow for the 16 interest areas we use in the lists. The descriptions are from the *New Guide for Occupational Exploration,* Fourth Edition. Some of them refer to jobs (as examples) that aren't included in this book.

Also note that we put each of the 300 best jobs into only one interest area list, the one it fit into best. However, many jobs could be included in more than one list, so consider reviewing several interest areas to find jobs that you might otherwise overlook.

❋ Agriculture and Natural Resources: *An interest in working with plants, animals, forests, or mineral resources for agriculture, horticulture, conservation, extraction, and other purposes.* You can satisfy this interest by working in farming, landscaping, forestry, fishing, mining, and related fields. You may like doing physical work outdoors, such as on a farm or ranch, in a forest, or on a drilling rig. If you have a scientific curiosity, you could study plants and animals or analyze biological or rock samples in a lab. If you have management ability, you could own, operate, or manage a fish hatchery, a landscaping business, or a greenhouse.

❋ Architecture and Construction: *An interest in designing, assembling, and maintaining components of buildings and other structures.* You may want to be part of the team of architects, drafters, and others who design buildings and render the plans. If construction interests you, you might find fulfillment in the many building projects that are being undertaken at all times. If you like to organize and plan, you can find careers in managing these projects. Or you can play a more direct role in putting up and finishing buildings by doing jobs such as plumbing, carpentry, masonry, painting, or roofing, either as a skilled craftsworker or as a helper. You can prepare the building site by operating heavy equipment or installing, maintaining, and repairing vital building equipment and systems such as electricity and heating.

❋ Arts and Communication: *An interest in creatively expressing feelings or ideas, in communicating news or information, or in performing.* You can satisfy this interest in creative, verbal, or performing activities. For example, if you enjoy literature, perhaps writing or editing would appeal to you. Journalism and public relations are other fields for people who like to use their writing or speaking skills. Do you prefer to work in the performing arts? If so, you could direct or perform in drama, music, or dance. If you especially enjoy the visual arts, you could create paintings, sculpture, or ceramics or design products or visual displays. A flair for technology might lead you to specialize in photography, broadcast production, or dispatching.

❋ Business and Administration: *An interest in making a business organization or function run smoothly.* You can satisfy this interest by working in a position of leadership or by specializing in a function that contributes to the overall effort in a business, a nonprofit organization, or a government agency. If you especially enjoy working with people, you may find fulfillment from working in human resources. An interest in numbers may lead you to consider accounting, finance, budgeting, billing, or financial record-keeping. A job as an administrative assistant may interest you if you like a variety of tasks in a busy environment. If you are good with details and word processing, you may enjoy a job as a secretary or data-entry clerk. Or perhaps you would do well as the manager of a business.

❋ Education and Training: *An interest in helping people learn.* You can satisfy this interest by teaching students, who may be preschoolers, retirees, or any age in between. You may specialize in a particular academic field or work with learners of a particular age, with a particular interest, or with a particular learning problem. Working in a library or museum may give you an opportunity to expand people's understanding of the world.

❋ Finance and Insurance: *An interest in helping businesses and people be assured of a financially secure future.* You can satisfy this interest by working in a financial or insurance business in a leadership or support role. If you like gathering and analyzing information, you may find fulfillment as an insurance adjuster or financial analyst. Or you may deal with information at the clerical level as a banking or insurance clerk or in person-to-person situations providing customer service. Another way to interact with people is to sell financial or insurance services that will meet their needs.

❋ Government and Public Administration: *An interest in helping a government agency serve the needs of the public.* You can satisfy this interest by working in a position of leadership or by specializing in a function that contributes to the role of government. You may help protect the public by working as an inspector or examiner to enforce standards. If you enjoy using clerical skills, you could work as a clerk in a law court or government office. Or perhaps you prefer the top-down perspective of a government executive or urban planner.

❋ Health Science: *An interest in helping people and animals be healthy.* You can satisfy this interest by working on a health-care team as a doctor, therapist, or nurse. You might specialize in one of the many different parts of the body (such as the teeth or eyes) or in one of the many different types of care. Or you may want to be a generalist who deals with the whole patient. If you like technology, you might find satisfaction working with X rays or new diagnostic methods. You might work with healthy people, helping them eat right. If you enjoy working with animals, you might care for them and keep them healthy.

❋ Hospitality, Tourism, and Recreation: *An interest in catering to the personal wishes and needs of others so that they can enjoy a clean environment, good food and drink, comfortable lodging away from home, and recreation.* You can satisfy this interest by providing services for the convenience, care, and pampering of others in hotels, restaurants, airplanes, beauty parlors, and so on. You may want to use your love of cooking as a chef. If you like working with people, you may want to provide personal services by being a travel guide, a flight attendant, a concierge, a hairdresser, or a waiter. You may want to work in cleaning and building services if you like a clean environment. If you enjoy sports or games, you could work for an athletic team or casino.

❋ Human Service: *An interest in improving people's social, mental, emotional, or spiritual well-being.* You can satisfy this interest as a counselor, social worker, or religious worker who helps people sort out their complicated lives or solve personal problems. You may work as a caretaker for very young people or the elderly. Or you may interview people to help identify the social services they need.

❋ Information Technology: *An interest in designing, developing, managing, and supporting information systems.* You can satisfy this interest by working with hardware, software, multimedia, or integrated systems. If you like to use your organizational skills, you might work as a systems or database administrator. Or you can solve complex problems as a software engineer or systems analyst. If you enjoy getting your hands on hardware, you might find work servicing computers, peripherals, and information-intense machines such as cash registers and ATMs.

❋ Law and Public Safety: *An interest in upholding people's rights or in protecting people and property by using authority, inspecting, or investigating.* You can satisfy this interest by working in law, law enforcement, fire fighting, the military, and related fields. For example, if you enjoy mental challenge and intrigue, you could investigate crimes or fires for a living. If you enjoy working with verbal skills and research skills, you may want to defend citizens in court or research deeds, wills, and other legal documents. If you want to help people in critical situations, you may want to fight fires, work as a police officer, or become a paramedic. Or, if you want more routine work in public safety, perhaps a job in guarding, patrolling, or inspecting would appeal to you. If you have management ability, you could seek a leadership position in law enforcement and the protective services. Work in the military gives you a chance to use technical and leadership skills while serving your country.

❋ Manufacturing: *An interest in processing materials into intermediate or final products or maintaining and repairing products by using machines or hand tools.* You can satisfy this interest by working in one of many industries that mass-produce goods or by working for a utility that distributes electric power or other resources. You might enjoy manual work, using your hands or hand tools in highly skilled jobs such as assembling engines or electronic equipment. If you enjoy making machines run efficiently or fixing them when they break down, you could seek a job installing or repairing such devices as copiers, aircraft engines, cars, or watches. Perhaps you prefer to set up or operate machines that are used to manufacture products made of food, glass, or paper. You could enjoy cutting and grinding metal and plastic parts to desired shapes and measurements. Or you may want to operate equipment in systems that provide water and process wastewater. You may like inspecting, sorting, counting, or weighing products. Another option is to work with your hands and machinery to move boxes and freight in a warehouse. If leadership appeals to you, you could manage people engaged in production and repair.

❋ Retail and Wholesale Sales and Service: *An interest in bringing others to a particular point of view by personal persuasion and by sales and promotional techniques.* You can satisfy this interest in various jobs that involve persuasion and selling. If you like using knowledge of science, you may enjoy selling pharmaceutical, medical, or electronic products or services. Real estate offers several kinds of sales jobs as well. If you like speaking on the phone, you could work as a telemarketer. Or you may enjoy selling apparel and other merchandise in a retail setting. If you prefer to help people, you may want a job in customer service.

❋ Scientific Research, Engineering, and Mathematics: *An interest in discovering, collecting, and analyzing information about the natural world; in applying scientific research findings to problems in medicine, the life sciences, human behavior, and the natural sciences; in imagining and manipulating quantitative data; and in applying technology to manufacturing, transportation, and other economic activities.* You can satisfy this interest by working with the knowledge and processes of the sciences. You may enjoy researching and developing new knowledge in mathematics, or perhaps solving problems in the physical, life, or social sciences would appeal to you. You may want to study engineering and help create new machines, processes, and structures. If you want to work with scientific equipment and procedures, you could seek a job in a research or testing laboratory.

❋ Transportation, Distribution, and Logistics: *An interest in operations that move people or materials.* You can satisfy this interest by managing a transportation service, by helping vehicles keep on their assigned schedules and routes, or by driving or piloting a vehicle. If you enjoy taking responsibility, perhaps managing a rail line would appeal to you. If you work well with details and can take pressure on the job, you might consider being an air traffic controller. Or would you rather get out on the highway, on the water, or up in the air? If so, you could drive a truck from state to state, be employed on a ship, or fly a crop duster over a cornfield. If you prefer to stay closer to home, you could drive a delivery van, taxi, or school bus. You can use your physical strength to load freight and arrange it so that it gets to its destination in one piece.

Best Jobs for People Interested in Agriculture and Natural Resources

Job	Annual Earnings	Percent Growth	Annual Openings
1. First-Line Supervisors/Managers of Construction Trades and Extraction Workers	$55,950	9.1%	82,923
2. First-Line Supervisors/Managers of Landscaping, Lawn Service, and Groundskeeping Workers	$38,720	17.6%	18,956
3. Environmental Science and Protection Technicians, Including Health	$39,370	28.0%	8,404
4. Landscaping and Groundskeeping Workers	$22,240	18.1%	307,138
5. First-Line Supervisors/Managers of Agricultural Crop and Horticultural Workers	$38,510	–0.4%	11,898
6. First-Line Supervisors/Managers of Animal Husbandry and Animal Care Workers	$38,510	–0.4%	11,898
7. First-Line Supervisors/Managers of Aquacultural Workers	$38,510	–0.4%	11,898
8. Geological Sample Test Technicians	$50,950	8.6%	1,895
9. Geophysical Data Technicians	$50,950	8.6%	1,895
10. Tree Trimmers and Pruners	$29,800	11.1%	9,621
11. Excavating and Loading Machine and Dragline Operators	$34,050	8.3%	6,562
12. Farmers and Ranchers	$33,360	–8.5%	129,552
13. Pest Control Workers	$29,030	15.5%	6,006
14. Pesticide Handlers, Sprayers, and Applicators, Vegetation	$28,560	14.0%	7,443
15. Agricultural Technicians	$33,630	6.6%	4,049
16. Food Science Technicians	$33,630	6.6%	4,049

Jobs 5, 6, and 7 share 11,898 openings with each other and with two other jobs not included in this list. Jobs 8 and 9 share 1,895 openings. Jobs 15 and 16 share 4,049 openings.

Best Jobs for People Interested in Architecture and Construction

Job	Annual Earnings	Percent Growth	Annual Openings
1. Pipe Fitters and Steamfitters	$44,090	10.6%	68,643
2. Plumbers	$44,090	10.6%	68,643
3. Construction Carpenters	$37,660	10.3%	223,225
4. Rough Carpenters	$37,660	10.3%	223,225
5. Electricians	$44,780	7.4%	79,083
6. Roofers	$33,240	14.3%	38,398
7. Tile and Marble Setters	$38,720	15.4%	9,066
8. Painters, Construction and Maintenance	$32,080	11.8%	101,140
9. Boilermakers	$50,700	14.0%	2,333
10. Brickmasons and Blockmasons	$44,070	9.7%	17,569
11. Construction Laborers	$27,310	10.9%	257,407
12. Cement Masons and Concrete Finishers	$33,840	11.4%	34,625
13. Operating Engineers and Other Construction Equipment Operators	$38,130	8.4%	55,468
14. Maintenance and Repair Workers, General	$32,570	10.1%	165,502
15. Commercial Divers	$41,610	17.7%	248
16. Heating and Air Conditioning Mechanics and Installers	$38,360	8.7%	29,719
17. Refrigeration Mechanics and Installers	$38,360	8.7%	29,719
18. Helpers—Installation, Maintenance, and Repair Workers	$22,920	11.8%	52,058
19. Elevator Installers and Repairers	$68,000	8.8%	2,850
20. Helpers—Carpenters	$24,340	11.7%	37,731
21. Security and Fire Alarm Systems Installers	$35,390	20.2%	5,729
22. Helpers—Pipelayers, Plumbers, Pipefitters, and Steamfitters	$25,350	11.9%	29,332
23. Glaziers	$35,230	11.9%	6,416
24. Reinforcing Iron and Rebar Workers	$37,890	11.5%	4,502
25. Sheet Metal Workers	$39,210	6.7%	31,677
26. Electrical Power-Line Installers and Repairers	$52,570	7.2%	6,401
27. Telecommunications Equipment Installers and Repairers, Except Line Installers	$54,070	2.5%	13,541
28. Architectural Drafters	$43,310	6.1%	16,238
29. Civil Drafters	$43,310	6.1%	16,238
30. Telecommunications Line Installers and Repairers	$47,220	4.6%	14,719
31. Helpers—Brickmasons, Blockmasons, Stonemasons, and Tile and Marble Setters	$26,260	11.0%	22,500
32. Drywall and Ceiling Tile Installers	$36,520	7.3%	30,945
33. Highway Maintenance Workers	$32,600	8.9%	24,774
34. Tapers	$42,050	7.1%	9,026
35. Pile-Driver Operators	$47,550	8.3%	701

Best Jobs for People Interested in Architecture and Construction

Job	Annual Earnings	Percent Growth	Annual Openings
36. Hazardous Materials Removal Workers	$36,330	11.2%	1,933
37. Structural Iron and Steel Workers	$42,130	6.0%	6,969
38. Stonemasons	$36,950	10.0%	2,657
39. Insulation Workers, Mechanical	$36,570	8.6%	5,787
40. Septic Tank Servicers and Sewer Pipe Cleaners	$32,740	10.2%	3,156
41. Pipelayers	$31,280	8.7%	8,902
42. Helpers—Electricians	$24,880	6.8%	35,109
43. Plasterers and Stucco Masons	$36,430	8.1%	4,509
44. Insulation Workers, Floor, Ceiling, and Wall	$31,280	8.4%	6,580

Jobs 1 and 2 share 68,643 openings. Jobs 3 and 4 share 223,225 openings. Jobs 16 and 17 share 29,719 openings. Jobs 28 and 29 share 16,238 openings.

Best Jobs for People Interested in Arts and Communication

Job	Annual Earnings	Percent Growth	Annual Openings
1. Interior Designers	$43,970	19.5%	8,434
2. Talent Directors	$61,090	11.1%	8,992
3. Technical Directors/Managers	$61,090	11.1%	8,992
4. Interpreters and Translators	$37,490	23.6%	6,630
5. Police, Fire, and Ambulance Dispatchers	$32,660	13.6%	17,628
6. Audio and Video Equipment Technicians	$36,050	24.2%	4,681
7. Camera Operators, Television, Video, and Motion Picture	$41,850	11.5%	3,496
8. Air Traffic Controllers	$112,930	10.2%	1,213
9. Makeup Artists, Theatrical and Performance	$35,250	39.8%	392
10. Dispatchers, Except Police, Fire, and Ambulance	$33,140	1.5%	29,793
11. Fashion Designers	$62,810	5.0%	1,968
12. Fine Artists, Including Painters, Sculptors, and Illustrators	$42,070	9.9%	3,830
13. Photographers	$27,720	10.3%	16,100
14. Merchandise Displayers and Window Trimmers	$24,830	10.7%	9,103
15. Airfield Operations Specialists	$38,320	11.8%	245
16. Broadcast Technicians	$32,230	12.1%	2,955
17. Sound Engineering Technicians	$46,550	9.1%	1,194

Jobs 2 and 3 share 8,992 openings with each other and with three other jobs not included in this list.

Best Jobs for People Interested in Business and Administration

Job	Annual Earnings	Percent Growth	Annual Openings
1. Executive Secretaries and Administrative Assistants	$38,640	14.8%	235,314
2. Bookkeeping, Accounting, and Auditing Clerks	$31,560	12.5%	286,854
3. First-Line Supervisors/Managers of Office and Administrative Support Workers	$44,650	5.8%	138,420
4. Brokerage Clerks	$37,360	20.0%	10,826
5. Legal Secretaries	$38,810	11.7%	38,682
6. Office Clerks, General	$24,460	12.6%	765,803
7. First-Line Supervisors/Managers of Housekeeping and Janitorial Workers	$32,850	12.7%	30,613
8. Industrial Engineering Technicians	$47,490	9.9%	6,172
9. Medical Secretaries	$28,950	16.7%	60,659
10. Production, Planning, and Expediting Clerks	$39,690	4.2%	52,735
11. Billing, Cost, and Rate Clerks	$29,970	4.4%	81,885
12. Billing, Posting, and Calculating Machine Operators	$29,970	4.4%	81,885
13. Human Resources Assistants, Except Payroll and Timekeeping	$34,970	11.3%	18,647
14. Statement Clerks	$29,970	4.4%	81,885
15. Secretaries, Except Legal, Medical, and Executive	$28,220	1.2%	239,630
16. Postal Service Clerks	$45,050	1.2%	3,703
17. Shipping, Receiving, and Traffic Clerks	$26,990	3.7%	138,967
18. Postal Service Mail Sorters, Processors, and Processing Machine Operators	$43,700	–8.4%	6,855
19. Correspondence Clerks	$29,500	12.0%	4,334
20. Payroll and Timekeeping Clerks	$33,810	3.1%	18,544

Jobs 11, 12, and 14 share 81,885 openings.

Best Jobs for People Interested in Education and Training

Job	Annual Earnings	Percent Growth	Annual Openings
1. Fitness Trainers and Aerobics Instructors	$27,680	26.8%	51,235
2. Self-Enrichment Education Teachers	$34,580	23.1%	64,449
3. Preschool Teachers, Except Special Education	$23,130	26.3%	78,172
4. Vocational Education Teachers, Postsecondary	$45,850	22.9%	19,313
5. Teacher Assistants	$21,580	10.4%	193,986
6. Library Technicians	$27,680	8.5%	29,075

Best Jobs for People Interested in Finance and Insurance

Job	Annual Earnings	Percent Growth	Annual Openings
1. Bill and Account Collectors	$29,990	22.9%	118,709
2. Claims Examiners, Property and Casualty Insurance	$53,560	8.9%	22,024
3. Insurance Adjusters, Examiners, and Investigators	$53,560	8.9%	22,024
4. Tellers	$22,920	13.5%	146,077
5. Insurance Appraisers, Auto Damage	$51,500	12.5%	1,030
6. Insurance Claims Clerks	$32,040	−1.3%	42,246
7. Insurance Policy Processing Clerks	$32,040	−1.3%	42,246
8. Loan Interviewers and Clerks	$31,680	−0.9%	40,217

Jobs 2 and 3 share 22,024 openings. Jobs 6 and 7 share 42,246 openings.

Best Jobs for People Interested in Government and Public Administration

Job	Annual Earnings	Percent Growth	Annual Openings
1. Immigration and Customs Inspectors	$59,930	17.3%	14,746
2. Aviation Inspectors	$51,440	16.4%	2,122
3. Freight and Cargo Inspectors	$51,440	16.4%	2,122
4. Transportation Vehicle, Equipment and Systems Inspectors, Except Aviation	$51,440	16.4%	2,122
5. Construction and Building Inspectors	$48,330	18.2%	12,606
6. Court Clerks	$32,330	8.8%	16,163
7. Court Reporters	$45,330	24.5%	2,620
8. Environmental Compliance Inspectors	$48,400	4.9%	15,841
9. Equal Opportunity Representatives and Officers	$48,400	4.9%	15,841
10. Government Property Inspectors and Investigators	$48,400	4.9%	15,841
11. License Clerks	$32,330	8.8%	16,163
12. Licensing Examiners and Inspectors	$48,400	4.9%	15,841
13. Municipal Clerks	$32,330	8.8%	16,163
14. Nuclear Monitoring Technicians	$66,140	6.7%	1,021
15. City and Regional Planning Aides	$35,870	12.4%	3,571
16. Fire Inspectors	$50,830	11.0%	644

Job 1 shares 14,746 openings with three other jobs not included in this list. Jobs 2, 3, and 4 share 2,122 openings. Jobs 6, 11, and 13 share 16,163 openings. Jobs 8, 9, 10, and 12 share 15,841 openings with each other and with another job not included in this list. Job 14 shares 1,021 openings with another job not included in this list. Job 15 shares 3,571 openings with another job not included in this list. Job 16 shares 644 openings with another job not included in this list.

Best Jobs for People Interested in Health Science

Job	Annual Earnings	Percent Growth	Annual Openings
1. Registered Nurses	$60,010	23.5%	233,499
2. Dental Hygienists	$64,740	30.1%	10,433
3. Medical Assistants	$27,430	35.4%	92,977
4. Dental Assistants	$31,550	29.2%	29,482
5. Pharmacy Technicians	$26,720	32.0%	54,453
6. Veterinary Technologists and Technicians	$27,970	41.0%	14,674
7. Physical Therapist Assistants	$44,130	32.4%	5,957
8. Surgical Technologists	$37,540	24.5%	15,365
9. Radiation Therapists	$70,010	24.8%	1,461
10. Radiologic Technicians	$50,260	15.1%	12,836
11. Radiologic Technologists	$50,260	15.1%	12,836
12. Cardiovascular Technologists and Technicians	$44,940	25.5%	3,550
13. Licensed Practical and Licensed Vocational Nurses	$37,940	14.0%	70,610
14. Occupational Therapist Assistants	$45,050	25.4%	2,634
15. Respiratory Therapists	$50,070	22.6%	5,563
16. Diagnostic Medical Sonographers	$59,860	19.1%	3,211
17. Medical Records and Health Information Technicians	$29,290	17.8%	39,048
18. Nursing Aides, Orderlies, and Attendants	$23,160	18.2%	321,036
19. Coroners	$48,400	4.9%	15,841
20. Massage Therapists	$34,870	20.3%	9,193
21. Medical and Clinical Laboratory Technicians	$34,270	15.0%	10,866
22. Nuclear Medicine Technologists	$64,670	14.8%	1,290
23. Medical Transcriptionists	$31,250	13.5%	18,080
24. Animal Trainers	$26,190	22.7%	6,713
25. Physical Therapist Aides	$22,990	24.4%	4,092
26. Embalmers	$36,800	14.3%	1,660
27. Medical Equipment Preparers	$27,040	14.2%	8,363

Jobs 10 and 11 share 12,836 openings. Job 19 shares 15,841 openings with four other jobs not included in this list.

Best Jobs for People Interested in Hospitality, Tourism, and Recreation

Job	Annual Earnings	Percent Growth	Annual Openings
1. Gaming Managers	$64,410	24.4%	549
2. First-Line Supervisors/Managers of Personal Service Workers	$33,900	15.5%	37,555

Best Jobs for People Interested in Hospitality, Tourism, and Recreation

Job	Annual Earnings	Percent Growth	Annual Openings
3. Gaming Supervisors	$42,980	23.4%	4,602
4. Coaches and Scouts	$27,840	14.6%	51,100
5. First-Line Supervisors/Managers of Food Preparation and Serving Workers	$28,040	11.3%	154,175
6. Food Service Managers	$44,570	5.0%	59,302
7. Skin Care Specialists	$27,190	34.3%	6,643
8. Flight Attendants	$61,120	10.6%	10,773
9. Athletes and Sports Competitors	$38,440	19.2%	4,293
10. Lodging Managers	$44,240	12.2%	5,529
11. Hairdressers, Hairstylists, and Cosmetologists	$22,210	12.4%	73,030
12. Tour Guides and Escorts	$22,110	21.2%	15,027
13. Cooks, Restaurant	$21,220	11.5%	238,542
14. Chefs and Head Cooks	$37,160	7.6%	9,401
15. Cooks, Institution and Cafeteria	$21,340	10.8%	111,898
16. Reservation and Transportation Ticket Agents and Travel Clerks	$29,820	1.1%	30,754
17. Concierges	$25,540	14.1%	4,893
18. Umpires, Referees, and Other Sports Officials	$24,770	16.0%	4,461

Best Jobs for People Interested in Human Service

Job	Annual Earnings	Percent Growth	Annual Openings
1. Social and Human Service Assistants	$26,630	33.6%	80,142
2. Interviewers, Except Eligibility and Loan	$27,320	9.5%	54,060
3. Eligibility Interviewers, Government Programs	$39,110	3.1%	11,337
4. Residential Advisors	$23,050	18.5%	8,053

Best Jobs for People Interested in Information Technology

Job	Annual Earnings	Percent Growth	Annual Openings
1. Computer Support Specialists	$42,400	12.9%	97,334
2. Computer, Automated Teller, and Office Machine Repairers	$37,100	3.0%	22,330

Best Jobs for People Interested in Law and Public Safety

Job	Annual Earnings	Percent Growth	Annual Openings
1. Criminal Investigators and Special Agents	$59,930	17.3%	14,746
2. Police Detectives	$59,930	17.3%	14,746
3. Police Identification and Records Officers	$59,930	17.3%	14,746
4. Paralegals and Legal Assistants	$44,990	22.2%	22,756
5. Correctional Officers and Jailers	$36,970	16.9%	56,579
6. Emergency Medical Technicians and Paramedics	$28,400	19.2%	19,513
7. Police Patrol Officers	$49,630	10.8%	37,842
8. Security Guards	$22,570	16.9%	222,085
9. Sheriffs and Deputy Sheriffs	$49,630	10.8%	37,842
10. First-Line Supervisors/Managers of Correctional Officers	$55,720	12.5%	4,180
11. Private Detectives and Investigators	$37,640	18.2%	7,329
12. Forest Fire Fighters	$43,170	12.1%	18,887
13. Forest Fire Fighting and Prevention Supervisors	$65,040	11.5%	3,771
14. Municipal Fire Fighters	$43,170	12.1%	18,887
15. Municipal Fire Fighting and Prevention Supervisors	$65,040	11.5%	3,771
16. First-Line Supervisors/Managers of Police and Detectives	$72,620	9.2%	9,373
17. Gaming Surveillance Officers and Gaming Investigators	$27,440	33.6%	2,124
18. Emergency Management Specialists	$48,380	12.3%	1,538
19. Animal Control Workers	$29,320	12.5%	3,377
20. Fire Investigators	$50,830	11.0%	644
21. Title Examiners, Abstractors, and Searchers	$37,200	−1.2%	6,880
22. Bailiffs	$36,900	11.2%	2,223

Jobs 1, 2, and 3 share 14,746 openings with each other and with another job not included in this list. Jobs 7 and 9 share 37,842 openings. Jobs 12 and 14 share 18,887 openings. Jobs 13 and 15 share 3,771 openings. Job 20 shares 644 openings with another job not included in this list.

Best Jobs for People Interested in Manufacturing

Job	Annual Earnings	Percent Growth	Annual Openings
1. Automotive Master Mechanics	$34,170	14.3%	97,350
2. Automotive Specialty Technicians	$34,170	14.3%	97,350
3. First-Line Supervisors/Managers of Mechanics, Installers, and Repairers	$55,380	7.3%	24,361
4. Automotive Body and Related Repairers	$35,690	11.6%	37,469
5. Bus and Truck Mechanics and Diesel Engine Specialists	$38,640	11.5%	25,428
6. Aircraft Mechanics and Service Technicians	$49,010	10.6%	9,708

Best Jobs for People Interested in Manufacturing

Job	Annual Earnings	Percent Growth	Annual Openings
7. Aircraft Structure, Surfaces, Rigging, and Systems Assemblers	$45,420	12.8%	6,550
8. First-Line Supervisors/Managers of Helpers, Laborers, and Material Movers, Hand	$40,640	12.5%	13,877
9. Industrial Machinery Mechanics	$42,350	9.0%	23,361
10. Mobile Heavy Equipment Mechanics, Except Engines	$41,450	12.3%	11,037
11. Water and Liquid Waste Treatment Plant and System Operators	$37,090	13.8%	9,575
12. First-Line Supervisors/Managers of Production and Operating Workers	$48,670	–4.8%	46,144
13. Ship Engineers	$56,090	14.1%	1,102
14. Medical Equipment Repairers	$40,320	21.7%	2,351
15. Motorboat Mechanics	$34,210	19.0%	4,326
16. Tire Repairers and Changers	$21,880	20.2%	18,829
17. Electrical and Electronics Repairers, Commercial and Industrial Equipment	$47,110	6.8%	6,607
18. Industrial Production Managers	$80,560	–5.9%	14,889
19. Locksmiths and Safe Repairers	$33,230	22.1%	3,545
20. Solderers and Brazers	$32,270	5.1%	61,125
21. Welders, Cutters, and Welder Fitters	$32,270	5.1%	61,125
22. Nuclear Power Reactor Operators	$70,410	10.6%	233
23. Millwrights	$46,090	5.8%	4,758
24. Machinists	$35,230	–3.1%	39,505
25. Refuse and Recyclable Material Collectors	$29,420	7.4%	37,785
26. Automotive Glass Installers and Repairers	$31,470	18.7%	3,457
27. Bakers	$22,590	10.0%	31,442
28. Slaughterers and Meat Packers	$22,500	12.7%	15,511
29. Recreational Vehicle Service Technicians	$31,760	18.2%	2,442
30. Avionics Technicians	$48,100	8.1%	1,193
31. Food Batchmakers	$23,730	10.9%	15,704
32. Power Plant Operators	$56,640	2.7%	1,796
33. Team Assemblers	$24,630	0.1%	264,135
34. Meat, Poultry, and Fish Cutters and Trimmers	$21,050	10.9%	17,920
35. Chemical Plant and System Operators	$50,860	–15.3%	5,620
36. Control and Valve Installers and Repairers, Except Mechanical Door	$46,140	0.3%	3,855
37. Mechanical Door Repairers	$31,880	14.9%	1,706

(continued)

(continued)

Best Jobs for People Interested in Manufacturing

Job	Annual Earnings	Percent Growth	Annual Openings
38. Petroleum Pump System Operators, Refinery Operators, and Gaugers	$53,010	−13.4%	4,477
39. Maintenance Workers, Machinery	$35,590	−1.1%	15,055
40. Painters, Transportation Equipment	$36,000	8.4%	3,268
41. Tank Car, Truck, and Ship Loaders	$33,140	9.2%	4,519
42. Industrial Truck and Tractor Operators	$28,010	−2.0%	89,547
43. Stationary Engineers and Boiler Operators	$47,640	3.4%	1,892
44. Rail Car Repairers	$44,970	5.1%	1,989
45. Inspectors, Testers, Sorters, Samplers, and Weighers	$30,310	−7.0%	75,361
46. Motorcycle Mechanics	$30,300	12.5%	3,564
47. Desktop Publishers	$35,510	1.0%	6,420
48. Structural Metal Fabricators and Fitters	$31,030	−0.2%	20,746
49. Multiple Machine Tool Setters, Operators, and Tenders, Metal and Plastic	$30,390	0.3%	15,709

Jobs 1 and 2 share 97,350 openings. Jobs 20 and 21 share 61,125 openings.

Best Jobs for People Interested in Retail and Wholesale Sales and Service

Job	Annual Earnings	Percent Growth	Annual Openings
1. Customer Service Representatives	$29,040	24.8%	600,937
2. Sales Representatives, Wholesale and Manufacturing, Technical and Scientific Products	$68,270	12.4%	43,469
3. Sales Representatives, Wholesale and Manufacturing, Except Technical and Scientific Products	$50,750	8.4%	156,215
4. Receptionists and Information Clerks	$23,710	17.2%	334,124
5. Advertising Sales Agents	$42,820	20.3%	29,233
6. First-Line Supervisors/Managers of Non-Retail Sales Workers	$67,020	3.7%	48,883
7. Real Estate Sales Agents	$40,600	10.6%	61,232
8. First-Line Supervisors/Managers of Retail Sales Workers	$34,470	4.2%	221,241
9. Real Estate Brokers	$58,860	11.1%	18,689
10. Funeral Directors	$50,370	12.5%	3,939

Best Jobs for People Interested in Retail and Wholesale Sales and Service

Job	Annual Earnings	Percent Growth	Annual Openings
11. Demonstrators and Product Promoters	$22,570	18.0%	32,779
12. Purchasing Agents, Except Wholesale, Retail, and Farm Products	$52,460	0.1%	22,349
13. Parts Salespersons	$28,130	–2.2%	52,414
14. Wholesale and Retail Buyers, Except Farm Products	$46,960	–0.1%	19,847

Best Jobs for People Interested in Scientific Research, Engineering, and Mathematics

Job	Annual Earnings	Percent Growth	Annual Openings
1. Electrical Engineering Technicians	$52,140	3.6%	12,583
2. Electronics Engineering Technicians	$52,140	3.6%	12,583
3. Mapping Technicians	$33,640	19.4%	8,299
4. Surveying Technicians	$33,640	19.4%	8,299
5. Civil Engineering Technicians	$42,580	10.2%	7,499
6. Aerospace Engineering and Operations Technicians	$54,930	10.4%	707
7. Mechanical Drafters	$44,740	5.2%	10,902
8. Nuclear Equipment Operation Technicians	$66,140	6.7%	1,021
9. Electrical Drafters	$49,250	4.1%	4,786
10. Electronic Drafters	$49,250	4.1%	4,786
11. Environmental Engineering Technicians	$40,690	24.8%	2,162
12. Mechanical Engineering Technicians	$47,280	6.4%	3,710
13. Social Science Research Assistants	$35,870	12.4%	3,571
14. Statistical Assistants	$32,540	7.6%	4,836
15. Chemical Technicians	$40,740	5.8%	4,010

Jobs 1 and 2 share 12,583 openings. Jobs 3 and 4 share 8,299 openings. Job 8 shares 1,021 openings with another job not included in this list. Jobs 9 and 10 share 4,786 openings. Job 13 shares 3,571 openings with another job not included in this list.

Best Jobs for People Interested in Transportation, Distribution, and Logistics

Job	Annual Earnings	Percent Growth	Annual Openings
1. Mates—Ship, Boat, and Barge	$57,210	17.9%	2,665
2. Pilots, Ship	$57,210	17.9%	2,665
3. Ship and Boat Captains	$57,210	17.9%	2,665
4. Storage and Distribution Managers	$76,310	8.3%	6,994
5. Transportation Managers	$76,310	8.3%	6,994
6. Cargo and Freight Agents	$37,060	16.5%	9,967
7. First-Line Supervisors/Managers of Transportation and Material-Moving Machine and Vehicle Operators	$49,850	10.2%	16,580
8. Truck Drivers, Heavy and Tractor-Trailer	$36,220	10.4%	279,032
9. Commercial Pilots	$61,640	13.2%	1,425
10. Bus Drivers, Transit and Intercity	$33,160	12.5%	27,100
11. Railroad Conductors and Yardmasters	$58,650	9.1%	3,235
12. Sailors and Marine Oilers	$32,570	15.7%	8,600
13. Locomotive Engineers	$57,520	2.9%	3,548
14. Bus Drivers, School	$25,860	9.3%	59,809
15. Truck Drivers, Light or Delivery Services	$26,380	8.4%	154,330
16. Aircraft Cargo Handling Supervisors	$37,760	23.3%	523
17. Postal Service Mail Carriers	$44,500	1.0%	16,710
18. Subway and Streetcar Operators	$50,520	12.1%	587
19. Locomotive Firers	$45,310	2.9%	3,548
20. Laborers and Freight, Stock, and Material Movers, Hand	$21,900	2.1%	630,487
21. Rail Yard Engineers, Dinkey Operators, and Hostlers	$39,020	2.9%	3,548
22. Postmasters and Mail Superintendents	$57,900	–0.8%	1,627

Jobs 1, 2, and 3 share 2,665 openings. Jobs 4 and 5 share 6,994 openings. Jobs 13, 19, and 21 share 3,548 openings.

Best Jobs Lists Based on Personality Types

These lists organize the 300 best jobs into groups matching six personality types. The personality types are Realistic, Investigative, Artistic, Social, Enterprising, and Conventional. This system was developed by John Holland and is used in the *Self-Directed Search (SDS)* and other career assessment inventories and information systems.

If you have used one of these career inventories or systems, the lists will help you identify jobs that most closely match these personality types. Even if you have not used one of these systems, the concept of personality types and the jobs that are related to them can help you identify jobs that suit the type of person you are.

As we did for the education levels, we have created only one list for each personality type. We've ranked the jobs within each personality type based on their total combined scores for earnings, growth, and annual job openings. Each job is listed in the one personality type it most closely matches, even though it might also fit into others. Consider reviewing the jobs for more than one personality type so you don't overlook possible jobs that would interest you.

Descriptions of the Six Personality Types

Following are brief descriptions for each of the six personality types used in the lists. Select the two or three descriptions that most closely describe you and then use the lists to identify jobs that best fit these personality types.

- **Realistic:** These occupations frequently involve work activities that include practical, hands-on problems and solutions. They often deal with plants; animals; and real-world materials such as wood, tools, and machinery. Many of the occupations require working outside and don't involve a lot of paperwork or working closely with others.

- **Investigative:** These occupations frequently involve working with ideas and require an extensive amount of thinking. These occupations can involve searching for facts and figuring out problems mentally.

- **Artistic:** These occupations frequently involve working with forms, designs, and patterns. They often require self-expression, and the work can be done without following a clear set of rules.

- **Social:** These occupations frequently involve working with, communicating with, and teaching people. These occupations often involve helping or providing service to others.

- **Enterprising:** These occupations frequently involve starting up and carrying out projects. These occupations can involve leading people and making many decisions. They sometimes require risk taking and often deal with business.

- **Conventional:** These occupations frequently involve following set procedures and routines. These occupations can include working with data and details more than with ideas. Usually there is a clear line of authority to follow.

Best Jobs for People with a Realistic Personality Type

Job	Annual Earnings	Percent Growth	Annual Openings
1. Construction and Building Inspectors	$48,330	18.2%	12,606
2. Computer Support Specialists	$42,400	12.9%	97,334
3. Radiologic Technicians	$50,260	15.1%	12,836
4. Radiologic Technologists	$50,260	15.1%	12,836
5. Correctional Officers and Jailers	$36,970	16.9%	56,579
6. Police Patrol Officers	$49,630	10.8%	37,842
7. Surgical Technologists	$37,540	24.5%	15,365
8. Pipe Fitters and Steamfitters	$44,090	10.6%	68,643
9. Plumbers	$44,090	10.6%	68,643
10. Automotive Master Mechanics	$34,170	14.3%	97,350
11. Automotive Specialty Technicians	$34,170	14.3%	97,350
12. Forest Fire Fighters	$43,170	12.1%	18,887
13. Municipal Fire Fighters	$43,170	12.1%	18,887
14. Pilots, Ship	$57,210	17.9%	2,665
15. Cardiovascular Technologists and Technicians	$44,940	25.5%	3,550
16. Construction Carpenters	$37,660	10.3%	223,225
17. Rough Carpenters	$37,660	10.3%	223,225
18. Roofers	$33,240	14.3%	38,398
19. Landscaping and Groundskeeping Workers	$22,240	18.1%	307,138
20. Truck Drivers, Heavy and Tractor-Trailer	$36,220	10.4%	279,032
21. Tile and Marble Setters	$38,720	15.4%	9,066
22. Bus and Truck Mechanics and Diesel Engine Specialists	$38,640	11.5%	25,428
23. Aviation Inspectors	$51,440	16.4%	2,122
24. Electricians	$44,780	7.4%	79,083
25. Freight and Cargo Inspectors	$51,440	16.4%	2,122
26. Transportation Vehicle, Equipment and Systems Inspectors, Except Aviation	$51,440	16.4%	2,122
27. Aircraft Structure, Surfaces, Rigging, and Systems Assemblers	$45,420	12.8%	6,550
28. Security Guards	$22,570	16.9%	222,085
29. Aircraft Mechanics and Service Technicians	$49,010	10.6%	9,708
30. Mobile Heavy Equipment Mechanics, Except Engines	$41,450	12.3%	11,037
31. Automotive Body and Related Repairers	$35,690	11.6%	37,469
32. Athletes and Sports Competitors	$38,440	19.2%	4,293
33. Painters, Construction and Maintenance	$32,080	11.8%	101,140
34. Audio and Video Equipment Technicians	$36,050	24.2%	4,681
35. Boilermakers	$50,700	14.0%	2,333

Best Jobs for People with a Realistic Personality Type

Job	Annual Earnings	Percent Growth	Annual Openings
36. Brickmasons and Blockmasons	$44,070	9.7%	17,569
37. Commercial Pilots	$61,640	13.2%	1,425
38. Industrial Machinery Mechanics	$42,350	9.0%	23,361
39. Surveying Technicians	$33,640	19.4%	8,299
40. Veterinary Technologists and Technicians	$27,970	41.0%	14,674
41. Environmental Engineering Technicians	$40,690	24.8%	2,162
42. Water and Liquid Waste Treatment Plant and System Operators	$37,090	13.8%	9,575
43. Security and Fire Alarm Systems Installers	$35,390	20.2%	5,729
44. Ship Engineers	$56,090	14.1%	1,102
45. Bus Drivers, Transit and Intercity	$33,160	12.5%	27,100
46. Medical Equipment Repairers	$40,320	21.7%	2,351
47. Medical and Clinical Laboratory Technicians	$34,270	15.0%	10,866
48. Operating Engineers and Other Construction Equipment Operators	$38,130	8.4%	55,468
49. Cement Masons and Concrete Finishers	$33,840	11.4%	34,625
50. Heating and Air Conditioning Mechanics and Installers	$38,360	8.7%	29,719
51. Refrigeration Mechanics and Installers	$38,360	8.7%	29,719
52. Maintenance and Repair Workers, General	$32,570	10.1%	165,502
53. Construction Laborers	$27,310	10.9%	257,407
54. Tire Repairers and Changers	$21,880	20.2%	18,829
55. Motorboat Mechanics	$34,210	19.0%	4,326
56. Electrical Engineering Technicians	$52,140	3.6%	12,583
57. Electronics Engineering Technicians	$52,140	3.6%	12,583
58. Sheet Metal Workers	$39,210	6.7%	31,677
59. Telecommunications Equipment Installers and Repairers, Except Line Installers	$54,070	2.5%	13,541
60. Sailors and Marine Oilers	$32,570	15.7%	8,600
61. Civil Engineering Technicians	$42,580	10.2%	7,499
62. Electrical Power-Line Installers and Repairers	$52,570	7.2%	6,401
63. Cooks, Restaurant	$21,220	11.5%	238,542
64. Elevator Installers and Repairers	$68,000	8.8%	2,850
65. Subway and Streetcar Operators	$50,520	12.1%	587
66. Telecommunications Line Installers and Repairers	$47,220	4.6%	14,719
67. Civil Drafters	$43,310	6.1%	16,238

(continued)

(continued)

Best Jobs for People with a Realistic Personality Type

Job	Annual Earnings	Percent Growth	Annual Openings
68. Animal Trainers	$26,190	22.7%	6,713
69. Locksmiths and Safe Repairers	$33,230	22.1%	3,545
70. Commercial Divers	$41,610	17.7%	248
71. Helpers—Installation, Maintenance, and Repair Workers	$22,920	11.8%	52,058
72. Nuclear Power Reactor Operators	$70,410	10.6%	233
73. Drywall and Ceiling Tile Installers	$36,520	7.3%	30,945
74. Helpers—Carpenters	$24,340	11.7%	37,731
75. Reinforcing Iron and Rebar Workers	$37,890	11.5%	4,502
76. Camera Operators, Television, Video, and Motion Picture	$41,850	11.5%	3,496
77. Helpers—Pipelayers, Plumbers, Pipefitters, and Steamfitters	$25,350	11.9%	29,332
78. Electrical and Electronics Repairers, Commercial and Industrial Equipment	$47,110	6.8%	6,607
79. Glaziers	$35,230	11.9%	6,416
80. Cooks, Institution and Cafeteria	$21,340	10.8%	111,898
81. Aerospace Engineering and Operations Technicians	$54,930	10.4%	707
82. Mechanical Drafters	$44,740	5.2%	10,902
83. Tapers	$42,050	7.1%	9,026
84. Truck Drivers, Light or Delivery Services	$26,380	8.4%	154,330
85. Highway Maintenance Workers	$32,600	8.9%	24,774
86. Pest Control Workers	$29,030	15.5%	6,006
87. Automotive Glass Installers and Repairers	$31,470	18.7%	3,457
88. Bus Drivers, School	$25,860	9.3%	59,809
89. Helpers—Brickmasons, Blockmasons, Stonemasons, and Tile and Marble Setters	$26,260	11.0%	22,500
90. Medical Equipment Preparers	$27,040	14.2%	8,363
91. Pesticide Handlers, Sprayers, and Applicators, Vegetation	$28,560	14.0%	7,443
92. Slaughterers and Meat Packers	$22,500	12.7%	15,511
93. Electrical Drafters	$49,250	4.1%	4,786
94. Embalmers	$36,800	14.3%	1,660
95. Locomotive Engineers	$57,520	2.9%	3,548
96. Geological Sample Test Technicians	$50,950	8.6%	1,895
97. Computer, Automated Teller, and Office Machine Repairers	$37,100	3.0%	22,330
98. Recreational Vehicle Service Technicians	$31,760	18.2%	2,442
99. Millwrights	$46,090	5.8%	4,758
100. Solderers and Brazers	$32,270	5.1%	61,125

Best Jobs for People with a Realistic Personality Type

Job	Annual Earnings	Percent Growth	Annual Openings
101. Welders, Cutters, and Welder Fitters	$32,270	5.1%	61,125
102. Structural Iron and Steel Workers	$42,130	6.0%	6,969
103. Gaming Surveillance Officers and Gaming Investigators	$27,440	33.6%	2,124
104. Farmers and Ranchers	$33,360	−8.5%	129,552
105. Mechanical Engineering Technicians	$47,280	6.4%	3,710
106. Refuse and Recyclable Material Collectors	$29,420	7.4%	37,785
107. Nuclear Equipment Operation Technicians	$66,140	6.7%	1,021
108. Nuclear Monitoring Technicians	$66,140	6.7%	1,021
109. Petroleum Pump System Operators, Refinery Operators, and Gaugers	$53,010	−13.4%	4,477
110. Tree Trimmers and Pruners	$29,800	11.1%	9,621
111. Chemical Plant and System Operators	$50,860	−15.3%	5,620
112. Machinists	$35,230	−3.1%	39,505
113. Bakers	$22,590	10.0%	31,442
114. Umpires, Referees, and Other Sports Officials	$24,770	16.0%	4,461
115. Food Batchmakers	$23,730	10.9%	15,704
116. Sound Engineering Technicians	$46,550	9.1%	1,194
117. Insulation Workers, Mechanical	$36,570	8.6%	5,787
118. Bailiffs	$36,900	11.2%	2,223
119. Meat, Poultry, and Fish Cutters and Trimmers	$21,050	10.9%	17,920
120. First-Line Supervisors/Managers of Agricultural Crop and Horticultural Workers	$38,510	−0.4%	11,898
121. Motorcycle Mechanics	$30,300	12.5%	3,564
122. Avionics Technicians	$48,100	8.1%	1,193
123. Broadcast Technicians	$32,230	12.1%	2,955
124. Hazardous Materials Removal Workers	$36,330	11.2%	1,933
125. Pile-Driver Operators	$47,550	8.3%	701
126. Power Plant Operators	$56,640	2.7%	1,796
127. Control and Valve Installers and Repairers, Except Mechanical Door	$46,140	0.3%	3,855
128. Helpers—Electricians	$24,880	6.8%	35,109
129. Locomotive Firers	$45,310	2.9%	3,548
130. Mechanical Door Repairers	$31,880	14.9%	1,706
131. Team Assemblers	$24,630	0.1%	264,135
132. Stonemasons	$36,950	10.0%	2,657

(continued)

(continued)

Best Jobs for People with a Realistic Personality Type

Job	Annual Earnings	Percent Growth	Annual Openings
133. Excavating and Loading Machine and Dragline Operators	$34,050	8.3%	6,562
134. Laborers and Freight, Stock, and Material Movers, Hand	$21,900	2.1%	630,487
135. Plasterers and Stucco Masons	$36,430	8.1%	4,509
136. Animal Control Workers	$29,320	12.5%	3,377
137. Pipelayers	$31,280	8.7%	8,902
138. Industrial Truck and Tractor Operators	$28,010	−2.0%	89,547
139. Maintenance Workers, Machinery	$35,590	−1.1%	15,055
140. Tank Car, Truck, and Ship Loaders	$33,140	9.2%	4,519
141. Rail Car Repairers	$44,970	5.1%	1,989
142. Stationary Engineers and Boiler Operators	$47,640	3.4%	1,892
143. Insulation Workers, Floor, Ceiling, and Wall	$31,280	8.4%	6,580
144. Painters, Transportation Equipment	$36,000	8.4%	3,268
145. Rail Yard Engineers, Dinkey Operators, and Hostlers	$39,020	2.9%	3,548
146. Septic Tank Servicers and Sewer Pipe Cleaners	$32,740	10.2%	3,156
147. Structural Metal Fabricators and Fitters	$31,030	−0.2%	20,746
148. Multiple Machine Tool Setters, Operators, and Tenders, Metal and Plastic	$30,390	0.3%	15,709
149. Agricultural Technicians	$33,630	6.6%	4,049
150. Food Science Technicians	$33,630	6.6%	4,049

Jobs 3 and 4 share 12,836 openings. Job 6 shares 37,842 openings with another job not included in this list. Jobs 8 and 9 share 68,643 openings. Jobs 10 and 11 share 97,350 openings. Jobs 12 and 13 share 18,887 openings. Job 14 shares 2,665 openings with two other jobs not included in this list. Jobs 16 and 17 share 223,225 openings. Jobs 23, 25, and 26 share 2,122 openings. Job 39 shares 8,299 openings with another job not included in this list. Jobs 50 and 51 share 29,719 openings. Jobs 56 and 57 share 12,583 openings. Job 67 shares 16,238 openings with another job not included in this list. Job 93 shares 4,786 openings with another job not included in this list. Job 95 shares 3,548 openings with two other jobs not included in this list. Job 96 shares 1,895 openings with another job not included in this list. Jobs 100 and 101 share 61,125 openings. Jobs 107 and 108 share 1,021 openings. Job 120 shares 11,898 openings with four other jobs not included in this list. Job 129 and 145 share 3,548 openings with each other and with another job not included in this list. Jobs 149 and 150 share 4,049 openings.

Best Jobs for People with an Investigative Personality Type

Job	Annual Earnings	Percent Growth	Annual Openings
1. Diagnostic Medical Sonographers	$59,860	19.1%	3,211
2. Environmental Science and Protection Technicians, Including Health	$39,370	28.0%	8,404

Best Jobs for People with an Investigative Personality Type

Job	Annual Earnings	Percent Growth	Annual Openings
3. Nuclear Medicine Technologists	$64,670	14.8%	1,290
4. Coroners	$48,400	4.9%	15,841
5. Industrial Engineering Technicians	$47,490	9.9%	6,172
6. Fire Investigators	$50,830	11.0%	644
7. Chemical Technicians	$40,740	5.8%	4,010

Job 4 shares 15,841 openings with four other jobs not included in this list. Job 6 shares 644 openings with another job not included in this list.

Best Jobs for People with an Artistic Personality Type

Job	Annual Earnings	Percent Growth	Annual Openings
1. Interior Designers	$43,970	19.5%	8,434
2. Architectural Drafters	$43,310	6.1%	16,238
3. Interpreters and Translators	$37,490	23.6%	6,630
4. Hairdressers, Hairstylists, and Cosmetologists	$22,210	12.4%	73,030
5. Photographers	$27,720	10.3%	16,100
6. Makeup Artists, Theatrical and Performance	$35,250	39.8%	392
7. Merchandise Displayers and Window Trimmers	$24,830	10.7%	9,103
8. Fashion Designers	$62,810	5.0%	1,968
9. Fine Artists, Including Painters, Sculptors, and Illustrators	$42,070	9.9%	3,830
10. Desktop Publishers	$35,510	1.0%	6,420

Job 2 shares 16,238 openings with another job not included in this list.

Best Jobs for People with a Social Personality Type

Job	Annual Earnings	Percent Growth	Annual Openings
1. Registered Nurses	$60,010	23.5%	233,499
2. Dental Hygienists	$64,740	30.1%	10,433
3. Medical Assistants	$27,430	35.4%	92,977
4. Fitness Trainers and Aerobics Instructors	$27,680	26.8%	51,235
5. Physical Therapist Assistants	$44,130	32.4%	5,957
6. Vocational Education Teachers, Postsecondary	$45,850	22.9%	19,313

(continued)

(continued)

Best Jobs for People with a Social Personality Type

Job	Annual Earnings	Percent Growth	Annual Openings
7. Preschool Teachers, Except Special Education	$23,130	26.3%	78,172
8. Self-Enrichment Education Teachers	$34,580	23.1%	64,449
9. Radiation Therapists	$70,010	24.8%	1,461
10. Respiratory Therapists	$50,070	22.6%	5,563
11. Occupational Therapist Assistants	$45,050	25.4%	2,634
12. Licensed Practical and Licensed Vocational Nurses	$37,940	14.0%	70,610
13. Nursing Aides, Orderlies, and Attendants	$23,160	18.2%	321,036
14. Emergency Medical Technicians and Paramedics	$28,400	19.2%	19,513
15. Equal Opportunity Representatives and Officers	$48,400	4.9%	15,841
16. Coaches and Scouts	$27,840	14.6%	51,100
17. Massage Therapists	$34,870	20.3%	9,193
18. Eligibility Interviewers, Government Programs	$39,110	3.1%	11,337
19. Teacher Assistants	$21,580	10.4%	193,986
20. Tour Guides and Escorts	$22,110	21.2%	15,027
21. Emergency Management Specialists	$48,380	12.3%	1,538
22. Physical Therapist Aides	$22,990	24.4%	4,092
23. Residential Advisors	$23,050	18.5%	8,053
24. Concierges	$25,540	14.1%	4,893

Job 15 shares 15,841 openings with four other jobs not included in this list.

Best Jobs for People with an Enterprising Personality Type

Job	Annual Earnings	Percent Growth	Annual Openings
1. Sales Representatives, Wholesale and Manufacturing, Technical and Scientific Products	$68,270	12.4%	43,469
2. Criminal Investigators and Special Agents	$59,930	17.3%	14,746
3. Customer Service Representatives	$29,040	24.8%	600,937
4. Police Detectives	$59,930	17.3%	14,746
5. Advertising Sales Agents	$42,820	20.3%	29,233
6. First-Line Supervisors/Managers of Non-Retail Sales Workers	$67,020	3.7%	48,883
7. First-Line Supervisors/Managers of Construction Trades and Extraction Workers	$55,950	9.1%	82,923
8. Gaming Managers	$64,410	24.4%	549

300 Best Jobs Without a Four-Year Degree © JIST Works

Best Jobs for People with an Enterprising Personality Type

Job	Annual Earnings	Percent Growth	Annual Openings
9. Real Estate Brokers	$58,860	11.1%	18,689
10. First-Line Supervisors/Managers of Landscaping, Lawn Service, and Groundskeeping Workers	$38,720	17.6%	18,956
11. Sheriffs and Deputy Sheriffs	$49,630	10.8%	37,842
12. First-Line Supervisors/Managers of Police and Detectives	$72,620	9.2%	9,373
13. Flight Attendants	$61,120	10.6%	10,773
14. Talent Directors	$61,090	11.1%	8,992
15. Technical Directors/Managers	$61,090	11.1%	8,992
16. Real Estate Sales Agents	$40,600	10.6%	61,232
17. First-Line Supervisors/Managers of Personal Service Workers	$33,900	15.5%	37,555
18. Forest Fire Fighting and Prevention Supervisors	$65,040	11.5%	3,771
19. Municipal Fire Fighting and Prevention Supervisors	$65,040	11.5%	3,771
20. Demonstrators and Product Promoters	$22,570	18.0%	32,779
21. Mates—Ship, Boat, and Barge	$57,210	17.9%	2,665
22. Ship and Boat Captains	$57,210	17.9%	2,665
23. First-Line Supervisors/Managers of Office and Administrative Support Workers	$44,650	5.8%	138,420
24. Storage and Distribution Managers	$76,310	8.3%	6,994
25. Transportation Managers	$76,310	8.3%	6,994
26. Gaming Supervisors	$42,980	23.4%	4,602
27. Industrial Production Managers	$80,560	–5.9%	14,889
28. First-Line Supervisors/Managers of Food Preparation and Serving Workers	$28,040	11.3%	154,175
29. First-Line Supervisors/Managers of Helpers, Laborers, and Material Movers, Hand	$40,640	12.5%	13,877
30. First-Line Supervisors/Managers of Housekeeping and Janitorial Workers	$32,850	12.7%	30,613
31. First-Line Supervisors/Managers of Correctional Officers	$55,720	12.5%	4,180
32. First-Line Supervisors/Managers of Transportation and Material-Moving Machine and Vehicle Operators	$49,850	10.2%	16,580
33. Food Service Managers	$44,570	5.0%	59,302
34. Air Traffic Controllers	$112,930	10.2%	1,213
35. First-Line Supervisors/Managers of Mechanics, Installers, and Repairers	$55,380	7.3%	24,361
36. Funeral Directors	$50,370	12.5%	3,939
37. Private Detectives and Investigators	$37,640	18.2%	7,329

(continued)

(continued)

Best Jobs for People with an Enterprising Personality Type

Job	Annual Earnings	Percent Growth	Annual Openings
38. First-Line Supervisors/Managers of Production and Operating Workers	$48,670	−4.8%	46,144
39. Skin Care Specialists	$27,190	34.3%	6,643
40. First-Line Supervisors/Managers of Retail Sales Workers	$34,470	4.2%	221,241
41. Lodging Managers	$44,240	12.2%	5,529
42. Wholesale and Retail Buyers, Except Farm Products	$46,960	−0.1%	19,847
43. Aircraft Cargo Handling Supervisors	$37,760	23.3%	523
44. Railroad Conductors and Yardmasters	$58,650	9.1%	3,235
45. Parts Salespersons	$28,130	−2.2%	52,414
46. First-Line Supervisors/Managers of Animal Husbandry and Animal Care Workers	$38,510	−0.4%	11,898
47. First-Line Supervisors/Managers of Aquacultural Workers	$38,510	−0.4%	11,898
48. Chefs and Head Cooks	$37,160	7.6%	9,401
49. Airfield Operations Specialists	$38,320	11.8%	245
50. Postmasters and Mail Superintendents	$57,900	−0.8%	1,627

Jobs 2 and 4 share 14,746 openings with each other and with two other jobs not included in this list. Job 11 shares 37,842 openings with another job not included in this list. Job 14 and 15 share 8,992 openings with each other and with three other jobs not included in this list. Jobs 18 and 19 share 3,771 openings. Jobs 21 and 22 share 2,665 openings with each other and with another job not included in this list. Jobs 24 and 25 share 6,994 openings. Job 46 and 47 share 11,898 openings with each other and with three other jobs not included in this list.

Best Jobs for People with a Conventional Personality Type

Job	Annual Earnings	Percent Growth	Annual Openings
1. Executive Secretaries and Administrative Assistants	$38,640	14.8%	235,314
2. Paralegals and Legal Assistants	$44,990	22.2%	22,756
3. Sales Representatives, Wholesale and Manufacturing, Except Technical and Scientific Products	$50,750	8.4%	156,215
4. Immigration and Customs Inspectors	$59,930	17.3%	14,746
5. Police Identification and Records Officers	$59,930	17.3%	14,746
6. Bill and Account Collectors	$29,990	22.9%	118,709
7. Bookkeeping, Accounting, and Auditing Clerks	$31,560	12.5%	286,854
8. Claims Examiners, Property and Casualty Insurance	$53,560	8.9%	22,024
9. Insurance Adjusters, Examiners, and Investigators	$53,560	8.9%	22,024
10. Legal Secretaries	$38,810	11.7%	38,682
11. Dental Assistants	$31,550	29.2%	29,482

Best Jobs for People with a Conventional Personality Type

Job	Annual Earnings	Percent Growth	Annual Openings
12. Social and Human Service Assistants	$26,630	33.6%	80,142
13. Receptionists and Information Clerks	$23,710	17.2%	334,124
14. Pharmacy Technicians	$26,720	32.0%	54,453
15. Brokerage Clerks	$37,360	20.0%	10,826
16. Court Reporters	$45,330	24.5%	2,620
17. Office Clerks, General	$24,460	12.6%	765,803
18. Medical Secretaries	$28,950	16.7%	60,659
19. Medical Records and Health Information Technicians	$29,290	17.8%	39,048
20. Production, Planning, and Expediting Clerks	$39,690	4.2%	52,735
21. Police, Fire, and Ambulance Dispatchers	$32,660	13.6%	17,628
22. Tellers	$22,920	13.5%	146,077
23. Cargo and Freight Agents	$37,060	16.5%	9,967
24. Insurance Appraisers, Auto Damage	$51,500	12.5%	1,030
25. Mapping Technicians	$33,640	19.4%	8,299
26. Human Resources Assistants, Except Payroll and Timekeeping	$34,970	11.3%	18,647
27. Purchasing Agents, Except Wholesale, Retail, and Farm Products	$52,460	0.1%	22,349
28. Environmental Compliance Inspectors	$48,400	4.9%	15,841
29. Government Property Inspectors and Investigators	$48,400	4.9%	15,841
30. Licensing Examiners and Inspectors	$48,400	4.9%	15,841
31. Medical Transcriptionists	$31,250	13.5%	18,080
32. Fire Inspectors	$50,830	11.0%	644
33. Billing, Cost, and Rate Clerks	$29,970	4.4%	81,885
34. Billing, Posting, and Calculating Machine Operators	$29,970	4.4%	81,885
35. Statement Clerks	$29,970	4.4%	81,885
36. Geophysical Data Technicians	$50,950	8.6%	1,895
37. Interviewers, Except Eligibility and Loan	$27,320	9.5%	54,060
38. City and Regional Planning Aides	$35,870	12.4%	3,571
39. Court Clerks	$32,330	8.8%	16,163
40. License Clerks	$32,330	8.8%	16,163
41. Municipal Clerks	$32,330	8.8%	16,163
42. Social Science Research Assistants	$35,870	12.4%	3,571
43. Dispatchers, Except Police, Fire, and Ambulance	$33,140	1.5%	29,793
44. Secretaries, Except Legal, Medical, and Executive	$28,220	1.2%	239,630
45. Postal Service Mail Carriers	$44,500	1.0%	16,710
46. Electronic Drafters	$49,250	4.1%	4,786

(continued)

(continued)

Best Jobs for People with a Conventional Personality Type			
Job	Annual Earnings	Percent Growth	Annual Openings
47. Payroll and Timekeeping Clerks	$33,810	3.1%	18,544
48. Shipping, Receiving, and Traffic Clerks	$26,990	3.7%	138,967
49. Insurance Claims Clerks	$32,040	−1.3%	42,246
50. Insurance Policy Processing Clerks	$32,040	−1.3%	42,246
51. Loan Interviewers and Clerks	$31,680	−0.9%	40,217
52. Inspectors, Testers, Sorters, Samplers, and Weighers	$30,310	−7.0%	75,361
53. Library Technicians	$27,680	8.5%	29,075
54. Postal Service Clerks	$45,050	1.2%	3,703
55. Statistical Assistants	$32,540	7.6%	4,836
56. Reservation and Transportation Ticket Agents and Travel Clerks	$29,820	1.1%	30,754
57. Correspondence Clerks	$29,500	12.0%	4,334
58. Postal Service Mail Sorters, Processors, and Processing Machine Operators	$43,700	−8.4%	6,855
59. Title Examiners, Abstractors, and Searchers	$37,200	−1.2%	6,880

Jobs 4 and 5 share 14,746 openings with each other and with two other jobs not included in this list. Jobs 8 and 9 share 22,024 openings. Job 25 shares 8,299 openings with another job not included in this list. Job 28, 29, and 30 share 15,841 openings with each other and with three other jobs not included in this list. Job 32 shares 644 openings with another job not included in this list. Jobs 33, 34, and 35 share 81,885 openings. Job 36 shares 1,895 openings with another job not included in this list. Jobs 38 and 42 share 3,571 openings. Jobs 39, 40, and 41 share 16,163 openings. Job 46 shares 4,786 openings with another job not included in this list. Jobs 49 and 50 share 42,246 openings.

Best Jobs Through Apprenticeship Training

Apprenticeship has many advantages over other methods of preparing for a rewarding career. Apprenticeship programs combine worksite learning with night classes. Apprentices earn while they learn but, unlike other people who get on-the-job training, they receive a credential (journey worker status) that is accepted anywhere. In some programs, the night classes generate academic credits that add up to an associate degree.

The following list shows the 50 best jobs for which a federally registered apprenticeship is an available entry route. They are ordered according to their rewards on the usual three economic measures.

The 50 Best Jobs Through Apprenticeship

Job	Annual Earnings	Percent Growth	Annual Openings
1. Paralegals and Legal Assistants	$44,990	22.2%	22,756
2. Computer Support Specialists	$42,400	12.9%	97,334
3. Construction and Building Inspectors	$48,330	18.2%	12,606
4. Radiologic Technologists	$50,260	15.1%	12,836
5. Police Patrol Officers	$49,630	10.8%	37,842
6. Correctional Officers and Jailers	$36,970	16.9%	56,579
7. Licensed Practical and Licensed Vocational Nurses	$37,940	14.0%	70,610
8. Pipe Fitters and Steamfitters	$44,090	10.6%	68,643
9. Plumbers	$44,090	10.6%	68,643
10. Surgical Technologists	$37,540	24.5%	15,365
11. Automotive Master Mechanics	$34,170	14.3%	97,350
12. Automotive Specialty Technicians	$34,170	14.3%	97,350
13. Interior Designers	$43,970	19.5%	8,434
14. Forest Fire Fighters	$43,170	12.1%	18,887
15. Municipal Fire Fighters	$43,170	12.1%	18,887
16. Legal Secretaries	$38,810	11.7%	38,682
17. Construction Carpenters	$37,660	10.3%	223,225
18. Rough Carpenters	$37,660	10.3%	223,225
19. Electricians	$44,780	7.4%	79,083
20. Environmental Science and Protection Technicians, Including Health	$39,370	28.0%	8,404
21. Truck Drivers, Heavy and Tractor-Trailer	$36,220	10.4%	279,032
22. Bus and Truck Mechanics and Diesel Engine Specialists	$38,640	11.5%	25,428
23. Bookkeeping, Accounting, and Auditing Clerks	$31,560	12.5%	286,854
24. Roofers	$33,240	14.3%	38,398
25. Dental Assistants	$31,550	29.2%	29,482
26. Aircraft Mechanics and Service Technicians	$49,010	10.6%	9,708
27. Automotive Body and Related Repairers	$35,690	11.6%	37,469
28. Tile and Marble Setters	$38,720	15.4%	9,066
29. Food Service Managers	$44,570	5.0%	59,302
30. Mobile Heavy Equipment Mechanics, Except Engines	$41,450	12.3%	11,037
31. Cargo and Freight Agents	$37,060	16.5%	9,967
32. Industrial Machinery Mechanics	$42,350	9.0%	23,361
33. Brickmasons and Blockmasons	$44,070	9.7%	17,569
34. Mates—Ship, Boat, and Barge	$57,210	17.9%	2,665
35. Medical Assistants	$27,430	35.4%	92,977

(continued)

(continued)

The 50 Best Jobs Through Apprenticeship			
Job	Annual Earnings	Percent Growth	Annual Openings
36. Pilots, Ship	$57,210	17.9%	2,665
37. Operating Engineers and Other Construction Equipment Operators	$38,130	8.4%	55,468
38. Aircraft Structure, Surfaces, Rigging, and Systems Assemblers	$45,420	12.8%	6,550
39. Painters, Construction and Maintenance	$32,080	11.8%	101,140
40. Private Detectives and Investigators	$37,640	18.2%	7,329
41. Social and Human Service Assistants	$26,630	33.6%	80,142
42. First-Line Supervisors/Managers of Housekeeping and Janitorial Workers	$32,850	12.7%	30,613
43. Heating and Air Conditioning Mechanics and Installers	$38,360	8.7%	29,719
44. Refrigeration Mechanics and Installers	$38,360	8.7%	29,719
45. Water and Liquid Waste Treatment Plant and System Operators	$37,090	13.8%	9,575
46. Medical Secretaries	$28,950	16.7%	60,659
47. Cement Masons and Concrete Finishers	$33,840	11.4%	34,625
48. Municipal Fire Fighting and Prevention Supervisors	$65,040	11.5%	3,771
49. Medical Records and Health Information Technicians	$29,290	17.8%	39,048
50. Pharmacy Technicians	$26,720	32.0%	54,453

Best Jobs Through Military Training

Many people launch successful careers by getting training in the military. They get free training, room and board, and benefits for further education. Of course, military service requires you to give up certain freedoms and can be hazardous. But it also gives you the satisfaction of serving your country and is an especially good way to learn teamwork and leadership skills.

To create the following list, we sorted the civilian jobs for which military training is an available entry route. (We did not include jobs that you must be trained for *before* entering the military, such as engineers or chaplains.) These 50 jobs have the best combination of earnings, job growth, and job openings.

The 50 Best Jobs Through Military Training

Job	Annual Earnings	Percent Growth	Annual Openings
1. Dental Hygienists	$64,740	30.1%	10,433
2. Criminal Investigators and Special Agents	$59,930	17.3%	14,746
3. Police Detectives	$59,930	17.3%	14,746
4. Paralegals and Legal Assistants	$44,990	22.2%	22,756
5. Executive Secretaries and Administrative Assistants	$38,640	14.8%	235,314
6. Computer Support Specialists	$42,400	12.9%	97,334
7. First-Line Supervisors/Managers of Construction Trades and Extraction Workers	$55,950	9.1%	82,923
8. Construction and Building Inspectors	$48,330	18.2%	12,606
9. Police Patrol Officers	$49,630	10.8%	37,842
10. Sheriffs and Deputy Sheriffs	$49,630	10.8%	37,842
11. Radiologic Technicians	$50,260	15.1%	12,836
12. Radiologic Technologists	$50,260	15.1%	12,836
13. Licensed Practical and Licensed Vocational Nurses	$37,940	14.0%	70,610
14. Pipe Fitters and Steamfitters	$44,090	10.6%	68,643
15. Plumbers	$44,090	10.6%	68,643
16. Correctional Officers and Jailers	$36,970	16.9%	56,579
17. Automotive Master Mechanics	$34,170	14.3%	97,350
18. Automotive Specialty Technicians	$34,170	14.3%	97,350
19. Physical Therapist Assistants	$44,130	32.4%	5,957
20. Surgical Technologists	$37,540	24.5%	15,365
21. Construction Carpenters	$37,660	10.3%	223,225
22. Rough Carpenters	$37,660	10.3%	223,225
23. Technical Directors/Managers	$61,090	11.1%	8,992
24. Legal Secretaries	$38,810	11.7%	38,682
25. Mates—Ship, Boat, and Barge	$57,210	17.9%	2,665
26. Pilots, Ship	$57,210	17.9%	2,665
27. Ship and Boat Captains	$57,210	17.9%	2,665
28. Electricians	$44,780	7.4%	79,083
29. Municipal Fire Fighters	$43,170	12.1%	18,887
30. Truck Drivers, Heavy and Tractor-Trailer	$36,220	10.4%	279,032
31. First-Line Supervisors/Managers of Mechanics, Installers, and Repairers	$55,380	7.3%	24,361
32. First-Line Supervisors/Managers of Transportation and Material-Moving Machine and Vehicle Operators	$49,850	10.2%	16,580
33. Cardiovascular Technologists and Technicians	$44,940	25.5%	3,550

(continued)

(continued)

The 50 Best Jobs Through Military Training

Job	Annual Earnings	Percent Growth	Annual Openings
34. First-Line Supervisors/Managers of Police and Detectives	$72,620	9.2%	9,373
35. Medical Assistants	$27,430	35.4%	92,977
36. First-Line Supervisors/Managers of Office and Administrative Support Workers	$44,650	5.8%	138,420
37. Municipal Fire Fighting and Prevention Supervisors	$65,040	11.5%	3,771
38. Social and Human Service Assistants	$26,630	33.6%	80,142
39. Bookkeeping, Accounting, and Auditing Clerks	$31,560	12.5%	286,854
40. Bus and Truck Mechanics and Diesel Engine Specialists	$38,640	11.5%	25,428
41. Nursing Aides, Orderlies, and Attendants	$23,160	18.2%	321,036
42. Dental Assistants	$31,550	29.2%	29,482
43. Occupational Therapist Assistants	$45,050	25.4%	2,634
44. Aircraft Mechanics and Service Technicians	$49,010	10.6%	9,708
45. Court Reporters	$45,330	24.5%	2,620
46. Roofers	$33,240	14.3%	38,398
47. Pharmacy Technicians	$26,720	32.0%	54,453
48. Aircraft Structure, Surfaces, Rigging, and Systems Assemblers	$45,420	12.8%	6,550
49. Automotive Body and Related Repairers	$35,690	11.6%	37,469
50. Storage and Distribution Managers	$76,310	8.3%	6,994

Bonus Lists: Jobs Employing a High Percentage of People Without a Four-Year Degree

Although this book focuses on jobs that don't require four years of college, many workers in these jobs actually hold bachelor's degrees. We thought you might be interested in a list of the jobs where *very few* workers have a bachelor's. In these jobs, a bachelor's probably provides little advantage for being hired or for advancement.

The first list shows the 104 jobs in which more than 90 percent of the workers don't have a four-year degree. The second list shows the 50 best jobs from this set, based on the usual three economic criteria.

Jobs Employing the Highest Percentage of Workers Without a Four-Year Degree

Job	Percent Without a Four-Year Degree
1. Boilermakers	100.0%
2. Industrial Truck and Tractor Operators	98.3%
3. Meat, Poultry, and Fish Cutters and Trimmers	98.2%
4. Slaughterers and Meat Packers	98.2%
5. Solderers and Brazers	98.1%
6. Welders, Cutters, and Welder Fitters	98.1%
7. Automotive Glass Installers and Repairers	98.1%
8. Drywall and Ceiling Tile Installers	98.0%
9. Tapers	98.0%
10. Cement Masons and Concrete Finishers	97.9%
11. Operating Engineers and Other Construction Equipment Operators	97.4%
12. Pile-Driver Operators	97.4%
13. Plasterers and Stucco Masons	97.3%
14. Reinforcing Iron and Rebar Workers	97.3%
15. Millwrights	97.2%
16. Roofers	97.1%
17. Glaziers	97.1%
18. Bus and Truck Mechanics and Diesel Engine Specialists	96.9%
19. Helpers—Brickmasons, Blockmasons, Stonemasons, and Tile and Marble Setters	96.9%
20. Helpers—Carpenters	96.9%
21. Helpers—Electricians	96.9%
22. Helpers—Pipelayers, Plumbers, Pipefitters, and Steamfitters	96.9%
23. Automotive Body and Related Repairers	96.8%
24. Machinists	96.8%
25. Mobile Heavy Equipment Mechanics, Except Engines	96.8%
26. Rail Car Repairers	96.8%
27. Refuse and Recyclable Material Collectors	96.8%
28. Brickmasons and Blockmasons	96.7%
29. Stonemasons	96.7%
30. Tile and Marble Setters	96.7%
31. Heating and Air Conditioning Mechanics and Installers	96.6%
32. Multiple Machine Tool Setters, Operators, and Tenders, Metal and Plastic	96.6%
33. Refrigeration Mechanics and Installers	96.6%
34. Excavating and Loading Machine and Dragline Operators	96.5%

(continued)

(continued)

Jobs Employing the Highest Percentage of Workers Without a Four-Year Degree	
Job	Percent Without a Four-Year Degree
35. Painters, Transportation Equipment	96.2%
36. Septic Tank Servicers and Sewer Pipe Cleaners	96.2%
37. Structural Iron and Steel Workers	96.2%
38. Automotive Master Mechanics	96.1%
39. Automotive Specialty Technicians	96.1%
40. Pipe Fitters and Steamfitters	96.1%
41. Pipelayers	96.1%
42. Plumbers	96.1%
43. Maintenance Workers, Machinery	95.9%
44. Truck Drivers, Heavy and Tractor-Trailer	95.9%
45. Truck Drivers, Light or Delivery Services	95.9%
46. Sheet Metal Workers	95.8%
47. Bus Drivers, School	95.7%
48. Bus Drivers, Transit and Intercity	95.7%
49. Insulation Workers, Floor, Ceiling, and Wall	95.6%
50. Insulation Workers, Mechanical	95.6%
51. Motorboat Mechanics	95.5%
52. Motorcycle Mechanics	95.5%
53. Avionics Technicians	95.4%
54. Food Batchmakers	95.4%
55. Laborers and Freight, Stock, and Material Movers, Hand	95.4%
56. Construction Laborers	95.3%
57. Team Assemblers	95.3%
58. Cooks, Institution and Cafeteria	95.2%
59. Cooks, Restaurant	95.2%
60. Highway Maintenance Workers	95.0%
61. Industrial Machinery Mechanics	94.7%
62. Helpers—Installation, Maintenance, and Repair Workers	94.6%
63. Tank Car, Truck, and Ship Loaders	94.5%
64. Construction Carpenters	94.4%
65. Rough Carpenters	94.4%
66. Landscaping and Groundskeeping Workers	94.2%
67. Pesticide Handlers, Sprayers, and Applicators, Vegetation	94.2%
68. Tree Trimmers and Pruners	94.2%
69. Electrical Power-Line Installers and Repairers	94.1%

Jobs Employing the Highest Percentage of Workers Without a Four-Year Degree

Job	Percent Without a Four-Year Degree
70. Parts Salespersons	94.1%
71. Recreational Vehicle Service Technicians	94.1%
72. Tire Repairers and Changers	94.1%
73. Aircraft Structure, Surfaces, Rigging, and Systems Assemblers	94.0%
74. Maintenance and Repair Workers, General	93.9%
75. Shipping, Receiving, and Traffic Clerks	93.9%
76. Painters, Construction and Maintenance	93.7%
77. Hairdressers, Hairstylists, and Cosmetologists	93.6%
78. Chemical Plant and System Operators	93.3%
79. Petroleum Pump System Operators, Refinery Operators, and Gaugers	93.3%
80. Mapping Technicians	93.2%
81. Surveying Technicians	93.2%
82. Control and Valve Installers and Repairers, Except Mechanical Door	93.1%
83. Electricians	93.1%
84. Mechanical Door Repairers	93.1%
85. Licensed Practical and Licensed Vocational Nurses	93.0%
86. Nursing Aides, Orderlies, and Attendants	92.6%
87. Electrical and Electronics Repairers, Commercial and Industrial Equipment	92.4%
88. Water and Liquid Waste Treatment Plant and System Operators	92.3%
89. Security and Fire Alarm Systems Installers	92.3%
90. Telecommunications Line Installers and Repairers	92.1%
91. Bakers	92.0%
92. Commercial Divers	91.2%
93. Dental Assistants	91.1%
94. Locomotive Engineers	91.1%
95. Locomotive Firers	91.1%
96. Rail Yard Engineers, Dinkey Operators, and Hostlers	91.1%
97. Pest Control Workers	90.8%
98. Hazardous Materials Removal Workers	90.5%
99. Structural Metal Fabricators and Fitters	90.5%
100. Elevator Installers and Repairers	90.2%
101. Makeup Artists, Theatrical and Performance	90.1%
102. Skin Care Specialists	90.1%
103. Subway and Streetcar Operators	89.5%
104. Locksmiths and Safe Repairers	88.7%

50 Best Jobs Overall Employing a High Percentage of Workers Without a Four-Year Degree

Job	Percent Without a Four-Year Degree	Annual Earnings	Percent Growth	Annual Openings
1. Licensed Practical and Licensed Vocational Nurses	93.0%	$37,940	14.0%	70,610
2. Automotive Master Mechanics	96.1%	$34,170	14.3%	97,350
3. Automotive Specialty Technicians	96.1%	$34,170	14.3%	97,350
4. Pipe Fitters and Steamfitters	96.1%	$44,090	10.6%	68,643
5. Plumbers	96.1%	$44,090	10.6%	68,643
6. Construction Carpenters	94.4%	$37,660	10.3%	223,225
7. Rough Carpenters	94.4%	$37,660	10.3%	223,225
8. Truck Drivers, Heavy and Tractor-Trailer	95.9%	$36,220	10.4%	279,032
9. Tile and Marble Setters	96.7%	$38,720	15.4%	9,066
10. Roofers	97.1%	$33,240	14.3%	38,398
11. Nursing Aides, Orderlies, and Attendants	92.6%	$23,160	18.2%	321,036
12. Aircraft Structure, Surfaces, Rigging, and Systems Assemblers	94.0%	$45,420	12.8%	6,550
13. Bus and Truck Mechanics and Diesel Engine Specialists	96.9%	$38,640	11.5%	25,428
14. Electricians	93.1%	$44,780	7.4%	79,083
15. Mobile Heavy Equipment Mechanics, Except Engines	96.8%	$41,450	12.3%	11,037
16. Dental Assistants	91.1%	$31,550	29.2%	29,482
17. Landscaping and Groundskeeping Workers	94.2%	$22,240	18.1%	307,138
18. Automotive Body and Related Repairers	96.8%	$35,690	11.6%	37,469
19. Painters, Construction and Maintenance	93.7%	$32,080	11.8%	101,140
20. Water and Liquid Waste Treatment Plant and System Operators	92.3%	$37,090	13.8%	9,575
21. Boilermakers	100.0%	$50,700	14.0%	2,333
22. Mapping Technicians	93.2%	$33,640	19.4%	8,299
23. Operating Engineers and Other Construction Equipment Operators	97.4%	$38,130	8.4%	55,468
24. Surveying Technicians	93.2%	$33,640	19.4%	8,299
25. Industrial Machinery Mechanics	94.7%	$42,350	9.0%	23,361
26. Security and Fire Alarm Systems Installers	92.3%	$35,390	20.2%	5,729
27. Brickmasons and Blockmasons	96.7%	$44,070	9.7%	17,569
28. Maintenance and Repair Workers, General	93.9%	$32,570	10.1%	165,502
29. Bus Drivers, Transit and Intercity	95.7%	$33,160	12.5%	27,100

50 Best Jobs Overall Employing a High Percentage of Workers Without a Four-Year Degree

Job	Percent Without a Four-Year Degree	Annual Earnings	Percent Growth	Annual Openings
30. Cement Masons and Concrete Finishers	97.9%	$33,840	11.4%	34,625
31. Heating and Air Conditioning Mechanics and Installers	96.6%	$38,360	8.7%	29,719
32. Refrigeration Mechanics and Installers	96.6%	$38,360	8.7%	29,719
33. Construction Laborers	95.3%	$27,310	10.9%	257,407
34. Subway and Streetcar Operators	89.5%	$50,520	12.1%	587
35. Commercial Divers	91.2%	$41,610	17.7%	248
36. Motorboat Mechanics	95.5%	$34,210	19.0%	4,326
37. Sheet Metal Workers	95.8%	$39,210	6.7%	31,677
38. Hairdressers, Hairstylists, and Cosmetologists	93.6%	$22,210	12.4%	73,030
39. Cooks, Restaurant	95.2%	$21,220	11.5%	238,542
40. Locksmiths and Safe Repairers	88.7%	$33,230	22.1%	3,545
41. Makeup Artists, Theatrical and Performance	90.1%	$35,250	39.8%	392
42. Glaziers	97.1%	$35,230	11.9%	6,416
43. Reinforcing Iron and Rebar Workers	97.3%	$37,890	11.5%	4,502
44. Skin Care Specialists	90.1%	$27,190	34.3%	6,643
45. Telecommunications Line Installers and Repairers	92.1%	$47,220	4.6%	14,719
46. Tire Repairers and Changers	94.1%	$21,880	20.2%	18,829
47. Drywall and Ceiling Tile Installers	98.0%	$36,520	7.3%	30,945
48. Electrical Power-Line Installers and Repairers	94.1%	$52,570	7.2%	6,401
49. Elevator Installers and Repairers	90.2%	$68,000	8.8%	2,850
50. Helpers—Installation, Maintenance, and Repair Workers	94.6%	$22,920	11.8%	52,058

Bonus Lists: Jobs with the Greatest Changes in Outlook Since the Previous Edition

The previous edition of this book, which came out in 2006, used job-growth figures from the Bureau of Labor Statistics (BLS) that were projected for the period from 2002 to 2012. Since that edition was prepared, BLS has updated its projections twice, based on the latest economic data and improvements to their forecasting models. Some jobs now are expected to have much better job growth than was previously projected; for other jobs, expectations for job growth have been scaled back.

We thought you might be interested in seeing which 25 jobs had the greatest *increases* and greatest *decreases* in job-growth projection, so we compiled the following two lists. We based the lists on those 256 jobs that were included in the best 300 jobs in both editions.

25 Jobs with the Greatest Increases in Job-Growth Projection

Job	Projected Job Growth 2002–2012	Projected Job Growth 2006–2016	Change in Forecast
1. Brokerage Clerks	−14.7%	20.0%	34.7%
2. Makeup Artists, Theatrical and Performance	18.2%	39.8%	21.6%
3. Ship and Boat Captains	2.4%	17.9%	15.5%
4. Mates—Ship, Boat, and Barge	2.4%	17.9%	15.5%
5. Skin Care Specialists	19.4%	34.3%	14.9%
6. Statistical Assistants	−7.2%	7.6%	14.8%
7. Loan Interviewers and Clerks	−14.3%	−0.9%	13.4%
8. Correspondence Clerks	−1.4%	12.0%	13.4%
9. Railroad Conductors and Yardmasters	−4.2%	9.1%	13.3%
10. Boilermakers	1.7%	14.0%	12.3%
11. Tire Repairers and Changers	8.0%	20.2%	12.2%
12. Farmers and Ranchers	−20.6%	−8.5%	12.1%
13. Court Reporters	12.7%	24.5%	11.8%
14. Tank Car, Truck, and Ship Loaders	−2.1%	9.2%	11.3%
15. Tour Guides and Escorts	11.0%	21.2%	10.2%
16. Rail Yard Engineers, Dinkey Operators, and Hostlers	−7.2%	2.9%	10.1%
17. Locomotive Engineers	−7.2%	2.9%	10.1%
18. Locomotive Firers	−7.2%	2.9%	10.1%
19. Ship Engineers	4.5%	14.1%	9.6%
20. Bookkeeping, Accounting, and Auditing Clerks	3.0%	12.5%	9.5%
21. Gaming Surveillance Officers and Gaming Investigators	24.6%	33.6%	9.0%
22. Aerospace Engineering and Operations Technicians	1.5%	10.4%	8.9%
23. Helpers—Brickmasons, Blockmasons, Stonemasons, and Tile and Marble Setters	2.2%	11.0%	8.8%
24. Cooks, Institution and Cafeteria	2.1%	10.8%	8.7%
25. Real Estate Brokers	2.4%	11.1%	8.7%

25 Jobs with the Greatest Decreases in Job-Growth Projections

Job	Projected Job Growth 2002–2012	Projected Job Growth 2006–2016	Change in Forecast
1. Hazardous Materials Removal Workers	43.1%	11.2%	–31.9%
2. Medical Records and Health Information Technicians	46.8%	17.8%	–29.0%
3. Desktop Publishers	29.2%	1.0%	–28.2%
4. Medical Assistants	58.9%	35.4%	–23.5%
5. Refrigeration Mechanics and Installers	31.8%	8.7%	–23.1%
6. Heating and Air Conditioning Mechanics and Installers	31.8%	8.7%	–23.1%
7. Physical Therapist Aides	46.4%	24.4%	–22.0%
8. Interviewers, Except Eligibility and Loan	28.0%	9.5%	–18.5%
9. Fitness Trainers and Aerobics Instructors	44.5%	26.8%	–17.7%
10. Computer Support Specialists	30.3%	12.9%	–17.4%
11. Self-Enrichment Education Teachers	40.1%	23.1%	–17.0%
12. Sound Engineering Technicians	25.5%	9.1%	–16.4%
13. Electricians	23.4%	7.4%	–16.0%
14. Emergency Management Specialists	28.2%	12.3%	–15.9%
15. Vocational Education Teachers, Postsecondary	38.1%	22.9%	–15.2%
16. Residential Advisors	33.6%	18.5%	–15.1%
17. Social and Human Service Assistants	48.7%	33.6%	–15.1%
18. Security Guards	31.9%	16.9%	–15.0%
19. Truck Drivers, Light or Delivery Services	23.2%	8.4%	–14.8%
20. Cement Masons and Concrete Finishers	26.1%	11.4%	–14.7%
21. First-Line Supervisors/Managers of Production and Operating Workers	9.5%	–4.8%	–14.3%
22. Telecommunications Line Installers and Repairers	18.8%	4.6%	–14.2%
23. Emergency Medical Technicians and Paramedics	33.1%	19.2%	–13.9%
24. Police Patrol Officers	24.7%	10.8%	–13.9%
25. Sheriffs and Deputy Sheriffs	24.7%	10.8%	–13.9%

PART II

The Job Descriptions

This part of the book provides descriptions for all the jobs included in one or more of the lists in Part I. The Introduction gives more details on how to use and interpret the job descriptions, but here is some additional information:

❋ Job descriptions are arranged in alphabetical order by job title. This approach allows you to quickly find a description if you know its correct title from one of the lists in Part I.

❋ If you are using this section to browse for interesting options, we suggest you begin with the Table of Contents. Part I features many interesting lists that will help you identify job titles to explore in more detail. If you have not browsed the lists in Part I, consider spending some time there. The lists are interesting and will help you identify job titles you can find described in the material that follows. The job titles in Part II are also listed in the Table of Contents.

Advertising Sales Agents

* ❋ Education/Training Required: Moderate-term on-the-job training
* ❋ Annual Earnings: $42,820
* ❋ Beginning Wage: $22,390
* ❋ Earnings Growth Potential: High
* ❋ Growth: 20.3%
* ❋ Annual Job Openings: 29,233
* ❋ Self-Employed: 5.6%
* ❋ Part-Time: 10.2%

Sell or solicit advertising, including graphic art, advertising space in publications, custom-made signs, or TV and radio advertising time. May obtain leases for outdoor advertising sites or persuade retailer to use sales promotion display items. Prepare and deliver sales presentations to new and existing customers to sell new advertising programs and to protect and increase existing advertising. Explain to customers how specific types of advertising will help promote their products or services in the most effective way possible. Maintain assigned account bases while developing new accounts. Process all correspondence and paperwork related to accounts. Deliver advertising or illustration proofs to customers for approval. Draw up contracts for advertising work and collect payments due. Locate and contact potential clients to offer advertising services. Provide clients with estimates of the costs of advertising products or services. Recommend appropriate sizes and formats for advertising, depending on medium being used. Inform customers of available options for advertisement artwork and provide samples. Obtain and study information about clients' products, needs, problems, advertising history, and business practices to offer effective sales presentations and appropriate product assistance. Determine advertising medium to be used and prepare sample advertisements within the selected medium for presentation to customers. Consult with company officials, sales departments, and advertising agencies to develop promotional plans. Prepare promotional plans, sales literature, media kits, and sales contracts, using computer. Identify new advertising markets and propose products to serve them. Write copy as part of layout. Attend sales meetings, industry trade shows, and training seminars to gather information, promote products, expand network of contacts, and increase knowledge. Gather all relevant material for bid processes and coordinate bidding and contract approval. Arrange for commercial taping sessions and accompany clients to sessions. Write sales outlines for use by staff.

Personality Type: Enterprising. These occupations frequently involve starting up and carrying out projects and can involve leading people and making many decisions. They sometimes require risk taking and often deal with business.

GOE—Interest Area/Cluster: 14. Retail and Wholesale Sales and Service. **Work Group:** 14.03. General Sales. **Other Jobs in This Work Group:** Insurance Sales Agents; Personal Financial Advisors; Sales Agents, Financial Services; Sales Agents, Securities and Commodities.

Skills—Negotiation: Bringing others together and trying to reconcile differences. **Management of Financial Resources:** Determining how money will be spent to get the work done and accounting for these expenditures. **Persuasion:** Persuading others to approach things differently. **Speaking:** Talking to others to effectively convey information. **Social Perceptiveness:** Being aware of others' reactions and understanding why they react the way they do. **Complex Problem Solving:** Identifying complex problems, reviewing the options, and implementing solutions. **Writing:** Communicating effectively with others in writing as indicated by the needs of the audience. **Service Orientation:** Actively looking for ways to help people.

Education and Training Program: Advertising. **Related Knowledge/Courses—Sales and Marketing:** Principles and methods involved in showing, promoting, and selling products or services. This includes marketing strategies and tactics, product demonstration and sales techniques, and sales control systems. **Economics and Accounting:** Economic and accounting principles and practices, the financial markets, banking, and the analysis and reporting of financial data. **Communications and Media:** Media production, communication, and dissemination techniques and methods, including alternative ways to inform and entertain via written, oral, and visual media. **Customer and Personal Service:** Principles and processes for providing customer and personal services, including needs assessment techniques, quality service standards, alternative delivery systems, and customer satisfaction evaluation techniques. **English Language:** The structure and content of the English language, including the meaning and spelling of words, rules of composition, and grammar.

Transportation: Principles and methods for moving people or goods by air, rail, sea, or road, including their relative costs, advantages, and limitations.

Work Environment: More often outdoors than indoors; standing.

Aerospace Engineering and Operations Technicians

- ❊ Education/Training Required: Associate degree
- ❊ Annual Earnings: $54,930
- ❊ Beginning Wage: $38,330
- ❊ Earnings Growth Potential: Low
- ❊ Growth: 10.4%
- ❊ Annual Job Openings: 707
- ❊ Self-Employed: 0.9%
- ❊ Part-Time: 5.9%

Operate, install, calibrate, and maintain integrated computer/communications systems consoles; simulators; and other data acquisition, test, and measurement instruments and equipment to launch, track, position, and evaluate air and space vehicles. May record and interpret test data. Inspect, diagnose, maintain, and operate test setups and equipment to detect malfunctions. Record and interpret test data on parts, assemblies, and mechanisms. Confer with engineering personnel regarding details and implications of test procedures and results. Adjust, repair, or replace faulty components of test setups and equipment. Identify required data, data acquisition plans, and test parameters, setting up equipment to conform to these specifications. Construct and maintain test facilities for aircraft parts and systems according to specifications. Operate and calibrate computer systems and devices to comply with test requirements and to perform data acquisition and analysis. Test aircraft systems under simulated operational conditions, performing systems readiness tests and pre- and post-operational checkouts, to establish design or fabrication parameters. Fabricate and install parts and systems to be tested in test equipment, using hand tools, power tools, and test instruments. Finish vehicle instrumentation and deinstrumentation. Exchange cooling system components in various vehicles.

Personality Type: Realistic. These occupations frequently involve work activities that include practical, hands-on problems and solutions. They often deal with plants; animals; and real-world materials such as wood, tools, and machinery. Many of the occupations require working outside and don't involve a lot of paperwork or working closely with others.

GOE—Interest Area/Cluster: 15. Scientific Research, Engineering, and Mathematics. **Work Group:** 15.09. Engineering Technology. **Other Jobs in This Work Group:** Cartographers and Photogrammetrists; Civil Engineering Technicians; Electrical and Electronic Engineering Technicians; Electrical and Electronics Drafters; Electrical Drafters; Electrical Engineering Technicians; Electro-Mechanical Technicians; Electronic Drafters; Electronics Engineering Technicians; Environmental Engineering Technicians; Mapping Technicians; Mechanical Drafters; Mechanical Engineering Technicians; Surveying and Mapping Technicians; Surveying Technicians.

Skills—Installation: Installing equipment, machines, wiring, or programs to meet specifications. **Technology Design:** Generating or adapting equipment and technology to serve user needs. **Operation Monitoring:** Watching gauges, dials, or other indicators to make sure a machine is working properly. **Science:** Using scientific methods to solve problems. **Troubleshooting:** Determining what is causing an operating error and deciding what to do about it. **Repairing:** Repairing machines or systems, using the needed tools. **Operations Analysis:** Analyzing needs and product requirements to create a design. **Operation and Control:** Controlling operations of equipment or systems.

Education and Training Program: Aeronautical/Aerospace Engineering Technology/Technician Training. **Related Knowledge/Courses—Engineering and Technology:** Equipment, tools, and mechanical devices and their uses to produce motion, light, power, technology, and other applications. **Mechanical Devices:** Machines and tools, including their designs, uses, benefits, repair, and maintenance. **Computers and Electronics:** Electric circuit boards, processors, chips, and computer hardware and software, including applications and programming. **Production and Processing:** Inputs, outputs, raw materials, waste, quality control, costs, and techniques for maximizing the manufacture and distribution of goods. **Public Safety and Security:** Weaponry; public safety; security operations, rules, regulations, precautions, and prevention;

and the protection of people, data, and property. **Design:** Design techniques, principles, tools, and instruments involved in the production and use of precision technical plans, blueprints, drawings, and models.

Work Environment: Indoors; noisy; sitting; using hands on objects, tools, or controls; repetitive motions.

Agricultural Technicians

- ❋ Education/Training Required: Associate degree
- ❋ Annual Earnings: $33,630
- ❋ Beginning Wage: $21,810
- ❋ Earnings Growth Potential: Medium
- ❋ Growth: 6.6%
- ❋ Annual Job Openings: 4,049
- ❋ Self-Employed: 0.7%
- ❋ Part-Time: 8.2%

The job openings listed here are shared with Food Science Technicians.

Set up and maintain laboratory equipment and collect samples from crops or animals. Prepare specimens and record data to assist scientist in biology or related science experiments. Receive and prepare laboratory samples for analysis, following proper protocols to ensure that they will be stored, prepared, and disposed of efficiently and effectively. Record data pertaining to experimentation, research, and animal care. Collect samples from crops or animals so testing can be performed. Prepare data summaries, reports, and analyses that include results, charts, and graphs to document research findings and results. Adjust testing equipment and prepare culture media, following standard procedures. Operate laboratory equipment such as spectrometers, nitrogen determination apparatus, air samplers, centrifuges, and potential hydrogen (pH) meters to perform tests. Measure or weigh ingredients used in testing or for purposes such as animal feed. Provide food and water to livestock and laboratory animals and record details of their food consumption. Plant seeds in specified areas and count the resulting plants to determine the percentage of seeds that germinated. Supervise pest or weed control operations, including locating and identifying pests or weeds, selecting chemicals and application methods, scheduling application, and training operators. Measure and mark plot

areas and plow, disc, level, and otherwise prepare land for cultivated crops, orchards, and vineyards. Conduct insect and plant disease surveys. Examine animals and specimens to determine the presence of diseases or other problems. Perform general nursery duties such as propagating standard varieties of plant materials, collecting and germinating seeds, maintaining cuttings of plants, and controlling environmental conditions. Operate farm machinery, including tractors, plows, mowers, combines, balers, sprayers, earthmoving equipment, and trucks. Perform crop production duties such as tilling, hoeing, pruning, weeding, and harvesting crops. Devise cultural methods and environmental controls for plants for which guidelines are sketchy or nonexistent. Maintain and repair agricultural facilities, equipment, and tools to ensure operational readiness, safety, and cleanliness. Provide routine animal care such as taking and recording body measurements, applying identification, and assisting in the birthing process.

Personality Type: Realistic. These occupations frequently involve work activities that include practical, hands-on problems and solutions. They often deal with plants; animals; and real-world materials such as wood, tools, and machinery. Many of the occupations require working outside and don't involve a lot of paperwork or working closely with others.

GOE—Interest Area/Cluster: 01. Agriculture and Natural Resources. **Work Group:** 01.03. Resource Technologies for Plants, Animals, and the Environment. **Other Jobs in This Work Group:** Agricultural and Food Science Technicians; Environmental Science and Protection Technicians, Including Health; Food Science Technicians; Food Scientists and Technologists; Geological and Petroleum Technicians; Geological Sample Test Technicians; Geophysical Data Technicians.

Skills—Science: Using scientific methods to solve problems. **Equipment Maintenance:** Performing routine maintenance and determining when and what kind of maintenance is needed. **Troubleshooting:** Determining what is causing an operating error and deciding what to do about it. **Operation Monitoring:** Watching gauges, dials, or other indicators to make sure a machine is working properly. **Operation and Control:** Controlling operations of equipment or systems. **Mathematics:** Using mathematics to solve problems. **Quality Control Analysis:** Evaluating the quality or performance of products, services, or processes. **Writing:** Communicating effectively with others in writing as indicated by the needs of the audience.

Education and Training Programs: Agricultural Animal Breeding; Agronomy and Crop Science; Animal Nutrition; Animal Sciences, General; Animal/Livestock Husbandry and Production; Crop Production; Dairy Science; Food Science. **Related Knowledge/Courses—Biology:** Plant and animal living tissue, cells, organisms, and entities, including their functions, interdependencies, and interactions with each other and the environment. **Food Production:** Techniques and equipment for planting, growing, and harvesting of food for consumption, including crop-rotation methods, animal husbandry, and food storage/handling techniques. **Chemistry:** The composition, structure, and properties of substances and of the chemical processes and transformations that they undergo. This includes uses of chemicals and their interactions, danger signs, production techniques, and disposal methods. **Mechanical Devices:** Machines and tools, including their designs, uses, benefits, repair, and maintenance. **Engineering and Technology:** Equipment, tools, and mechanical devices and their uses to produce motion, light, power, technology, and other applications. **Production and Processing:** Inputs, outputs, raw materials, waste, quality control, costs, and techniques for maximizing the manufacture and distribution of goods.

Work Environment: Indoors; contaminants; hazardous conditions; standing; using hands on objects, tools, or controls.

Air Traffic Controllers

- ❋ Education/Training Required: Long-term on-the-job training
- ❋ Annual Earnings: $112,930
- ❋ Beginning Wage: $47,290
- ❋ Earnings Growth Potential: Very high
- ❋ Growth: 10.2%
- ❋ Annual Job Openings: 1,213
- ❋ Self-Employed: 0.0%
- ❋ Part-Time: 2.1%

Control air traffic on and within vicinity of airport and movement of air traffic between altitude sectors and control centers according to established procedures and policies. Authorize, regulate, and control commercial airline flights according to government or company regulations to expedite and ensure flight safety. Issue landing and take-off authorizations and instructions. Monitor and direct the movement of aircraft within an assigned airspace and on the ground at airports to minimize delays and maximize safety. Monitor aircraft within a specific airspace, using radar, computer equipment, and visual references. Inform pilots about nearby planes as well as potentially hazardous conditions such as weather, speed and direction of wind, and visibility problems. Provide flight path changes or directions to emergency landing fields for pilots traveling in bad weather or in emergency situations. Alert airport emergency services in cases of emergency and when aircraft experience difficulties. Direct pilots to runways when space is available, or direct them to maintain a traffic pattern until there is space for them to land. Transfer control of departing flights to traffic control centers and accept control of arriving flights. Direct ground traffic, including taxiing aircraft, maintenance and baggage vehicles, and airport workers. Determine the timing and procedures for flight vector changes. Maintain radio and telephone contact with adjacent control towers, terminal control units, and other area control centers in order to coordinate aircraft movement. Contact pilots by radio to provide meteorological, navigational, and other information. Initiate and coordinate searches for missing aircraft. Check conditions and traffic at different altitudes in response to pilots' requests for altitude changes. Relay to control centers air traffic information such as courses, altitudes, and expected arrival times. Compile information about flights from flight plans, pilot reports, radar, and observations. Inspect, adjust, and control radio equipment and airport lights. Conduct preflight briefings on weather conditions, suggested routes, altitudes, indications of turbulence, and other flight safety information. Analyze factors such as weather reports, fuel requirements, and maps in order to determine air routes. Organize flight plans and traffic management plans to prepare for planes about to enter assigned airspace.

Personality Type: Enterprising. These occupations frequently involve starting up and carrying out projects and can involve leading people and making many decisions. They sometimes require risk taking and often deal with business.

GOE—Interest Area/Cluster: 03. Arts and Communication. **Work Group:** 03.10. Communications Technology. **Other Jobs in This Work Group:** Airfield Operations

Specialists; Dispatchers, Except Police, Fire, and Ambulance; Police, Fire, and Ambulance Dispatchers; Telephone Operators.

Skills—Operation and Control: Controlling operations of equipment or systems. **Operation Monitoring:** Watching gauges, dials, or other indicators to make sure a machine is working properly. **Coordination:** Adjusting actions in relation to others' actions. **Complex Problem Solving:** Identifying complex problems, reviewing the options, and implementing solutions. **Active Listening:** Listening to what other people are saying and asking questions as appropriate. **Instructing:** Teaching others how to do something. **Judgment and Decision Making:** Weighing the relative costs and benefits of a potential action. **Monitoring:** Assessing how well one is doing when learning or doing something.

Education and Training Program: Air Traffic Controller Training. **Related Knowledge/Courses—Transportation:** Principles and methods for moving people or goods by air, rail, sea, or road, including their relative costs, advantages, and limitations. **Geography:** Various methods for describing the location and distribution of land, sea, and air masses, including their physical locations, relationships, and characteristics. **Telecommunications:** Transmission, broadcasting, switching, control, and operation of telecommunications systems. **Public Safety and Security:** Weaponry; public safety; security operations, rules, regulations, precautions, and prevention; and the protection of people, data, and property. **Physics:** Physical principles, laws, and applications, including air, water, material dynamics, light, atomic principles, heat, electric theory, earth formations, and meteorological and related natural phenomena. **Education and Training:** Instructional methods and training techniques, including curriculum design principles, learning theory, group and individual teaching techniques, design of individual development plans, and test design principles.

Work Environment: Indoors; noisy; sitting; using hands on objects, tools, or controls; repetitive motions.

Aircraft Cargo Handling Supervisors

- ❋ Education/Training Required: Work experience in a related occupation
- ❋ Annual Earnings: $37,760
- ❋ Beginning Wage: $24,030
- ❋ Earnings Growth Potential: Medium
- ❋ Growth: 23.3%
- ❋ Annual Job Openings: 523
- ❋ Self-Employed: 2.0%
- ❋ Part-Time: 5.3%

Direct ground crew in the loading, unloading, securing, and staging of aircraft cargo or baggage. Determine the quantity and orientation of cargo and compute aircraft center of gravity. May accompany aircraft as member of flight crew, monitor and handle cargo in flight, and assist and brief passengers on safety and emergency procedures. Calculate load weights for different aircraft compartments, using charts and computers. Distribute cargo in such a manner that space use is maximized.

Personality Type: Enterprising. These occupations frequently involve starting up and carrying out projects and can involve leading people and making many decisions. They sometimes require risk taking and often deal with business.

GOE—Interest Area/Cluster: 16. Transportation, Distribution, and Logistics. **Work Group:** 16.01. Managerial Work in Transportation. **Other Jobs in This Work Group:** First-Line Supervisors/Managers of Transportation and Material-Moving Machine and Vehicle Operators; Postmasters and Mail Superintendents; Railroad Conductors and Yardmasters; Storage and Distribution Managers; Transportation Managers; Transportation, Storage, and Distribution Managers.

Skills—Equipment Maintenance: Performing routine maintenance and determining when and what kind of maintenance is needed. **Service Orientation:** Actively looking for ways to help people. **Operation and Control:** Controlling operations of equipment or systems. **Operation Monitoring:** Watching gauges, dials, or other indicators to make sure a machine is working properly. **Management of Personnel Resources:** Motivating, developing, and directing people as they work; identifying the best people for the job. **Operations Analysis:** Analyzing needs and product requirements to create a design. **Systems Evaluation:** Looking at many indicators of system performance and taking into account their accuracy. **Social Perceptiveness:** Being aware of others' reactions and understanding why they react the way they do.

Education and Training Program: Aviation/Airway Management and Operations. **Related Knowledge/Courses—Transportation:** Principles and methods for moving people or goods by air, rail, sea, or road, including their relative costs, advantages, and limitations. **Public Safety and Security:** Weaponry; public safety; security operations, rules, regulations, precautions, and prevention; and the protection of people, data, and property. **Geography:** Various methods for describing the location and distribution of land, sea, and air masses, including their physical locations, relationships, and characteristics. **Personnel and Human Resources:** Principles and procedures for personnel recruitment; selection; training; compensation and benefits; labor relations and negotiation; and personnel information systems. **Psychology:** Human behavior and performance, mental processes, psychological research methods, and the assessment and treatment of behavioral and affective disorders. **Customer and Personal Service:** Principles and processes for providing customer and personal services, including needs assessment techniques, quality service standards, alternative delivery systems, and customer satisfaction evaluation techniques.

Work Environment: Outdoors; noisy; very hot or cold; contaminants; hazardous equipment; standing.

Aircraft Mechanics and Service Technicians

- ❋ Education/Training Required: Postsecondary vocational training
- ❋ Annual Earnings: $49,010
- ❋ Beginning Wage: $32,160
- ❋ Earnings Growth Potential: Low
- ❋ Growth: 10.6%
- ❋ Annual Job Openings: 9,708
- ❋ Self-Employed: 0.4%
- ❋ Part-Time: 2.1%

Diagnose, adjust, repair, or overhaul aircraft engines and assemblies, such as hydraulic and pneumatic systems. Read and interpret maintenance manuals, service bulletins, and other specifications to determine the feasibility and method of repairing or replacing malfunctioning or damaged components. Inspect completed work to certify that maintenance meets standards and that aircraft are ready for operation. Maintain repair logs, documenting all preventive and corrective aircraft maintenance. Conduct routine and special inspections as required by regulations. Examine and inspect aircraft components, including landing gear, hydraulic systems, and de-icers, to locate cracks, breaks, leaks, or other problem. Inspect airframes for wear or other defects. Maintain, repair, and rebuild aircraft structures; functional components; and parts such as wings and fuselage, rigging, hydraulic units, oxygen systems, fuel systems, electrical systems, gaskets, and seals. Measure the tension of control cables. Replace or repair worn, defective, or damaged components, using hand tools, gauges, and testing equipment. Measure parts for wear, using precision instruments. Assemble and install electrical, plumbing, mechanical, hydraulic, and structural components and accessories, using hand tools and power tools. Test operation of engines and other systems, using test equipment such as ignition analyzers, compression checkers, distributor timers, and ammeters. Obtain fuel and oil samples and check them for contamination. Reassemble engines following repair or inspection and re-install engines in aircraft. Read and interpret pilots' descriptions of problems to diagnose causes. Modify aircraft structures, space vehicles, systems, or components, following drawings, schematics, charts, engineering orders, and technical publications. Install and align repaired or replacement parts for subsequent riveting or welding, using clamps and wrenches. Locate and mark dimensions and reference lines on defective or replacement parts, using templates, scribes, compasses, and steel rules. Clean, strip, prime, and sand structural surfaces and materials to prepare them for bonding. Service and maintain aircraft and related apparatus by performing activities such as flushing crankcases, cleaning screens, and lubricating moving parts.

Personality Type: Realistic. These occupations frequently involve work activities that include practical, hands-on problems and solutions. They often deal with plants; animals; and real-world materials such as wood, tools, and machinery. Many of the occupations require working

outside and don't involve a lot of paperwork or working closely with others.

GOE—Interest Area/Cluster: 13. Manufacturing. **Work Group:** 13.14. Vehicle and Facility Mechanical Work. **Other Jobs in This Work Group:** Aircraft Structure, Surfaces, Rigging, and Systems Assemblers; Automotive Body and Related Repairers; Automotive Glass Installers and Repairers; Automotive Master Mechanics; Automotive Service Technicians and Mechanics; Automotive Specialty Technicians; Bus and Truck Mechanics and Diesel Engine Specialists; Farm Equipment Mechanics; Fiberglass Laminators and Fabricators; Mobile Heavy Equipment Mechanics, Except Engines; Motorboat Mechanics; Motorcycle Mechanics; Outdoor Power Equipment and Other Small Engine Mechanics; Rail Car Repairers; Recreational Vehicle Service Technicians; Tire Repairers and Changers.

Skills—Repairing: Repairing machines or systems, using the needed tools. **Equipment Maintenance:** Performing routine maintenance and determining when and what kind of maintenance is needed. **Installation:** Installing equipment, machines, wiring, or programs to meet specifications. **Operation Monitoring:** Watching gauges, dials, or other indicators to make sure a machine is working properly. **Troubleshooting:** Determining what is causing an operating error and deciding what to do about it. **Operation and Control:** Controlling operations of equipment or systems. **Quality Control Analysis:** Evaluating the quality or performance of products, services, or processes. Complex Problem Solving;

Education and Training Programs: Agricultural Mechanics and Equipment/Machine Technology; Aircraft Powerplant Technology/Technician Training; Airframe Mechanics and Aircraft Maintenance Technology/Technician Training. **Related Knowledge/Courses—Mechanical Devices:** Machines and tools, including their designs, uses, benefits, repair, and maintenance. **Design:** Design techniques, principles, tools, and instruments involved in the production and use of precision technical plans, blueprints, drawings, and models. **Physics:** Physical principles, laws, and applications, including air, water, material dynamics, light, atomic principles, heat, electric theory, earth formations, and meteorological and related natural phenomena. **Chemistry:** The composition, structure, and properties of substances and of the chemical processes and transformations that they undergo. This includes uses of chemicals and their interactions, danger signs, production

techniques, and disposal methods. **Engineering and Technology:** Equipment, tools, and mechanical devices and their uses to produce motion, light, power, technology, and other applications. **Transportation:** Principles and methods for moving people or goods by air, rail, sea, or road, including their relative costs, advantages, and limitations.

Work Environment: Noisy; contaminants; cramped work space, awkward positions; standing; using hands on objects, tools, or controls; bending or twisting the body.

Aircraft Structure, Surfaces, Rigging, and Systems Assemblers

- ❋ Education/Training Required: Moderate-term on-the-job training
- ❋ Annual Earnings: $45,420
- ❋ Beginning Wage: $25,050
- ❋ Earnings Growth Potential: High
- ❋ Growth: 12.8%
- ❋ Annual Job Openings: 6,550
- ❋ Self-Employed: 0.0%
- ❋ Part-Time: 1.9%

Assemble, fit, fasten, and install parts of airplanes, space vehicles, or missiles, such as tails, wings, fuselage, bulkheads, stabilizers, landing gear, rigging and control equipment, or heating and ventilating systems. Form loops or splices in cables, using clamps and fittings, or reweave cable strands. Align and fit structural assemblies manually or signal crane operators to position assemblies for joining. Align, fit, assemble, connect, and install system components, using jigs, fixtures, measuring instruments, hand tools, and power tools. Assemble and fit prefabricated parts to form subassemblies. Assemble, install, and connect parts, fittings, and assemblies on aircraft, using layout tools; hand tools; power tools; and fasteners such as bolts, screws, rivets, and clamps. Attach brackets, hinges, or clips to secure or support components and subassemblies, using bolts, screws, rivets, chemical bonding, or welding. Select and install accessories in swaging machines, using hand tools. Fit and fasten sheet metal coverings to surface areas and other sections of aircraft prior to welding or riveting. Lay out and mark reference points and locations for installation of parts and components, using jigs, templates, and measuring and marking instruments.

Inspect and test installed units, parts, systems, and assemblies for fit, alignment, performance, defects, and compliance with standards, using measuring instruments and test equipment. Install mechanical linkages and actuators and verify tension of cables, using tensiometers. Join structural assemblies such as wings, tails, and fuselage. Measure and cut cables and tubing, using master templates, measuring instruments, and cable cutters or saws. Read and interpret blueprints, illustrations, and specifications to determine layouts, sequences of operations, or identities and relationships of parts. Prepare and load live ammunition, missiles, and bombs onto aircraft according to established procedures. Adjust, repair, rework, or replace parts and assemblies to eliminate malfunctions and to ensure proper operation. Cut, trim, file, bend, and smooth parts and verify sizes and fitting tolerances in order to ensure proper fit and clearance of parts. Install and connect control cables to electronically controlled units, using hand tools, ring locks, cotter keys, threaded connectors, turnbuckles, and related devices.

Personality Type: Realistic. These occupations frequently involve work activities that include practical, hands-on problems and solutions. They often deal with plants; animals; and real-world materials such as wood, tools, and machinery. Many of the occupations require working outside and don't involve a lot of paperwork or working closely with others.

GOE—Interest Area/Cluster: 13. Manufacturing. **Work Group:** 13.14. Vehicle and Facility Mechanical Work. **Other Jobs in This Work Group:** Aircraft Mechanics and Service Technicians; Automotive Body and Related Repairers; Automotive Glass Installers and Repairers; Automotive Master Mechanics; Automotive Service Technicians and Mechanics; Automotive Specialty Technicians; Bus and Truck Mechanics and Diesel Engine Specialists; Farm Equipment Mechanics; Fiberglass Laminators and Fabricators; Mobile Heavy Equipment Mechanics, Except Engines; Motorboat Mechanics; Motorcycle Mechanics; Outdoor Power Equipment and Other Small Engine Mechanics; Rail Car Repairers; Recreational Vehicle Service Technicians; Tire Repairers and Changers.

Skills—Installation: Installing equipment, machines, wiring, or programs to meet specifications. **Equipment Maintenance:** Performing routine maintenance and determining when and what kind of maintenance is needed. **Repairing:** Repairing machines or systems, using the needed tools. **Quality Control Analysis:** Evaluating the quality or performance of products, services, or processes. **Equipment Selection:** Determining the kind of tools and equipment needed to do a job. **Operation Monitoring:** Watching gauges, dials, or other indicators to make sure a machine is working properly. **Mathematics:** Using mathematics to solve problems. **Troubleshooting:** Determining what is causing an operating error and deciding what to do about it.

Education and Training Programs: Aircraft Powerplant Technology/Technician Training; Airframe Mechanics and Aircraft Maintenance Technology/Technician Training; Avionics Maintenance Technology/Technician Training. **Related Knowledge/Courses—Mechanical Devices:** Machines and tools, including their designs, uses, benefits, repair, and maintenance. **Design:** Design techniques, principles, tools, and instruments involved in the production and use of precision technical plans, blueprints, drawings, and models. **Chemistry:** The composition, structure, and properties of substances and of the chemical processes and transformations that they undergo. This includes uses of chemicals and their interactions, danger signs, production techniques, and disposal methods. **Public Safety and Security:** Weaponry; public safety; security operations, rules, regulations, precautions, and prevention; and the protection of people, data, and property. **Production and Processing:** Inputs, outputs, raw materials, waste, quality control, costs, and techniques for maximizing the manufacture and distribution of goods.

Work Environment: Noisy; contaminants; hazardous conditions; hazardous equipment; standing; using hands on objects, tools, or controls.

Airfield Operations Specialists

- ❋ Education/Training Required: Long-term on-the-job training
- ❋ Annual Earnings: $38,320
- ❋ Beginning Wage: $19,470
- ❋ Earnings Growth Potential: High
- ❋ Growth: 11.8%
- ❋ Annual Job Openings: 245
- ❋ Self-Employed: 0.0%
- ❋ Part-Time: 2.1%

Ensure the safe takeoff and landing of commercial and military aircraft. Duties include coordination between air traffic control and maintenance personnel; dispatching; using airfield landing and navigational aids; implementing airfield safety procedures; monitoring and maintaining flight records; and applying knowledge of weather information. Implement airfield safety procedures to ensure a safe operating environment for personnel and aircraft operation. Plan and coordinate airfield construction. Coordinate with agencies such as air traffic control, civil engineers, and command posts to ensure support of airfield management activities. Monitor the arrival, parking, refueling, loading, and departure of all aircraft. Maintain air-to-ground and point-to-point radio contact with aircraft commanders. Train operations staff. Relay departure, arrival, delay, aircraft and airfield status, and other pertinent information to upline controlling agencies. Procure, produce, and provide information on the safe operation of aircraft, such as flight-planning publications, operations publications, charts and maps, and weather information. Coordinate communications between air traffic control and maintenance personnel. Perform and supervise airfield management activities, which may include mobile airfield management functions. Receive, transmit, and control message traffic. Receive and post weather information and flight plan data such as air routes and arrival and departure times. Maintain flight and events logs, air crew flying records, and flight operations records of incoming and outgoing flights. Coordinate with agencies to meet aircrew requirements for billeting, messing, refueling, ground transportation, and transient aircraft maintenance. Collaborate with others to plan flight schedules and air crew assignments. Coordinate changes to flight itineraries with appropriate Air Traffic Control (ATC) agencies. Anticipate aircraft equipment needs for air evacuation and cargo flights. Provide air crews with information and services needed for airfield management and flight planning. Conduct departure and arrival briefings. Use airfield landing and navigational aids and digital data terminal communications equipment to perform duties. Post visual display boards and status boards. Check military flight plans with civilian agencies.

Personality Type: Enterprising. These occupations frequently involve starting up and carrying out projects and can involve leading people and making many decisions. They sometimes require risk taking and often deal with business.

GOE—Interest Area/Cluster: 03. Arts and Communication. **Work Group:** 03.10. Communications Technology. **Other Jobs in This Work Group:** Air Traffic Controllers; Dispatchers, Except Police, Fire, and Ambulance; Police, Fire, and Ambulance Dispatchers; Telephone Operators.

Skills—Operation Monitoring: Watching gauges, dials, or other indicators to make sure a machine is working properly. **Operations Analysis:** Analyzing needs and product requirements to create a design. **Science:** Using scientific methods to solve problems. **Instructing:** Teaching others how to do something. **Writing:** Communicating effectively with others in writing as indicated by the needs of the audience. **Active Learning:** Working with new material or information to grasp its implications. **Management of Personnel Resources:** Motivating, developing, and directing people as they work; identifying the best people for the job. **Operation and Control:** Controlling operations of equipment or systems.

Education and Training Program: Air Traffic Controller Training. **Related Knowledge/Courses—Transportation:** Principles and methods for moving people or goods by air, rail, sea, or road, including their relative costs, advantages, and limitations. **Geography:** Various methods for describing the location and distribution of land, sea, and air masses, including their physical locations, relationships, and characteristics. **Telecommunications:** Transmission, broadcasting, switching, control, and operation of telecommunications systems. **Customer and Personal Service:** Principles and processes for providing customer and personal services, including needs assessment techniques, quality service standards, alternative delivery systems, and customer satisfaction evaluation techniques. **Physics:** Physical principles, laws, and applications, including air, water, material dynamics, light, atomic principles, heat, electric theory, earth formations, and meteorological and related natural phenomena. **Computers and Electronics:** Electric circuit boards, processors, chips, and computer hardware and software, including applications and programming.

Work Environment: More often indoors than outdoors; noisy; very hot or cold; contaminants; sitting.

Animal Control Workers

- ❋ Education/Training Required: Moderate-term on-the-job training
- ❋ Annual Earnings: $29,320
- ❋ Beginning Wage: $18,370
- ❋ Earnings Growth Potential: Medium
- ❋ Growth: 12.5%
- ❋ Annual Job Openings: 3,377
- ❋ Self-Employed: 0.1%
- ❋ Part-Time: 15.1%

Handle animals for the purpose of investigations of mistreatment or control of abandoned, dangerous, or unattended animals. Investigate reports of animal attacks or animal cruelty, interviewing witnesses, collecting evidence, and writing reports. Capture and remove stray, uncontrolled, or abused animals from undesirable conditions, using nets, nooses, or tranquilizer darts as necessary. Examine animals for injuries or malnutrition and arrange for any necessary medical treatment. Remove captured animals from animal-control service vehicles and place animals in shelter cages or other enclosures. Euthanize rabid, unclaimed, or severely injured animals. Supply animals with food, water, and personal care. Clean facilities and equipment such as dog pens and animal control trucks. Prepare for prosecutions related to animal treatment and give evidence in court. Contact animal owners to inform them that their pets are at animal holding facilities. Educate the public about animal welfare and animal control laws and regulations. Write reports of activities and maintain files of impoundments and dispositions of animals. Issue warnings or citations in connection with animal-related offenses or contact police to report violations and request arrests. Answer inquiries from the public concerning animal control operations. Examine animal licenses and inspect establishments housing animals for compliance with laws. Organize the adoption of unclaimed animals. Train police officers in dog handling and training techniques for tracking, crowd control, and narcotics and bomb detection.

Personality Type: Realistic. These occupations frequently involve work activities that include practical, hands-on problems and solutions. They often deal with plants; animals; and real-world materials such as wood, tools, and machinery. Many of the occupations require working outside and don't involve a lot of paperwork or working closely with others.

GOE—Interest Area/Cluster: 12. Law and Public Safety. **Work Group:** 12.05. Safety and Security. **Other Jobs in This Work Group:** Crossing Guards; Gaming Surveillance Officers and Gaming Investigators; Lifeguards, Ski Patrol, and Other Recreational Protective Service Workers; Private Detectives and Investigators; Security Guards; Transportation Security Screeners.

Skills—Negotiation: Bringing others together and trying to reconcile differences. **Active Listening:** Listening to what other people are saying and asking questions as appropriate. **Writing:** Communicating effectively with others in writing as indicated by the needs of the audience. **Reading Comprehension:** Understanding written sentences and paragraphs in work-related documents. **Equipment Maintenance:** Performing routine maintenance and determining when and what kind of maintenance is needed. **Equipment Selection:** Determining the kind of tools and equipment needed to do a job. **Social Perceptiveness:** Being aware of others' reactions and understanding why they react the way they do.

Education and Training Program: Security and Protective Services, Other. **Related Knowledge/Courses—Public Safety and Security:** Weaponry; public safety; security operations, rules, regulations, precautions, and prevention; and the protection of people, data, and property. **Law and Government:** Laws, legal codes, court procedures, precedents, government regulations, executive orders, agency rules, and the democratic political process. **Biology:** Plant and animal living tissue, cells, organisms, and entities, including their functions, interdependencies, and interactions with each other and the environment. **Customer and Personal Service:** Principles and processes for providing customer and personal services, including needs assessment techniques, quality service standards, alternative delivery systems, and customer satisfaction evaluation techniques. **Telecommunications:** Transmission, broadcasting, switching, control, and operation of telecommunications systems. **Transportation:** Principles and methods for moving people or goods by air, rail, sea, or road, including their relative costs, advantages, and limitations.

Work Environment: More often outdoors than indoors; contaminants; disease or infections; minor burns, cuts, bites, or stings; using hands on objects, tools, or controls.

Animal Trainers

- ❀ Education/Training Required: Moderate-term on-the-job training
- ❀ Annual Earnings: $26,190
- ❀ Beginning Wage: $16,510
- ❀ Earnings Growth Potential: Medium
- ❀ Growth: 22.7%
- ❀ Annual Job Openings: 6,713
- ❀ Self-Employed: 56.9%
- ❀ Part-Time: 21.3%

Train animals for riding, harness, security, performance, or obedience or assisting persons with disabilities. Accustom animals to human voice and contact and condition animals to respond to commands. Train animals according to prescribed standards for show or competition. May train animals to carry pack loads or work as part of pack team. Observe animals' physical conditions to detect illness or unhealthy conditions requiring medical care. Cue or signal animals during performances. Administer prescribed medications to animals. Evaluate animals to determine their temperaments, abilities, and aptitude for training. Feed and exercise animals and provide other general care such as cleaning and maintaining holding and performance areas. Talk to and interact with animals in order to familiarize them to human voices and contact. Conduct training programs to develop and maintain desired animal behaviors for competition, entertainment, obedience, security, riding, and related areas. Keep records documenting animal health, diet, and behavior. Advise animal owners regarding the purchase of specific animals. Instruct jockeys in handling specific horses during races. Train horses or other equines for riding, harness, show, racing, or other work, using knowledge of breed characteristics, training methods, performance standards, and the peculiarities of each animal. Use oral, spur, rein, and hand commands to condition horses to carry riders or to pull horse-drawn equipment. Place tack or harnesses on horses to accustom horses to the feel of equipment. Train dogs in human-assistance or property protection duties. Retrain horses to break bad habits, such as kicking, bolting, and resisting bridling and grooming. Train and rehearse animals, according to scripts, for motion picture, television, film, stage, or circus performances. Organize and conduct animal shows. Arrange for mating of stallions and mares and assist mares during foaling.

Personality Type: Realistic. These occupations frequently involve work activities that include practical, hands-on problems and solutions. They often deal with plants; animals; and real-world materials such as wood, tools, and machinery. Many of the occupations require working outside and don't involve a lot of paperwork or working closely with others.

GOE—Interest Area/Cluster: 08. Health Science. **Work Group:** 08.05. Animal Care. **Other Jobs in This Work Group:** Animal Breeders; Nonfarm Animal Caretakers; Veterinarians; Veterinary Assistants and Laboratory Animal Caretakers; Veterinary Technologists and Technicians.

Skills—Management of Financial Resources: Determining how money will be spent to get the work done and accounting for these expenditures. **Persuasion:** Persuading others to approach things differently. **Service Orientation:** Actively looking for ways to help people. **Instructing:** Teaching others how to do something. **Learning Strategies:** Using multiple approaches when learning or teaching new things. **Monitoring:** Assessing how well one is doing when learning or doing something. **Management of Material Resources:** Obtaining and seeing to the appropriate use of equipment, facilities, and materials needed to do certain work. **Social Perceptiveness:** Being aware of others' reactions and understanding why they react the way they do.

Education and Training Programs: Animal Training; Equestrian/Equine Studies. **Related Knowledge/Courses—Sales and Marketing:** Principles and methods involved in showing, promoting, and selling products or services. This includes marketing strategies and tactics, product demonstration and sales techniques, and sales control systems. **Biology:** Plant and animal living tissue, cells, organisms, and entities, including their functions, interdependencies, and interactions with each other and the environment. **Economics and Accounting:** Economic and accounting principles and practices, the financial markets, banking, and the analysis and reporting of financial data. **Communications and Media:** Media production, communication, and dissemination techniques and methods, including alternative ways to inform and entertain via written, oral, and visual media. **Customer and Personal Service:** Principles and processes for providing customer and personal services, including needs assessment techniques, quality service standards, alternative delivery systems, and customer satisfaction evaluation techniques. **Clerical Studies:** Administrative and clerical procedures and systems such as word-processing systems, filing and records management systems, stenography and transcription, forms, design principles, and other office procedures and terminology.

Work Environment: Outdoors; noisy; standing; walking and running; using hands on objects, tools, or controls; repetitive motions.

Architectural Drafters

- ❋ Education/Training Required: Postsecondary vocational training
- ❋ Annual Earnings: $43,310
- ❋ Beginning Wage: $27,680
- ❋ Earnings Growth Potential: Medium
- ❋ Growth: 6.1%
- ❋ Annual Job Openings: 16,238
- ❋ Self-Employed: 5.0%
- ❋ Part-Time: 5.9%

The job openings listed here are shared with Civil Drafters.

Prepare detailed drawings of architectural designs and plans for buildings and structures according to specifications provided by architect. Analyze building codes, by-laws, space and site requirements, and other technical documents and reports to determine their effect on architectural designs. Operate computer-aided drafting (CAD) equipment or conventional drafting station to produce designs, working drawings, charts, forms, and records. Coordinate structural, electrical, and mechanical designs and determine a method of presentation to graphically represent building plans. Obtain and assemble data to complete architectural designs, visiting job sites to compile measurements as necessary. Lay out and plan interior room arrangements for commercial buildings, using computer-assisted drafting (CAD) equipment and software. Draw rough and detailed scale plans for foundations, buildings, and structures based on preliminary concepts, sketches, engineering calculations, specification sheets, and other data. Supervise, coordinate, and inspect the work of draftspersons, technicians, and technologists on construction projects. Represent architect on construction site, ensuring builder compliance with design specifications and advising on design corrections under architect's supervision. Check dimensions of materials to be used and assign numbers to lists of materials. Determine procedures and instructions to be followed according to design specifications and quantity of required materials. Analyze technical implications of architect's design concept, calculating weights, volumes, and stress factors. Create freehand drawings and lettering to accompany drawings. Prepare colored drawings of landscape and interior designs for presentation to client. Reproduce drawings on copy machines or trace copies of plans and drawings, using transparent paper or cloth, ink, pencil, and standard drafting instruments. Prepare cost estimates, contracts, bidding documents, and technical reports for specific projects under an architect's supervision. Calculate heat loss and gain of buildings and structures to determine required equipment specifications, following standard procedures. Build landscape, architectural, and display models.

Personality Type: Artistic. These occupations frequently involve working with forms, designs, and patterns. They often require self-expression, and the work can be done without following a clear set of rules.

GOE—Interest Area/Cluster: 02. Architecture and Construction. **Work Group:** 02.03. Architecture/Construction Engineering Technologies. **Other Jobs in This Work Group:** Architectural and Civil Drafters; Civil Drafters; Surveyors.

Skills—Operations Analysis: Analyzing needs and product requirements to create a design. **Coordination:** Adjusting actions in relation to others' actions. **Active Learning:** Working with new material or information to grasp its implications. **Technology Design:** Generating or adapting equipment and technology to serve user needs. **Mathematics:** Using mathematics to solve problems. **Complex Problem Solving:** Identifying complex problems, reviewing the options, and implementing solutions. **Science:** Using scientific methods to solve problems. **Monitoring:** Assessing how well one is doing when learning or doing something.

Education and Training Programs: Architectural Drafting and Architectural CAD/CADD; Architectural Technology/Technician Training; CAD/CADD Drafting and/or Design Technology/Technician Training; Civil

Drafting and Civil Engineering CAD/CADD; Drafting and Design Technology/Technician Training, General. **Related Knowledge/Courses—Design:** Design techniques, principles, tools, and instruments involved in the production and use of precision technical plans, blueprints, drawings, and models. **Building and Construction:** Materials, methods, and the appropriate tools to construct objects, structures, and buildings. **Engineering and Technology:** Equipment, tools, and mechanical devices and their uses to produce motion, light, power, technology, and other applications. **Computers and Electronics:** Electric circuit boards, processors, chips, and computer hardware and software, including applications and programming. **Mathematics:** Numbers and their operations and interrelationships, including arithmetic, algebra, geometry, calculus, and statistics and their applications. **Physics:** Physical principles, laws, and applications, including air, water, material dynamics, light, atomic principles, heat, electric theory, earth formations, and meteorological and related natural phenomena.

Work Environment: Indoors; noisy; sitting; using hands on objects, tools, or controls; repetitive motions.

Athletes and Sports Competitors

- ❋ Education/Training Required: Long-term on-the-job training
- ❋ Annual Earnings: $38,440
- ❋ Beginning Wage: $15,210
- ❋ Earnings Growth Potential: Very high
- ❋ Growth: 19.2%
- ❋ Annual Job Openings: 4,293
- ❋ Self-Employed: 27.0%
- ❋ Part-Time: 39.1%

Compete in athletic events. Assess performance following athletic competition, identifying strengths and weaknesses and making adjustments to improve future performance. Receive instructions from coaches and other sports staff prior to events and discuss performance afterwards. Lead teams by serving as captains. Maintain equipment used in a particular sport. Represent teams or professional sports clubs, performing such activities as meeting with members of the media, making speeches, or participating in charity events. Participate in athletic events and competitive sports according to established rules and regulations. Attend scheduled practice and training sessions. Exercise and practice under the direction of athletic trainers or professional coaches in order to develop skills, improve physical condition, and prepare for competitions. Maintain optimum physical fitness levels by training regularly, following nutrition plans, and consulting with health professionals.

Personality Type: Realistic. These occupations frequently involve work activities that include practical, hands-on problems and solutions. They often deal with plants; animals; and real-world materials such as wood, tools, and machinery. Many of the occupations require working outside and don't involve a lot of paperwork or working closely with others.

GOE—Interest Area/Cluster: 09. Hospitality, Tourism, and Recreation. **Work Group:** 09.06. Sports. **Other Jobs in This Work Group:** Coaches and Scouts; Umpires, Referees, and Other Sports Officials.

Skills—Equipment Maintenance: Performing routine maintenance and determining when and what kind of maintenance is needed. **Equipment Selection:** Determining the kind of tools and equipment needed to do a job. **Troubleshooting:** Determining what is causing an operating error and deciding what to do about it. **Time Management:** Managing one's own time and the time of others. **Learning Strategies:** Using multiple approaches when learning or teaching new things. **Active Learning:** Working with new material or information to grasp its implications. **Judgment and Decision Making:** Weighing the relative costs and benefits of a potential action. **Repairing:** Repairing machines or systems, using the needed tools.

Education and Training Program: Health and Physical Education, General. **Related Knowledge/Courses—Therapy and Counseling:** Information and techniques needed to rehabilitate physical and mental ailments and to provide career guidance, including alternative treatments, rehabilitation equipment and its proper use, and methods to evaluate treatment effects. **Communications and Media:** Media production, communication, and dissemination techniques and methods, including alternative ways to inform and entertain via written, oral, and visual media. **Psychology:** Human behavior and performance, mental processes, psychological research methods, and the assessment and treatment of behavioral and affective disorders. **Sales and Marketing:** Principles and methods involved in showing, promoting, and selling products or services. This includes marketing strategies and tactics, product demonstration and sales techniques, and sales control systems. **Personnel and Human Resources:** Principles and procedures for personnel recruitment; selection; training; compensation and benefits; labor relations and negotiation; and personnel information systems.

Work Environment: Indoors; very hot or cold; keeping or regaining balance; using hands on objects, tools, or controls; bending or twisting the body; repetitive motions.

Audio and Video Equipment Technicians

- ❊ Education/Training Required: Long-term on-the-job training
- ❊ Annual Earnings: $36,050
- ❊ Beginning Wage: $20,450
- ❊ Earnings Growth Potential: High
- ❊ Growth: 24.2%
- ❊ Annual Job Openings: 4,681
- ❊ Self-Employed: 12.8%
- ❊ Part-Time: 12.9%

Set up or set up and operate audio and video equipment, including microphones, sound speakers, video screens, projectors, video monitors, recording equipment, connecting wires and cables, sound and mixing boards, and related electronic equipment for concerts, sports events, meetings and conventions, presentations, and news conferences. May also set up and operate associated spotlights and other custom lighting systems. Notify supervisors when major equipment repairs are needed. Monitor incoming and outgoing pictures and sound feeds to ensure quality; notify directors of any possible problems. Mix and regulate sound inputs and feeds or coordinate audio feeds with television pictures. Install, adjust, and operate electronic equipment used to record, edit, and transmit radio and television programs, cable programs, and motion pictures. Design layouts of audio and video equipment and perform upgrades and maintenance. Perform minor repairs and routine cleaning of audio and video equipment. Diagnose and resolve media system problems in classrooms. Switch sources of video input from one camera or studio to another, from film to live programming, or from network to local programming. Meet with

directors and senior members of camera crews to discuss assignments and determine filming sequences, camera movements, and picture composition. Construct and position properties, sets, lighting equipment, and other equipment. Compress, digitize, duplicate, and store audio and video data. Obtain, set up, and load videotapes for scheduled productions or broadcasts. Edit videotapes by erasing and removing portions of programs and adding video or sound as required. Direct and coordinate activities of assistants and other personnel during production. Plan and develop pre-production ideas into outlines, scripts, storyboards, and graphics, using own ideas or specifications of assignments. Maintain inventories of audiotapes and videotapes and related supplies. Determine formats, approaches, content, levels, and media to effectively meet objectives within budgetary constraints, utilizing research, knowledge, and training. Record and edit audio material such as movie soundtracks, using audio recording and editing equipment. Inform users of audiotaping and videotaping service policies and procedures. Obtain and preview musical performance programs prior to events to become familiar with the order and approximate times of pieces. Produce rough and finished graphics and graphic designs. Locate and secure settings, properties, effects, and other production necessities.

Personality Type: Realistic. These occupations frequently involve work activities that include practical, hands-on problems and solutions. They often deal with plants; animals; and real-world materials such as wood, tools, and machinery. Many of the occupations require working outside and don't involve a lot of paperwork or working closely with others.

GOE—Interest Area/Cluster: 03. Arts and Communication. **Work Group:** 03.09. Media Technology. **Other Jobs in This Work Group:** Broadcast Technicians; Camera Operators, Television, Video, and Motion Picture; Film and Video Editors; Multi-Media Artists and Animators; Photographers; Radio Operators; Sound Engineering Technicians.

Skills—Installation: Installing equipment, machines, wiring, or programs to meet specifications. **Operation and Control:** Controlling operations of equipment or systems. **Equipment Maintenance:** Performing routine maintenance and determining when and what kind of maintenance is needed. **Troubleshooting:** Determining what is causing an operating error and deciding what to do about it. **Operation Monitoring:** Watching gauges, dials, or other indicators to make sure a machine is working properly. **Repairing:** Repairing machines or systems, using the needed tools. **Equipment Selection:** Determining the kind of tools and equipment needed to do a job. **Technology Design:** Generating or adapting equipment and technology to serve user needs.

Education and Training Programs: Agricultural Communication/Journalism; Photographic and Film/Video Technology/Technician and Assistant Training; Recording Arts Technology/Technician Training. **Related Knowledge/Courses—Computers and Electronics:** Electric circuit boards, processors, chips, and computer hardware and software, including applications and programming. **Telecommunications:** Transmission, broadcasting, switching, control, and operation of telecommunications systems. **Engineering and Technology:** Equipment, tools, and mechanical devices and their uses to produce motion, light, power, technology, and other applications. **Communications and Media:** Media production, communication, and dissemination techniques and methods, including alternative ways to inform and entertain via written, oral, and visual media. **Mechanical Devices:** Machines and tools, including their designs, uses, benefits, repair, and maintenance. **Physics:** Physical principles, laws, and applications, including air, water, material dynamics, light, atomic principles, heat, electric theory, earth formations, and meteorological and related natural phenomena.

Work Environment: Indoors; standing; using hands on objects, tools, or controls.

Automotive Body and Related Repairers

* Education/Training Required: Long-term on-the-job training
* Annual Earnings: $35,690
* Beginning Wage: $21,480
* Earnings Growth Potential: Medium
* Growth: 11.6%
* Annual Job Openings: 37,469
* Self-Employed: 14.1%
* Part-Time: 5.6%

Repair and refinish automotive vehicle bodies and straighten vehicle frames. File, grind, sand, and smooth filled or repaired surfaces, using power tools and hand tools. Sand body areas to be painted and cover bumpers, windows, and trim with masking tape or paper to protect them from the paint. Follow supervisors' instructions as to which parts to restore or replace and how much time a job should take. Remove damaged sections of vehicles, using metal-cutting guns, air grinders, and wrenches, and install replacement parts, using wrenches or welding equipment. Cut and tape plastic separating film to outside repair areas to avoid damaging surrounding surfaces during repair procedure and remove tape and wash surfaces after repairs are complete. Prime and paint repaired surfaces, using paint spray guns and motorized sanders. Inspect repaired vehicles for dimensional accuracy and test-drive them to ensure proper alignment and handling. Mix polyester resins and hardeners to be used in restoring damaged areas. Chain or clamp frames and sections to alignment machines that use hydraulic pressure to align damaged components. Fill small dents that cannot be worked out with plastic or solder. Fit and weld replacement parts into place, using wrenches and welding equipment, and grind down welds to smooth them, using power grinders and other tools. Position dolly blocks against surfaces of dented areas and beat opposite surfaces to remove dents, using hammers. Remove damaged panels and identify the family and properties of the plastic used on a vehicle. Review damage reports, prepare or review repair cost estimates, and plan work to be performed. Remove small pits and dimples in body metal, using pick hammers and punches. Remove upholstery, accessories, electrical window- and seat-operating equipment, and trim to gain access to vehicle bodies and fenders. Clean work areas, using air hoses, to remove damaged material and discarded fiberglass strips used in repair procedures. Adjust or align headlights, wheels, and brake systems. Apply heat to plastic panels, using hot-air welding guns or immersion in hot water, and press the softened panels back into shape by hand. Soak fiberglass matting in resin mixtures and apply layers of matting over repair areas to specified thicknesses.

Personality Type: Realistic. These occupations frequently involve work activities that include practical, hands-on problems and solutions. They often deal with plants; animals; and real-world materials such as wood, tools, and machinery. Many of the occupations require working outside and don't involve a lot of paperwork or working closely with others.

GOE—Interest Area/Cluster: 13. Manufacturing. **Work Group:** 13.14. Vehicle and Facility Mechanical Work. **Other Jobs in This Work Group:** Aircraft Mechanics and Service Technicians; Aircraft Structure, Surfaces, Rigging, and Systems Assemblers; Automotive Glass Installers and Repairers; Automotive Master Mechanics; Automotive Service Technicians and Mechanics; Automotive Specialty Technicians; Bus and Truck Mechanics and Diesel Engine Specialists; Farm Equipment Mechanics; Fiberglass Laminators and Fabricators; Mobile Heavy Equipment Mechanics, Except Engines; Motorboat Mechanics; Motorcycle Mechanics; Outdoor Power Equipment and Other Small Engine Mechanics; Rail Car Repairers; Recreational Vehicle Service Technicians; Tire Repairers and Changers.

Skills—Repairing: Repairing machines or systems, using the needed tools. **Installation:** Installing equipment, machines, wiring, or programs to meet specifications. **Equipment Maintenance:** Performing routine maintenance and determining when and what kind of maintenance is needed. **Troubleshooting:** Determining what is causing an operating error and deciding what to do about it. **Equipment Selection:** Determining the kind of tools and equipment needed to do a job. **Management of Financial Resources:** Determining how money will be spent to get the work done and accounting for these expenditures.

Education and Training Program: Autobody/Collision and Repair Technology/Technician Training. **Related Knowledge/Courses—Mechanical Devices:** Machines and tools, including their designs, uses, benefits, repair, and maintenance. **Building and Construction:** Materials, methods, and the appropriate tools to construct objects, structures, and buildings. **Chemistry:** The composition, structure, and properties of substances and of the chemical processes and transformations that they undergo. This includes uses of chemicals and their interactions, danger signs, production techniques, and disposal methods. **Production and Processing:** Inputs, outputs, raw materials, waste, quality control, costs, and techniques for maximizing the manufacture and distribution of goods. **Administration and Management:** Principles and processes involved in business and organizational planning, coordination, and execution. This includes strategic planning, resource allocation, manpower modeling, leadership techniques, and production methods. **Transportation:** Principles and methods for moving people or goods by air, rail, sea, or road, including their relative costs, advantages, and limitations.

Work Environment: Noisy; contaminants; hazardous equipment; standing; using hands on objects, tools, or controls; repetitive motions.

Automotive Glass Installers and Repairers

- ❋ Education/Training Required: Long-term on-the-job training
- ❋ Annual Earnings: $31,470
- ❋ Beginning Wage: $19,730
- ❋ Earnings Growth Potential: Medium
- ❋ Growth: 18.7%
- ❋ Annual Job Openings: 3,457
- ❋ Self-Employed: 20.7%
- ❋ Part-Time: 4.5%

Replace or repair broken windshields and window glass in motor vehicles. Remove all dirt, foreign matter, and loose glass from damaged areas; then apply primer along windshield or window edges and allow it to dry. Install replacement glass in vehicles after old glass has been removed and all necessary preparations have been made. Allow all glass parts installed with urethane ample time to cure, taking temperature and humidity into account. Prime all scratches on pinch welds with primer and allow primed scratches to dry. Obtain windshields or windows for specific automobile makes and models from stock and examine them for defects before installation. Apply a bead of urethane around the perimeter of each pinch weld and dress the remaining urethane on the pinch welds so that it is of uniform level and thickness all the way around. Check for moisture or contamination in damaged areas, dry out any moisture before making repairs, and keep damaged areas dry until repairs are complete. Select appropriate tools, safety equipment, and parts according to job requirements. Remove broken or damaged glass windshields or window glass from motor vehicles, using hand tools to remove screws from frames holding glass. Remove all moldings, clips, windshield wipers, screws, bolts, and inside A-pillar moldings; then lower headliners before beginning installation or repair work. Install, repair, and replace safety glass and related materials, such as back glass heating elements, on vehicles and equipment. Install rubber channeling strips around edges of glass or frames to weatherproof windows or to prevent rattling. Hold cut or uneven edges of glass against automated abrasive belts to shape or smooth edges. Cut flat safety glass according to specified patterns or perform precision pattern-making and glass-cutting to custom-fit replacement windows. Replace or adjust motorized or manual window-raising mechanisms. Install new foam dams on pinch welds if required. Cool or warm glass in the event of temperature extremes. Replace all moldings, clips, windshield wipers, and other parts that were removed before glass replacement or repair.

Personality Type: Realistic. These occupations frequently involve work activities that include practical, hands-on problems and solutions. They often deal with plants; animals; and real-world materials such as wood, tools, and machinery. Many of the occupations require working outside and don't involve a lot of paperwork or working closely with others.

GOE—Interest Area/Cluster: 13. Manufacturing. **Work Group:** 13.14. Vehicle and Facility Mechanical Work. **Other Jobs in This Work Group:** Aircraft Mechanics and Service Technicians; Aircraft Structure, Surfaces, Rigging, and Systems Assemblers; Automotive Body and Related Repairers; Automotive Master Mechanics; Automotive Service Technicians and Mechanics; Automotive Specialty Technicians; Bus and Truck Mechanics and Diesel Engine Specialists; Farm Equipment Mechanics; Fiberglass Laminators and Fabricators; Mobile Heavy Equipment Mechanics, Except Engines; Motorboat Mechanics; Motorcycle Mechanics; Outdoor Power Equipment and Other Small Engine Mechanics; Rail Car Repairers; Recreational Vehicle Service Technicians; Tire Repairers and Changers.

Skills—Installation: Installing equipment, machines, wiring, or programs to meet specifications. **Equipment Maintenance:** Performing routine maintenance and determining when and what kind of maintenance is needed. **Repairing:** Repairing machines or systems, using the needed tools. **Equipment Selection:** Determining the kind of tools and equipment needed to do a job. **Management of Material Resources:** Obtaining and seeing to the appropriate use of equipment, facilities, and materials needed to do certain work. **Quality Control Analysis:** Evaluating the quality or performance of products, services, or processes. **Operation and Control:** Controlling operations of equipment or systems.

Education and Training Program: Autobody/Collision and Repair Technology/Technician Training. **Related**

Knowledge/Courses—Mechanical Devices: Machines and tools, including their designs, uses, benefits, repair, and maintenance. **Production and Processing:** Inputs, outputs, raw materials, waste, quality control, costs, and techniques for maximizing the manufacture and distribution of goods. **Customer and Personal Service:** Principles and processes for providing customer and personal services, including needs assessment techniques, quality service standards, alternative delivery systems, and customer satisfaction evaluation techniques. **Administration and Management:** Principles and processes involved in business and organizational planning, coordination, and execution. This includes strategic planning, resource allocation, manpower modeling, leadership techniques, and production methods. **Sales and Marketing:** Principles and methods involved in showing, promoting, and selling products or services. This includes marketing strategies and tactics, product demonstration and sales techniques, and sales control systems. **Transportation:** Principles and methods for moving people or goods by air, rail, sea, or road, including their relative costs, advantages, and limitations.

Work Environment: Outdoors; very hot or cold; contaminants; cramped work space, awkward positions; standing; using hands on objects, tools, or controls.

Automotive Master Mechanics

- ✳ Education/Training Required: Postsecondary vocational training
- ✳ Annual Earnings: $34,170
- ✳ Beginning Wage: $19,240
- ✳ Earnings Growth Potential: High
- ✳ Growth: 14.3%
- ✳ Annual Job Openings: 97,350
- ✳ Self-Employed: 16.8%
- ✳ Part-Time: 5.6%

The job openings listed here are shared with Automotive Specialty Technicians.

Repair automobiles, trucks, buses, and other vehicles. Master mechanics repair virtually any part on the vehicle or specialize in the transmission system. Examine vehicles to determine extent of damage or malfunctions. Test-drive vehicles and test components and systems, using equipment such as infrared engine analyzers, compression gauges, and computerized diagnostic devices. Repair, reline, replace, and adjust brakes. Review work orders and discuss work with supervisors. Follow checklists to ensure all important parts are examined, including belts, hoses, steering systems, spark plugs, brake and fuel systems, wheel bearings, and other potentially troublesome areas. Plan work procedures, using charts, technical manuals, and experience. Test and adjust repaired systems to meet manufacturers' performance specifications. Confer with customers to obtain descriptions of vehicle problems and to discuss work to be performed and future repair requirements. Perform routine and scheduled maintenance services such as oil changes, lubrications, and tune-ups. Disassemble units and inspect parts for wear, using micrometers, calipers, and gauges. Overhaul or replace carburetors, blowers, generators, distributors, starters, and pumps. Repair and service air conditioning, heating, engine-cooling, and electrical systems. Repair or replace parts such as pistons, rods, gears, valves, and bearings. Tear down, repair, and rebuild faulty assemblies such as power systems, steering systems, and linkages. Rewire ignition systems, lights, and instrument panels. Repair radiator leaks. Install and repair accessories such as radios, heaters, mirrors, and windshield wipers. Repair manual and automatic transmissions. Repair or replace shock absorbers. Align vehicles' front ends. Rebuild parts such as crankshafts and cylinder blocks. Repair damaged automobile bodies. Replace and adjust headlights.

Personality Type: Realistic. These occupations frequently involve work activities that include practical, hands-on problems and solutions. They often deal with plants; animals; and real-world materials such as wood, tools, and machinery. Many of the occupations require working outside and don't involve a lot of paperwork or working closely with others.

GOE—Interest Area/Cluster: 13. Manufacturing. **Work Group:** 13.14. Vehicle and Facility Mechanical Work. **Other Jobs in This Work Group:** Aircraft Mechanics and Service Technicians; Aircraft Structure, Surfaces, Rigging, and Systems Assemblers; Automotive Body and Related Repairers; Automotive Glass Installers and Repairers; Automotive Service Technicians and Mechanics; Automotive Specialty Technicians; Bus and Truck Mechanics and Diesel Engine Specialists; Farm Equipment Mechanics; Fiberglass Laminators and Fabricators; Mobile Heavy Equipment Mechanics, Except Engines; Motorboat Mechanics; Motorcycle Mechanics; Outdoor Power

Equipment and Other Small Engine Mechanics; Rail Car Repairers; Recreational Vehicle Service Technicians; Tire Repairers and Changers.

Skills—Repairing: Repairing machines or systems, using the needed tools. **Troubleshooting:** Determining what is causing an operating error and deciding what to do about it. **Installation:** Installing equipment, machines, wiring, or programs to meet specifications. **Equipment Maintenance:** Performing routine maintenance and determining when and what kind of maintenance is needed. **Equipment Selection:** Determining the kind of tools and equipment needed to do a job. **Operation Monitoring:** Watching gauges, dials, or other indicators to make sure a machine is working properly. **Complex Problem Solving:** Identifying complex problems, reviewing the options, and implementing solutions. **Technology Design:** Generating or adapting equipment and technology to serve user needs.

Education and Training Programs: Automobile/Automotive Mechanics Technology/Technician Training; Automotive Engineering Technology/Technician Training; Medium/Heavy Vehicle and Truck Technology/Technician Training. **Related Knowledge/Courses—Mechanical Devices:** Machines and tools, including their designs, uses, benefits, repair, and maintenance. **Physics:** Physical principles, laws, and applications, including air, water, material dynamics, light, atomic principles, heat, electric theory, earth formations, and meteorological and related natural phenomena. **Computers and Electronics:** Electric circuit boards, processors, chips, and computer hardware and software, including applications and programming. **Engineering and Technology:** Equipment, tools, and mechanical devices and their uses to produce motion, light, power, technology, and other applications. **Chemistry:** The composition, structure, and properties of substances and of the chemical processes and transformations that they undergo. This includes uses of chemicals and their interactions, danger signs, production techniques, and disposal methods. **Public Safety and Security:** Weaponry; public safety; security operations, rules, regulations, precautions, and prevention; and the protection of people, data, and property.

Work Environment: Noisy; contaminants; hazardous equipment; minor burns, cuts, bites, or stings; standing; using hands on objects, tools, or controls.

Automotive Specialty Technicians

- ❋ Education/Training Required: Postsecondary vocational training
- ❋ Annual Earnings: $34,170
- ❋ Beginning Wage: $19,240
- ❋ Earnings Growth Potential: High
- ❋ Growth: 14.3%
- ❋ Annual Job Openings: 97,350
- ❋ Self-Employed: 16.8%
- ❋ Part-Time: 5.6%

The job openings listed here are shared with Automotive Master Mechanics.

Repair only one system or component on a vehicle, such as brakes, suspension, or radiator. Examine vehicles, compile estimates of repair costs, and secure customers' approval to perform repairs. Repair, overhaul, and adjust automobile brake systems. Use electronic test equipment to locate and correct malfunctions in fuel, ignition, and emissions control systems. Repair and replace defective ball joint suspensions, brake shoes, and wheel bearings. Inspect and test new vehicles for damage; then record findings so that necessary repairs can be made. Test electronic computer components in automobiles to ensure that they are working properly. Tune automobile engines to ensure proper and efficient functioning. Install and repair air conditioners and service components such as compressors, condensers, and controls. Repair, replace, and adjust defective carburetor parts and gasoline filters. Remove and replace defective mufflers and tailpipes. Repair and replace automobile leaf springs. Rebuild, repair, and test automotive fuel injection units. Align and repair wheels, axles, frames, torsion bars, and steering mechanisms of automobiles, using special alignment equipment and wheel-balancing machines. Repair, install, and adjust hydraulic and electromagnetic automatic lift mechanisms used to raise and lower automobile windows, seats, and tops. Repair and rebuild clutch systems. Convert vehicle fuel systems from gasoline to butane gas operations and repair and service operating butane fuel units.

Personality Type: Realistic. These occupations frequently involve work activities that include practical, hands-on problems and solutions. They often deal with plants; animals; and real-world materials such as wood, tools, and machinery. Many of the occupations require working outside and don't involve a lot of paperwork or working closely with others.

GOE—Interest Area/Cluster: 13. Manufacturing. **Work Group:** 13.14. Vehicle and Facility Mechanical Work. **Other Jobs in This Work Group:** Aircraft Mechanics and Service Technicians; Aircraft Structure, Surfaces, Rigging, and Systems Assemblers; Automotive Body and Related Repairers; Automotive Glass Installers and Repairers; Automotive Master Mechanics; Automotive Service Technicians and Mechanics; Bus and Truck Mechanics and Diesel Engine Specialists; Farm Equipment Mechanics; Fiberglass Laminators and Fabricators; Mobile Heavy Equipment Mechanics, Except Engines; Motorboat Mechanics; Motorcycle Mechanics; Outdoor Power Equipment and Other Small Engine Mechanics; Rail Car Repairers; Recreational Vehicle Service Technicians; Tire Repairers and Changers.

Skills—Repairing: Repairing machines or systems, using the needed tools. **Troubleshooting:** Determining what is causing an operating error and deciding what to do about it. **Operation Monitoring:** Watching gauges, dials, or other indicators to make sure a machine is working properly. **Equipment Maintenance:** Performing routine maintenance and determining when and what kind of maintenance is needed. **Installation:** Installing equipment, machines, wiring, or programs to meet specifications. **Equipment Selection:** Determining the kind of tools and equipment needed to do a job. **Active Learning:** Working with new material or information to grasp its implications. **Operation and Control:** Controlling operations of equipment or systems.

Education and Training Programs: Alternative Fuel Vehicle Technology/Technician Training; Automotive Engineering Technology/Technician Training; Vehicle Emissions Inspection and Maintenance Technology/Technician Training. **Related Knowledge/Courses— Mechanical Devices:** Machines and tools, including their designs, uses, benefits, repair, and maintenance. **Physics:** Physical principles, laws, and applications, including air, water, material dynamics, light, atomic principles, heat, electric theory, earth formations, and meteorological and related natural phenomena. **Engineering and Technology:** Equipment, tools, and mechanical devices and their uses to produce motion, light, power, technology, and other applications. **Customer and Personal Service:** Principles and processes for providing customer and personal services, including needs assessment techniques, quality service standards, alternative delivery systems, and customer satisfaction evaluation techniques. **Sales and Marketing:** Principles and methods involved in showing, promoting, and selling products or services. This includes marketing strategies and tactics, product demonstration and sales techniques, and sales control systems. **Administration and Management:** Principles and processes involved in business and organizational planning, coordination, and execution. This includes strategic planning, resource allocation, manpower modeling, leadership techniques, and production methods.

Work Environment: Contaminants; cramped work space, awkward positions; minor burns, cuts, bites, or stings; standing; using hands on objects, tools, or controls; bending or twisting the body.

Aviation Inspectors

- ❈ Education/Training Required: Work experience in a related occupation
- ❈ Annual Earnings: $51,440
- ❈ Beginning Wage: $27,340
- ❈ Earnings Growth Potential: High
- ❈ Growth: 16.4%
- ❈ Annual Job Openings: 2,122
- ❈ Self-Employed: 5.9%
- ❈ Part-Time: 3.7%

The job openings listed here are shared with Freight and Cargo Inspectors and with Transportation Vehicle, Equipment, and Systems Inspectors, Except Aviation.

Inspect aircraft, maintenance procedures, air navigational aids, air traffic controls, and communications equipment to ensure conformance with federal safety regulations. Inspect work of aircraft mechanics performing maintenance, modification, or repair and overhaul of aircraft and aircraft mechanical systems to ensure adherence to standards and procedures. Start aircraft and observe gauges, meters, and other instruments to detect evidence of malfunctions. Examine aircraft access plates and doors for security. Examine landing gear, tires, and exteriors of fuselage, wings, and engines for evidence of damage or corrosion and to determine whether repairs are needed.

Prepare and maintain detailed repair, inspection, investigation, and certification records and reports. Inspect new, repaired, or modified aircraft to identify damage or defects and to assess airworthiness and conformance to standards, using checklists, hand tools, and test instruments. Examine maintenance records and flight logs to determine if service and maintenance checks and overhauls were performed at prescribed intervals. Recommend replacement, repair, or modification of aircraft equipment. Recommend changes in rules, policies, standards, and regulations based on knowledge of operating conditions, aircraft improvements, and other factors. Issue pilots' licenses to individuals meeting standards. Investigate air accidents and complaints to determine causes. Observe flight activities of pilots to assess flying skills and to ensure conformance to flight and safety regulations. Conduct flight test programs to test equipment, instruments, and systems under a variety of conditions, using both manual and automatic controls. Approve or deny issuance of certificates of airworthiness. Analyze training programs and conduct oral and written examinations to ensure the competency of persons operating, installing, and repairing aircraft equipment. Schedule and coordinate in-flight testing programs with ground crews and air traffic control to ensure availability of ground tracking, equipment monitoring, and related services.

Personality Type: Realistic. These occupations frequently involve work activities that include practical, hands-on problems and solutions. They often deal with plants; animals; and real-world materials such as wood, tools, and machinery. Many of the occupations require working outside and don't involve a lot of paperwork or working closely with others.

GOE—Interest Area/Cluster: 07. Government and Public Administration. **Work Group:** 07.03. Regulations Enforcement. **Other Jobs in This Work Group:** Agricultural Inspectors; Compliance Officers, Except Agriculture, Construction, Health and Safety, and Transportation; Construction and Building Inspectors; Environmental Compliance Inspectors; Equal Opportunity Representatives and Officers; Financial Examiners; Fire Inspectors; Fish and Game Wardens; Forest Fire Inspectors and Prevention Specialists; Freight and Cargo Inspectors; Government Property Inspectors and Investigators; Immigration and Customs Inspectors; Licensing Examiners and Inspectors; Nuclear Monitoring Technicians; Occupational Health and Safety Specialists; Occupational Health and

Safety Technicians; Tax Examiners, Collectors, and Revenue Agents; Transportation Vehicle, Equipment, and Systems Inspectors, Except Aviation.

Skills—Systems Analysis: Determining how a system should work and how changes will affect outcomes. **Systems Evaluation:** Looking at many indicators of system performance and taking into account their accuracy. **Quality Control Analysis:** Evaluating the quality or performance of products, services, or processes. **Operation Monitoring:** Watching gauges, dials, or other indicators to make sure a machine is working properly. **Troubleshooting:** Determining what is causing an operating error and deciding what to do about it. **Operation and Control:** Controlling operations of equipment or systems. **Reading Comprehension:** Understanding written sentences and paragraphs in work-related documents. **Judgment and Decision Making:** Weighing the relative costs and benefits of a potential action.

Education and Training Program: Avionics Maintenance Technology/Technician Training. **Related Knowledge/ Courses—Physics:** Physical principles, laws, and applications, including air, water, material dynamics, light, atomic principles, heat, electric theory, earth formations, and meteorological and related natural phenomena. **Mechanical Devices:** Machines and tools, including their designs, uses, benefits, repair, and maintenance. **Transportation:** Principles and methods for moving people or goods by air, rail, sea, or road, including their relative costs, advantages, and limitations. **Chemistry:** The composition, structure, and properties of substances and of the chemical processes and transformations that they undergo. This includes uses of chemicals and their interactions, danger signs, production techniques, and disposal methods. **Design:** Design techniques, principles, tools, and instruments involved in the production and use of precision technical plans, blueprints, drawings, and models. **Law and Government:** Laws, legal codes, court procedures, precedents, government regulations, executive orders, agency rules, and the democratic political process.

Work Environment: More often indoors than outdoors; noisy; sitting.

Avionics Technicians

- ❋ Education/Training Required: Postsecondary vocational training
- ❋ Annual Earnings: $48,100
- ❋ Beginning Wage: $33,050
- ❋ Earnings Growth Potential: Low
- ❋ Growth: 8.1%
- ❋ Annual Job Openings: 1,193
- ❋ Self-Employed: 0.0%
- ❋ Part-Time: 0.0%

Install, inspect, test, adjust, or repair avionics equipment, such as radar, radio, navigation, and missile control systems in aircraft or space vehicles. Set up and operate ground support and test equipment to perform functional flight tests of electrical and electronic systems. Test and troubleshoot instruments, components, and assemblies, using circuit testers, oscilloscopes, and voltmeters. Keep records of maintenance and repair work. Coordinate work with that of engineers, technicians, and other aircraft maintenance personnel. Interpret flight test data to diagnose malfunctions and systemic performance problems. Install electrical and electronic components, assemblies, and systems in aircraft, using hand tools, power tools, and soldering irons. Adjust, repair, or replace malfunctioning components or assemblies, using hand tools and soldering irons. Connect components to assemblies such as radio systems, instruments, magnetos, inverters, and in-flight refueling systems, using hand tools and soldering irons. Assemble components such as switches, electrical controls, and junction boxes, using hand tools and soldering irons. Fabricate parts and test aids as required. Lay out installation of aircraft assemblies and systems, following documentation such as blueprints, manuals, and wiring diagrams. Assemble prototypes or models of circuits, instruments, and systems so that they can be used for testing. Operate computer-aided drafting and design applications to design avionics system modifications.

Personality Type: Realistic. These occupations frequently involve work activities that include practical, hands-on problems and solutions. They often deal with plants; animals; and real-world materials such as wood, tools, and machinery. Many of the occupations require working outside and don't involve a lot of paperwork or working closely with others.

GOE—Interest Area/Cluster: 13. Manufacturing. **Work Group:** 13.12. Electrical and Electronic Repair. **Other Jobs in This Work Group:** Electric Motor, Power Tool, and Related Repairers; Electrical and Electronics Installers and Repairers, Transportation Equipment; Electrical and Electronics Repairers, Commercial and Industrial Equipment; Electronic Equipment Installers and Repairers, Motor Vehicles; Electronic Home Entertainment Equipment Installers and Repairers; Radio Mechanics.

Skills—Installation: Installing equipment, machines, wiring, or programs to meet specifications. **Repairing:** Repairing machines or systems, using the needed tools. **Equipment Maintenance:** Performing routine maintenance and determining when and what kind of maintenance is needed. **Troubleshooting:** Determining what is causing an operating error and deciding what to do about it. **Operation and Control:** Controlling operations of equipment or systems. **Operation Monitoring:** Watching gauges, dials, or other indicators to make sure a machine is working properly. **Quality Control Analysis:** Evaluating the quality or performance of products, services, or processes. **Science:** Using scientific methods to solve problems.

Education and Training Programs: Airframe Mechanics and Aircraft Maintenance Technology/Technician Training; Avionics Maintenance Technology/Technician Training. **Related Knowledge/Courses—Engineering and Technology:** Equipment, tools, and mechanical devices and their uses to produce motion, light, power, technology, and other applications. **Mechanical Devices:** Machines and tools, including their designs, uses, benefits, repair, and maintenance. **Computers and Electronics:** Electric circuit boards, processors, chips, and computer hardware and software, including applications and programming. **Telecommunications:** Transmission, broadcasting, switching, control, and operation of telecommunications systems. **Production and Processing:** Inputs, outputs, raw materials, waste, quality control, costs, and techniques for maximizing the manufacture and distribution of goods. **Design:** Design techniques, principles, tools, and instruments involved in the production and use of precision technical plans, blueprints, drawings, and models.

Work Environment: Indoors; noisy; contaminants; hazardous conditions; sitting; using hands on objects, tools, or controls.

Bailiffs

* Education/Training Required: Moderate-term on-the-job training
* Annual Earnings: $36,900
* Beginning Wage: $19,130
* Earnings Growth Potential: High
* Growth: 11.2%
* Annual Job Openings: 2,223
* Self-Employed: 0.0%
* Part-Time: 1.8%

Maintain order in courts of law. Collect and retain unauthorized firearms from persons entering courtroom. Maintain order in courtroom during trial and guard jury from outside contact. Guard lodging of sequestered jury. Provide jury escort to restaurant and other areas outside of courtroom to prevent jury contact with public. Enforce courtroom rules of behavior and warn persons not to smoke or disturb court procedure. Report need for police or medical assistance to sheriff's office. Check courtroom for security and cleanliness and assure availability of sundry supplies for use of judge. Announce entrance of judge. Stop people from entering courtroom while judge charges jury.

Personality Type: Realistic. These occupations frequently involve work activities that include practical, hands-on problems and solutions. They often deal with plants; animals; and real-world materials such as wood, tools, and machinery. Many of the occupations require working outside and don't involve a lot of paperwork or working closely with others.

GOE—Interest Area/Cluster: 12. Law and Public Safety. **Work Group:** 12.04. Law Enforcement and Public Safety. **Other Jobs in This Work Group:** Correctional Officers and Jailers; Criminal Investigators and Special Agents; Detectives and Criminal Investigators; Fire Investigators; Forensic Science Technicians; Parking Enforcement Workers; Police and Sheriff's Patrol Officers; Police Detectives; Police Identification and Records Officers; Police Patrol Officers; Sheriffs and Deputy Sheriffs; Transit and Railroad Police.

Skills—Persuasion: Persuading others to approach things differently. **Social Perceptiveness:** Being aware of others' reactions and understanding why they react the way they do.

Education and Training Program: Criminal Justice/ Police Science. **Related Knowledge/Courses—Public Safety and Security:** Weaponry; public safety; security operations, rules, regulations, precautions, and prevention; and the protection of people, data, and property. **Law and Government:** Laws, legal codes, court procedures, precedents, government regulations, executive orders, agency rules, and the democratic political process. **Philosophy and Theology:** Different philosophical systems and religions, including their basic principles, values, ethics, ways of thinking, customs, and practices and their impact on human culture. **Customer and Personal Service:** Principles and processes for providing customer and personal services, including needs assessment techniques, quality service standards, alternative delivery systems, and customer satisfaction evaluation techniques. **Psychology:** Human behavior and performance, mental processes, psychological research methods, and the assessment and treatment of behavioral and affective disorders. **Sociology and Anthropology:** Group behavior and dynamics; societal trends and influences; and cultures and their history, migrations, ethnicity, and origins.

Work Environment: Indoors; contaminants; disease or infections; sitting.

Bakers

- ❋ Education/Training Required: Long-term on-the-job training
- ❋ Annual Earnings: $22,590
- ❋ Beginning Wage: $15,760
- ❋ Earnings Growth Potential: Low
- ❋ Growth: 10.0%
- ❋ Annual Job Openings: 31,442
- ❋ Self-Employed: 4.3%
- ❋ Part-Time: 22.1%

Mix and bake ingredients according to recipes to produce breads, rolls, cookies, cakes, pies, pastries, or other baked goods. Observe color of products being baked and adjust oven temperatures, humidity, and conveyor speeds accordingly. Set oven temperatures and place items into hot ovens for baking. Combine measured ingredients in bowls of mixing, blending, or cooking machinery. Measure and weigh flour and other ingredients to prepare batters, doughs, fillings, and icings, using scales and graduated containers. Roll, knead, cut, and shape dough to form sweet rolls, pie crusts, tarts, cookies, and other products. Place dough in pans, in molds, or on sheets and bake in production ovens or on grills. Adapt the quantity of ingredients to match the amount of items to be baked. Check the quality of raw materials to ensure that standards and specifications are met. Apply glazes, icings, or other toppings to baked goods, using spatulas or brushes. Check equipment to ensure that it meets health and safety regulations and perform maintenance or cleaning as necessary. Decorate baked goods such as cakes and pastries. Set time and speed controls for mixing machines, blending machines, or steam kettles so that ingredients will be mixed or cooked according to instructions. Prepare and maintain inventory and production records. Direct and coordinate bakery deliveries. Order and receive supplies and equipment. Operate slicing and wrapping machines. Develop new recipes for baked goods.

Personality Type: Realistic. These occupations frequently involve work activities that include practical, hands-on problems and solutions. They often deal with plants; animals; and real-world materials such as wood, tools, and machinery. Many of the occupations require working outside and don't involve a lot of paperwork or working closely with others.

GOE—Interest Area/Cluster: 13. Manufacturing. **Work Group:** 13.03. Production Work, Assorted Materials Processing. **Other Jobs in This Work Group:** Cementing and Gluing Machine Operators and Tenders; Chemical Equipment Operators and Tenders; Cleaning, Washing, and Metal Pickling Equipment Operators and Tenders; Coating, Painting, and Spraying Machine Setters, Operators, and Tenders; Cooling and Freezing Equipment Operators and Tenders; Cutting and Slicing Machine Setters, Operators, and Tenders; Extruding and Forming Machine Setters, Operators, and Tenders, Synthetic and Glass Fibers; Extruding, Forming, Pressing, and Compacting Machine Setters, Operators, and Tenders; Food and Tobacco Roasting, Baking, and Drying Machine Operators and Tenders; Food Batchmakers; Food Cooking Machine Operators and Tenders; Furnace, Kiln, Oven, Drier, and Kettle Operators and Tenders; Heat Treating Equipment Setters, Operators, and Tenders, Metal and Plastic; Helpers—Production Workers; Meat, Poultry, and Fish Cutters and Trimmers; Metal-Refining Furnace Operators and Tenders; Mixing and Blending Machine Setters, Operators, and Tenders;

Packaging and Filling Machine Operators and Tenders; Plating and Coating Machine Setters, Operators, and Tenders, Metal and Plastic; Pourers and Casters, Metal; Sawing Machine Setters, Operators, and Tenders, Wood; Separating, Filtering, Clarifying, Precipitating, and Still Machine Setters, Operators, and Tenders; Sewing Machine Operators; Shoe Machine Operators and Tenders; Slaughterers and Meat Packers; Team Assemblers; Textile Bleaching and Dyeing Machine Operators and Tenders; Tire Builders; Woodworking Machine Setters, Operators, and Tenders, Except Sawing.

Skills—Quality Control Analysis: Evaluating the quality or performance of products, services, or processes. **Systems Evaluation:** Looking at many indicators of system performance and taking into account their accuracy. **Equipment Maintenance:** Performing routine maintenance and determining when and what kind of maintenance is needed. **Operation and Control:** Controlling operations of equipment or systems. **Troubleshooting:** Determining what is causing an operating error and deciding what to do about it. **Systems Analysis:** Determining how a system should work and how changes will affect outcomes. **Management of Personnel Resources:** Motivating, developing, and directing people as they work; identifying the best people for the job. **Operation Monitoring:** Watching gauges, dials, or other indicators to make sure a machine is working properly.

Education and Training Program: Baking and Pastry Arts/Baker/Pastry Chef Training. **Related Knowledge/Courses—Food Production:** Techniques and equipment for planting, growing, and harvesting of food for consumption, including crop-rotation methods, animal husbandry, and food storage/handling techniques. **Production and Processing:** Inputs, outputs, raw materials, waste, quality control, costs, and techniques for maximizing the manufacture and distribution of goods. **Personnel and Human Resources:** Principles and procedures for personnel recruitment; selection; training; compensation and benefits; labor relations and negotiation; and personnel information systems. **Mathematics:** Numbers and their operations and interrelationships, including arithmetic, algebra, geometry, calculus, and statistics and their applications. **Sales and Marketing:** Principles and methods involved in showing, promoting, and selling products or services. This includes marketing strategies and tactics, product demonstration and sales techniques, and sales control systems.

Administration and Management: Principles and processes involved in business and organizational planning, coordination, and execution. This includes strategic planning, resource allocation, manpower modeling, leadership techniques, and production methods.

Work Environment: Indoors; very hot or cold; minor burns, cuts, bites, or stings; standing; walking and running; using hands on objects, tools, or controls.

Bill and Account Collectors

- ✹ Education/Training Required: Short-term on-the-job training
- ✹ Annual Earnings: $29,990
- ✹ Beginning Wage: $20,630
- ✹ Earnings Growth Potential: Low
- ✹ Growth: 22.9%
- ✹ Annual Job Openings: 118,709
- ✹ Self-Employed: 1.0%
- ✹ Part-Time: 10.7%

Locate and notify customers of delinquent accounts by mail, telephone, or personal visit to solicit payment. Duties include receiving payment and posting amount to customer's account, preparing statements to credit department if customer fails to respond, initiating repossession proceedings or service disconnection, and keeping records of collection and status of accounts. Receive payments and post amounts paid to customer accounts. Locate and monitor overdue accounts, using computers and a variety of automated systems. Record information about financial status of customers and status of collection efforts. Locate and notify customers of delinquent accounts by mail, telephone, or personal visits to solicit payment. Confer with customers by telephone or in person to determine reasons for overdue payments and to review the terms of sales, service, or credit contracts. Advise customers of necessary actions and strategies for debt repayment. Persuade customers to pay amounts due on credit accounts, damage claims, or nonpayable checks or to return merchandise. Sort and file correspondence and perform miscellaneous clerical duties such as answering correspondence and writing reports. Perform various administrative functions for assigned accounts, such as recording address changes and purging the records of deceased customers. Arrange for debt repayment or establish repayment schedules based on customers' financial situations. Negotiate credit extensions when necessary. Trace delinquent customers to new addresses by inquiring at post offices, telephone companies, or credit bureaus or through the questioning of neighbors. Notify credit departments, order merchandise repossession or service disconnection, and turn over account records to attorneys when customers fail to respond to collection attempts. Drive vehicles to visit customers, return merchandise to creditors, or deliver bills.

Personality Type: Conventional. These occupations frequently involve following set procedures and routines and can include working with data and details more than with ideas. Usually there is a clear line of authority to follow.

GOE—Interest Area/Cluster: 06. Finance and Insurance. **Work Group:** 06.04. Finance/Insurance Customer Service. **Other Jobs in This Work Group:** Loan Interviewers and Clerks; New Accounts Clerks; Tellers.

Skills—Management of Financial Resources: Determining how money will be spent to get the work done and accounting for these expenditures. **Speaking:** Talking to others to effectively convey information. **Management of Personnel Resources:** Motivating, developing, and directing people as they work; identifying the best people for the job. **Social Perceptiveness:** Being aware of others' reactions and understanding why they react the way they do. **Operations Analysis:** Analyzing needs and product requirements to create a design. **Time Management:** Managing one's own time and the time of others. **Service Orientation:** Actively looking for ways to help people. **Judgment and Decision Making:** Weighing the relative costs and benefits of a potential action.

Education and Training Program: Banking and Financial Support Services. **Related Knowledge/Courses— Clerical Studies:** Administrative and clerical procedures and systems such as word-processing systems, filing and records management systems, stenography and transcription, forms, design principles, and other office procedures and terminology. **Economics and Accounting:** Economic and accounting principles and practices, the financial markets, banking, and the analysis and reporting of financial data. **Law and Government:** Laws, legal codes, court procedures, precedents, government regulations, executive orders, agency rules, and the democratic political process.

Customer and Personal Service: Principles and processes for providing customer and personal services, including needs assessment techniques, quality service standards, alternative delivery systems, and customer satisfaction evaluation techniques. **Computers and Electronics:** Electric circuit boards, processors, chips, and computer hardware and software, including applications and programming. **Personnel and Human Resources:** Principles and procedures for personnel recruitment; selection; training; compensation and benefits; labor relations and negotiation; and personnel information systems.

Work Environment: Indoors; sitting; using hands on objects, tools, or controls; repetitive motions.

Billing, Cost, and Rate Clerks

- ❋ Education/Training Required: Moderate-term on-the-job training
- ❋ Annual Earnings: $29,970
- ❋ Beginning Wage: $20,930
- ❋ Earnings Growth Potential: Low
- ❋ Growth: 4.4%
- ❋ Annual Job Openings: 81,885
- ❋ Self-Employed: 1.6%
- ❋ Part-Time: 14.3%

The job openings listed here are shared with Billing, Posting, and Calculating Machine Operators and with Statement Clerks.

Compile data, compute fees and charges, and prepare invoices for billing purposes. Duties include computing costs and calculating rates for goods, services, and shipment of goods; posting data; and keeping other relevant records. May involve use of computer or typewriter, calculator, and adding and bookkeeping machines. Verify accuracy of billing data and revise any errors. Operate typing, adding, calculating, and billing machines. Prepare itemized statements, bills, or invoices and record amounts due for items purchased or services rendered. Review documents such as purchase orders, sales tickets, charge slips, or hospital records to compute fees and charges due. Perform bookkeeping work, including posting data and keeping other records concerning costs of goods and services and the shipment of goods. Keep records of invoices and support documents. Resolve discrepancies in accounting records. Type billing documents, shipping labels, credit memorandums, and credit forms, using typewriters or computers. Contact customers to obtain or relay account information. Compute credit terms, discounts, shipment charges, and rates for goods and services to complete billing documents. Answer mail and telephone inquiries regarding rates, routing, and procedures. Track accumulated hours and dollar amounts charged to each client job to calculate client fees for professional services such as legal and accounting services. Review compiled data on operating costs and revenues to set rates. Compile reports of cost factors, such as labor, production, storage, and equipment. Consult sources such as rate books, manuals, and insurance company representatives to determine specific charges and information such as rules, regulations, and government tax and tariff information. Update manuals when rates, rules, or regulations are amended. Estimate market value of products or services.

Personality Type: Conventional. These occupations frequently involve following set procedures and routines and can include working with data and details more than with ideas. Usually there is a clear line of authority to follow.

GOE—Interest Area/Cluster: 04. Business and Administration. **Work Group:** 04.06. Mathematical Clerical Support. **Other Jobs in This Work Group:** Billing and Posting Clerks and Machine Operators; Bookkeeping, Accounting, and Auditing Clerks; Brokerage Clerks; Payroll and Timekeeping Clerks; Statement Clerks; Tax Preparers.

Skills—Writing: Communicating effectively with others in writing as indicated by the needs of the audience. **Active Listening:** Listening to what other people are saying and asking questions as appropriate. **Service Orientation:** Actively looking for ways to help people. **Reading Comprehension:** Understanding written sentences and paragraphs in work-related documents. **Instructing:** Teaching others how to do something. **Speaking:** Talking to others to effectively convey information. **Social Perceptiveness:** Being aware of others' reactions and understanding why they react the way they do.

Education and Training Program: Accounting Technology/Technician Training and Bookkeeping. **Related Knowledge/Courses—Clerical Studies:** Administrative and clerical procedures and systems such as word-processing systems, filing and records management systems, stenography and transcription, forms, design principles, and

other office procedures and terminology. **Economics and Accounting:** Economic and accounting principles and practices, the financial markets, banking, and the analysis and reporting of financial data. **Computers and Electronics:** Electric circuit boards, processors, chips, and computer hardware and software, including applications and programming. **Mathematics:** Numbers and their operations and interrelationships, including arithmetic, algebra, geometry, calculus, and statistics and their applications.

Work Environment: Indoors; sitting.

Billing, Posting, and Calculating Machine Operators

* Education/Training Required: Moderate-term on-the-job training
* Annual Earnings: $29,970
* Beginning Wage: $20,930
* Earnings Growth Potential: Low
* Growth: 4.4%
* Annual Job Openings: 81,885
* Self-Employed: 1.6%
* Part-Time: 14.3%

The job openings listed here are shared with Billing, Cost, and Rate Clerks and with Statement Clerks.

Operate machines that automatically perform mathematical processes, such as addition, subtraction, multiplication, and division, to calculate and record billing, accounting, statistical, and other numerical data. Duties include operating special billing machines to prepare statements, bills, and invoices and operating bookkeeping machines to copy and post data, make computations, and compile records of transactions. Enter into machines all information needed for bill generation. Train other calculating machine operators and review their work. Operate special billing machines to prepare statements, bills, and invoices. Operate bookkeeping machines to copy and post data, make computations, and compile records of transactions. Reconcile and post receipts for cash received by various departments. Prepare transmittal reports for changes to assessment and tax rolls; redemption file changes; and warrants, deposits, and invoices. Encode and add amounts of transaction documents, such as checks or money orders, using encoding machines. Balance and reconcile batch control totals with source documents or computer listings to locate errors, encode correct amounts, or prepare correction records. Compute payroll and retirement amounts, applying knowledge of payroll deductions, actuarial tables, disability factors, and survivor allowances. Maintain ledgers and registers, posting charges and refunds to individual funds and computing and verifying balances. Compute monies due on personal and real property, inventories, redemption payments, and other amounts, applying specialized knowledge of tax rates, formulas, interest rates, and other relevant information. Verify and post to ledgers purchase orders, reports of goods received, invoices, paid vouchers, and other information. Assign purchase order numbers to invoices, requisitions, and formal and informal bids. Verify completeness and accuracy of original documents such as business property statements, tax rolls, invoices, bonds and coupons, and redemption certificates. Bundle sorted documents to prepare those drawn on other banks for collection. Transcribe data from office records, using specified forms, billing machines, and transcribing machines. Sort and list items for proof or collection. Send completed bills to billing clerks for information verification. Transfer data from machines, such as encoding machines, to computers. Sort and microfilm transaction documents, such as checks, using sorting machines. Observe operation of sorters to locate documents that machines cannot read and manually record amounts of these documents.

Personality Type: Conventional. These occupations frequently involve following set procedures and routines and can include working with data and details more than with ideas. Usually there is a clear line of authority to follow.

GOE—Interest Area/Cluster: 04. Business and Administration. **Work Group:** 04.08. Clerical Machine Operation. **Other Jobs in This Work Group:** Data Entry Keyers; Mail Clerks and Mail Machine Operators, Except Postal Service; Office Machine Operators, Except Computer; Switchboard Operators, Including Answering Service; Word Processors and Typists.

Skills—Speaking: Talking to others to effectively convey information. **Active Listening:** Listening to what other people are saying and asking questions as appropriate. **Writing:** Communicating effectively with others in writing as indicated by the needs of the audience.

Education and Training Program: Accounting Technology/Technician Training and Bookkeeping. **Related Knowledge/Courses—Economics and Accounting:** Economic and accounting principles and practices, the financial markets, banking, and the analysis and reporting of financial data. **Clerical Studies:** Administrative and clerical procedures and systems such as word-processing systems, filing and records management systems, stenography and transcription, forms, design principles, and other office procedures and terminology. **Personnel and Human Resources:** Principles and procedures for personnel recruitment; selection; training; compensation and benefits; labor relations and negotiation; and personnel information systems.

Work Environment: Indoors; noisy; contaminants; sitting; using hands on objects, tools, or controls; repetitive motions.

Boilermakers

- ❋ Education/Training Required: Long-term on-the-job training
- ❋ Annual Earnings: $50,700
- ❋ Beginning Wage: $32,910
- ❋ Earnings Growth Potential: Medium
- ❋ Growth: 14.0%
- ❋ Annual Job Openings: 2,333
- ❋ Self-Employed: 0.2%
- ❋ Part-Time: 2.6%

Construct, assemble, maintain, and repair stationary steam boilers and boiler house auxiliaries. Align structures or plate sections to assemble boiler frame tanks or vats, following blueprints. Work involves use of hand and power tools, plumb bobs, levels, wedges, dogs, or turnbuckles. Assist in testing assembled vessels. Direct cleaning of boilers and boiler furnaces. Inspect and repair boiler fittings, such as safety valves, regulators, automatic-control mechanisms, water columns, and auxiliary machines. Examine boilers, pressure vessels, tanks, and vats to locate defects such as leaks, weak spots, and defective sections so that they can be repaired. Bolt or arc-weld pressure vessel structures and parts together, using wrenches and welding equipment. Inspect assembled vessels and individual components, such as tubes, fittings, valves, controls, and auxiliary mechanisms, to locate any defects. Repair or replace defective pressure vessel parts, such as safety valves and regulators, using torches, jacks, caulking hammers, power saws, threading dies, welding equipment, and metalworking machinery. Attach rigging and signal crane or hoist operators to lift heavy frame and plate sections and other parts into place. Bell, bead with power hammers, or weld pressure vessel tube ends in order to ensure leakproof joints. Lay out plate, sheet steel, or other heavy metal and locate and mark bending and cutting lines, using protractors, compasses, and drawing instruments or templates. Install manholes, handholes, taps, tubes, valves, gauges, and feedwater connections in drums of water tube boilers, using hand tools. Study blueprints to determine locations, relationships, and dimensions of parts. Straighten or reshape bent pressure vessel plates and structure parts, using hammers, jacks, and torches. Shape seams, joints, and irregular edges of pressure vessel sections and structural parts in order to attain specified fit of parts, using cutting torches, hammers, files, and metalworking machines. Position, align, and secure structural parts and related assemblies to boiler frames, tanks, or vats of pressure vessels, following blueprints. Locate and mark reference points for columns or plates on boiler foundations, following blueprints and using straightedges, squares, transits, and measuring instruments. Shape and fabricate parts, such as stacks, uptakes, and chutes, in order to adapt pressure vessels, heat exchangers, and piping to premises, using heavy-metalworking machines such as brakes, rolls, and drill presses. Clean pressure vessel equipment, using scrapers, wire brushes, and cleaning solvents.

Personality Type: Realistic. These occupations frequently involve work activities that include practical, hands-on problems and solutions. They often deal with plants; animals; and real-world materials such as wood, tools, and machinery. Many of the occupations require working outside and don't involve a lot of paperwork or working closely with others.

GOE—Interest Area/Cluster: 02. Architecture and Construction. **Work Group:** 02.04. Construction Crafts. **Other Jobs in This Work Group:** Brickmasons and Blockmasons; Carpet Installers; Cement Masons and Concrete Finishers; Commercial Divers; Construction Carpenters; Crane and Tower Operators; Drywall and Ceiling Tile Installers; Electricians; Fence Erectors; Floor Layers, Except Carpet, Wood, and Hard Tiles; Floor Sanders and Finishers; Glaziers; Hazardous Materials Removal Workers; Insulation Workers, Floor, Ceiling, and Wall; Insulation Workers, Mechanical; Manufactured Building and Mobile Home Installers; Operating Engineers and Other Construction Equipment Operators; Painters, Construction and Maintenance; Paperhangers; Paving, Surfacing, and Tamping Equipment Operators; Pile-Driver Operators; Pipe Fitters and Steamfitters; Pipelayers; Plasterers and Stucco Masons; Plumbers; Plumbers, Pipefitters, and Steamfitters; Rail-Track Laying and Maintenance Equipment Operators; Refractory Materials Repairers, Except Brickmasons; Reinforcing Iron and Rebar Workers; Riggers; Roofers; Rough Carpenters; Security and Fire Alarm Systems Installers; Segmental Pavers; Sheet Metal Workers; Stone Cutters and Carvers, Manufacturing; Stonemasons; Structural Iron and Steel Workers; Tapers; Terrazzo Workers and Finishers; Tile and Marble Setters.

Skills—Repairing: Repairing machines or systems, using the needed tools. **Installation:** Installing equipment, machines, wiring, or programs to meet specifications. **Equipment Maintenance:** Performing routine maintenance and determining when and what kind of maintenance is needed. **Operation Monitoring:** Watching gauges, dials, or other indicators to make sure a machine is working properly. **Mathematics:** Using mathematics to solve problems. **Troubleshooting:** Determining what is causing an operating error and deciding what to do about it. **Operation and Control:** Controlling operations of equipment or systems. **Equipment Selection:** Determining the kind of tools and equipment needed to do a job.

Education and Training Program: Boilermaking/Boilermaker Training. **Related Knowledge/Courses—Building and Construction:** Materials, methods, and the appropriate tools to construct objects, structures, and buildings. **Mechanical Devices:** Machines and tools, including their designs, uses, benefits, repair, and maintenance. **Engineering and Technology:** Equipment, tools, and mechanical devices and their uses to produce motion, light, power, technology, and other applications. **Design:** Design techniques, principles, tools, and instruments involved in the production and use of precision technical plans, blueprints, drawings, and models. **Physics:** Physical principles, laws, and applications, including air, water, material dynamics, light, atomic principles, heat, electric theory, earth formations, and meteorological and related natural phenomena. **Transportation:** Principles and methods for moving people or goods by air, rail, sea, or road, including their relative costs, advantages, and limitations.

Work Environment: Noisy; very hot or cold; contaminants; minor burns, cuts, bites, or stings; standing; using hands on objects, tools, or controls.

Bookkeeping, Accounting, and Auditing Clerks

- ❋ Education/Training Required: Moderate-term on-the-job training
- ❋ Annual Earnings: $31,560
- ❋ Beginning Wage: $20,310
- ❋ Earnings Growth Potential: Medium
- ❋ Growth: 12.5%
- ❋ Annual Job Openings: 286,854
- ❋ Self-Employed: 6.6%
- ❋ Part-Time: 24.8%

Compute, classify, and record numerical data to keep financial records complete. Perform any combination of routine calculating, posting, and verifying duties to obtain primary financial data for use in maintaining accounting records. May also check the accuracy of figures, calculations, and postings pertaining to business transactions recorded by other workers. Operate computers programmed with accounting software to record, store, and analyze information. Check figures, postings, and documents for correct entry, mathematical accuracy, and proper codes. Comply with federal, state, and company policies, procedures, and regulations. Debit, credit, and total accounts on computer spreadsheets and databases, using specialized accounting software. Classify, record, and summarize numerical and financial data to compile and keep financial records, using journals and ledgers or computers. Calculate, prepare, and issue bills, invoices, account statements, and other financial statements according to established procedures. Code documents according to company procedures. Compile statistical, financial, accounting, or auditing reports and tables pertaining to such matters as cash receipts, expenditures, accounts payable and receivable, and profits and losses. Operate 10-key calculators, typewriters, and copy machines to perform calculations and produce documents. Access computerized financial information to answer general questions as well as those related to specific accounts. Reconcile or note and report discrepancies found in records. Perform financial calculations such as amounts due, interest charges, balances, discounts, equity, and principal. Perform general office duties such as filing, answering telephones, and handling routine correspondence. Prepare bank deposits by compiling data from cashiers; verifying and balancing receipts; and sending cash, checks, or other forms of payment to banks. Receive, record, and bank cash, checks, and vouchers. Calculate and prepare checks for utilities, taxes, and other payments. Compare computer printouts to manually maintained journals to determine if they match. Reconcile records of bank transactions. Prepare trial balances of books. Monitor status of loans and accounts to ensure that payments are up to date. Transfer details from separate journals to general ledgers or data-processing sheets. Compile budget data and documents based on estimated revenues and expenses and previous budgets. Calculate costs of materials, overhead, and other expenses, based on estimates, quotations, and price lists.

Personality Type: Conventional. These occupations frequently involve following set procedures and routines and can include working with data and details more than with ideas. Usually there is a clear line of authority to follow.

GOE—Interest Area/Cluster: 04. Business and Administration. **Work Group:** 04.06. Mathematical Clerical Support. **Other Jobs in This Work Group:** Billing and Posting Clerks and Machine Operators; Billing, Cost, and Rate Clerks; Brokerage Clerks; Payroll and Timekeeping Clerks; Statement Clerks; Tax Preparers.

Skills—Management of Financial Resources: Determining how money will be spent to get the work done and accounting for these expenditures. **Mathematics:** Using mathematics to solve problems. **Time Management:** Managing one's own time and the time of others.

Education and Training Programs: Accounting and Related Services, Other; Accounting Technology/Technician Training and Bookkeeping. **Related Knowledge/Courses—Clerical Studies:** Administrative and clerical procedures and systems such as word-processing systems, filing and records management systems, stenography and transcription, forms, design principles, and other office procedures and terminology. **Economics and Accounting:** Economic and accounting principles and practices, the financial markets, banking, and the analysis and reporting of financial data. **Mathematics:** Numbers and their operations and interrelationships, including arithmetic, algebra, geometry, calculus, and statistics and their applications. **Computers and Electronics:** Electric circuit boards, processors, chips, and computer hardware and software, including applications and programming.

Work Environment: Indoors; sitting; repetitive motions.

Brickmasons and Blockmasons

- ❋ Education/Training Required: Long-term on-the-job training
- ❋ Annual Earnings: $44,070
- ❋ Beginning Wage: $26,370
- ❋ Earnings Growth Potential: High
- ❋ Growth: 9.7%
- ❋ Annual Job Openings: 17,569
- ❋ Self-Employed: 24.5%
- ❋ Part-Time: 7.9%

Lay and bind building materials, such as brick, structural tile, concrete block, cinderblock, glass block, and terra-cotta block, with mortar and other substances to construct or repair walls, partitions, arches, sewers, and other structures. Construct corners by fastening in plumb position a corner pole or building a corner pyramid of bricks and filling in between the corners, using a line from corner to corner to guide each course, or layer, of brick. Measure distance from reference points and mark guidelines to lay out work, using plumb bobs and levels. Fasten or fuse brick or other building material to structure with wire clamps, anchor holes, torch, or cement. Calculate angles and courses and determine vertical and horizontal alignment of courses. Break or cut bricks, tiles, or blocks to size, using trowel edge, hammer, or power saw. Remove excess mortar with trowels and hand tools and finish mortar joints with jointing tools for a sealed, uniform appearance. Interpret blueprints and drawings to determine specifications and to calculate the materials required. Apply and smooth mortar or other mixture over work surface. Mix specified amounts of sand, clay, dirt, or mortar powder with water to form refractory mixtures. Examine brickwork or structure to determine need for repair. Clean working surface to remove scale, dust, soot, or chips of brick and mortar, using broom, wire brush, or scraper. Lay and align bricks, blocks, or tiles to build or repair structures or high-temperature equipment, such as cupola, kilns, ovens, or furnaces. Remove burned or damaged brick or mortar, using sledgehammer, crowbar, chipping gun, or chisel. Spray or spread refractory material over brickwork to protect against deterioration.

Personality Type: Realistic. These occupations frequently involve work activities that include practical, hands-on problems and solutions. They often deal with plants; animals; and real-world materials such as wood, tools, and machinery. Many of the occupations require working outside and don't involve a lot of paperwork or working closely with others.

GOE—Interest Area/Cluster: 02. Architecture and Construction. **Work Group:** 02.04. Construction Crafts. **Other Jobs in This Work Group:** Boilermakers; Carpet Installers; Cement Masons and Concrete Finishers; Commercial Divers; Construction Carpenters; Crane and Tower Operators; Drywall and Ceiling Tile Installers; Electricians; Fence Erectors; Floor Layers, Except Carpet, Wood, and Hard Tiles; Floor Sanders and Finishers; Glaziers; Hazardous Materials Removal Workers; Insulation Workers, Floor, Ceiling, and Wall; Insulation Workers, Mechanical; Manufactured Building and Mobile Home Installers; Operating Engineers and Other Construction Equipment Operators; Painters, Construction and Maintenance; Paperhangers; Paving, Surfacing, and Tamping Equipment Operators; Pile-Driver Operators; Pipe Fitters and Steamfitters; Pipelayers; Plasterers and Stucco Masons; Plumbers; Plumbers, Pipefitters, and Steamfitters; Rail-Track Laying and Maintenance Equipment Operators; Refractory Materials Repairers, Except Brickmasons; Reinforcing Iron and Rebar Workers; Riggers; Roofers; Rough Carpenters; Security and Fire Alarm Systems Installers; Segmental Pavers; Sheet Metal Workers; Stone Cutters and Carvers, Manufacturing; Stonemasons; Structural Iron and Steel Workers; Tapers; Terrazzo Workers and Finishers; Tile and Marble Setters.

Skills—Equipment Maintenance: Performing routine maintenance and determining when and what kind of maintenance is needed. **Mathematics:** Using mathematics to solve problems. **Installation:** Installing equipment, machines, wiring, or programs to meet specifications. **Repairing:** Repairing machines or systems, using the needed tools. **Technology Design:** Generating or adapting equipment and technology to serve user needs.

Education and Training Program: Mason Training/ Masonry. **Related Knowledge/Courses—Building and Construction:** Materials, methods, and the appropriate tools to construct objects, structures, and buildings. **Design:** Design techniques, principles, tools, and instruments involved in the production and use of precision technical plans, blueprints, drawings, and models. **Mechanical Devices:** Machines and tools, including their designs, uses, benefits, repair, and maintenance. **Production and Processing:** Inputs, outputs, raw materials, waste, quality control, costs, and techniques for maximizing the manufacture and distribution of goods. **Public Safety and Security:** Weaponry; public safety; security operations, rules, regulations, precautions, and prevention; and the protection of people, data, and property. **Mathematics:** Numbers and their operations and interrelationships, including arithmetic, algebra, geometry, calculus, and statistics and their applications.

Work Environment: Outdoors; very hot or cold; hazardous equipment; standing; using hands on objects, tools, or controls; bending or twisting the body.

Broadcast Technicians

- ❋ Education/Training Required: Associate degree
- ❋ Annual Earnings: $32,230
- ❋ Beginning Wage: $17,060
- ❋ Earnings Growth Potential: High
- ❋ Growth: 12.1%
- ❋ Annual Job Openings: 2,955
- ❋ Self-Employed: 12.4%
- ❋ Part-Time: 12.9%

Set up, operate, and maintain the electronic equipment used to transmit radio and television programs. Control audio equipment to regulate volume level and quality of sound during radio and television broadcasts. Operate radio transmitter to broadcast radio and television programs. Maintain programming logs as required by station management and the Federal Communications Commission. Control audio equipment to regulate the volume and sound quality during radio and television broadcasts. Monitor strength, clarity, and reliability of incoming and outgoing signals and adjust equipment as necessary to maintain quality broadcasts. Regulate the fidelity, brightness, and contrast of video transmissions, using video console control panels. Observe monitors and converse with station personnel to determine audio and video levels and to ascertain that programs are airing. Preview scheduled programs to ensure that signals are functioning and programs are ready for transmission. Select sources from which programming will be received or through which programming will be transmitted. Report equipment problems, ensure that repairs are made; make emergency repairs to equipment when necessary and possible. Record sound onto tape or film for radio or television, checking its quality and making adjustments where necessary. Align antennae with receiving dishes to obtain the clearest signal for transmission of broadcasts from field locations. Substitute programs in cases where signals fail. Organize recording sessions and prepare areas such as radio booths and television stations for recording. Perform preventive and minor equipment maintenance, using hand tools. Instruct trainees in how to use television production equipment, how to film events, and how to copy and edit graphics or sound onto videotape. Schedule programming or read television programming logs to determine which programs are to be recorded or aired. Edit broadcast material electronically, using computers. Give technical directions to other personnel during filming. Set up and operate portable field transmission equipment outside the studio. Determine the number, type, and approximate location of microphones needed for best sound recording or transmission quality and position them appropriately. Design and modify equipment to employer specifications. Prepare reports outlining past and future programs, including content.

Personality Type: Realistic. These occupations frequently involve work activities that include practical, hands-on problems and solutions. They often deal with plants; animals; and real-world materials such as wood, tools, and machinery. Many of the occupations require working outside and don't involve a lot of paperwork or working closely with others.

GOE—Interest Area/Cluster: 03. Arts and Communication. **Work Group:** 03.09. Media Technology. **Other Jobs in This Work Group:** Audio and Video Equipment Technicians; Camera Operators, Television, Video, and Motion Picture; Film and Video Editors; Multi-Media Artists and Animators; Photographers; Radio Operators; Sound Engineering Technicians.

Skills—Operation Monitoring: Watching gauges, dials, or other indicators to make sure a machine is working properly. **Operation and Control:** Controlling operations of equipment or systems. **Installation:** Installing equipment, machines, wiring, or programs to meet specifications. **Troubleshooting:** Determining what is causing an operating error and deciding what to do about it. **Equipment Maintenance:** Performing routine maintenance and determining when and what kind of maintenance is needed. **Repairing:** Repairing machines or systems, using the needed tools. **Operations Analysis:** Analyzing needs and product requirements to create a design. **Technology Design:** Generating or adapting equipment and technology to serve user needs.

Education and Training Programs: Audiovisual Communications Technologies/Technician Training, Other; Communications Technology/Technician Training; Radio and Television Broadcasting Technology/Technician Training. **Related Knowledge/Courses—Telecommunications:** Transmission, broadcasting, switching, control, and operation of telecommunications systems. **Communications and Media:** Media production, communication, and dissemination techniques and methods, including alternative ways to inform and entertain via written, oral, and visual media. **Engineering and Technology:** Equipment, tools, and mechanical devices and their uses to produce motion, light, power, technology, and other applications. **Computers and Electronics:** Electric circuit boards, processors, chips, and computer hardware and software, including applications and programming. **Mechanical Devices:** Machines and tools, including their designs, uses, benefits, repair, and maintenance. **Production and Processing:** Inputs, outputs, raw materials, waste, quality control, costs, and techniques for maximizing the manufacture and distribution of goods.

Work Environment: Indoors; noisy; sitting; using hands on objects, tools, or controls.

Brokerage Clerks

- Education/Training Required: Moderate-term on-the-job training
- Annual Earnings: $37,360
- Beginning Wage: $25,710
- Earnings Growth Potential: Low
- Growth: 20.0%
- Annual Job Openings: 10,826
- Self-Employed: 0.0%
- Part-Time: 19.4%

Perform clerical duties involving the purchase or sale of securities. Duties include writing orders for stock purchases and sales, computing transfer taxes, verifying stock transactions, accepting and delivering securities, tracking stock price fluctuations, computing equity, distributing dividends, and keeping records of daily transactions and holdings. Correspond with customers and confer with co-workers to answer inquiries, discuss market fluctuations, and resolve account problems. Record and document security transactions, such as purchases, sales, conversions, redemptions, and payments, using computers, accounting ledgers, and certificate records. Schedule and coordinate transfer and delivery of security certificates between companies, departments, and customers. Prepare forms, such as receipts, withdrawal orders, transmittal papers, and transfer confirmations, based on transaction requests from stockholders. File, type, and operate standard office machines. Monitor daily stock prices and compute fluctuations to determine the need for additional collateral to secure loans. Prepare reports summarizing daily transactions and earnings for individual customer accounts. Compute total holdings, dividends, interest, transfer taxes, brokerage fees, and commissions and allocate appropriate payments to customers. Verify ownership and transaction information and dividend distribution instructions to ensure conformance with governmental regulations, using stock records and reports.

Personality Type: Conventional. These occupations frequently involve following set procedures and routines and can include working with data and details more than with ideas. Usually there is a clear line of authority to follow.

GOE—Interest Area/Cluster: 04. Business and Administration. **Work Group:** 04.06. Mathematical Clerical

Support. **Other Jobs in This Work Group:** Billing and Posting Clerks and Machine Operators; Billing, Cost, and Rate Clerks; Bookkeeping, Accounting, and Auditing Clerks; Payroll and Timekeeping Clerks; Statement Clerks; Tax Preparers.

Skills—Service Orientation: Actively looking for ways to help people. **Mathematics:** Using mathematics to solve problems. **Speaking:** Talking to others to effectively convey information. **Active Listening:** Listening to what other people are saying and asking questions as appropriate. **Systems Evaluation:** Looking at many indicators of system performance and taking into account their accuracy.

Education and Training Program: Accounting Technology/Technician Training and Bookkeeping. **Related Knowledge/Courses—Economics and Accounting:** Economic and accounting principles and practices, the financial markets, banking, and the analysis and reporting of financial data. **Clerical Studies:** Administrative and clerical procedures and systems such as word-processing systems, filing and records management systems, stenography and transcription, forms, design principles, and other office procedures and terminology. **Customer and Personal Service:** Principles and processes for providing customer and personal services, including needs assessment techniques, quality service standards, alternative delivery systems, and customer satisfaction evaluation techniques. **Sales and Marketing:** Principles and methods involved in showing, promoting, and selling products or services. This includes marketing strategies and tactics, product demonstration and sales techniques, and sales control systems. **Computers and Electronics:** Electric circuit boards, processors, chips, and computer hardware and software, including applications and programming. **Mathematics:** Numbers and their operations and interrelationships, including arithmetic, algebra, geometry, calculus, and statistics and their applications.

Work Environment: Indoors; sitting; repetitive motions.

Bus and Truck Mechanics and Diesel Engine Specialists

- ❋ Education/Training Required: Postsecondary vocational training
- ❋ Annual Earnings: $38,640
- ❋ Beginning Wage: $25,210
- ❋ Earnings Growth Potential: Low
- ❋ Growth: 11.5%
- ❋ Annual Job Openings: 25,428
- ❋ Self-Employed: 5.8%
- ❋ Part-Time: 2.8%

Diagnose, adjust, repair, or overhaul trucks, buses, and all types of diesel engines. Includes mechanics working primarily with automobile diesel engines. Use hand tools such as screwdrivers, pliers, wrenches, pressure gauges, and precision instruments, as well as power tools such as pneumatic wrenches, lathes, welding equipment, and jacks and hoists. Inspect brake systems, steering mechanisms, wheel bearings, and other important parts to ensure that they are in proper operating condition. Perform routine maintenance such as changing oil, checking batteries, and lubricating equipment and machinery. Adjust and reline brakes, align wheels, tighten bolts and screws, and reassemble equipment. Raise trucks, buses, and heavy parts or equipment, using hydraulic jacks or hoists. Test drive trucks and buses to diagnose malfunctions or to ensure that they are working properly. Inspect, test, and listen to defective equipment to diagnose malfunctions, using test instruments such as handheld computers, motor analyzers, chassis charts, and pressure gauges. Examine and adjust protective guards, loose bolts, and specified safety devices. Inspect and verify dimensions and clearances of parts to ensure conformance to factory specifications. Specialize in repairing and maintaining parts of the engine, such as fuel injection systems. Attach test instruments to equipment and read dials and gauges to diagnose malfunctions. Rewire ignition systems, lights, and instrument panels. Recondition and replace parts, pistons, bearings, gears, and valves. Repair and adjust seats, doors, and windows and install and repair accessories. Inspect, repair, and maintain automotive and mechanical equipment and machinery such as pumps and compressors. Disassemble and overhaul internal combustion engines, pumps, generators, transmissions, clutches, and differential units. Rebuild gas or diesel engines. Align front ends and suspension systems. Operate valve-grinding machines to grind and reset valves.

Personality Type: Realistic. These occupations frequently involve work activities that include practical, hands-on problems and solutions. They often deal with plants; animals; and real-world materials such as wood, tools, and machinery. Many of the occupations require working outside and don't involve a lot of paperwork or working closely with others.

GOE—Interest Area/Cluster: 13. Manufacturing. **Work Group:** 13.14. Vehicle and Facility Mechanical Work. **Other Jobs in This Work Group:** Aircraft Mechanics and Service Technicians; Aircraft Structure, Surfaces, Rigging, and Systems Assemblers; Automotive Body and Related Repairers; Automotive Glass Installers and Repairers; Automotive Master Mechanics; Automotive Service Technicians and Mechanics; Automotive Specialty Technicians; Farm Equipment Mechanics; Fiberglass Laminators and Fabricators; Mobile Heavy Equipment Mechanics, Except Engines; Motorboat Mechanics; Motorcycle Mechanics; Outdoor Power Equipment and Other Small Engine Mechanics; Rail Car Repairers; Recreational Vehicle Service Technicians; Tire Repairers and Changers.

Skills—Repairing: Repairing machines or systems, using the needed tools. **Equipment Maintenance:** Performing routine maintenance and determining when and what kind of maintenance is needed. **Troubleshooting:** Determining what is causing an operating error and deciding what to do about it. **Installation:** Installing equipment, machines, wiring, or programs to meet specifications. **Science:** Using scientific methods to solve problems. **Technology Design:** Generating or adapting equipment and technology to serve user needs. **Equipment Selection:** Determining the kind of tools and equipment needed to do a job.

Education and Training Programs: Diesel Mechanics Technology/Technician Training; Medium/Heavy Vehicle and Truck Technology/Technician Training. **Related Knowledge/Courses—Mechanical Devices:** Machines and tools, including their designs, uses, benefits, repair, and maintenance. **Transportation:** Principles and methods for moving people or goods by air, rail, sea, or road, including their relative costs, advantages, and limitations. **Public Safety and Security:** Weaponry; public safety; security operations, rules, regulations, precautions, and prevention; and the protection of people, data, and property. **Physics:**

Physical principles, laws, and applications, including air, water, material dynamics, light, atomic principles, heat, electric theory, earth formations, and meteorological and related natural phenomena. **Engineering and Technology:** Equipment, tools, and mechanical devices and their uses to produce motion, light, power, technology, and other applications. **Law and Government:** Laws, legal codes, court procedures, precedents, government regulations, executive orders, agency rules, and the democratic political process.

Work Environment: Noisy; very bright or dim lighting; contaminants; hazardous equipment; standing; using hands on objects, tools, or controls.

Bus Drivers, School

- ❋ Education/Training Required: Moderate-term on-the-job training
- ❋ Annual Earnings: $25,860
- ❋ Beginning Wage: $14,480
- ❋ Earnings Growth Potential: High
- ❋ Growth: 9.3%
- ❋ Annual Job Openings: 59,809
- ❋ Self-Employed: 1.4%
- ❋ Part-Time: 34.1%

Transport students or special clients, such as the elderly or persons with disabilities. Ensure adherence to safety rules. May assist passengers in boarding or exiting. Follow safety rules as students board and exit buses and as they cross streets near bus stops. Comply with traffic regulations to operate vehicles safely and courteously. Check the condition of a vehicle's tires, brakes, windshield wipers, lights, oil, fuel, water, and safety equipment to ensure that everything is in working order. Maintain order among pupils during trips to ensure safety. Pick up and drop off students at regularly scheduled neighborhood locations, following strict time schedules. Report any bus malfunctions or needed repairs. Drive gasoline, diesel, or electrically powered multi-passenger vehicles to transport students between neighborhoods, schools, and school activities. Prepare and submit reports that may include the number of passengers or trips, hours worked, mileage, fuel consumption, and fares received. Maintain knowledge of first-aid procedures. Keep bus interiors clean for passengers. Read maps and follow written and verbal geographic directions. Report delays, accidents, or other traffic and transportation situations, using telephones or mobile two-way radios. Regulate heating, lighting, and ventilation systems for passenger comfort. Escort small children across roads and highways. Make minor repairs to vehicles.

Personality Type: Realistic. These occupations frequently involve work activities that include practical, hands-on problems and solutions. They often deal with plants; animals; and real-world materials such as wood, tools, and machinery. Many of the occupations require working outside and don't involve a lot of paperwork or working closely with others.

GOE—Interest Area/Cluster: 16. Transportation, Distribution, and Logistics. **Work Group:** 16.06. Other Services Requiring Driving. **Other Jobs in This Work Group:** Ambulance Drivers and Attendants, Except Emergency Medical Technicians; Bus Drivers, Transit and Intercity; Couriers and Messengers; Driver/Sales Workers; Parking Lot Attendants; Postal Service Mail Carriers; Taxi Drivers and Chauffeurs.

Skills—Operation Monitoring: Watching gauges, dials, or other indicators to make sure a machine is working properly. **Equipment Maintenance:** Performing routine maintenance and determining when and what kind of maintenance is needed. **Operation and Control:** Controlling operations of equipment or systems. **Social Perceptiveness:** Being aware of others' reactions and understanding why they react the way they do. **Persuasion:** Persuading others to approach things differently. **Negotiation:** Bringing others together and trying to reconcile differences.

Education and Training Program: Truck and Bus Driver Training/Commercial Vehicle Operation. **Related Knowledge/Courses—Transportation:** Principles and methods for moving people or goods by air, rail, sea, or road, including their relative costs, advantages, and limitations. **Psychology:** Human behavior and performance, mental processes, psychological research methods, and the assessment and treatment of behavioral and affective disorders. **Public Safety and Security:** Weaponry; public safety; security operations, rules, regulations, precautions, and prevention; and the protection of people, data, and property.

Work Environment: Noisy; contaminants; disease or infections; sitting; using hands on objects, tools, or controls; repetitive motions.

Bus Drivers, Transit and Intercity

- ❋ Education/Training Required: Moderate-term on-the-job training
- ❋ Annual Earnings: $33,160
- ❋ Beginning Wage: $19,660
- ❋ Earnings Growth Potential: High
- ❋ Growth: 12.5%
- ❋ Annual Job Openings: 27,100
- ❋ Self-Employed: 1.3%
- ❋ Part-Time: 34.1%

Drive bus or motor coach, including regular route operations, charters, and private carriage. May assist passengers with baggage. May collect fares or tickets. Inspect vehicles and check gas, oil, and water levels prior to departure. Drive vehicles over specified routes or to specified destinations according to time schedules to transport passengers, complying with traffic regulations. Park vehicles at loading areas so that passengers can board. Assist passengers with baggage and collect tickets or cash fares. Report delays or accidents. Advise passengers to be seated and orderly while on vehicles. Regulate heating, lighting, and ventilating systems for passenger comfort. Load and unload baggage in baggage compartments. Record cash receipts and ticket fares. Make minor repairs to vehicle and change tires.

Personality Type: Realistic. These occupations frequently involve work activities that include practical, hands-on problems and solutions. They often deal with plants; animals; and real-world materials such as wood, tools, and machinery. Many of the occupations require working outside and don't involve a lot of paperwork or working closely with others.

GOE—Interest Area/Cluster: 16. Transportation, Distribution, and Logistics. **Work Group:** 16.06. Other Services Requiring Driving. **Other Jobs in This Work Group:** Ambulance Drivers and Attendants, Except Emergency Medical Technicians; Bus Drivers, School; Couriers and Messengers; Driver/Sales Workers; Parking Lot Attendants; Postal Service Mail Carriers; Taxi Drivers and Chauffeurs.

Skills—Equipment Maintenance: Performing routine maintenance and determining when and what kind of maintenance is needed. **Operation and Control:** Controlling operations of equipment or systems. **Social Perceptiveness:** Being aware of others' reactions and understanding why they react the way they do. **Operation Monitoring:** Watching gauges, dials, or other indicators to make sure a machine is working properly. **Troubleshooting:** Determining what is causing an operating error and deciding what to do about it. **Repairing:** Repairing machines or systems, using the needed tools.

Education and Training Program: Truck and Bus Driver Training/Commercial Vehicle Operation. **Related Knowledge/Courses—Transportation:** Principles and methods for moving people or goods by air, rail, sea, or road, including their relative costs, advantages, and limitations. **Geography:** Various methods for describing the location and distribution of land, sea, and air masses, including their physical locations, relationships, and characteristics. **Public Safety and Security:** Weaponry; public safety; security operations, rules, regulations, precautions, and prevention; and the protection of people, data, and property. **Psychology:** Human behavior and performance, mental processes, psychological research methods, and the assessment and treatment of behavioral and affective disorders. **Law and Government:** Laws, legal codes, court procedures, precedents, government regulations, executive orders, agency rules, and the democratic political process. **Customer and Personal Service:** Principles and processes for providing customer and personal services, including needs assessment techniques, quality service standards, alternative delivery systems, and customer satisfaction evaluation techniques.

Work Environment: Outdoors; noisy; contaminants; sitting; using hands on objects, tools, or controls; repetitive motions.

Camera Operators, Television, Video, and Motion Picture

* Education/Training Required: Postsecondary vocational training
* Annual Earnings: $41,850
* Beginning Wage: $21,050
* Earnings Growth Potential: High
* Growth: 11.5%
* Annual Job Openings: 3,496
* Self-Employed: 16.9%
* Part-Time: 18.9%

Operate television, video, or motion picture camera to photograph images or scenes for various purposes, such as TV broadcasts, advertising, video production, or motion pictures. Operate television or motion picture cameras to record scenes for television broadcasts, advertising, or motion pictures. Compose and frame each shot, applying the technical aspects of light, lenses, film, filters, and camera settings to achieve the effects sought by directors. Operate zoom lenses, changing images according to specifications and rehearsal instructions. Use cameras in any of several different camera mounts, such as stationary, track-mounted, or crane-mounted. Test, clean, and maintain equipment to ensure proper working condition. Adjust positions and controls of cameras, printers, and related equipment to change focus, exposure, and lighting. Gather and edit raw footage on location to send to television affiliates for broadcast, using electronic news-gathering or film-production equipment. Confer with directors, sound and lighting technicians, electricians, and other crew members to discuss assignments and determine filming sequences, desired effects, camera movements, and lighting requirements. Observe sets or locations for potential problems and to determine filming and lighting requirements. Instruct camera operators regarding camera setups, angles, distances, movement, and variables and cues for starting and stopping filming. Select and assemble cameras, accessories, equipment, and film stock to be used during filming, using knowledge of filming techniques, requirements, and computations. Label and record contents of exposed film and note details on report forms. Read charts and compute ratios to determine variables such as lighting, shutter angles, filter factors, and camera distances. Set up cameras, optical printers, and related equipment to produce photographs and special effects. View films to resolve problems of exposure control, subject and camera movement, changes in subject distance, and related variables. Reload camera magazines with fresh raw film stock. Read and analyze work orders and specifications to determine locations of subject material, work procedures, sequences of operations, and machine setups. Receive raw film stock and maintain film inventories.

Personality Type: Realistic. These occupations frequently involve work activities that include practical, hands-on problems and solutions. They often deal with plants; animals; and real-world materials such as wood, tools, and machinery. Many of the occupations require working outside and don't involve a lot of paperwork or working closely with others.

GOE—Interest Area/Cluster: 03. Arts and Communication. **Work Group:** 03.09. Media Technology. **Other Jobs in This Work Group:** Audio and Video Equipment Technicians; Broadcast Technicians; Film and Video Editors; Multi-Media Artists and Animators; Photographers; Radio Operators; Sound Engineering Technicians.

Skills—Operation Monitoring: Watching gauges, dials, or other indicators to make sure a machine is working properly. **Operation and Control:** Controlling operations of equipment or systems. **Equipment Maintenance:** Performing routine maintenance and determining when and what kind of maintenance is needed. **Troubleshooting:** Determining what is causing an operating error and deciding what to do about it. **Equipment Selection:** Determining the kind of tools and equipment needed to do a job. **Operations Analysis:** Analyzing needs and product requirements to create a design. **Active Listening:** Listening to what other people are saying and asking questions as appropriate. **Installation:** Installing equipment, machines, wiring, or programs to meet specifications.

Education and Training Programs: Audiovisual Communications Technologies/Technician Training, Other; Cinematography and Film/Video Production; Radio and Television Broadcasting Technology/Technician Training. **Related Knowledge/Courses—Communications and Media:** Media production, communication, and dissemination techniques and methods, including alternative ways to inform and entertain via written, oral, and visual media. **Telecommunications:** Transmission, broadcasting, switching, control, and operation of telecommunications

systems. **Computers and Electronics:** Electric circuit boards, processors, chips, and computer hardware and software, including applications and programming. **Engineering and Technology:** Equipment, tools, and mechanical devices and their uses to produce motion, light, power, technology, and other applications.

Work Environment: More often indoors than outdoors; very bright or dim lighting; standing; using hands on objects, tools, or controls.

Cardiovascular Technologists and Technicians

- ❋ Education/Training Required: Associate degree
- ❋ Annual Earnings: $44,940
- ❋ Beginning Wage: $24,650
- ❋ Earnings Growth Potential: High
- ❋ Growth: 25.5%
- ❋ Annual Job Openings: 3,550
- ❋ Self-Employed: 1.1%
- ❋ Part-Time: 17.3%

Conduct tests on pulmonary or cardiovascular systems of patients for diagnostic purposes. May conduct or assist in electrocardiograms, cardiac catheterizations, pulmonary-functions, lung capacity, and similar tests. Monitor patients' blood pressures and heart rates, using electrocardiogram (EKG) equipment during diagnostic and therapeutic procedures to notify physicians if something appears wrong. Explain testing procedures to patients to obtain cooperation and reduce anxiety. Observe gauges, recorders, and video screens of data analysis systems during imaging of cardiovascular systems. Monitor patients' comfort and safety during tests, alerting physicians to abnormalities or changes in patient responses. Obtain and record patients' identities, medical histories, or test results. Attach electrodes to patients' chests, arms, and legs; connect electrodes to leads from electrocardiogram (EKG) machines; and operate EKG machines to obtain readings. Adjust equipment and controls according to physicians' orders or established protocol. Prepare and position patients for testing. Check, test, and maintain cardiology equipment, making minor repairs when necessary, to ensure proper operation. Supervise and train other cardiology technologists and students. Perform general administrative tasks, such as scheduling appointments or ordering supplies and equipment. Maintain a proper sterile field during surgical procedures. Assist physicians in the diagnosis and treatment of cardiac and peripheral vascular treatments, such as implanting pacemakers or assisting with balloon angioplasties to treat blood vessel blockages. Inject contrast medium into patients' blood vessels. Assess cardiac physiology and calculate valve areas from blood flow velocity measurements. Operate diagnostic imaging equipment to produce contrast enhanced radiographs of hearts and cardiovascular systems. Observe ultrasound display screens and listen to signals to record vascular information such as blood pressure, limb volume changes, oxygen saturation, and cerebral circulation. Transcribe, type, and distribute reports of diagnostic procedures for interpretation by physician. Conduct electrocardiogram (EKG), phonocardiogram, echocardiogram, stress testing, or other cardiovascular tests to record patients' cardiac activities, using specialized electronic test equipment, recording devices, and laboratory instruments.

Personality Type: Realistic. These occupations frequently involve work activities that include practical, hands-on problems and solutions. They often deal with plants; animals; and real-world materials such as wood, tools, and machinery. Many of the occupations require working outside and don't involve a lot of paperwork or working closely with others.

GOE—Interest Area/Cluster: 08. Health Science. **Work Group:** 08.06. Medical Technology. **Other Jobs in This Work Group:** Biological Technicians; Diagnostic Medical Sonographers; Medical and Clinical Laboratory Technicians; Medical and Clinical Laboratory Technologists; Medical Equipment Preparers; Medical Records and Health Information Technicians; Nuclear Medicine Technologists; Opticians, Dispensing; Orthotists and Prosthetists; Radiologic Technicians; Radiologic Technologists; Radiologic Technologists and Technicians.

Skills—Operation Monitoring: Watching gauges, dials, or other indicators to make sure a machine is working properly. **Management of Personnel Resources:** Motivating, developing, and directing people as they work; identifying the best people for the job. **Systems Analysis:** Determining how a system should work and how changes will affect outcomes. **Quality Control Analysis:** Evaluating the quality or performance of products, services, or

processes. **Management of Material Resources:** Obtaining and seeing to the appropriate use of equipment, facilities, and materials needed to do certain work.

Education and Training Programs: Cardiopulmonary Technology/Technologist Training; Cardiovascular Technology/Technologist Training; Electrocardiograph Technology/Technician Training; Perfusion Technology/Perfusionist Training. **Related Knowledge/Courses— Medicine and Dentistry:** The information and techniques needed to diagnose and treat injuries, diseases, and deformities. This includes symptoms, treatment alternatives, drug properties and interactions, and preventive healthcare measures. **Biology:** Plant and animal living tissue, cells, organisms, and entities, including their functions, interdependencies, and interactions with each other and the environment. **Psychology:** Human behavior and performance, mental processes, psychological research methods, and the assessment and treatment of behavioral and affective disorders. **Customer and Personal Service:** Principles and processes for providing customer and personal services, including needs assessment techniques, quality service standards, alternative delivery systems, and customer satisfaction evaluation techniques. **Sociology and Anthropology:** Group behavior and dynamics; societal trends and influences; and cultures and their history, migrations, ethnicity, and origins. **Chemistry:** The composition, structure, and properties of substances and of the chemical processes and transformations that they undergo. This includes uses of chemicals and their interactions, danger signs, production techniques, and disposal methods.

Work Environment: Indoors; radiation; disease or infections; standing; using hands on objects, tools, or controls; repetitive motions.

Cargo and Freight Agents

* Education/Training Required: Moderate-term on-the-job training
* Annual Earnings: $37,060
* Beginning Wage: $22,720
* Earnings Growth Potential: Medium
* Growth: 16.5%
* Annual Job Openings: 9,967
* Self-Employed: 1.1%
* Part-Time: 6.1%

Expedite and route movement of incoming and outgoing cargo and freight shipments in airline, train, and trucking terminals and shipping docks. Take orders from customers and arrange pickup of freight and cargo for delivery to loading platform. Prepare and examine bills of lading to determine shipping charges and tariffs. Negotiate and arrange transport of goods with shipping or freight companies. Notify consignees, passengers, or customers of the arrival of freight or baggage and arrange for delivery. Advise clients on transportation and payment methods. Prepare manifests showing baggage, mail, and freight weights and number of passengers on airplanes and transmit data to destinations. Determine method of shipment and prepare bills of lading, invoices, and other shipping documents. Check import/export documentation to determine cargo contents and classify goods into different fee or tariff groups, using a tariff coding system. Estimate freight or postal rates and record shipment costs and weights. Enter shipping information into a computer by hand or by using a hand-held scanner that reads bar codes on goods. Retrieve stored items and trace lost shipments as necessary. Pack goods for shipping, using tools such as staplers, strapping machines, and hammers. Direct delivery trucks to shipping doors or designated marshalling areas and help load and unload goods safely. Inspect and count items received and check them against invoices or other documents, recording shortages and rejecting damaged goods. Install straps, braces, and padding to loads to prevent shifting or damage during shipment. Keep records of all goods shipped, received, and stored. Coordinate and supervise activities of workers engaged in packing and shipping merchandise. Arrange insurance coverage for goods. Direct or participate in cargo loading to ensure completeness of load and even distribution of weight. Open cargo containers and unwrap contents, using steel cutters, crowbars, or other hand tools. Attach address labels, identification codes, and shipping instructions to containers. Contact vendors or claims adjustment departments to resolve problems with shipments or contact service depots to arrange for repairs. Route received goods to first available flight or to appropriate storage areas or departments, using forklifts, handtrucks, or other equipment. Maintain a supply of packing materials.

Personality Type: Conventional. These occupations frequently involve following set procedures and routines and can include working with data and details more than with ideas. Usually there is a clear line of authority to follow.

GOE—Interest Area/Cluster: 16. Transportation, Distribution, and Logistics. **Work Group:** 16.07. Transportation Support Work. **Other Jobs in This Work Group:** Bridge and Lock Tenders; Cleaners of Vehicles and Equipment; Laborers and Freight, Stock, and Material Movers, Hand; Railroad Brake, Signal, and Switch Operators; Traffic Technicians.

Skills—Negotiation: Bringing others together and trying to reconcile differences. **Instructing:** Teaching others how to do something. **Writing:** Communicating effectively with others in writing as indicated by the needs of the audience. **Service Orientation:** Actively looking for ways to help people. **Monitoring:** Assessing how well one is doing when learning or doing something. **Speaking:** Talking to others to effectively convey information. **Learning Strategies:** Using multiple approaches when learning or teaching new things.

Education and Training Program: General Office Occupations and Clerical Services. **Related Knowledge/Courses—Transportation:** Principles and methods for moving people or goods by air, rail, sea, or road, including their relative costs, advantages, and limitations. **Geography:** Various methods for describing the location and distribution of land, sea, and air masses, including their physical locations, relationships, and characteristics. **Customer and Personal Service:** Principles and processes for providing customer and personal services, including needs assessment techniques, quality service standards, alternative delivery systems, and customer satisfaction evaluation techniques. **Clerical Studies:** Administrative and clerical procedures and systems such as word-processing systems, filing and records management systems, stenography and transcription, forms, design principles, and other office procedures and terminology. **Computers and Electronics:** Electric circuit boards, processors, chips, and computer hardware and software, including applications and programming. **Administration and Management:** Principles and processes involved in business and organizational planning, coordination, and execution. This includes strategic planning, resource allocation, manpower modeling, leadership techniques, and production methods.

Work Environment: Indoors; sitting; repetitive motions.

Cement Masons and Concrete Finishers

* Education/Training Required: Moderate-term on-the-job training
* Annual Earnings: $33,840
* Beginning Wage: $21,980
* Earnings Growth Potential: Medium
* Growth: 11.4%
* Annual Job Openings: 34,625
* Self-Employed: 2.0%
* Part-Time: 6.0%

Smooth and finish surfaces of poured concrete, such as floors, walks, sidewalks, roads, or curbs, using a variety of hand and power tools. Align forms for sidewalks, curbs, or gutters; patch voids; and use saws to cut expansion joints. Check the forms that hold the concrete to see that they are properly constructed. Set the forms that hold concrete to the desired pitch and depth and align them. Spread, level, and smooth concrete, using rake, shovel, hand or power trowel, hand or power screed, and float. Mold expansion joints and edges, using edging tools, jointers, and straightedge. Monitor how the wind, heat, or cold affect the curing of the concrete throughout the entire process. Signal truck driver to position truck to facilitate pouring concrete and move chute to direct concrete on forms. Produce rough concrete surface, using broom. Operate power vibrator to compact concrete. Direct the casting of the concrete and supervise laborers who use shovels or special tools to spread it. Mix cement, sand, and water to produce concrete, grout, or slurry, using hoe, trowel, tamper, scraper, or concrete-mixing machine. Cut out damaged areas, drill holes for reinforcing rods, and position reinforcing rods to repair concrete, using power saw and drill. Wet surface to prepare for bonding, fill holes and cracks with grout or slurry, and smooth, using trowel. Wet concrete surface and rub with stone to smooth surface and obtain specified finish. Clean chipped area, using wire brush, and feel and observe surface to determine if it is rough or uneven. Apply hardening and sealing compounds to cure surface of concrete and waterproof or restore surface. Chip, scrape, and grind high spots, ridges, and rough projections to finish concrete, using pneumatic chisels, power grinders, or hand tools. Spread roofing paper on surface of foundation and spread concrete onto roofing paper with trowel to form terrazzo base. Build wooden molds and clamp molds around area to be repaired, using hand tools. Sprinkle colored marble or stone chips, powdered steel, or coloring powder over surface to produce prescribed finish. Cut metal division strips and press them into terrazzo base so that top edges form desired design or pattern. Fabricate concrete beams, columns, and panels. Waterproof or restore concrete surfaces, using appropriate compounds.

Personality Type: Realistic. These occupations frequently involve work activities that include practical, hands-on problems and solutions. They often deal with plants; animals; and real-world materials such as wood, tools, and machinery. Many of the occupations require working outside and don't involve a lot of paperwork or working closely with others.

GOE—Interest Area/Cluster: 02. Architecture and Construction. **Work Group:** 02.04. Construction Crafts. **Other Jobs in This Work Group:** Boilermakers; Brickmasons and Blockmasons; Carpet Installers; Commercial Divers; Construction Carpenters; Crane and Tower Operators; Drywall and Ceiling Tile Installers; Electricians; Fence Erectors; Floor Layers, Except Carpet, Wood, and Hard Tiles; Floor Sanders and Finishers; Glaziers; Hazardous Materials Removal Workers; Insulation Workers, Floor, Ceiling, and Wall; Insulation Workers, Mechanical; Manufactured Building and Mobile Home Installers; Operating Engineers and Other Construction Equipment Operators; Painters, Construction and Maintenance; Paperhangers; Paving, Surfacing, and Tamping Equipment Operators; Pile-Driver Operators; Pipe Fitters and Steamfitters; Pipelayers; Plasterers and Stucco Masons; Plumbers; Plumbers, Pipefitters, and Steamfitters; Rail-Track Laying and Maintenance Equipment Operators; Refractory Materials Repairers, Except Brickmasons; Reinforcing Iron and Rebar Workers; Riggers; Roofers; Rough Carpenters; Security and Fire Alarm Systems Installers; Segmental Pavers; Sheet Metal Workers; Stone Cutters and Carvers, Manufacturing; Stonemasons; Structural Iron and Steel Workers; Tapers; Terrazzo Workers and Finishers; Tile and Marble Setters.

Skills—Mathematics: Using mathematics to solve problems. **Installation:** Installing equipment, machines, wiring, or programs to meet specifications. **Repairing:** Repairing machines or systems, using the needed tools. **Equipment Maintenance:** Performing routine maintenance and determining when and what kind of maintenance is needed.

Equipment Selection: Determining the kind of tools and equipment needed to do a job. **Coordination:** Adjusting actions in relation to others' actions.

Education and Training Program: Concrete Finishing/Concrete Finisher Training. **Related Knowledge/Courses—Building and Construction:** Materials, methods, and the appropriate tools to construct objects, structures, and buildings. **Public Safety and Security:** Weaponry; public safety; security operations, rules, regulations, precautions, and prevention; and the protection of people, data, and property. **Mechanical Devices:** Machines and tools, including their designs, uses, benefits, repair, and maintenance. **Design:** Design techniques, principles, tools, and instruments involved in the production and use of precision technical plans, blueprints, drawings, and models. **Engineering and Technology:** Equipment, tools, and mechanical devices and their uses to produce motion, light, power, technology, and other applications.

Work Environment: Outdoors; noisy; hazardous equipment; standing; using hands on objects, tools, or controls; bending or twisting the body.

Chefs and Head Cooks

- ❋ Education/Training Required: Work experience in a related occupation
- ❋ Annual Earnings: $37,160
- ❋ Beginning Wage: $21,560
- ❋ Earnings Growth Potential: High
- ❋ Growth: 7.6%
- ❋ Annual Job Openings: 9,401
- ❋ Self-Employed: 7.2%
- ❋ Part-Time: 7.8%

Direct the preparation, seasoning, and cooking of salads, soups, fish, meats, vegetables, desserts, or other foods. May plan and price menu items, order supplies, and keep records and accounts. May participate in cooking. Check the quality of raw and cooked food products to ensure that standards are met. Monitor sanitation practices to ensure that employees follow standards and regulations. Check the quantity and quality of received products. Order or requisition food and other supplies needed to ensure efficient operation. Inspect supplies, equipment, and work areas to ensure conformance to established standards.

Supervise and coordinate activities of cooks and workers engaged in food preparation. Determine how food should be presented and create decorative food displays. Instruct cooks and other workers in the preparation, cooking, garnishing, and presentation of food. Estimate amounts and costs of required supplies, such as food and ingredients. Collaborate with other personnel to plan and develop recipes and menus, taking into account such factors as seasonal availability of ingredients and the likely number of customers. Analyze recipes to assign prices to menu items, based on food, labor, and overhead costs. Prepare and cook foods of all types, either on a regular basis or for special guests or functions. Determine production schedules and staff requirements necessary to ensure timely delivery of services. Recruit and hire staff, including cooks and other kitchen workers. Meet with customers to discuss menus for special occasions such as weddings, parties, and banquets. Demonstrate new cooking techniques and equipment to staff. Meet with sales representatives in order to negotiate prices and order supplies. Arrange for equipment purchases and repairs. Record production and operational data on specified forms. Plan, direct, and supervise the food preparation and cooking activities of multiple kitchens or restaurants in an establishment such as a restaurant chain, hospital, or hotel. Coordinate planning, budgeting, and purchasing for all the food operations within establishments such as clubs, hotels, or restaurant chains.

Personality Type: Enterprising. These occupations frequently involve starting up and carrying out projects and can involve leading people and making many decisions. They sometimes require risk taking and often deal with business.

GOE—Interest Area/Cluster: 09. Hospitality, Tourism, and Recreation. **Work Group:** 09.04. Food and Beverage Preparation. **Other Jobs in This Work Group:** Butchers and Meat Cutters; Cooks, Fast Food; Cooks, Institution and Cafeteria; Cooks, Private Household; Cooks, Restaurant; Cooks, Short Order; Dishwashers; Food Preparation Workers.

Skills—Equipment Maintenance: Performing routine maintenance and determining when and what kind of maintenance is needed. **Management of Financial Resources:** Determining how money will be spent to get the work done and accounting for these expenditures. **Repairing:** Repairing machines or systems, using the needed tools. **Management of Personnel Resources:**

Motivating, developing, and directing people as they work; identifying the best people for the job. **Service Orientation:** Actively looking for ways to help people. **Negotiation:** Bringing others together and trying to reconcile differences. **Quality Control Analysis:** Evaluating the quality or performance of products, services, or processes. **Systems Analysis:** Determining how a system should work and how changes will affect outcomes.

Education and Training Programs: Cooking and Related Culinary Arts, General; Culinary Arts/Chef Training. **Related Knowledge/Courses—Food Production:** Techniques and equipment for planting, growing, and harvesting of food for consumption, including crop-rotation methods, animal husbandry, and food storage/handling techniques. **Production and Processing:** Inputs, outputs, raw materials, waste, quality control, costs, and techniques for maximizing the manufacture and distribution of goods. **Administration and Management:** Principles and processes involved in business and organizational planning, coordination, and execution. This includes strategic planning, resource allocation, manpower modeling, leadership techniques, and production methods. **Chemistry:** The composition, structure, and properties of substances and of the chemical processes and transformations that they undergo. This includes uses of chemicals and their interactions, danger signs, production techniques, and disposal methods. **Education and Training:** Instructional methods and training techniques, including curriculum design principles, learning theory, group and individual teaching techniques, design of individual development plans, and test design principles. **Personnel and Human Resources:** Principles and procedures for personnel recruitment; selection; training; compensation and benefits; labor relations and negotiation; and personnel information systems.

Work Environment: Minor burns, cuts, bites, or stings; standing; walking and running; using hands on objects, tools, or controls; bending or twisting the body; repetitive motions.

Chemical Plant and System Operators

- ❋ Education/Training Required: Long-term on-the-job training
- ❋ Annual Earnings: $50,860
- ❋ Beginning Wage: $33,600
- ❋ Earnings Growth Potential: Low
- ❋ Growth: –15.3%
- ❋ Annual Job Openings: 5,620
- ❋ Self-Employed: 0.1%
- ❋ Part-Time: 0.6%

Control or operate an entire chemical process or system of machines. Move control settings to make necessary adjustments on equipment units affecting speeds of chemical reactions, quality, and yields. Monitor recording instruments, flowmeters, panel lights, and other indicators and listen for warning signals to verify conformity of process conditions. Control or operate chemical processes or systems of machines, using panelboards, control boards, or semi-automatic equipment. Record operating data such as process conditions, test results, and instrument readings. Confer with technical and supervisory personnel to report or resolve conditions affecting safety, efficiency, and product quality. Draw samples of products and conduct quality control tests to monitor processing and to ensure that standards are met. Regulate or shut down equipment during emergency situations as directed by supervisory personnel. Start pumps to wash and rinse reactor vessels; to exhaust gases and vapors; to regulate the flow of oil, steam, air, and perfume to towers; and to add products to converter or blending vessels. Interpret chemical reactions visible through sight glasses or on television monitors and review laboratory test reports for process adjustments. Patrol work areas to ensure that solutions in tanks and troughs are not in danger of overflowing. Notify maintenance, stationary-engineering, and other auxiliary personnel to correct equipment malfunctions and to adjust power, steam, water, or air supplies. Direct workers engaged in operating machinery that regulates the flow of materials and products. Inspect operating units such as towers, soap-spray storage tanks, scrubbers, collectors, and driers to ensure that all are functioning and to maintain maximum efficiency. Turn valves to regulate flow of products or byproducts through agitator tanks, storage drums, or neutralizer tanks. Calculate material requirements or yields according to formulas. Gauge tank levels, using calibrated rods. Repair and replace damaged equipment. Defrost frozen valves, using steam hoses. Supervise the cleaning of towers, strainers, and spray tips.

Personality Type: Realistic. These occupations frequently involve work activities that include practical, hands-on problems and solutions. They often deal with plants; animals; and real-world materials such as wood, tools, and machinery. Many of the occupations require working outside and don't involve a lot of paperwork or working closely with others.

GOE—Interest Area/Cluster: 13. Manufacturing. **Work Group:** 13.16. Utility Operation and Energy Distribution. **Other Jobs in This Work Group:** Gas Compressor and Gas Pumping Station Operators; Gas Plant Operators; Nuclear Power Reactor Operators; Petroleum Pump System Operators, Refinery Operators, and Gaugers; Power Distributors and Dispatchers; Power Plant Operators; Ship Engineers; Stationary Engineers and Boiler Operators; Water and Liquid Waste Treatment Plant and System Operators.

Skills—Operation Monitoring: Watching gauges, dials, or other indicators to make sure a machine is working properly. **Operation and Control:** Controlling operations of equipment or systems. **Troubleshooting:** Determining what is causing an operating error and deciding what to do about it. **Science:** Using scientific methods to solve problems. **Equipment Maintenance:** Performing routine maintenance and determining when and what kind of maintenance is needed. **Operations Analysis:** Analyzing needs and product requirements to create a design. **Systems Analysis:** Determining how a system should work and how changes will affect outcomes. **Quality Control Analysis:** Evaluating the quality or performance of products, services, or processes.

Education and Training Program: Chemical Technology/Technician Training. **Related Knowledge/Courses—Production and Processing:** Inputs, outputs, raw materials, waste, quality control, costs, and techniques for maximizing the manufacture and distribution of goods. **Chemistry:** The composition, structure, and properties of substances and of the chemical processes and transformations that they undergo. This includes uses of chemicals and their interactions, danger signs, production techniques, and disposal methods. **Mechanical Devices:** Machines

and tools, including their designs, uses, benefits, repair, and maintenance. **Physics:** Physical principles, laws, and applications, including air, water, material dynamics, light, atomic principles, heat, electric theory, earth formations, and meteorological and related natural phenomena. **Engineering and Technology:** Equipment, tools, and mechanical devices and their uses to produce motion, light, power, technology, and other applications. **Public Safety and Security:** Weaponry; public safety; security operations, rules, regulations, precautions, and prevention; and the protection of people, data, and property.

Work Environment: More often indoors than outdoors; noisy; very hot or cold; contaminants; hazardous conditions.

Chemical Technicians

- ❋ Education/Training Required: Associate degree
- ❋ Annual Earnings: $40,740
- ❋ Beginning Wage: $25,380
- ❋ Earnings Growth Potential: Medium
- ❋ Growth: 5.8%
- ❋ Annual Job Openings: 4,010
- ❋ Self-Employed: 0.4%
- ❋ Part-Time: 3.9%

Conduct chemical and physical laboratory tests to assist scientists in making qualitative and quantitative analyses of solids, liquids, and gaseous materials for purposes such as research and development of new products or processes; quality control; maintenance of environmental standards; and other work involving experimental, theoretical, or practical application of chemistry and related sciences. Monitor product quality to ensure compliance to standards and specifications. Set up and conduct chemical experiments, tests, and analyses using techniques such as chromatography, spectroscopy, physical and chemical separation techniques, and microscopy. Conduct chemical and physical laboratory tests to assist scientists in making qualitative and quantitative analyses of solids, liquids, and gaseous materials. Compile and interpret results of tests and analyses. Provide technical support and assistance to chemists and engineers. Prepare chemical solutions for products and processes following standardized formulas or create experimental formulas. Maintain, clean, and sterilize laboratory instruments and equipment. Write technical reports or prepare graphs and charts to document experimental results. Order and inventory materials to maintain supplies. Develop and conduct programs of sampling and analysis to maintain quality standards of raw materials, chemical intermediates, and products. Direct or monitor other workers producing chemical products. Operate experimental pilot plants, assisting with experimental design. Develop new chemical engineering processes or production techniques. Design and fabricate experimental apparatus to develop new products and processes.

Personality Type: Investigative. These occupations frequently involve working with ideas and require an extensive amount of thinking. They can involve searching for facts and figuring out problems mentally.

GOE—Interest Area/Cluster: 15. Scientific Research, Engineering, and Mathematics. **Work Group:** 15.05. Physical Science Laboratory Technology. **Other Jobs in This Work Group:** Nuclear Equipment Operation Technicians; Nuclear Technicians.

Skills—Science: Using scientific methods to solve problems. **Operation Monitoring:** Watching gauges, dials, or other indicators to make sure a machine is working properly. **Quality Control Analysis:** Evaluating the quality or performance of products, services, or processes. **Equipment Maintenance:** Performing routine maintenance and determining when and what kind of maintenance is needed. **Operation and Control:** Controlling operations of equipment or systems. **Repairing:** Repairing machines or systems, using the needed tools. **Mathematics:** Using mathematics to solve problems. **Troubleshooting:** Determining what is causing an operating error and deciding what to do about it.

Education and Training Programs: Chemical Technology/Technician Training; Food Science. **Related Knowledge/Courses—Chemistry:** The composition, structure, and properties of substances and of the chemical processes and transformations that they undergo. This includes uses of chemicals and their interactions, danger signs, production techniques, and disposal methods. **Mechanical Devices:** Machines and tools, including their designs, uses, benefits, repair, and maintenance. **Computers and Electronics:** Electric circuit boards, processors, chips,

and computer hardware and software, including applications and programming. **Mathematics:** Numbers and their operations and interrelationships, including arithmetic, algebra, geometry, calculus, and statistics and their applications.

Work Environment: Indoors; noisy; contaminants; hazardous conditions; standing.

City and Regional Planning Aides

- ❋ Education/Training Required: Associate degree
- ❋ Annual Earnings: $35,870
- ❋ Beginning Wage: $21,940
- ❋ Earnings Growth Potential: Medium
- ❋ Growth: 12.4%
- ❋ Annual Job Openings: 3,571
- ❋ Self-Employed: 1.7%
- ❋ Part-Time: 19.4%

The job openings listed here are shared with Social Science Research Assistants.

Compile data from various sources, such as maps, reports, and field and file investigations, for use by city planner in making planning studies. Participate in and support team planning efforts. Prepare reports, using statistics, charts, and graphs, to illustrate planning studies in areas such as population, land use, or zoning. Research, compile, analyze, and organize information from maps, reports, investigations, and books for use in reports and special projects. Provide and process zoning and project permits and applications. Respond to public inquiries and complaints. Serve as liaison between planning department and other departments and agencies. Inspect sites and review plans for minor development permit applications. Conduct interviews, surveys, and site inspections concerning factors that affect land usage, such as zoning, traffic flow, and housing. Prepare, maintain, and update files and records, including land use data and statistics. Prepare, develop, and maintain maps and databases. Perform clerical duties such as composing, typing, and proofreading documents; scheduling appointments and meetings; handling mail; and posting public notices. Perform code enforcement tasks.

Personality Type: Conventional. These occupations frequently involve following set procedures and routines and can include working with data and details more than with ideas. Usually there is a clear line of authority to follow.

GOE—Interest Area/Cluster: 07. Government and Public Administration. **Work Group:** 07.02. Public Planning. **Other Jobs in This Work Group:** Urban and Regional Planners.

Skill: Systems Analysis: Determining how a system should work and how changes will affect outcomes.

Education and Training Program: Social Sciences, General. **Related Knowledge/Courses—Geography:** Various methods for describing the location and distribution of land, sea, and air masses, including their physical locations, relationships, and characteristics. **History and Archeology:** Historical events and their causes, indicators, and impact on particular civilizations and cultures. **Design:** Design techniques, principles, tools, and instruments involved in the production and use of precision technical plans, blueprints, drawings, and models. **Law and Government:** Laws, legal codes, court procedures, precedents, government regulations, executive orders, agency rules, and the democratic political process. **Building and Construction:** Materials, methods, and the appropriate tools to construct objects, structures, and buildings. **Sociology and Anthropology:** Group behavior and dynamics; societal trends and influences; and cultures and their history, migrations, ethnicity, and origins.

Work Environment: Indoors; sitting.

Civil Drafters

- ❋ Education/Training Required: Postsecondary vocational training
- ❋ Annual Earnings: $43,310
- ❋ Beginning Wage: $27,680
- ❋ Earnings Growth Potential: Medium
- ❋ Growth: 6.1%
- ❋ Annual Job Openings: 16,238
- ❋ Self-Employed: 5.0%
- ❋ Part-Time: 5.9%

The job openings listed here are shared with Architectural Drafters.

Prepare drawings and topographical and relief maps used in civil engineering projects such as highways, bridges, pipelines, flood control projects, and water and sewerage control systems. Produce drawings by using computer-assisted drafting systems (CAD) or drafting machines or by hand, using compasses, dividers, protractors, triangles, and other drafting devices. Draw maps, diagrams, and profiles, using cross-sections and surveys, to represent elevations, topographical contours, subsurface formations, and structures. Draft plans and detailed drawings for structures, installations, and construction projects such as highways, sewage disposal systems, and dikes, working from sketches or notes. Determine the order of work and method of presentation such as orthographic or isometric drawing. Finish and duplicate drawings and documentation packages according to required mediums and specifications for reproduction, using blueprinting, photography, or other duplication methods. Review rough sketches, drawings, specifications, and other engineering data received from civil engineers to ensure that they conform to design concepts. Calculate excavation tonnage and prepare graphs and fill-hauling diagrams for use in earth-moving operations. Supervise and train other technologists, technicians, and drafters. Correlate, interpret, and modify data obtained from topographical surveys, well logs, and geophysical prospecting reports. Determine quality, cost, strength, and quantity of required materials and enter figures on materials lists. Locate and identify symbols located on topographical surveys to denote geological and geophysical formations or oil field installations. Calculate weights, volumes, and stress factors and their implications for technical aspects of designs. Supervise or conduct field surveys, inspections, or technical investigations to obtain data required to revise construction drawings. Explain drawings to production or construction teams and provide adjustments as necessary. Plot characteristics of boreholes for oil and gas wells from photographic subsurface survey recordings and other data, representing depth, degree, and direction of inclination.

Personality Type: Realistic. These occupations frequently involve work activities that include practical, hands-on problems and solutions. They often deal with plants; animals; and real-world materials such as wood, tools, and machinery. Many of the occupations require working outside and don't involve a lot of paperwork or working closely with others.

GOE—**Interest Area/Cluster:** 02. Architecture and Construction. **Work Group:** 02.03. Architecture/Construction Engineering Technologies. **Other Jobs in This Work Group:** Architectural and Civil Drafters; Architectural Drafters; Surveyors.

Skills—Programming: Writing computer programs for various purposes. **Systems Analysis:** Determining how a system should work and how changes will affect outcomes. **Mathematics:** Using mathematics to solve problems. **Quality Control Analysis:** Evaluating the quality or performance of products, services, or processes. **Systems Evaluation:** Looking at many indicators of system performance and taking into account their accuracy.

Education and Training Programs: Architectural Drafting and Architectural CAD/CADD; Architectural Technology/Technician Training; CAD/CADD Drafting and/or Design Technology/Technician Training; Civil Drafting and Civil Engineering CAD/CADD; Drafting and Design Technology/Technician Training, General. **Related Knowledge/Courses—Design:** Design techniques, principles, tools, and instruments involved in the production and use of precision technical plans, blueprints, drawings, and models. **Engineering and Technology:** Equipment, tools, and mechanical devices and their uses to produce motion, light, power, technology, and other applications. **Building and Construction:** Materials, methods, and the appropriate tools to construct objects, structures, and buildings. **Geography:** Various methods for describing the location and distribution of land, sea, and air masses, including their physical locations, relationships, and characteristics. **Mathematics:** Using mathematics to solve problems. **Physics:** Physical principles, laws, and applications, including air, water, material dynamics, light, atomic principles, heat, electric theory, earth formations, and meteorological and related natural phenomena.

Work Environment: Indoors; sitting; using hands on objects, tools, or controls; repetitive motions.

Civil Engineering Technicians

- ✳ Education/Training Required: Associate degree
- ✳ Annual Earnings: $42,580
- ✳ Beginning Wage: $25,390
- ✳ Earnings Growth Potential: High
- ✳ Growth: 10.2%
- ✳ Annual Job Openings: 7,499
- ✳ Self-Employed: 0.9%
- ✳ Part-Time: 5.9%

Apply theory and principles of civil engineering in planning, designing, and overseeing construction and maintenance of structures and facilities under the direction of engineering staff or physical scientists. Calculate dimensions, square footage, profile and component specifications, and material quantities, using calculator or computer. Draft detailed dimensional drawings and design layouts for projects and to ensure conformance to specifications. Analyze proposed site factors and design maps, graphs, tracings, and diagrams to illustrate findings. Read and review project blueprints and structural specifications to determine dimensions of structure or system and material requirements. Prepare reports and document project activities and data. Confer with supervisor to determine project details such as plan preparation, acceptance testing, and evaluation of field conditions. Inspect project site and evaluate contractor work to detect design malfunctions and ensure conformance to design specifications and applicable codes. Plan and conduct field surveys to locate new sites and analyze details of project sites. Develop plans and estimate costs for installation of systems, utilization of facilities, or construction of structures. Report maintenance problems occurring at project site to supervisor and negotiate changes to resolve system conflicts. Conduct materials test and analysis, using tools and equipment and applying engineering knowledge. Respond to public suggestions and complaints. Evaluate facility to determine suitability for occupancy and square footage availability.

Personality Type: Realistic. These occupations frequently involve work activities that include practical, hands-on problems and solutions. They often deal with plants; animals; and real-world materials such as wood, tools, and machinery. Many of the occupations require working

outside and don't involve a lot of paperwork or working closely with others.

GOE—Interest Area/Cluster: 15. Scientific Research, Engineering, and Mathematics. **Work Group:** 15.09. Engineering Technology. **Other Jobs in This Work Group:** Aerospace Engineering and Operations Technicians; Cartographers and Photogrammetrists; Electrical and Electronic Engineering Technicians; Electrical and Electronics Drafters; Electrical Drafters; Electrical Engineering Technicians; Electro-Mechanical Technicians; Electronic Drafters; Electronics Engineering Technicians; Environmental Engineering Technicians; Mapping Technicians; Mechanical Drafters; Mechanical Engineering Technicians; Surveying and Mapping Technicians; Surveying Technicians.

Skills—Mathematics: Using mathematics to solve problems. **Science:** Using scientific methods to solve problems. **Operations Analysis:** Analyzing needs and product requirements to create a design. **Writing:** Communicating effectively with others in writing as indicated by the needs of the audience. **Complex Problem Solving:** Identifying complex problems, reviewing the options, and implementing solutions. **Reading Comprehension:** Understanding written sentences and paragraphs in work-related documents. **Technology Design:** Generating or adapting equipment and technology to serve user needs. **Active Learning:** Working with new material or information to grasp its implications.

Education and Training Programs: Civil Engineering Technology/Technician Training; Construction Engineering Technology/Technician Training. **Related Knowledge/Courses—Building and Construction:** Materials, methods, and the appropriate tools to construct objects, structures, and buildings. **Design:** Design techniques, principles, tools, and instruments involved in the production and use of precision technical plans, blueprints, drawings, and models. **Engineering and Technology:** Equipment, tools, and mechanical devices and their uses to produce motion, light, power, technology, and other applications. **Mathematics:** Numbers and their operations and interrelationships, including arithmetic, algebra, geometry, calculus, and statistics and their applications. **Computers and Electronics:** Electric circuit boards, processors, chips, and computer hardware and software, including applications and programming. **Transportation:** Principles and methods for moving people or goods by air, rail, sea, or road, including their relative costs, advantages, and limitations.

Work Environment: More often indoors than outdoors; sitting.

Claims Examiners, Property and Casualty Insurance

- ❋ Education/Training Required: Long-term on-the-job training
- ❋ Annual Earnings: $53,560
- ❋ Beginning Wage: $33,010
- ❋ Earnings Growth Potential: Medium
- ❋ Growth: 8.9%
- ❋ Annual Job Openings: 22,024
- ❋ Self-Employed: 3.5%
- ❋ Part-Time: 4.0%

The job openings listed here are shared with Insurance Adjusters, Examiners, and Investigators.

Review settled insurance claims to determine that payments and settlements have been made in accordance with company practices and procedures. Report overpayments, underpayments, and other irregularities. Confer with legal counsel on claims requiring litigation. Investigate, evaluate, and settle claims, applying technical knowledge and human relations skills to effect fair and prompt disposal of cases and to contribute to a reduced loss ratio. Pay and process claims within designated authority level. Adjust reserves or provide reserve recommendations to ensure that reserve activities are consistent with corporate policies. Enter claim payments, reserves, and new claims on computer system, inputting concise yet sufficient file documentation. Resolve complex severe exposure claims, using high-service-oriented file handling. Maintain claim files such as records of settled claims and an inventory of claims requiring detailed analysis. Verify and analyze data used in settling claims to ensure that claims are valid and that settlements are made according to company practices and procedures. Examine claims investigated by insurance adjusters, further investigating questionable claims to determine whether to authorize payments. Present cases and participate in their discussion at claim committee meetings. Contact or interview claimants, doctors, medical specialists, or employers to get additional information. Confer with legal counsel on claims requiring litigation. Report overpayments, underpayments, and other irregularities. Communicate with reinsurance brokers to obtain information necessary for processing claims. Supervise claims adjusters to ensure that adjusters have followed proper methods. Conduct detailed bill reviews to implement sound litigation management and expense control. Prepare reports to be submitted to company's data-processing department.

Personality Type: Conventional. These occupations frequently involve following set procedures and routines and can include working with data and details more than with ideas. Usually there is a clear line of authority to follow.

GOE—Interest Area/Cluster: 06. Finance and Insurance. **Work Group:** 06.02. Finance/Insurance Investigation and Analysis. **Other Jobs in This Work Group:** Appraisers and Assessors of Real Estate; Appraisers, Real Estate; Assessors; Claims Adjusters, Examiners, and Investigators; Cost Estimators; Credit Analysts; Financial Analysts; Insurance Adjusters, Examiners, and Investigators; Insurance Appraisers, Auto Damage; Insurance Underwriters; Loan Counselors; Loan Officers; Market Research Analysts; Survey Researchers.

Skills—Judgment and Decision Making: Weighing the relative costs and benefits of a potential action. **Writing:** Communicating effectively with others in writing as indicated by the needs of the audience. **Persuasion:** Persuading others to approach things differently. **Negotiation:** Bringing others together and trying to reconcile differences. **Reading Comprehension:** Understanding written sentences and paragraphs in work-related documents. **Critical Thinking:** Using logic and analysis to identify the strengths and weaknesses of different approaches. **Instructing:** Teaching others how to do something. **Active Listening:** Listening to what other people are saying and asking questions as appropriate.

Education and Training Program: Health/Medical Claims Examiner Training. **Related Knowledge/ Courses—Customer and Personal Service:** Principles and processes for providing customer and personal services, including needs assessment techniques, quality service standards, alternative delivery systems, and customer satisfaction evaluation techniques. **Medicine and Dentistry:** The information and techniques needed to diagnose and treat injuries, diseases, and deformities. This includes symptoms, treatment alternatives, drug properties and interactions, and preventive health-care measures. **Clerical**

Studies: Administrative and clerical procedures and systems such as word-processing systems, filing and records management systems, stenography and transcription, forms, design principles, and other office procedures and terminology. **Law and Government:** Laws, legal codes, court procedures, precedents, government regulations, executive orders, agency rules, and the democratic political process. **Computers and Electronics:** Electric circuit boards, processors, chips, and computer hardware and software, including applications and programming. **English Language:** The structure and content of the English language, including the meaning and spelling of words, rules of composition, and grammar.

Work Environment: Indoors; sitting; using hands on objects, tools, or controls; repetitive motions.

Coaches and Scouts

- ❋ Education/Training Required: Long-term on-the-job training
- ❋ Annual Earnings: $27,840
- ❋ Beginning Wage: $14,860
- ❋ Earnings Growth Potential: High
- ❋ Growth: 14.6%
- ❋ Annual Job Openings: 51,100
- ❋ Self-Employed: 22.7%
- ❋ Part-Time: 39.1%

Instruct or coach groups or individuals in the fundamentals of sports. Demonstrate techniques and methods of participation. May evaluate athletes' strengths and weaknesses as possible recruits or to improve the athletes' technique to prepare them for competition. Plan, organize, and conduct practice sessions. Provide training direction, encouragement, and motivation to prepare athletes for games, competitive events, or tours. Identify and recruit potential athletes, arranging and offering incentives such as athletic scholarships. Plan strategies and choose team members for individual games or sports seasons. Plan and direct physical conditioning programs that will enable athletes to achieve maximum performance. Adjust coaching techniques based on the strengths and weaknesses of athletes. File scouting reports that detail player assessments, provide recommendations on athlete recruitment, and identify locations and individuals to be targeted for future recruitment efforts. Keep records of athlete, team, and opposing team performance. Instruct individuals or groups in sports rules, game strategies, and performance principles such as specific ways of moving the body, hands, and feet in order to achieve desired results. Analyze the strengths and weaknesses of opposing teams to develop game strategies. Evaluate athletes' skills and review performance records to determine their fitness and potential in a particular area of athletics. Keep abreast of changing rules, techniques, technologies, and philosophies relevant to their sport. Monitor athletes' use of equipment to ensure safe and proper use. Explain and enforce safety rules and regulations. Develop and arrange competition schedules and programs. Serve as organizer, leader, instructor, or referee for outdoor and indoor games such as volleyball, football, and soccer. Explain and demonstrate the use of sports and training equipment, such as trampolines or weights. Perform activities that support a team or a specific sport, such as meeting with media representatives and appearing at fundraising events. Arrange and conduct sports-related activities such as training camps, skill-improvement courses, clinics, or pre-season try-outs. Select, acquire, store, and issue equipment and other materials as necessary. Negotiate with professional athletes or their representatives to obtain services and arrange contracts.

Personality Type: Social. These occupations frequently involve working with, communicating with, and teaching people and often involve helping or providing service to others.

GOE—Interest Area/Cluster: 09. Hospitality, Tourism, and Recreation. **Work Group:** 09.06. Sports. **Other Jobs in This Work Group:** Athletes and Sports Competitors; Umpires, Referees, and Other Sports Officials.

Skills—Social Perceptiveness: Being aware of others' reactions and understanding why they react the way they do. **Management of Personnel Resources:** Motivating, developing, and directing people as they work; identifying the best people for the job. **Management of Financial Resources:** Determining how money will be spent to get the work done and accounting for these expenditures. **Persuasion:** Persuading others to approach things differently. **Negotiation:** Bringing others together and trying to reconcile differences. **Instructing:** Teaching others how to do something. **Monitoring:** Assessing how well one is doing when learning or doing something. **Time Management:** Managing one's own time and the time of others.

Education and Training Programs: Physical Education Teaching and Coaching; Sport and Fitness Administration/Management. **Related Knowledge/Courses—Psychology:** Human behavior and performance, mental processes, psychological research methods, and the assessment and treatment of behavioral and affective disorders. **Therapy and Counseling:** Information and techniques needed to rehabilitate physical and mental ailments and to provide career guidance, including alternative treatments, rehabilitation equipment and its proper use, and methods to evaluate treatment effects. **Education and Training:** Instructional methods and training techniques, including curriculum design principles, learning theory, group and individual teaching techniques, design of individual development plans, and test design principles. **Sales and Marketing:** Principles and methods involved in showing, promoting, and selling products or services. This includes marketing strategies and tactics, product demonstration and sales techniques, and sales control systems. **Personnel and Human Resources:** Principles and procedures for personnel recruitment; selection; training; compensation and benefits; labor relations and negotiation; and personnel information systems. **Sociology and Anthropology:** Group behavior and dynamics; societal trends and influences; and cultures and their history, migrations, ethnicity, and origins.

Work Environment: More often indoors than outdoors; noisy; standing; walking and running.

Commercial Divers

- Education/Training Required: Postsecondary vocational training
- Annual Earnings: $41,610
- Beginning Wage: $28,640
- Earnings Growth Potential: Low
- Growth: 17.7%
- Annual Job Openings: 248
- Self-Employed: 12.7%
- Part-Time: 9.8%

Work below surface of water, using scuba gear to inspect, repair, remove, or install equipment and structures. May use a variety of power and hand tools such as drills, sledgehammers, torches, and welding equipment.

May conduct tests or experiments, rig explosives, or photograph structures or marine life. Perform activities related to underwater search and rescue, salvage, recovery, and cleanup operations. Take appropriate safety precautions, such as monitoring dive lengths and depths and registering with authorities before diving expeditions begin. Set or guide placement of pilings and sandbags to provide support for structures such as docks, bridges, cofferdams, and platforms. Salvage wrecked ships and/or their cargoes, using pneumatic power velocity and hydraulic tools and explosive charges when necessary. Repair ships, bridge foundations, and other structures below the water line, using caulk, bolts, and hand tools. Remove obstructions from strainers and marine railway or launching ways, using pneumatic and power hand tools. Inspect and test docks; ships; buoyage systems; plant intakes and outflows; and underwater pipelines, cables, and sewers, using closed-circuit television, still photography, and testing equipment. Perform offshore oil and gas exploration and extraction duties such as conducting underwater surveys and repairing and maintaining drilling rigs and platforms. Install, inspect, clean, and repair piping and valves. Carry out non-destructive testing such as tests for cracks on the legs of oil rigs at sea. Check and maintain diving equipment such as helmets, masks, air tanks, harnesses, and gauges. Communicate with workers on the surface while underwater, using signal lines or telephones. Cut and weld steel, using underwater welding equipment, jigs, and supports. Descend into water with the aid of diver helpers, using scuba gear or diving suits. Recover objects by placing rigging around sunken objects; hooking rigging to crane lines; and operating winches, derricks, or cranes to raise objects. Install pilings or footings for piers and bridges. Supervise and train other divers, including hobby divers. Obtain information about diving tasks and environmental conditions. Remove rubbish and pollution from the sea. Cultivate and harvest marine species and perform routine work on fish farms. Set up dive sites for recreational instruction. Drill holes in rock and rig explosives for underwater demolitions.

Personality Type: Realistic. These occupations frequently involve work activities that include practical, hands-on problems and solutions. They often deal with plants; animals; and real-world materials such as wood, tools, and machinery. Many of the occupations require working outside and don't involve a lot of paperwork or working closely with others.

GOE—Interest Area/Cluster: 02. Architecture and Construction. **Work Group:** 02.04. Construction Crafts. **Other Jobs in This Work Group:** Boilermakers; Brickmasons and Blockmasons; Carpet Installers; Cement Masons and Concrete Finishers; Construction Carpenters; Crane and Tower Operators; Drywall and Ceiling Tile Installers; Electricians; Fence Erectors; Floor Layers, Except Carpet, Wood, and Hard Tiles; Floor Sanders and Finishers; Glaziers; Hazardous Materials Removal Workers; Insulation Workers, Floor, Ceiling, and Wall; Insulation Workers, Mechanical; Manufactured Building and Mobile Home Installers; Operating Engineers and Other Construction Equipment Operators; Painters, Construction and Maintenance; Paperhangers; Paving, Surfacing, and Tamping Equipment Operators; Pile-Driver Operators; Pipe Fitters and Steamfitters; Pipelayers; Plasterers and Stucco Masons; Plumbers; Plumbers, Pipefitters, and Steamfitters; Rail-Track Laying and Maintenance Equipment Operators; Refractory Materials Repairers, Except Brickmasons; Reinforcing Iron and Rebar Workers; Riggers; Roofers; Rough Carpenters; Security and Fire Alarm Systems Installers; Segmental Pavers; Sheet Metal Workers; Stone Cutters and Carvers, Manufacturing; Stonemasons; Structural Iron and Steel Workers; Tapers; Terrazzo Workers and Finishers; Tile and Marble Setters.

Skills—Repairing: Repairing machines or systems, using the needed tools. **Equipment Maintenance:** Performing routine maintenance and determining when and what kind of maintenance is needed. **Installation:** Installing equipment, machines, wiring, or programs to meet specifications. **Operation Monitoring:** Watching gauges, dials, or other indicators to make sure a machine is working properly. **Operation and Control:** Controlling operations of equipment or systems. **Equipment Selection:** Determining the kind of tools and equipment needed to do a job. **Troubleshooting:** Determining what is causing an operating error and deciding what to do about it. **Technology Design:** Generating or adapting equipment and technology to serve user needs.

Education and Training Program: Diver, Professional and Instructor Training. **Related Knowledge/Courses—Building and Construction:** Materials, methods, and the appropriate tools to construct objects, structures, and buildings. **Mechanical Devices:** Machines and tools, including their designs, uses, benefits, repair, and maintenance. **Physics:** Physical principles, laws, and applications, including air, water, material dynamics, light, atomic principles, heat, electric theory, earth formations, and meteorological and related natural phenomena. **Engineering and Technology:** Equipment, tools, and mechanical devices and their uses to produce motion, light, power, technology, and other applications. **Design:** Design techniques, principles, tools, and instruments involved in the production and use of precision technical plans, blueprints, drawings, and models. **Biology:** Plant and animal living tissue, cells, organisms, and entities, including their functions, interdependencies, and interactions with each other and the environment.

Work Environment: Outdoors; noisy; very hot or cold; hazardous equipment; standing; using hands on objects, tools, or controls.

Commercial Pilots

- ❀ Education/Training Required: Postsecondary vocational training
- ❀ Annual Earnings: $61,640
- ❀ Beginning Wage: $30,460
- ❀ Earnings Growth Potential: Very high
- ❀ Growth: 13.2%
- ❀ Annual Job Openings: 1,425
- ❀ Self-Employed: 1.9%
- ❀ Part-Time: 14.2%

Pilot and navigate the flight of small fixed or rotary winged aircraft primarily for the transport of cargo and passengers. Requires Commercial Rating. Check aircraft prior to flights to ensure that the engines, controls, instruments, and other systems are functioning properly. Start engines, operate controls, and pilot airplanes to transport passengers, mail, or freight while adhering to flight plans, regulations, and procedures. Contact control towers for takeoff clearances, arrival instructions, and other information, using radio equipment. Monitor engine operation, fuel consumption, and functioning of aircraft systems during flights. Consider airport altitudes, outside temperatures, plane weights, and wind speeds and directions to calculate the speed needed to become airborne. Order changes in fuel supplies, loads, routes, or schedules to ensure safety of flights. Obtain and review data such as load weights, fuel supplies, weather conditions, and flight

schedules to determine flight plans and to see if changes might be necessary. Plan flights, following government and company regulations, using aeronautical charts and navigation instruments. Use instrumentation to pilot aircraft when visibility is poor. Check baggage or cargo to ensure that it has been loaded correctly. Request changes in altitudes or routes as circumstances dictate. Choose routes, altitudes, and speeds that will provide the fastest, safest, and smoothest flights. Coordinate flight activities with ground crews and air-traffic control and inform crew members of flight and test procedures. Write specified information in flight records, such as flight times, altitudes flown, and fuel consumption. Teach company regulations and procedures to other pilots. Instruct other pilots and student pilots in aircraft operations. Co-pilot aircraft or perform captain's duties if required. File instrument flight plans with air traffic control so that flights can be coordinated with other air traffic. Conduct in-flight tests and evaluations at specified altitudes and in all types of weather to determine the receptivity and other characteristics of equipment and systems. Rescue and evacuate injured persons. Supervise other crew members. Perform minor aircraft maintenance and repair work or arrange for major maintenance.

Personality Type: Realistic. These occupations frequently involve work activities that include practical, hands-on problems and solutions. They often deal with plants; animals; and real-world materials such as wood, tools, and machinery. Many of the occupations require working outside and don't involve a lot of paperwork or working closely with others.

GOE—Interest Area/Cluster: 16. Transportation, Distribution, and Logistics. **Work Group:** 16.02. Air Vehicle Operation. **Other Jobs in This Work Group:** Airline Pilots, Copilots, and Flight Engineers.

Skills—Operation Monitoring: Watching gauges, dials, or other indicators to make sure a machine is working properly. **Operation and Control:** Controlling operations of equipment or systems. **Troubleshooting:** Determining what is causing an operating error and deciding what to do about it. **Judgment and Decision Making:** Weighing the relative costs and benefits of a potential action. **Systems Evaluation:** Looking at many indicators of system performance and taking into account their accuracy. **Critical Thinking:** Using logic and analysis to identify the strengths and weaknesses of different approaches. **Systems Analysis:** Determining how a system should work and how changes will affect outcomes. **Mathematics:** Using mathematics to solve problems.

Education and Training Programs: Airline/Commercial/Professional Pilot and Flight Crew Training; Flight Instructor Training. **Related Knowledge/Courses—Transportation:** Principles and methods for moving people or goods by air, rail, sea, or road, including their relative costs, advantages, and limitations. **Geography:** Various methods for describing the location and distribution of land, sea, and air masses, including their physical locations, relationships, and characteristics. **Mechanical Devices:** Machines and tools, including their designs, uses, benefits, repair, and maintenance. **Physics:** Physical principles, laws, and applications, including air, water, material dynamics, light, atomic principles, heat, electric theory, earth formations, and meteorological and related natural phenomena. **Telecommunications:** Transmission, broadcasting, switching, control, and operation of telecommunications systems. **Psychology:** Human behavior and performance, mental processes, psychological research methods, and the assessment and treatment of behavioral and affective disorders.

Work Environment: Outdoors; noisy; very hot or cold; contaminants; sitting; using hands on objects, tools, or controls.

Computer Support Specialists

- ❋ Education/Training Required: Associate degree
- ❋ Annual Earnings: $42,400
- ❋ Beginning Wage: $25,950
- ❋ Earnings Growth Potential: Medium
- ❋ Growth: 12.9%
- ❋ Annual Job Openings: 97,334
- ❋ Self-Employed: 1.3%
- ❋ Part-Time: 6.9%

Provide technical assistance to computer system users. Answer questions or resolve computer problems for clients in person, via telephone, or from remote locations. May provide assistance concerning the use of computer hardware and software, including printing, installation, word processing, e-mail, and operating systems. Oversee the daily performance of computer systems. Answer user inquiries regarding computer software or hardware operation to resolve problems. Enter commands and observe system functioning to verify correct operations and detect errors. Set up equipment for employee use, performing or ensuring proper installation of cables, operating systems, or appropriate software. Install and perform minor repairs to hardware, software, or peripheral equipment, following design or installation specifications. Maintain records of daily data communication transactions, problems and remedial actions taken, or installation activities. Read technical manuals, confer with users, or conduct computer diagnostics to investigate and resolve problems or to provide technical assistance and support. Refer major hardware or software problems or defective products to vendors or technicians for service. Develop training materials and procedures or train users in the proper use of hardware or software. Confer with staff, users, and management to establish requirements for new systems or modifications. Prepare evaluations of software or hardware and recommend improvements or upgrades. Read trade magazines and technical manuals or attend conferences and seminars to maintain knowledge of hardware and software. Hire, supervise, and direct workers engaged in special project work, problem solving, monitoring, and installing data communication equipment and software. Inspect equipment and read order sheets to prepare for delivery to users. Modify and customize commercial programs for internal needs. Conduct office automation feasibility studies, including workflow analysis, space design, or cost comparison analysis.

Personality Type: Realistic. These occupations frequently involve work activities that include practical, hands-on problems and solutions. They often deal with plants; animals; and real-world materials such as wood, tools, and machinery. Many of the occupations require working outside and don't involve a lot of paperwork or working closely with others.

GOE—Interest Area/Cluster: 11. Information Technology. **Work Group:** 11.02. Information Technology Specialties. **Other Jobs in This Work Group:** Computer and Information Scientists, Research; Computer Operators; Computer Programmers; Computer Security Specialists; Computer Software Engineers, Applications; Computer Software Engineers, Systems Software; Computer Systems Analysts; Computer Systems Engineers/Architects; Database Administrators; Network Designers; Network Systems and Data Communications Analysts; Software

Quality Assurance Engineers and Testers; Web Administrators; Web Developers.

Skills—Programming: Writing computer programs for various purposes. **Installation:** Installing equipment, machines, wiring, or programs to meet specifications. **Systems Analysis:** Determining how a system should work and how changes will affect outcomes. **Operation Monitoring:** Watching gauges, dials, or other indicators to make sure a machine is working properly. **Repairing:** Repairing machines or systems, using the needed tools. **Systems Evaluation:** Looking at many indicators of system performance and taking into account their accuracy. **Troubleshooting:** Determining what is causing an operating error and deciding what to do about it. **Operation and Control:** Controlling operations of equipment or systems.

Education and Training Programs: Accounting and Computer Science; Agricultural Business Technology; Computer Hardware Technology/Technician Training; Computer Software Technology/Technician Training; Data Processing and Data Processing Technology/Technician Training; Medical Office Computer Specialist/Assistant Training. **Related Knowledge/Courses—Computers and Electronics:** Electric circuit boards, processors, chips, and computer hardware and software, including applications and programming. **Telecommunications:** Transmission, broadcasting, switching, control, and operation of telecommunications systems. **Engineering and Technology:** Equipment, tools, and mechanical devices and their uses to produce motion, light, power, technology, and other applications. **Clerical Studies:** Administrative and clerical procedures and systems such as word-processing systems, filing and records management systems, stenography and transcription, forms, design principles, and other office procedures and terminology. **Customer and Personal Service:** Principles and processes for providing customer and personal services, including needs assessment techniques, quality service standards, alternative delivery systems, and customer satisfaction evaluation techniques. **Communications and Media:** Media production, communication, and dissemination techniques and methods, including alternative ways to inform and entertain via written, oral, and visual media.

Work Environment: Indoors; sitting; using hands on objects, tools, or controls.

Computer, Automated Teller, and Office Machine Repairers

- ❋ Education/Training Required: Postsecondary vocational training
- ❋ Annual Earnings: $37,100
- ❋ Beginning Wage: $22,640
- ❋ Earnings Growth Potential: Medium
- ❋ Growth: 3.0%
- ❋ Annual Job Openings: 22,330
- ❋ Self-Employed: 19.7%
- ❋ Part-Time: 9.0%

Repair, maintain, or install computers, word-processing systems, automated teller machines, and electronic office machines such as duplicating and fax machines. Converse with customers in order to determine details of equipment problems. Reassemble machines after making repairs or replacing parts. Travel to customers' stores or offices to service machines or to provide emergency repair service. Reinstall software programs or adjust settings on existing software in order to fix machine malfunctions. Advise customers concerning equipment operation, maintenance, and programming. Assemble machines according to specifications, using hand tools, power tools, and measuring devices. Test new systems in order to ensure that they are in working order. Operate machines in order to test functioning of parts and mechanisms. Maintain records of equipment maintenance work and repairs. Install and configure new equipment, including operating software and peripheral equipment. Maintain parts inventories and order any additional parts needed for repairs. Update existing equipment, performing tasks such as installing updated circuit boards or additional memory. Test components and circuits of faulty equipment in order to locate defects, using oscilloscopes, signal generators, ammeters, voltmeters, or special diagnostic software programs. Align, adjust, and calibrate equipment according to specifications. Repair, adjust, or replace electrical and mechanical components and parts, using hand tools, power tools, and soldering or welding equipment. Complete repair bills, shop records, time cards, and expense reports. Disassemble machine to examine parts such as wires, gears, and bearings for wear and defects, using hand tools, power tools, and measuring devices. Clean, oil, and adjust mechanical parts to maintain machines' operating efficiency and to prevent breakdowns. Read specifications such as blueprints, charts, and schematics in order to determine machine settings and adjustments. Enter information into computers to copy programs from one electronic component to another or to draw, modify, or store schematics. Lay cable and hook up electrical connections between machines, power sources, and phone lines. Analyze equipment performance records in order to assess equipment functioning.

Personality Type: Realistic. These occupations frequently involve work activities that include practical, hands-on problems and solutions. They often deal with plants; animals; and real-world materials such as wood, tools, and machinery. Many of the occupations require working outside and don't involve a lot of paperwork or working closely with others.

GOE—Interest Area/Cluster: 11. Information Technology. **Work Group:** 11.03. Digital Equipment Repair. **Other Jobs in This Work Group:** Coin, Vending, and Amusement Machine Servicers and Repairers.

Skills—Installation: Installing equipment, machines, wiring, or programs to meet specifications. **Repairing:** Repairing machines or systems, using the needed tools. **Troubleshooting:** Determining what is causing an operating error and deciding what to do about it. **Equipment Maintenance:** Performing routine maintenance and determining when and what kind of maintenance is needed. **Management of Material Resources:** Obtaining and seeing to the appropriate use of equipment, facilities, and materials needed to do certain work. **Programming:** Writing computer programs for various purposes. **Technology Design:** Generating or adapting equipment and technology to serve user needs. **Systems Evaluation:** Looking at many indicators of system performance and taking into account their accuracy.

Education and Training Programs: Business Machine Repair; Computer Installation and Repair Technology/Technician Training. **Related Knowledge/Courses—Computers and Electronics:** Electric circuit boards, processors, chips, and computer hardware and software, including applications and programming. **Telecommunications:** Transmission, broadcasting, switching, control, and operation of telecommunications systems. **Mechanical Devices:** Machines and tools, including their designs, uses, benefits, repair, and maintenance. **Customer and Personal Service:** Principles and processes for providing customer and personal services, including needs assessment techniques, quality service standards, alternative delivery systems, and customer satisfaction evaluation techniques. **Engineering and Technology:** Equipment, tools, and mechanical devices and their uses to produce motion, light, power, technology, and other applications. **Sales and Marketing:** Principles and methods involved in showing, promoting, and selling products or services. This includes marketing strategies and tactics, product demonstration and sales techniques, and sales control systems.

Work Environment: Indoors; sitting; using hands on objects, tools, or controls; repetitive motions.

Concierges

* Education/Training Required: Moderate-term on-the-job training
* Annual Earnings: $25,540
* Beginning Wage: $16,910
* Earnings Growth Potential: Low
* Growth: 14.1%
* Annual Job Openings: 4,893
* Self-Employed: 0.3%
* Part-Time: 16.9%

Assist patrons at hotel, apartment, or office building with personal services. May take messages; arrange or give advice on transportation, business services, or entertainment; or monitor guest requests for housekeeping and maintenance. Make dining and other reservations for patrons and obtain tickets for events. Provide information about local features such as shopping, dining, nightlife, and recreational destinations. Make travel arrangements for sightseeing and other tours. Receive, store, and deliver luggage and mail. Perform office duties on a temporary basis when needed. Pick up and deliver items or run errands for guests. Carry out unusual requests such as searching for hard-to-find items and arranging for exotic services such as hot-air balloon rides. Arrange for the replacement of items lost by travelers. Arrange for interpreters or translators when patrons require such services. Plan special events, parties, and meetings, which may include booking musicians or celebrities to appear.

Personality Type: Social. These occupations frequently involve working with, communicating with, and teaching people and often involve helping or providing service to others.

GOE—Interest Area/Cluster: 09. Hospitality, Tourism, and Recreation. **Work Group:** 09.03. Hospitality and Travel Services. **Other Jobs in This Work Group:** Baggage Porters and Bellhops; Flight Attendants; Hotel, Motel, and Resort Desk Clerks; Janitors and Cleaners, Except Maids and Housekeeping Cleaners; Maids and Housekeeping Cleaners; Reservation and Transportation Ticket Agents and Travel Clerks; Tour Guides and Escorts; Transportation Attendants, Except Flight Attendants and Baggage Porters; Travel Agents; Travel Guides.

Skills—Service Orientation: Actively looking for ways to help people. **Social Perceptiveness:** Being aware of others' reactions and understanding why they react the way they do. **Management of Personnel Resources:** Motivating, developing, and directing people as they work; identifying the best people for the job. **Critical Thinking:** Using logic and analysis to identify the strengths and weaknesses of different approaches.

Education and Training Programs: No related CIP programs; this job is learned through informal moderate-term on-the-job training. **Related Knowledge/Courses—Customer and Personal Service:** Principles and processes for providing customer and personal services, including needs assessment techniques, quality service standards, alternative delivery systems, and customer satisfaction evaluation techniques. **Philosophy and Theology:** Different philosophical systems and religions, including their basic principles, values, ethics, ways of thinking, customs, and practices and their impact on human culture. **Clerical Studies:** Administrative and clerical procedures and systems such as word-processing systems, filing and records management systems, stenography and transcription, forms, design principles, and other office procedures and terminology. **Communications and Media:** Media production, communication, and dissemination techniques and methods, including alternative ways to inform and entertain via written, oral, and visual media. **Psychology:** Human behavior and performance, mental processes, psychological research methods, and the assessment and treatment of behavioral and affective disorders. **Public Safety and Security:** Weaponry; public safety; security operations, rules, regulations, precautions, and prevention; and the protection of people, data, and property.

Work Environment: Indoors; noisy; standing; repetitive motions.

Construction and Building Inspectors

* Education/Training Required: Work experience in a related occupation
* Annual Earnings: $48,330
* Beginning Wage: $30,450
* Earnings Growth Potential: Medium
* Growth: 18.2%
* Annual Job Openings: 12,606
* Self-Employed: 9.4%
* Part-Time: 4.6%

Inspect structures, using engineering skills to determine structural soundness and compliance with specifications, building codes, and other regulations. Inspections may be general in nature or may be limited to a specific area, such as electrical systems or plumbing. Issue violation notices and stop-work orders, conferring with owners, violators, and authorities to explain regulations and recommend rectifications. Inspect bridges, dams, highways, buildings, wiring, plumbing, electrical circuits, sewers, heating systems, and foundations during and after construction for structural quality, general safety, and conformance to specifications and codes. Approve and sign plans that meet required specifications. Review and interpret plans, blueprints, site layouts, specifications, and construction methods to ensure compliance to legal requirements and safety regulations. Monitor installation of plumbing, wiring, equipment, and appliances to ensure that installation is performed properly and is in compliance with applicable regulations. Inspect and monitor construction sites to ensure adherence to safety standards, building codes, and specifications. Measure dimensions and verify level, alignment, and elevation of structures and fixtures to ensure compliance to building plans and codes. Maintain daily logs and supplement inspection records with photographs. Use survey instruments, metering devices, tape measures, and test equipment such as concrete strength measurers to perform inspections. Train, direct, and supervise other construction inspectors. Issue permits for construction, relocation, demolition, and occupancy. Examine lifting and conveying devices such as elevators, escalators,

C

moving sidewalks, lifts and hoists, inclined railways, ski lifts, and amusement rides to ensure safety and proper functioning. Compute estimates of work completed or of needed renovations or upgrades and approve payment for contractors. Evaluate premises for cleanliness, including proper garbage disposal and lack of vermin infestation.

Personality Type: Realistic. These occupations frequently involve work activities that include practical, hands-on problems and solutions. They often deal with plants; animals; and real-world materials such as wood, tools, and machinery. Many of the occupations require working outside and don't involve a lot of paperwork or working closely with others.

GOE—Interest Area/Cluster: 07. Government and Public Administration. **Work Group:** 07.03. Regulations Enforcement. **Other Jobs in This Work Group:** Agricultural Inspectors; Aviation Inspectors; Compliance Officers, Except Agriculture, Construction, Health and Safety, and **Transportation:** Principles and methods for moving people or goods by air, rail, sea, or road, including their relative costs, advantages, and limitations. Environmental Compliance Inspectors; Equal Opportunity Representatives and Officers; Financial Examiners; Fire Inspectors; Fish and Game Wardens; Forest Fire Inspectors and Prevention Specialists; Freight and Cargo Inspectors; Government Property Inspectors and Investigators; Immigration and Customs Inspectors; Licensing Examiners and Inspectors; Nuclear Monitoring Technicians; Occupational Health and Safety Specialists; Occupational Health and Safety Technicians; Tax Examiners, Collectors, and Revenue Agents; Transportation Vehicle, Equipment, and Systems Inspectors, Except Aviation.

Skills—Quality Control Analysis: Evaluating the quality or performance of products, services, or processes. **Systems Analysis:** Determining how a system should work and how changes will affect outcomes. **Systems Evaluation:** Looking at many indicators of system performance and taking into account their accuracy. **Management of Personnel Resources:** Motivating, developing, and directing people as they work; identifying the best people for the job. **Operation Monitoring:** Watching gauges, dials, or other indicators to make sure a machine is working properly.

Education and Training Program: Building/Home/Construction Inspection/Inspector Training. **Related Knowledge/Courses—Building and Construction:** Materials,

methods, and the appropriate tools to construct objects, structures, and buildings. **Engineering and Technology:** Equipment, tools, and mechanical devices and their uses to produce motion, light, power, technology, and other applications. **Design:** Design techniques, principles, tools, and instruments involved in the production and use of precision technical plans, blueprints, drawings, and models. **Physics:** Physical principles, laws, and applications, including air, water, material dynamics, light, atomic principles, heat, electric theory, earth formations, and meteorological and related natural phenomena. **Public Safety and Security:** Weaponry; public safety; security operations, rules, regulations, precautions, and prevention; and the protection of people, data, and property. **Mechanical Devices:** Machines and tools, including their designs, uses, benefits, repair, and maintenance.

Work Environment: More often outdoors than indoors; very hot or cold; very bright or dim lighting; contaminants; cramped work space, awkward positions.

Construction Carpenters

- ❋ Education/Training Required: Long-term on-the-job training
- ❋ Annual Earnings: $37,660
- ❋ Beginning Wage: $23,370
- ❋ Earnings Growth Potential: Medium
- ❋ Growth: 10.3%
- ❋ Annual Job Openings: 223,225
- ❋ Self-Employed: 31.8%
- ❋ Part-Time: 6.1%

The job openings listed here are shared with Rough Carpenters.

Construct, erect, install, and repair structures and fixtures of wood, plywood, and wallboard, using carpenter's hand tools and power tools. Measure and mark cutting lines on materials, using ruler, pencil, chalk, and marking gauge. Follow established safety rules and regulations and maintain a safe and clean environment. Verify trueness of structure, using plumb bob and level. Shape or cut materials to specified measurements, using hand tools, machines, or power saw. Study specifications in blueprints, sketches, or building plans to prepare project layout and determine dimensions and materials required. Assemble and fasten materials to make framework or props, using hand tools and wood screws, nails, dowel pins, or glue. Build or repair cabinets, doors, frameworks, floors, and other wooden fixtures used in buildings, using woodworking machines, carpenter's hand tools, and power tools. Erect scaffolding and ladders for assembling structures above ground level. Remove damaged or defective parts or sections of structures and repair or replace, using hand tools. Install structures and fixtures, such as windows, frames, floorings, and trim, or hardware, using carpenter's hand and power tools. Select and order lumber and other required materials. Maintain records, document actions, and present written progress reports. Finish surfaces of woodwork or wallboard in houses and buildings, using paint, hand tools, and paneling. Prepare cost estimates for clients or employers. Arrange for subcontractors to deal with special areas such as heating and electrical wiring work. Inspect ceiling or floor tile, wall coverings, siding, glass, or woodwork to detect broken or damaged structures. Work with or remove hazardous material. Construct forms and chutes for pouring concrete. Cover subfloors with building paper to keep out moisture and lay hardwood, parquet, and wood-strip-block floors by nailing floors to subfloor or cementing them to mastic or asphalt base. Fill cracks and other defects in plaster or plasterboard and sand patch, using patching plaster, trowel, and sanding tool. Perform minor plumbing, welding, or concrete mixing work. Apply shock-absorbing, sound-deadening, and decorative paneling to ceilings and walls.

Personality Type: Realistic. These occupations frequently involve work activities that include practical, hands-on problems and solutions. They often deal with plants; animals; and real-world materials such as wood, tools, and machinery. Many of the occupations require working outside and don't involve a lot of paperwork or working closely with others.

GOE—Interest Area/Cluster: 02. Architecture and Construction. **Work Group:** 02.04. Construction Crafts. **Other Jobs in This Work Group:** Boilermakers; Brickmasons and Blockmasons; Carpet Installers; Cement Masons and Concrete Finishers; Commercial Divers; Crane and Tower Operators; Drywall and Ceiling Tile Installers; Electricians; Fence Erectors; Floor Layers, Except Carpet, Wood, and Hard Tiles; Floor Sanders and Finishers; Glaziers; Hazardous Materials Removal Workers; Insulation Workers, Floor, Ceiling, and Wall; Insulation Workers,

Mechanical; Manufactured Building and Mobile Home Installers; Operating Engineers and Other Construction Equipment Operators; Painters, Construction and Maintenance; Paperhangers; Paving, Surfacing, and Tamping Equipment Operators; Pile-Driver Operators; Pipe Fitters and Steamfitters; Pipelayers; Plasterers and Stucco Masons; Plumbers; Plumbers, Pipefitters, and Steamfitters; Rail-Track Laying and Maintenance Equipment Operators; Refractory Materials Repairers, Except Brickmasons; Reinforcing Iron and Rebar Workers; Riggers; Roofers; Rough Carpenters; Security and Fire Alarm Systems Installers; Segmental Pavers; Sheet Metal Workers; Stone Cutters and Carvers, Manufacturing; Stonemasons; Structural Iron and Steel Workers; Tapers; Terrazzo Workers and Finishers; Tile and Marble Setters.

Skills—Management of Personnel Resources: Motivating, developing, and directing people as they work; identifying the best people for the job. **Management of Material Resources:** Obtaining and seeing to the appropriate use of equipment, facilities, and materials needed to do certain work. **Management of Financial Resources:** Determining how money will be spent to get the work done and accounting for these expenditures. **Repairing:** Repairing machines or systems, using the needed tools. **Equipment Maintenance:** Performing routine maintenance and determining when and what kind of maintenance is needed. **Quality Control Analysis:** Evaluating the quality or performance of products, services, or processes. **Installation:** Installing equipment, machines, wiring, or programs to meet specifications. **Mathematics:** Using mathematics to solve problems.

Education and Training Program: Carpentry/Carpenter Training. **Related Knowledge/Courses—Building and Construction:** Materials, methods, and the appropriate tools to construct objects, structures, and buildings. **Mechanical Devices:** Machines and tools, including their designs, uses, benefits, repair, and maintenance. **Design:** Design techniques, principles, tools, and instruments involved in the production and use of precision technical plans, blueprints, drawings, and models. **Engineering and Technology:** Equipment, tools, and mechanical devices and their uses to produce motion, light, power, technology, and other applications. **Production and Processing:** Inputs, outputs, raw materials, waste, quality control, costs, and techniques for maximizing the manufacture and distribution of goods. **Public Safety and Security:**

Weaponry; public safety; security operations, rules, regulations, precautions, and prevention; and the protection of people, data, and property.

Work Environment: Outdoors; noisy; hazardous equipment; standing; walking and running; using hands on objects, tools, or controls.

Construction Laborers

- ❋ Education/Training Required: Moderate-term on-the-job training
- ❋ Annual Earnings: $27,310
- ❋ Beginning Wage: $17,410
- ❋ Earnings Growth Potential: Medium
- ❋ Growth: 10.9%
- ❋ Annual Job Openings: 257,407
- ❋ Self-Employed: 16.4%
- ❋ Part-Time: 8.7%

Perform tasks involving physical labor at building, highway, and heavy construction projects; tunnel and shaft excavations; and demolition sites. May operate hand and power tools of all types: air hammers, earth tampers, cement mixers, small mechanical hoists, surveying and measuring equipment, and various other types of equipment and instruments. May clean and prepare sites; dig trenches; set braces to support the sides of excavations; erect scaffolding; clean up rubble and debris; and remove asbestos, lead, and other hazardous waste materials. May assist other craft workers. Clean and prepare construction sites to eliminate possible hazards. Read and interpret plans, instructions, and specifications to determine work activities. Control traffic passing near, in, and around work zones. Signal equipment operators to facilitate alignment, movement, and adjustment of machinery, equipment, and materials. Dig ditches or trenches, backfill excavations, and compact and level earth to grade specifications, using picks, shovels, pneumatic tampers, and rakes. Measure, mark, and record openings and distances to lay out areas where construction work will be performed. Position, join, align, and seal structural components, such as concrete wall sections and pipes. Load, unload, and identify building materials, machinery, and tools and distribute them to the appropriate locations according to project plans and specifications. Erect and disassemble scaffolding, shoring, braces, traffic barricades, ramps, and other temporary structures. Build and position forms for pouring concrete and dismantle forms after use, using saws, hammers, nails, or bolts. Lubricate, clean, and repair machinery, equipment, and tools. Operate jackhammers and drills to break up concrete or pavement. Smooth and finish freshly poured cement or concrete, using floats, trowels, screeds, or powered cement finishing tools. Operate, read, and maintain air monitoring and other sampling devices in confined or hazardous environments. Install sewer, water, and storm drain pipes, using pipe-laying machinery and laser guidance equipment. Transport and set explosives for tunnel, shaft, and road construction. Provide assistance to craft workers, such as carpenters, plasterers, and masons. Tend pumps, compressors, and generators to provide power for tools, machinery, and equipment or to heat and move materials such as asphalt. Mop, brush, or spread paints, cleaning solutions, or other compounds over surfaces to clean them or to provide protection. Place, consolidate, and protect case-in-place concrete or masonry structures. Identify, pack, and transport hazardous and/or radioactive materials. Use computers and other input devices to control robotic pipe cutters and cleaners.

Personality Type: Realistic. These occupations frequently involve work activities that include practical, hands-on problems and solutions. They often deal with plants; animals; and real-world materials such as wood, tools, and machinery. Many of the occupations require working outside and don't involve a lot of paperwork or working closely with others.

GOE—Interest Area/Cluster: 02. Architecture and Construction. **Work Group:** 02.06. Construction Support/Labor. **Other Jobs in This Work Group:** Helpers—Brickmasons, Blockmasons, Stonemasons, and Tile and Marble Setters; Helpers—Carpenters; Helpers—Electricians; Helpers—Installation, Maintenance, and Repair Workers; Helpers—Painters, Paperhangers, Plasterers, and Stucco Masons; Helpers—Pipelayers, Plumbers, Pipefitters, and Steamfitters; Helpers—Roofers; Highway Maintenance Workers; Septic Tank Servicers and Sewer Pipe Cleaners.

Skills—Equipment Maintenance: Performing routine maintenance and determining when and what kind of maintenance is needed. **Repairing:** Repairing machines or systems, using the needed tools. **Equipment Selection:** Determining the kind of tools and equipment needed to do a job. **Installation:** Installing equipment, machines, wiring, or programs to meet specifications.

Education and Training Program: Construction Trades, Other. **Related Knowledge/Courses—Building and Construction:** Materials, methods, and the appropriate tools to construct objects, structures, and buildings. **Design:** Design techniques, principles, tools, and instruments involved in the production and use of precision technical plans, blueprints, drawings, and models. **Mechanical Devices:** Machines and tools, including their designs, uses, benefits, repair, and maintenance. **Transportation:** Principles and methods for moving people or goods by air, rail, sea, or road, including their relative costs, advantages, and limitations. **Engineering and Technology:** Equipment, tools, and mechanical devices and their uses to produce motion, light, power, technology, and other applications. **Public Safety and Security:** Weaponry; public safety; security operations, rules, regulations, precautions, and prevention; and the protection of people, data, and property.

Work Environment: Outdoors; noisy; very hot or cold; contaminants; standing; using hands on objects, tools, or controls.

Control and Valve Installers and Repairers, Except Mechanical Door

- ❋ Education/Training Required: Moderate-term on-the-job training
- ❋ Annual Earnings: $46,140
- ❋ Beginning Wage: $25,830
- ❋ Earnings Growth Potential: High
- ❋ Growth: 0.3%
- ❋ Annual Job Openings: 3,855
- ❋ Self-Employed: 0.3%
- ❋ Part-Time: 0.5%

Install, repair, and maintain mechanical regulating and controlling devices such as electric meters, gas regulators, thermostats, safety and flow valves, and other mechanical governors. Turn meters on or off to establish or close service. Turn valves to allow measured amounts of air or gas to pass through meters at specified flow rates. Report hazardous field situations and damaged or missing meters. Record meter readings and installation data on meter cards, work orders, or field service orders or enter data into handheld computers. Connect regulators to test stands and turn screw adjustments until gauges indicate that inlet and outlet pressures meet specifications. Disassemble and repair mechanical control devices or valves, such as regulators, thermostats, or hydrants, using power tools, hand tools, and cutting torches. Record maintenance information, including test results, material usage, and repairs made. Disconnect or remove defective or unauthorized meters, using hand tools. Lubricate wearing surfaces of mechanical parts, using oils or other lubricants. Test valves and regulators for leaks and accurate temperature and pressure settings, using precision testing equipment. Install regulators and related equipment such as gas meters, odorization units, and gas pressure telemetering equipment. Shut off service and notify repair crews when major repairs are required, such as the replacement of underground pipes or wiring. Examine valves or mechanical control device parts for defects, dents, or loose attachments and mark malfunctioning areas of defective units. Attach air hoses to meter inlets; then plug outlets and observe gauges for pressure losses in order to test internal seams for leaks. Dismantle meters and replace or adjust defective parts such as cases, shafts, gears, disks, and recording mechanisms, using soldering irons and hand tools. Advise customers on proper installation of valves or regulators and related equipment. Connect hoses from provers to meter inlets and outlets and raise prover bells until prover gauges register zero. Make adjustments to meter components, such as setscrews or timing mechanisms, so that they conform to specifications. Replace defective parts, such as bellows, range springs, and toggle switches, and reassemble units according to blueprints, using cam presses and hand tools.

Personality Type: Realistic. These occupations frequently involve work activities that include practical, hands-on problems and solutions. They often deal with plants; animals; and real-world materials such as wood, tools, and machinery. Many of the occupations require working outside and don't involve a lot of paperwork or working closely with others.

GOE—Interest Area/Cluster: 13. Manufacturing. **Work Group:** 13.13. Machinery Repair. **Other Jobs in This Work Group:** Bicycle Repairers; Home Appliance Repairers; Industrial Machinery Mechanics; Locksmiths and Safe Repairers; Maintenance Workers, Machinery; Mechanical Door Repairers; Millwrights; Signal and Track Switch Repairers.

Skills—Installation: Installing equipment, machines, wiring, or programs to meet specifications. **Repairing:** Repairing machines or systems, using the needed tools. **Equipment Maintenance:** Performing routine maintenance and determining when and what kind of maintenance is needed. **Operation Monitoring:** Watching gauges, dials, or other indicators to make sure a machine is working properly. **Troubleshooting:** Determining what is causing an operating error and deciding what to do about it. **Quality Control Analysis:** Evaluating the quality or performance of products, services, or processes. **Science:** Using scientific methods to solve problems. **Operation and Control:** Controlling operations of equipment or systems.

Education and Training Program: Instrumentation Technology/Technician Training. **Related Knowledge/Courses—Mechanical Devices:** Machines and tools, including their designs, uses, benefits, repair, and maintenance. **Transportation:** Principles and methods for moving people or goods by air, rail, sea, or road, including their relative costs, advantages, and limitations. **Physics:** Physical principles, laws, and applications, including air, water, material dynamics, light, atomic principles, heat, electric theory, earth formations, and meteorological and related natural phenomena. **Public Safety and Security:** Weaponry; public safety; security operations, rules, regulations, precautions, and prevention; and the protection of people, data, and property. **Design:** Design techniques, principles, tools, and instruments involved in the production and use of precision technical plans, blueprints, drawings, and models. **Chemistry:** The composition, structure, and properties of substances and of the chemical processes and transformations that they undergo. This includes uses of chemicals and their interactions, danger signs, production techniques, and disposal methods.

Work Environment: Outdoors; very hot or cold; very bright or dim lighting; contaminants; cramped work space, awkward positions; hazardous conditions.

Cooks, Institution and Cafeteria

* Education/Training Required: Moderate-term on-the-job training
* Annual Earnings: $21,340
* Beginning Wage: $14,300
* Earnings Growth Potential: Low
* Growth: 10.8%
* Annual Job Openings: 111,898
* Self-Employed: 1.4%
* Part-Time: 29.9%

Prepare and cook large quantities of food for institutions, such as schools, hospitals, or cafeterias. Clean and inspect galley equipment, kitchen appliances, and work areas to ensure cleanliness and functional operation. Apportion and serve food to facility residents, employees, or patrons. Cook foodstuffs according to menus, special dietary or nutritional restrictions, and numbers of portions to be served. Clean, cut, and cook meat, fish, and poultry. Monitor use of government food commodities to ensure that proper procedures are followed. Wash pots, pans, dishes, utensils, and other cooking equipment. Compile and maintain records of food use and expenditures. Direct activities of one or more workers who assist in preparing and serving meals. Bake breads, rolls, and other pastries. Train new employees. Take inventory of supplies and equipment. Monitor menus and spending to ensure that meals are prepared economically. Plan menus that are varied, nutritionally balanced, and appetizing, taking advantage of foods in season and local availability. Requisition food supplies, kitchen equipment, and appliances based on estimates of future needs. Determine meal prices based on calculations of ingredient prices.

Personality Type: Realistic. These occupations frequently involve work activities that include practical, hands-on problems and solutions. They often deal with plants; animals; and real-world materials such as wood, tools, and machinery. Many of the occupations require working outside and don't involve a lot of paperwork or working closely with others.

GOE—Interest Area/Cluster: 09. Hospitality, Tourism, and Recreation. **Work Group:** 09.04. Food and Beverage Preparation. **Other Jobs in This Work Group:** Butchers and Meat Cutters; Chefs and Head Cooks; Cooks,

Fast Food; Cooks, Private Household; Cooks, Restaurant; Cooks, Short Order; Dishwashers; Food Preparation Workers.

Skills—Equipment Selection: Determining the kind of tools and equipment needed to do a job. **Instructing:** Teaching others how to do something. **Service Orientation:** Actively looking for ways to help people.

Education and Training Programs: Cooking and Related Culinary Arts, General; Culinary Arts and Related Services, Other; Food Preparation/Professional Cooking/Kitchen Assistant Training; Foodservice Systems Administration/Management; Institutional Food Worker Training. **Related Knowledge/Courses—Food Production:** Techniques and equipment for planting, growing, and harvesting of food for consumption, including crop-rotation methods, animal husbandry, and food storage/handling techniques. **Public Safety and Security:** Weaponry; public safety; security operations, rules, regulations, precautions, and prevention; and the protection of people, data, and property.

Work Environment: Indoors; very hot or cold; minor burns, cuts, bites, or stings; standing; walking and running; repetitive motions.

Cooks, Restaurant

- ✽ Education/Training Required: Long-term on-the-job training
- ✽ Annual Earnings: $21,220
- ✽ Beginning Wage: $15,120
- ✽ Earnings Growth Potential: Low
- ✽ Growth: 11.5%
- ✽ Annual Job Openings: 238,542
- ✽ Self-Employed: 1.2%
- ✽ Part-Time: 29.9%

Prepare, season, and cook soups, meats, vegetables, desserts, or other foodstuffs in restaurants. May order supplies, keep records and accounts, price items on menu, or plan menu. Inspect food preparation and serving areas to ensure observance of safe, sanitary food-handling practices. Turn or stir foods to ensure even cooking. Season and cook food according to recipes or personal judgment and experience. Observe and test foods to determine if they have been cooked sufficiently, using methods such as tasting them, smelling them, or piercing them with utensils. Weigh, measure, and mix ingredients according to recipes or personal judgment, using various kitchen utensils and equipment. Portion, arrange, and garnish food and serve food to waiters or patrons. Regulate temperature of ovens, broilers, grills, and roasters. Substitute for or assist other cooks during emergencies or rush periods. Bake, roast, broil, and steam meats, fish, vegetables, and other foods. Wash, peel, cut, and seed fruits and vegetables to prepare them for consumption. Estimate expected food consumption, requisition or purchase supplies, or procure food from storage. Carve and trim meats such as beef, veal, ham, pork, and lamb for hot or cold service or for sandwiches. Coordinate and supervise work of kitchen staff. Consult with supervisory staff to plan menus, taking into consideration factors such as costs and special event needs. Butcher and dress animals, fowl, or shellfish or cut and bone meat prior to cooking. Prepare relishes and hors d'oeuvres. Bake breads, rolls, cakes, and pastries. Keep records and accounts. Plan and price menu items.

Personality Type: Realistic. These occupations frequently involve work activities that include practical, hands-on problems and solutions. They often deal with plants; animals; and real-world materials such as wood, tools, and machinery. Many of the occupations require working outside and don't involve a lot of paperwork or working closely with others.

GOE—Interest Area/Cluster: 09. Hospitality, Tourism, and Recreation. **Work Group:** 09.04. Food and Beverage Preparation. **Other Jobs in This Work Group:** Butchers and Meat Cutters; Chefs and Head Cooks; Cooks, Fast Food; Cooks, Institution and Cafeteria; Cooks, Private Household; Cooks, Short Order; Dishwashers; Food Preparation Workers.

Skill: Equipment Maintenance: Performing routine maintenance and determining when and what kind of maintenance is needed.

Education and Training Programs: Cooking and Related Culinary Arts, General; Culinary Arts/Chef Training. **Related Knowledge/Courses—Food Production:** Techniques and equipment for planting, growing, and harvesting of food for consumption, including crop-rotation methods, animal husbandry, and food storage/handling techniques. **Production and Processing:** Inputs;

outputs, raw materials, waste, quality control, costs, and techniques for maximizing the manufacture and distribution of goods.

Work Environment: Indoors; very hot or cold; minor burns, cuts, bites, or stings; standing; using hands on objects, tools, or controls; repetitive motions.

Coroners

* Education/Training Required: Work experience in a related occupation
* Annual Earnings: $48,400
* Beginning Wage: $28,980
* Earnings Growth Potential: High
* Growth: 4.9%
* Annual Job Openings: 15,841
* Self-Employed: 0.4%
* Part-Time: 5.0%

The job openings listed here are shared with Environmental Compliance Inspectors; Equal Opportunity Representatives and Officers; Government Property Inspectors and Investigators; and Licensing Examiners and Inspectors.

Direct activities such as autopsies, pathological and toxicological analyses, and inquests relating to the investigation of deaths occurring within a legal jurisdiction to determine cause of death or to fix responsibility for accidental, violent, or unexplained deaths. Perform medico-legal examinations and autopsies, conducting preliminary examinations of the body in order to identify victims, to locate signs of trauma, and to identify factors that would indicate time of death. Inquire into the cause, manner, and circumstances of human deaths and establish the identities of deceased persons. Direct activities of workers who conduct autopsies, perform pathological and toxicological analyses, and prepare documents for permanent records. Complete death certificates, including the assignment of a cause and manner of death. Observe and record the positions and conditions of bodies and of related evidence. Collect and document any pertinent medical history information. Observe, record, and preserve any objects or personal property related to deaths, including objects such as medication containers and suicide notes. Complete reports and forms required to finalize cases.

Remove or supervise removal of bodies from death scenes, using the proper equipment and supplies, and arrange for transportation to morgues. Testify at inquests, hearings, and court trials. Interview persons present at death scenes to obtain information useful in determining the manner of death. Provide information concerning the circumstances of death to relatives of the deceased. Locate and document information regarding the next of kin, including their relationship to the deceased and the status of notification attempts. Confer with officials of public health and law enforcement agencies in order to coordinate interdepartmental activities. Inventory personal effects, such as jewelry or wallets, that are recovered from bodies. Coordinate the release of personal effects to authorized persons and facilitate the disposition of unclaimed corpses and personal effects. Arrange for the next of kin to be notified of deaths. Record the disposition of minor children, as well as details of arrangements made for their care. Collect wills, burial instructions, and other documentation needed for investigations and for handling of the remains. Witness and certify deaths that are the result of a judicial order.

Personality Type: Investigative. These occupations frequently involve working with ideas and require an extensive amount of thinking. They can involve searching for facts and figuring out problems mentally.

GOE—Interest Area/Cluster: 08. Health Science. **Work Group:** 08.01. Managerial Work in Medical and Health Services. **Other Jobs in This Work Group:** Medical and Health Services Managers.

Skills—Science: Using scientific methods to solve problems. **Management of Financial Resources:** Determining how money will be spent to get the work done and accounting for these expenditures. **Reading Comprehension:** Understanding written sentences and paragraphs in work-related documents. **Critical Thinking:** Using logic and analysis to identify the strengths and weaknesses of different approaches. **Management of Personnel Resources:** Motivating, developing, and directing people as they work; identifying the best people for the job. **Speaking:** Talking to others to effectively convey information. **Management of Material Resources:** Obtaining and seeing to the appropriate use of equipment, facilities, and materials needed to do certain work. **Writing:** Communicating effectively with others in writing as indicated by the needs of the audience.

Education and Training Program: Public Administration. **Related Knowledge/Courses—Medicine and Dentistry:** The information and techniques needed to diagnose and treat injuries, diseases, and deformities. This includes symptoms, treatment alternatives, drug properties and interactions, and preventive health-care measures. **Biology:** Plant and animal living tissue, cells, organisms, and entities, including their functions, interdependencies, and interactions with each other and the environment. **Psychology:** Human behavior and performance, mental processes, psychological research methods, and the assessment and treatment of behavioral and affective disorders. **Therapy and Counseling:** Information and techniques needed to rehabilitate physical and mental ailments and to provide career guidance, including alternative treatments, rehabilitation equipment and its proper use, and methods to evaluate treatment effects. **Chemistry:** The composition, structure, and properties of substances and of the chemical processes and transformations that they undergo. This includes uses of chemicals and their interactions, danger signs, production techniques, and disposal methods. **Law and Government:** Laws, legal codes, court procedures, precedents, government regulations, executive orders, agency rules, and the democratic political process.

Work Environment: More often indoors than outdoors; contaminants; disease or infections; hazardous equipment; using hands on objects, tools, or controls.

Correctional Officers and Jailers

* Education/Training Required: Moderate-term on-the-job training
* Annual Earnings: $36,970
* Beginning Wage: $24,820
* Earnings Growth Potential: Low
* Growth: 16.9%
* Annual Job Openings: 56,579
* Self-Employed: 0.0%
* Part-Time: 1.8%

Guard inmates in penal or rehabilitative institution in accordance with established regulations and procedures. May guard prisoners in transit between jail, courtroom, prison, or other point. Includes deputy sheriffs and police who spend the majority of their time guarding prisoners in correctional institutions. Conduct head counts to ensure that each prisoner is present. Monitor conduct of prisoners in housing unit or during work or recreational activities according to established policies, regulations, and procedures to prevent escape or violence. Inspect conditions of locks, window bars, grills, doors, and gates at correctional facilities to ensure security and help prevent escapes. Record information such as prisoner identification, charges, and incidences of inmate disturbance and keep daily logs of prisoner activities. Search prisoners and vehicles and conduct shakedowns of cells for valuables and contraband, such as weapons or drugs. Use weapons, handcuffs, and physical force to maintain discipline and order among prisoners. Guard facility entrances to screen visitors. Inspect mail for the presence of contraband. Maintain records of prisoners' identification and charges. Process or book convicted individuals into prison. Settle disputes between inmates. Conduct fire, safety, and sanitation inspections. Provide to supervisors oral and written reports of the quality and quantity of work performed by inmates, inmate disturbances and rule violations, and unusual occurrences. Participate in required job training. Take prisoners into custody and escort to locations within and outside of facility, such as visiting room, courtroom, or airport. Serve meals, distribute commissary items, and dispense prescribed medication to prisoners. Counsel inmates and respond to legitimate questions, concerns, and requests. Drive passenger vehicles and trucks used to transport inmates to other institutions, courtrooms, hospitals, and work sites. Use nondisciplinary tools and equipment such as a computer. Assign duties to inmates, providing instructions as needed. Investigate crimes that have occurred within an institution or assist police in their investigations of crimes and inmates. Issue clothing, tools, and other authorized items to inmates. Arrange daily schedules for prisoners, including library visits, work assignments, family visits, and counseling appointments. Search for and recapture escapees.

Personality Type: Realistic. These occupations frequently involve work activities that include practical, hands-on problems and solutions. They often deal with plants; animals; and real-world materials such as wood, tools, and machinery. Many of the occupations require working outside and don't involve a lot of paperwork or working closely with others.

GOE—Interest Area/Cluster: 12. Law and Public Safety. **Work Group:** 12.04. Law Enforcement and Public Safety. **Other Jobs in This Work Group:** Bailiffs; Criminal Investigators and Special Agents; Detectives and Criminal Investigators; Fire Investigators; Forensic Science Technicians; Parking Enforcement Workers; Police and Sheriff's Patrol Officers; Police Detectives; Police Identification and Records Officers; Police Patrol Officers; Sheriffs and Deputy Sheriffs; Transit and Railroad Police.

Skills: None met the criteria.

Education and Training Programs: Corrections; Corrections and Criminal Justice, Other; Juvenile Corrections. **Related Knowledge/Courses—Public Safety and Security:** Weaponry; public safety; security operations, rules, regulations, precautions, and prevention; and the protection of people, data, and property. **Psychology:** Human behavior and performance, mental processes, psychological research methods, and the assessment and treatment of behavioral and affective disorders. **Therapy and Counseling:** Information and techniques needed to rehabilitate physical and mental ailments and to provide career guidance, including alternative treatments, rehabilitation equipment and its proper use, and methods to evaluate treatment effects. **Law and Government:** Laws, legal codes, court procedures, precedents, government regulations, executive orders, agency rules, and the democratic political process. **Medicine and Dentistry:** The information and techniques needed to diagnose and treat injuries, diseases, and deformities. This includes symptoms, treatment alternatives, drug properties and interactions, and preventive health-care measures. **Sociology and Anthropology:** Group behavior and dynamics; societal trends and influences; and cultures and their history, migrations, ethnicity, and origins.

Work Environment: Indoors; noisy; disease or infections; standing; walking and running; using hands on objects, tools, or controls.

Correspondence Clerks

- ❈ Education/Training Required: Short-term on-the-job training
- ❈ Annual Earnings: $29,500
- ❈ Beginning Wage: $20,350
- ❈ Earnings Growth Potential: Low
- ❈ Growth: 12.0%
- ❈ Annual Job Openings: 4,334
- ❈ Self-Employed: 0.0%
- ❈ Part-Time: 12.4%

Compose letters in reply to requests for merchandise, damage claims, credit and other information, delinquent accounts, incorrect billings, or unsatisfactory services. Duties may include gathering data to formulate reply and typing correspondence. Prepare documents and correspondence such as damage claims, credit and billing inquiries, invoices, and service complaints. Compile data from records to prepare periodic reports. Present clear and concise explanations of governing rules and regulations. Read incoming correspondence to ascertain nature of writers' concerns and to determine disposition of correspondence. Type acknowledgment letters to persons sending correspondence. Review correspondence for format and typographical accuracy, assemble the information into a prescribed form with the correct number of copies, and submit it to an authorized official for signature. Maintain files and control records to show correspondence activities. Gather records pertinent to specific problems, review them for completeness and accuracy, and attach records to correspondence as necessary. Complete form letters in response to requests or problems identified by correspondence. Route correspondence to other departments for reply. Compose letters in reply to correspondence concerning such items as requests for merchandise, damage claims, credit information requests, delinquent accounts, incorrect billing, or unsatisfactory service. Ensure that money collected is properly recorded and secured. Respond to internal and external requests for the release of information contained in medical records, copying medical records, and selective extracts in accordance with laws and regulations. Compute costs of records furnished to requesters and write letters to obtain payment. Compose correspondence requesting medical information and records. Prepare records for shipment by certified mail. Obtain written authorization to access required medical information. Confer with company personnel regarding feasibility of complying with writers' requests. Submit completed documents to typists for typing in final form and instruct typists in matters such as format, addresses, addressees, and the necessary number of copies. Process orders for goods requested in correspondence. Compile data pertinent to manufacture of special products for customers.

Personality Type: Conventional. These occupations frequently involve following set procedures and routines and can include working with data and details more than with ideas. Usually there is a clear line of authority to follow.

GOE—Interest Area/Cluster: 04. Business and Administration. **Work Group:** 04.07. Records and Materials Processing. **Other Jobs in This Work Group:** File Clerks; Human Resources Assistants, Except Payroll and Timekeeping; Marking Clerks; Meter Readers, Utilities; Office Clerks, General; Order Fillers, Wholesale and Retail Sales; Postal Service Clerks; Postal Service Mail Sorters, Processors, and Processing Machine Operators; Procurement Clerks; Production, Planning, and Expediting Clerks; Shipping, Receiving, and Traffic Clerks; Stock Clerks and Order Fillers; Stock Clerks, Sales Floor; Stock Clerks—Stockroom, Warehouse, or Storage Yard; Weighers, Measurers, Checkers, and Samplers, Recordkeeping.

Skills—Writing: Communicating effectively with others in writing as indicated by the needs of the audience. **Reading Comprehension:** Understanding written sentences and paragraphs in work-related documents. **Instructing:** Teaching others how to do something. **Active Listening:** Listening to what other people are saying and asking questions as appropriate.

Education and Training Program: General Office Occupations and Clerical Services. **Related Knowledge/ Courses—Clerical Studies:** Administrative and clerical procedures and systems such as word-processing systems, filing and records management systems, stenography and transcription, forms, design principles, and other office procedures and terminology. **Economics and Accounting:** Economic and accounting principles and practices, the financial markets, banking, and the analysis and reporting of financial data. **Therapy and Counseling:** Information and techniques needed to rehabilitate physical and mental ailments and to provide career guidance, including alternative treatments, rehabilitation equipment and its proper use, and methods to evaluate treatment effects. **Medicine and Dentistry:** The information and techniques needed to diagnose and treat injuries, diseases, and deformities. This includes symptoms, treatment alternatives, drug properties and interactions, and preventive health-care measures. **Personnel and Human Resources:** Principles and procedures for personnel recruitment; selection; training; compensation and benefits; labor relations and negotiation; and personnel information systems. **Customer and Personal Service:** Principles and processes for providing customer and personal services, including needs assessment techniques, quality service standards, alternative delivery systems, and customer satisfaction evaluation techniques.

Work Environment: Indoors; sitting; repetitive motions.

Court Clerks

* Education/Training Required: Short-term on-the-job training
* Annual Earnings: $32,330
* Beginning Wage: $21,050
* Earnings Growth Potential: Low
* Growth: 8.8%
* Annual Job Openings: 16,163
* Self-Employed: 2.7%
* Part-Time: 9.6%

The job openings listed here are shared with License Clerks and with Municipal Clerks.

Perform clerical duties in court of law; prepare docket of cases to be called; secure information for judges; and contact witnesses, attorneys, and litigants to obtain information for court. Prepare dockets or calendars of cases to be called, using typewriters or computers. Record case dispositions, court orders, and arrangements made for payment of court fees. Answer inquiries from the general public regarding judicial procedures, court appearances, trial dates, adjournments, outstanding warrants, summonses, subpoenas, witness fees, and payment of fines. Prepare and issue orders of the court, including probation orders, release documentation, sentencing information, and summonses. Prepare documents recording the outcomes of court proceedings. Instruct parties about timing of court appearances. Explain procedures or forms to parties in cases or to the general public. Search files and contact witnesses, attorneys, and litigants to obtain information for the court. Follow procedures to secure courtrooms and exhibits such as money, drugs, and weapons. Amend indictments when necessary and endorse indictments with pertinent information. Read charges and related information to the court and, if necessary, record defendants' pleas. Swear in jury members, interpreters, witnesses, and defendants. Collect court fees or fines and record amounts collected. Direct support staff in handling of paperwork processed by clerks' offices. Examine legal documents submitted to courts for adherence to laws or court procedures. Prepare and mark all applicable court exhibits and evidence. Record court proceedings, using recording equipment, or record minutes of court proceedings, using stenotype machines or shorthand. Prepare courtrooms with paper, pens, water, easels, and electronic equipment and ensure that recording equipment is working. Conduct roll calls and poll jurors. Meet with judges, lawyers, parole officers, police, and social agency officials to coordinate the functions of the court. Open courts, calling them to order and announcing judges.

Personality Type: Conventional. These occupations frequently involve following set procedures and routines and can include working with data and details more than with ideas. Usually there is a clear line of authority to follow.

GOE—Interest Area/Cluster: 07. Government and Public Administration. **Work Group:** 07.04. Public Administration Clerical Support. **Other Jobs in This Work Group:** Court Reporters; Court, Municipal, and License Clerks; License Clerks; Municipal Clerks.

Skills—Active Listening: Listening to what other people are saying and asking questions as appropriate. **Writing:** Communicating effectively with others in writing as indicated by the needs of the audience. **Instructing:** Teaching others how to do something. **Service Orientation:** Actively looking for ways to help people. **Coordination:** Adjusting actions in relation to others' actions.

Education and Training Program: General Office Occupations and Clerical Services. **Related Knowledge/Courses—Clerical Studies:** Administrative and clerical procedures and systems such as word-processing systems, filing and records management systems, stenography and transcription, forms, design principles, and other office procedures and terminology. **Law and Government:** Laws, legal codes, court procedures, precedents, government regulations, executive orders, agency rules, and the democratic

political process. **Computers and Electronics:** Electric circuit boards, processors, chips, and computer hardware and software, including applications and programming.

Work Environment: Indoors; noisy; sitting; using hands on objects, tools, or controls; repetitive motions.

Court Reporters

- ❋ Education/Training Required: Postsecondary vocational training
- ❋ Annual Earnings: $45,330
- ❋ Beginning Wage: $23,810
- ❋ Earnings Growth Potential: High
- ❋ Growth: 24.5%
- ❋ Annual Job Openings: 2,620
- ❋ Self-Employed: 7.9%
- ❋ Part-Time: 13.6%

Use verbatim methods and equipment to capture, store, retrieve, and transcribe pretrial and trial proceedings or other information. Includes stenocaptioners who operate computerized stenographic captioning equipment to provide captions of live or prerecorded broadcasts for hearing-impaired viewers. Take notes in shorthand or use a stenotype or shorthand machine that prints letters on a paper tape. Provide transcripts of proceedings upon request of judges, lawyers, or the public. Record verbatim proceedings of courts, legislative assemblies, committee meetings, and other proceedings, using computerized recording equipment, electronic stenograph machines, or stenomasks. Transcribe recorded proceedings in accordance with established formats. Ask speakers to clarify inaudible statements. File a legible transcript of records of a court case with the court clerk's office. File and store shorthand notes of court session. Respond to requests during court sessions to read portions of the proceedings already recorded. Record depositions and other proceedings for attorneys. Verify accuracy of transcripts by checking copies against original records of proceedings and accuracy of rulings by checking with judges. Record symbols on computer disks or CD-ROM; then translate and display them as text in computer-aided transcription process.

Personality Type: Conventional. These occupations frequently involve following set procedures and routines and can include working with data and details more than with ideas. Usually there is a clear line of authority to follow.

GOE—Interest Area/Cluster: 07. Government and Public Administration. **Work Group:** 07.04. Public Administration Clerical Support. **Other Jobs in This Work Group:** Court Clerks; Court, Municipal, and License Clerks; License Clerks; Municipal Clerks.

Skills—Reading Comprehension: Understanding written sentences and paragraphs in work-related documents. **Active Listening:** Listening to what other people are saying and asking questions as appropriate. **Equipment Selection:** Determining the kind of tools and equipment needed to do a job. **Operation and Control:** Controlling operations of equipment or systems. **Equipment Maintenance:** Performing routine maintenance and determining when and what kind of maintenance is needed. **Operation Monitoring:** Watching gauges, dials, or other indicators to make sure a machine is working properly. **Operations Analysis:** Analyzing needs and product requirements to create a design. **Installation:** Installing equipment, machines, wiring, or programs to meet specifications.

Education and Training Program: Court Reporting/Court Reporter Training. **Related Knowledge/Courses—Clerical Studies:** Administrative and clerical procedures and systems such as word-processing systems, filing and records management systems, stenography and transcription, forms, design principles, and other office procedures and terminology. **English Language:** The structure and content of the English language, including the meaning and spelling of words, rules of composition, and grammar. **Law and Government:** Laws, legal codes, court procedures, precedents, government regulations, executive orders, agency rules, and the democratic political process. **Computers and Electronics:** Electric circuit boards, processors, chips, and computer hardware and software, including applications and programming. **Production and Processing:** Inputs, outputs, raw materials, waste, quality control, costs, and techniques for maximizing the manufacture and distribution of goods. **Customer and Personal Service:** Principles and processes for providing customer and personal services, including needs assessment techniques, quality service standards, alternative delivery systems, and customer satisfaction evaluation techniques.

Work Environment: Indoors; noisy; sitting; using hands on objects, tools, or controls; repetitive motions.

Criminal Investigators and Special Agents

- ✳ Education/Training Required: Work experience in a related occupation
- ✳ Annual Earnings: $59,930
- ✳ Beginning Wage: $35,600
- ✳ Earnings Growth Potential: High
- ✳ Growth: 17.3%
- ✳ Annual Job Openings: 14,746
- ✳ Self-Employed: 0.3%
- ✳ Part-Time: 2.2%

The job openings listed here are shared with Immigration and Customs Inspectors; Police Detectives; and Police Identification and Records Officers.

Investigate alleged or suspected criminal violations of federal, state, or local laws to determine if evidence is sufficient to recommend prosecution. Record evidence and documents, using equipment such as cameras and photocopy machines. Obtain and verify evidence by interviewing and observing suspects and witnesses or by analyzing records. Examine records to locate links in chains of evidence or information. Prepare reports that detail investigation findings. Determine scope, timing, and direction of investigations. Collaborate with other offices and agencies to exchange information and coordinate activities. Testify before grand juries concerning criminal activity investigations. Analyze evidence in laboratories or in the field. Investigate organized crime, public corruption, financial crime, copyright infringement, civil rights violations, bank robbery, extortion, kidnapping, and other violations of federal or state statutes. Identify case issues and evidence needed, based on analysis of charges, complaints, or allegations of law violations. Obtain and use search and arrest warrants. Serve subpoenas or other official papers. Collaborate with other authorities on activities such as surveillance, transcription, and research. Develop relationships with informants to obtain information related to cases. Search for and collect evidence such as fingerprints, using investigative equipment. Collect and record physical information about arrested suspects, including fingerprints, height and weight measurements, and photographs. Compare crime scene fingerprints with those from suspects or fingerprint files to identify perpetrators, using computers. Administer counter-terrorism and counter-narcotics reward programs. Provide protection for individuals such as government leaders, political candidates, and visiting foreign dignitaries. Perform undercover assignments and maintain surveillance, including monitoring authorized wiretaps. Manage security programs designed to protect personnel, facilities, and information. Issue security clearances.

Personality Type: Enterprising. These occupations frequently involve starting up and carrying out projects and can involve leading people and making many decisions. They sometimes require risk taking and often deal with business.

GOE—Interest Area/Cluster: 12. Law and Public Safety. **Work Group:** 12.04. Law Enforcement and Public Safety. **Other Jobs in This Work Group:** Bailiffs; Correctional Officers and Jailers; Detectives and Criminal Investigators; Fire Investigators; Forensic Science Technicians; Parking Enforcement Workers; Police and Sheriff's Patrol Officers; Police Detectives; Police Identification and Records Officers; Police Patrol Officers; Sheriffs and Deputy Sheriffs; Transit and Railroad Police.

Skills—Negotiation: Bringing others together and trying to reconcile differences. **Operations Analysis:** Analyzing needs and product requirements to create a design. **Programming:** Writing computer programs for various purposes. **Judgment and Decision Making:** Weighing the relative costs and benefits of a potential action. **Service Orientation:** Actively looking for ways to help people. **Complex Problem Solving:** Identifying complex problems, reviewing the options, and implementing solutions. **Equipment Selection:** Determining the kind of tools and equipment needed to do a job. **Persuasion:** Persuading others to approach things differently.

Education and Training Programs: Criminal Justice/Police Science; Criminalistics and Criminal Science. **Related Knowledge/Courses—Law and Government:** Laws, legal codes, court procedures, precedents, government regulations, executive orders, agency rules, and the democratic political process. **Psychology:** Human behavior and performance, mental processes, psychological research methods, and the assessment and treatment of behavioral and affective disorders. **Geography:** Various methods for describing the location and distribution of land, sea, and air masses, including their physical locations, relationships, and characteristics. **Public Safety and Security:**

Weaponry; public safety; security operations, rules, regulations, precautions, and prevention; and the protection of people, data, and property. **Clerical Studies:** Administrative and clerical procedures and systems such as word-processing systems, filing and records management systems, stenography and transcription, forms, design principles, and other office procedures and terminology. **Telecommunications:** Transmission, broadcasting, switching, control, and operation of telecommunications systems.

Work Environment: More often outdoors than indoors; noisy; very hot or cold; standing.

Customer Service Representatives

- ❋ Education/Training Required: Moderate-term on-the-job training
- ❋ Annual Earnings: $29,040
- ❋ Beginning Wage: $18,490
- ❋ Earnings Growth Potential: Medium
- ❋ Growth: 24.8%
- ❋ Annual Job Openings: 600,937
- ❋ Self-Employed: 0.4%
- ❋ Part-Time: 16.5%

Interact with customers to provide information in response to inquiries about products and services and to handle and resolve complaints. Confer with customers by telephone or in person to provide information about products and services, to take orders or cancel accounts, or to obtain details of complaints. Keep records of customer interactions and transactions, recording details of inquiries, complaints, and comments, as well as actions taken. Resolve customers' service or billing complaints by performing activities such as exchanging merchandise, refunding money, and adjusting bills. Check to ensure that appropriate changes were made to resolve customers' problems. Contact customers to respond to inquiries or to notify them of claim investigation results and any planned adjustments. Refer unresolved customer grievances to designated departments for further investigation. Determine charges for services requested, collect deposits or payments, or arrange for billing. Complete contract forms, prepare change of address records, and issue service discontinuance orders, using computers. Obtain and examine all relevant information to assess validity of complaints and to determine possible causes, such as extreme weather conditions, that could increase utility bills. Solicit sale of new or additional services or products. Review insurance policy terms to determine whether a particular loss is covered by insurance. Review claims adjustments with dealers, examining parts claimed to be defective and approving or disapproving dealers' claims. Compare disputed merchandise with original requisitions and information from invoices and prepare invoices for returned goods. Order tests that could determine the causes of product malfunctions. Recommend improvements in products, packaging, shipping, service, or billing methods and procedures to prevent future problems.

Personality Type: Enterprising. These occupations frequently involve starting up and carrying out projects and can involve leading people and making many decisions. They sometimes require risk taking and often deal with business.

GOE—Interest Area/Cluster: 14. Retail and Wholesale Sales and Service. **Work Group:** 14.06. Customer Service. **Other Jobs in This Work Group:** Cashiers; Counter and Rental Clerks; Gaming Cage Workers; Gaming Change Persons and Booth Cashiers; Order Clerks; Receptionists and Information Clerks.

Skills—Service Orientation: Actively looking for ways to help people. **Monitoring:** Assessing how well one is doing when learning or doing something. **Reading Comprehension:** Understanding written sentences and paragraphs in work-related documents. **Active Listening:** Listening to what other people are saying and asking questions as appropriate. **Social Perceptiveness:** Being aware of others' reactions and understanding why they react the way they do.

Education and Training Programs: Customer Service Support/Call Center/Teleservice Operation; Receptionist Training. **Related Knowledge/Courses—Customer and Personal Service:** Principles and processes for providing customer and personal services, including needs assessment techniques, quality service standards, alternative delivery systems, and customer satisfaction evaluation techniques. **Clerical Studies:** Administrative and clerical procedures and systems such as word-processing systems, filing and records management systems, stenography and transcription, forms, design principles, and other office procedures and terminology. **Sales and Marketing:** Principles and methods involved in showing, promoting, and selling products or services. This includes marketing strategies and tactics, product demonstration and sales techniques, and sales control systems.

Work Environment: Indoors; sitting; using hands on objects, tools, or controls; repetitive motions.

Demonstrators and Product Promoters

- ❀ Education/Training Required: Moderate-term on-the-job training
- ❀ Annual Earnings: $22,570
- ❀ Beginning Wage: $16,440
- ❀ Earnings Growth Potential: Low
- ❀ Growth: 18.0%
- ❀ Annual Job Openings: 32,779
- ❀ Self-Employed: 20.8%
- ❀ Part-Time: 56.1%

Demonstrate merchandise and answer questions for the purpose of creating public interest in buying the product. May sell demonstrated merchandise. Demonstrate and explain products, methods, or services in order to persuade customers to purchase products or utilize services. Learn about competitors' products and consumers' interests and concerns in order to answer questions and provide more complete information. Recommend product or service improvements to employers. Train demonstrators to present a company's products or services. Give tours of plants where specific products are made. Develop lists of prospective clients from sources such as newspaper items, company records, local merchants, and customers. Contact businesses and civic establishments to arrange to exhibit and sell merchandise. Visit trade shows, stores, community organizations, and other venues to demonstrate products or services and to answer questions from potential customers. Write articles and pamphlets about products. Transport, assemble, and disassemble materials used in presentations. Instruct customers in alteration of products. Collect fees or accept donations. Identify interested and qualified customers in order to provide them with additional information. Work as part of a team of demonstrators to accommodate large crowds. Wear costumes or sign boards and walk in public to promote merchandise, services, or events. Provide product information, using lectures, films, charts, and/or slide shows. Prepare and alter presentation contents to target specific audiences. Keep areas neat while working and return items to correct locations following demonstrations. Record and report demonstration-related information such as the number of questions asked by the audience and the number of coupons distributed. Research and investigate products to be presented to prepare for demonstrations. Sell products being promoted and keep records of sales. Set up and arrange displays and demonstration areas to attract the attention of prospective customers. Stock shelves with products. Suggest specific product purchases to meet customers' needs. Provide product samples, coupons, informational brochures, and other incentives to persuade people to buy products. Practice demonstrations to ensure that they will run smoothly.

Personality Type: Enterprising. These occupations frequently involve starting up and carrying out projects and can involve leading people and making many decisions. They sometimes require risk taking and often deal with business.

GOE—Interest Area/Cluster: 14. Retail and Wholesale Sales and Service. **Work Group:** 14.04. Personal Soliciting. **Other Jobs in This Work Group:** Door-To-Door Sales Workers, News and Street Vendors, and Related Workers; Models; Telemarketers.

Skill: Persuasion: Persuading others to approach things differently.

Education and Training Program: Retailing and Retail Operations. **Related Knowledge/Courses—Sales and Marketing:** Principles and methods involved in showing, promoting, and selling products or services. This includes marketing strategies and tactics, product demonstration and sales techniques, and sales control systems. **Customer and Personal Service:** Principles and processes for providing customer and personal services, including needs assessment techniques, quality service standards, alternative delivery systems, and customer satisfaction evaluation techniques.

Work Environment: Standing.

Dental Assistants

- ✸ Education/Training Required: Moderate-term on-the-job training
- ✸ Annual Earnings: $31,550
- ✸ Beginning Wage: $21,550
- ✸ Earnings Growth Potential: Low
- ✸ Growth: 29.2%
- ✸ Annual Job Openings: 29,482
- ✸ Self-Employed: 0.0%
- ✸ Part-Time: 35.7%

Assist dentist, set up patient and equipment, and keep records. Prepare patient, sterilize and disinfect instruments, set up instrument trays, prepare materials, and assist dentist during dental procedures. Expose dental diagnostic X rays. Record treatment information in patient records. Take and record medical and dental histories and vital signs of patients. Provide postoperative instructions prescribed by dentist. Assist dentist in management of medical and dental emergencies. Pour, trim, and polish study casts. Instruct patients in oral hygiene and plaque control programs. Make preliminary impressions for study casts and occlusal registrations for mounting study casts. Clean and polish removable appliances. Clean teeth, using dental instruments. Apply protective coating of fluoride to teeth. Fabricate temporary restorations and custom impressions from preliminary impressions. Schedule appointments, prepare bills, and receive payment for dental services; complete insurance forms; and maintain records, manually or using computer.

Personality Type: Conventional. These occupations frequently involve following set procedures and routines and can include working with data and details more than with ideas. Usually there is a clear line of authority to follow.

GOE—Interest Area/Cluster: 08. Health Science. **Work Group:** 08.03. Dentistry. **Other Jobs in This Work Group:** Dental Hygienists; Dentists, General; Oral and Maxillofacial Surgeons; Orthodontists; Prosthodontists.

Skills—Equipment Maintenance: Performing routine maintenance and determining when and what kind of maintenance is needed. **Operation and Control:** Controlling operations of equipment or systems. **Social Perceptiveness:** Being aware of others' reactions and understanding why they react the way they do. **Management of Material

Resources: Obtaining and seeing to the appropriate use of equipment, facilities, and materials needed to do certain work. **Operation Monitoring:** Watching gauges, dials, or other indicators to make sure a machine is working properly. **Equipment Selection:** Determining the kind of tools and equipment needed to do a job. **Installation:** Installing equipment, machines, wiring, or programs to meet specifications. **Repairing:** Repairing machines or systems, using the needed tools.

Education and Training Program: Dental Assisting/Assistant Training. **Related Knowledge/Courses—Medicine and Dentistry:** The information and techniques needed to diagnose and treat injuries, diseases, and deformities. This includes symptoms, treatment alternatives, drug properties and interactions, and preventive healthcare measures. **Chemistry:** The composition, structure, and properties of substances and of the chemical processes and transformations that they undergo. This includes uses of chemicals and their interactions, danger signs, production techniques, and disposal methods. **Clerical Studies:** Administrative and clerical procedures and systems such as word-processing systems, filing and records management systems, stenography and transcription, forms, design principles, and other office procedures and terminology. **Customer and Personal Service:** Principles and processes for providing customer and personal services, including needs assessment techniques, quality service standards, alternative delivery systems, and customer satisfaction evaluation techniques. **Psychology:** Human behavior and performance, mental processes, psychological research methods, and the assessment and treatment of behavioral and affective disorders.

Work Environment: Indoors; contaminants; disease or infections; using hands on objects, tools, or controls; bending or twisting the body; repetitive motions.

Dental Hygienists

- Education/Training Required: Associate degree
- Annual Earnings: $64,740
- Beginning Wage: $42,480
- Earnings Growth Potential: Low
- Growth: 30.1%
- Annual Job Openings: 10,433
- Self-Employed: 0.1%
- Part-Time: 58.7%

Clean teeth and examine oral areas, head, and neck for signs of oral disease. May educate patients on oral hygiene, take and develop X rays, or apply fluoride or sealants. Clean calcareous deposits, accretions, and stains from teeth and beneath margins of gums, using dental instruments. Feel and visually examine gums for sores and signs of disease. Chart conditions of decay and disease for diagnosis and treatment by dentist. Feel lymph nodes under patient's chin to detect swelling or tenderness that could indicate presence of oral cancer. Apply fluorides and other cavity-preventing agents to arrest dental decay. Examine gums, using probes, to locate periodontal recessed gums and signs of gum disease. Expose and develop X-ray film. Provide clinical services and health education to improve and maintain oral health of schoolchildren. Remove excess cement from coronal surfaces of teeth. Make impressions for study casts. Place, carve, and finish amalgam restorations. Administer local anesthetic agents. Conduct dental health clinics for community groups to augment services of dentist. Remove sutures and dressings. Place and remove rubber dams, matrices, and temporary restorations.

Personality Type: Social. These occupations frequently involve working with, communicating with, and teaching people and often involve helping or providing service to others.

GOE—Interest Area/Cluster: 08. Health Science. **Work Group:** 08.03. Dentistry. **Other Jobs in This Work Group:** Dental Assistants; Dentists, General; Oral and Maxillofacial Surgeons; Orthodontists; Prosthodontists.

Skills—Science: Using scientific methods to solve problems. **Active Learning:** Working with new material or information to grasp its implications. **Reading Comprehension:** Understanding written sentences and paragraphs in work-related documents. **Time Management:** Managing one's own time and the time of others. **Equipment Selection:** Determining the kind of tools and equipment needed to do a job. **Persuasion:** Persuading others to approach things differently. **Social Perceptiveness:** Being aware of others' reactions and understanding why they react the way they do. **Writing:** Communicating effectively with others in writing as indicated by the needs of the audience.

Education and Training Program: Dental Hygiene/Hygienist Training. **Related Knowledge/Courses—Biology:** Plant and animal living tissue, cells, organisms, and entities, including their functions, interdependencies, and interactions with each other and the environment. **Medicine and Dentistry:** The information and techniques needed to diagnose and treat injuries, diseases, and deformities. This includes symptoms, treatment alternatives, drug properties and interactions, and preventive health-care measures. **Chemistry:** The composition, structure, and properties of substances and of the chemical processes and transformations that they undergo. This includes uses of chemicals and their interactions, danger signs, production techniques, and disposal methods. **Psychology:** Human behavior and performance, mental processes, psychological research methods, and the assessment and treatment of behavioral and affective disorders. **Therapy and Counseling:** Information and techniques needed to rehabilitate physical and mental ailments and to provide career guidance, including alternative treatments, rehabilitation equipment and its proper use, and methods to evaluate treatment effects. **Sales and Marketing:** Principles and methods involved in showing, promoting, and selling products or services. This includes marketing strategies and tactics, product demonstration and sales techniques, and sales control systems.

Work Environment: Indoors; radiation; disease or infections; sitting; using hands on objects, tools, or controls; repetitive motions.

Desktop Publishers

- ❀ Education/Training Required: Postsecondary vocational training
- ❀ Annual Earnings: $35,510
- ❀ Beginning Wage: $20,960
- ❀ Earnings Growth Potential: High
- ❀ Growth: 1.0%
- ❀ Annual Job Openings: 6,420
- ❀ Self-Employed: 2.2%
- ❀ Part-Time: 13.9%

Format typescript and graphic elements, using computer software to produce publication-ready material. Check preliminary and final proofs for errors and make necessary corrections. Operate desktop publishing software and equipment to design, lay out, and produce camera-ready copy. View monitors for visual representation of work in progress and for instructions and feedback throughout process, making modifications as necessary. Enter text into computer keyboard and select the size and style of type, column width, and appropriate spacing for printed materials. Store copies of publications on paper, magnetic tape, CD, or DVD. Position text and art elements from a variety of databases in a visually appealing way to design print or Web pages, using knowledge of type styles and size and layout patterns. Enter digitized data into electronic prepress system computer memory, using scanner, camera, keyboard, or mouse. Edit graphics and photos, using pixel or bitmap editing, airbrushing, masking, or image retouching. Import text and art elements such as electronic clip art or electronic files from photographs that have been scanned or produced with a digital camera, using computer software. Prepare sample layouts for approval, using computer software. Study layout or other design instructions to determine work to be done and sequence of operations. Load CDs, DVDs, or tapes containing information into system. Convert various types of files for printing or for the Internet, using computer software. Enter data, such as coordinates of images and color specifications, into system to retouch and make color corrections. Select number of colors and determine color separations. Transmit, deliver, or mail publication master to printer for production into film and plates. Collaborate with graphic artists, editors, and writers to produce master copies according to design specifications. Create special effects such as vignettes, mosaics, and image combining and add elements such as sound and animation to electronic publications.

Personality Type: Artistic. These occupations frequently involve working with forms, designs, and patterns. They often require self-expression, and the work can be done without following a clear set of rules.

GOE—Interest Area/Cluster: 13. Manufacturing. **Work Group:** 13.08. Graphic Arts Production. **Other Jobs in This Work Group:** Bindery Workers; Etchers and Engravers; Job Printers; Photographic Process Workers; Photographic Processing Machine Operators; Prepress Technicians and Workers; Printing Machine Operators.

Skills—Operation and Control: Controlling operations of equipment or systems. **Operations Analysis:** Analyzing needs and product requirements to create a design. **Writing:** Communicating effectively with others in writing as indicated by the needs of the audience. **Reading Comprehension:** Understanding written sentences and paragraphs in work-related documents. **Time Management:** Managing one's own time and the time of others. **Active Listening:** Listening to what other people are saying and asking questions as appropriate. **Equipment Selection:** Determining the kind of tools and equipment needed to do a job. **Service Orientation:** Actively looking for ways to help people.

Education and Training Program: Prepress/Desktop Publishing and Digital Imaging Design. **Related Knowledge/Courses—Computers and Electronics:** Electric circuit boards, processors, chips, and computer hardware and software, including applications and programming. **Production and Processing:** Inputs, outputs, raw materials, waste, quality control, costs, and techniques for maximizing the manufacture and distribution of goods.

Work Environment: Indoors; sitting; repetitive motions.

Diagnostic Medical Sonographers

- ❋ Education/Training Required: Associate degree
- ❋ Annual Earnings: $59,860
- ❋ Beginning Wage: $42,250
- ❋ Earnings Growth Potential: Low
- ❋ Growth: 19.1%
- ❋ Annual Job Openings: 3,211
- ❋ Self-Employed: 1.1%
- ❋ Part-Time: 17.3%

Produce ultrasonic recordings of internal organs for use by physicians. Provide sonograms and oral or written summaries of technical findings to physicians for use in medical diagnosis. Decide which images to include, looking for differences between healthy and pathological areas. Operate ultrasound equipment to produce and record images of the motion, shape, and composition of blood, organs, tissues, and bodily masses such as fluid accumulations. Select appropriate equipment settings and adjust patient positions to obtain the best sites and angles. Observe screens during scans to ensure that images produced are satisfactory for diagnostic purposes, making adjustments to equipment as required. Prepare patients for exams by explaining procedures, transferring them to ultrasound tables, scrubbing skin and applying gel, and positioning them properly. Observe and care for patients throughout examinations to ensure their safety and comfort. Obtain and record accurate patient histories, including prior test results and information from physical examinations. Determine whether scope of exams should be extended, based on findings. Maintain records that include patient information; sonographs and interpretations; files of correspondence; publications and regulations; or quality assurance records such as pathology, biopsy, or post-operative reports. Record and store suitable images, using camera unit connected to the ultrasound equipment. Coordinate work with physicians and other health-care team members, including providing assistance during invasive procedures. Perform clerical duties such as scheduling exams and special procedures, keeping records, and archiving computerized images. Perform legal and ethical duties, including preparing safety and accident reports, obtaining written consent from patients to perform invasive procedures, and reporting symptoms of abuse and neglect. Clean, check, and

D

maintain sonographic equipment, submitting maintenance requests or performing minor repairs as necessary. Supervise and train students and other medical sonographers. Maintain stock and supplies, preparing supplies for special examinations and ordering supplies when necessary. Process and code film from procedures and complete appropriate documentation.

Personality Type: Investigative. These occupations frequently involve working with ideas and require an extensive amount of thinking. They can involve searching for facts and figuring out problems mentally.

GOE—Interest Area/Cluster: 08. Health Science. **Work Group:** 08.06. Medical Technology. **Other Jobs in This Work Group:** Biological Technicians; Cardiovascular Technologists and Technicians; Medical and Clinical Laboratory Technicians; Medical and Clinical Laboratory Technologists; Medical Equipment Preparers; Medical Records and Health Information Technicians; Nuclear Medicine Technologists; Opticians, Dispensing; Orthotists and Prosthetists; Radiologic Technicians; Radiologic Technologists; Radiologic Technologists and Technicians.

Skills—Operation Monitoring: Watching gauges, dials, or other indicators to make sure a machine is working properly. **Service Orientation:** Actively looking for ways to help people. **Systems Analysis:** Determining how a system should work and how changes will affect outcomes. **Systems Evaluation:** Looking at many indicators of system performance and taking into account their accuracy.

Education and Training Programs: Allied Health Diagnostic, Intervention, and Treatment Professions, Other; Diagnostic Medical Sonography/Sonographer and Ultrasound Technician Training. **Related Knowledge/Courses—Medicine and Dentistry:** The information and techniques needed to diagnose and treat injuries, diseases, and deformities. This includes symptoms, treatment alternatives, drug properties and interactions, and preventive health-care measures. **Physics:** Physical principles, laws, and applications, including air, water, material dynamics, light, atomic principles, heat, electric theory, earth formations, and meteorological and related natural phenomena. **Biology:** Plant and animal living tissue, cells, organisms, and entities, including their functions, interdependencies, and interactions with each other and the environment. **Psychology:** Human behavior and performance, mental processes, psychological research methods, and the assessment and treatment of behavioral and affective disorders. **Customer and Personal Service:** Principles and processes for providing customer and personal services, including needs assessment techniques, quality service standards, alternative delivery systems, and customer satisfaction evaluation techniques. **Clerical Studies:** Administrative and clerical procedures and systems such as word-processing systems, filing and records management systems, stenography and transcription, forms, design principles, and other office procedures and terminology.

Work Environment: Indoors; disease or infections; standing; using hands on objects, tools, or controls; bending or twisting the body; repetitive motions.

Dispatchers, Except Police, Fire, and Ambulance

* Education/Training Required: Moderate-term on-the-job training
* Annual Earnings: $33,140
* Beginning Wage: $20,410
* Earnings Growth Potential: Medium
* Growth: 1.5%
* Annual Job Openings: 29,793
* Self-Employed: 1.1%
* Part-Time: 6.3%

Schedule and dispatch workers, work crews, equipment, or service vehicles for conveyance of materials, freight, or passengers or for normal installation, service, or emergency repairs rendered outside the place of business. Duties may include using radio, telephone, or computer to transmit assignments and compiling statistics and reports on work progress. Schedule and dispatch workers, work crews, equipment, or service vehicles to appropriate locations according to customer requests, specifications, or needs, using radios or telephones. Arrange for necessary repairs to restore service and schedules. Relay work orders, messages, and information to or from work crews, supervisors, and field inspectors, using telephones or two-way radios. Confer with customers or supervising personnel to address questions, problems, and requests for service or equipment. Prepare daily work and run schedules. Receive or prepare work orders. Oversee all communications within specifically assigned territories. Monitor personnel or equipment locations and utilization to coordinate service and schedules. Record and maintain files and records of customer requests, work or services performed, charges, expenses, inventory, and other dispatch information. Determine types or amounts of equipment, vehicles, materials, or personnel required according to work orders or specifications. Advise personnel about traffic problems such as construction areas, accidents, congestion, weather conditions, and other hazards. Ensure timely and efficient movement of trains according to train orders and schedules. Order supplies and equipment and issue them to personnel.

Personality Type: Conventional. These occupations frequently involve following set procedures and routines and can include working with data and details more than with ideas. Usually there is a clear line of authority to follow.

GOE—Interest Area/Cluster: 03. Arts and Communication. **Work Group:** 03.10. Communications Technology. **Other Jobs in This Work Group:** Air Traffic Controllers; Airfield Operations Specialists; Police, Fire, and Ambulance Dispatchers; Telephone Operators.

Skills—Operations Analysis: Analyzing needs and product requirements to create a design. **Service Orientation:** Actively looking for ways to help people. **Systems Evaluation:** Looking at many indicators of system performance and taking into account their accuracy. **Management of Personnel Resources:** Motivating, developing, and directing people as they work; identifying the best people for the job. **Troubleshooting:** Determining what is causing an operating error and deciding what to do about it. **Systems Analysis:** Determining how a system should work and how changes will affect outcomes. **Judgment and Decision Making:** Weighing the relative costs and benefits of a potential action. **Critical Thinking:** Using logic and analysis to identify the strengths and weaknesses of different approaches.

Education and Training Program: Logistics and Materials Management. **Related Knowledge/Courses—Transportation:** Principles and methods for moving people or goods by air, rail, sea, or road, including their relative costs, advantages, and limitations. **Clerical Studies:** Administrative and clerical procedures and systems such as word-processing systems, filing and records management systems, stenography and transcription, forms, design principles, and other office procedures and terminology. **Public Safety**

and Security: Weaponry; public safety; security operations, rules, regulations, precautions, and prevention; and the protection of people, data, and property. **Communications and Media:** Media production, communication, and dissemination techniques and methods, including alternative ways to inform and entertain via written, oral, and visual media.

Work Environment: Indoors; noisy; sitting; using hands on objects, tools, or controls; repetitive motions.

Drywall and Ceiling Tile Installers

- ❋ Education/Training Required: Moderate-term on-the-job training
- ❋ Annual Earnings: $36,520
- ❋ Beginning Wage: $23,480
- ❋ Earnings Growth Potential: Medium
- ❋ Growth: 7.3%
- ❋ Annual Job Openings: 30,945
- ❋ Self-Employed: 23.0%
- ❋ Part-Time: 6.1%

Apply plasterboard or other wallboard to ceilings or interior walls of buildings. Apply or mount acoustical tiles or blocks, strips, or sheets of shock-absorbing materials to ceilings and walls of buildings to reduce or reflect sound. Materials may be of decorative quality. Includes lathers who fasten wooden, metal, or rockboard lath to walls, ceilings, or partitions of buildings to provide support base for plaster, fireproofing, or acoustical material. Inspect furrings, mechanical mountings, and masonry surface for plumbness and level, using spirit or water levels. Install metal lath where plaster applications will be exposed to weather or water or for curved or irregular surfaces. Install blanket insulation between studs and tack plastic moisture barriers over insulation. Coordinate work with drywall finishers who cover the seams between drywall panels. Trim rough edges from wallboard to maintain even joints, using knives. Seal joints between ceiling tiles and walls. Scribe and cut edges of tile to fit walls where wall molding is not specified. Read blueprints and other specifications to determine methods of installation, work procedures, and material and tool requirements. Nail channels or wood furring strips to surfaces to provide mounting for tile. Mount tile, using adhesives, or by

D

nailing, screwing, stapling, or wire-tying lath directly to structural frameworks. Measure and mark surfaces to lay out work according to blueprints and drawings, using tape measures, straightedges or squares, and marking devices. Hang drywall panels on metal frameworks of walls and ceilings in offices, schools, and other large buildings, using lifts or hoists to adjust panel heights when necessary. Install horizontal and vertical metal or wooden studs to frames so that wallboard can be attached to interior walls. Fasten metal or rockboard lath to the structural framework of walls, ceilings, and partitions of buildings, using nails, screws, staples, or wire-ties. Apply or mount acoustical tile or blocks, strips, or sheets of shock-absorbing materials to ceilings and walls of buildings to reduce reflection of sound or to decorate rooms. Apply cement to backs of tiles and press tiles into place, aligning them with layout marks or joints of previously laid tile. Hang dry lines (stretched string) to wall moldings in order to guide positioning of main runners. Assemble and install metal framing and decorative trim for windows, doorways, and vents. Fit and fasten wallboard or drywall into position on wood or metal frameworks, using glue, nails, or screws.

Personality Type: Realistic. These occupations frequently involve work activities that include practical, hands-on problems and solutions. They often deal with plants; animals; and real-world materials such as wood, tools, and machinery. Many of the occupations require working outside and don't involve a lot of paperwork or working closely with others.

GOE—Interest Area/Cluster: 02. Architecture and Construction. **Work Group:** 02.04. Construction Crafts. **Other Jobs in This Work Group:** Boilermakers; Brickmasons and Blockmasons; Carpet Installers; Cement Masons and Concrete Finishers; Commercial Divers; Construction Carpenters; Crane and Tower Operators; Electricians; Fence Erectors; Floor Layers, Except Carpet, Wood, and Hard Tiles; Floor Sanders and Finishers; Glaziers; Hazardous Materials Removal Workers; Insulation Workers, Floor, Ceiling, and Wall; Insulation Workers, Mechanical; Manufactured Building and Mobile Home Installers; Operating Engineers and Other Construction Equipment Operators; Painters, Construction and Maintenance; Paperhangers; Paving, Surfacing, and Tamping Equipment Operators; Pile-Driver Operators; Pipe Fitters and Steamfitters; Pipelayers; Plasterers and Stucco Masons; Plumbers; Plumbers, Pipefitters, and Steamfitters; Rail-Track Laying

and Maintenance Equipment Operators; Refractory Materials Repairers, Except Brickmasons; Reinforcing Iron and Rebar Workers; Riggers; Roofers; Rough Carpenters; Security and Fire Alarm Systems Installers; Segmental Pavers; Sheet Metal Workers; Stone Cutters and Carvers, Manufacturing; Stonemasons; Structural Iron and Steel Workers; Tapers; Terrazzo Workers and Finishers; Tile and Marble Setters.

Skills—Installation: Installing equipment, machines, wiring, or programs to meet specifications. **Management of Personnel Resources:** Motivating, developing, and directing people as they work; identifying the best people for the job. **Management of Material Resources:** Obtaining and seeing to the appropriate use of equipment, facilities, and materials needed to do certain work. **Management of Financial Resources:** Determining how money will be spent to get the work done and accounting for these expenditures. **Mathematics:** Using mathematics to solve problems. **Repairing:** Repairing machines or systems, using the needed tools. **Science:** Using scientific methods to solve problems. **Equipment Selection:** Determining the kind of tools and equipment needed to do a job.

Education and Training Program: Drywall Installation/Drywaller Training. **Related Knowledge/Courses— Building and Construction:** Materials, methods, and the appropriate tools to construct objects, structures, and buildings. **Design:** Design techniques, principles, tools, and instruments involved in the production and use of precision technical plans, blueprints, drawings, and models. **Mechanical Devices:** Machines and tools, including their designs, uses, benefits, repair, and maintenance. **Mathematics:** Numbers and their operations and interrelationships, including arithmetic, algebra, geometry, calculus, and statistics and their applications. **Production and Processing:** Inputs, outputs, raw materials, waste, quality control, costs, and techniques for maximizing the manufacture and distribution of goods. **Public Safety and Security:** Weaponry; public safety; security operations, rules, regulations, precautions, and prevention; and the protection of people, data, and property.

Work Environment: High places; standing; walking and running; using hands on objects, tools, or controls; bending or twisting the body; repetitive motions.

Electrical and Electronics Repairers, Commercial and Industrial Equipment

- ❋ Education/Training Required:
  Postsecondary vocational training
- ❋ Annual Earnings: $47,110
- ❋ Beginning Wage: $28,830
- ❋ Earnings Growth Potential: Medium
- ❋ Growth: 6.8%
- ❋ Annual Job Openings: 6,607
- ❋ Self-Employed: 0.0%
- ❋ Part-Time: 0.6%

Repair, test, adjust, or install electronic equipment, such as industrial controls, transmitters, and antennas. Perform scheduled preventive maintenance tasks, such as checking, cleaning, and repairing equipment, to detect and prevent problems. Examine work orders and converse with equipment operators to detect equipment problems and to ascertain whether mechanical or human errors contributed to the problems. Operate equipment to demonstrate proper use and to analyze malfunctions. Set up and test industrial equipment to ensure that it functions properly. Test faulty equipment to diagnose malfunctions, using test equipment and software and applying knowledge of the functional operation of electronic units and systems. Repair and adjust equipment, machines, and defective components, replacing worn parts such as gaskets and seals in watertight electrical equipment. Calibrate testing instruments and installed or repaired equipment to prescribed specifications. Advise management regarding customer satisfaction, product performance, and suggestions for product improvements. Study blueprints, schematics, manuals, and other specifications to determine installation procedures. Inspect components of industrial equipment for accurate assembly and installation and for defects such as loose connections and frayed wires. Maintain equipment logs that record performance problems, repairs, calibrations, and tests. Coordinate efforts with other workers involved in installing and maintaining equipment or components. Maintain inventory of spare parts. Consult with customers, supervisors, and engineers to plan layout of equipment and to resolve problems in system operation and maintenance. Install repaired equipment in various settings, such as industrial or military establishments. Send defective units to the manufacturer or to a specialized repair shop for repair. Determine feasibility of using standardized equipment and develop specifications for equipment required to perform additional functions. Enter information into computer to copy program or to draw, modify, or store schematics, applying knowledge of software package used. Sign overhaul documents for equipment replaced or repaired. Develop or modify industrial electronic devices, circuits, and equipment according to available specifications.

Personality Type: Realistic. These occupations frequently involve work activities that include practical, hands-on problems and solutions. They often deal with plants; animals; and real-world materials such as wood, tools, and machinery. Many of the occupations require working outside and don't involve a lot of paperwork or working closely with others.

GOE—Interest Area/Cluster: 13. Manufacturing. **Work Group:** 13.12. Electrical and Electronic Repair. **Other Jobs in This Work Group:** Avionics Technicians; Electric Motor, Power Tool, and Related Repairers; Electrical and Electronics Installers and Repairers, Transportation Equipment; Electronic Equipment Installers and Repairers, Motor Vehicles; Electronic Home Entertainment Equipment Installers and Repairers; Radio Mechanics.

Skills—Installation: Installing equipment, machines, wiring, or programs to meet specifications. **Repairing:** Repairing machines or systems, using the needed tools. **Operation Monitoring:** Watching gauges, dials, or other indicators to make sure a machine is working properly. **Troubleshooting:** Determining what is causing an operating error and deciding what to do about it. **Equipment Maintenance:** Performing routine maintenance and determining when and what kind of maintenance is needed. **Operation and Control:** Controlling operations of equipment or systems. **Systems Analysis:** Determining how a system should work and how changes will affect outcomes. **Science:** Using scientific methods to solve problems.

Education and Training Programs: Computer Installation and Repair Technology/Technician Training; Industrial Electronics Technology/Technician Training. **Related Knowledge/Courses—Mechanical Devices:** Machines and tools, including their designs, uses, benefits, repair, and maintenance. **Computers and Electronics:** Electric circuit boards, processors, chips, and computer hardware and software, including applications and programming. **Telecommunications:** Transmission, broadcasting, switching, control, and operation of telecommunications systems. **Engineering and Technology:** Equipment, tools, and mechanical devices and their uses to produce motion, light, power, technology, and other applications.

Work Environment: Indoors; noisy; cramped work space, awkward positions; hazardous conditions; standing; using hands on objects, tools, or controls.

Electrical Drafters

- ❋ Education/Training Required: Postsecondary vocational training
- ❋ Annual Earnings: $49,250
- ❋ Beginning Wage: $30,490
- ❋ Earnings Growth Potential: Medium
- ❋ Growth: 4.1%
- ❋ Annual Job Openings: 4,786
- ❋ Self-Employed: 5.7%
- ❋ Part-Time: 5.9%

The job openings listed here are shared with Electronic Drafters.

Develop specifications and instructions for installation of voltage transformers, overhead or underground cables, and related electrical equipment used to conduct electrical energy from transmission lines or high-voltage distribution lines to consumers. Use computer-aided drafting equipment and/or conventional drafting stations; technical handbooks; tables; calculators; and traditional drafting tools such as boards, pencils, protractors, and T-squares. Draft working drawings, wiring diagrams, wiring connection specifications, or cross-sections of underground cables as required for instructions to installation crew. Confer with engineering staff and other personnel to resolve problems. Draw master sketches to scale, showing relation of proposed installations to existing facilities and exact specifications and dimensions. Measure factors that affect installation and arrangement of equipment, such as distances to be spanned by wire and cable. Assemble documentation packages and produce drawing sets, which are then checked by an engineer or an architect. Review completed construction drawings and cost estimates for

accuracy and conformity to standards and regulations. Prepare and interpret specifications, calculating weights, volumes, and stress factors. Explain drawings to production or construction teams and provide adjustments as necessary. Supervise and train other technologists, technicians, and drafters. Study work order requests to determine type of service, such as lighting or power, demanded by installation. Visit proposed installation sites and draw rough sketches of location. Determine the order of work and the method of presentation, such as orthographic or isometric drawing. Reproduce working drawings on copy machines or trace drawings in ink. Write technical reports and draw charts that display statistics and data.

Personality Type: Realistic. These occupations frequently involve work activities that include practical, hands-on problems and solutions. They often deal with plants; animals; and real-world materials such as wood, tools, and machinery. Many of the occupations require working outside and don't involve a lot of paperwork or working closely with others.

GOE—Interest Area/Cluster: 15. Scientific Research, Engineering, and Mathematics. **Work Group:** 15.09. Engineering Technology. **Other Jobs in This Work Group:** Aerospace Engineering and Operations Technicians; Cartographers and Photogrammetrists; Civil Engineering Technicians; Electrical and Electronic Engineering Technicians; Electrical and Electronics Drafters; Electrical Engineering Technicians; Electro-Mechanical Technicians; Electronic Drafters; Electronics Engineering Technicians; Environmental Engineering Technicians; Mapping Technicians; Mechanical Drafters; Mechanical Engineering Technicians; Surveying and Mapping Technicians; Surveying Technicians.

Skills—Mathematics: Using mathematics to solve problems. **Installation:** Installing equipment, machines, wiring, or programs to meet specifications. **Active Learning:** Working with new material or information to grasp its implications. **Critical Thinking:** Using logic and analysis to identify the strengths and weaknesses of different approaches. **Quality Control Analysis:** Evaluating the quality or performance of products, services, or processes. **Technology Design:** Generating or adapting equipment and technology to serve user needs. **Equipment Selection:** Determining the kind of tools and equipment needed to do a job. **Operations Analysis:** Analyzing needs and product requirements to create a design.

Education and Training Program: Electrical/Electronics Drafting and Electrical/Electronics CAD/CADD. **Related Knowledge/Courses—Design:** Design techniques, principles, tools, and instruments involved in the production and use of precision technical plans, blueprints, drawings, and models. **Engineering and Technology:** Equipment, tools, and mechanical devices and their uses to produce motion, light, power, technology, and other applications. **Building and Construction:** Materials, methods, and the appropriate tools to construct objects, structures, and buildings. **Computers and Electronics:** Electric circuit boards, processors, chips, and computer hardware and software, including applications and programming. **Telecommunications:** Transmission, broadcasting, switching, control, and operation of telecommunications systems. **Clerical Studies:** Administrative and clerical procedures and systems such as word-processing systems, filing and records management systems, stenography and transcription, forms, design principles, and other office procedures and terminology.

Work Environment: Indoors; sitting.

Electrical Engineering Technicians

- ❋ Education/Training Required: Associate degree
- ❋ Annual Earnings: $52,140
- ❋ Beginning Wage: $31,310
- ❋ Earnings Growth Potential: High
- ❋ Growth: 3.6%
- ❋ Annual Job Openings: 12,583
- ❋ Self-Employed: 0.9%
- ❋ Part-Time: 5.9%

The job openings listed here are shared with Electronics Engineering Technicians.

Apply electrical theory and related knowledge to test and modify developmental or operational electrical machinery and electrical control equipment and circuitry in industrial or commercial plants and laboratories. Usually work under direction of engineering staff. Assemble electrical and electronic systems and prototypes according to engineering data and knowledge of electrical principles, using hand tools and measuring instruments. Provide technical assistance and resolution when electrical or engineering problems are encountered before, during, and after construction. Install and maintain electrical control systems and solid state equipment. Modify electrical prototypes, parts, assemblies, and systems to correct functional deviations. Set up and operate test equipment to evaluate performance of developmental parts, assemblies, or systems under simulated operating conditions and record results. Collaborate with electrical engineers and other personnel to identify, define, and solve developmental problems. Build, calibrate, maintain, troubleshoot, and repair electrical instruments or testing equipment. Analyze and interpret test information to resolve design-related problems. Write commissioning procedures for electrical installations. Prepare project cost and work-time estimates. Evaluate engineering proposals, shop drawings, and design comments for sound electrical engineering practice and conformance with established safety and design criteria and recommend approval or disapproval. Draw or modify diagrams and write engineering specifications to clarify design details and functional criteria of experimental electronics units. Conduct inspections for quality control and assurance programs, reporting findings and recommendations. Prepare contracts and initiate, review, and coordinate modifications to contract specifications and plans throughout the construction process. Plan, schedule, and monitor work of support personnel to assist supervisor. Review existing electrical engineering criteria to identify necessary revisions, deletions, or amendments to outdated material. Perform supervisory duties such as recommending work assignments, approving leaves, and completing performance evaluations. Plan method and sequence of operations for developing and testing experimental electronic and electrical equipment. Visit construction sites to observe conditions impacting design and to identify solutions to technical design problems involving electrical systems equipment that arise during construction.

Personality Type: Realistic. These occupations frequently involve work activities that include practical, hands-on problems and solutions. They often deal with plants; animals; and real-world materials such as wood, tools, and machinery. Many of the occupations require working outside and don't involve a lot of paperwork or working closely with others.

GOE—Interest Area/Cluster: 15. Scientific Research, Engineering, and Mathematics. **Work Group:** 15.09. Engineering Technology. **Other Jobs in This Work**

Group: Aerospace Engineering and Operations Technicians; Cartographers and Photogrammetrists; Civil Engineering Technicians; Electrical and Electronic Engineering Technicians; Electrical and Electronics Drafters; Electrical Drafters; Electro-Mechanical Technicians; Electronic Drafters; Electronics Engineering Technicians; Environmental Engineering Technicians; Mapping Technicians; Mechanical Drafters; Mechanical Engineering Technicians; Surveying and Mapping Technicians; Surveying Technicians.

Skills—Repairing: Repairing machines or systems, using the needed tools. **Installation:** Installing equipment, machines, wiring, or programs to meet specifications. **Troubleshooting:** Determining what is causing an operating error and deciding what to do about it. **Science:** Using scientific methods to solve problems. **Operations Analysis:** Analyzing needs and product requirements to create a design. **Technology Design:** Generating or adapting equipment and technology to serve user needs. **Mathematics:** Using mathematics to solve problems. **Equipment Maintenance:** Performing routine maintenance and determining when and what kind of maintenance is needed.

Education and Training Programs: Computer Engineering Technology/Technician Training; Computer Technology/Computer Systems Technology; Electrical and Electronic Engineering Technologies/Technician Training, Other; Electrical, Electronic, and Communications Engineering Technology/Technician Training; Telecommunications Technology/Technician Training. **Related Knowledge/Courses—Engineering and Technology:** Equipment, tools, and mechanical devices and their uses to produce motion, light, power, technology, and other applications. **Design:** Design techniques, principles, tools, and instruments involved in the production and use of precision technical plans, blueprints, drawings, and models. **Computers and Electronics:** Electric circuit boards, processors, chips, and computer hardware and software, including applications and programming. **Physics:** Physical principles, laws, and applications, including air, water, material dynamics, light, atomic principles, heat, electric theory, earth formations, and meteorological and related natural phenomena. **Mechanical Devices:** Machines and tools, including their designs, uses, benefits, repair, and maintenance. **Telecommunications:** Transmission, broadcasting, switching, control, and operation of telecommunications systems.

Work Environment: Indoors; noisy; sitting; using hands on objects, tools, or controls.

Electrical Power-Line Installers and Repairers

- ❋ Education/Training Required: Long-term on-the-job training
- ❋ Annual Earnings: $52,570
- ❋ Beginning Wage: $29,780
- ❋ Earnings Growth Potential: High
- ❋ Growth: 7.2%
- ❋ Annual Job Openings: 6,401
- ❋ Self-Employed: 0.6%
- ❋ Part-Time: 1.3%

Install or repair cables or wires used in electrical power or distribution systems. May erect poles and light- or heavy-duty transmission towers. Adhere to safety practices and procedures, such as checking equipment regularly and erecting barriers around work areas. Open switches or attach grounding devices to remove electrical hazards from disturbed or fallen lines or to facilitate repairs. Climb poles or use truck-mounted buckets to access equipment. Place insulating or fireproofing materials over conductors and joints. Install, maintain, and repair electrical distribution and transmission systems, including conduits; cables; wires; and related equipment such as transformers, circuit breakers, and switches. Identify defective sectionalizing devices, circuit breakers, fuses, voltage regulators, transformers, switches, relays, or wiring, using wiring diagrams and electrical-testing instruments. Drive vehicles equipped with tools and materials to job sites. Coordinate work assignment preparation and completion with other workers. String wire conductors and cables between poles, towers, trenches, pylons, and buildings, setting lines in place and using winches to adjust tension. Inspect and test power lines and auxiliary equipment to locate and identify problems, using reading and testing instruments. Test conductors according to electrical diagrams and specifications to identify corresponding conductors and to prevent incorrect connections. Replace damaged poles with new poles and straighten the poles. Install watt-hour meters and connect service drops between power lines and consumers' facilities. Attach crossarms, insulators, and auxiliary equipment to poles prior to installing them. Travel in trucks, helicopters, and airplanes to inspect lines for freedom from obstruction and adequacy of insulation. Dig holes, using augers, and set poles, using cranes and power equipment. Trim trees that could be hazardous to the functioning of cables or wires. Splice or solder cables together or to overhead transmission lines, customer service lines, or street light lines, using hand tools, epoxies, or specialized equipment. Cut and peel lead sheathing and insulation from defective or newly installed cables and conduits prior to splicing.

Personality Type: Realistic. These occupations frequently involve work activities that include practical, hands-on problems and solutions. They often deal with plants; animals; and real-world materials such as wood, tools, and machinery. Many of the occupations require working outside and don't involve a lot of paperwork or working closely with others.

GOE—Interest Area/Cluster: 02. Architecture and Construction. **Work Group:** 02.05. Systems and Equipment Installation, Maintenance, and Repair. **Other Jobs in This Work Group:** Electrical and Electronics Repairers, Powerhouse, Substation, and Relay; Elevator Installers and Repairers; Heating and Air Conditioning Mechanics and Installers; Maintenance and Repair Workers, General; Refrigeration Mechanics and Installers; Telecommunications Equipment Installers and Repairers, Except Line Installers; Telecommunications Line Installers and Repairers.

Skills—Repairing: Repairing machines or systems, using the needed tools. **Installation:** Installing equipment, machines, wiring, or programs to meet specifications. **Equipment Maintenance:** Performing routine maintenance and determining when and what kind of maintenance is needed. **Operation Monitoring:** Watching gauges, dials, or other indicators to make sure a machine is working properly. **Troubleshooting:** Determining what is causing an operating error and deciding what to do about it. **Operation and Control:** Controlling operations of equipment or systems. **Equipment Selection:** Determining the kind of tools and equipment needed to do a job. **Technology Design:** Generating or adapting equipment and technology to serve user needs.

Education and Training Programs: Electrical and Power Transmission Installation/Installer Training, General; Electrical and Power Transmission Installer Training, Other; Lineworker Training. **Related Knowledge/**

Courses—Building and Construction: Materials, methods, and the appropriate tools to construct objects, structures, and buildings. **Mechanical Devices:** Machines and tools, including their designs, uses, benefits, repair, and maintenance. **Customer and Personal Service:** Principles and processes for providing customer and personal services, including needs assessment techniques, quality service standards, alternative delivery systems, and customer satisfaction evaluation techniques. **Engineering and Technology:** Equipment, tools, and mechanical devices and their uses to produce motion, light, power, technology, and other applications. **Transportation:** Principles and methods for moving people or goods by air, rail, sea, or road, including their relative costs, advantages, and limitations. **Design:** Design techniques, principles, tools, and instruments involved in the production and use of precision technical plans, blueprints, drawings, and models.

Work Environment: Outdoors; very hot or cold; high places; hazardous conditions; hazardous equipment; using hands on objects, tools, or controls.

Electricians

⌘ Education/Training Required: Long-term on-the-job training
⌘ Annual Earnings: $44,780
⌘ Beginning Wage: $27,330
⌘ Earnings Growth Potential: Medium
⌘ Growth: 7.4%
⌘ Annual Job Openings: 79,083
⌘ Self-Employed: 10.7%
⌘ Part-Time: 2.3%

Install, maintain, and repair electrical wiring, equipment, and fixtures. Ensure that work is in accordance with relevant codes. May install or service street lights, intercom systems, or electrical control systems. Maintain current electrician's license or identification card to meet governmental regulations. Connect wires to circuit breakers, transformers, or other components. Repair or replace wiring, equipment, and fixtures, using hand tools and power tools. Assemble, install, test, and maintain electrical or electronic wiring, equipment, appliances, apparatus, and fixtures, using hand tools and power tools. Test electrical systems and continuity of circuits in electrical wiring, equipment, and fixtures, using testing devices such as ohmmeters, voltmeters, and oscilloscopes, to ensure compatibility and safety of system. Use a variety of tools and equipment such as power construction equipment, measuring devices, power tools, and testing equipment, including oscilloscopes, ammeters, and test lamps. Plan layout and installation of electrical wiring, equipment, and fixtures based on job specifications and local codes. Inspect electrical systems, equipment, and components to identify hazards, defects, and the need for adjustment or repair and to ensure compliance with codes. Direct and train workers to install, maintain, or repair electrical wiring, equipment, and fixtures. Diagnose malfunctioning systems, apparatus, and components, using test equipment and hand tools, to locate the cause of a breakdown and correct the problem. Prepare sketches or follow blueprints to determine the location of wiring and equipment and to ensure conformance to building and safety codes. Install ground leads and connect power cables to equipment such as motors. Work from ladders, scaffolds, and roofs to install, maintain, or repair electrical wiring, equipment, and fixtures. Perform business management duties such as maintaining records and files, preparing reports, and ordering supplies and equipment. Fasten small metal or plastic boxes to walls to house electrical switches or outlets. Place conduit, pipes, or tubing inside designated partitions, walls, or other concealed areas and pull insulated wires or cables through the conduit to complete circuits between boxes. Advise management on whether continued operation of equipment could be hazardous.

Personality Type: Realistic. These occupations frequently involve work activities that include practical, hands-on problems and solutions. They often deal with plants; animals; and real-world materials such as wood, tools, and machinery. Many of the occupations require working outside and don't involve a lot of paperwork or working closely with others.

GOE—Interest Area/Cluster: 02. Architecture and Construction. **Work Group:** 02.04. Construction Crafts. **Other Jobs in This Work Group:** Boilermakers; Brickmasons and Blockmasons; Carpet Installers; Cement Masons and Concrete Finishers; Commercial Divers; Construction Carpenters; Crane and Tower Operators; Drywall and Ceiling Tile Installers; Fence Erectors; Floor Layers, Except Carpet, Wood, and Hard Tiles; Floor Sanders and Finishers; Glaziers; Hazardous Materials Removal Workers;

Insulation Workers, Floor, Ceiling, and Wall; Insulation Workers, Mechanical; Manufactured Building and Mobile Home Installers; Operating Engineers and Other Construction Equipment Operators; Painters, Construction and Maintenance; Paperhangers; Paving, Surfacing, and Tamping Equipment Operators; Pile-Driver Operators; Pipe Fitters and Steamfitters; Pipelayers; Plasterers and Stucco Masons; Plumbers; Plumbers, Pipefitters, and Steamfitters; Rail-Track Laying and Maintenance Equipment Operators; Refractory Materials Repairers, Except Brickmasons; Reinforcing Iron and Rebar Workers; Riggers; Roofers; Rough Carpenters; Security and Fire Alarm Systems Installers; Segmental Pavers; Sheet Metal Workers; Stone Cutters and Carvers, Manufacturing; Stonemasons; Structural Iron and Steel Workers; Tapers; Terrazzo Workers and Finishers; Tile and Marble Setters.

Skills—Repairing: Repairing machines or systems, using the needed tools. **Operation Monitoring:** Watching gauges, dials, or other indicators to make sure a machine is working properly. **Installation:** Installing equipment, machines, wiring, or programs to meet specifications. **Equipment Maintenance:** Performing routine maintenance and determining when and what kind of maintenance is needed. **Troubleshooting:** Determining what is causing an operating error and deciding what to do about it. **Operation and Control:** Controlling operations of equipment or systems. **Quality Control Analysis:** Evaluating the quality or performance of products, services, or processes.

Education and Training Program: Electrician Training. **Related Knowledge/Courses—Building and Construction:** Materials, methods, and the appropriate tools to construct objects, structures, and buildings. **Mechanical Devices:** Machines and tools, including their designs, uses, benefits, repair, and maintenance. **Design:** Design techniques, principles, tools, and instruments involved in the production and use of precision technical plans, blueprints, drawings, and models. **Physics:** Physical principles, laws, and applications, including air, water, material dynamics, light, atomic principles, heat, electric theory, earth formations, and meteorological and related natural phenomena. **Telecommunications:** Transmission, broadcasting, switching, control, and operation of telecommunications systems. **Engineering and Technology:** Equipment, tools, and mechanical devices and their uses to produce motion, light, power, technology, and other applications.

Work Environment: Noisy; cramped work space, awkward positions; hazardous conditions; hazardous equipment; standing; using hands on objects, tools, or controls.

Electronic Drafters

- ✸ Education/Training Required: Postsecondary vocational training
- ✸ Annual Earnings: $49,250
- ✸ Beginning Wage: $30,490
- ✸ Earnings Growth Potential: Medium
- ✸ Growth: 4.1%
- ✸ Annual Job Openings: 4,786
- ✸ Self-Employed: 5.7%
- ✸ Part-Time: 5.9%

The job openings listed here are shared with Electrical Drafters.

Draw wiring diagrams, circuit board assembly diagrams, schematics, and layout drawings used for manufacture, installation, and repair of electronic equipment. Draft detail and assembly drawings of design components, circuitry, and printed circuit boards, using computer-assisted equipment or standard drafting techniques and devices. Consult with engineers to discuss and interpret design concepts and determine requirements of detailed working drawings. Locate files relating to specified design project in database library, load program into computer, and record completed job data. Examine electronic schematics and supporting documents to develop, compute, and verify specifications for drafting data, such as configuration of parts, dimensions, and tolerances. Supervise and coordinate work activities of workers engaged in drafting, designing layouts, assembling, and testing printed circuit boards. Compare logic element configuration on display screen with engineering schematics and calculate figures to convert, redesign, and modify element. Review work orders and procedural manuals and confer with vendors and design staff to resolve problems and modify design. Review blueprints to determine customer requirements and consult with assembler regarding schematics, wiring procedures, and conductor paths. Train students to use drafting machines and to prepare schematic diagrams, block diagrams, control drawings, logic diagrams, integrated circuit drawings, and interconnection diagrams. Generate computer tapes of final layout design to produce layered photo masks and photo plotting design onto film. Select drill size to drill test head, according to test design and specifications, and submit guide layout to designated department. Key and program specified commands and engineering specifications into computer system to change functions and test final layout. Copy drawings of printed circuit board fabrication, using print machine or blueprinting procedure. Plot electrical test points on layout sheets and draw schematics for wiring test fixture heads to frames.

Personality Type: Conventional. These occupations frequently involve following set procedures and routines and can include working with data and details more than with ideas. Usually there is a clear line of authority to follow.

GOE—Interest Area/Cluster: 15. Scientific Research, Engineering, and Mathematics. **Work Group:** 15.09. Engineering Technology. **Other Jobs in This Work Group:** Aerospace Engineering and Operations Technicians; Cartographers and Photogrammetrists; Civil Engineering Technicians; Electrical and Electronic Engineering Technicians; Electrical and Electronics Drafters; Electrical Drafters; Electrical Engineering Technicians; Electro-Mechanical Technicians; Electronics Engineering Technicians; Environmental Engineering Technicians; Mapping Technicians; Mechanical Drafters; Mechanical Engineering Technicians; Surveying and Mapping Technicians; Surveying Technicians.

Skills—Technology Design: Generating or adapting equipment and technology to serve user needs. **Operations Analysis:** Analyzing needs and product requirements to create a design. **Installation:** Installing equipment, machines, wiring, or programs to meet specifications. **Equipment Selection:** Determining the kind of tools and equipment needed to do a job. **Mathematics:** Using mathematics to solve problems. **Coordination:** Adjusting actions in relation to others' actions. **Negotiation:** Bringing others together and trying to reconcile differences. **Complex Problem Solving:** Identifying complex problems, reviewing the options, and implementing solutions.

Education and Training Program: Electrical/Electronics Drafting and Electrical/Electronics CAD/CADD. **Related Knowledge/Courses—Design:** Design techniques, principles, tools, and instruments involved in the production and use of precision technical plans, blueprints, drawings, and models. **Engineering and Technology:** Equipment, tools, and mechanical devices and their uses to produce motion, light, power, technology, and other applications. **Mechanical Devices:** Machines and tools, including their designs, uses, benefits, repair, and maintenance. **Physics:** Physical principles, laws, and applications, including air, water, material dynamics, light, atomic principles, heat, electric theory, earth formations, and meteorological and related natural phenomena. **Telecommunications:** Transmission, broadcasting, switching, control, and operation of telecommunications systems. **Mathematics:** Numbers and their operations and interrelationships, including arithmetic, algebra, geometry, calculus, and statistics and their applications.

Work Environment: Indoors; noisy; sitting; using hands on objects, tools, or controls; repetitive motions.

Electronics Engineering Technicians

- ❋ Education/Training Required: Associate degree
- ❋ Annual Earnings: $52,140
- ❋ Beginning Wage: $31,310
- ❋ Earnings Growth Potential: High
- ❋ Growth: 3.6%
- ❋ Annual Job Openings: 12,583
- ❋ Self-Employed: 0.9%
- ❋ Part-Time: 5.9%

The job openings listed here are shared with Electrical Engineering Technicians.

Lay out, build, test, troubleshoot, repair, and modify developmental and production electronic components, parts, equipment, and systems, such as computer equipment, missile control instrumentation, electron tubes, test equipment, and machine tool numerical controls, applying principles and theories of electronics, electrical circuitry, engineering mathematics, electronic and electrical testing, and physics. Usually work under direction of engineering staff. Read blueprints, wiring diagrams, schematic drawings, and engineering instructions for assembling electronics units, applying knowledge of electronic theory and components. Test

electronics units, using standard test equipment, and analyze results to evaluate performance and determine need for adjustment. Perform preventative maintenance and calibration of equipment and systems. Assemble, test, and maintain circuitry or electronic components according to engineering instructions, technical manuals, and knowledge of electronics, using hand and power tools. Adjust and replace defective or improperly functioning circuitry and electronics components, using hand tools and soldering iron. Write reports and record data on testing techniques, laboratory equipment, and specifications to assist engineers. Identify and resolve equipment malfunctions, working with manufacturers and field representatives as necessary to procure replacement parts. Provide user applications and engineering support and recommendations for new and existing equipment with regard to installation, upgrades, and enhancement. Maintain system logs and manuals to document testing and operation of equipment. Provide customer support and education, working with users to identify needs, determine sources of problems, and to provide information on product use. Maintain working knowledge of state-of-the-art tools or software by reading or attending conferences, workshops, or other training. Build prototypes from rough sketches or plans. Design basic circuitry and draft sketches for clarification of details and design documentation under engineers' direction, using drafting instruments and computer aided design (CAD) equipment. Procure parts and maintain inventory and related documentation. Research equipment and component needs, sources, competitive prices, delivery times, and ongoing operational costs. Write computer or microprocessor software programs. Fabricate parts such as coils, terminal boards, and chassis, using bench lathes, drills, or other machine tools. Develop and upgrade preventative maintenance procedures for components, equipment, parts, and systems.

Personality Type: Realistic. These occupations frequently involve work activities that include practical, hands-on problems and solutions. They often deal with plants; animals; and real-world materials such as wood, tools, and machinery. Many of the occupations require working outside and don't involve a lot of paperwork or working closely with others.

GOE—Interest Area/Cluster: 15. Scientific Research, Engineering, and Mathematics. **Work Group:** 15.09. Engineering Technology. **Other Jobs in This Work**

Group: Aerospace Engineering and Operations Technicians; Cartographers and Photogrammetrists; Civil Engineering Technicians; Electrical and Electronic Engineering Technicians; Electrical and Electronics Drafters; Electrical Drafters; Electrical Engineering Technicians; Electro-Mechanical Technicians; Electronic Drafters; Environmental Engineering Technicians; Mapping Technicians; Mechanical Drafters; Mechanical Engineering Technicians; Surveying and Mapping Technicians; Surveying Technicians.

Skills—Repairing: Repairing machines or systems, using the needed tools. **Troubleshooting:** Determining what is causing an operating error and deciding what to do about it. **Operation Monitoring:** Watching gauges, dials, or other indicators to make sure a machine is working properly. **Equipment Maintenance:** Performing routine maintenance and determining when and what kind of maintenance is needed. **Systems Analysis:** Determining how a system should work and how changes will affect outcomes. **Quality Control Analysis:** Evaluating the quality or performance of products, services, or processes. **Systems Evaluation:** Looking at many indicators of system performance and taking into account their accuracy. **Operation and Control:** Controlling operations of equipment or systems.

Education and Training Programs: Computer Engineering Technology/Technician Training; Electrical and Electronic Engineering Technologies/Technician Training, Other; Electrical, Electronic, and Communications Engineering Technology/Technician Training; Telecommunications Technology/Technician Training. **Related Knowledge/Courses—Telecommunications:** Transmission, broadcasting, switching, control, and operation of telecommunications systems. **Engineering and Technology:** Equipment, tools, and mechanical devices and their uses to produce motion, light, power, technology, and other applications. **Design:** Design techniques, principles, tools, and instruments involved in the production and use of precision technical plans, blueprints, drawings, and models. **Mechanical Devices:** Machines and tools, including their designs, uses, benefits, repair, and maintenance. **Computers and Electronics:** Electric circuit boards, processors, chips, and computer hardware and software, including applications and programming. **Physics:** Physical principles, laws, and applications, including air, water, material dynamics, light, atomic principles, heat, electric theory, earth formations, and meteorological and related natural phenomena.

Work Environment: Indoors; noisy; sitting; using hands on objects, tools, or controls.

Elevator Installers and Repairers

* Education/Training Required: Long-term on-the-job training
* Annual Earnings: $68,000
* Beginning Wage: $39,120
* Earnings Growth Potential: High
* Growth: 8.8%
* Annual Job Openings: 2,850
* Self-Employed: 0.0%
* Part-Time: 0.4%

Assemble, install, repair, or maintain electric or hydraulic freight or passenger elevators, escalators, or dumbwaiters. Assemble, install, repair, and maintain elevators, escalators, moving sidewalks, and dumbwaiters, using hand and power tools and testing devices such as test lamps, ammeters, and voltmeters. Test newly installed equipment to ensure that it meets specifications such as stopping at floors for set amounts of time. Check that safety regulations and building codes are met and complete service reports verifying conformance to standards. Locate malfunctions in brakes, motors, switches, and signal and control systems, using test equipment. Connect electrical wiring to control panels and electric motors. Read and interpret blueprints to determine the layout of system components, frameworks, and foundations, and to select installation equipment. Adjust safety controls, counterweights, door mechanisms, and components such as valves, ratchets, seals, and brake linings. Inspect wiring connections, control panel hookups, door installations, and alignments and clearances of cars and hoistways to ensure that equipment will operate properly. Disassemble defective units, and repair or replace parts such as locks, gears, cables, and electric wiring. Maintain log books that detail all repairs and checks performed. Participate in additional training to keep skills up-to-date. Attach guide shoes and rollers to minimize the lateral motion of cars as they travel through shafts. Connect car frames to counterweights, using steel cables. Bolt or weld steel rails to the walls of shafts to guide

E

elevators, working from scaffolding or platforms. Assemble elevator cars, installing each car's platform, walls, and doors. Install outer doors and door frames at elevator entrances on each floor of a structure. Install electrical wires and controls by attaching conduit along shaft walls from floor to floor, then pulling plastic-covered wires through the conduit. Cut prefabricated sections of framework, rails, and other components to specified dimensions. Operate elevators to determine power demands, and test power consumption to detect overload factors. Assemble electrically powered stairs, steel frameworks, and tracks, and install associated motors and electrical wiring.

Personality Type: Realistic. These occupations frequently involve work activities that include practical, hands-on problems and solutions. They often deal with plants; animals; and real-world materials such as wood, tools, and machinery. Many of the occupations require working outside and don't involve a lot of paperwork or working closely with others.

GOE—Interest Area/Cluster: 02. Architecture and Construction. **Work Group:** 02.05. Systems and Equipment Installation, Maintenance, and Repair. **Other Jobs in This Work Group:** Electrical and Electronics Repairers, Powerhouse, Substation, and Relay; Electrical Power-Line Installers and Repairers; Heating and Air Conditioning Mechanics and Installers; Maintenance and Repair Workers, General; Refrigeration Mechanics and Installers; Telecommunications Equipment Installers and Repairers, Except Line Installers; Telecommunications Line Installers and Repairers.

Skills—Installation: Installing equipment, machines, wiring, or programs to meet specifications. **Repairing:** Repairing machines or systems, using the needed tools. **Equipment Maintenance:** Performing routine maintenance and determining when and what kind of maintenance is needed. **Troubleshooting:** Determining what is causing an operating error and deciding what to do about it. **Quality Control Analysis:** Evaluating the quality or performance of products, services, or processes. **Technology Design:** Generating or adapting equipment and technology to serve user needs. **Equipment Selection:** Determining the kind of tools and equipment needed to do a job. **Science:** Using scientific methods to solve problems.

Education and Training Program: Industrial Mechanics and Maintenance Technology. **Related Knowledge/**

Courses—Building and Construction: Materials, methods, and the appropriate tools to construct objects, structures, and buildings. **Mechanical Devices:** Machines and tools, including their designs, uses, benefits, repair, and maintenance. **Physics:** Physical principles, laws, and applications, including air, water, material dynamics, light, atomic principles, heat, electric theory, earth formations, and meteorological and related natural phenomena. **Design:** Design techniques, principles, tools, and instruments involved in the production and use of precision technical plans, blueprints, drawings, and models. **Engineering and Technology:** Equipment, tools, and mechanical devices and their uses to produce motion, light, power, technology, and other applications. **Public Safety and Security:** Weaponry; public safety; security operations, rules, regulations, precautions, and prevention; and the protection of people, data, and property.

Work Environment: Very bright or dim lighting; contaminants; high places; hazardous conditions; hazardous equipment; using hands on objects, tools, or controls.

Eligibility Interviewers, Government Programs

- ❋ Education/Training Required: Moderate-term on-the-job training
- ❋ Annual Earnings: $39,110
- ❋ Beginning Wage: $26,410
- ❋ Earnings Growth Potential: Low
- ❋ Growth: 3.1%
- ❋ Annual Job Openings: 11,337
- ❋ Self-Employed: 0.0%
- ❋ Part-Time: 4.7%

Determine eligibility of persons applying to receive assistance from government programs and agency resources, such as welfare, unemployment benefits, social security, and public housing. Answer applicants' questions about benefits and claim procedures. Interview benefits recipients at specified intervals to certify their eligibility for continuing benefits. Interpret and explain information such as eligibility requirements, application details, payment methods, and applicants' legal rights. Initiate procedures to grant, modify, deny, or terminate assistance or refer applicants to other agencies for assistance. Compile, record, and evaluate personal and financial data to verify completeness and accuracy and to determine eligibility status. Interview and investigate applicants for public assistance to gather information pertinent to their applications. Check with employers or other references to verify answers and obtain further information. Keep records of assigned cases and prepare required reports. Schedule benefits claimants for adjudication interviews to address questions of eligibility. Prepare applications and forms for applicants for such purposes as school enrollment, employment, and medical services. Refer applicants to job openings or to interviews with other staff in accordance with administrative guidelines or office procedures. Provide social workers with pertinent information gathered during applicant interviews. Compute and authorize amounts of assistance for programs such as grants, monetary payments, and food stamps. Monitor the payments of benefits throughout the duration of a claim. Provide applicants with assistance in completing application forms such as those for job referrals or unemployment compensation claims. Investigate claimants for the possibility of fraud or abuse. Conduct annual, interim, and special housing reviews and home visits to ensure conformance to regulations.

Personality Type: Social. These occupations frequently involve working with, communicating with, and teaching people and often involve helping or providing service to others.

GOE—Interest Area/Cluster: 10. Human Service. **Work Group:** 10.04. Client Interviewing. **Other Jobs in This Work Group:** Interviewers, Except Eligibility and Loan.

Skills—Service Orientation: Actively looking for ways to help people. **Speaking:** Talking to others to effectively convey information. **Active Listening:** Listening to what other people are saying and asking questions as appropriate. **Social Perceptiveness:** Being aware of others' reactions and understanding why they react the way they do. **Writing:** Communicating effectively with others in writing as indicated by the needs of the audience. **Active Learning:** Working with new material or information to grasp its implications. **Time Management:** Managing one's own time and the time of others. **Reading Comprehension:** Understanding written sentences and paragraphs in work-related documents.

Education and Training Program: Community Organization and Advocacy. **Related Knowledge/**

Courses—Clerical Studies: Administrative and clerical procedures and systems such as word-processing systems, filing and records management systems, stenography and transcription, forms, design principles, and other office procedures and terminology. **Customer and Personal Service:** Principles and processes for providing customer and personal services, including needs assessment techniques, quality service standards, alternative delivery systems, and customer satisfaction evaluation techniques. **Law and Government:** Laws, legal codes, court procedures, precedents, government regulations, executive orders, agency rules, and the democratic political process. **Psychology:** Human behavior and performance, mental processes, psychological research methods, and the assessment and treatment of behavioral and affective disorders. **Sociology and Anthropology:** Group behavior and dynamics; societal trends and influences; and cultures and their history, migrations, ethnicity, and origins. **Computers and Electronics:** Electric circuit boards, processors, chips, and computer hardware and software, including applications and programming.

Work Environment: Indoors; contaminants; sitting; using hands on objects, tools, or controls; repetitive motions.

Embalmers

- ❋ Education/Training Required: Postsecondary vocational training
- ❋ Annual Earnings: $36,800
- ❋ Beginning Wage: $20,470
- ❋ Earnings Growth Potential: High
- ❋ Growth: 14.3%
- ❋ Annual Job Openings: 1,660
- ❋ Self-Employed: 0.7%
- ❋ Part-Time: 21.6%

Prepare bodies for interment in conformity with legal requirements. Conform to laws of health and sanitation and ensure that legal requirements concerning embalming are met. Apply cosmetics to impart lifelike appearance to the deceased. Incise stomach and abdominal walls and probe internal organs, using trocar, to withdraw blood and waste matter from organs. Close incisions, using needles and sutures. Reshape or reconstruct disfigured or maimed bodies when necessary, using derma-surgery techniques and materials such as clay, cotton, plaster of paris, and wax.

Make incisions in arms or thighs and drain blood from circulatory system and replace it with embalming fluid, using pump. Dress bodies and place them in caskets. Join lips, using needles and thread or wire. Conduct interviews to arrange for the preparation of obituary notices, to assist with the selection of caskets or urns, and to determine the location and time of burials or cremations. Perform the duties of funeral directors, including coordinating funeral activities. Attach trocar to pump-tube, start pump, and repeat probing to force embalming fluid into organs. Perform special procedures necessary for remains that are to be transported to other states or overseas or where death was caused by infectious disease. Maintain records such as itemized lists of clothing or valuables delivered with body and names of persons embalmed. Insert convex celluloid or cotton between eyeballs and eyelids to prevent slipping and sinking of eyelids. Wash and dry bodies, using germicidal soap and towels or hot air dryers. Arrange for transporting the deceased to another state for interment. Supervise funeral attendants and other funeral home staff. Pack body orifices with cotton saturated with embalming fluid to prevent escape of gases or waste matter. Assist with placing caskets in hearses and organize cemetery processions. Serve as pallbearers, attend visiting rooms, and provide other assistance to the bereaved. Direct casket and floral display placement and arrange guest seating. Arrange funeral home equipment and perform general maintenance. Assist coroners at death scenes or at autopsies, file police reports, and testify at inquests or in court if employed by a coroner.

Personality Type: Realistic. These occupations frequently involve work activities that include practical, hands-on problems and solutions. They often deal with plants; animals; and real-world materials such as wood, tools, and machinery. Many of the occupations require working outside and don't involve a lot of paperwork or working closely with others.

GOE—Interest Area/Cluster: 08. Health Science. **Work Group:** 08.09. Health Protection and Promotion. **Other Jobs in This Work Group:** Athletic Trainers; Dietetic Technicians; Dietitians and Nutritionists.

Skills—Science: Using scientific methods to solve problems. **Service Orientation:** Actively looking for ways to help people. **Management of Financial Resources:** Determining how money will be spent to get the work done and accounting for these expenditures. **Management of Material Resources:** Obtaining and seeing to the appropriate use of equipment, facilities, and materials needed to do certain work. **Social Perceptiveness:** Being aware of others' reactions and understanding why they react the way they do. **Equipment Maintenance:** Performing routine maintenance and determining when and what kind of maintenance is needed. **Operation Monitoring:** Watching gauges, dials, or other indicators to make sure a machine is working properly. **Equipment Selection:** Determining the kind of tools and equipment needed to do a job.

Education and Training Programs: Funeral Service and Mortuary Science, General; Mortuary Science and Embalming/Embalmer Training. **Related Knowledge/Courses—Chemistry:** The composition, structure, and properties of substances and of the chemical processes and transformations that they undergo. This includes uses of chemicals and their interactions, danger signs, production techniques, and disposal methods. **Biology:** Plant and animal living tissue, cells, organisms, and entities, including their functions, interdependencies, and interactions with each other and the environment. **Philosophy and Theology:** Different philosophical systems and religions, including their basic principles, values, ethics, ways of thinking, customs, and practices and their impact on human culture. **Customer and Personal Service:** Principles and processes for providing customer and personal services, including needs assessment techniques, quality service standards, alternative delivery systems, and customer satisfaction evaluation techniques. **Therapy and Counseling:** Information and techniques needed to rehabilitate physical and mental ailments and to provide career guidance, including alternative treatments, rehabilitation equipment and its proper use, and methods to evaluate treatment effects. **Medicine and Dentistry:** The information and techniques needed to diagnose and treat injuries, diseases, and deformities. This includes symptoms, treatment alternatives, drug properties and interactions, and preventive health-care measures.

Work Environment: Indoors; contaminants; disease or infections; hazardous conditions; standing; using hands on objects, tools, or controls.

Emergency Management Specialists

* Education/Training Required: Work experience in a related occupation
* Annual Earnings: $48,380
* Beginning Wage: $26,340
* Earnings Growth Potential: High
* Growth: 12.3%
* Annual Job Openings: 1,538
* Self-Employed: 0.1%
* Part-Time: 9.6%

Coordinate disaster response or crisis management activities, provide disaster-preparedness training, and prepare emergency plans and procedures for natural (e.g., hurricanes, floods, earthquakes), wartime, or technological (e.g., nuclear power plant emergencies, hazardous materials spills) disasters or hostage situations. Keep informed of activities or changes that could affect the likelihood of an emergency, as well as those that could affect response efforts and details of plan implementation. Prepare plans that outline operating procedures to be used in response to disasters or emergencies such as hurricanes, nuclear accidents, and terrorist attacks and in recovery from these events. Propose alteration of emergency response procedures based on regulatory changes, technological changes, or knowledge gained from outcomes of previous emergency situations. Maintain and update all resource materials associated with emergency-preparedness plans. Coordinate disaster response or crisis management activities such as ordering evacuations, opening public shelters, and implementing special needs plans and programs. Develop and maintain liaisons with municipalities, county departments, and similar entities in order to facilitate plan development, response effort coordination, and exchanges of personnel and equipment. Keep informed of federal, state, and local regulations affecting emergency plans and ensure that plans adhere to these regulations. Design and administer emergency and disaster-preparedness training courses that teach people how to effectively respond to major emergencies and disasters. Prepare emergency situation status reports that describe response and recovery efforts, needs, and preliminary damage assessments. Inspect facilities and equipment such as emergency management centers and communications equipment to determine their operational and functional capabilities in emergency situations. Consult with officials of local and area governments, schools, hospitals, and other institutions in order to determine their needs and capabilities in the event of a natural disaster or other emergency. Develop and perform tests and evaluations of emergency management plans in accordance with state and federal regulations. Attend meetings, conferences, and workshops related to emergency management to learn new information and to develop working relationships with other emergency management specialists.

Personality Type: Social. These occupations frequently involve working with, communicating with, and teaching people and often involve helping or providing service to others.

GOE—Interest Area/Cluster: 12. Law and Public Safety. **Work Group:** 12.01. Managerial Work in Law and Public Safety. **Other Jobs in This Work Group:** First-Line Supervisors/Managers of Correctional Officers; First-Line Supervisors/Managers of Fire Fighting and Prevention Workers; First-Line Supervisors/Managers of Police and Detectives; Forest Fire Fighting and Prevention Supervisors; Municipal Fire Fighting and Prevention Supervisors.

Skills—Management of Material Resources: Obtaining and seeing to the appropriate use of equipment, facilities, and materials needed to do certain work. **Service Orientation:** Actively looking for ways to help people. **Judgment and Decision Making:** Weighing the relative costs and benefits of a potential action. **Complex Problem Solving:** Identifying complex problems, reviewing the options, and implementing solutions. **Coordination:** Adjusting actions in relation to others' actions. **Operations Analysis:** Analyzing needs and product requirements to create a design. **Management of Financial Resources:** Determining how money will be spent to get the work done and accounting for these expenditures. **Writing:** Communicating effectively with others in writing as indicated by the needs of the audience.

Education and Training Programs: Community Organization and Advocacy; Public Administration. **Related Knowledge/Courses—Public Safety and Security:** Weaponry; public safety; security operations, rules, regulations, precautions, and prevention; and the protection of people, data, and property. **Customer and Personal Service:** Principles and processes for providing customer and personal services, including needs assessment techniques, quality service standards, alternative delivery systems, and customer satisfaction evaluation techniques. **Education and Training:** Instructional methods and training techniques, including curriculum design principles, learning theory, group and individual teaching techniques, design of individual development plans, and test design principles. **Law and Government:** Laws, legal codes, court procedures, precedents, government regulations, executive orders, agency rules, and the democratic political process. **Physics:** Physical principles, laws, and applications, including air, water, material dynamics, light, atomic principles, heat, electric theory, earth formations, and meteorological and related natural phenomena. **Telecommunications:** Transmission, broadcasting, switching, control, and operation of telecommunications systems.

Work Environment: Indoors; sitting.

Emergency Medical Technicians and Paramedics

- ⊛ Education/Training Required: Postsecondary vocational training
- ⊛ Annual Earnings: $28,400
- ⊛ Beginning Wage: $18,150
- ⊛ Earnings Growth Potential: Medium
- ⊛ Growth: 19.2%
- ⊛ Annual Job Openings: 19,513
- ⊛ Self-Employed: 0.2%
- ⊛ Part-Time: 10.5%

Assess injuries, administer emergency medical care, and extricate trapped individuals. Transport injured or sick persons to medical facilities. Administer first-aid treatment and life-support care to sick or injured persons in prehospital setting. Perform emergency diagnostic and treatment procedures, such as stomach suction, airway management, or heart monitoring, during ambulance ride. Observe, record, and report to physician the patient's condition or injury, the treatment provided, and reactions to drugs and treatment. Immobilize patient for placement on stretcher and ambulance transport, using backboard or other spinal immobilization device. Maintain vehicles and medical and communication equipment, and replenish first-aid equipment and supplies. Assess nature and extent of illness or injury to establish and prioritize medical

procedures. Communicate with dispatchers and treatment center personnel to provide information about situation, to arrange reception of victims, and to receive instructions for further treatment. Comfort and reassure patients. Decontaminate ambulance interior following treatment of patient with infectious disease and report case to proper authorities. Operate equipment such as electrocardiograms (EKGs), external defibrillators, and bag-valve mask resuscitators in advanced life-support environments. Drive mobile intensive care unit to specified location, following instructions from emergency medical dispatcher. Coordinate with treatment center personnel to obtain patients' vital statistics and medical history, to determine the circumstances of the emergency, and to administer emergency treatment. Coordinate work with other emergency medical team members and police and fire department personnel. Attend training classes to maintain certification licensure, keep abreast of new developments in the field, or maintain existing knowledge. Administer drugs, orally or by injection, and perform intravenous procedures under a physician's direction.

Personality Type: Social. These occupations frequently involve working with, communicating with, and teaching people and often involve helping or providing service to others.

GOE—Interest Area/Cluster: 12. Law and Public Safety. **Work Group:** 12.06. Emergency Responding. **Other Jobs in This Work Group:** Fire Fighters; Forest Fire Fighters; Municipal Fire Fighters.

Skills—Operation Monitoring: Watching gauges, dials, or other indicators to make sure a machine is working properly. **Operation and Control:** Controlling operations of equipment or systems. **Management of Personnel Resources:** Motivating, developing, and directing people as they work; identifying the best people for the job. **Systems Analysis:** Determining how a system should work and how changes will affect outcomes. **Systems Evaluation:** Looking at many indicators of system performance and taking into account their accuracy. **Service Orientation:** Actively looking for ways to help people.

Education and Training Programs: Emergency Care Attendant Training (EMT Ambulance); Emergency Medical Technology/Technician Training (EMT Paramedic). **Related Knowledge/Courses—Medicine and Dentistry:** The information and techniques needed to diagnose and treat injuries, diseases, and deformities. This includes symptoms, treatment alternatives, drug properties and interactions, and preventive health-care measures. **Customer and Personal Service:** Principles and processes for providing customer and personal services, including needs assessment techniques, quality service standards, alternative delivery systems, and customer satisfaction evaluation techniques. **Therapy and Counseling:** Information and techniques needed to rehabilitate physical and mental ailments and to provide career guidance, including alternative treatments, rehabilitation equipment and its proper use, and methods to evaluate treatment effects. **Psychology:** Human behavior and performance, mental processes, psychological research methods, and the assessment and treatment of behavioral and affective disorders. **Transportation:** Principles and methods for moving people or goods by air, rail, sea, or road, including their relative costs, advantages, and limitations. **Education and Training:** Instructional methods and training techniques, including curriculum design principles, learning theory, group and individual teaching techniques, design of individual development plans, and test design principles.

Work Environment: More often outdoors than indoors; noisy; very hot or cold; very bright or dim lighting; disease or infections.

Environmental Compliance Inspectors

- ❋ Education/Training Required: Long-term on-the-job training
- ❋ Annual Earnings: $48,400
- ❋ Beginning Wage: $28,980
- ❋ Earnings Growth Potential: High
- ❋ Growth: 4.9%
- ❋ Annual Job Openings: 15,841
- ❋ Self-Employed: 0.4%
- ❋ Part-Time: 5.0%

The job openings listed here are shared with Coroners, with Equal Opportunity Representatives and Officers, with Government Property Inspectors and Investigators, and with Licensing Examiners and Inspectors.

Inspect and investigate sources of pollution to protect the public and environment and ensure conformance with federal, state, and local regulations and ordinances. Determine the nature of code violations and actions to be taken, and issue written notices of violation; participate in enforcement hearings as necessary. Examine permits, licenses, applications, and records to ensure compliance with licensing requirements. Prepare, organize, and maintain inspection records. Interview individuals to determine the nature of suspected violations and to obtain evidence of violations. Prepare written, oral, tabular, and graphic reports summarizing requirements and regulations, including enforcement and chain of custody documentation. Monitor follow-up actions in cases where violations were found, and review compliance monitoring reports. Investigate complaints and suspected violations regarding illegal dumping, pollution, pesticides, product quality, or labeling laws. Inspect waste pretreatment, treatment, and disposal facilities and systems for conformance to federal, state, or local regulations. Inform individuals and groups of pollution control regulations and inspection findings, and explain how problems can be corrected. Determine sampling locations and methods, and collect water or wastewater samples for analysis, preserving samples with appropriate containers and preservation methods. Verify that hazardous chemicals are handled, stored, and disposed of in accordance with regulations. Research and keep informed of pertinent information and developments in areas such as EPA laws and regulations. Determine which sites and violation reports to investigate, and coordinate compliance and enforcement activities with other government agencies. Observe and record field conditions, gathering, interpreting, and reporting data such as flow meter readings and chemical levels. Learn and observe proper safety precautions, rules, regulations, and practices so that unsafe conditions can be recognized and proper safety protocols implemented. Evaluate label information for accuracy and conformance to regulatory requirements. Inform health professionals, property owners, and the public about harmful properties and related problems of water pollution and contaminated wastewater.

Personality Type: Conventional. These occupations frequently involve following set procedures and routines and can include working with data and details more than with ideas. Usually there is a clear line of authority to follow.

GOE—Interest Area/Cluster: 07. Government and Public Administration. **Work Group:** 07.03. Regulations Enforcement. **Other Jobs in This Work Group:**

E

Agricultural Inspectors; Aviation Inspectors; Compliance Officers, Except Agriculture, Construction, Health and Safety, and **Transportation:** Principles and methods for moving people or goods by air, rail, sea, or road, including their relative costs, advantages, and limitations. Construction and Building Inspectors; Equal Opportunity Representatives and Officers; Financial Examiners; Fire Inspectors; Fish and Game Wardens; Forest Fire Inspectors and Prevention Specialists; Freight and Cargo Inspectors; Government Property Inspectors and Investigators; Immigration and Customs Inspectors; Licensing Examiners and Inspectors; Nuclear Monitoring Technicians; Occupational Health and Safety Specialists; Occupational Health and Safety Technicians; Tax Examiners, Collectors, and Revenue Agents; Transportation Vehicle, Equipment, and Systems Inspectors, Except Aviation.

Skills—Science: Using scientific methods to solve problems. **Negotiation:** Bringing others together and trying to reconcile differences. **Writing:** Communicating effectively with others in writing as indicated by the needs of the audience. **Reading Comprehension:** Understanding written sentences and paragraphs in work-related documents. **Mathematics:** Using mathematics to solve problems. **Active Listening:** Listening to what other people are saying and asking questions as appropriate. **Persuasion:** Persuading others to approach things differently. **Operation Monitoring:** Watching gauges, dials, or other indicators to make sure a machine is working properly.

Education and Training Program: Natural Resources Management and Policy, Other. **Related Knowledge/Courses—Biology:** Plant and animal living tissue, cells, organisms, and entities, including their functions, interdependencies, and interactions with each other and the environment. **Chemistry:** The composition, structure, and properties of substances and of the chemical processes and transformations that they undergo. This includes uses of chemicals and their interactions, danger signs, production techniques, and disposal methods. **Law and Government:** Laws, legal codes, court procedures, precedents, government regulations, executive orders, agency rules, and the democratic political process. **Geography:** Various methods for describing the location and distribution of land, sea, and air masses, including their physical locations, relationships, and characteristics. **Physics:** Physical principles, laws, and applications, including air, water, material dynamics, light, atomic principles, heat, electric theory, earth formations,

and meteorological and related natural phenomena. **Engineering and Technology:** Equipment, tools, and mechanical devices and their uses to produce motion, light, power, technology, and other applications.

Work Environment: More often indoors than outdoors; contaminants; sitting.

Environmental Engineering Technicians

* Education/Training Required: Associate degree
* Annual Earnings: $40,690
* Beginning Wage: $25,360
* Earnings Growth Potential: Medium
* Growth: 24.8%
* Annual Job Openings: 2,162
* Self-Employed: 0.8%
* Part-Time: 5.9%

Apply theory and principles of environmental engineering to modify, test, and operate equipment and devices used in the prevention, control, and remediation of environmental pollution, including waste treatment and site remediation. May assist in the development of environmental pollution remediation devices under direction of engineer. Receive, set up, test, and decontaminate equipment. Maintain project logbook records and computer program files. Perform environmental quality work in field and office settings. Conduct pollution surveys, collecting and analyzing samples such as air and groundwater. Review technical documents to ensure completeness and conformance to requirements. Perform laboratory work such as logging numerical and visual observations, preparing and packaging samples, recording test results, and performing photo documentation. Review work plans to schedule activities. Obtain product information, identify vendors and suppliers, and order materials and equipment to maintain inventory. Arrange for the disposal of lead, asbestos, and other hazardous materials. Inspect facilities to monitor compliance with regulations governing substances such as asbestos, lead, and wastewater. Provide technical engineering support in the planning of projects such as wastewater treatment plants to ensure compliance with environmental regulations and policies. Improve chemical processes to reduce toxic emissions. Oversee support staff. Assist in the cleanup of hazardous material spills. Produce environmental assessment reports, tabulating data and preparing charts, graphs, and sketches. Maintain process parameters and evaluate process anomalies. Work with customers to assess the environmental impact of proposed construction and to develop pollution prevention programs. Perform statistical analysis and correction of air or water pollution data submitted by industry and other agencies. Develop work plans, including writing specifications and establishing material, manpower, and facilities needs.

Personality Type: Realistic. These occupations frequently involve work activities that include practical, hands-on problems and solutions. They often deal with plants; animals; and real-world materials such as wood, tools, and machinery. Many of the occupations require working outside and don't involve a lot of paperwork or working closely with others.

GOE—Interest Area/Cluster: 15. Scientific Research, Engineering, and Mathematics. **Work Group:** 15.09. Engineering Technology. **Other Jobs in This Work Group:** Aerospace Engineering and Operations Technicians; Cartographers and Photogrammetrists; Civil Engineering Technicians; Electrical and Electronic Engineering Technicians; Electrical and Electronics Drafters; Electrical Drafters; Electrical Engineering Technicians; Electro-Mechanical Technicians; Electronic Drafters; Electronics Engineering Technicians; Mapping Technicians; Mechanical Drafters; Mechanical Engineering Technicians; Surveying and Mapping Technicians; Surveying Technicians.

Skills—Science: Using scientific methods to solve problems. **Repairing:** Repairing machines or systems, using the needed tools. **Troubleshooting:** Determining what is causing an operating error and deciding what to do about it. **Equipment Maintenance:** Performing routine maintenance and determining when and what kind of maintenance is needed. **Operation Monitoring:** Watching gauges, dials, or other indicators to make sure a machine is working properly. **Mathematics:** Using mathematics to solve problems. **Quality Control Analysis:** Evaluating the quality or performance of products, services, or processes. **Installation:** Installing equipment, machines, wiring, or programs to meet specifications.

Education and Training Programs: Environmental Engineering Technology/Environmental Technology; Hazardous Materials Information Systems Technology/Technician Training. **Related Knowledge/Courses— Engineering and Technology:** Equipment, tools, and mechanical devices and their uses to produce motion, light, power, technology, and other applications. **Building and Construction:** Materials, methods, and the appropriate tools to construct objects, structures, and buildings. **Physics:** Physical principles, laws, and applications, including air, water, material dynamics, light, atomic principles, heat, electric theory, earth formations, and meteorological and related natural phenomena. **Design:** Design techniques, principles, tools, and instruments involved in the production and use of precision technical plans, blueprints, drawings, and models. **Biology:** Plant and animal living tissue, cells, organisms, and entities, including their functions, interdependencies, and interactions with each other and the environment. **Chemistry:** The composition, structure, and properties of substances and of the chemical processes and transformations that they undergo. This includes uses of chemicals and their interactions, danger signs, production techniques, and disposal methods.

Work Environment: More often indoors than outdoors; contaminants; hazardous conditions; hazardous equipment; standing.

Environmental Science and Protection Technicians, Including Health

- ❊ Education/Training Required: Associate degree
- ❊ Annual Earnings: $39,370
- ❊ Beginning Wage: $25,090
- ❊ Earnings Growth Potential: Medium
- ❊ Growth: 28.0%
- ❊ Annual Job Openings: 8,404
- ❊ Self-Employed: 1.5%
- ❊ Part-Time: 19.4%

Perform laboratory and field tests to monitor the environment and investigate sources of pollution, including those that affect health. Under direction of environmental scientists or specialists, may collect samples of gases,

soil, water, and other materials for testing and take corrective actions as assigned. Collect samples of gases, soils, water, industrial wastewater, and asbestos products to conduct tests on pollutant levels and identify sources of pollution. Record test data and prepare reports, summaries, and charts that interpret test results. Develop and implement programs for monitoring of environmental pollution and radiation. Discuss test results and analyses with customers. Set up equipment or stations to monitor and collect pollutants from sites such as smoke stacks, manufacturing plants, or mechanical equipment. Maintain files such as hazardous waste databases, chemical usage data, personnel exposure information, and diagrams showing equipment locations. Develop testing procedures or direct activities of workers in laboratory. Prepare samples or photomicrographs for testing and analysis. Calibrate microscopes and test instruments. Examine and analyze material for presence and concentration of contaminants such as asbestos, using variety of microscopes. Calculate amount of pollutant in samples or compute air pollution or gas flow in industrial processes, using chemical and mathematical formulas. Make recommendations to control or eliminate unsafe conditions at workplaces or public facilities. Weigh, analyze, and measure collected sample particles such as lead, coal dust, or rock, to determine concentration of pollutants. Provide information and technical and program assistance to government representatives, employers, and the general public on the issues of public health, environmental protection, or workplace safety. Conduct standardized tests to ensure materials and supplies used throughout power supply systems meet processing and safety specifications. Perform statistical analysis of environmental data. Respond to and investigate hazardous conditions or spills or outbreaks of disease or food poisoning, collecting samples for analysis. Determine amounts and kinds of chemicals to use in destroying harmful organisms and removing impurities from purification systems. Inspect sanitary conditions at public facilities. Inspect workplaces to ensure the absence of health and safety hazards such as high noise levels, radiation, or potential lighting hazards.

Personality Type: Investigative. These occupations frequently involve working with ideas and require an extensive amount of thinking. They can involve searching for facts and figuring out problems mentally.

GOE—Interest Area/Cluster: 01. Agriculture and Natural Resources. **Work Group:** 01.03. Resource Technologies

for Plants, Animals, and the Environment. **Other Jobs in This Work Group:** Agricultural and Food Science Technicians; Agricultural Technicians; Food Science Technicians; Food Scientists and Technologists; Geological and Petroleum Technicians; Geological Sample Test Technicians; Geophysical Data Technicians.

Skills—Quality Control Analysis: Evaluating the quality or performance of products, services, or processes. **Systems Analysis:** Determining how a system should work and how changes will affect outcomes. **Systems Evaluation:** Looking at many indicators of system performance and taking into account their accuracy. **Operation Monitoring:** Watching gauges, dials, or other indicators to make sure a machine is working properly. **Operation and Control:** Controlling operations of equipment or systems. **Science:** Using scientific methods to solve problems.

Education and Training Programs: Environmental Science; Environmental Studies; Physical Science Technologies/Technician Training, Other; Science Technologies/Technician Training, Other. **Related Knowledge/Courses—Biology:** Plant and animal living tissue, cells, organisms, and entities, including their functions, interdependencies, and interactions with each other and the environment. **Chemistry:** The composition, structure, and properties of substances and of the chemical processes and transformations that they undergo. This includes uses of chemicals and their interactions, danger signs, production techniques, and disposal methods. **Geography:** Various methods for describing the location and distribution of land, sea, and air masses, including their physical locations, relationships, and characteristics. **Physics:** Physical principles, laws, and applications, including air, water, material dynamics, light, atomic principles, heat, electric theory, earth formations, and meteorological and related natural phenomena. **Computers and Electronics:** Electric circuit boards, processors, chips, and computer hardware and software, including applications and programming. **Building and Construction:** Materials, methods, and the appropriate tools to construct objects, structures, and buildings.

Work Environment: More often outdoors than indoors; very hot or cold; contaminants; hazardous equipment; standing.

Equal Opportunity Representatives and Officers

* Education/Training Required: Long-term on-the-job training
* Annual Earnings: $48,400
* Beginning Wage: $28,980
* Earnings Growth Potential: High
* Growth: 4.9%
* Annual Job Openings: 15,841
* Self-Employed: 0.4%
* Part-Time: 5.0%

The job openings listed here are shared with Coroners, with Environmental Compliance Inspectors, with Government Property Inspectors and Investigators, and with Licensing Examiners and Inspectors.

Monitor and evaluate compliance with equal opportunity laws, guidelines, and policies to ensure that employment practices and contracting arrangements give equal opportunity without regard to race, religion, color, national origin, sex, age, or disability. Investigate employment practices and alleged violations of laws, in order to document and correct discriminatory factors. Interpret civil rights laws and equal opportunity regulations for individuals and employers. Study equal opportunity complaints in order to clarify issues. Meet with persons involved in equal opportunity complaints in order to verify case information, and to arbitrate and settle disputes. Coordinate, monitor, and revise complaint procedures to ensure timely processing and review of complaints. Prepare reports of selection, survey, and other statistics, and recommendations for corrective action. Conduct surveys and evaluate findings in order to determine if systematic discrimination exists. Develop guidelines for non-discriminatory employment practices, and monitor their implementation and impact. Review company contracts to determine actions required to meet governmental equal opportunity provisions. Counsel newly hired members of minority and disadvantaged groups, informing them about details of civil rights laws. Provide information, technical assistance, and training to supervisors, managers, and employees on topics such as employee supervision, hiring, grievance procedures, and staff development. Verify that all job descriptions are submitted for review and approval, and that descriptions meet regulatory standards. Act as liaisons between minority placement agencies and employers, or between job search committees and other equal opportunity administrators. Consult with community representatives to develop technical assistance agreements in accordance with governmental regulations. Meet with job search committees or coordinators to explain the role of the equal opportunity coordinator, to provide resources for advertising, and to explain expectations for future contacts. Participate in the recruitment of employees through job fairs, career days, and advertising plans.

Personality Type: Social. These occupations frequently involve working with, communicating with, and teaching people and often involve helping or providing service to others.

GOE—Interest Area/Cluster: 07. Government and Public Administration. **Work Group:** 07.03. Regulations Enforcement. **Other Jobs in This Work Group:** Agricultural Inspectors; Aviation Inspectors; Compliance Officers, Except Agriculture, Construction, Health and Safety, and Transportation; Construction and Building Inspectors; Environmental Compliance Inspectors; Financial Examiners; Fire Inspectors; Fish and Game Wardens; Forest Fire Inspectors and Prevention Specialists; Freight and Cargo Inspectors; Government Property Inspectors and Investigators; Immigration and Customs Inspectors; Licensing Examiners and Inspectors; Nuclear Monitoring Technicians; Occupational Health and Safety Specialists; Occupational Health and Safety Technicians; Tax Examiners, Collectors, and Revenue Agents; Transportation Vehicle, Equipment, and Systems Inspectors, Except Aviation.

Skills—Negotiation: Bringing others together and trying to reconcile differences. **Persuasion:** Persuading others to approach things differently. **Social Perceptiveness:** Being aware of others' reactions and understanding why they react the way they do. **Service Orientation:** Actively looking for ways to help people. **Complex Problem Solving:** Identifying complex problems, reviewing the options, and implementing solutions. **Judgment and Decision Making:** Weighing the relative costs and benefits of a potential action. **Active Listening:** Listening to what other people are saying and asking questions as appropriate. **Writing:** Communicating effectively with others in writing as indicated by the needs of the audience.

Education and Training Program: Public Administration and Social Service Professions, Other. **Related**

Knowledge/Courses—**Law and Government:** Laws, legal codes, court procedures, precedents, government regulations, executive orders, agency rules, and the democratic political process. **Personnel and Human Resources:** Principles and procedures for personnel recruitment; selection; training; compensation and benefits; labor relations and negotiation; and personnel information systems. **Clerical Studies:** Administrative and clerical procedures and systems such as word-processing systems, filing and records management systems, stenography and transcription, forms, design principles, and other office procedures and terminology. **English Language:** The structure and content of the English language, including the meaning and spelling of words, rules of composition, and grammar. **Customer and Personal Service:** Principles and processes for providing customer and personal services, including needs assessment techniques, quality service standards, alternative delivery systems, and customer satisfaction evaluation techniques. **Administration and Management:** Principles and processes involved in business and organizational planning, coordination, and execution. This includes strategic planning, resource allocation, manpower modeling, leadership techniques, and production methods.

Work Environment: Indoors; sitting; repetitive motions.

Excavating and Loading Machine and Dragline Operators

* Education/Training Required: Moderate-term on-the-job training
* Annual Earnings: $34,050
* Beginning Wage: $23,140
* Earnings Growth Potential: Low
* Growth: 8.3%
* Annual Job Openings: 6,562
* Self-Employed: 14.9%
* Part-Time: 3.2%

Operate or tend machinery equipped with scoops, shovels, or buckets to excavate and load loose materials. Move levers, depress foot pedals, and turn dials to operate power machinery such as power shovels, stripping-shovels, scraper loaders, or backhoes. Set up and inspect equipment prior to operation. Observe hand signals, grade stakes, and other markings when operating machines so that work can be performed to specifications. Become familiar with digging plans, machine capabilities and limitations, and with efficient and safe digging procedures in a given application. Operate machinery to perform activities such as backfilling excavations, vibrating or breaking rock or concrete, and making winter roads. Lubricate, adjust, and repair machinery, and replace parts such as gears, bearings, and bucket teeth. Create and maintain inclines and ramps, and handle slides, mud, and pit cleanings and maintenance. Move materials over short distances such as around a construction site, factory, or warehouse. Measure and verify levels of rock or gravel, bases, and other excavated material. Receive written or oral instructions regarding material movement or excavation. Adjust dig face angles for varying overburden depths and set lengths. Drive machines to work sites. Perform manual labor to prepare or finish sites, such as shoveling materials by hand. Direct ground workers engaged in activities such as moving stakes or markers or changing positions of towers. Direct workers engaged in placing blocks and outriggers in order to prevent capsizing of machines when lifting heavy loads.

Personality Type: Realistic. These occupations frequently involve work activities that include practical, hands-on problems and solutions. They often deal with plants; animals; and real-world materials such as wood, tools, and machinery. Many of the occupations require working outside and don't involve a lot of paperwork or working closely with others.

GOE—Interest Area/Cluster: 01. Agriculture and Natural Resources. **Work Group:** 01.08. Mining and Drilling. **Other Jobs in This Work Group:** Continuous Mining Machine Operators; Derrick Operators, Oil and Gas; Earth Drillers, Except Oil and Gas; Explosives Workers, Ordnance Handling Experts, and Blasters; Helpers—Extraction Workers; Loading Machine Operators, Underground Mining; Mine Cutting and Channeling Machine Operators; Rock Splitters, Quarry; Roof Bolters, Mining; Rotary Drill Operators, Oil and Gas; Roustabouts, Oil and Gas; Service Unit Operators, Oil, Gas, and Mining; Shuttle Car Operators; Wellhead Pumpers.

Skills—Repairing: Repairing machines or systems, using the needed tools. **Equipment Maintenance:** Performing routine maintenance and determining when and what kind of maintenance is needed. **Operation and Control:** Controlling operations of equipment or systems. **Operation Monitoring:** Watching gauges, dials, or other indicators to make sure a machine is working properly. **Installation:** Installing equipment, machines, wiring, or programs to meet specifications. **Equipment Selection:** Determining the kind of tools and equipment needed to do a job. **Systems Analysis:** Determining how a system should work and how changes will affect outcomes. **Technology Design:** Generating or adapting equipment and technology to serve user needs.

Education and Training Program: Construction/Heavy Equipment/Earthmoving Equipment Operation. **Related Knowledge/Courses—Building and Construction:** Materials, methods, and the appropriate tools to construct objects, structures, and buildings. **Mechanical Devices:** Machines and tools, including their designs, uses, benefits, repair, and maintenance. **Transportation:** Principles and methods for moving people or goods by air, rail, sea, or road, including their relative costs, advantages, and limitations. **Production and Processing:** Inputs, outputs, raw materials, waste, quality control, costs, and techniques for maximizing the manufacture and distribution of goods. **Public Safety and Security:** Weaponry; public safety; security operations, rules, regulations, precautions, and prevention; and the protection of people, data, and property. **Engineering and Technology:** Equipment, tools, and mechanical devices and their uses to produce motion, light, power, technology, and other applications.

Work Environment: Outdoors; noisy; contaminants; whole-body vibration; sitting; using hands on objects, tools, or controls.

Executive Secretaries and Administrative Assistants

- ❋ Education/Training Required: Work experience in a related occupation
- ❋ Annual Earnings: $38,640
- ❋ Beginning Wage: $26,060
- ❋ Earnings Growth Potential: Low
- ❋ Growth: 14.8%
- ❋ Annual Job Openings: 235,314
- ❋ Self-Employed: 1.4%
- ❋ Part-Time: 18.9%

Provide high-level administrative support by conducting research; preparing statistical reports; handling information requests; and performing clerical functions such as preparing correspondence, receiving visitors, arranging conference calls, and scheduling meetings. May also train and supervise lower-level clerical staff. Manage and maintain executives' schedules. Prepare invoices, reports, memos, letters, financial statements, and other documents, using word-processing, spreadsheet, database, or presentation software. Open, sort, and distribute incoming correspondence, including faxes and e-mail. Read and analyze incoming memos, submissions, and reports to determine their significance and plan their distribution. File and retrieve corporate documents, records, and reports. Greet visitors and determine whether they should be given access to specific individuals. Prepare responses to correspondence containing routine inquiries. Perform general office duties such as ordering supplies, maintaining records management systems, and performing basic bookkeeping work. Prepare agendas and make arrangements for committee, board, and other meetings. Make travel arrangements for executives. Conduct research, compile data, and prepare papers for consideration and presentation by executives, committees, and boards of directors. Compile, transcribe, and distribute minutes of meetings. Attend meetings to record minutes. Coordinate and direct office services, such as records and budget preparation, personnel, and housekeeping, to aid executives. Meet with individuals, special-interest groups, and others on behalf of executives, committees, and boards of directors. Set up and oversee administrative policies and procedures for offices or organizations. Supervise and train other clerical staff. Review operating practices and procedures to determine whether improvements can be made in areas such as workflow, reporting procedures, or expenditures. Interpret administrative and operating policies and procedures for employees.

Personality Type: Conventional. These occupations frequently involve following set procedures and routines and can include working with data and details more than with ideas. Usually there is a clear line of authority to follow.

GOE—Interest Area/Cluster: 04. Business and Administration. **Work Group:** 04.04. Secretarial Support. **Other Jobs in This Work Group:** Legal Secretaries; Medical Secretaries; Secretaries, Except Legal, Medical, and Executive.

Skills—Writing: Communicating effectively with others in writing as indicated by the needs of the audience. **Active**

Listening: Listening to what other people are saying and asking questions as appropriate. **Speaking:** Talking to others to effectively convey information. **Management of Financial Resources:** Determining how money will be spent to get the work done and accounting for these expenditures.

Education and Training Programs: Administrative Assistant and Secretarial Science, General; Executive Assistant/Executive Secretary Training; Medical Administrative/Executive Assistant and Medical Secretary Training. **Related Knowledge/Courses—Clerical Studies:** Administrative and clerical procedures and systems such as word-processing systems, filing and records management systems, stenography and transcription, forms, design principles, and other office procedures and terminology. **Customer and Personal Service:** Principles and processes for providing customer and personal services, including needs assessment techniques, quality service standards, alternative delivery systems, and customer satisfaction evaluation techniques. **English Language:** The structure and content of the English language, including the meaning and spelling of words, rules of composition, and grammar. **Computers and Electronics:** Electric circuit boards, processors, chips, and computer hardware and software, including applications and programming. **Communications and Media:** Media production, communication, and dissemination techniques and methods, including alternative ways to inform and entertain via written, oral, and visual media. **Personnel and Human Resources:** Principles and procedures for personnel recruitment; selection; training; compensation and benefits; labor relations and negotiation; and personnel information systems.

Work Environment: Indoors; sitting; repetitive motions.

Farmers and Ranchers

- ❈ Education/Training Required: Long-term on-the-job training
- ❈ Annual Earnings: $33,360
- ❈ Beginning Wage: $21,230
- ❈ Earnings Growth Potential: Medium
- ❈ Growth: –8.5%
- ❈ Annual Job Openings: 129,552
- ❈ Self-Employed: 100.0%
- ❈ Part-Time: 18.8%

On an ownership or rental basis, operate farms, ranches, greenhouses, nurseries, timber tracts, or other agricultural production establishments that produce crops, horticultural specialties, livestock, poultry, finfish, shellfish, or animal specialties. May plant, cultivate, harvest, perform post-harvest activities on, and market crops and livestock; may hire, train, and supervise farm workers or supervise a farm labor contractor; may prepare cost, production, and other records. May maintain and operate machinery and perform physical work. Breed and raise stock such as cattle, poultry, and honeybees, using recognized breeding practices to ensure continued improvement in stock. Lubricate, adjust, and make minor repairs to farm equipment, using oilcans, grease guns, and hand tools. Assist in animal births, and care for newborn livestock. Assemble, position, and secure structures such as trellises, beehives, or fences, using hand tools. Operate dairy farms that produce bulk milk. Manage and oversee the day-to-day running of farms raising poultry or pigs for the production of meat and breeding stock. Maintain colonies of bees to produce honey and hive byproducts, pollinate crops, and/or produce queens and bees for sale. Keep hens in order to produce table eggs for eating or fertile eggs for breeding. Maintain financial, tax, production, and employee records. Maintain facilities such as fencing, water supplies, and outdoor housing and wind shelters. Hire, train, and direct workers engaged in planting, cultivating, irrigating, harvesting, and marketing crops, and in raising livestock. Grow out-of-season or early crops in greenhouses or cold-frame beds, or bud and graft plant stock. Herd cattle, using horses or all-terrain vehicles. Buy or sell futures contracts, or price products in advance of future sales so that risk is limited and/or profit is increased. Clean and disinfect buildings and yards, and remove manure. Transport grain to silos for storage, and burn or bale any straw that is left behind. Set up and operate farm machinery to cultivate, harvest, and haul crops. Select animals for market, and provide transportation of livestock to market. Select and purchase supplies and equipment such as seed, fertilizers, and farm machinery. Remove lower quality or older animals from herds and purchase other livestock to replace culled animals. Purchase and store livestock feed. Control the spread of disease and parasites in herds by using vaccination and medication and by separating sick animals. Clean, grade, and package crops for marketing. Clean and sanitize milking equipment, storage tanks, collection cups, and cows' udders, or ensure that procedures are followed to maintain sanitary conditions for handling of milk.

Personality Type: Realistic. These occupations frequently involve work activities that include practical, hands-on problems and solutions. They often deal with plants; animals; and real-world materials such as wood, tools, and machinery. Many of the occupations require working outside and don't involve a lot of paperwork or working closely with others.

GOE—Interest Area/Cluster: 01. Agriculture and Natural Resources. **Work Group:** 01.01. Managerial Work in Agriculture and Natural Resources. **Other Jobs in This Work Group:** Aquacultural Managers; Crop and Livestock Managers; Farm Labor Contractors; Farm, Ranch, and Other Agricultural Managers; First-Line Supervisors/Managers of Agricultural Crop and Horticultural Workers; First-Line Supervisors/Managers of Animal Husbandry and Animal Care Workers; First-Line Supervisors/Managers of Aquacultural Workers; First-Line Supervisors/Managers of Construction Trades and Extraction Workers; First-Line Supervisors/Managers of Farming, Fishing, and Forestry Workers; First-Line Supervisors/Managers of Landscaping, Lawn Service, and Groundskeeping Workers; First-Line Supervisors/Managers of Logging Workers; Nursery and Greenhouse Managers; Park Naturalists; Purchasing Agents and Buyers, Farm Products.

Skills—Repairing: Repairing machines or systems, using the needed tools. **Equipment Maintenance:** Performing routine maintenance and determining when and what kind of maintenance is needed. **Management of Financial Resources:** Determining how money will be spent to get the work done and accounting for these expenditures. **Installation:** Installing equipment, machines, wiring, or programs to meet specifications. **Operation Monitoring:** Watching gauges, dials, or other indicators to make sure a machine is working properly. **Operation and Control:** Controlling operations of equipment or systems. **Management of Material Resources:** Obtaining and seeing to the appropriate use of equipment, facilities, and materials needed to do certain work. **Troubleshooting:** Determining what is causing an operating error and deciding what to do about it.

Education and Training Programs: Agribusiness/Agricultural Business Operations; Agricultural Animal Breeding; Agricultural Business and Management, General;

Agronomy and Crop Science; Animal Nutrition; Animal Sciences, General; Aquaculture; Crop Production; Dairy Science; Farm/Farm and Ranch Management; Greenhouse Operations and Management; Horticultural Science; Livestock Management; Ornamental Horticulture; Plant Nursery Operations and Management; Poultry Science; Range Science and Management; others. **Related Knowledge/Courses—Food Production:** Techniques and equipment for planting, growing, and harvesting of food for consumption, including crop-rotation methods, animal husbandry, and food storage/handling techniques. **Building and Construction:** Materials, methods, and the appropriate tools to construct objects, structures, and buildings. **Biology:** Plant and animal living tissue, cells, organisms, and entities, including their functions, interdependencies, and interactions with each other and the environment. **Mechanical Devices:** Machines and tools, including their designs, uses, benefits, repair, and maintenance. **Sales and Marketing:** Principles and methods involved in showing, promoting, and selling products or services. This includes marketing strategies and tactics, product demonstration and sales techniques, and sales control systems. **Economics and Accounting:** Economic and accounting principles and practices, the financial markets, banking, and the analysis and reporting of financial data.

Work Environment: Outdoors; noisy; very hot or cold; contaminants; hazardous equipment; using hands on objects, tools, or controls.

Fashion Designers

- ❊ Education/Training Required: Associate degree
- ❊ Annual Earnings: $62,810
- ❊ Beginning Wage: $31,340
- ❊ Earnings Growth Potential: Very high
- ❊ Growth: 5.0%
- ❊ Annual Job Openings: 1,968
- ❊ Self-Employed: 23.6%
- ❊ Part-Time: 16.7%

Design clothing and accessories. Create original garments or design garments that follow well-established fashion trends. May develop the line of color and kinds of materials. Examine sample garments on and off models;

then modify designs to achieve desired effects. Determine prices for styles. Select materials and production techniques to be used for products. Draw patterns for articles designed; then cut patterns, and cut material according to patterns, using measuring instruments and scissors. Design custom clothing and accessories for individuals, retailers, or theatrical, television, or film productions. Attend fashion shows and review garment magazines and manuals in order to gather information about fashion trends and consumer preferences. Develop a group of products and/or accessories, and market them through venues such as boutiques or mail-order catalogs. Test fabrics or oversee testing so that garment care labels can be created. Visit textile showrooms to keep up-to-date on the latest fabrics. Sew together sections of material to form mockups or samples of garments or articles, using sewing equipment. Research the styles and periods of clothing needed for film or theatrical productions. Direct and coordinate workers involved in drawing and cutting patterns and constructing samples or finished garments. Purchase new or used clothing and accessory items as needed to complete designs. Provide sample garments to agents and sales representatives, and arrange for showings of sample garments at sales meetings or fashion shows. Identify target markets for designs, looking at factors such as age, gender, and socioeconomic status. Read scripts and consult directors and other production staff in order to develop design concepts and plan productions. Confer with sales and management executives or with clients in order to discuss design ideas. Collaborate with other designers to coordinate special products and designs. Sketch rough and detailed drawings of apparel or accessories, and write specifications such as color schemes, construction, material types, and accessory requirements. Adapt other designers' ideas for the mass market.

Personality Type: Artistic. These occupations frequently involve working with forms, designs, and patterns. They often require self-expression, and the work can be done without following a clear set of rules.

GOE—Interest Area/Cluster: 03. Arts and Communication. **Work Group:** 03.05. Design. **Other Jobs in This Work Group:** Commercial and Industrial Designers; Floral Designers; Graphic Designers; Interior Designers; Merchandise Displayers and Window Trimmers; Set and Exhibit Designers.

Skills—Technology Design: Generating or adapting equipment and technology to serve user needs. **Operations Analysis:** Analyzing needs and product requirements to create a design. **Quality Control Analysis:** Evaluating the quality or performance of products, services, or processes. **Negotiation:** Bringing others together and trying to reconcile differences. **Time Management:** Managing one's own time and the time of others. **Systems Evaluation:** Looking at many indicators of system performance and taking into account their accuracy. **Mathematics:** Using mathematics to solve problems. **Active Learning:** Working with new material or information to grasp its implications.

Education and Training Programs: Apparel and Textile Manufacture; Fashion and Fabric Consultant; Fashion/Apparel Design; Textile Science. **Related Knowledge/Courses—Fine Arts:** Theory and techniques required to produce, compose, and perform works of music, dance, visual arts, drama, and sculpture. **Design:** Design techniques, principles, tools, and instruments involved in the production and use of precision technical plans, blueprints, drawings, and models. **Sales and Marketing:** Principles and methods involved in showing, promoting, and selling products or services. This includes marketing strategies and tactics, product demonstration and sales techniques, and sales control systems. **Production and Processing:** Inputs, outputs, raw materials, waste, quality control, costs, and techniques for maximizing the manufacture and distribution of goods. **Communications and Media:** Media production, communication, and dissemination techniques and methods, including alternative ways to inform and entertain via written, oral, and visual media. **Administration and Management:** Principles and processes involved in business and organizational planning, coordination, and execution. This includes strategic planning, resource allocation, manpower modeling, leadership techniques, and production methods.

Work Environment: Indoors; noisy; cramped work space, awkward positions; sitting; using hands on objects, tools, or controls; repetitive motions.

Fine Artists, Including Painters, Sculptors, and Illustrators

- ❀ Education/Training Required: Long-term on-the-job training
- ❀ Annual Earnings: $42,070
- ❀ Beginning Wage: $18,650
- ❀ Earnings Growth Potential: Very high
- ❀ Growth: 9.9%
- ❀ Annual Job Openings: 3,830
- ❀ Self-Employed: 62.6%
- ❀ Part-Time: 22.5%

Create original artwork, using any of a wide variety of mediums and techniques such as painting and sculpture. Use materials such as pens and ink, watercolors, charcoal, oil, or computer software to create artwork. Integrate and develop visual elements such as line, space, mass, color, and perspective, in order to produce desired effects such as the illustration of ideas, emotions, or moods. Confer with clients, editors, writers, art directors, and other interested parties regarding the nature and content of artwork to be produced. Submit preliminary or finished artwork or project plans to clients for approval, incorporating changes as necessary. Maintain portfolios of artistic work to demonstrate styles, interests, and abilities. Create finished artwork as decoration or to elucidate or substitute for spoken or written messages. Cut, bend, laminate, arrange, and fasten individual or mixed raw and manufactured materials and products to form works of art. Monitor events, trends, and other circumstances, research specific subject areas, attend art exhibitions, and read art publications in order to develop ideas and keep current on art world activities. Study different techniques to learn how to apply them to artistic endeavors. Render drawings, illustrations, and sketches of buildings, manufactured products, or models, working from sketches, blueprints, memory, models, or reference materials. Create sculptures, statues, and other three-dimensional artwork by using abrasives and tools to shape, carve, and fabricate materials such as clay, stone, wood, or metal. Create sketches, profiles, or likenesses of posed subjects or photographs, using any combination of freehand drawing, mechanical assembly kits, and computer imaging. Develop project budgets for approval, estimating time lines and material costs. Study styles, techniques, colors, textures, and materials used in works

undergoing restoration to ensure consistency during the restoration process. Shade and fill in sketch outlines and backgrounds, using a variety of media such as water colors, markers, and transparent washes, labeling designated colors when necessary. Collaborate with engineers, mechanics, and other technical experts as necessary to build and install creations.

Personality Type: Artistic. These occupations frequently involve working with forms, designs, and patterns. They often require self-expression, and the work can be done without following a clear set of rules.

GOE—Interest Area/Cluster: 03. Arts and Communication. **Work Group:** 03.04. Studio Art. **Other Jobs in This Work Group:** Craft Artists; Potters, Manufacturing.

Skills—Management of Financial Resources: Determining how money will be spent to get the work done and accounting for these expenditures. **Equipment Selection:** Determining the kind of tools and equipment needed to do a job. **Operations Analysis:** Analyzing needs and product requirements to create a design. **Repairing:** Repairing machines or systems, using the needed tools. **Equipment Maintenance:** Performing routine maintenance and determining when and what kind of maintenance is needed. **Installation:** Installing equipment, machines, wiring, or programs to meet specifications. **Complex Problem Solving:** Identifying complex problems, reviewing the options, and implementing solutions. **Mathematics:** Using mathematics to solve problems.

Education and Training Programs: Art/Art Studies, General; Drawing; Fine Arts and Art Studies, Other; Fine/Studio Arts, General; Painting; Visual and Performing Arts, General. **Related Knowledge/Courses—Fine Arts:** Theory and techniques required to produce, compose, and perform works of music, dance, visual arts, drama, and sculpture. **Design:** Design techniques, principles, tools, and instruments involved in the production and use of precision technical plans, blueprints, drawings, and models. **Sales and Marketing:** Principles and methods involved in showing, promoting, and selling products or services. This includes marketing strategies and tactics, product demonstration and sales techniques, and sales control systems. **Production and Processing:** Inputs, outputs, raw materials, waste, quality control, costs, and techniques for maximizing the manufacture and distribution of goods. **Economics and Accounting:** Economic and accounting principles and practices, the financial markets, banking, and the analysis and reporting of financial data. **Communications and Media:** Media production, communication, and dissemination techniques and methods, including alternative ways to inform and entertain via written, oral, and visual media.

Work Environment: Indoors; contaminants; standing; using hands on objects, tools, or controls; repetitive motions.

Fire Inspectors

- ❋ Education/Training Required: Work experience in a related occupation
- ❋ Annual Earnings: $50,830
- ❋ Beginning Wage: $31,170
- ❋ Earnings Growth Potential: Medium
- ❋ Growth: 11.0%
- ❋ Annual Job Openings: 644
- ❋ Self-Employed: 0.0%
- ❋ Part-Time: 2.2%

The job openings listed here are shared with Fire Investigators.

Inspect buildings and equipment to detect fire hazards and enforce state and local regulations. Inspect buildings to locate hazardous conditions and fire code violations such as accumulations of combustible material, electrical wiring problems, and inadequate or non-functional fire exits. Identify corrective actions necessary to bring properties into compliance with applicable fire codes, laws, regulations, and standards and explain these measures to property owners or their representatives. Conduct inspections and acceptance testing of newly installed fire protection systems. Inspect and test fire protection or fire detection systems to verify that such systems are installed in accordance with appropriate laws, codes, ordinances, regulations, and standards. Conduct fire code compliance follow-ups to ensure that corrective actions have been taken in cases where violations were found. Inspect properties that store, handle, and use hazardous materials to ensure compliance with laws, codes, and regulations; issue hazardous materials permits to facilities found in compliance. Write detailed reports of fire inspections performed, fire code violations observed, and corrective recommendations offered. Review blueprints and plans for new or remodeled buildings to ensure the structures meet fire safety codes. Develop or review fire exit plans. Attend training classes to maintain current knowledge of fire prevention, safety, and firefighting procedures. Present and explain fire code requirements and fire prevention information to architects, contractors, attorneys, engineers, developers, fire service personnel, and the general public. Conduct fire exit drills to monitor and evaluate evacuation procedures. Inspect liquefied petroleum installations, storage containers, and transportation and delivery systems for compliance with fire laws. Search for clues as to the cause of a fire after the fire is completely extinguished. Develop and coordinate fire prevention programs such as false alarm billing, fire inspection reporting, and hazardous materials management. Testify in court regarding fire code and fire safety issues. Recommend changes to fire prevention, inspection, and fire code endorsement procedures.

Personality Type: Conventional. These occupations frequently involve following set procedures and routines and can include working with data and details more than with ideas. Usually there is a clear line of authority to follow.

GOE—Interest Area/Cluster: 07. Government and Public Administration. **Work Group:** 07.03. Regulations Enforcement. **Other Jobs in This Work Group:** Agricultural Inspectors; Aviation Inspectors; Compliance Officers, Except Agriculture, Construction, Health and Safety, and Transportation; Construction and Building Inspectors; Environmental Compliance Inspectors; Equal Opportunity Representatives and Officers; Financial Examiners; Fish and Game Wardens; Forest Fire Inspectors and Prevention Specialists; Freight and Cargo Inspectors; Government Property Inspectors and Investigators; Immigration and Customs Inspectors; Licensing Examiners and Inspectors; Nuclear Monitoring Technicians; Occupational Health and Safety Specialists; Occupational Health and Safety Technicians; Tax Examiners, Collectors, and Revenue Agents; Transportation Vehicle, Equipment, and Systems Inspectors, Except Aviation.

Skills—Science: Using scientific methods to solve problems. **Persuasion:** Persuading others to approach things differently. **Operations Analysis:** Analyzing needs and product requirements to create a design. **Service Orientation:** Actively looking for ways to help people. **Negotiation:** Bringing others together and trying to reconcile differences. **Operation Monitoring:** Watching gauges, dials, or other indicators to make sure a machine is working properly. **Writing:** Communicating effectively with others in writing as indicated by the needs of the audience. **Complex Problem Solving:** Identifying complex problems, reviewing the options, and implementing solutions.

Education and Training Programs: Fire Protection and Safety Technology/Technician Training; Fire Science/Firefighting. **Related Knowledge/Courses—Building and Construction:** Materials, methods, and the appropriate tools to construct objects, structures, and buildings. **Public Safety and Security:** Weaponry; public safety; security operations, rules, regulations, precautions, and prevention; and the protection of people, data, and property. **Physics:** Physical principles, laws, and applications, including air, water, material dynamics, light, atomic principles, heat, electric theory, earth formations, and meteorological and related natural phenomena. **Customer and Personal Service:** Principles and processes for providing customer and personal services, including needs assessment techniques, quality service standards, alternative delivery systems, and customer satisfaction evaluation techniques. **Law and Government:** Laws, legal codes, court procedures, precedents, government regulations, executive orders, agency rules, and the democratic political process. **Design:** Design techniques, principles, tools, and instruments involved in the production and use of precision technical plans, blueprints, drawings, and models.

Work Environment: More often outdoors than indoors; noisy; very hot or cold; very bright or dim lighting; hazardous equipment.

Fire Investigators

- ❋ Education/Training Required: Work experience in a related occupation
- ❋ Annual Earnings: $50,830
- ❋ Beginning Wage: $31,170
- ❋ Earnings Growth Potential: Medium
- ❋ Growth: 11.0%
- ❋ Annual Job Openings: 644
- ❋ Self-Employed: 0.0%
- ❋ Part-Time: 2.2%

The job openings listed here are shared with Fire Inspectors.

Conduct investigations to determine causes of fires and explosions. Package collected pieces of evidence in securely closed containers such as bags, crates, or boxes to protect them. Examine fire sites and collect evidence such as glass, metal fragments, charred wood, and accelerant residue for use in determining the cause of a fire. Instruct children about the dangers of fire. Analyze evidence and other information to determine probable cause of fire or explosion. Photograph damage and evidence related to causes of fires or explosions to document investigation findings. Subpoena and interview witnesses, property owners, and building occupants to obtain information and sworn testimony. Swear out warrants and arrest and process suspected arsonists. Testify in court cases involving fires, suspected arson, and false alarms. Prepare and maintain reports of investigation results and records of convicted arsonists and arson suspects. Test sites and materials to establish facts such as burn patterns and flash points of materials, using test equipment. Conduct internal investigation to determine negligence and violation of laws and regulations by fire department employees. Dust evidence or portions of fire scenes for latent fingerprints.

Personality Type: Investigative. These occupations frequently involve working with ideas and require an extensive amount of thinking. They can involve searching for facts and figuring out problems mentally.

GOE—Interest Area/Cluster: 12. Law and Public Safety. **Work Group:** 12.04. Law Enforcement and Public Safety. **Other Jobs in This Work Group:** Bailiffs; Correctional Officers and Jailers; Criminal Investigators and Special Agents; Detectives and Criminal Investigators; Forensic Science Technicians; Parking Enforcement Workers; Police and Sheriff's Patrol Officers; Police Detectives; Police Identification and Records Officers; Police Patrol Officers; Sheriffs and Deputy Sheriffs; Transit and Railroad Police.

Skills—Science: Using scientific methods to solve problems. **Equipment Maintenance:** Performing routine maintenance and determining when and what kind of maintenance is needed. **Management of Personnel Resources:** Motivating, developing, and directing people as they work; identifying the best people for the job. **Operation and Control:** Controlling operations of equipment or systems. **Equipment Selection:** Determining the kind of tools and equipment needed to do a job. **Repairing:** Repairing machines or systems, using the needed tools. **Judgment and Decision Making:** Weighing the relative costs and benefits of a potential action. **Operations Analysis:** Analyzing needs and product requirements to create a design.

Education and Training Programs: Fire Protection and Safety Technology/Technician Training; Fire Science/Firefighting. **Related Knowledge/Courses—Building and Construction:** Materials, methods, and the appropriate tools to construct objects, structures, and buildings. **Public Safety and Security:** Weaponry; public safety; security operations, rules, regulations, precautions, and prevention; and the protection of people, data, and property. **Physics:** Physical principles, laws, and applications, including air, water, material dynamics, light, atomic principles, heat, electric theory, earth formations, and meteorological and related natural phenomena. **Chemistry:** The composition, structure, and properties of substances and of the chemical processes and transformations that they undergo. This includes uses of chemicals and their interactions, danger signs, production techniques, and disposal methods. **Mechanical Devices:** Machines and tools, including their designs, uses, benefits, repair, and maintenance. **Law and Government:** Laws, legal codes, court procedures, precedents, government regulations, executive orders, agency rules, and the democratic political process.

Work Environment: Indoors; noisy; contaminants; hazardous conditions; hazardous equipment; using hands on objects, tools, or controls.

First-Line Supervisors/Managers of Agricultural Crop and Horticultural Workers

- ❋ Education/Training Required: Associate degree
- ❋ Annual Earnings: $38,510
- ❋ Beginning Wage: $20,540
- ❋ Earnings Growth Potential: High
- ❋ Growth: –0.4%
- ❋ Annual Job Openings: 11,898
- ❋ Self-Employed: 24.8%
- ❋ Part-Time: 7.2%

The job openings listed here are shared with Farm Labor Contractors, with First-Line Supervisors/Managers of Animal Husbandry and Animal Care Workers, with First-Line Supervisors/Managers of Aquacultural Workers, and with First-Line Supervisors/Managers of Logging Workers.

Directly supervise and coordinate activities of agricultural crop or horticultural workers. Prepare and maintain time and payroll reports, as well as details of personnel actions such as performance evaluations, hires, promotions, and disciplinary actions. Monitor and oversee construction projects such as horticultural buildings and irrigation systems. Calculate and monitor budgets for maintenance and development of collections, grounds, and infrastructure. Perform hardscape activities, including installation and repair of irrigation systems, resurfacing and grading of paths, rockwork, or erosion control. Prepare reports regarding farm conditions, crop yields, machinery breakdowns, or labor problems. Requisition and purchase supplies such as insecticides, machine parts or lubricants, and tools. Investigate grievances and settle disputes to maintain harmony among workers. Issue equipment such as farm implements, machinery, ladders, or containers to workers and collect equipment when work is complete. Confer with managers to evaluate weather and soil conditions, to develop plans and procedures, and to discuss issues such as changes in fertilizers, herbicides, or cultivating techniques. Estimate labor requirements for jobs and plan work schedules accordingly. Inspect crops, fields, and plant stock to determine conditions and need for cultivating, spraying, weeding, or harvesting. Observe workers to detect inefficient and unsafe work procedures or to identify problems, initiating corrective action as necessary. Assign duties such as cultivation, irrigation, and harvesting of crops or plants; product packaging and grading; and equipment maintenance. Recruit, hire, and discharge workers. Read inventory records, customer orders, and shipping schedules to determine required activities. Review employees' work to evaluate quality and quantity. Train workers in techniques such as planting, harvesting, weeding, and insect identification and in the use of safety measures. Arrange for transportation, equipment, and living quarters for seasonal workers. Contract with seasonal workers and farmers to provide employment. Direct or assist with the adjustment and repair of farm equipment and machinery.

Personality Type: Realistic. These occupations frequently involve work activities that include practical, hands-on problems and solutions. They often deal with plants; animals; and real-world materials such as wood, tools, and machinery. Many of the occupations require working outside and don't involve a lot of paperwork or working closely with others.

GOE—Interest Area/Cluster: 01. Agriculture and Natural Resources. **Work Group:** 01.01. Managerial Work in Agriculture and Natural Resources. **Other Jobs in This Work Group:** Aquacultural Managers; Crop and Livestock Managers; Farm Labor Contractors; Farm, Ranch, and Other Agricultural Managers; Farmers and Ranchers; First-Line Supervisors/Managers of Animal Husbandry and Animal Care Workers; First-Line Supervisors/Managers of Aquacultural Workers; First-Line Supervisors/Managers of Construction Trades and Extraction Workers; First-Line Supervisors/Managers of Farming, Fishing, and Forestry Workers; First-Line Supervisors/Managers of Landscaping, Lawn Service, and Groundskeeping Workers; First-Line Supervisors/Managers of Logging Workers; Nursery and Greenhouse Managers; Park Naturalists; Purchasing Agents and Buyers, Farm Products.

Skills—Management of Personnel Resources: Motivating, developing, and directing people as they work; identifying the best people for the job. **Repairing:** Repairing machines or systems, using the needed tools. **Equipment Maintenance:** Performing routine maintenance and determining when and what kind of maintenance is needed. **Operation Monitoring:** Watching gauges, dials, or other indicators to make sure a machine is working properly. **Management of Financial Resources:** Determining how money will be spent to get the work done and accounting for these expenditures. **Management of Material Resources:** Obtaining and seeing to the appropriate use of equipment, facilities, and materials needed to do certain work. **Operation and Control:** Controlling operations of equipment or systems. **Installation:** Installing equipment, machines, wiring, or programs to meet specifications.

Education and Training Programs: Agricultural Business and Management, Other; Agricultural Production Operations, General; Agricultural Production Operations, Other; Agriculture, Agriculture Operations, and Related Sciences, Other; Agronomy and Crop Science; Crop Production; Farm/Farm and Ranch Management; Plant Sciences, General; Range Science and Management. **Related Knowledge/Courses—Food Production:** Techniques and equipment for planting, growing, and harvesting of food for consumption, including crop-rotation methods, animal husbandry, and food storage/handling techniques.

Mechanical Devices: Machines and tools, including their designs, uses, benefits, repair, and maintenance. **Foreign Language:** The structure and content of a foreign (non-English) language, including the meaning and spelling of words, rules of composition and grammar, and pronunciation. **Production and Processing:** Inputs, outputs, raw materials, waste, quality control, costs, and techniques for maximizing the manufacture and distribution of goods. **Personnel and Human Resources:** Principles and procedures for personnel recruitment; selection; training; compensation and benefits; labor relations and negotiation; and personnel information systems. **Education and Training:** Instructional methods and training techniques, including curriculum design principles, learning theory, group and individual teaching techniques, design of individual development plans, and test design principles.

Work Environment: More often outdoors than indoors; noisy; very hot or cold; contaminants; using hands on objects, tools, or controls.

First-Line Supervisors/Managers of Animal Husbandry and Animal Care Workers

- ❋ Education/Training Required: Associate degree
- ❋ Annual Earnings: $38,510
- ❋ Beginning Wage: $20,540
- ❋ Earnings Growth Potential: High
- ❋ Growth: –0.4%
- ❋ Annual Job Openings: 11,898
- ❋ Self-Employed: 24.8%
- ❋ Part-Time: 7.2%

The job openings listed here are shared with Farm Labor Contractors, with First-Line Supervisors/Managers of Agricultural Crop and Horticultural Workers, with First-Line Supervisors/Managers of Aquacultural Workers, and with First-Line Supervisors/Managers of Logging Workers.

Directly supervise and coordinate activities of animal husbandry or animal care workers. Study feed, weight, health, genetic, or milk production records in order to determine feed formulas and rations and breeding schedules. Inspect buildings, fences, fields or ranges, supplies, and equipment in order to determine work to be performed. Monitor animal care, maintenance, breeding, or packing and transfer activities to ensure work is done correctly. Train workers in animal care procedures, maintenance duties, and safety precautions. Perform the same animal care duties as subordinates. Observe animals for signs of illness, injury, or unusual behavior, notifying veterinarians or managers as warranted. Plan budgets and arrange for purchase of animals, feed, or supplies. Direct and assist workers in maintenance and repair of facilities. Recruit, hire, and pay workers. Confer with managers to determine production requirements, conditions of equipment and supplies, and work schedules. Transport or arrange for transport of animals, equipment, food, animal feed, and other supplies to and from worksites. Treat animal illnesses or injuries, following experience or instructions of veterinarians. Inseminate livestock artificially to produce desired offspring. Investigate complaints of animal neglect or cruelty and follow up on complaints appearing to require prosecution. Monitor eggs and adjust incubator thermometers and gauges to facilitate hatching progress and to maintain specified conditions. Operate euthanasia equipment to destroy animals. Prepare reports concerning facility activities, employees' time records, and animal treatment. Assign tasks such as feeding and treatment of animals and cleaning and maintenance of animal quarters. Establish work schedules and procedures.

Personality Type: Enterprising. These occupations frequently involve starting up and carrying out projects and can involve leading people and making many decisions. They sometimes require risk taking and often deal with business.

GOE—Interest Area/Cluster: 01. Agriculture and Natural Resources. **Work Group:** 01.01. Managerial Work in Agriculture and Natural Resources. **Other Jobs in This Work Group:** Aquacultural Managers; Crop and Livestock Managers; Farm Labor Contractors; Farm, Ranch, and Other Agricultural Managers; Farmers and Ranchers; First-Line Supervisors/Managers of Agricultural Crop and Horticultural Workers; First-Line Supervisors/Managers of Aquacultural Workers; First-Line Supervisors/Managers of Construction Trades and Extraction Workers; First-Line Supervisors/Managers of Farming, Fishing, and Forestry Workers; First-Line Supervisors/Managers of Landscaping, Lawn Service, and Groundskeeping Workers; First-Line Supervisors/Managers of Logging Workers; Nursery and Greenhouse Managers; Park Naturalists; Purchasing Agents and Buyers, Farm Products.

Skills—Repairing: Repairing machines or systems, using the needed tools. **Management of Financial Resources:** Determining how money will be spent to get the work done and accounting for these expenditures. **Operation Monitoring:** Watching gauges, dials, or other indicators to make sure a machine is working properly. **Monitoring:** Assessing how well one is doing when learning or doing something. **Equipment Maintenance:** Performing routine maintenance and determining when and what kind of maintenance is needed. **Troubleshooting:** Determining what is causing an operating error and deciding what to do about it. **Science:** Using scientific methods to solve problems. **Management of Personnel Resources:** Motivating, developing, and directing people as they work; identifying the best people for the job.

Education and Training Programs: Agricultural Animal Breeding; Agriculture, Agriculture Operations, and Related Sciences, Other; Animal Nutrition; Animal Sciences, General; Animal/Livestock Husbandry and Production; Dairy Husbandry and Production; Dairy Science; Horse Husbandry/Equine Science and Management; Livestock Management; Poultry Science. **Related Knowledge/Courses—Food Production:** Techniques and equipment for planting, growing, and harvesting of food for consumption, including crop-rotation methods, animal husbandry, and food storage/handling techniques. **Biology:** Plant and animal living tissue, cells, organisms, and entities, including their functions, interdependencies, and interactions with each other and the environment. **Chemistry:** The composition, structure, and properties of substances and of the chemical processes and transformations that they undergo. This includes uses of chemicals and their interactions, danger signs, production techniques, and disposal methods. **Mechanical Devices:** Machines and tools, including their designs, uses, benefits, repair, and maintenance. **Transportation:** Principles and methods for moving people or goods by air, rail, sea, or road, including their relative costs, advantages, and limitations. **Personnel and Human Resources:** Principles and procedures for personnel recruitment; selection; training; compensation and benefits; labor relations and negotiation; and personnel information systems.

Work Environment: Outdoors; very hot or cold; contaminants; minor burns, cuts, bites, or stings; standing; walking and running.

First-Line Supervisors/Managers of Aquacultural Workers

❋ Education/Training Required: Associate degree
❋ Annual Earnings: $38,510
❋ Beginning Wage: $20,540
❋ Earnings Growth Potential: High
❋ Growth: –0.4%
❋ Annual Job Openings: 11,898
❋ Self-Employed: 24.8%
❋ Part-Time: 7.2%

The job openings listed here are shared with Farm Labor Contractors, with First-Line Supervisors/Managers of Agricultural Crop and Horticultural Workers, with First-Line Supervisors/Managers of Animal Husbandry and Animal Care Workers, and with First-Line Supervisors/Managers of Logging Workers.

Directly supervise and coordinate activities of aquacultural workers. Observe fish and beds or ponds to detect diseases, monitor fish growth, determine quality of fish, or determine completeness of harvesting. Record the numbers and types of fish or shellfish reared, harvested, released, sold, and shipped. Assign to workers duties such as fertilizing and incubating spawn; feeding and transferring fish; and planting, cultivating, and harvesting shellfish beds. Confer with managers to determine times and places of seed planting and cultivating, feeding, or harvesting of fish or shellfish. Direct and monitor worker activities such as treatment and rearing of fingerlings, maintenance of equipment, and harvesting of fish or shellfish. Prepare or direct the preparation of fish food and specify medications to be added to food and water to treat fish for diseases. Engage in the same fishery work as workers supervised. Train workers in spawning, rearing, cultivating, and harvesting methods and in the use of equipment. Direct workers to correct problems such as disease, quality of seed distribution, or adequacy of cultivation. Plan work schedules according to personnel and equipment availability, tidal levels, feeding schedules, or transfer and harvest needs. Interview and select new employees. Maintain workers' time records. Perform both supervisory and management functions, such as accounting, marketing, and personnel work. Requisition supplies. Supervise the artificial spawning of various salmon and trout species. Select and ship eggs to other hatcheries.

Personality Type: Enterprising. These occupations frequently involve starting up and carrying out projects and can involve leading people and making many decisions. They sometimes require risk taking and often deal with business.

GOE—Interest Area/Cluster: 01. Agriculture and Natural Resources. **Work Group:** 01.01. Managerial Work in Agriculture and Natural Resources. **Other Jobs in This Work Group:** Aquacultural Managers; Crop and Livestock Managers; Farm Labor Contractors; Farm, Ranch, and Other Agricultural Managers; Farmers and Ranchers; First-Line Supervisors/Managers of Agricultural Crop and Horticultural Workers; First-Line Supervisors/Managers of Animal Husbandry and Animal Care Workers; First-Line Supervisors/Managers of Construction Trades and Extraction Workers; First-Line Supervisors/Managers of Farming, Fishing, and Forestry Workers; First-Line Supervisors/Managers of Landscaping, Lawn Service, and Groundskeeping Workers; First-Line Supervisors/Managers of Logging Workers; Nursery and Greenhouse Managers; Park Naturalists; Purchasing Agents and Buyers, Farm Products.

Skills—Science: Using scientific methods to solve problems. **Management of Financial Resources:** Determining how money will be spent to get the work done and accounting for these expenditures. **Management of Personnel Resources:** Motivating, developing, and directing people as they work; identifying the best people for the job. **Management of Material Resources:** Obtaining and seeing to the appropriate use of equipment, facilities, and materials needed to do certain work. **Mathematics:** Using mathematics to solve problems. **Repairing:** Repairing machines or systems, using the needed tools. **Quality Control Analysis:** Evaluating the quality or performance of products, services, or processes. **Operations Analysis:** Analyzing needs and product requirements to create a design.

Education and Training Programs: Agricultural Business and Management, Other; Aquaculture; Fishing and Fisheries Sciences and Management. **Related Knowledge/ Courses—Biology:** Plant and animal living tissue, cells, organisms, and entities, including their functions, interdependencies, and interactions with each other and the environment. **Building and Construction:** Materials, methods, and the appropriate tools to construct objects, structures, and buildings. **Food Production:** Techniques and equipment for planting, growing, and harvesting of food for consumption, including crop-rotation methods, animal husbandry, and food storage/handling techniques. **Chemistry:** The composition, structure, and properties of substances and of the chemical processes and transformations that they undergo. This includes uses of chemicals and their interactions, danger signs, production techniques, and disposal methods. **Engineering and Technology:** Equipment, tools, and mechanical devices and their uses to produce motion, light, power, technology, and other applications. **Mechanical Devices:** Machines and tools, including their designs, uses, benefits, repair, and maintenance.

Work Environment: Outdoors; noisy; very hot or cold; contaminants; minor burns, cuts, bites, or stings; standing.

First-Line Supervisors/Managers of Construction Trades and Extraction Workers

* Education/Training Required: Work experience in a related occupation
* Annual Earnings: $55,950
* Beginning Wage: $34,870
* Earnings Growth Potential: Medium
* Growth: 9.1%
* Annual Job Openings: 82,923
* Self-Employed: 24.4%
* Part-Time: 3.0%

Directly supervise and coordinate activities of construction or extraction workers. Examine and inspect work progress, equipment, and construction sites to verify safety and to ensure that specifications are met. Read specifications such as blueprints to determine construction requirements and to plan procedures. Estimate material and worker requirements to complete jobs. Supervise, coordinate, and schedule the activities of construction or extractive workers. Confer with managerial and technical personnel, other departments, and contractors in order to resolve problems and to coordinate activities. Coordinate work activities with other construction project activities. Locate, measure, and mark site locations and placement of structures and equipment, using measuring and marking equipment. Order or requisition materials and supplies. Record information such as personnel, production, and operational data on specified forms and reports. Assign work to employees, based on material and worker requirements of specific jobs. Provide assistance to workers engaged in construction or extraction activities, using hand tools and equipment. Train workers in construction methods, operation of equipment, safety procedures, and company policies. Analyze worker and production problems and recommend solutions such as improving production methods or implementing motivational plans. Arrange for repairs of equipment and machinery. Suggest or initiate personnel actions such as promotions, transfers, and hires.

Personality Type: Enterprising. These occupations frequently involve starting up and carrying out projects and can involve leading people and making many decisions. They sometimes require risk taking and often deal with business.

GOE—Interest Area/Cluster: 01. Agriculture and Natural Resources. **Work Group:** 01.01. Managerial Work in Agriculture and Natural Resources. **Other Jobs in This Work Group:** Aquacultural Managers; Crop and Livestock Managers; Farm Labor Contractors; Farm, Ranch, and Other Agricultural Managers; Farmers and Ranchers; First-Line Supervisors/Managers of Agricultural Crop and Horticultural Workers; First-Line Supervisors/Managers of Animal Husbandry and Animal Care Workers; First-Line Supervisors/Managers of Aquacultural Workers; First-Line Supervisors/Managers of Farming, Fishing, and Forestry Workers; First-Line Supervisors/Managers of Landscaping, Lawn Service, and Groundskeeping Workers; First-Line Supervisors/Managers of Logging Workers; Nursery and Greenhouse Managers; Park Naturalists; Purchasing Agents and Buyers, Farm Products.

Skills—Management of Material Resources: Obtaining and seeing to the appropriate use of equipment, facilities, and materials needed to do certain work. **Installation:** Installing equipment, machines, wiring, or programs to meet specifications. **Equipment Maintenance:** Performing routine maintenance and determining when and what kind of maintenance is needed. **Repairing:** Repairing machines or systems, using the needed tools. **Coordination:** Adjusting actions in relation to others' actions. **Equipment Selection:** Determining the kind of tools and equipment needed to do a job. **Management of Personnel Resources:** Motivating, developing, and directing people as they work; identifying the best people for the job. **Mathematics:** Using mathematics to solve problems.

Education and Training Programs: Blasting/Blaster Training; Building/Construction Site Management/Manager Training; Building/Home/Construction Inspection/Inspector Training; Building/Property Maintenance and Management; Carpentry; Concrete Finishing; Drywall Installation; Electrical and Power Transmission Installation, General; Electrician Training; Glazier Training; Lineworker Training; Masonry; Painting; Plumbing Technology; Roofer Training; Well Drilling. **Related Knowledge/Courses—Building and Construction:** Materials, methods, and the appropriate tools to construct objects, structures, and buildings. **Mechanical Devices:** Machines and tools, including their designs, uses, benefits, repair, and maintenance. **Design:** Design techniques, principles, tools, and instruments involved in the production and use of precision technical plans, blueprints, drawings, and models. **Engineering and Technology:** Equipment, tools, and mechanical devices and their uses to produce motion, light, power, technology, and other applications. **Production and Processing:** Inputs, outputs, raw materials, waste, quality control, costs, and techniques for maximizing the manufacture and distribution of goods. **Administration and Management:** Principles and processes involved in business and organizational planning, coordination, and execution. This includes strategic planning, resource allocation, manpower modeling, leadership techniques, and production methods.

Work Environment: Outdoors; noisy; very hot or cold; contaminants; hazardous equipment; standing.

First-Line Supervisors/Managers of Correctional Officers

- ✸ Education/Training Required: Work experience in a related occupation
- ✸ Annual Earnings: $55,720
- ✸ Beginning Wage: $31,780
- ✸ Earnings Growth Potential: High
- ✸ Growth: 12.5%
- ✸ Annual Job Openings: 4,180
- ✸ Self-Employed: 0.0%
- ✸ Part-Time: 0.0%

Supervise and coordinate activities of correctional officers and jailers. Take, receive, and check periodic inmate counts. Maintain order, discipline, and security within assigned areas in accordance with relevant rules, regulations, policies, and laws. Respond to emergencies such as escapes. Maintain knowledge of, comply with, and enforce all institutional policies, rules, procedures, and regulations. Supervise and direct the work of correctional officers to ensure the safe custody, discipline, and welfare of inmates. Restrain, secure, and control offenders, using chemical agents, firearms, and other weapons of force as necessary. Supervise and perform searches of inmates and their quarters to locate contraband items. Monitor behavior of subordinates to ensure alert, courteous, and professional behavior toward inmates, parolees, fellow employees, visitors, and the public. Complete administrative paperwork and supervise the preparation and maintenance of records, forms, and reports. Instruct employees and provide on-the-job training. Conduct roll calls of correctional officers. Supervise activities such as searches, shakedowns, riot control, and institutional tours. Carry injured offenders or employees to safety and provide emergency first aid when necessary. Supervise and provide security for offenders performing tasks such as construction, maintenance, laundry, food service, and other industrial or agricultural operations. Develop work and security procedures. Set up employee work schedules. Resolve problems between inmates. Read and review offender information to identify issues that require special attention. Rate behavior of inmates, promoting acceptable attitudes and behaviors to those with low ratings. Transfer and transport offenders on foot or by driving vehicles such as trailers, vans, and buses. Examine incoming and outgoing mail to ensure conformance with regulations. Convey correctional officers' and inmates' complaints to superiors.

Personality Type: Enterprising. These occupations frequently involve starting up and carrying out projects and can involve leading people and making many decisions. They sometimes require risk taking and often deal with business.

GOE—Interest Area/Cluster: 12. Law and Public Safety. **Work Group:** 12.01. Managerial Work in Law and Public Safety. **Other Jobs in This Work Group:** Emergency Management Specialists; First-Line Supervisors/Managers of Fire Fighting and Prevention Workers; First-Line Supervisors/Managers of Police and Detectives; Forest Fire Fighting and Prevention Supervisors; Municipal Fire Fighting and Prevention Supervisors.

Skills—Social Perceptiveness: Being aware of others' reactions and understanding why they react the way they do. **Negotiation:** Bringing others together and trying to reconcile differences. **Management of Personnel Resources:** Motivating, developing, and directing people as they work; identifying the best people for the job. **Persuasion:** Persuading others to approach things differently. **Monitoring:** Assessing how well one is doing when learning or doing something. **Writing:** Communicating effectively with others in writing as indicated by the needs of the audience. **Service Orientation:** Actively looking for ways to help people. **Complex Problem Solving:** Identifying complex problems, reviewing the options, and implementing solutions.

Education and Training Programs: Corrections; Corrections Administration. **Related Knowledge/Courses—Public Safety and Security:** Weaponry; public safety; security operations, rules, regulations, precautions, and prevention; and the protection of people, data, and property. **Psychology:** Human behavior and performance, mental processes, psychological research methods, and the assessment and treatment of behavioral and affective disorders. **Therapy and Counseling:** Information and techniques needed to rehabilitate physical and mental ailments and to provide career guidance, including alternative treatments, rehabilitation equipment and its proper use, and methods to evaluate treatment effects. **Personnel and Human Resources:** Principles and procedures for personnel recruitment; selection; training; compensation and benefits; labor relations and negotiation; and personnel

information systems. **Clerical Studies:** Administrative and clerical procedures and systems such as word-processing systems, filing and records management systems, stenography and transcription, forms, design principles, and other office procedures and terminology. **Law and Government:** Laws, legal codes, court procedures, precedents, government regulations, executive orders, agency rules, and the democratic political process.

Work Environment: More often indoors than outdoors; noisy; very bright or dim lighting; contaminants; disease or infections.

First-Line Supervisors/Managers of Food Preparation and Serving Workers

* Education/Training Required: Work experience in a related occupation
* Annual Earnings: $28,040
* Beginning Wage: $17,920
* Earnings Growth Potential: Medium
* Growth: 11.3%
* Annual Job Openings: 154,175
* Self-Employed: 4.1%
* Part-Time: 14.5%

Supervise workers engaged in preparing and serving food. Compile and balance cash receipts at the end of the day or shift. Resolve customer complaints regarding food service. Inspect supplies, equipment, and work areas to ensure efficient service and conformance to standards. Train workers in food preparation and in service, sanitation, and safety procedures. Control inventories of food, equipment, smallware, and liquor and report shortages to designated personnel. Observe and evaluate workers and work procedures to ensure quality standards and service. Assign duties, responsibilities, and workstations to employees in accordance with work requirements. Estimate ingredients and supplies required to prepare a recipe. Perform personnel actions such as hiring and firing staff, consulting with other managers as necessary. Analyze operational problems, such as theft and wastage, and establish procedures to alleviate these problems. Specify food portions and courses, production and time sequences, and workstation and equipment arrangements. Recommend measures for improving work procedures and worker performance to increase service quality and enhance job safety. Greet and seat guests and present menus and wine lists. Present bills and accept payments. Forecast staff, equipment, and supply requirements based on a master menu. Record production and operational data on specified forms. Perform serving duties such as carving meat, preparing flambé dishes, or serving wine and liquor. Purchase or requisition supplies and equipment needed to ensure quality and timely delivery of services. Collaborate with other personnel to plan menus, serving arrangements, and related details. Supervise and check the assembly of regular and special diet trays and the delivery of food trolleys to hospital patients. Schedule parties and take reservations. Develop departmental objectives, budgets, policies, procedures, and strategies. Develop equipment maintenance schedules and arrange for repairs. Evaluate new products for usefulness and suitability.

Personality Type: Enterprising. These occupations frequently involve starting up and carrying out projects and can involve leading people and making many decisions. They sometimes require risk taking and often deal with business.

GOE—Interest Area/Cluster: 09. Hospitality, Tourism, and Recreation. **Work Group:** 09.01. Managerial Work in Hospitality and Tourism. **Other Jobs in This Work Group:** First-Line Supervisors/Managers of Personal Service Workers; Food Service Managers; Gaming Managers; Gaming Supervisors; Lodging Managers.

Skills—Equipment Maintenance: Performing routine maintenance and determining when and what kind of maintenance is needed. **Management of Financial Resources:** Determining how money will be spent to get the work done and accounting for these expenditures. **Management of Personnel Resources:** Motivating, developing, and directing people as they work; identifying the best people for the job. **Operation Monitoring:** Watching gauges, dials, or other indicators to make sure a machine is working properly. **Management of Material Resources:** Obtaining and seeing to the appropriate use of equipment, facilities, and materials needed to do certain work. **Monitoring:** Assessing how well one is doing when learning or doing something.

Education and Training Programs: Cooking and Related Culinary Arts, General; Foodservice Systems Administration/Management; Restaurant, Culinary, and Catering

Management/Manager Training. **Related Knowledge/Courses—Food Production:** Techniques and equipment for planting, growing, and harvesting of food for consumption, including crop-rotation methods, animal husbandry, and food storage/handling techniques. **Administration and Management:** Principles and processes involved in business and organizational planning, coordination, and execution. This includes strategic planning, resource allocation, manpower modeling, leadership techniques, and production methods. **Customer and Personal Service:** Principles and processes for providing customer and personal services, including needs assessment techniques, quality service standards, alternative delivery systems, and customer satisfaction evaluation techniques. **Economics and Accounting:** Economic and accounting principles and practices, the financial markets, banking, and the analysis and reporting of financial data. **Sales and Marketing:** Principles and methods involved in showing, promoting, and selling products or services. This includes marketing strategies and tactics, product demonstration and sales techniques, and sales control systems. **Production and Processing:** Inputs, outputs, raw materials, waste, quality control, costs, and techniques for maximizing the manufacture and distribution of goods.

Work Environment: Indoors; minor burns, cuts, bites, or stings; standing; walking and running; using hands on objects, tools, or controls; repetitive motions.

First-Line Supervisors/Managers of Helpers, Laborers, and Material Movers, Hand

* Education/Training Required: Work experience in a related occupation
* Annual Earnings: $40,640
* Beginning Wage: $25,430
* Earnings Growth Potential: Medium
* Growth: 12.5%
* Annual Job Openings: 13,877
* Self-Employed: 1.4%
* Part-Time: 5.3%

Supervise and coordinate the activities of helpers, laborers, or material movers. Plan work schedules and assign duties to maintain adequate staffing levels, to ensure that activities are performed effectively, and to respond to fluctuating workloads. Collaborate with workers and managers to solve work-related problems. Review work throughout the work process and at completion to ensure that it has been performed properly. Transmit and explain work orders to laborers. Check specifications of materials loaded or unloaded against information contained in work orders. Inform designated employees or departments of items loaded and problems encountered. Examine freight to determine loading sequences. Evaluate employee performance and prepare performance appraisals. Perform the same work duties as those whom they supervise or perform more difficult or skilled tasks or assist in their performance. Prepare and maintain work records and reports that include information such as employee time and wages, daily receipts, and inspection results. Counsel employees in work-related activities, personal growth, and career development. Conduct staff meetings to relay general information or to address specific topics such as safety. Inspect equipment for wear and for conformance to specifications. Resolve personnel problems, complaints, and formal grievances when possible or refer them to higher-level supervisors for resolution. Recommend or initiate personnel actions such as promotions, transfers, and disciplinary measures. Assess training needs of staff; then arrange for or provide appropriate instruction. Schedule times of shipment and modes of transportation for materials. Quote prices to customers. Estimate material, time, and staffing requirements for a given project based on work orders, job specifications, and experience. Provide assistance in balancing books; tracking, monitoring, and projecting a unit's budget needs; and developing unit policies and procedures. Inspect job sites to determine the extent of maintenance or repairs needed. Participate in the hiring process by reviewing credentials, conducting interviews, and making hiring decisions or recommendations.

Personality Type: Enterprising. These occupations frequently involve starting up and carrying out projects and can involve leading people and making many decisions. They sometimes require risk taking and often deal with business.

GOE—Interest Area/Cluster: 13. Manufacturing. **Work Group:** 13.01. Managerial Work in Manufacturing. **Other Jobs in This Work Group:** First-Line Supervisors/Managers of Mechanics, Installers, and Repairers; First-Line Supervisors/Managers of Production and Operating Workers; Industrial Production Managers.

Skills—Management of Personnel Resources: Motivating, developing, and directing people as they work; identifying the best people for the job. **Monitoring:** Assessing how well one is doing when learning or doing something. **Persuasion:** Persuading others to approach things differently. **Time Management:** Managing one's own time and the time of others. **Social Perceptiveness:** Being aware of others' reactions and understanding why they react the way they do. **Quality Control Analysis:** Evaluating the quality or performance of products, services, or processes. **Systems Evaluation:** Looking at many indicators of system performance and taking into account their accuracy. **Judgment and Decision Making:** Weighing the relative costs and benefits of a potential action.

Education and Training Programs: No related CIP programs; this job is learned through work experience in a related occupation. **Related Knowledge/Courses—Production and Processing:** Inputs, outputs, raw materials, waste, quality control, costs, and techniques for maximizing the manufacture and distribution of goods. **Transportation:** Principles and methods for moving people or goods by air, rail, sea, or road, including their relative costs, advantages, and limitations. **Personnel and Human Resources:** Principles and procedures for personnel recruitment; selection; training; compensation and benefits; labor relations and negotiation; and personnel information systems. **Administration and Management:** Principles and processes involved in business and organizational planning, coordination, and execution. This includes strategic planning, resource allocation, manpower modeling, leadership techniques, and production methods. **Public Safety and Security:** Weaponry; public safety; security operations, rules, regulations, precautions, and prevention; and the protection of people, data, and property. **Psychology:** Human behavior and performance, mental processes, psychological research methods, and the assessment and treatment of behavioral and affective disorders.

Work Environment: Indoors; noisy; very hot or cold; contaminants; standing; walking and running.

First-Line Supervisors/Managers of Housekeeping and Janitorial Workers

* Education/Training Required: Work experience in a related occupation
* Annual Earnings: $32,850
* Beginning Wage: $20,650
* Earnings Growth Potential: Medium
* Growth: 12.7%
* Annual Job Openings: 30,613
* Self-Employed: 30.7%
* Part-Time: 10.8%

Supervise work activities of cleaning personnel in hotels, hospitals, offices, and other establishments. Direct activities for stopping the spread of infections in facilities such as hospitals. Inspect work performed to ensure that it meets specifications and established standards. Plan and prepare employee work schedules. Perform or assist with cleaning duties as necessary. Investigate complaints about service and equipment and take corrective action. Coordinate activities with other departments to ensure that services are provided in an efficient and timely manner. Check equipment to ensure that it is in working order. Inspect and evaluate the physical condition of facilities to determine the type of work required. Select the most suitable cleaning materials for different types of linens, furniture, flooring, and surfaces. Instruct staff in work policies and procedures and the use and maintenance of equipment. Issue supplies and equipment to workers. Forecast necessary levels of staffing and stock at different times to facilitate effective scheduling and ordering. Inventory stock to ensure that supplies and equipment are available in adequate amounts. Evaluate employee performance and recommend personnel actions such as promotions, transfers, and dismissals. Confer with staff to resolve performance and personnel problems and to discuss company policies. Establish and implement operational standards and procedures for the departments they supervise. Recommend or arrange for additional services such as painting, repair work, renovations, and the replacement of furnishings and equipment. Select and order or purchase new equipment, supplies, and furnishings. Recommend changes that could improve service and increase operational efficiency. Maintain required records of work hours, budgets, payrolls, and other information. Screen job applicants and hire new employees. Supervise in-house services such as laundries, maintenance and repair, dry cleaning, and valet services. Advise managers, desk clerks, or admitting personnel of rooms ready for occupancy. Perform financial tasks such as estimating costs and preparing and managing budgets. Prepare activity and personnel reports and reports containing information such as occupancy, hours worked, facility usage, work performed, and departmental expenses.

Personality Type: Enterprising. These occupations frequently involve starting up and carrying out projects and can involve leading people and making many decisions. They sometimes require risk taking and often deal with business.

GOE—Interest Area/Cluster: 04. Business and Administration. **Work Group:** 04.02. Managerial Work in Business Detail. **Other Jobs in This Work Group:** Administrative Services Managers; First-Line Supervisors/Managers of Office and Administrative Support Workers; Meeting and Convention Planners.

Skills—Management of Personnel Resources: Motivating, developing, and directing people as they work; identifying the best people for the job. **Monitoring:** Assessing how well one is doing when learning or doing something. **Equipment Maintenance:** Performing routine maintenance and determining when and what kind of maintenance is needed. **Equipment Selection:** Determining the kind of tools and equipment needed to do a job. **Service Orientation:** Actively looking for ways to help people. **Writing:** Communicating effectively with others in writing as indicated by the needs of the audience. **Systems Evaluation:** Looking at many indicators of system performance and taking into account their accuracy. **Science:** Using scientific methods to solve problems.

Education and Training Programs: No related CIP programs; this job is learned through work experience in a related occupation. **Related Knowledge/Courses— Chemistry:** The composition, structure, and properties of substances and of the chemical processes and transformations that they undergo. This includes uses of chemicals and their interactions, danger signs, production techniques, and disposal methods. **Building and Construction:** Materials, methods, and the appropriate tools to construct objects, structures, and buildings. **Public Safety**

and Security: Weaponry; public safety; security operations, rules, regulations, precautions, and prevention; and the protection of people, data, and property. **Physics:** Physical principles, laws, and applications, including air, water, material dynamics, light, atomic principles, heat, electric theory, earth formations, and meteorological and related natural phenomena. **Mechanical Devices:** Machines and tools, including their designs, uses, benefits, repair, and maintenance. **Administration and Management:** Principles and processes involved in business and organizational planning, coordination, and execution. This includes strategic planning, resource allocation, manpower modeling, leadership techniques, and production methods.

Work Environment: Indoors; contaminants; disease or infections; standing; walking and running.

First-Line Supervisors/Managers of Landscaping, Lawn Service, and Groundskeeping Workers

* Education/Training Required: Work experience in a related occupation
* Annual Earnings: $38,720
* Beginning Wage: $25,270
* Earnings Growth Potential: Low
* Growth: 17.6%
* Annual Job Openings: 18,956
* Self-Employed: 44.1%
* Part-Time: 6.1%

Plan, organize, direct, or coordinate activities of workers engaged in landscaping or groundskeeping activities such as planting and maintaining ornamental trees, shrubs, flowers, and lawns and applying fertilizers, pesticides, and other chemicals, according to contract specifications. May also coordinate activities of workers engaged in terracing hillsides, building retaining walls, constructing pathways, installing patios, and similar activities in following a landscape design plan. Work may involve reviewing contracts to ascertain service, machine, and work force requirements; answering inquiries from potential customers regarding methods, material, and price ranges; and preparing estimates according to labor, material, and machine costs. Establish and enforce operating procedures and work standards that will ensure adequate performance and personnel safety. Inspect completed work to ensure conformance to specifications, standards, and contract requirements. Direct activities of workers who perform duties such as landscaping, cultivating lawns, or pruning trees and shrubs. Schedule work for crews depending on work priorities, crew and equipment availability, and weather conditions. Plant and maintain vegetation through activities such as mulching, fertilizing, watering, mowing, and pruning. Monitor project activities to ensure that instructions are followed, deadlines are met, and schedules are maintained. Train workers in tasks such as transplanting and pruning trees and shrubs, finishing cement, using equipment, and caring for turf. Provide workers with assistance in performing duties as necessary to meet deadlines. Inventory supplies of tools, equipment, and materials to ensure that sufficient supplies are available and items are in usable condition. Confer with other supervisors to coordinate work activities with those of other departments or units. Perform personnel-related activities such as hiring workers, evaluating staff performance, and taking disciplinary actions when performance problems occur. Direct or perform mixing and application of fertilizers, insecticides, herbicides, and fungicides. Review contracts or work assignments to determine service, machine, and workforce requirements for jobs. Maintain required records such as personnel information and project records. Prepare and maintain required records such as work activity and personnel reports. Order the performance of corrective work when problems occur, and recommend procedural changes to avoid such problems. Identify diseases and pests affecting landscaping, and order appropriate treatments. Investigate work-related complaints in order to verify problems, and to determine responses. Direct and assist workers engaged in the maintenance and repair of equipment such as power tools and motorized equipment. Install and maintain landscaped areas, performing tasks such as removing snow, pouring cement curbs, and repairing sidewalks.

Personality Type: Enterprising. These occupations frequently involve starting up and carrying out projects and can involve leading people and making many decisions. They sometimes require risk taking and often deal with business.

GOE—Interest Area/Cluster: 01. Agriculture and Natural Resources. **Work Group:** 01.01. Managerial Work in Agriculture and Natural Resources. **Other Jobs in This**

Work Group: Aquacultural Managers; Crop and Livestock Managers; Farm Labor Contractors; Farm, Ranch, and Other Agricultural Managers; Farmers and Ranchers; First-Line Supervisors/Managers of Agricultural Crop and Horticultural Workers; First-Line Supervisors/Managers of Animal Husbandry and Animal Care Workers; First-Line Supervisors/Managers of Aquacultural Workers; First-Line Supervisors/Managers of Construction Trades and Extraction Workers; First-Line Supervisors/Managers of Farming, Fishing, and Forestry Workers; First-Line Supervisors/ Managers of Logging Workers; Nursery and Greenhouse Managers; Park Naturalists; Purchasing Agents and Buyers, Farm Products.

Skills—Repairing: Repairing machines or systems, using the needed tools. **Equipment Maintenance:** Performing routine maintenance and determining when and what kind of maintenance is needed. **Systems Analysis:** Determining how a system should work and how changes will affect outcomes. **Operations Analysis:** Analyzing needs and product requirements to create a design. **Management of Personnel Resources:** Motivating, developing, and directing people as they work; identifying the best people for the job. **Equipment Selection:** Determining the kind of tools and equipment needed to do a job. **Monitoring:** Assessing how well one is doing when learning or doing something. **Operation and Control:** Controlling operations of equipment or systems.

Education and Training Programs: Landscaping and Groundskeeping; Ornamental Horticulture; Turf and Turfgrass Management. **Related Knowledge/Courses— Mechanical Devices:** Machines and tools, including their designs, uses, benefits, repair, and maintenance. **Building and Construction:** Materials, methods, and the appropriate tools to construct objects, structures, and buildings. **Biology:** Plant and animal living tissue, cells, organisms, and entities, including their functions, interdependencies, and interactions with each other and the environment. **Design:** Design techniques, principles, tools, and instruments involved in the production and use of precision technical plans, blueprints, drawings, and models. **Chemistry:** The composition, structure, and properties of substances and of the chemical processes and transformations that they undergo. This includes uses of chemicals and their interactions, danger signs, production techniques, and disposal methods. **Education and Training:** Instructional methods and training techniques, including curriculum design

principles, learning theory, group and individual teaching techniques, design of individual development plans, and test design principles.

Work Environment: Outdoors; noisy; very hot or cold; contaminants; minor burns, cuts, bites, or stings; standing.

First-Line Supervisors/Managers of Mechanics, Installers, and Repairers

- ❊ Education/Training Required: Work experience in a related occupation
- ❊ Annual Earnings: $55,380
- ❊ Beginning Wage: $33,620
- ❊ Earnings Growth Potential: Medium
- ❊ Growth: 7.3%
- ❊ Annual Job Openings: 24,361
- ❊ Self-Employed: 1.5%
- ❊ Part-Time: 0.9%

Supervise and coordinate the activities of mechanics, installers, and repairers. Determine schedules, sequences, and assignments for work activities, based on work priority, quantity of equipment, and skill of personnel. Monitor employees' work levels and review work performance. Monitor tool and part inventories and the condition and maintenance of shops to ensure adequate working conditions. Recommend or initiate personnel actions such as hires, promotions, transfers, discharges, and disciplinary measures. Investigate accidents and injuries, and prepare reports of findings. Compile operational and personnel records such as time and production records, inventory data, repair and maintenance statistics, and test results. Develop, implement, and evaluate maintenance policies and procedures. Counsel employees about work-related issues and assist employees to correct job-skill deficiencies. Examine objects, systems, or facilities, and analyze information to determine needed installations, services, or repairs. Conduct or arrange for worker training in safety, repair, and maintenance techniques, operational procedures, or equipment use. Inspect and monitor work areas, examine tools and equipment, and provide employee safety training to prevent, detect, and correct unsafe conditions or violations of procedures and safety rules. Inspect, test, and measure completed work, using devices such as hand tools and gauges to verify conformance to standards and repair requirements. Requisition materials and supplies such as tools, equipment, and replacement parts. Participate in budget preparation and administration, coordinating purchasing and documentation, and monitoring departmental expenditures. Perform skilled repair and maintenance operations, using equipment such as hand and power tools, hydraulic presses and shears, and welding equipment. Meet with vendors and suppliers to discuss products used in repair work. Compute estimates and actual costs of factors such as materials, labor, and outside contractors. Review, evaluate, accept, and coordinate completion of work bid from contractors. Confer with personnel such as management, engineering, quality control, customer, and union workers' representatives, to coordinate work activities, resolve employee grievances, and identify and review resource needs.

Personality Type: Enterprising. These occupations frequently involve starting up and carrying out projects and can involve leading people and making many decisions. They sometimes require risk taking and often deal with business.

GOE—Interest Area/Cluster: 13. Manufacturing. **Work Group:** 13.01. Managerial Work in Manufacturing. **Other Jobs in This Work Group:** First-Line Supervisors/Managers of Helpers, Laborers, and Material Movers, Hand; First-Line Supervisors/Managers of Production and Operating Workers; Industrial Production Managers.

Skills—Repairing: Repairing machines or systems, using the needed tools. **Operation Monitoring:** Watching gauges, dials, or other indicators to make sure a machine is working properly. **Management of Personnel Resources:** Motivating, developing, and directing people as they work; identifying the best people for the job. **Equipment Maintenance:** Performing routine maintenance and determining when and what kind of maintenance is needed. **Management of Financial Resources:** Determining how money will be spent to get the work done and accounting for these expenditures. **Systems Analysis:** Determining how a system should work and how changes will affect outcomes. **Operation and Control:** Controlling operations of equipment or systems. **Quality Control Analysis:** Evaluating the quality or performance of products, services, or processes.

Education and Training Program: Operations Management and Supervision. **Related Knowledge/Courses—Mechanical Devices:** Machines and tools, including their designs, uses, benefits, repair, and maintenance. **Personnel and Human Resources:** Principles and procedures for personnel recruitment; selection; training; compensation and benefits; labor relations and negotiation; and personnel information systems. **Production and Processing:** Inputs, outputs, raw materials, waste, quality control, costs, and techniques for maximizing the manufacture and distribution of goods. **Engineering and Technology:** Equipment, tools, and mechanical devices and their uses to produce motion, light, power, technology, and other applications. **Building and Construction:** Materials, methods, and the appropriate tools to construct objects, structures, and buildings. **Economics and Accounting:** Economic and accounting principles and practices, the financial markets, banking, and the analysis and reporting of financial data.

Work Environment: More often indoors than outdoors; noisy; contaminants; hazardous conditions; standing.

First-Line Supervisors/Managers of Non-Retail Sales Workers

- Education/Training Required: Work experience in a related occupation
- Annual Earnings: $67,020
- Beginning Wage: $36,120
- Earnings Growth Potential: High
- Growth: 3.7%
- Annual Job Openings: 48,883
- Self-Employed: 45.4%
- Part-Time: 5.3%

Directly supervise and coordinate activities of sales workers other than retail sales workers. May perform duties such as budgeting, accounting, and personnel work in addition to supervisory duties. Listen to and resolve customer complaints regarding services, products, or personnel. Monitor sales staff performance to ensure that goals are met. Hire, train, and evaluate personnel. Confer with company officials to develop methods and procedures to increase sales, expand markets, and promote business. Direct and supervise employees engaged in sales, inventory-taking, reconciling cash receipts, or performing specific services such as pumping gasoline for customers. Provide staff with assistance in performing difficult or complicated duties. Plan and prepare work schedules and assign employees to specific duties. Attend company meetings to exchange product information and coordinate work activities with other departments. Prepare sales and inventory reports for management and budget departments. Formulate pricing policies on merchandise according to profitability requirements. Examine merchandise to ensure correct pricing and display and ensure that it functions as advertised. Analyze details of sales territories to assess their growth potential and to set quotas. Visit retailers and sales representatives to promote products and gather information. Keep records pertaining to purchases, sales, and requisitions. Coordinate sales promotion activities and prepare merchandise displays and advertising copy. Prepare rental or lease agreements, specifying charges and payment procedures for use of machinery, tools, or other items. Inventory stock and reorder when inventories drop to specified levels. Examine products purchased for resale or received for storage to determine product condition.

Personality Type: Enterprising. These occupations frequently involve starting up and carrying out projects and can involve leading people and making many decisions. They sometimes require risk taking and often deal with business.

GOE—Interest Area/Cluster: 14. Retail and Wholesale Sales and Service. **Work Group:** 14.01. Managerial Work in Retail/Wholesale Sales and Service. **Other Jobs in This Work Group:** Advertising and Promotions Managers; First-Line Supervisors/Managers of Retail Sales Workers; Funeral Directors; Marketing Managers; Property, Real Estate, and Community Association Managers; Purchasing Managers; Sales Managers.

Skills—Management of Personnel Resources: Motivating, developing, and directing people as they work; identifying the best people for the job. **Negotiation:** Bringing others together and trying to reconcile differences. **Persuasion:** Persuading others to approach things differently. **Time Management:** Managing one's own time and the time of others. **Social Perceptiveness:** Being aware of others' reactions and understanding why they react the way they do. **Operations Analysis:** Analyzing needs and product requirements to create a design. **Monitoring:** Assessing how well one is doing when learning or doing something.

Judgment and Decision Making: Weighing the relative costs and benefits of a potential action.

Education and Training Programs: Business, Management, Marketing, and Related Support Services, Other; General Merchandising, Sales, and Related Marketing Operations, Other; Special Products Marketing Operations; Specialized Merchandising, Sales, and Related Marketing Operations, Other. **Related Knowledge/Courses—Sales and Marketing:** Principles and methods involved in showing, promoting, and selling products or services. This includes marketing strategies and tactics, product demonstration and sales techniques, and sales control systems. **Economics and Accounting:** Economic and accounting principles and practices, the financial markets, banking, and the analysis and reporting of financial data. **Personnel and Human Resources:** Principles and procedures for personnel recruitment; selection; training; compensation and benefits; labor relations and negotiation; and personnel information systems. **Administration and Management:** Principles and processes involved in business and organizational planning, coordination, and execution. This includes strategic planning, resource allocation, manpower modeling, leadership techniques, and production methods. **Mathematics:** Numbers and their operations and interrelationships, including arithmetic, algebra, geometry, calculus, and statistics and their applications. **Education and Training:** Instructional methods and training techniques, including curriculum design principles, learning theory, group and individual teaching techniques, design of individual development plans, and test design principles.

Work Environment: Indoors; noisy.

First-Line Supervisors/Managers of Office and Administrative Support Workers

- ❋ Education/Training Required: Work experience in a related occupation
- ❋ Annual Earnings: $44,650
- ❋ Beginning Wage: $27,190
- ❋ Earnings Growth Potential: Medium
- ❋ Growth: 5.8%
- ❋ Annual Job Openings: 138,420
- ❋ Self-Employed: 1.6%
- ❋ Part-Time: 7.9%

Supervise and coordinate the activities of clerical and administrative support workers. Resolve customer complaints and answer customers' questions regarding policies and procedures. Supervise the work of office, administrative, or customer service employees to ensure adherence to quality standards, deadlines, and proper procedures, correcting errors or problems. Provide employees with guidance in handling difficult or complex problems and in resolving escalated complaints or disputes. Implement corporate and departmental policies, procedures, and service standards in conjunction with management. Discuss job performance problems with employees to identify causes and issues and to work on resolving problems. Train and instruct employees in job duties and company policies or arrange for training to be provided. Evaluate employees' job performance and conformance to regulations and recommend appropriate personnel action. Recruit, interview, and select employees. Review records and reports pertaining to activities such as production, payroll, and shipping to verify details, monitor work activities, and evaluate performance. Interpret and communicate work procedures and company policies to staff. Prepare and issue work schedules, deadlines, and duty assignments of office or administrative staff. Maintain records pertaining to inventory, personnel, orders, supplies, and machine maintenance. Compute figures such as balances, totals, and commissions. Research, compile, and prepare reports, manuals, correspondence, and other information required by management or governmental agencies. Coordinate activities with other supervisory personnel and with other work units or departments. Analyze financial activities of establishments or departments and provide input into budget planning and preparation processes. Develop or update procedures, policies, and standards. Make recommendations to management concerning such issues as staffing decisions and procedural changes. Consult with managers and other personnel to resolve problems in areas such as equipment performance, output quality, and work schedules. Participate in the work of subordinates to facilitate productivity or to overcome difficult aspects of work.

Personality Type: Enterprising. These occupations frequently involve starting up and carrying out projects and can involve leading people and making many decisions. They sometimes require risk taking and often deal with business.

GOE—Interest Area/Cluster: 04. Business and Administration. **Work Group:** 04.02. Managerial Work in Business Detail. **Other Jobs in This Work Group:** Administrative Services Managers; First-Line Supervisors/Managers of Housekeeping and Janitorial Workers; Meeting and Convention Planners.

Skills—Management of Personnel Resources: Motivating, developing, and directing people as they work; identifying the best people for the job. **Management of Financial Resources:** Determining how money will be spent to get the work done and accounting for these expenditures. **Negotiation:** Bringing others together and trying to reconcile differences. **Management of Material Resources:** Obtaining and seeing to the appropriate use of equipment, facilities, and materials needed to do certain work. **Monitoring:** Assessing how well one is doing when learning or doing something. **Service Orientation:** Actively looking for ways to help people. **Persuasion:** Persuading others to approach things differently. **Judgment and Decision Making:** Weighing the relative costs and benefits of a potential action.

Education and Training Programs: No related CIP programs; this job is learned through work experience in a related occupation. **Related Knowledge/Courses— Clerical Studies:** Administrative and clerical procedures and systems such as word-processing systems, filing and records management systems, stenography and transcription, forms, design principles, and other office procedures and terminology. **Economics and Accounting:** Economic and accounting principles and practices, the financial markets, banking, and the analysis and reporting of financial data. **Administration and Management:** Principles and processes involved in business and organizational planning, coordination, and execution. This includes strategic planning, resource allocation, manpower modeling, leadership techniques, and production methods. **Personnel and Human Resources:** Principles and procedures for personnel recruitment; selection; training; compensation and benefits; labor relations and negotiation; and personnel information systems. **Customer and Personal Service:** Principles and processes for providing customer and personal services, including needs assessment techniques, quality service standards, alternative delivery systems, and customer satisfaction evaluation techniques. **Education and Training:** Instructional methods and training techniques, including curriculum design principles, learning theory, group and individual teaching techniques, design of individual development plans, and test design principles.

Work Environment: Indoors; noisy; sitting.

First-Line Supervisors/Managers of Personal Service Workers

- ✳ Education/Training Required: Work experience in a related occupation
- ✳ Annual Earnings: $33,900
- ✳ Beginning Wage: $20,820
- ✳ Earnings Growth Potential: Medium
- ✳ Growth: 15.5%
- ✳ Annual Job Openings: 37,555
- ✳ Self-Employed: 38.6%
- ✳ Part-Time: 15.8%

Supervise and coordinate activities of personal service workers such as flight attendants, hairdressers, or caddies. Requisition necessary supplies, equipment, and services. Inform workers about interests and special needs of specific groups. Participate in continuing education to stay abreast of industry trends and developments. Meet with managers and other supervisors to stay informed of changes affecting operations. Collaborate with staff members to plan and develop programs of events, schedules of activities, or menus. Train workers in proper operational procedures and functions, and explain company policies. Furnish customers with information on events and activities. Resolve customer complaints regarding worker performance and services rendered. Analyze and record personnel and operational data, and write related activity reports. Observe and evaluate workers' appearance and performance to ensure quality service and compliance with specifications. Inspect work areas and operating equipment to ensure conformance to established standards in areas such as cleanliness and maintenance. Direct and coordinate the activities of workers such as flight attendants, hotel staff, or hair stylists. Assign work schedules, following work requirements, to ensure quality and timely delivery of service. Apply customer/guest feedback to service improvement efforts. Direct marketing, advertising, and other customer recruitment efforts. Take disciplinary action to address performance problems. Recruit and hire staff members.

Personality Type: Enterprising. These occupations frequently involve starting up and carrying out projects and can involve leading people and making many decisions. They sometimes require risk taking and often deal with business.

GOE—Interest Area/Cluster: 09. Hospitality, Tourism, and Recreation. **Work Group:** 09.01. Managerial Work in Hospitality and Tourism. **Other Jobs in This Work Group:** First-Line Supervisors/Managers of Food Preparation and Serving Workers; Food Service Managers; Gaming Managers; Gaming Supervisors; Lodging Managers.

Skills—Management of Personnel Resources: Motivating, developing, and directing people as they work; identifying the best people for the job. **Social Perceptiveness:** Being aware of others' reactions and understanding why they react the way they do. **Service Orientation:** Actively looking for ways to help people. **Learning Strategies:** Using multiple approaches when learning or teaching new things. **Coordination:** Adjusting actions in relation to others' actions. **Judgment and Decision Making:** Weighing the relative costs and benefits of a potential action. **Writing:** Communicating effectively with others in writing as indicated by the needs of the audience. **Time Management:** Managing one's own time and the time of others.

Education and Training Program: Personal and Culinary Services, Other. **Related Knowledge/Courses— Psychology:** Human behavior and performance, mental processes, psychological research methods, and the assessment and treatment of behavioral and affective disorders. **Therapy and Counseling:** Information and techniques needed to rehabilitate physical and mental ailments and to provide career guidance, including alternative treatments, rehabilitation equipment and its proper use, and methods to evaluate treatment effects. **Education and Training:** Instructional methods and training techniques, including curriculum design principles, learning theory, group and individual teaching techniques, design of individual development plans, and test design principles. **Philosophy and Theology:** Different philosophical systems and religions, including their basic principles, values, ethics, ways of thinking, customs, and practices and their impact on human culture. **Medicine and Dentistry:** The information and techniques needed to diagnose and treat injuries, diseases, and deformities. This includes symptoms, treatment alternatives, drug properties and interactions, and preventive health-care measures. **Public Safety and Security:** Weaponry; public safety; security operations, rules, regulations, precautions, and prevention; and the protection of people, data, and property.

Work Environment: Indoors; noisy; contaminants; standing; walking and running; using hands on objects, tools, or controls.

First-Line Supervisors/Managers of Police and Detectives

- ✳ Education/Training Required: Work experience in a related occupation
- ✳ Annual Earnings: $72,620
- ✳ Beginning Wage: $43,720
- ✳ Earnings Growth Potential: Medium
- ✳ Growth: 9.2%
- ✳ Annual Job Openings: 9,373
- ✳ Self-Employed: 0.0%
- ✳ Part-Time: 0.8%

Supervise and coordinate activities of members of police force. Supervise and coordinate the investigation of criminal cases, offering guidance and expertise to investigators, and ensuring that procedures are conducted in accordance with laws and regulations. Maintain logs, prepare reports, and direct the preparation, handling, and maintenance of departmental records. Explain police operations to subordinates to assist them in performing their job duties. Cooperate with court personnel and officials from other

law enforcement agencies and testify in court as necessary. Review contents of written orders to ensure adherence to legal requirements. Investigate and resolve personnel problems within organization and charges of misconduct against staff. Direct collection, preparation, and handling of evidence and personal property of prisoners. Inform personnel of changes in regulations and policies, implications of new or amended laws, and new techniques of police work. Train staff in proper police work procedures. Monitor and evaluate the job performance of subordinates, and authorize promotions and transfers. Prepare work schedules and assign duties to subordinates. Conduct raids and order detention of witnesses and suspects for questioning. Discipline staff for violation of departmental rules and regulations. Develop, implement, and revise departmental policies and procedures. Inspect facilities, supplies, vehicles, and equipment to ensure conformance to standards. Requisition and issue equipment and supplies. Meet with civic, educational, and community groups to develop community programs and events, and to discuss law enforcement subjects. Prepare news releases and respond to police correspondence. Prepare budgets and manage expenditures of department funds. Direct release or transfer of prisoners.

Personality Type: Enterprising. These occupations frequently involve starting up and carrying out projects and can involve leading people and making many decisions. They sometimes require risk taking and often deal with business.

GOE—Interest Area/Cluster: 12. Law and Public Safety. **Work Group:** 12.01. Managerial Work in Law and Public Safety. **Other Jobs in This Work Group:** Emergency Management Specialists; First-Line Supervisors/Managers of Correctional Officers; First-Line Supervisors/Managers of Fire Fighting and Prevention Workers; Forest Fire Fighting and Prevention Supervisors; Municipal Fire Fighting and Prevention Supervisors.

Skills—Management of Personnel Resources: Motivating, developing, and directing people as they work; identifying the best people for the job. **Systems Analysis:** Determining how a system should work and how changes will affect outcomes. **Negotiation:** Bringing others together and trying to reconcile differences. **Systems Evaluation:** Looking at many indicators of system performance and taking into account their accuracy. **Operation Monitoring:** Watching gauges, dials, or other indicators to make sure a machine is working properly. **Writing:**

Communicating effectively with others in writing as indicated by the needs of the audience. **Social Perceptiveness:** Being aware of others' reactions and understanding why they react the way they do. **Persuasion:** Persuading others to approach things differently.

Education and Training Programs: Corrections; Criminal Justice/Law Enforcement Administration; Criminal Justice/Safety Studies. **Related Knowledge/Courses— Public Safety and Security:** Weaponry; public safety; security operations, rules, regulations, precautions, and prevention; and the protection of people, data, and property. **Law and Government:** Laws, legal codes, court procedures, precedents, government regulations, executive orders, agency rules, and the democratic political process. **Psychology:** Human behavior and performance, mental processes, psychological research methods, and the assessment and treatment of behavioral and affective disorders. **Sociology and Anthropology:** Group behavior and dynamics; societal trends and influences; and cultures and their history, migrations, ethnicity, and origins. **Therapy and Counseling:** Information and techniques needed to rehabilitate physical and mental ailments and to provide career guidance, including alternative treatments, rehabilitation equipment and its proper use, and methods to evaluate treatment effects. **Personnel and Human Resources:** Principles and procedures for personnel recruitment; selection; training; compensation and benefits; labor relations and negotiation; and personnel information systems.

Work Environment: More often indoors than outdoors; noisy; very hot or cold; contaminants; sitting.

First-Line Supervisors/Managers of Production and Operating Workers

- ❋ Education/Training Required: Work experience in a related occupation
- ❋ Annual Earnings: $48,670
- ❋ Beginning Wage: $29,830
- ❋ Earnings Growth Potential: Medium
- ❋ Growth: –4.8%
- ❋ Annual Job Openings: 46,144
- ❋ Self-Employed: 2.4%
- ❋ Part-Time: 1.9%

Supervise and coordinate the activities of production and operating workers, such as inspectors, precision workers, machine setters and operators, assemblers, fabricators, and plant and system operators. Enforce safety and sanitation regulations. Direct and coordinate the activities of employees engaged in the production or processing of goods, such as inspectors, machine setters, and fabricators. Read and analyze charts, work orders, production schedules, and other records and reports to determine production requirements and to evaluate current production estimates and outputs. Confer with other supervisors to coordinate operations and activities within or between departments. Plan and establish work schedules, assignments, and production sequences to meet production goals. Inspect materials, products, or equipment to detect defects or malfunctions. Demonstrate equipment operations and work and safety procedures to new employees or assign employees to experienced workers for training. Observe work and monitor gauges, dials, and other indicators to ensure that operators conform to production or processing standards. Interpret specifications, blueprints, job orders, and company policies and procedures for workers. Confer with management or subordinates to resolve worker problems, complaints, or grievances. Maintain operations data such as time, production, and cost records and prepare management reports of production results. Recommend or implement measures to motivate employees and to improve production methods, equipment performance, product quality, or efficiency. Determine standards, budgets, production goals, and rates based on company policies, equipment and labor availability, and workloads. Requisition materials, supplies, equipment parts, or repair services. Recommend personnel actions such as hirings and promotions. Set up and adjust machines and equipment. Calculate labor and equipment requirements and production specifications, using standard formulas. Plan and develop new products and production processes.

Personality Type: Enterprising. These occupations frequently involve starting up and carrying out projects and can involve leading people and making many decisions. They sometimes require risk taking and often deal with business.

GOE—Interest Area/Cluster: 13. Manufacturing. **Work Group:** 13.01. Managerial Work in Manufacturing. **Other Jobs in This Work Group:** First-Line Supervisors/Managers of Helpers, Laborers, and Material Movers, Hand; First-

Line Supervisors/Managers of Mechanics, Installers, and Repairers; Industrial Production Managers.

Skills—Management of Personnel Resources: Motivating, developing, and directing people as they work; identifying the best people for the job. **Operation Monitoring:** Watching gauges, dials, or other indicators to make sure a machine is working properly. **Operation and Control:** Controlling operations of equipment or systems. **Quality Control Analysis:** Evaluating the quality or performance of products, services, or processes. **Operations Analysis:** Analyzing needs and product requirements to create a design. **Systems Analysis:** Determining how a system should work and how changes will affect outcomes. **Monitoring:** Assessing how well one is doing when learning or doing something. **Systems Evaluation:** Looking at many indicators of system performance and taking into account their accuracy.

Education and Training Program: Operations Management and Supervision. **Related Knowledge/Courses—Production and Processing:** Inputs, outputs, raw materials, waste, quality control, costs, and techniques for maximizing the manufacture and distribution of goods. **Mechanical Devices:** Machines and tools, including their designs, uses, benefits, repair, and maintenance. **Personnel and Human Resources:** Principles and procedures for personnel recruitment; selection; training; compensation and benefits; labor relations and negotiation; and personnel information systems. **Engineering and Technology:** Equipment, tools, and mechanical devices and their uses to produce motion, light, power, technology, and other applications. **Administration and Management:** Principles and processes involved in business and organizational planning, coordination, and execution. This includes strategic planning, resource allocation, manpower modeling, leadership techniques, and production methods. **Psychology:** Human behavior and performance, mental processes, psychological research methods, and the assessment and treatment of behavioral and affective disorders.

Work Environment: Indoors; noisy; contaminants; hazardous equipment; standing; walking and running.

First-Line Supervisors/Managers of Retail Sales Workers

* Education/Training Required: Work experience in a related occupation
* Annual Earnings: $34,470
* Beginning Wage: $21,760
* Earnings Growth Potential: Medium
* Growth: 4.2%
* Annual Job Openings: 221,241
* Self-Employed: 34.2%
* Part-Time: 7.8%

Directly supervise sales workers in a retail establishment or department. Duties may include management functions, such as purchasing, budgeting, accounting, and personnel work, in addition to supervisory duties. Provide customer service by greeting and assisting customers and responding to customer inquiries and complaints. Assign employees to specific duties. Monitor sales activities to ensure that customers receive satisfactory service and quality goods. Direct and supervise employees engaged in sales, inventory-taking, reconciling cash receipts, or performing services for customers. Inventory stock and reorder when inventory drops to a specified level. Keep records of purchases, sales, and requisitions. Enforce safety, health, and security rules. Examine products purchased for resale or received for storage to assess the condition of each product or item. Hire, train, and evaluate personnel in sales or marketing establishments, promoting or firing workers when appropriate. Perform work activities of subordinates, such as cleaning and organizing shelves and displays and selling merchandise. Establish and implement policies, goals, objectives, and procedures for their department. Instruct staff on how to handle difficult and complicated sales. Formulate pricing policies for merchandise according to profitability requirements. Estimate consumer demand and determine the types and amounts of goods to be sold. Examine merchandise to ensure that it is correctly priced and displayed and that it functions as advertised. Plan and prepare work schedules and keep records of employees' work schedules and time cards. Review inventory and sales records to prepare reports for management and budget departments. Plan and coordinate advertising campaigns and sales promotions and prepare merchandise displays and advertising copy. Confer with company officials to develop methods and procedures to increase sales, expand markets, and promote business. Establish credit policies and operating procedures. Plan budgets and authorize payments and merchandise returns.

Personality Type: Enterprising. These occupations frequently involve starting up and carrying out projects and can involve leading people and making many decisions. They sometimes require risk taking and often deal with business.

GOE—Interest Area/Cluster: 14. Retail and Wholesale Sales and Service. **Work Group:** 14.01. Managerial Work in Retail/Wholesale Sales and Service. **Other Jobs in This Work Group:** Advertising and Promotions Managers; First-Line Supervisors/Managers of Non-Retail Sales Workers; Funeral Directors; Marketing Managers; Property, Real Estate, and Community Association Managers; Purchasing Managers; Sales Managers.

Skills—Management of Personnel Resources: Motivating, developing, and directing people as they work; identifying the best people for the job. **Management of Financial Resources:** Determining how money will be spent to get the work done and accounting for these expenditures. **Persuasion:** Persuading others to approach things differently. **Repairing:** Repairing machines or systems, using the needed tools. **Equipment Maintenance:** Performing routine maintenance and determining when and what kind of maintenance is needed. **Monitoring:** Assessing how well one is doing when learning or doing something. **Troubleshooting:** Determining what is causing an operating error and deciding what to do about it. **Social Perceptiveness:** Being aware of others' reactions and understanding why they react the way they do.

Education and Training Programs: Business, Management, Marketing, and Related Support Services, Other; Consumer Merchandising/Retailing Management; E-Commerce/Electronic Commerce; Floriculture/Floristry Operations and Management; Retailing and Retail Operations; Selling Skills and Sales Operations; Special Products Marketing Operations; Specialized Merchandising, Sales, and Related Marketing Operations, Other. **Related Knowledge/Courses—Sales and Marketing:** Principles and methods involved in showing, promoting, and selling products or services. This includes marketing strategies and tactics, product demonstration and sales techniques, and sales control systems. **Personnel and Human Resources:**

Principles and procedures for personnel recruitment; selection; training; compensation and benefits; labor relations and negotiation; and personnel information systems. **Administration and Management:** Principles and processes involved in business and organizational planning, coordination, and execution. This includes strategic planning, resource allocation, manpower modeling, leadership techniques, and production methods. **Economics and Accounting:** Economic and accounting principles and practices, the financial markets, banking, and the analysis and reporting of financial data. **Customer and Personal Service:** Principles and processes for providing customer and personal services, including needs assessment techniques, quality service standards, alternative delivery systems, and customer satisfaction evaluation techniques.

Work Environment: Indoors; hazardous equipment; standing; walking and running; using hands on objects, tools, or controls.

First-Line Supervisors/Managers of Transportation and Material-Moving Machine and Vehicle Operators

- ❋ Education/Training Required: Work experience in a related occupation
- ❋ Annual Earnings: $49,850
- ❋ Beginning Wage: $29,760
- ❋ Earnings Growth Potential: High
- ❋ Growth: 10.2%
- ❋ Annual Job Openings: 16,580
- ❋ Self-Employed: 1.5%
- ❋ Part-Time: 5.3%

Directly supervise and coordinate activities of transportation and material-moving machine and vehicle operators and helpers. Enforce safety rules and regulations. Plan work assignments and equipment allocations to meet transportation, operations, or production goals. Confer with customers, supervisors, contractors, and other personnel to exchange information and to resolve problems. Direct workers in transportation or related services, such as pumping, moving, storing, and loading and unloading of materials or people. Resolve worker problems or collaborate with employees to assist in problem resolution. Review orders, production schedules, blueprints, and shipping and receiving notices to determine work sequences and material shipping dates, types, volumes, and destinations. Monitor fieldwork to ensure that it is being performed properly and that materials are being used as they should be. Recommend and implement measures to improve worker motivation, equipment performance, work methods, and customer services. Maintain or verify records of time, materials, expenditures, and crew activities. Interpret transportation and tariff regulations, shipping orders, safety regulations, and company policies and procedures for workers. Explain and demonstrate work tasks to new workers or assign workers to more experienced workers for further training. Prepare, compile, and submit reports on work activities, operations, production, and work-related accidents. Recommend or implement personnel actions such as employee selection, evaluation, and rewards or disciplinary actions. Requisition needed personnel, supplies, equipment, parts, or repair services. Inspect or test materials, stock, vehicles, equipment, and facilities to ensure that they are safe, are free of defects, and meet specifications. Plan and establish transportation routes. Compute and estimate cash, payroll, transportation, personnel, and storage requirements. Dispatch personnel and vehicles in response to telephone or radio reports of emergencies. Perform or schedule repairs and preventive maintenance of vehicles and other equipment. Examine, measure, and weigh cargo or materials to determine specific handling requirements. Provide workers with assistance in performing tasks such as coupling railroad cars or loading vehicles.

Personality Type: Enterprising. These occupations frequently involve starting up and carrying out projects and can involve leading people and making many decisions. They sometimes require risk taking and often deal with business.

GOE—Interest Area/Cluster: 16. Transportation, Distribution, and Logistics. **Work Group:** 16.01. Managerial Work in Transportation. **Other Jobs in This Work Group:** Aircraft Cargo Handling Supervisors; Postmasters and Mail Superintendents; Railroad Conductors and Yardmasters; Storage and Distribution Managers; Transportation Managers; Transportation, Storage, and Distribution Managers.

Skills—Management of Personnel Resources: Motivating, developing, and directing people as they work; identifying the best people for the job. **Management of Financial Resources:** Determining how money will be spent to get the work done and accounting for these expenditures. **Management of Material Resources:** Obtaining and seeing to the appropriate use of equipment, facilities, and materials needed to do certain work. **Social Perceptiveness:** Being aware of others' reactions and understanding why they react the way they do. **Operations Analysis:** Analyzing needs and product requirements to create a design. **Equipment Selection:** Determining the kind of tools and equipment needed to do a job. **Systems Evaluation:** Looking at many indicators of system performance and taking into account their accuracy. **Monitoring:** Assessing how well one is doing when learning or doing something.

Education and Training Programs: No related CIP programs; this job is learned through work experience in a related occupation. **Related Knowledge/Courses—Transportation:** Principles and methods for moving people or goods by air, rail, sea, or road, including their relative costs, advantages, and limitations. **Production and Processing:** Inputs, outputs, raw materials, waste, quality control, costs, and techniques for maximizing the manufacture and distribution of goods. **Personnel and Human Resources:** Principles and procedures for personnel recruitment; selection; training; compensation and benefits; labor relations and negotiation; and personnel information systems. **Customer and Personal Service:** Principles and processes for providing customer and personal services, including needs assessment techniques, quality service standards, alternative delivery systems, and customer satisfaction evaluation techniques. **Public Safety and Security:** Weaponry; public safety; security operations, rules, regulations, precautions, and prevention; and the protection of people, data, and property. **Administration and Management:** Principles and processes involved in business and organizational planning, coordination, and execution. This includes strategic planning, resource allocation, manpower modeling, leadership techniques, and production methods.

Work Environment: Indoors; noisy; contaminants; sitting.

Fitness Trainers and Aerobics Instructors

* ❋ Education/Training Required:
  Postsecondary vocational training
* ❋ Annual Earnings: $27,680
* ❋ Beginning Wage: $15,550
* ❋ Earnings Growth Potential: High
* ❋ Growth: 26.8%
* ❋ Annual Job Openings: 51,235
* ❋ Self-Employed: 7.6%
* ❋ Part-Time: 38.2%

Instruct or coach groups or individuals in exercise activities and the fundamentals of sports. Demonstrate techniques and methods of participation. Observe participants and inform them of corrective measures necessary to improve their skills. Explain and enforce safety rules and regulations governing sports, recreational activities, and the use of exercise equipment. Offer alternatives during classes to accommodate different levels of fitness. Plan routines, choose appropriate music, and choose different movements for each set of muscles, depending on participants' capabilities and limitations. Observe participants and inform them of corrective measures necessary for skill improvement. Teach proper breathing techniques used during physical exertion. Teach and demonstrate use of gymnastic and training equipment such as trampolines and weights. Instruct participants in maintaining exertion levels to maximize benefits from exercise routines. Maintain fitness equipment. Conduct therapeutic, recreational, or athletic activities. Monitor participants' progress and adapt programs as needed. Evaluate individuals' abilities, needs, and physical conditions and develop suitable training programs to meet any special requirements. Plan physical education programs to promote development of participants' physical attributes and social skills. Provide students with information and resources regarding nutrition, weight control, and lifestyle issues. Administer emergency first aid, wrap injuries, treat minor chronic disabilities, or refer injured persons to physicians. Advise clients about proper clothing and shoes. Wrap ankles, fingers, wrists, or other body parts with synthetic skin, gauze, or adhesive tape to support muscles and ligaments. Teach individual and team sports to participants through instruction and demonstration, utilizing knowledge of sports techniques and of participants' physical capabilities. Promote health clubs through membership sales and record member information. Organize, lead, and referee indoor and outdoor games such as volleyball, baseball, and basketball. Maintain equipment inventories and select, store, or issue equipment as needed. Organize and conduct competitions and tournaments. Advise participants in use of heat or ultraviolet treatments and hot baths. Massage body parts to relieve soreness, strains, and bruises.

Personality Type: Social. These occupations frequently involve working with, communicating with, and teaching people and often involve helping or providing service to others.

GOE—Interest Area/Cluster: 05. Education and Training. **Work Group:** 05.06. Counseling, Health, and Fitness Education. **Other Jobs in This Work Group:** Educational, Vocational, and School Counselors; Health Educators.

Skills—Instructing: Teaching others how to do something. **Equipment Selection:** Determining the kind of tools and equipment needed to do a job. **Monitoring:** Assessing how well one is doing when learning or doing something. **Service Orientation:** Actively looking for ways to help people. **Coordination:** Adjusting actions in relation to others' actions. **Science:** Using scientific methods to solve problems. **Social Perceptiveness:** Being aware of others' reactions and understanding why they react the way they do. **Time Management:** Managing one's own time and the time of others.

Education and Training Programs: Health and Physical Education, General; Physical Education Teaching and Coaching; Sport and Fitness Administration/Management. **Related Knowledge/Courses—Customer and Personal Service:** Principles and processes for providing customer and personal services, including needs assessment techniques, quality service standards, alternative delivery systems, and customer satisfaction evaluation techniques. **Psychology:** Human behavior and performance, mental processes, psychological research methods, and the assessment and treatment of behavioral and affective disorders. **Sociology and Anthropology:** Group behavior and dynamics; societal trends and influences; and cultures and their history, migrations, ethnicity, and origins. **Education and Training:** Instructional methods and training techniques, including curriculum design principles, learning theory, group and individual teaching techniques, design of individual development plans, and test design principles. **Sales and Marketing:** Principles and methods involved in showing, promoting, and selling products or services. This includes marketing strategies and tactics, product demonstration and sales techniques, and sales control systems. **Personnel and Human Resources:** Principles and procedures for personnel recruitment; selection; training; compensation and benefits; labor relations and negotiation; and personnel information systems.

Work Environment: Indoors; standing; walking and running; repetitive motions.

Flight Attendants

- ❋ Education/Training Required: Long-term on-the-job training
- ❋ Annual Earnings: $61,120
- ❋ Beginning Wage: $28,880
- ❋ Earnings Growth Potential: Very high
- ❋ Growth: 10.6%
- ❋ Annual Job Openings: 10,773
- ❋ Self-Employed: 0.0%
- ❋ Part-Time: 24.9%

Provide personal services to ensure the safety and comfort of airline passengers during flight. Greet passengers, verify tickets, explain use of safety equipment, and serve food or beverages. Direct and assist passengers in the event of an emergency, such as directing passengers to evacuate a plane following an emergency landing. Announce and demonstrate safety and emergency procedures such as the use of oxygen masks, seat belts, and life jackets. Walk aisles of planes to verify that passengers have complied with federal regulations prior to takeoffs and landings. Verify that first aid kits and other emergency equipment, including fire extinguishers and oxygen bottles, are in working order. Administer first aid to passengers in distress. Attend preflight briefings concerning weather, altitudes, routes, emergency procedures, crew coordination, lengths of flights, food and beverage services offered, and numbers of passengers. Prepare passengers and aircraft for landing, following procedures. Determine special assistance needs of passengers such as small children, the elderly, or disabled persons. Check to ensure that food, beverages, blankets, reading material, emergency equipment,

and other supplies are aboard and are in adequate supply. Reassure passengers when situations such as turbulence are encountered. Announce flight delays and descent preparations. Inspect passenger tickets to verify information and to obtain destination information. Answer passengers' questions about flights, aircraft, weather, travel routes and services, arrival times, and schedules. Assist passengers while entering or disembarking the aircraft. Inspect and clean cabins, checking for any problems and making sure that cabins are in order. Greet passengers boarding aircraft and direct them to assigned seats. Conduct periodic trips through the cabin to ensure passenger comfort and to distribute reading material, headphones, pillows, playing cards, and blankets. Take inventory of headsets, alcoholic beverages, and money collected. Operate audio and video systems. Assist passengers in placing carry-on luggage in overhead, garment, or under-seat storage. Prepare reports showing places of departure and destination, passenger ticket numbers, meal and beverage inventories, the conditions of cabin equipment, and any problems encountered by passengers.

Personality Type: Enterprising. These occupations frequently involve starting up and carrying out projects and can involve leading people and making many decisions. They sometimes require risk taking and often deal with business.

GOE—Interest Area/Cluster: 09. Hospitality, Tourism, and Recreation. **Work Group:** 09.03. Hospitality and Travel Services. **Other Jobs in This Work Group:** Baggage Porters and Bellhops; Concierges; Hotel, Motel, and Resort Desk Clerks; Janitors and Cleaners, Except Maids and Housekeeping Cleaners; Maids and Housekeeping Cleaners; Reservation and Transportation Ticket Agents and Travel Clerks; Tour Guides and Escorts; Transportation Attendants, Except Flight Attendants and Baggage Porters; Travel Agents; Travel Guides.

Skills—Service Orientation: Actively looking for ways to help people. **Social Perceptiveness:** Being aware of others' reactions and understanding why they react the way they do. **Reading Comprehension:** Understanding written sentences and paragraphs in work-related documents. **Critical Thinking:** Using logic and analysis to identify the strengths and weaknesses of different approaches.

Education and Training Program: Airline Flight Attendant Training. **Related Knowledge/Courses—Customer**

and **Personal Service:** Principles and processes for providing customer and personal services, including needs assessment techniques, quality service standards, alternative delivery systems, and customer satisfaction evaluation techniques. **Psychology:** Human behavior and performance, mental processes, psychological research methods, and the assessment and treatment of behavioral and affective disorders. **Geography:** Various methods for describing the location and distribution of land, sea, and air masses, including their physical locations, relationships, and characteristics. **Transportation:** Principles and methods for moving people or goods by air, rail, sea, or road, including their relative costs, advantages, and limitations. **Philosophy and Theology:** Different philosophical systems and religions, including their basic principles, values, ethics, ways of thinking, customs, and practices and their impact on human culture. **Public Safety and Security:** Weaponry; public safety; security operations, rules, regulations, precautions, and prevention; and the protection of people, data, and property.

Work Environment: Indoors; noisy; contaminants; disease or infections; high places; standing.

Food Batchmakers

- ❊ Education/Training Required: Short-term on-the-job training
- ❊ Annual Earnings: $23,730
- ❊ Beginning Wage: $15,670
- ❊ Earnings Growth Potential: Low
- ❊ Growth: 10.9%
- ❊ Annual Job Openings: 15,704
- ❊ Self-Employed: 1.7%
- ❊ Part-Time: 15.7%

Set up and operate equipment that mixes or blends ingredients used in the manufacturing of food products. Includes candy makers and cheese makers. Record production and test data for each food product batch, such as the ingredients used, temperature, test results, and time cycle. Observe gauges and thermometers to determine if the mixing chamber temperature is within specified limits and turn valves to control the temperature. Clean and sterilize vats and factory processing areas. Press switches and turn knobs to start, adjust, and regulate equipment

such as beaters, extruders, discharge pipes, and salt pumps. Observe and listen to equipment to detect possible malfunctions, such as leaks or plugging, and report malfunctions or undesirable tastes to supervisors. Set up, operate, and tend equipment that cooks, mixes, blends, or processes ingredients in the manufacturing of food products according to formulas or recipes. Mix or blend ingredients according to recipes by using a paddle or an agitator or by controlling vats that heat and mix ingredients. Select and measure or weigh ingredients, using English or metric measures and balance scales. Follow recipes to produce food products of specified flavor, texture, clarity, bouquet, or color. Turn valve controls to start equipment and to adjust operation to maintain product quality. Determine mixing sequences, based on knowledge of temperature effects and of the solubility of specific ingredients. Fill processing or cooking containers, such as kettles, rotating cookers, pressure cookers, or vats, with ingredients by opening valves, by starting pumps or injectors, or by hand. Give directions to other workers who are assisting in the batchmaking process. Homogenize or pasteurize material to prevent separation or to obtain prescribed butterfat content, using a homogenizing device. Inspect vats after cleaning to ensure that fermentable residue has been removed. Examine, feel, and taste product samples during production to evaluate quality, color, texture, flavor, and bouquet and document the results. Test food product samples for moisture content, acidity level, specific gravity, or butterfat content and continue processing until desired levels are reached. Formulate or modify recipes for specific kinds of food products.

Personality Type: Realistic. These occupations frequently involve work activities that include practical, hands-on problems and solutions. They often deal with plants; animals; and real-world materials such as wood, tools, and machinery. Many of the occupations require working outside and don't involve a lot of paperwork or working closely with others.

GOE—Interest Area/Cluster: 13. Manufacturing. **Work Group:** 13.03. Production Work, Assorted Materials Processing. **Other Jobs in This Work Group:** Bakers; Cementing and Gluing Machine Operators and Tenders; Chemical Equipment Operators and Tenders; Cleaning, Washing, and Metal Pickling Equipment Operators and Tenders; Coating, Painting, and Spraying Machine Setters, Operators, and Tenders; Cooling and Freezing Equipment Operators and Tenders; Cutting and Slicing Machine

Setters, Operators, and Tenders; Extruding and Forming Machine Setters, Operators, and Tenders, Synthetic and Glass Fibers; Extruding, Forming, Pressing, and Compacting Machine Setters, Operators, and Tenders; Food and Tobacco Roasting, Baking, and Drying Machine Operators and Tenders; Food Cooking Machine Operators and Tenders; Furnace, Kiln, Oven, Drier, and Kettle Operators and Tenders; Heat Treating Equipment Setters, Operators, and Tenders, Metal and Plastic; Helpers—Production Workers; Meat, Poultry, and Fish Cutters and Trimmers; Metal-Refining Furnace Operators and Tenders; Mixing and Blending Machine Setters, Operators, and Tenders; Packaging and Filling Machine Operators and Tenders; Plating and Coating Machine Setters, Operators, and Tenders, Metal and Plastic; Pourers and Casters, Metal; Sawing Machine Setters, Operators, and Tenders, Wood; Separating, Filtering, Clarifying, Precipitating, and Still Machine Setters, Operators, and Tenders; Sewing Machine Operators; Shoe Machine Operators and Tenders; Slaughterers and Meat Packers; Team Assemblers; Textile Bleaching and Dyeing Machine Operators and Tenders; Tire Builders; Woodworking Machine Setters, Operators, and Tenders, Except Sawing.

Skills—Operation Monitoring: Watching gauges, dials, or other indicators to make sure a machine is working properly. **Operation and Control:** Controlling operations of equipment or systems. **Equipment Maintenance:** Performing routine maintenance and determining when and what kind of maintenance is needed. **Repairing:** Repairing machines or systems, using the needed tools. **Quality Control Analysis:** Evaluating the quality or performance of products, services, or processes. **Troubleshooting:** Determining what is causing an operating error and deciding what to do about it.

Education and Training Program: Foodservice Systems Administration/Management. **Related Knowledge/ Courses—Production and Processing:** Inputs, outputs, raw materials, waste, quality control, costs, and techniques for maximizing the manufacture and distribution of goods. **Public Safety and Security:** Weaponry; public safety; security operations, rules, regulations, precautions, and prevention; and the protection of people, data, and property. **Chemistry:** The composition, structure, and properties of substances and of the chemical processes and transformations that they undergo. This includes uses of chemicals and their interactions, danger signs, production techniques, and disposal methods.

Work Environment: Noisy; contaminants; standing; using hands on objects, tools, or controls; bending or twisting the body; repetitive motions.

Food Science Technicians

- ❋ Education/Training Required: Associate degree
- ❋ Annual Earnings: $33,630
- ❋ Beginning Wage: $21,810
- ❋ Earnings Growth Potential: Medium
- ❋ Growth: 6.6%
- ❋ Annual Job Openings: 4,049
- ❋ Self-Employed: 0.7%
- ❋ Part-Time: 8.2%

The job openings listed here are shared with Agricultural Technicians.

Perform standardized qualitative and quantitative tests to determine physical or chemical properties of food or beverage products. Conduct standardized tests on food, beverages, additives, and preservatives in order to ensure compliance with standards and regulations regarding factors such as color, texture, and nutrients. Provide assistance to food scientists and technologists in research and development, production technology, and quality control. Compute moisture or salt content, percentages of ingredients, formulas, or other product factors, using mathematical and chemical procedures. Record and compile test results and prepare graphs, charts, and reports. Clean and sterilize laboratory equipment. Analyze test results to classify products or compare results with standard tables. Taste or smell foods or beverages in order to ensure that flavors meet specifications or to select samples with specific characteristics. Examine chemical and biological samples in order to identify cell structures and to locate bacteria or extraneous material, using microscope. Mix, blend, or cultivate ingredients in order to make reagents or to manufacture food or beverage products. Measure, test, and weigh bottles, cans, and other containers in order to ensure hardness, strength, and dimensions that meet specifications. Prepare slides and incubate slides with cell cultures. Order supplies needed to maintain inventories in laboratories or in storage facilities of food or beverage processing plants.

Personality Type: Realistic. These occupations frequently involve work activities that include practical, hands-on problems and solutions. They often deal with plants; animals; and real-world materials such as wood, tools, and machinery. Many of the occupations require working outside and don't involve a lot of paperwork or working closely with others.

GOE—Interest Area/Cluster: 01. Agriculture and Natural Resources. **Work Group:** 01.03. Resource Technologies for Plants, Animals, and the Environment. **Other Jobs in This Work Group:** Agricultural and Food Science Technicians; Agricultural Technicians; Environmental Science and Protection Technicians, Including Health; Food Scientists and Technologists; Geological and Petroleum Technicians; Geological Sample Test Technicians; Geophysical Data Technicians.

Skills—Science: Using scientific methods to solve problems. **Quality Control Analysis:** Evaluating the quality or performance of products, services, or processes. **Operation Monitoring:** Watching gauges, dials, or other indicators to make sure a machine is working properly. **Technology Design:** Generating or adapting equipment and technology to serve user needs. **Equipment Maintenance:** Performing routine maintenance and determining when and what kind of maintenance is needed. **Troubleshooting:** Determining what is causing an operating error and deciding what to do about it. **Reading Comprehension:** Understanding written sentences and paragraphs in work-related documents. **Installation:** Installing equipment, machines, wiring, or programs to meet specifications.

Education and Training Programs: Agricultural Animal Breeding; Animal Nutrition; Animal Sciences, General; Animal/Livestock Husbandry and Production; Crop Production; Dairy Science; Food Science. **Related Knowledge/Courses—Food Production:** Techniques and equipment for planting, growing, and harvesting of food for consumption, including crop-rotation methods, animal husbandry, and food storage/handling techniques. **Chemistry:** The composition, structure, and properties of substances and of the chemical processes and transformations that they undergo. This includes uses of chemicals and their interactions, danger signs, production techniques, and disposal methods. **Biology:** Plant and animal living tissue, cells, organisms, and entities, including their functions, interdependencies, and interactions with each other and the environment. **Production and Processing:** Inputs, outputs, raw materials, waste, quality control, costs, and techniques for maximizing the manufacture and distribution of goods. **Mathematics:** Using mathematics to solve problems. **English Language:** The structure and content of the English language, including the meaning and spelling of words, rules of composition, and grammar.

Work Environment: Indoors; noisy; contaminants; hazardous conditions; standing; using hands on objects, tools, or controls.

Food Service Managers

- Education/Training Required: Work experience in a related occupation
- Annual Earnings: $44,570
- Beginning Wage: $28,240
- Earnings Growth Potential: Medium
- Growth: 5.0%
- Annual Job Openings: 59,302
- Self-Employed: 44.8%
- Part-Time: 8.0%

Plan, direct, or coordinate activities of an organization or department that serves food and beverages. Monitor compliance with health and fire regulations regarding food preparation and serving, and building maintenance in lodging and dining facilities. Monitor food preparation methods, portion sizes, and garnishing and presentation of food to ensure that food is prepared and presented in an acceptable manner. Count money and make bank deposits. Investigate and resolve complaints regarding food quality, service, or accommodations. Coordinate assignments of cooking personnel to ensure economical use of food and timely preparation. Schedule and receive food and beverage deliveries, checking delivery contents to verify product quality and quantity. Monitor budgets and payroll records, and review financial transactions to ensure that expenditures are authorized and budgeted. Schedule staff hours and assign duties. Maintain food and equipment inventories, and keep inventory records. Establish standards for personnel performance and customer service. Perform some food preparation or service tasks such as cooking, clearing tables, and serving food and drinks when necessary. Plan menus and food utilization based on anticipated number of guests, nutritional value, palatability, popularity, and costs. Keep records required by government agencies regarding sanitation, and food subsidies when appropriate. Test cooked food by tasting and smelling it to ensure palatability and flavor conformity. Organize and direct worker training programs, resolve personnel problems, hire new staff, and evaluate employee performance in dining and lodging facilities. Order and purchase equipment and supplies. Review work procedures and operational problems to determine ways to improve service, performance, or safety. Assess staffing needs, and recruit staff using methods such as newspaper advertisements or attendance at job fairs. Arrange for equipment maintenance and repairs, and coordinate a variety of services such as waste removal and pest control. Record the number, type, and cost of items sold to determine which items may be unpopular or less profitable. Review menus and analyze recipes to determine labor and overhead costs, and assign prices to menu items.

Personality Type: Enterprising. These occupations frequently involve starting up and carrying out projects and can involve leading people and making many decisions. They sometimes require risk taking and often deal with business.

GOE—Interest Area/Cluster: 09. Hospitality, Tourism, and Recreation. **Work Group:** 09.01. Managerial Work in Hospitality and Tourism. **Other Jobs in This Work Group:** First-Line Supervisors/Managers of Food Preparation and Serving Workers; First-Line Supervisors/Managers of Personal Service Workers; Gaming Managers; Gaming Supervisors; Lodging Managers.

Skills—Management of Financial Resources: Determining how money will be spent to get the work done and accounting for these expenditures. **Management of Personnel Resources:** Motivating, developing, and directing people as they work; identifying the best people for the job. **Systems Evaluation:** Looking at many indicators of system performance and taking into account their accuracy. **Management of Material Resources:** Obtaining and seeing to the appropriate use of equipment, facilities, and materials needed to do certain work. **Systems Analysis:** Determining how a system should work and how changes will affect outcomes. **Negotiation:** Bringing others together and trying to reconcile differences. **Service Orientation:** Actively looking for ways to help people. **Persuasion:** Persuading others to approach things differently.

Education and Training Programs: Hospitality Administration/Management, General; Hotel/Motel Administration/Management; Restaurant, Culinary, and Catering Management/Manager Training; Restaurant/Food Services Management. **Related Knowledge/Courses—Food Production:** Techniques and equipment for planting, growing, and harvesting of food for consumption, including crop-rotation methods, animal husbandry, and food storage/handling techniques. **Sales and Marketing:** Principles and methods involved in showing, promoting, and selling products or services. This includes marketing strategies and tactics, product demonstration and sales techniques, and sales control systems. **Personnel and Human Resources:** Principles and procedures for personnel recruitment; selection; training; compensation and benefits; labor relations and negotiation; and personnel information systems. **Production and Processing:** Inputs, outputs, raw materials, waste, quality control, costs, and techniques for maximizing the manufacture and distribution of goods. **Education and Training:** Instructional methods and training techniques, including curriculum design principles, learning theory, group and individual teaching techniques, design of individual development plans, and test design principles. **Administration and Management:** Principles and processes involved in business and organizational planning, coordination, and execution. This includes strategic planning, resource allocation, manpower modeling, leadership techniques, and production methods.

Work Environment: Indoors; noisy; standing; walking and running; using hands on objects, tools, or controls; repetitive motions.

Forest Fire Fighters

- ❈ Education/Training Required: Long-term on-the-job training
- ❈ Annual Earnings: $43,170
- ❈ Beginning Wage: $21,530
- ❈ Earnings Growth Potential: Very high
- ❈ Growth: 12.1%
- ❈ Annual Job Openings: 18,887
- ❈ Self-Employed: 0.0%
- ❈ Part-Time: 1.3%

The job openings listed here are shared with Municipal Fire Fighters.

Control and suppress fires in forests or vacant public land. Maintain contact with fire dispatchers at all times to notify them of the need for additional firefighters and supplies or to detail any difficulties encountered. Rescue fire victims and administer emergency medical aid. Collaborate with other firefighters as a member of a firefighting crew. Patrol burned areas after fires to locate and eliminate hot spots that may restart fires. Extinguish flames and embers to suppress fires, using shovels or engine- or hand-driven water or chemical pumps. Fell trees, cut and clear brush, and dig trenches to create firelines, using axes, chain saws, or shovels. Maintain knowledge of current firefighting practices by participating in drills and by attending seminars, conventions, and conferences. Operate pumps connected to high-pressure hoses. Participate in physical training to maintain high levels of physical fitness. Establish water supplies, connect hoses, and direct water onto fires. Maintain fire equipment and firehouse living quarters. Inform and educate the public about fire prevention. Take action to contain any hazardous chemicals that could catch fire, leak, or spill. Organize fire caches, positioning equipment for the most effective response. Transport personnel and cargo to and from fire areas. Participate in fire prevention and inspection programs. Perform forest maintenance and improvement tasks such as cutting brush, planting trees, building trails, and marking timber. Test and maintain tools, equipment, jump gear, and parachutes to ensure readiness for fire-suppression activities. Observe forest areas from fire lookout towers to spot potential problems. Orient self in relation to fire, using compass and map, and collect supplies and equipment dropped by parachute. Serve as fully trained lead helicopter crewmember and as helispot manager. Drop weighted paper streamers from aircraft to determine the speed and direction of the wind at fire sites.

Personality Type: Realistic. These occupations frequently involve work activities that include practical, hands-on problems and solutions. They often deal with plants; animals; and real-world materials such as wood, tools, and machinery. Many of the occupations require working outside and don't involve a lot of paperwork or working closely with others.

GOE—Interest Area/Cluster: 12. Law and Public Safety. **Work Group:** 12.06. Emergency Responding. **Other Jobs in This Work Group:** Emergency Medical Technicians and Paramedics; Fire Fighters; Municipal Fire Fighters.

Skills—Repairing: Repairing machines or systems, using the needed tools. **Equipment Maintenance:** Performing routine maintenance and determining when and what kind of maintenance is needed. **Management of Personnel Resources:** Motivating, developing, and directing people as they work; identifying the best people for the job. **Operation Monitoring:** Watching gauges, dials, or other indicators to make sure a machine is working properly. **Equipment Selection:** Determining the kind of tools and equipment needed to do a job. **Operation and Control:** Controlling operations of equipment or systems. **Systems Analysis:** Determining how a system should work and how changes will affect outcomes. **Operations Analysis:** Analyzing needs and product requirements to create a design.

Education and Training Programs: Fire Protection, Other; Fire Science/Firefighting. **Related Knowledge/Courses—Geography:** Various methods for describing the location and distribution of land, sea, and air masses, including their physical locations, relationships, and characteristics. **Customer and Personal Service:** Principles and processes for providing customer and personal services, including needs assessment techniques, quality service standards, alternative delivery systems, and customer satisfaction evaluation techniques. **Mechanical Devices:** Machines and tools, including their designs, uses, benefits, repair, and maintenance. **Public Safety and Security:** Weaponry; public safety; security operations, rules, regulations, precautions, and prevention; and the protection of people, data, and property. **Education and Training:** Instructional methods and training techniques, including curriculum design principles, learning theory, group and individual teaching techniques, design of individual development plans, and test design principles. **Psychology:** Human behavior and performance, mental processes, psychological research methods, and the assessment and treatment of behavioral and affective disorders.

Work Environment: Outdoors; very hot or cold; contaminants; hazardous conditions; minor burns, cuts, bites, or stings; using hands on objects, tools, or controls.

Forest Fire Fighting and Prevention Supervisors

- ❋ Education/Training Required: Work experience in a related occupation
- ❋ Annual Earnings: $65,040
- ❋ Beginning Wage: $37,930
- ❋ Earnings Growth Potential: High
- ❋ Growth: 11.5%
- ❋ Annual Job Openings: 3,771
- ❋ Self-Employed: 0.0%
- ❋ Part-Time: 0.4%

The job openings listed here are shared with Municipal Fire Fighting and Prevention Supervisors.

Supervise fire fighters who control and suppress fires in forests or vacant public land. Communicate fire details to superiors, subordinates, and interagency dispatch centers, using two-way radios. Serve as working leader of an engine, hand, helicopter, or prescribed fire crew of three or more firefighters. Maintain fire suppression equipment in good condition, checking equipment periodically to ensure that it is ready for use. Evaluate size, location, and condition of forest fires in order to request and dispatch crews and position equipment so fires can be contained safely and effectively. Operate wildland fire engines and hoselays. Direct and supervise prescribed burn projects and prepare post-burn reports analyzing burn conditions and results. Monitor prescribed burns to ensure that they are conducted safely and effectively. Identify staff training and development needs to ensure that appropriate training can be arranged. Maintain knowledge of forest fire laws and fire prevention techniques and tactics. Recommend equipment modifications or new equipment purchases. Perform administrative duties such as compiling and maintaining records, completing forms, preparing reports, and composing correspondence. Recruit and hire forest fire-fighting personnel. Train workers in such skills as parachute jumping, fire suppression, aerial observation, and radio communication, both in the classroom and on the job. Review and evaluate employee performance. Observe fires and crews from air to determine fire-fighting force requirements and to note changing conditions that will affect fire-fighting efforts. Inspect all stations, uniforms, equipment, and recreation areas to ensure compliance with safety standards, taking corrective action as necessary. Schedule employee work assignments and set work priorities. Regulate open burning by issuing burning permits, inspecting problem sites, issuing citations for violations of laws and ordinances, and educating the public in proper burning practices. Direct investigations of suspected arsons in wildfires, working closely with other investigating agencies. Monitor fire suppression expenditures to ensure that they are necessary and reasonable.

Personality Type: Enterprising. These occupations frequently involve starting up and carrying out projects and can involve leading people and making many decisions. They sometimes require risk taking and often deal with business.

GOE—Interest Area/Cluster: 12. Law and Public Safety. **Work Group:** 12.01. Managerial Work in Law and Public Safety. **Other Jobs in This Work Group:** Emergency Management Specialists; First-Line Supervisors/Managers of Correctional Officers; First-Line Supervisors/Managers of Fire Fighting and Prevention Workers; First-Line Supervisors/Managers of Police and Detectives; Municipal Fire Fighting and Prevention Supervisors.

Skills—Equipment Maintenance: Performing routine maintenance and determining when and what kind of maintenance is needed. **Repairing:** Repairing machines or systems, using the needed tools. **Operation Monitoring:** Watching gauges, dials, or other indicators to make sure a machine is working properly. **Management of Personnel Resources:** Motivating, developing, and directing people as they work; identifying the best people for the job. **Operation and Control:** Controlling operations of equipment or systems. **Science:** Using scientific methods to solve problems. **Management of Material Resources:** Obtaining and seeing to the appropriate use of equipment, facilities, and materials needed to do certain work. **Equipment Selection:** Determining the kind of tools and equipment needed to do a job.

Education and Training Programs: Fire Protection and Safety Technology/Technician Training; Fire Services Administration. **Related Knowledge/Courses—Public Safety and Security:** Weaponry; public safety; security operations, rules, regulations, precautions, and prevention; and the protection of people, data, and property. **Building and Construction:** Materials, methods, and the appropriate tools to construct objects, structures, and buildings.

Mechanical Devices: Machines and tools, including their designs, uses, benefits, repair, and maintenance. **Customer and Personal Service:** Principles and processes for providing customer and personal services, including needs assessment techniques, quality service standards, alternative delivery systems, and customer satisfaction evaluation techniques. **Personnel and Human Resources:** Principles and procedures for personnel recruitment; selection; training; compensation and benefits; labor relations and negotiation; and personnel information systems. **Transportation:** Principles and methods for moving people or goods by air, rail, sea, or road, including their relative costs, advantages, and limitations.

Work Environment: Outdoors; noisy; very hot or cold; hazardous equipment; minor burns, cuts, bites, or stings; standing.

Freight and Cargo Inspectors

- ❀ Education/Training Required: Work experience in a related occupation
- ❀ Annual Earnings: $51,440
- ❀ Beginning Wage: $27,340
- ❀ Earnings Growth Potential: High
- ❀ Growth: 16.4%
- ❀ Annual Job Openings: 2,122
- ❀ Self-Employed: 5.9%
- ❀ Part-Time: 3.7%

The job openings listed here are shared with Aviation Inspectors and with Transportation Vehicle, Equipment, and Systems Inspectors, Except Aviation.

Inspect the handling, storage, and stowing of freight and cargoes. Prepare and submit reports after completion of freight shipments. Inspect shipments to ensure that freight is securely braced and blocked. Record details about freight conditions, handling of freight, and any problems encountered. Advise crews in techniques of stowing dangerous and heavy cargo. Observe loading of freight to ensure that crews comply with procedures. Recommend remedial procedures to correct any violations found during inspections. Inspect loaded cargo, cargo lashed to decks or in storage facilities, and cargo handling devices to determine compliance with health and safety regulations and need for maintenance. Measure ships' holds and depths of fuel and water in tanks, using sounding lines and tape measures. Notify workers of any special treatment required for shipments. Direct crews to reload freight or to insert additional bracing or packing as necessary. Check temperatures and humidities of shipping and storage areas to ensure that they are at appropriate levels to protect cargo. Determine cargo transportation capabilities by reading documents that set forth cargo loading and securing procedures, capacities, and stability factors. Read draft markings to determine depths of vessels in water. Issue certificates of compliance for vessels without violations. Write certificates of admeasurement that list details such as designs, lengths, depths, and breadths of vessels, and methods of propulsion. Calculate gross and net tonnage, hold capacities, volumes of stored fuel and water, cargo weights, and ship stability factors, using mathematical formulas. Post warning signs on vehicles containing explosives or flammable or radioactive materials. Measure heights and widths of loads to ensure they will pass over bridges or through tunnels on scheduled routes. Time rolls of ships, using stopwatches. Determine types of licenses and safety equipment required, and compute applicable fees such as tolls and wharfage fees.

Personality Type: Realistic. These occupations frequently involve work activities that include practical, hands-on problems and solutions. They often deal with plants; animals; and real-world materials such as wood, tools, and machinery. Many of the occupations require working outside and don't involve a lot of paperwork or working closely with others.

GOE—Interest Area/Cluster: 07. Government and Public Administration. **Work Group:** 07.03. Regulations Enforcement. **Other Jobs in This Work Group:** Agricultural Inspectors; Aviation Inspectors; Compliance Officers, Except Agriculture, Construction, Health and Safety, and **Transportation:** Principles and methods for moving people or goods by air, rail, sea, or road, including their relative costs, advantages, and limitations. Construction and Building Inspectors; Environmental Compliance Inspectors; Equal Opportunity Representatives and Officers; Financial Examiners; Fire Inspectors; Fish and Game Wardens; Forest Fire Inspectors and Prevention Specialists; Government Property Inspectors and Investigators; Immigration and Customs Inspectors; Licensing Examiners and Inspectors; Nuclear Monitoring Technicians; Occupational Health and Safety Specialists; Occupational Health and Safety Technicians; Tax Examiners, Collectors, and

Revenue Agents; Transportation Vehicle, Equipment, and Systems Inspectors, Except Aviation.

Skills—Operation Monitoring: Watching gauges, dials, or other indicators to make sure a machine is working properly. **Quality Control Analysis:** Evaluating the quality or performance of products, services, or processes. **Science:** Using scientific methods to solve problems. **Mathematics:** Using mathematics to solve problems. **Writing:** Communicating effectively with others in writing as indicated by the needs of the audience. **Service Orientation:** Actively looking for ways to help people. **Equipment Selection:** Determining the kind of tools and equipment needed to do a job. **Troubleshooting:** Determining what is causing an operating error and deciding what to do about it.

Education and Training Programs: No related CIP programs; this job is learned through work experience in a related occupation. **Related Knowledge/Courses— Transportation:** Principles and methods for moving people or goods by air, rail, sea, or road, including their relative costs, advantages, and limitations. **Engineering and Technology:** Equipment, tools, and mechanical devices and their uses to produce motion, light, power, technology, and other applications. **Public Safety and Security:** Weaponry; public safety; security operations, rules, regulations, precautions, and prevention; and the protection of people, data, and property. **Physics:** Physical principles, laws, and applications, including air, water, material dynamics, light, atomic principles, heat, electric theory, earth formations, and meteorological and related natural phenomena. **Geography:** Various methods for describing the location and distribution of land, sea, and air masses, including their physical locations, relationships, and characteristics. **Mechanical Devices:** Machines and tools, including their designs, uses, benefits, repair, and maintenance.

Work Environment: More often outdoors than indoors; noisy; very hot or cold; very bright or dim lighting; contaminants.

Funeral Directors

* Education/Training Required: Associate degree
* Annual Earnings: $50,370
* Beginning Wage: $28,890
* Earnings Growth Potential: High
* Growth: 12.5%
* Annual Job Openings: 3,939
* Self-Employed: 19.7%
* Part-Time: 8.5%

Perform various tasks to arrange and direct funeral services, such as coordinating transportation of bodies to mortuaries for embalming, interviewing families or other authorized people to arrange details, selecting pallbearers, procuring officials for religious rites, and providing transportation for mourners. Obtain information needed to complete legal documents such as death certificates and burial permits. Oversee the preparation and care of the remains of people who have died. Consult with families or friends of the deceased to arrange funeral details such as obituary notice wording, casket selection, and plans for services. Plan, schedule, and coordinate funerals, burials, and cremations, arranging details such as floral delivery and the time and place of services. Perform embalming duties as necessary. Arrange for clergy members to perform needed services. Contact cemeteries to schedule the opening and closing of graves. Provide information on funeral service options, products, and merchandise, and maintain a casket display area. Close caskets and lead funeral corteges to churches or burial sites. Offer counsel and comfort to bereaved families and friends. Inform survivors of benefits for which they may be eligible. Discuss and negotiate prearranged funerals with clients. Maintain financial records, order merchandise, and prepare accounts. Provide or arrange transportation between sites for the remains, mourners, pallbearers, clergy, and flowers. Plan placement of caskets at funeral sites, and place and adjust lights, fixtures, and floral displays. Direct preparations and shipment of bodies for out-of-state burials. Manage funeral home operations, including the hiring, training, and supervision of embalmers, funeral attendants, or other staff. Clean funeral home facilities and grounds. Arrange for pallbearers, and inform pallbearers and honorary groups of their duties. Receive and usher people to their seats for services.

Participate in community activities for funeral home promotion or other purposes.

Personality Type: Enterprising. These occupations frequently involve starting up and carrying out projects and can involve leading people and making many decisions. They sometimes require risk taking and often deal with business.

GOE—Interest Area/Cluster: 14. Retail and Wholesale Sales and Service. **Work Group:** 14.01. Managerial Work in Retail/Wholesale Sales and Service. **Other Jobs in This Work Group:** Advertising and Promotions Managers; First-Line Supervisors/Managers of Non-Retail Sales Workers; First-Line Supervisors/Managers of Retail Sales Workers; Marketing Managers; Property, Real Estate, and Community Association Managers; Purchasing Managers; Sales Managers.

Skills—Management of Personnel Resources: Motivating, developing, and directing people as they work; identifying the best people for the job. **Social Perceptiveness:** Being aware of others' reactions and understanding why they react the way they do. **Negotiation:** Bringing others together and trying to reconcile differences. **Management of Financial Resources:** Determining how money will be spent to get the work done and accounting for these expenditures. **Service Orientation:** Actively looking for ways to help people.

Education and Training Programs: Funeral Direction/Service; Funeral Service and Mortuary Science, General. **Related Knowledge/Courses—Chemistry:** The composition, structure, and properties of substances and of the chemical processes and transformations that they undergo. This includes uses of chemicals and their interactions, danger signs, production techniques, and disposal methods. **Philosophy and Theology:** Different philosophical systems and religions, including their basic principles, values, ethics, ways of thinking, customs, and practices and their impact on human culture. **Therapy and Counseling:** Information and techniques needed to rehabilitate physical and mental ailments and to provide career guidance, including alternative treatments, rehabilitation equipment and its proper use, and methods to evaluate treatment effects. **Customer and Personal Service:** Principles and processes for providing customer and personal services, including needs assessment techniques, quality service standards, alternative delivery systems, and customer satisfaction evaluation techniques. **Biology:** Plant and animal living tissue, cells, organisms, and entities, including their functions, interdependencies, and interactions with each other and the environment. **Sales and Marketing:** Principles and methods involved in showing, promoting, and selling products or services. This includes marketing strategies and tactics, product demonstration and sales techniques, and sales control systems.

Work Environment: More often indoors than outdoors; contaminants; disease or infections; standing; using hands on objects, tools, or controls.

Gaming Managers

- ❋ Education/Training Required: Work experience in a related occupation
- ❋ Annual Earnings: $64,410
- ❋ Beginning Wage: $36,740
- ❋ Earnings Growth Potential: High
- ❋ Growth: 24.4%
- ❋ Annual Job Openings: 549
- ❋ Self-Employed: 16.3%
- ❋ Part-Time: 4.5%

Plan, organize, direct, control, or coordinate gaming operations in a casino. Formulate gaming policies for their area of responsibility. Resolve customer complaints regarding problems such as payout errors. Remove suspected cheaters, such as card counters and other players who may have systems that shift the odds of winning to their favor. Maintain familiarity with all games used at a facility, as well as strategies and tricks employed in those games. Train new workers and evaluate their performance. Circulate among gaming tables to ensure that operations are conducted properly, that dealers follow house rules, and that players are not cheating. Explain and interpret house rules, such as game rules and betting limits. Monitor staffing levels to ensure that games and tables are adequately staffed for each shift, arranging for staff rotations and breaks and locating substitute employees as necessary. Interview and hire workers. Prepare work schedules and station assignments and keep attendance records. Direct the distribution of complimentary hotel rooms, meals, and other discounts or free items given to players based on their length of play and betting totals. Establish policies on issues such as the type of gambling offered and the odds, the extension of credit, and the serving of food and beverages. Track supplies of money to tables and perform any required paperwork. Set and maintain a bank and table limit for each game. Monitor credit extended to players. Review operational expenses, budget estimates, betting accounts, and collection reports for accuracy. Record, collect, and pay off bets, issuing receipts as necessary. Direct workers compiling summary sheets that show wager amounts and payoffs for races and events. Notify board attendants of table vacancies so that waiting patrons can play.

Personality Type: Enterprising. These occupations frequently involve starting up and carrying out projects and can involve leading people and making many decisions. They sometimes require risk taking and often deal with business.

GOE—Interest Area/Cluster: 09. Hospitality, Tourism, and Recreation. **Work Group:** 09.01. Managerial Work in Hospitality and Tourism. **Other Jobs in This Work Group:** First-Line Supervisors/Managers of Food Preparation and Serving Workers; First-Line Supervisors/Managers of Personal Service Workers; Food Service Managers; Gaming Supervisors; Lodging Managers.

Skills—Management of Personnel Resources: Motivating, developing, and directing people as they work; identifying the best people for the job. **Management of Financial Resources:** Determining how money will be spent to get the work done and accounting for these expenditures. **Systems Evaluation:** Looking at many indicators of system performance and taking into account their accuracy. **Service Orientation:** Actively looking for ways to help people. **Negotiation:** Bringing others together and trying to reconcile differences. **Operations Analysis:** Analyzing needs and product requirements to create a design. **Social Perceptiveness:** Being aware of others' reactions and understanding why they react the way they do. **Mathematics:** Using mathematics to solve problems.

Education and Training Program: Personal and Culinary Services, Other. **Related Knowledge/Courses—Sales and Marketing:** Principles and methods involved in showing, promoting, and selling products or services. This includes marketing strategies and tactics, product demonstration and sales techniques, and sales control systems. **Personnel and Human Resources:** Principles and procedures for personnel recruitment; selection; training;

compensation and benefits; labor relations and negotiation; and personnel information systems. **Customer and Personal Service:** Principles and processes for providing customer and personal services, including needs assessment techniques, quality service standards, alternative delivery systems, and customer satisfaction evaluation techniques. **Administration and Management:** Principles and processes involved in business and organizational planning, coordination, and execution. This includes strategic planning, resource allocation, manpower modeling, leadership techniques, and production methods. **Economics and Accounting:** Economic and accounting principles and practices, the financial markets, banking, and the analysis and reporting of financial data. **Mathematics:** Numbers and their operations and interrelationships, including arithmetic, algebra, geometry, calculus, and statistics and their applications.

Work Environment: Indoors; noisy; contaminants; standing; walking and running.

Gaming Supervisors

- ❋ Education/Training Required: Work experience in a related occupation
- ❋ Annual Earnings: $42,980
- ❋ Beginning Wage: $26,310
- ❋ Earnings Growth Potential: Medium
- ❋ Growth: 23.4%
- ❋ Annual Job Openings: 4,602
- ❋ Self-Employed: 29.2%
- ❋ Part-Time: 12.8%

Supervise gaming operations and personnel in an assigned area. Circulate among tables and observe operations. Ensure that stations and games are covered for each shift. May explain and interpret operating rules of house to patrons. May plan and organize activities and create friendly atmosphere for guests in hotels/casinos. May adjust service complaints. Monitor game operations to ensure that house rules are followed, that tribal, state, and federal regulations are adhered to, and that employees provide prompt and courteous service. Observe gamblers' behavior for signs of cheating such as marking, switching, or counting cards; notify security staff of suspected cheating. Maintain familiarity with the games at a facility and with strategies and tricks used by cheaters at such games. Perform paperwork required for monetary transactions. Resolve customer and employee complaints. Greet customers and ask about the quality of service they are receiving. Establish and maintain banks and table limits for each game. Report customer-related incidents occurring in gaming areas to supervisors. Monitor stations and games and move dealers from game to game to ensure adequate staffing. Explain and interpret house rules, such as game rules and betting limits, for patrons. Supervise the distribution of complimentary meals, hotel rooms, discounts, and other items given to players based on length of play and amount bet. Evaluate workers' performance and prepare written performance evaluations. Monitor patrons for signs of compulsive gambling, offering assistance if necessary. Record, issue receipts for, and pay off bets. Monitor and verify the counting, wrapping, weighing, and distribution of currency and coins. Direct workers compiling summary sheets for each race or event to record amounts wagered and amounts to be paid to winners. Determine how many gaming tables to open each day and schedule staff accordingly. Establish policies on types of gambling offered, odds, and extension of credit. Interview, hire, and train workers. Provide fire protection and first-aid assistance when necessary. Review operational expenses, budget estimates, betting accounts, and collection reports for accuracy.

Personality Type: Enterprising. These occupations frequently involve starting up and carrying out projects and can involve leading people and making many decisions. They sometimes require risk taking and often deal with business.

GOE—Interest Area/Cluster: 09. Hospitality, Tourism, and Recreation. **Work Group:** 09.01. Managerial Work in Hospitality and Tourism. **Other Jobs in This Work Group:** First-Line Supervisors/Managers of Food Preparation and Serving Workers; First-Line Supervisors/Managers of Personal Service Workers; Food Service Managers; Gaming Managers; Lodging Managers.

Skills—Management of Personnel Resources: Motivating, developing, and directing people as they work; identifying the best people for the job. **Instructing:** Teaching others how to do something. **Service Orientation:** Actively looking for ways to help people. **Monitoring:** Assessing how well one is doing when learning or doing something. **Social Perceptiveness:** Being aware of others' reactions and

understanding why they react the way they do. **Mathematics:** Using mathematics to solve problems. **Critical Thinking:** Using logic and analysis to identify the strengths and weaknesses of different approaches. **Judgment and Decision Making:** Weighing the relative costs and benefits of a potential action.

Education and Training Program: Personal and Culinary Services, Other. **Related Knowledge/Courses— Customer and Personal Service:** Principles and processes for providing customer and personal services, including needs assessment techniques, quality service standards, alternative delivery systems, and customer satisfaction evaluation techniques. **Psychology:** Human behavior and performance, mental processes, psychological research methods, and the assessment and treatment of behavioral and affective disorders. **Mathematics:** Numbers and their operations and interrelationships, including arithmetic, algebra, geometry, calculus, and statistics and their applications. **Law and Government:** Laws, legal codes, court procedures, precedents, government regulations, executive orders, agency rules, and the democratic political process. **Sales and Marketing:** Principles and methods involved in showing, promoting, and selling products or services. This includes marketing strategies and tactics, product demonstration and sales techniques, and sales control systems. **Personnel and Human Resources:** Principles and procedures for personnel recruitment; selection; training; compensation and benefits; labor relations and negotiation; and personnel information systems.

Work Environment: Indoors; noisy; contaminants; standing; walking and running.

Gaming Surveillance Officers and Gaming Investigators

- ❊ Education/Training Required: Moderate-term on-the-job training
- ❊ Annual Earnings: $27,440
- ❊ Beginning Wage: $19,170
- ❊ Earnings Growth Potential: Low
- ❊ Growth: 33.6%
- ❊ Annual Job Openings: 2,124
- ❊ Self-Employed: 0.7%
- ❊ Part-Time: 15.5%

Act as oversight and security agent for management and customers. Observe casino or casino hotel operation for irregular activities such as cheating or theft by either employees or patrons. May utilize one-way mirrors above the casino floor and cashier's cage and from desk. Use of audio/video equipment is also common to observe operation of the business. Usually required to provide verbal and written reports of all violations and suspicious behavior to supervisor. Report all violations and suspicious behaviors to supervisors, verbally or in writing. Monitor establishment activities to ensure adherence to all state gaming regulations and company policies and procedures. Act as oversight or security agents for management or customers. Supervise or train surveillance observers.

Personality Type: Realistic. These occupations frequently involve work activities that include practical, hands-on problems and solutions. They often deal with plants; animals; and real-world materials such as wood, tools, and machinery. Many of the occupations require working outside and don't involve a lot of paperwork or working closely with others.

GOE—Interest Area/Cluster: 12. Law and Public Safety. **Work Group:** 12.05. Safety and Security. **Other Jobs in This Work Group:** Animal Control Workers; Crossing Guards; Lifeguards, Ski Patrol, and Other Recreational Protective Service Workers; Private Detectives and Investigators; Security Guards; Transportation Security Screeners.

Skills—Management of Personnel Resources: Motivating, developing, and directing people as they work; identifying the best people for the job. **Active Listening:** Listening to what other people are saying and asking questions as appropriate. **Writing:** Communicating effectively with others in writing as indicated by the needs of the audience. **Negotiation:** Bringing others together and trying to reconcile differences. **Learning Strategies:** Using multiple approaches when learning or teaching new things. **Social Perceptiveness:** Being aware of others' reactions and understanding why they react the way they do. **Installation:** Installing equipment, machines, wiring, or programs to meet specifications. **Critical Thinking:** Using logic and analysis to identify the strengths and weaknesses of different approaches.

Education and Training Program: Personal and Culinary Services, Other. **Related Knowledge/Courses— Public Safety and Security:** Weaponry; public safety; security operations, rules, regulations, precautions, and prevention; and the protection of people, data, and property. **Computers and Electronics:** Electric circuit boards, processors, chips, and computer hardware and software, including applications and programming. **Telecommunications:** Transmission, broadcasting, switching, control, and operation of telecommunications systems. **Law and Government:** Laws, legal codes, court procedures, precedents, government regulations, executive orders, agency rules, and the democratic political process. **Clerical Studies:** Administrative and clerical procedures and systems such as word-processing systems, filing and records management systems, stenography and transcription, forms, design principles, and other office procedures and terminology. **Education and Training:** Instructional methods and training techniques, including curriculum design principles, learning theory, group and individual teaching techniques, design of individual development plans, and test design principles.

Work Environment: Indoors; contaminants; sitting; using hands on objects, tools, or controls; repetitive motions.

Geological Sample Test Technicians

- ❋ Education/Training Required: Associate degree
- ❋ Annual Earnings: $50,950
- ❋ Beginning Wage: $25,160
- ❋ Earnings Growth Potential: Very high
- ❋ Growth: 8.6%
- ❋ Annual Job Openings: 1,895
- ❋ Self-Employed: 0.0%
- ❋ Part-Time: 1.0%

The job openings listed here are shared with Geophysical Data Technicians.

Test and analyze geological samples, crude oil, or petroleum products to detect presence of petroleum, gas, or mineral deposits indicating potential for exploration and production or to determine physical and chemical properties to ensure that products meet quality standards. Test and analyze samples in order to determine their content and characteristics, using laboratory apparatus and testing equipment. Collect and prepare solid and fluid samples for analysis. Assemble, operate, and maintain field and laboratory testing, measuring, and mechanical equipment, working as part of a crew when required. Compile and record testing and operational data for review and further analysis. Adjust and repair testing, electrical, and mechanical equipment and devices. Supervise well exploration and drilling activities and well completions. Inspect engines for wear and defective parts, using equipment and measuring devices. Prepare notes, sketches, geological maps, and cross sections. Participate in geological, geophysical, geochemical, hydrographic, or oceanographic surveys; prospecting field trips; exploratory drilling; well logging; or underground mine survey programs. Plot information from aerial photographs, well logs, section descriptions, and other databases. Assess the environmental impacts of development projects on subsurface materials. Collaborate with hydrogeologists to evaluate groundwater and well circulation. Prepare, transcribe, and/or analyze seismic, gravimetric, well log, or other geophysical and survey data. Participate in the evaluation of possible mining locations.

Personality Type: Realistic. These occupations frequently involve work activities that include practical, hands-on problems and solutions. They often deal with plants; animals; and real-world materials such as wood, tools, and machinery. Many of the occupations require working outside and don't involve a lot of paperwork or working closely with others.

GOE—Interest Area/Cluster: 01. Agriculture and Natural Resources. **Work Group:** 01.03. Resource Technologies for Plants, Animals, and the Environment. **Other Jobs in This Work Group:** Agricultural and Food Science Technicians; Agricultural Technicians; Environmental Science and Protection Technicians, Including Health; Food Science Technicians; Food Scientists and Technologists; Geological and Petroleum Technicians; Geophysical Data Technicians.

Skills—Science: Using scientific methods to solve problems. **Equipment Maintenance:** Performing routine maintenance and determining when and what kind of maintenance is needed. **Operation Monitoring:** Watching gauges, dials, or other indicators to make sure a machine is working properly. **Quality Control Analysis:** Evaluating the quality or performance of products, services, or processes. **Mathematics:** Using mathematics to solve problems. **Operations Analysis:** Analyzing needs and product requirements to create a design. **Installation:** Installing equipment, machines, wiring, or programs to meet specifications. **Operation and Control:** Controlling operations of equipment or systems.

Education and Training Program: Petroleum Technology/Technician Training. **Related Knowledge/Courses—Chemistry:** The composition, structure, and properties of substances and of the chemical processes and transformations that they undergo. This includes uses of chemicals and their interactions, danger signs, production techniques, and disposal methods. **Geography:** Various methods for describing the location and distribution of land, sea, and air masses, including their physical locations, relationships, and characteristics. **Physics:** Physical principles, laws, and applications, including air, water, material dynamics, light, atomic principles, heat, electric theory, earth formations, and meteorological and related natural phenomena. **Mechanical Devices:** Machines and tools, including their designs, uses, benefits, repair, and maintenance. **Mathematics:** Numbers and their operations and interrelationships, including arithmetic, algebra, geometry, calculus, and statistics and their applications. **Computers and Electronics:** Electric circuit boards, processors, chips, and computer hardware and software, including applications and programming.

Work Environment: Indoors; noisy; contaminants; more often standing than sitting; using hands on objects, tools, or controls.

Geophysical Data Technicians

* Education/Training Required: Associate degree
* Annual Earnings: $50,950
* Beginning Wage: $25,160
* Earnings Growth Potential: Very high
* Growth: 8.6%
* Annual Job Openings: 1,895
* Self-Employed: 0.0%
* Part-Time: 1.0%

The job openings listed here are shared with Geological Sample Test Technicians.

Measure, record, and evaluate geological data by using sonic, electronic, electrical, seismic, or gravity-measuring instruments to prospect for oil or gas. May collect and evaluate core samples and cuttings. Prepare notes, sketches, geological maps, and cross-sections. Read and study reports in order to compile information and data for geological and geophysical prospecting. Interview individuals, and research public databases in order to obtain information. Assemble, maintain, and distribute information for library or record systems. Operate and adjust equipment and apparatus used to obtain geological data. Plan and direct activities of workers who operate equipment to collect data. Set up, or direct set-up of instruments used to collect geological data. Record readings in order to compile data used in prospecting for oil or gas. Supervise oil, water, and gas well drilling activities. Collect samples and cuttings, using equipment and hand tools. Develop and print photographic recordings of information, using equipment. Measure geological characteristics used in prospecting for oil or gas, using measuring instruments. Evaluate and interpret core samples and cuttings, and other geological data used in prospecting for oil or gas. Diagnose and repair malfunctioning instruments and equipment, using manufacturers' manuals and hand tools. Prepare and attach packing instructions to shipping containers. Develop and design packing materials and handling procedures for shipping of objects.

Personality Type: Conventional. These occupations frequently involve following set procedures and routines and can include working with data and details more than with ideas. Usually there is a clear line of authority to follow.

GOE—Interest Area/Cluster: 01. Agriculture and Natural Resources. **Work Group:** 01.03. Resource Technologies for Plants, Animals, and the Environment. **Other Jobs in This Work Group:** Agricultural and Food Science Technicians; Agricultural Technicians; Environmental Science and Protection Technicians, Including Health; Food Science Technicians; Food Scientists and Technologists; Geological and Petroleum Technicians; Geological Sample Test Technicians.

Skills—Science: Using scientific methods to solve problems. **Technology Design:** Generating or adapting equipment and technology to serve user needs. **Mathematics:** Using mathematics to solve problems. **Operations Analysis:** Analyzing needs and product requirements to create a design. **Operation Monitoring:** Watching gauges,

dials, or other indicators to make sure a machine is working properly. **Persuasion:** Persuading others to approach things differently. **Equipment Selection:** Determining the kind of tools and equipment needed to do a job. **Management of Financial Resources:** Determining how money will be spent to get the work done and accounting for these expenditures.

Education and Training Program: Petroleum Technology/Technician Training. **Related Knowledge/Courses— Geography:** Various methods for describing the location and distribution of land, sea, and air masses, including their physical locations, relationships, and characteristics. **Engineering and Technology:** Equipment, tools, and mechanical devices and their uses to produce motion, light, power, technology, and other applications. **Physics:** Physical principles, laws, and applications, including air, water, material dynamics, light, atomic principles, heat, electric theory, earth formations, and meteorological and related natural phenomena. **Computers and Electronics:** Electric circuit boards, processors, chips, and computer hardware and software, including applications and programming. **Mathematics:** Numbers and their operations and interrelationships, including arithmetic, algebra, geometry, calculus, and statistics and their applications. **Chemistry:** The composition, structure, and properties of substances and of the chemical processes and transformations that they undergo. This includes uses of chemicals and their interactions, danger signs, production techniques, and disposal methods.

Work Environment: Indoors; sitting.

Glaziers

* Education/Training Required: Long-term on-the-job training
* Annual Earnings: $35,230
* Beginning Wage: $21,670
* Earnings Growth Potential: Medium
* Growth: 11.9%
* Annual Job Openings: 6,416
* Self-Employed: 5.3%
* Part-Time: 2.7%

Install glass in windows, skylights, storefronts, and display cases or on surfaces such as building fronts,

interior walls, ceilings, and tabletops. Read and interpret blueprints and specifications to determine size, shape, color, type, and thickness of glass; location of framing; installation procedures; and staging and scaffolding materials required. Determine plumb of walls or ceilings, using plumb-lines and levels. Fabricate and install metal sashes and moldings for glass installation, using aluminum or steel framing. Measure mirrors and dimensions of areas to be covered in order to determine work procedures. Fasten glass panes into wood sashes or frames with clips, points, or moldings, adding weather seals or putty around pane edges to seal joints. Secure mirrors in position, using mastic cement, putty, bolts, or screws. Cut, fit, install, repair, and replace glass and glass substitutes such as plastic and aluminum, in building interiors or exteriors and in furniture or other products. Cut and remove broken glass prior to installing replacement glass. Set glass doors into frames, and bolt metal hinges, handles, locks, and other hardware to attach doors to frames and walls. Score glass with cutters' wheels, breaking off excess glass by hand or with notched tools. Cut, assemble, fit, and attach metal-framed glass enclosures for showers, bathtubs, display cases, skylights, solariums, and other structures. Drive trucks to installation sites, and unload mirrors, glass equipment, and tools. Install pre-assembled metal or wood frameworks for windows or doors to be fitted with glass panels, using hand tools. Cut and attach mounting strips, metal or wood moldings, rubber gaskets, or metal clips to surfaces in preparation for mirror installation. Assemble, erect, and dismantle scaffolds, rigging, and hoisting equipment. Load and arrange glass and mirrors onto delivery trucks, using suction cups or cranes to lift glass. Measure and mark outlines or patterns on glass to indicate cutting lines. Grind and polish glass, and smooth edges when necessary. Prepare glass for cutting by resting it on rack edges or against cutting tables, and brushing a thin layer of oil along cutting lines or dipping cutting tools in oil. Pack spaces between moldings and glass with glazing compounds, and trim excess material with glazing knives.

Personality Type: Realistic. These occupations frequently involve work activities that include practical, hands-on problems and solutions. They often deal with plants; animals; and real-world materials such as wood, tools, and machinery. Many of the occupations require working outside and don't involve a lot of paperwork or working closely with others.

GOE—Interest Area/Cluster: 02. Architecture and Construction. **Work Group:** 02.04. Construction Crafts. **Other Jobs in This Work Group:** Boilermakers; Brickmasons and Blockmasons; Carpet Installers; Cement Masons and Concrete Finishers; Commercial Divers; Construction Carpenters; Crane and Tower Operators; Drywall and Ceiling Tile Installers; Electricians; Fence Erectors; Floor Layers, Except Carpet, Wood, and Hard Tiles; Floor Sanders and Finishers; Hazardous Materials Removal Workers; Insulation Workers, Floor, Ceiling, and Wall; Insulation Workers, Mechanical; Manufactured Building and Mobile Home Installers; Operating Engineers and Other Construction Equipment Operators; Painters, Construction and Maintenance; Paperhangers; Paving, Surfacing, and Tamping Equipment Operators; Pile-Driver Operators; Pipe Fitters and Steamfitters; Pipelayers; Plasterers and Stucco Masons; Plumbers; Plumbers, Pipefitters, and Steamfitters; Rail-Track Laying and Maintenance Equipment Operators; Refractory Materials Repairers, Except Brickmasons; Reinforcing Iron and Rebar Workers; Riggers; Roofers; Rough Carpenters; Security and Fire Alarm Systems Installers; Segmental Pavers; Sheet Metal Workers; Stone Cutters and Carvers, Manufacturing; Stonemasons; Structural Iron and Steel Workers; Tapers; Terrazzo Workers and Finishers; Tile and Marble Setters.

Skills—Installation: Installing equipment, machines, wiring, or programs to meet specifications. **Mathematics:** Using mathematics to solve problems. **Repairing:** Repairing machines or systems, using the needed tools.

Education and Training Program: Glazier Training. **Related Knowledge/Courses—Building and Construction:** Materials, methods, and the appropriate tools to construct objects, structures, and buildings. **Mechanical Devices:** Machines and tools, including their designs, uses, benefits, repair, and maintenance. **Design:** Design techniques, principles, tools, and instruments involved in the production and use of precision technical plans, blueprints, drawings, and models. **Engineering and Technology:** Equipment, tools, and mechanical devices and their uses to produce motion, light, power, technology, and other applications. **Mathematics:** Numbers and their operations and interrelationships, including arithmetic, algebra, geometry, calculus, and statistics and their applications. **Public Safety and Security:** Weaponry; public safety; security operations, rules, regulations, precautions, and prevention; and the protection of people, data, and property.

Work Environment: Outdoors; noisy; very hot or cold; contaminants; standing; using hands on objects, tools, or controls.

Government Property Inspectors and Investigators

- ✳ Education/Training Required: Long-term on-the-job training
- ✳ Annual Earnings: $48,400
- ✳ Beginning Wage: $28,980
- ✳ Earnings Growth Potential: High
- ✳ Growth: 4.9%
- ✳ Annual Job Openings: 15,841
- ✳ Self-Employed: 0.4%
- ✳ Part-Time: 5.0%

The job openings listed here are shared with Coroners; with Environmental Compliance Inspectors; with Equal Opportunity Representatives and Officers; and with Licensing Examiners and Inspectors.

Investigate or inspect government property to ensure compliance with contract agreements and government regulations. Prepare correspondence, reports of inspections or investigations, and recommendations for action. Inspect government-owned equipment and materials in the possession of private contractors in order to ensure compliance with contracts and regulations and to prevent misuse. Examine records, reports, and documents in order to establish facts and detect discrepancies. Inspect manufactured or processed products to ensure compliance with contract specifications and legal requirements. Locate and interview plaintiffs, witnesses, or representatives of business or government in order to gather facts relevant to inspections or alleged violations. Recommend legal or administrative action to protect government property. Submit samples of products to government laboratories for testing as required. Coordinate with and assist law enforcement agencies in matters of mutual concern. Testify in court or at administrative proceedings concerning investigation findings. Collect, identify, evaluate, and preserve case evidence. Monitor investigations of suspected offenders to ensure that they are conducted in accordance with constitutional requirements. Investigate applications for special licenses or permits, as well as alleged license or permit violations.

Personality Type: Conventional. These occupations frequently involve following set procedures and routines and can include working with data and details more than with ideas. Usually there is a clear line of authority to follow.

GOE—Interest Area/Cluster: 07. Government and Public Administration. **Work Group:** 07.03. Regulations Enforcement. **Other Jobs in This Work Group:** Agricultural Inspectors; Aviation Inspectors; Compliance Officers, Except Agriculture, Construction, Health and Safety, and Transportation; Construction and Building Inspectors; Environmental Compliance Inspectors; Equal Opportunity Representatives and Officers; Financial Examiners; Fire Inspectors; Fish and Game Wardens; Forest Fire Inspectors and Prevention Specialists; Freight and Cargo Inspectors; Immigration and Customs Inspectors; Licensing Examiners and Inspectors; Nuclear Monitoring Technicians; Occupational Health and Safety Specialists; Occupational Health and Safety Technicians; Tax Examiners, Collectors, and Revenue Agents; Transportation Vehicle, Equipment, and Systems Inspectors, Except Aviation.

Skills—Quality Control Analysis: Evaluating the quality or performance of products, services, or processes. **Technology Design:** Generating or adapting equipment and technology to serve user needs. **Science:** Using scientific methods to solve problems. **Troubleshooting:** Determining what is causing an operating error and deciding what to do about it. **Equipment Selection:** Determining the kind of tools and equipment needed to do a job. **Coordination:** Adjusting actions in relation to others' actions. **Operation and Control:** Controlling operations of equipment or systems. **Service Orientation:** Actively looking for ways to help people.

Education and Training Program: Building/Home/Construction Inspection/Inspector Training. **Related Knowledge/Courses—Building and Construction:** Materials, methods, and the appropriate tools to construct objects, structures, and buildings. **Engineering and Technology:** Equipment, tools, and mechanical devices and their uses to produce motion, light, power, technology, and other applications. **Public Safety and Security:** Weaponry; public safety; security operations, rules, regulations, precautions, and prevention; and the protection of people, data, and property. **Mechanical Devices:** Machines and tools, including their designs, uses, benefits, repair, and maintenance. **Computers and Electronics:** Electric circuit boards, processors, chips, and computer hardware and software, including applications and programming. **Transportation:** Principles and methods for moving people or goods by air, rail, sea, or road, including their relative costs, advantages, and limitations.

Work Environment: More often outdoors than indoors; noisy; very hot or cold; contaminants; sitting.

Hairdressers, Hairstylists, and Cosmetologists

- ❋ Education/Training Required: Postsecondary vocational training
- ❋ Annual Earnings: $22,210
- ❋ Beginning Wage: $14,790
- ❋ Earnings Growth Potential: Low
- ❋ Growth: 12.4%
- ❋ Annual Job Openings: 73,030
- ❋ Self-Employed: 44.5%
- ❋ Part-Time: 31.1%

Provide beauty services, such as shampooing, cutting, coloring, and styling hair and massaging and treating scalp. May also apply makeup, dress wigs, perform hair removal, and provide nail and skin care services. Keep work stations clean and sanitize tools such as scissors and combs. Cut, trim, and shape hair or hairpieces based on customers' instructions, hair type, and facial features, using clippers, scissors, trimmers, and razors. Analyze patrons' hair and other physical features to determine and recommend beauty treatment or suggest hairstyles. Schedule client appointments. Bleach, dye, or tint hair, using applicator or brush. Update and maintain customer information records, such as beauty services provided. Shampoo, rinse, condition, and dry hair and scalp or hairpieces with water, liquid soap, or other solutions. Operate cash registers to receive payments from patrons. Demonstrate and sell hair care products and cosmetics. Apply water, setting, straightening, or waving solutions to hair and use curlers, rollers, hot combs, and curling irons to press and curl hair. Develop new styles and techniques. Comb, brush, and spray hair or wigs to set style. Shape eyebrows and remove facial hair, using depilatory cream, tweezers, electrolysis, or wax. Administer therapeutic medication and advise patron to seek medical treatment for chronic or contagious scalp conditions. Massage and treat scalp for hygienic and remedial purposes, using hands, fingers, or vibrating equipment. Shave, trim, and shape beards and moustaches. Train or supervise other hairstylists, hairdressers, and assistants. Recommend and explain the use of cosmetics, lotions, and creams to soften and lubricate skin and enhance and restore natural appearance. Give facials to patrons, using special compounds such as lotions and creams. Clean, shape, and polish fingernails and toenails, using files and nail polish. Apply artificial fingernails. Attach wigs or hairpieces to model heads and dress wigs and hairpieces according to instructions, samples, sketches, or photographs.

Personality Type: Artistic. These occupations frequently involve working with forms, designs, and patterns. They often require self-expression, and the work can be done without following a clear set of rules.

GOE—Interest Area/Cluster: 09. Hospitality, Tourism, and Recreation. **Work Group:** 09.07. Barber and Beauty Services. **Other Jobs in This Work Group:** Barbers; Manicurists and Pedicurists; Shampooers; Skin Care Specialists.

Skills—Science: Using scientific methods to solve problems. **Operations Analysis:** Analyzing needs and product requirements to create a design. **Equipment Selection:** Determining the kind of tools and equipment needed to do a job. **Management of Financial Resources:** Determining how money will be spent to get the work done and accounting for these expenditures. **Equipment Maintenance:** Performing routine maintenance and determining when and what kind of maintenance is needed. **Learning Strategies:** Using multiple approaches when learning or teaching new things. **Social Perceptiveness:** Being aware of others' reactions and understanding why they react the way they do. **Management of Material Resources:** Obtaining and seeing to the appropriate use of equipment, facilities, and materials needed to do certain work.

Education and Training Programs: Cosmetology and Related Personal Grooming Arts, Other; Cosmetology, Barber/Styling, and Nail Instructor Training; Cosmetology/CosmetologistTraining, General; Electrolysis/Electrology and Electrolysis Technician Training; Hair Styling/Stylist and Hair Design; Make-Up Artist/Specialist Training; Permanent Cosmetics/Makeup and Tattooing; Salon/Beauty Salon Management/Manager Training. **Related Knowledge/Courses—Chemistry:** The composition, structure, and properties of substances and of the chemical processes and transformations that they undergo. This includes uses of chemicals and their interactions, danger signs, production techniques, and disposal methods. **Sales and Marketing:** Principles and methods involved in showing, promoting, and selling products or services. This includes marketing strategies and tactics, product demonstration and sales techniques, and sales control systems. **Customer and Personal Service:** Principles and processes for providing customer and personal services, including needs assessment techniques, quality service standards, alternative delivery systems, and customer satisfaction evaluation techniques.

Work Environment: Indoors; contaminants; minor burns, cuts, bites, or stings; standing; using hands on objects, tools, or controls; repetitive motions.

Hazardous Materials Removal Workers

- ❋ Education/Training Required: Moderate-term on-the-job training
- ❋ Annual Earnings: $36,330
- ❋ Beginning Wage: $23,200
- ❋ Earnings Growth Potential: Medium
- ❋ Growth: 11.2%
- ❋ Annual Job Openings: 1,933
- ❋ Self-Employed: 1.6%
- ❋ Part-Time: 5.7%

Identify, remove, pack, transport, or dispose of hazardous materials, including asbestos, lead-based paint, waste oil, fuel, transmission fluid, radioactive materials, contaminated soil, and so on. Specialized training and certification in hazardous materials handling or a confined entry permit are generally required. May operate earth-moving equipment or trucks. Follow prescribed safety procedures, and comply with federal laws regulating waste disposal methods. Record numbers of containers stored at disposal sites, and specify amounts and types of equipment and waste disposed. Drive trucks or other heavy equipment to convey contaminated waste to designated sea or ground locations. Operate machines and equipment to remove, package, store, or transport loads of waste materials. Load and unload materials into containers

and onto trucks, using hoists or forklifts. Clean contaminated equipment or areas for reuse, using detergents and solvents, sandblasters, filter pumps, and steam cleaners. Construct scaffolding or build containment areas prior to beginning abatement or decontamination work. Remove asbestos and/or lead from surfaces, using hand and power tools such as scrapers, vacuums, and high-pressure sprayers. Unload baskets of irradiated elements onto packaging machines that automatically insert fuel elements into canisters and secure lids. Apply chemical compounds to lead-based paint, allow compounds to dry, then scrape the hazardous material into containers for removal and/or storage. Identify asbestos, lead, or other hazardous materials that need to be removed, using monitoring devices. Pull tram cars along underwater tracks, and position cars to receive irradiated fuel elements; then pull loaded cars to mechanisms that automatically unload elements onto underwater tables. Package, store, and move irradiated fuel elements in the underwater storage basin of a nuclear reactor plant, using machines and equipment. Organize and track the locations of hazardous items in landfills. Operate cranes to move and load baskets, casks, and canisters. Manipulate handgrips of mechanical arms to place irradiated fuel elements into baskets. Mix and pour concrete into forms to encase waste material for disposal.

Personality Type: Realistic. These occupations frequently involve work activities that include practical, hands-on problems and solutions. They often deal with plants; animals; and real-world materials such as wood, tools, and machinery. Many of the occupations require working outside and don't involve a lot of paperwork or working closely with others.

GOE—Interest Area/Cluster: 02. Architecture and Construction. **Work Group:** 02.04. Construction Crafts. **Other Jobs in This Work Group:** Boilermakers; Brickmasons and Blockmasons; Carpet Installers; Cement Masons and Concrete Finishers; Commercial Divers; Construction Carpenters; Crane and Tower Operators; Drywall and Ceiling Tile Installers; Electricians; Fence Erectors; Floor Layers, Except Carpet, Wood, and Hard Tiles; Floor Sanders and Finishers; Glaziers; Insulation Workers, Floor, Ceiling, and Wall; Insulation Workers, Mechanical; Manufactured Building and Mobile Home Installers; Operating Engineers and Other Construction Equipment Operators; Painters, Construction and Maintenance; Paperhangers; Paving, Surfacing, and Tamping Equipment

Operators; Pile-Driver Operators; Pipe Fitters and Steam-fitters; Pipelayers; Plasterers and Stucco Masons; Plumbers; Plumbers, Pipefitters, and Steamfitters; Rail-Track Laying and Maintenance Equipment Operators; Refractory Materials Repairers, Except Brickmasons; Reinforcing Iron and Rebar Workers; Riggers; Roofers; Rough Carpenters; Security and Fire Alarm Systems Installers; Segmental Pavers; Sheet Metal Workers; Stone Cutters and Carvers, Manufacturing; Stonemasons; Structural Iron and Steel Workers; Tapers; Terrazzo Workers and Finishers; Tile and Marble Setters.

Skills—Equipment Maintenance: Performing routine maintenance and determining when and what kind of maintenance is needed. **Operation Monitoring:** Watching gauges, dials, or other indicators to make sure a machine is working properly. **Repairing:** Repairing machines or systems, using the needed tools. **Operation and Control:** Controlling operations of equipment or systems. **Science:** Using scientific methods to solve problems. **Troubleshooting:** Determining what is causing an operating error and deciding what to do about it. **Quality Control Analysis:** Evaluating the quality or performance of products, services, or processes. **Systems Analysis:** Determining how a system should work and how changes will affect outcomes.

Education and Training Programs: Hazardous Materials Management and Waste Technology/Technician Training; Mechanic and Repair Technologies/Technician Training, Other. **Related Knowledge/Courses—Chemistry:** The composition, structure, and properties of substances and of the chemical processes and transformations that they undergo. This includes uses of chemicals and their interactions, danger signs, production techniques, and disposal methods. **Mechanical Devices:** Machines and tools, including their designs, uses, benefits, repair, and maintenance. **Building and Construction:** Materials, methods, and the appropriate tools to construct objects, structures, and buildings. **Transportation:** Principles and methods for moving people or goods by air, rail, sea, or road, including their relative costs, advantages, and limitations. **Physics:** Physical principles, laws, and applications, including air, water, material dynamics, light, atomic principles, heat, electric theory, earth formations, and meteorological and related natural phenomena. **Public Safety and Security:** Weaponry; public safety; security operations, rules, regulations, precautions, and prevention; and the protection of people, data, and property.

Work Environment: Outdoors; very hot or cold; contaminants; hazardous conditions; using hands on objects, tools, or controls; repetitive motions.

Heating and Air Conditioning Mechanics and Installers

- ❀ Education/Training Required: Long-term on-the-job training
- ❀ Annual Earnings: $38,360
- ❀ Beginning Wage: $24,240
- ❀ Earnings Growth Potential: Medium
- ❀ Growth: 8.7%
- ❀ Annual Job Openings: 29,719
- ❀ Self-Employed: 12.7%
- ❀ Part-Time: 3.6%

The job openings listed here are shared with Refrigeration Mechanics and Installers.

Install, service, and repair heating and air conditioning systems in residences and commercial establishments. Obtain and maintain required certifications. Comply with all applicable standards, policies, and procedures, including safety procedures and the maintenance of a clean work area. Repair or replace defective equipment, components, or wiring. Test electrical circuits and components for continuity, using electrical test equipment. Reassemble and test equipment following repairs. Inspect and test system to verify system compliance with plans and specifications and to detect and locate malfunctions. Discuss heating-cooling system malfunctions with users to isolate problems or to verify that malfunctions have been corrected. Test pipe or tubing joints and connections for leaks, using pressure gauge or soap-and-water solution. Record and report all faults, deficiencies, and other unusual occurrences, as well as the time and materials expended on work orders. Adjust system controls to setting recommended by manufacturer to balance system, using hand tools. Recommend, develop, and perform preventive and general maintenance procedures such as cleaning, power-washing, and vacuuming equipment; oiling parts; and changing filters. Lay out and connect electrical wiring between controls and equipment according to wiring diagram, using electrician's hand tools. Install auxiliary components to heating-cooling equipment, such as expansion and discharge valves, air ducts, pipes, blowers, dampers, flues, and stokers, following blueprints. Assist with other work in coordination with repair and maintenance teams. Install, connect, and adjust thermostats, humidistats, and timers, using hand tools. Generate work orders that address deficiencies in need of correction. Join pipes or tubing to equipment and to fuel, water, or refrigerant source to form complete circuit. Assemble, position, and mount heating or cooling equipment, following blueprints. Study blueprints, design specifications, and manufacturers' recommendations to ascertain the configuration of heating or cooling equipment components and to ensure the proper installation of components. Cut and drill holes in floors, walls, and roof to install equipment, using power saws and drills.

Personality Type: Realistic. These occupations frequently involve work activities that include practical, hands-on problems and solutions. They often deal with plants; animals; and real-world materials such as wood, tools, and machinery. Many of the occupations require working outside and don't involve a lot of paperwork or working closely with others.

GOE—Interest Area/Cluster: 02. Architecture and Construction. **Work Group:** 02.05. Systems and Equipment Installation, Maintenance, and Repair. **Other Jobs in This Work Group:** Electrical and Electronics Repairers, Powerhouse, Substation, and Relay; Electrical Power-Line Installers and Repairers; Elevator Installers and Repairers; Maintenance and Repair Workers, General; Refrigeration Mechanics and Installers; Telecommunications Equipment Installers and Repairers, Except Line Installers; Telecommunications Line Installers and Repairers.

Skills—Repairing: Repairing machines or systems, using the needed tools. **Installation:** Installing equipment, machines, wiring, or programs to meet specifications. **Equipment Maintenance:** Performing routine maintenance and determining when and what kind of maintenance is needed. **Troubleshooting:** Determining what is causing an operating error and deciding what to do about it. **Systems Evaluation:** Looking at many indicators of system performance and taking into account their accuracy. **Science:** Using scientific methods to solve problems. **Systems Analysis:** Determining how a system should work and how changes will affect outcomes. **Coordination:** Adjusting actions in relation to others' actions.

Education and Training Programs: Heating, Air Conditioning, and Refrigeration Technology/Technician Training (ACH/ACR/ACHR/HRAC/HVAC); Heating, Air Conditioning, Ventilation, and Refrigeration Maintenance Technology/Technician Training; Solar Energy Technology/Technician Training. **Related Knowledge/Courses—Mechanical Devices:** Machines and tools, including their designs, uses, benefits, repair, and maintenance. **Building and Construction:** Materials, methods, and the appropriate tools to construct objects, structures, and buildings. **Design:** Design techniques, principles, tools, and instruments involved in the production and use of precision technical plans, blueprints, drawings, and models. **Physics:** Physical principles, laws, and applications, including air, water, material dynamics, light, atomic principles, heat, electric theory, earth formations, and meteorological and related natural phenomena. **Engineering and Technology:** Equipment, tools, and mechanical devices and their uses to produce motion, light, power, technology, and other applications. **Sales and Marketing:** Principles and methods involved in showing, promoting, and selling products or services. This includes marketing strategies and tactics, product demonstration and sales techniques, and sales control systems.

Work Environment: Outdoors; contaminants; hazardous conditions; minor burns, cuts, bites, or stings; standing; using hands on objects, tools, or controls.

Helpers—Brickmasons, Blockmasons, Stonemasons, and Tile and Marble Setters

- ❋ Education/Training Required: Short-term on-the-job training
- ❋ Annual Earnings: $26,260
- ❋ Beginning Wage: $18,340
- ❋ Earnings Growth Potential: Low
- ❋ Growth: 11.0%
- ❋ Annual Job Openings: 22,500
- ❋ Self-Employed: 3.0%
- ❋ Part-Time: 10.4%

Help brickmasons, blockmasons, stonemasons, or tile and marble setters by performing duties of lesser skill. Duties include using, supplying, or holding materials or

tools and cleaning work area and equipment. Transport materials, tools, and machines to installation sites, manually or using conveyance equipment. Move or position materials such as marble slabs, using cranes, hoists, or dollies. Modify material moving, mixing, grouting, grinding, polishing, or cleaning procedures according to installation or material requirements. Correct surface imperfections or fill chipped, cracked, or broken bricks or tiles, using fillers, adhesives, and grouting materials. Arrange and store materials, machines, tools, and equipment. Apply caulk, sealants, or other agents to installed surfaces. Select or locate and supply materials to masons for installation, following drawings or numbered sequences. Remove excess grout and residue from tile or brick joints, using sponges or trowels. Remove damaged tile, brick, or mortar, and clean and prepare surfaces, using pliers, hammers, chisels, drills, wire brushes, and metal wire anchors. Provide assistance in the preparation, installation, repair, and/or rebuilding of tile, brick, or stone surfaces. Mix mortar, plaster, and grout, manually or using machines, according to standard formulas. Erect scaffolding or other installation structures. Cut materials to specified sizes for installation, using power saws or tile cutters. Clean installation surfaces, equipment, tools, work sites, and storage areas, using water, chemical solutions, oxygen lances, or polishing machines. Apply grout between joints of bricks or tiles, using grouting trowels.

Personality Type: Realistic. These occupations frequently involve work activities that include practical, hands-on problems and solutions. They often deal with plants; animals; and real-world materials such as wood, tools, and machinery. Many of the occupations require working outside and don't involve a lot of paperwork or working closely with others.

GOE—Interest Area/Cluster: 02. Architecture and Construction. **Work Group:** 02.06. Construction Support/Labor. **Other Jobs in This Work Group:** Construction Laborers; Helpers—Carpenters; Helpers—Electricians; Helpers—Installation, Maintenance, and Repair Workers; Helpers—Painters, Paperhangers, Plasterers, and Stucco Masons; Helpers—Pipelayers, Plumbers, Pipefitters, and Steamfitters; Helpers—Roofers; Highway Maintenance Workers; Septic Tank Servicers and Sewer Pipe Cleaners.

Skills—Repairing: Repairing machines or systems, using the needed tools. **Equipment Maintenance:** Performing routine maintenance and determining when and what kind of maintenance is needed. **Installation:** Installing equipment, machines, wiring, or programs to meet specifications. **Management of Material Resources:** Obtaining and seeing to the appropriate use of equipment, facilities, and materials needed to do certain work. **Operation and Control:** Controlling operations of equipment or systems. **Mathematics:** Using mathematics to solve problems. **Operations Analysis:** Analyzing needs and product requirements to create a design.

Education and Training Program: Mason Training/Masonry. **Related Knowledge/Courses—Building and Construction:** Materials, methods, and the appropriate tools to construct objects, structures, and buildings. **Chemistry:** The composition, structure, and properties of substances and of the chemical processes and transformations that they undergo. This includes uses of chemicals and their interactions, danger signs, production techniques, and disposal methods. **Transportation:** Principles and methods for moving people or goods by air, rail, sea, or road, including their relative costs, advantages, and limitations. **Production and Processing:** Inputs, outputs, raw materials, waste, quality control, costs, and techniques for maximizing the manufacture and distribution of goods. **Mechanical Devices:** Machines and tools, including their designs, uses, benefits, repair, and maintenance. **Design:** Design techniques, principles, tools, and instruments involved in the production and use of precision technical plans, blueprints, drawings, and models.

Work Environment: Outdoors; noisy; very hot or cold; high places; using hands on objects, tools, or controls; repetitive motions.

Helpers—Carpenters

* Education/Training Required: Short-term on-the-job training
* Annual Earnings: $24,340
* Beginning Wage: $16,790
* Earnings Growth Potential: Low
* Growth: 11.7%
* Annual Job Openings: 37,731
* Self-Employed: 3.2%
* Part-Time: 10.4%

Help carpenters by performing duties of lesser skill. Duties include using, supplying, or holding materials or tools and cleaning work area and equipment. Position and hold timbers, lumber, and paneling in place for fastening or cutting. Erect scaffolding, shoring, and braces. Select tools, equipment, and materials from storage and transport items to worksite. Fasten timbers or lumber with glue, screws, pegs, or nails and install hardware. Clean work areas, machines, and equipment to maintain a clean and safe jobsite. Align, straighten, plumb, and square forms for installation. Hold plumb bobs, sighting rods, and other equipment to aid in establishing reference points and lines. Cut timbers, lumber, or paneling to specified dimensions and drill holes in timbers or lumber. Smooth and sand surfaces to remove ridges, tool marks, glue, or caulking. Perform tie spacing layout; then measure, mark, drill, and cut. Secure stakes to grids for constructions of footings, nail scabs to footing forms, and vibrate and float concrete. Construct forms; then assist in raising them to the required elevation. Install handrails under the direction of a carpenter. Glue and clamp edges or joints of assembled parts. Cut and install insulating or sound-absorbing material. Cut tile or linoleum to fit and spread adhesives on flooring to install tile or linoleum. Cover surfaces with laminated-plastic covering material.

Personality Type: Realistic. These occupations frequently involve work activities that include practical, hands-on problems and solutions. They often deal with plants; animals; and real-world materials such as wood, tools, and machinery. Many of the occupations require working outside and don't involve a lot of paperwork or working closely with others.

GOE—Interest Area/Cluster: 02. Architecture and Construction. **Work Group:** 02.06. Construction Support/Labor. **Other Jobs in This Work Group:** Construction Laborers; Helpers—Brickmasons, Blockmasons, Stonemasons, and Tile and Marble Setters; Helpers—Electricians; Helpers—Installation, Maintenance, and Repair Workers; Helpers—Painters, Paperhangers, Plasterers, and Stucco Masons; Helpers—Pipelayers, Plumbers, Pipefitters, and Steamfitters; Helpers—Roofers; Highway Maintenance Workers; Septic Tank Servicers and Sewer Pipe Cleaners.

Skills—Installation: Installing equipment, machines, wiring, or programs to meet specifications. **Repairing:** Repairing machines or systems, using the needed tools. **Equipment Maintenance:** Performing routine maintenance and determining when and what kind of maintenance is needed. **Management of Material Resources:** Obtaining and seeing to the appropriate use of equipment, facilities, and materials needed to do certain work. **Troubleshooting:** Determining what is causing an operating error and deciding what to do about it. **Equipment Selection:** Determining the kind of tools and equipment needed to do a job. **Mathematics:** Using mathematics to solve problems. **Operation and Control:** Controlling operations of equipment or systems.

Education and Training Program: Carpentry/Carpenter Training. **Related Knowledge/Courses—Building and Construction:** Materials, methods, and the appropriate tools to construct objects, structures, and buildings. **Design:** Design techniques, principles, tools, and instruments involved in the production and use of precision technical plans, blueprints, drawings, and models. **Engineering and Technology:** Equipment, tools, and mechanical devices and their uses to produce motion, light, power, technology, and other applications.

Work Environment: Noisy; very hot or cold; hazardous equipment; standing; walking and running; using hands on objects, tools, or controls.

Helpers—Electricians

- ❋ Education/Training Required: Short-term on-the-job training
- ❋ Annual Earnings: $24,880
- ❋ Beginning Wage: $17,580
- ❋ Earnings Growth Potential: Low
- ❋ Growth: 6.8%
- ❋ Annual Job Openings: 35,109
- ❋ Self-Employed: 2.9%
- ❋ Part-Time: 10.4%

Help electricians by performing duties of lesser skill. Duties include using, supplying, or holding materials or tools and cleaning work area and equipment. Trace out short circuits in wiring, using test meter. Measure, cut, and bend wire and conduit, using measuring instruments and hand tools. Maintain tools, vehicles, and equipment and keep parts and supplies in order. Drill holes and pull or push wiring through openings, using hand and power tools. Perform semi-skilled and unskilled laboring duties related to the installation, maintenance, and repair of a wide variety of electrical systems and equipment. Disassemble defective electrical equipment, replace defective or worn parts, and reassemble equipment, using hand tools. Transport tools, materials, equipment, and supplies to worksite by hand; handtruck; or heavy, motorized truck. Examine electrical units for loose connections and broken insulation and tighten connections, using hand tools. Strip insulation from wire ends, using wire-stripping pliers, and attach wires to terminals for subsequent soldering. Construct controllers and panels, using power drills, drill presses, taps, saws, and punches. Thread conduit ends, connect couplings, and fabricate and secure conduit support brackets, using hand tools. String transmission lines or cables through ducts or conduits, under the ground, through equipment, or to towers. Clean work area and wash parts. Erect electrical system components and barricades and rig scaffolds, hoists, and shoring. Install copper-clad ground rods, using a manual post driver. Raise, lower, or position equipment, tools, and materials, using hoist, hand line, or block and tackle. Dig trenches or holes for installation of conduit or supports. Requisition materials, using warehouse requisition or release forms. Bolt component parts together to form tower assemblies, using hand tools. Paint a variety of objects related to electrical functions. Operate cutting torches and welding equipment while working with conduit and metal components to construct devices associated with electrical functions. Break up concrete, using air hammer, to facilitate installation, construction, or repair of equipment. Solder electrical connections, using soldering iron. Trim trees and clear undergrowth along right-of-way.

Personality Type: Realistic. These occupations frequently involve work activities that include practical, hands-on problems and solutions. They often deal with plants; animals; and real-world materials such as wood, tools, and machinery. Many of the occupations require working outside and don't involve a lot of paperwork or working closely with others.

GOE—Interest Area/Cluster: 02. Architecture and Construction. **Work Group:** 02.06. Construction Support/Labor. **Other Jobs in This Work Group:** Construction Laborers; Helpers—Brickmasons, Blockmasons, Stonemasons, and Tile and Marble Setters; Helpers—Carpenters; Helpers—Installation, Maintenance, and Repair Workers; Helpers—Painters, Paperhangers, Plasterers, and Stucco Masons; Helpers—Pipelayers, Plumbers, Pipefitters, and Steamfitters; Helpers—Roofers; Highway Maintenance Workers; Septic Tank Servicers and Sewer Pipe Cleaners.

Skills—Installation: Installing equipment, machines, wiring, or programs to meet specifications. **Troubleshooting:** Determining what is causing an operating error and deciding what to do about it. **Repairing:** Repairing machines or systems, using the needed tools. **Mathematics:** Using mathematics to solve problems. **Equipment Selection:** Determining the kind of tools and equipment needed to do a job. **Complex Problem Solving:** Identifying complex problems, reviewing the options, and implementing solutions. **Operation and Control:** Controlling operations of equipment or systems. **Science:** Using scientific methods to solve problems.

Education and Training Program: Electrician Training. **Related Knowledge/Courses—Building and Construction:** Materials, methods, and the appropriate tools to construct objects, structures, and buildings. **Mechanical Devices:** Machines and tools, including their designs, uses, benefits, repair, and maintenance. **Design:** Design techniques, principles, tools, and instruments involved in the production and use of precision technical plans, blueprints, drawings, and models. **Engineering and Technology:** Equipment, tools, and mechanical devices and their uses to produce motion, light, power, technology, and other applications. **Mathematics:** Numbers and their operations and interrelationships, including arithmetic, algebra, geometry, calculus, and statistics and their applications. **Public Safety and Security:** Weaponry; public safety; security operations, rules, regulations, precautions, and prevention; and the protection of people, data, and property.

Work Environment: Outdoors; very hot or cold; contaminants; high places; standing; using hands on objects, tools, or controls.

Helpers—Installation, Maintenance, and Repair Workers

- ❋ Education/Training Required: Short-term on-the-job training
- ❋ Annual Earnings: $22,920
- ❋ Beginning Wage: $15,530
- ❋ Earnings Growth Potential: Low
- ❋ Growth: 11.8%
- ❋ Annual Job Openings: 52,058
- ❋ Self-Employed: 0.1%
- ❋ Part-Time: 22.7%

Help installation, maintenance, and repair workers in maintenance, parts replacement, and repair of vehicles, industrial machinery, and electrical and electronic equipment. Perform duties such as furnishing tools, materials, and supplies to other workers; cleaning work area, machines, and tools; and holding materials or tools for other workers. Tend and observe equipment and machinery to verify efficient and safe operation. Examine and test machinery, equipment, components, and parts for defects and to ensure proper functioning. Adjust, connect, or disconnect wiring, piping, tubing, and other parts, using hand tools or power tools. Install or replace machinery, equipment, and new or replacement parts and instruments, using hand tools or power tools. Clean or lubricate vehicles, machinery, equipment, instruments, tools, work areas, and other objects, using hand tools, power tools, and cleaning equipment. Apply protective materials to equipment, components, and parts to prevent defects and corrosion. Transfer tools, parts, equipment, and supplies to and from workstations and other areas. Disassemble broken or defective equipment in order to facilitate repair; reassemble equipment when repairs are complete. Assemble and maintain physical structures, using hand tools or power tools. Provide assistance to more skilled workers involved in the adjustment, maintenance, part replacement, and repair of tools, equipment, and machines. Position vehicles, machinery, equipment, physical structures, and other objects for assembly or installation, using hand tools, power tools, and moving equipment. Hold or supply tools, parts, equipment, and supplies for other workers. Prepare work stations so mechanics and repairers can conduct work.

Personality Type: Realistic. These occupations frequently involve work activities that include practical, hands-on problems and solutions. They often deal with plants; animals; and real-world materials such as wood, tools, and machinery. Many of the occupations require working outside and don't involve a lot of paperwork or working closely with others.

GOE—Interest Area/Cluster: 02. Architecture and Construction. **Work Group:** 02.06. Construction Support/Labor. **Other Jobs in This Work Group:** Construction Laborers; Helpers—Brickmasons, Blockmasons, Stonemasons, and Tile and Marble Setters; Helpers—Carpenters; Helpers—Electricians; Helpers—Painters, Paperhangers, Plasterers, and Stucco Masons; Helpers—Pipelayers, Plumbers, Pipefitters, and Steamfitters; Helpers—Roofers; Highway Maintenance Workers; Septic Tank Servicers and Sewer Pipe Cleaners.

Skills—Installation: Installing equipment, machines, wiring, or programs to meet specifications. **Operation Monitoring:** Watching gauges, dials, or other indicators to make sure a machine is working properly. **Repairing:** Repairing machines or systems, using the needed tools. **Equipment Maintenance:** Performing routine maintenance and determining when and what kind of maintenance is needed. **Troubleshooting:** Determining what is causing an operating error and deciding what to do about it. **Operations Analysis:** Analyzing needs and product requirements to create a design. **Operation and Control:** Controlling operations of equipment or systems. **Science:** Using scientific methods to solve problems.

Education and Training Program: Industrial Mechanics and Maintenance Technology. **Related Knowledge/Courses—Mechanical Devices:** Machines and tools, including their designs, uses, benefits, repair, and maintenance. **Engineering and Technology:** Equipment, tools, and mechanical devices and their uses to produce motion, light, power, technology, and other applications. **Building and Construction:** Materials, methods, and the appropriate tools to construct objects, structures, and buildings. **Chemistry:** The composition, structure, and properties of substances and of the chemical processes and transformations that they undergo. This includes uses of chemicals and their interactions, danger signs, production techniques, and disposal methods. **Design:** Design techniques, principles, tools, and instruments involved in the production and use of precision technical plans, blueprints, drawings, and models. **Public Safety and Security:** Weaponry; public safety; security operations, rules, regulations, precautions, and prevention; and the protection of people, data, and property.

Work Environment: Noisy; hazardous conditions; hazardous equipment; standing; using hands on objects, tools, or controls; bending or twisting the body.

Helpers—Pipelayers, Plumbers, Pipefitters, and Steamfitters

- ❋ Education/Training Required: Short-term on-the-job training
- ❋ Annual Earnings: $25,350
- ❋ Beginning Wage: $17,700
- ❋ Earnings Growth Potential: Low
- ❋ Growth: 11.9%
- ❋ Annual Job Openings: 29,332
- ❋ Self-Employed: 2.9%
- ❋ Part-Time: 10.4%

Help plumbers, pipefitters, steamfitters, or pipelayers by performing duties of lesser skill. Duties include using, supplying, or holding materials or tools and cleaning work area and equipment. Assist plumbers by performing rough-ins, repairing and replacing fixtures, and locating and repairing leaking or broken pipes. Cut or drill holes in walls or floors to accommodate the passage of pipes. Measure, cut, thread, and assemble new pipe, placing the assembled pipe in hangers or other supports. Mount brackets and hangers on walls and ceilings to hold pipes and set sleeves or inserts to provide support for pipes. Requisition tools and equipment, select type and size of pipe, and collect and transport materials and equipment to worksite. Fit or assist in fitting valves, couplings, or assemblies to tanks, pumps, or systems, using hand tools. Assist pipe fitters in the layout, assembly, and installation of piping for air, ammonia, gas, and water systems. Excavate and grade ditches and lay and join pipe for water and sewer service. Cut pipe and lift up to fitters. Disassemble and remove damaged or worn pipe. Clean shop, work area, and machines, using solvent and rags. Install gas burners to convert furnaces from wood, coal, or oil. Immerse pipe in chemical solution to remove dirt, oil, and scale. Clean and

renew steam traps. Fill pipes with sand or resin to prevent distortion and hold pipes during bending and installation.

Personality Type: Realistic. These occupations frequently involve work activities that include practical, hands-on problems and solutions. They often deal with plants; animals; and real-world materials such as wood, tools, and machinery. Many of the occupations require working outside and don't involve a lot of paperwork or working closely with others.

GOE—Interest Area/Cluster: 02. Architecture and Construction. **Work Group:** 02.06. Construction Support/ Labor. **Other Jobs in This Work Group:** Construction Laborers; Helpers—Brickmasons, Blockmasons, Stonemasons, and Tile and Marble Setters; Helpers—Carpenters; Helpers—Electricians; Helpers—Installation, Maintenance, and Repair Workers; Helpers—Painters, Paperhangers, Plasterers, and Stucco Masons; Helpers—Roofers; Highway Maintenance Workers; Septic Tank Servicers and Sewer Pipe Cleaners.

Skills—Installation: Installing equipment, machines, wiring, or programs to meet specifications. **Repairing:** Repairing machines or systems, using the needed tools. **Equipment Maintenance:** Performing routine maintenance and determining when and what kind of maintenance is needed. **Troubleshooting:** Determining what is causing an operating error and deciding what to do about it. **Mathematics:** Using mathematics to solve problems. **Quality Control Analysis:** Evaluating the quality or performance of products, services, or processes. **Equipment Selection:** Determining the kind of tools and equipment needed to do a job. **Negotiation:** Bringing others together and trying to reconcile differences.

Education and Training Program: Plumbing Technology/Plumber Training. **Related Knowledge/Courses— Building and Construction:** Materials, methods, and the appropriate tools to construct objects, structures, and buildings. **Mechanical Devices:** Machines and tools, including their designs, uses, benefits, repair, and maintenance. **Design:** Design techniques, principles, tools, and instruments involved in the production and use of precision technical plans, blueprints, drawings, and models. **Public Safety and Security:** Weaponry; public safety; security operations, rules, regulations, precautions, and prevention; and the protection of people, data, and property. **Engineering and Technology:** Equipment, tools, and mechanical devices and their uses to produce motion, light, power, technology, and other applications. **Law and Government:** Laws, legal codes, court procedures, precedents, government regulations, executive orders, agency rules, and the democratic political process.

Work Environment: Outdoors; noisy; contaminants; hazardous equipment; standing; using hands on objects, tools, or controls.

Highway Maintenance Workers

- ❋ Education/Training Required: Moderate-term on-the-job training
- ❋ Annual Earnings: $32,600
- ❋ Beginning Wage: $20,960
- ❋ Earnings Growth Potential: Medium
- ❋ Growth: 8.9%
- ❋ Annual Job Openings: 24,774
- ❋ Self-Employed: 0.9%
- ❋ Part-Time: 1.9%

Maintain highways, municipal and rural roads, airport runways, and rights-of-way. Duties include patching broken or eroded pavement and repairing guardrails, highway markers, and snow fences. May also mow or clear brush from along road or plow snow from roadway. Flag motorists to warn them of obstacles or repair work ahead. Set out signs and cones around work areas to divert traffic. Drive trucks or tractors with adjustable attachments to sweep debris from paved surfaces, mow grass and weeds, and remove snow and ice. Dump, spread, and tamp asphalt, using pneumatic tampers, to repair joints and patch broken pavement. Drive trucks to transport crews and equipment to worksites. Inspect, clean, and repair drainage systems, bridges, tunnels, and other structures. Haul and spread sand, gravel, and clay to fill washouts and repair road shoulders. Erect, install, or repair guardrails, road shoulders, berms, highway markers, warning signals, and highway lighting, using hand tools and power tools. Remove litter and debris from roadways, including debris from rock slides and mudslides. Clean and clear debris from culverts, catch basins, drop inlets, ditches, and other drain structures. Perform roadside landscaping work, such as clearing weeds and brush and planting and trimming trees. Paint traffic control lines and place pavement traffic messages by

hand or using machines. Inspect markers to verify accurate installation. Apply poisons along roadsides and in animal burrows to eliminate unwanted roadside vegetation and rodents. Measure and mark locations for installation of markers, using tape, string, or chalk. Apply oil to road surfaces, using sprayers. Blend compounds to form adhesive mixtures used for marker installation. Place and remove snow fences used to prevent the accumulation of drifting snow on highways.

Personality Type: Realistic. These occupations frequently involve work activities that include practical, hands-on problems and solutions. They often deal with plants; animals; and real-world materials such as wood, tools, and machinery. Many of the occupations require working outside and don't involve a lot of paperwork or working closely with others.

GOE—Interest Area/Cluster: 02. Architecture and Construction. **Work Group:** 02.06. Construction Support/Labor. **Other Jobs in This Work Group:** Construction Laborers; Helpers—Brickmasons, Blockmasons, Stonemasons, and Tile and Marble Setters; Helpers—Carpenters; Helpers—Electricians; Helpers—Installation, Maintenance, and Repair Workers; Helpers—Painters, Paperhangers, Plasterers, and Stucco Masons; Helpers—Pipelayers, Plumbers, Pipefitters, and Steamfitters; Helpers—Roofers; Septic Tank Servicers and Sewer Pipe Cleaners.

Skills—Equipment Maintenance: Performing routine maintenance and determining when and what kind of maintenance is needed. **Repairing:** Repairing machines or systems, using the needed tools. **Installation:** Installing equipment, machines, wiring, or programs to meet specifications. **Operation and Control:** Controlling operations of equipment or systems. **Management of Material Resources:** Obtaining and seeing to the appropriate use of equipment, facilities, and materials needed to do certain work. **Equipment Selection:** Determining the kind of tools and equipment needed to do a job. **Troubleshooting:** Determining what is causing an operating error and deciding what to do about it. **Technology Design:** Generating or adapting equipment and technology to serve user needs.

Education and Training Program: Construction/Heavy Equipment/Earthmoving Equipment Operation. **Related Knowledge/Courses—Building and Construction:** Materials, methods, and the appropriate tools to construct objects, structures, and buildings. **Transportation:** Principles and methods for moving people or goods by air, rail, sea, or road, including their relative costs, advantages, and limitations. **Mechanical Devices:** Machines and tools, including their designs, uses, benefits, repair, and maintenance. **Public Safety and Security:** Weaponry; public safety; security operations, rules, regulations, precautions, and prevention; and the protection of people, data, and property. **Customer and Personal Service:** Principles and processes for providing customer and personal services, including needs assessment techniques, quality service standards, alternative delivery systems, and customer satisfaction evaluation techniques. **Geography:** Various methods for describing the location and distribution of land, sea, and air masses, including their physical locations, relationships, and characteristics.

Work Environment: Outdoors; noisy; very hot or cold; contaminants; hazardous equipment; using hands on objects, tools, or controls.

Human Resources Assistants, Except Payroll and Timekeeping

- ❋ Education/Training Required: Short-term on-the-job training
- ❋ Annual Earnings: $34,970
- ❋ Beginning Wage: $23,750
- ❋ Earnings Growth Potential: Low
- ❋ Growth: 11.3%
- ❋ Annual Job Openings: 18,647
- ❋ Self-Employed: 0.0%
- ❋ Part-Time: 9.3%

Compile and keep personnel records. Record data for each employee, such as address, weekly earnings, absences, amount of sales or production, supervisory reports on ability, and date of and reason for termination. Compile and type reports from employment records. File employment records. Search employee files and furnish information to authorized persons. Explain company personnel policies, benefits, and procedures to employees or job applicants. Process, verify, and maintain documentation relating to personnel activities such as staffing, recruitment, training, grievances, performance evaluations, and classifications. Record data for each employee, including such information as addresses, weekly earnings, absences, amount of sales or production, supervisory reports on performance, and dates of and reasons for terminations. Process and review employment applications to evaluate qualifications or eligibility of applicants. Answer questions regarding examinations, eligibility, salaries, benefits, and other pertinent information. Examine employee files to answer inquiries and provide information for personnel actions. Gather personnel records from other departments or employees. Search employee files to obtain information for authorized persons and organizations such as credit bureaus and finance companies. Interview job applicants to obtain and verify information used to screen and evaluate them. Request information from law enforcement officials, previous employers, and other references to determine applicants' employment acceptability. Compile and prepare reports and documents pertaining to personnel activities. Inform job applicants of their acceptance or rejection of employment. Select applicants meeting specified job requirements and refer them to hiring personnel. Arrange for in-house and external training activities. Arrange for advertising or posting of job vacancies and notify eligible workers of position availability. Provide assistance in administering employee benefit programs and worker's compensation plans. Prepare badges, passes, and identification cards and perform other security-related duties. Administer and score applicant and employee aptitude, personality, and interest assessment instruments.

Personality Type: Conventional. These occupations frequently involve following set procedures and routines and can include working with data and details more than with ideas. Usually there is a clear line of authority to follow.

GOE—Interest Area/Cluster: 04. Business and Administration. **Work Group:** 04.07. Records and Materials Processing. **Other Jobs in This Work Group:** Correspondence Clerks; File Clerks; Marking Clerks; Meter Readers, Utilities; Office Clerks, General; Order Fillers, Wholesale and Retail Sales; Postal Service Clerks; Postal Service Mail Sorters, Processors, and Processing Machine Operators; Procurement Clerks; Production, Planning, and Expediting Clerks; Shipping, Receiving, and Traffic Clerks; Stock Clerks and Order Fillers; Stock Clerks, Sales Floor; Stock Clerks—Stockroom, Warehouse, or Storage Yard; Weighers, Measurers, Checkers, and Samplers, Recordkeeping.

Skills—Writing: Communicating effectively with others in writing as indicated by the needs of the audience. **Active**

Listening: Listening to what other people are saying and asking questions as appropriate. **Management of Personnel Resources:** Motivating, developing, and directing people as they work; identifying the best people for the job.

Education and Training Program: General Office Occupations and Clerical Services. **Related Knowledge/Courses—Clerical Studies:** Administrative and clerical procedures and systems such as word-processing systems, filing and records management systems, stenography and transcription, forms, design principles, and other office procedures and terminology. **Personnel and Human Resources:** Principles and procedures for personnel recruitment; selection; training; compensation and benefits; labor relations and negotiation; and personnel information systems. **Customer and Personal Service:** Principles and processes for providing customer and personal services, including needs assessment techniques, quality service standards, alternative delivery systems, and customer satisfaction evaluation techniques. **Computers and Electronics:** Electric circuit boards, processors, chips, and computer hardware and software, including applications and programming. **Economics and Accounting:** Economic and accounting principles and practices, the financial markets, banking, and the analysis and reporting of financial data. **Sociology and Anthropology:** Group behavior and dynamics; societal trends and influences; and cultures and their history, migrations, ethnicity, and origins.

Work Environment: Indoors; noisy; sitting.

Immigration and Customs Inspectors

- ❋ Education/Training Required: Work experience in a related occupation
- ❋ Annual Earnings: $59,930
- ❋ Beginning Wage: $35,600
- ❋ Earnings Growth Potential: High
- ❋ Growth: 17.3%
- ❋ Annual Job Openings: 14,746
- ❋ Self-Employed: 0.3%
- ❋ Part-Time: 2.2%

The job openings listed here are shared with Criminal Investigators and Special Agents; with Police Detectives; and with Police Identification and Records Officers.

Investigate and inspect persons, common carriers, goods, and merchandise arriving in or departing from the United States or moving between states to detect violations of immigration and customs laws and regulations. Examine immigration applications, visas, and passports and interview persons to determine eligibility for admission, residence, and travel in U.S. Detain persons found to be in violation of customs or immigration laws and arrange for legal action such as deportation. Locate and seize contraband or undeclared merchandise and vehicles, aircraft, or boats that contain such merchandise. Interpret and explain laws and regulations to travelers, prospective immigrants, shippers, and manufacturers. Inspect cargo, baggage, and personal articles entering or leaving U.S. for compliance with revenue laws and U.S. Customs Service regulations. Record and report job-related activities, findings, transactions, violations, discrepancies, and decisions. Institute civil and criminal prosecutions and cooperate with other law enforcement agencies in the investigation and prosecution of those in violation of immigration or customs laws. Testify regarding decisions at immigration appeals or in federal court. Determine duty and taxes to be paid on goods. Collect samples of merchandise for examination, appraisal, or testing. Investigate applications for duty refunds and petition for remission or mitigation of penalties when warranted.

Personality Type: Conventional. These occupations frequently involve following set procedures and routines and can include working with data and details more than with ideas. Usually there is a clear line of authority to follow.

GOE—Interest Area/Cluster: 07. Government and Public Administration. **Work Group:** 07.03. Regulations Enforcement. **Other Jobs in This Work Group:** Agricultural Inspectors; Aviation Inspectors; Compliance Officers, Except Agriculture, Construction, Health and Safety, and Transportation; Construction and Building Inspectors; Environmental Compliance Inspectors; Equal Opportunity Representatives and Officers; Financial Examiners; Fire Inspectors; Fish and Game Wardens; Forest Fire Inspectors and Prevention Specialists; Freight and Cargo Inspectors; Government Property Inspectors and Investigators; Licensing Examiners and Inspectors; Nuclear Monitoring Technicians; Occupational Health and Safety Specialists; Occupational Health and Safety Technicians; Tax Examiners, Collectors, and Revenue Agents; Transportation Vehicle, Equipment, and Systems Inspectors, Except Aviation.

Skills—**Persuasion:** Persuading others to approach things differently. **Operations Analysis:** Analyzing needs and product requirements to create a design. **Equipment Selection:** Determining the kind of tools and equipment needed to do a job. **Negotiation:** Bringing others together and trying to reconcile differences. **Speaking:** Talking to others to effectively convey information. **Social Perceptiveness:** Being aware of others' reactions and understanding why they react the way they do. **Active Listening:** Listening to what other people are saying and asking questions as appropriate. **Judgment and Decision Making:** Weighing the relative costs and benefits of a potential action.

Education and Training Programs: Criminal Justice/Police Science; Criminalistics and Criminal Science. **Related Knowledge/Courses—Public Safety and Security:** Weaponry; public safety; security operations, rules, regulations, precautions, and prevention; and the protection of people, data, and property. **Law and Government:** Laws, legal codes, court procedures, precedents, government regulations, executive orders, agency rules, and the democratic political process. **Foreign Language:** The structure and content of a foreign (non-English) language, including the meaning and spelling of words, rules of composition and grammar, and pronunciation. **Geography:** Various methods for describing the location and distribution of land, sea, and air masses, including their physical locations, relationships, and characteristics. **Customer and Personal Service:** Principles and processes for providing customer and personal services, including needs assessment techniques, quality service standards, alternative delivery systems, and customer satisfaction evaluation techniques. **Philosophy and Theology:** Different philosophical systems and religions, including their basic principles, values, ethics, ways of thinking, customs, and practices and their impact on human culture.

Work Environment: More often outdoors than indoors; noisy; contaminants; radiation; hazardous equipment.

Industrial Engineering Technicians

- Education/Training Required: Associate degree
- Annual Earnings: $47,490
- Beginning Wage: $31,130
- Earnings Growth Potential: Low
- Growth: 9.9%
- Annual Job Openings: 6,172
- Self-Employed: 0.8%
- Part-Time: 5.9%

Apply engineering theory and principles to problems of industrial layout or manufacturing production, usually under the direction of engineering staff. May study and record time, motion, method, and speed involved in performance of production, maintenance, clerical, and other worker operations for such purposes as establishing standard production rates or improving efficiency. Recommend revision to methods of operation, material handling, equipment layout, or other changes to increase production or improve standards. Study time, motion, methods, and speed involved in maintenance, production, and other operations to establish standard production rate and improve efficiency. Interpret engineering drawings, schematic diagrams, or formulas and confer with management or engineering staff to determine quality and reliability standards. Recommend modifications to existing quality or production standards to achieve optimum quality within limits of equipment capability. Aid in planning work assignments in accordance with worker performance, machine capacity, production schedules, and anticipated delays. Observe workers using equipment to verify that equipment is being operated and maintained according to quality assurance standards. Observe workers operating equipment or performing tasks to determine time involved and fatigue rate, using timing devices. Prepare charts, graphs, and diagrams to illustrate workflow, routing, floor layouts, material handling, and machine utilization. Evaluate data and write reports to validate or indicate deviations from existing standards. Read worker logs, product processing sheets, and specification sheets to verify that records adhere to quality assurance specifications. Prepare graphs or charts of data or enter data into computer for analysis. Record test data, applying statistical quality control procedures. Select products for tests at specified stages in production process and test products for performance characteristics and adherence to specifications. Compile and evaluate statistical data to determine and maintain quality and reliability of products.

Personality Type: Investigative. These occupations frequently involve working with ideas and require an extensive amount of thinking. They can involve searching for facts and figuring out problems mentally.

GOE—Interest Area/Cluster: 04. Business and Administration. **Work Group:** 04.05. Accounting, Auditing, and Analytical Support. **Other Jobs in This Work Group:** Accountants; Accountants and Auditors; Auditors; Budget Analysts; Logisticians; Management Analysts; Operations Research Analysts.

Skills—Operations Analysis: Analyzing needs and product requirements to create a design. **Technology Design:** Generating or adapting equipment and technology to serve user needs. **Repairing:** Repairing machines or systems, using the needed tools. **Troubleshooting:** Determining what is causing an operating error and deciding what to do about it. **Systems Evaluation:** Looking at many indicators of system performance and taking into account their accuracy. **Systems Analysis:** Determining how a system should work and how changes will affect outcomes. **Quality Control Analysis:** Evaluating the quality or performance of products, services, or processes. **Mathematics:** Using mathematics to solve problems.

Education and Training Programs: Engineering/Industrial Management; Industrial Production Technologies/Technician Training, Other; Industrial Technology/Technician Training; Manufacturing Technology/Technician Training. **Related Knowledge/Courses—Production and Processing:** Inputs, outputs, raw materials, waste, quality control, costs, and techniques for maximizing the manufacture and distribution of goods. **Engineering and Technology:** Equipment, tools, and mechanical devices and their uses to produce motion, light, power, technology, and other applications. **Design:** Design techniques, principles, tools, and instruments involved in the production and use of precision technical plans, blueprints, drawings, and models. **Clerical Studies:** Administrative and clerical procedures and systems such as word-processing systems, filing and records management systems, stenography and transcription, forms, design principles, and other office procedures and terminology. **Mathematics:** Numbers and their

operations and interrelationships, including arithmetic, algebra, geometry, calculus, and statistics and their applications. **Mechanical Devices:** Machines and tools, including their designs, uses, benefits, repair, and maintenance.

Work Environment: Indoors; noisy; contaminants; hazardous equipment; standing; walking and running.

Industrial Machinery Mechanics

- ❋ Education/Training Required: Long-term on-the-job training
- ❋ Annual Earnings: $42,350
- ❋ Beginning Wage: $27,650
- ❋ Earnings Growth Potential: Low
- ❋ Growth: 9.0%
- ❋ Annual Job Openings: 23,361
- ❋ Self-Employed: 2.5%
- ❋ Part-Time: 1.7%

Repair, install, adjust, or maintain industrial production and processing machinery or refinery and pipeline distribution systems. Disassemble machinery and equipment to remove parts and make repairs. Repair and replace broken or malfunctioning components of machinery and equipment. Repair and maintain the operating condition of industrial production and processing machinery and equipment. Examine parts for defects such as breakage and excessive wear. Reassemble equipment after completion of inspections, testing, or repairs. Observe and test the operation of machinery and equipment in order to diagnose malfunctions, using voltmeters and other testing devices. Operate newly repaired machinery and equipment to verify the adequacy of repairs. Clean, lubricate, and adjust parts, equipment, and machinery. Analyze test results, machine error messages, and information obtained from operators in order to diagnose equipment problems. Record repairs and maintenance performed. Study blueprints and manufacturers' manuals to determine correct installation and operation of machinery. Record parts and materials used, and order or requisition new parts and materials as necessary. Cut and weld metal to repair broken metal parts, fabricate new parts, and assemble new equipment. Demonstrate equipment functions and features to machine operators. Enter codes and instructions to program computer-controlled machinery.

Personality Type: Realistic. These occupations frequently involve work activities that include practical, hands-on problems and solutions. They often deal with plants; animals; and real-world materials such as wood, tools, and machinery. Many of the occupations require working outside and don't involve a lot of paperwork or working closely with others.

GOE—Interest Area/Cluster: 13. Manufacturing. **Work Group:** 13.13. Machinery Repair. **Other Jobs in This Work Group:** Bicycle Repairers; Control and Valve Installers and Repairers, Except Mechanical Door; Home Appliance Repairers; Locksmiths and Safe Repairers; Maintenance Workers, Machinery; Mechanical Door Repairers; Millwrights; Signal and Track Switch Repairers.

Skills—Installation: Installing equipment, machines, wiring, or programs to meet specifications. **Repairing:** Repairing machines or systems, using the needed tools. **Equipment Maintenance:** Performing routine maintenance and determining when and what kind of maintenance is needed. **Operation Monitoring:** Watching gauges, dials, or other indicators to make sure a machine is working properly. **Troubleshooting:** Determining what is causing an operating error and deciding what to do about it. **Technology Design:** Generating or adapting equipment and technology to serve user needs. **Equipment Selection:** Determining the kind of tools and equipment needed to do a job. **Operation and Control:** Controlling operations of equipment or systems.

Education and Training Programs: Heavy/Industrial Equipment Maintenance Technologies, Other; Industrial Mechanics and Maintenance Technology. **Related Knowledge/Courses—Mechanical Devices:** Machines and tools, including their designs, uses, benefits, repair, and maintenance. **Engineering and Technology:** Equipment, tools, and mechanical devices and their uses to produce motion, light, power, technology, and other applications. **Building and Construction:** Materials, methods, and the appropriate tools to construct objects, structures, and buildings. **Design:** Design techniques, principles, tools, and instruments involved in the production and use of precision technical plans, blueprints, drawings, and models. **Chemistry:** The composition, structure, and properties of substances and of the chemical processes and transformations that they undergo. This includes uses of chemicals and their interactions, danger signs, production techniques, and disposal methods. **Physics:** Physical principles, laws, and applications, including air, water, material dynamics, light, atomic principles, heat, electric theory, earth formations, and meteorological and related natural phenomena.

Work Environment: Noisy; contaminants; hazardous conditions; hazardous equipment; standing; using hands on objects, tools, or controls.

Industrial Production Managers

- ❋ Education/Training Required: Work experience in a related occupation
- ❋ Annual Earnings: $80,560
- ❋ Beginning Wage: $48,670
- ❋ Earnings Growth Potential: Medium
- ❋ Growth: –5.9%
- ❋ Annual Job Openings: 14,889
- ❋ Self-Employed: 2.0%
- ❋ Part-Time: 1.6%

Plan, direct, or coordinate the work activities and resources necessary for manufacturing products in accordance with cost, quality, and quantity specifications. Direct and coordinate production, processing, distribution, and marketing activities of industrial organization. Review processing schedules and production orders to make decisions concerning inventory requirements, staffing requirements, work procedures, and duty assignments, considering budgetary limitations and time constraints. Review operations and confer with technical or administrative staff to resolve production or processing problems. Develop and implement production tracking and quality control systems, analyzing production, quality control, maintenance, and other operational reports, to detect production problems. Hire, train, evaluate, and discharge staff, and resolve personnel grievances. Set and monitor product standards, examining samples of raw products or directing testing during processing, to ensure finished products are of prescribed quality. Prepare and maintain production reports and personnel records. Coordinate and recommend procedures for facility and equipment maintenance or modification, including the replacement of machines. Initiate and coordinate inventory and cost control programs. Institute employee suggestion or involvement programs. Maintain current knowledge of the quality control field, relying on current literature pertaining to materials use, technological advances, and statistical studies. Review plans and confer with research and support staff to develop new products and processes. Develop budgets and approve expenditures for supplies, materials, and human resources, ensuring that materials, labor, and equipment are used efficiently to meet production targets. Negotiate prices of materials with suppliers.

Personality Type: Enterprising. These occupations frequently involve starting up and carrying out projects and can involve leading people and making many decisions. They sometimes require risk taking and often deal with business.

GOE—Interest Area/Cluster: 13. Manufacturing. **Work Group:** 13.01. Managerial Work in Manufacturing. **Other Jobs in This Work Group:** First-Line Supervisors/Managers of Helpers, Laborers, and Material Movers, Hand; First-Line Supervisors/Managers of Mechanics, Installers, and Repairers; First-Line Supervisors/Managers of Production and Operating Workers.

Skills—Management of Personnel Resources: Motivating, developing, and directing people as they work; identifying the best people for the job. **Systems Analysis:** Determining how a system should work and how changes will affect outcomes. **Systems Evaluation:** Looking at many indicators of system performance and taking into account their accuracy. **Management of Financial Resources:** Determining how money will be spent to get the work done and accounting for these expenditures. **Management of Material Resources:** Obtaining and seeing to the appropriate use of equipment, facilities, and materials needed to do certain work. **Negotiation:** Bringing others together and trying to reconcile differences. **Operation Monitoring:** Watching gauges, dials, or other indicators to make sure a machine is working properly. **Monitoring:** Assessing how well one is doing when learning or doing something.

Education and Training Programs: Business Administration and Management, General; Business/Commerce, General; Operations Management and Supervision. **Related Knowledge/Courses—Production and Processing:** Inputs, outputs, raw materials, waste, quality control, costs, and techniques for maximizing the manufacture and distribution of goods. **Mechanical Devices:** Machines and tools, including their designs, uses, benefits, repair, and maintenance. **Administration and Management:**

Principles and processes involved in business and organizational planning, coordination, and execution. This includes strategic planning, resource allocation, manpower modeling, leadership techniques, and production methods. **Design:** Design techniques, principles, tools, and instruments involved in the production and use of precision technical plans, blueprints, drawings, and models. **Personnel and Human Resources:** Principles and procedures for personnel recruitment; selection; training; compensation and benefits; labor relations and negotiation; and personnel information systems. **Engineering and Technology:** Equipment, tools, and mechanical devices and their uses to produce motion, light, power, technology, and other applications.

Work Environment: Indoors; noisy; contaminants; hazardous equipment; minor burns, cuts, bites, or stings; standing.

Industrial Truck and Tractor Operators

* Education/Training Required: Short-term on-the-job training
* Annual Earnings: $28,010
* Beginning Wage: $19,510
* Earnings Growth Potential: Low
* Growth: –2.0%
* Annual Job Openings: 89,547
* Self-Employed: 0.3%
* Part-Time: 2.7%

Operate industrial trucks or tractors equipped to move materials around a warehouse, storage yard, factory, construction site, or similar location. Inspect product load for accuracy, and safely move it around the warehouse or facility to ensure timely and complete delivery. Move controls to drive gasoline- or electric-powered trucks, cars, or tractors and transport materials between loading, processing, and storage areas. Move levers and controls that operate lifting devices such as forklifts, lift beams and swivel-hooks, hoists, and elevating platforms, to load, unload, transport, and stack material. Position lifting devices under, over, or around loaded pallets, skids, and boxes, and secure material or products for transport to designated areas. Manually or mechanically load and unload materials from pallets, skids, platforms, cars, lifting devices, or other transport vehicles. Perform routine maintenance on vehicles and auxiliary equipment, such as cleaning, lubricating, recharging batteries, fueling, or replacing liquefied-gas tank. Weigh materials or products, and record weight and other production data on tags or labels. Operate or tend automatic stacking, loading, packaging, or cutting machines. Turn valves and open chutes to dump, spray, or release materials from dump cars or storage bins into hoppers. Signal workers to discharge, dump, or level materials. Hook tow trucks to trailer hitches and fasten attachments such as graders, plows, rollers, and winch cables to tractors, using hitchpins.

Personality Type: Realistic. These occupations frequently involve work activities that include practical, hands-on problems and solutions. They often deal with plants; animals; and real-world materials such as wood, tools, and machinery. Many of the occupations require working outside and don't involve a lot of paperwork or working closely with others.

GOE—Interest Area/Cluster: 13. Manufacturing. **Work Group:** 13.17. Loading, Moving, Hoisting, and Conveying. **Other Jobs in This Work Group:** Conveyor Operators and Tenders; Hoist and Winch Operators; Machine Feeders and Offbearers; Packers and Packagers, Hand; Pump Operators, Except Wellhead Pumpers; Refuse and Recyclable Material Collectors; Tank Car, Truck, and Ship Loaders.

Skills—Operation Monitoring: Watching gauges, dials, or other indicators to make sure a machine is working properly. **Operation and Control:** Controlling operations of equipment or systems.

Education and Training Program: Ground Transportation, Other. **Related Knowledge/Course: Production and Processing:** Inputs, outputs, raw materials, waste, quality control, costs, and techniques for maximizing the manufacture and distribution of goods.

Work Environment: Very hot or cold; contaminants; sitting; using hands on objects, tools, or controls; bending or twisting the body; repetitive motions.

Inspectors, Testers, Sorters, Samplers, and Weighers

- ❋ Education/Training Required: Moderate-term on-the-job training
- ❋ Annual Earnings: $30,310
- ❋ Beginning Wage: $18,630
- ❋ Earnings Growth Potential: Medium
- ❋ Growth: –7.0%
- ❋ Annual Job Openings: 75,361
- ❋ Self-Employed: 1.5%
- ❋ Part-Time: 4.9%

Inspect, test, sort, sample, or weigh nonagricultural raw materials or processed, machined, fabricated, or assembled parts or products for defects, wear, and deviations from specifications. May use precision measuring instruments and complex test equipment. Discard or reject products, materials, and equipment not meeting specifications. Analyze and interpret blueprints, data, manuals, and other materials to determine specifications, inspection and testing procedures, adjustment and certification methods, formulas, and measuring instruments required. Inspect, test, or measure materials, products, installations, and work for conformance to specifications. Notify supervisors and other personnel of production problems, and assist in identifying and correcting these problems. Discuss inspection results with those responsible for products, and recommend necessary corrective actions. Record inspection or test data such as weights, temperatures, grades, or moisture content, and quantities inspected or graded. Mark items with details such as grade and acceptance or rejection status. Observe and monitor production operations and equipment to ensure conformance to specifications and make or order necessary process or assembly adjustments. Measure dimensions of products to verify conformance to specifications, using measuring instruments such as rulers, calipers, gauges, or micrometers. Analyze test data and make computations as necessary to determine test results. Collect or select samples for testing or for use as models. Check arriving materials to ensure that they match purchase orders and submit discrepancy reports when problems are found. Compare colors, shapes, textures, or grades of products or materials with color charts, templates, or samples to verify conformance to standards. Write test and inspection reports describing results, recommendations, and needed repairs. Read dials and meters to verify that equipment is functioning at specified levels. Remove defects such as chips and burrs, and lap corroded or pitted surfaces. Clean, maintain, repair, and calibrate measuring instruments and test equipment such as dial indicators, fixed gauges, and height gauges. Adjust, clean, or repair products or processing equipment to correct defects found during inspections. Stack and arrange tested products for further processing, shipping, or packaging and transport products to other work stations as necessary.

Personality Type: Conventional. These occupations frequently involve following set procedures and routines and can include working with data and details more than with ideas. Usually there is a clear line of authority to follow.

GOE—Interest Area/Cluster: 13. Manufacturing. **Work Group:** 13.07. Production Quality Control. **Other Jobs in This Work Group:** Graders and Sorters, Agricultural Products.

Skills—Quality Control Analysis: Evaluating the quality or performance of products, services, or processes. **Operation Monitoring:** Watching gauges, dials, or other indicators to make sure a machine is working properly. **Operation and Control:** Controlling operations of equipment or systems. **Repairing:** Repairing machines or systems, using the needed tools. **Systems Evaluation:** Looking at many indicators of system performance and taking into account their accuracy. **Troubleshooting:** Determining what is causing an operating error and deciding what to do about it.

Education and Training Program: Quality Control Technology/Technician. **Related Knowledge/Course: Production and Processing:** Inputs, outputs, raw materials, waste, quality control, costs, and techniques for maximizing the manufacture and distribution of goods.

Work Environment: Noisy; standing; using hands on objects, tools, or controls; repetitive motions.

Insulation Workers, Floor, Ceiling, and Wall

* Education/Training Required: Moderate-term on-the-job training
* Annual Earnings: $31,280
* Beginning Wage: $19,650
* Earnings Growth Potential: Medium
* Growth: 8.4%
* Annual Job Openings: 6,580
* Self-Employed: 1.3%
* Part-Time: 3.1%

Line and cover structures with insulating materials. May work with batt, roll, or blown insulation materials. Move controls, buttons, or levers to start blowers and regulate flow of materials through nozzles. Cover and line structures with blown or rolled forms of materials to insulate against cold, heat, or moisture, using saws, knives, rasps, trowels, blowers, and other tools and implements. Cover, seal, or finish insulated surfaces or access holes with plastic covers, canvas strips, sealants, tape, cement, or asphalt mastic. Distribute insulating materials evenly into small spaces within floors, ceilings, or walls, using blowers and hose attachments or cement mortars. Fill blower hoppers with insulating materials. Fit, wrap, staple, or glue insulating materials to structures or surfaces, using hand tools or wires. Read blueprints and select appropriate insulation based on space characteristics and the heat-retaining or -excluding characteristics of the material. Remove old insulation such as asbestos, following safety procedures. Measure and cut insulation for covering surfaces, using tape measures, handsaws, power saws, knives, or scissors. Prepare surfaces for insulation application by brushing or spreading on adhesives, cement, or asphalt or by attaching metal pins to surfaces.

Personality Type: Realistic. These occupations frequently involve work activities that include practical, hands-on problems and solutions. They often deal with plants; animals; and real-world materials such as wood, tools, and machinery. Many of the occupations require working outside and don't involve a lot of paperwork or working closely with others.

GOE—Interest Area/Cluster: 02. Architecture and Construction. **Work Group:** 02.04. Construction Crafts. **Other Jobs in This Work Group:** Boilermakers; Brickmasons and Blockmasons; Carpet Installers; Cement Masons and Concrete Finishers; Commercial Divers; Construction Carpenters; Crane and Tower Operators; Drywall and Ceiling Tile Installers; Electricians; Fence Erectors; Floor Layers, Except Carpet, Wood, and Hard Tiles; Floor Sanders and Finishers; Glaziers; Hazardous Materials Removal Workers; Insulation Workers, Mechanical; Manufactured Building and Mobile Home Installers; Operating Engineers and Other Construction Equipment Operators; Painters, Construction and Maintenance; Paperhangers; Paving, Surfacing, and Tamping Equipment Operators; Pile-Driver Operators; Pipe Fitters and Steamfitters; Pipelayers; Plasterers and Stucco Masons; Plumbers; Plumbers, Pipefitters, and Steamfitters; Rail-Track Laying and Maintenance Equipment Operators; Refractory Materials Repairers, Except Brickmasons; Reinforcing Iron and Rebar Workers; Riggers; Roofers; Rough Carpenters; Security and Fire Alarm Systems Installers; Segmental Pavers; Sheet Metal Workers; Stone Cutters and Carvers, Manufacturing; Stonemasons; Structural Iron and Steel Workers; Tapers; Terrazzo Workers and Finishers; Tile and Marble Setters.

Skills—Installation: Installing equipment, machines, wiring, or programs to meet specifications. **Repairing:** Repairing machines or systems, using the needed tools. **Management of Material Resources:** Obtaining and seeing to the appropriate use of equipment, facilities, and materials needed to do certain work. **Equipment Maintenance:** Performing routine maintenance and determining when and what kind of maintenance is needed. **Mathematics:** Using mathematics to solve problems. **Equipment Selection:** Determining the kind of tools and equipment needed to do a job.

Education and Training Program: Construction Trades, Other. **Related Knowledge/Courses—Building and Construction:** Materials, methods, and the appropriate tools to construct objects, structures, and buildings. **Production and Processing:** Inputs, outputs, raw materials, waste, quality control, costs, and techniques for maximizing the manufacture and distribution of goods. **Transportation:** Principles and methods for moving people or goods by air, rail, sea, or road, including their relative costs, advantages, and limitations. **Personnel and Human Resources:**

Principles and procedures for personnel recruitment; selection; training; compensation and benefits; labor relations and negotiation; and personnel information systems. **Design:** Design techniques, principles, tools, and instruments involved in the production and use of precision technical plans, blueprints, drawings, and models. **Economics and Accounting:** Economic and accounting principles and practices, the financial markets, banking, and the analysis and reporting of financial data.

Work Environment: Outdoors; contaminants; standing; using hands on objects, tools, or controls; bending or twisting the body; repetitive motions.

Insulation Workers, Mechanical

- Education/Training Required: Moderate-term on-the-job training
- Annual Earnings: $36,570
- Beginning Wage: $22,840
- Earnings Growth Potential: Medium
- Growth: 8.6%
- Annual Job Openings: 5,787
- Self-Employed: 0.7%
- Part-Time: 3.1%

Apply insulating materials to pipes or ductwork or other mechanical systems to help control and maintain temperature. Cover, seal, or finish insulated surfaces or access holes with plastic covers, canvas strips, sealants, tape, cement, or asphalt mastic. Measure and cut insulation for covering surfaces, using tape measures, handsaws, knives, and scissors. Prepare surfaces for insulation application by brushing or spreading on adhesives, cement, or asphalt, or by attaching metal pins to surfaces. Select appropriate insulation such as fiberglass, Styrofoam, or cork, based on the heat retaining or excluding characteristics of the material. Read blueprints and specifications to determine job requirements. Install sheet metal around insulated pipes with screws in order to protect the insulation from weather conditions or physical damage. Determine the amounts and types of insulation needed, and methods of installation, based on factors such as location, surface shape, and equipment use. Apply, remove, and repair insulation on industrial equipment, pipes, ductwork, or other mechanical systems such as heat exchangers, tanks, and vessels, to help control noise and maintain temperatures. Remove or seal off old asbestos insulation, following safety procedures. Move controls, buttons, or levers to start blowers and to regulate flow of materials through nozzles. Fill blower hoppers with insulating materials. Distribute insulating materials evenly into small spaces within floors, ceilings, or walls, using blowers and hose attachments or cement mortar. Fit insulation around obstructions, and shape insulating materials and protective coverings as required.

Personality Type: Realistic. These occupations frequently involve work activities that include practical, hands-on problems and solutions. They often deal with plants; animals; and real-world materials such as wood, tools, and machinery. Many of the occupations require working outside and don't involve a lot of paperwork or working closely with others.

GOE—Interest Area/Cluster: 02. Architecture and Construction. **Work Group:** 02.04. Construction Crafts. **Other Jobs in This Work Group:** Boilermakers; Brickmasons and Blockmasons; Carpet Installers; Cement Masons and Concrete Finishers; Commercial Divers; Construction Carpenters; Crane and Tower Operators; Drywall and Ceiling Tile Installers; Electricians; Fence Erectors; Floor Layers, Except Carpet, Wood, and Hard Tiles; Floor Sanders and Finishers; Glaziers; Hazardous Materials Removal Workers; Insulation Workers, Floor, Ceiling, and Wall; Manufactured Building and Mobile Home Installers; Operating Engineers and Other Construction Equipment Operators; Painters, Construction and Maintenance; Paperhangers; Paving, Surfacing, and Tamping Equipment Operators; Pile-Driver Operators; Pipe Fitters and Steamfitters; Pipelayers; Plasterers and Stucco Masons; Plumbers; Plumbers, Pipefitters, and Steamfitters; Rail-Track Laying and Maintenance Equipment Operators; Refractory Materials Repairers, Except Brickmasons; Reinforcing Iron and Rebar Workers; Riggers; Roofers; Rough Carpenters; Security and Fire Alarm Systems Installers; Segmental Pavers; Sheet Metal Workers; Stone Cutters and Carvers, Manufacturing; Stonemasons; Structural Iron and Steel Workers; Tapers; Terrazzo Workers and Finishers; Tile and Marble Setters.

Skills—Installation: Installing equipment, machines, wiring, or programs to meet specifications. **Repairing:** Repairing machines or systems, using the needed tools. **Mathematics:** Using mathematics to solve problems. **Coordination:** Adjusting actions in relation to others'

actions. **Management of Personnel Resources:** Motivating, developing, and directing people as they work; identifying the best people for the job. **Equipment Selection:** Determining the kind of tools and equipment needed to do a job. **Management of Material Resources:** Obtaining and seeing to the appropriate use of equipment, facilities, and materials needed to do certain work. **Equipment Maintenance:** Performing routine maintenance and determining when and what kind of maintenance is needed.

Education and Training Program: Construction Trades, Other. **Related Knowledge/Courses—Building and Construction:** Materials, methods, and the appropriate tools to construct objects, structures, and buildings. **Design:** Design techniques, principles, tools, and instruments involved in the production and use of precision technical plans, blueprints, drawings, and models. **Mechanical Devices:** Machines and tools, including their designs, uses, benefits, repair, and maintenance. **Transportation:** Principles and methods for moving people or goods by air, rail, sea, or road, including their relative costs, advantages, and limitations. **Education and Training:** Instructional methods and training techniques, including curriculum design principles, learning theory, group and individual teaching techniques, design of individual development plans, and test design principles. **Public Safety and Security:** Weaponry; public safety; security operations, rules, regulations, precautions, and prevention; and the protection of people, data, and property.

Work Environment: Noisy; contaminants; cramped work space, awkward positions; high places; standing; using hands on objects, tools, or controls.

Insurance Adjusters, Examiners, and Investigators

- ❋ Education/Training Required: Long-term on-the-job training
- ❋ Annual Earnings: $53,560
- ❋ Beginning Wage: $33,010
- ❋ Earnings Growth Potential: Medium
- ❋ Growth: 8.9%
- ❋ Annual Job Openings: 22,024
- ❋ Self-Employed: 3.5%
- ❋ Part-Time: 4.0%

The job openings listed here are shared with Claims Examiners, Property and Casualty Insurance.

Investigate, analyze, and determine the extent of insurance company's liability concerning personal, casualty, or property loss or damages and attempt to effect settlement with claimants. Correspond with or interview medical specialists, agents, witnesses, or claimants to compile information. Calculate benefit payments and approve payment of claims within a certain monetary limit. Interview or correspond with claimant and witnesses, consult police and hospital records, and inspect property damage to determine extent of liability. Investigate and assess damage to property. Examine claims forms and other records to determine insurance coverage. Analyze information gathered by investigation and report findings and recommendations. Negotiate claim settlements and recommend litigation when settlement cannot be negotiated. Collect evidence to support contested claims in court. Prepare report of findings of investigation. Interview or correspond with agents and claimants to correct errors or omissions and to investigate questionable claims. Refer questionable claims to investigator or claims adjuster for investigation or settlement. Examine titles to property to determine validity and act as company agent in transactions with property owners. Obtain credit information from banks and other credit services. Communicate with former associates to verify employment record and to obtain background information regarding persons or businesses applying for credit.

Personality Type: Conventional. These occupations frequently involve following set procedures and routines and can include working with data and details more than with ideas. Usually there is a clear line of authority to follow.

GOE—Interest Area/Cluster: 06. Finance and Insurance. **Work Group:** 06.02. Finance/Insurance Investigation and Analysis. **Other Jobs in This Work Group:** Appraisers and Assessors of Real Estate; Appraisers, Real Estate; Assessors; Claims Adjusters, Examiners, and Investigators; Claims Examiners, Property and Casualty Insurance; Cost Estimators; Credit Analysts; Financial Analysts; Insurance Appraisers, Auto Damage; Insurance Underwriters; Loan Counselors; Loan Officers; Market Research Analysts; Survey Researchers.

Skills—Negotiation: Bringing others together and trying to reconcile differences. **Persuasion:** Persuading others to approach things differently. **Judgment and Decision Making:** Weighing the relative costs and benefits of a potential action. **Time Management:** Managing one's own time and the time of others. **Management of Financial Resources:** Determining how money will be spent to get the work done and accounting for these expenditures. **Reading Comprehension:** Understanding written sentences and paragraphs in work-related documents. **Writing:** Communicating effectively with others in writing as indicated by the needs of the audience. **Critical Thinking:** Using logic and analysis to identify the strengths and weaknesses of different approaches.

Education and Training Program: Insurance. **Related Knowledge/Courses—Customer and Personal Service:** Principles and processes for providing customer and personal services, including needs assessment techniques, quality service standards, alternative delivery systems, and customer satisfaction evaluation techniques. **Clerical Studies:** Administrative and clerical procedures and systems such as word-processing systems, filing and records management systems, stenography and transcription, forms, design principles, and other office procedures and terminology. **Computers and Electronics:** Electric circuit boards, processors, chips, and computer hardware and software, including applications and programming. **Law and Government:** Laws, legal codes, court procedures, precedents, government regulations, executive orders, agency rules, and the democratic political process. **Medicine and Dentistry:** The information and techniques needed to diagnose and treat injuries, diseases, and deformities. This includes symptoms, treatment alternatives, drug properties and interactions, and preventive health-care measures. **Therapy and Counseling:** Information and techniques needed to rehabilitate physical and mental ailments and to provide career guidance, including alternative treatments, rehabilitation equipment and its proper use, and methods to evaluate treatment effects.

Work Environment: Indoors; noisy; sitting; using hands on objects, tools, or controls; repetitive motions.

Insurance Appraisers, Auto Damage

- ❋ Education/Training Required:
  Postsecondary vocational training
- ❋ Annual Earnings: $51,500
- ❋ Beginning Wage: $35,750
- ❋ Earnings Growth Potential: Low
- ❋ Growth: 12.5%
- ❋ Annual Job Openings: 1,030
- ❋ Self-Employed: 4.1%
- ❋ Part-Time: 4.0%

Appraise automobile or other vehicle damage to determine cost of repair for insurance claim settlement and seek agreement with automotive repair shop on cost of repair. Prepare insurance forms to indicate repair cost or cost estimates and recommendations. Estimate parts and labor to repair damage, using standard automotive labor and parts-cost manuals and knowledge of automotive repair. Review repair-cost estimates with automobile-repair shop to secure agreement on cost of repairs. Examine damaged vehicle to determine extent of structural, body, mechanical, electrical, or interior damage. Evaluate practicality of repair as opposed to payment of market value of vehicle before accident. Determine salvage value on total-loss vehicle. Prepare insurance forms to indicate repair-cost estimates and recommendations. Arrange to have damage appraised by another appraiser to resolve disagreement with shop on repair cost.

Personality Type: Conventional. These occupations frequently involve following set procedures and routines and can include working with data and details more than with ideas. Usually there is a clear line of authority to follow.

GOE—Interest Area/Cluster: 06. Finance and Insurance. **Work Group:** 06.02. Finance/Insurance Investigation and Analysis. **Other Jobs in This Work Group:** Appraisers and Assessors of Real Estate; Appraisers, Real Estate; Assessors; Claims Adjusters, Examiners, and Investigators; Claims Examiners, Property and Casualty Insurance; Cost Estimators; Credit Analysts; Financial Analysts; Insurance Adjusters, Examiners, and Investigators; Insurance Underwriters; Loan Counselors; Loan Officers; Market Research Analysts; Survey Researchers.

Skills—Negotiation: Bringing others together and trying to reconcile differences. **Service Orientation:** Actively looking for ways to help people. **Persuasion:** Persuading others to approach things differently. **Judgment and Decision Making:** Weighing the relative costs and benefits of a potential action. **Active Listening:** Listening to what other people are saying and asking questions as appropriate. **Time Management:** Managing one's own time and the time of others. **Equipment Selection:** Determining the kind of tools and equipment needed to do a job. **Speaking:** Talking to others to effectively convey information.

Education and Training Program: Insurance. **Related Knowledge/Courses—Customer and Personal Service:** Principles and processes for providing customer and personal services, including needs assessment techniques, quality service standards, alternative delivery systems, and customer satisfaction evaluation techniques. **Law and Government:** Laws, legal codes, court procedures, precedents, government regulations, executive orders, agency rules, and the democratic political process. **Medicine and Dentistry:** The information and techniques needed to diagnose and treat injuries, diseases, and deformities. This includes symptoms, treatment alternatives, drug properties and interactions, and preventive health-care measures. **Computers and Electronics:** Electric circuit boards, processors, chips, and computer hardware and software, including applications and programming. **Transportation:** Principles and methods for moving people or goods by air, rail, sea, or road, including their relative costs, advantages, and limitations. **Telecommunications:** Transmission, broadcasting, switching, control, and operation of telecommunications systems.

Work Environment: More often indoors than outdoors; noisy; very hot or cold; contaminants; sitting.

Insurance Claims Clerks

- ❋ Education/Training Required: Moderate-term on-the-job training
- ❋ Annual Earnings: $32,040
- ❋ Beginning Wage: $21,950
- ❋ Earnings Growth Potential: Low
- ❋ Growth: –1.3%
- ❋ Annual Job Openings: 42,246
- ❋ Self-Employed: 0.4%
- ❋ Part-Time: 9.7%

The job openings listed here are shared with Insurance Policy Processing Clerks.

Obtain information from insured or designated persons for purpose of settling claim with insurance carrier. Review insurance policy to determine coverage. Prepare and review insurance-claim forms and related documents for completeness. Provide customer service, such as giving limited instructions on how to proceed with claims or providing referrals to auto repair facilities or local contractors. Organize and work with detailed office or warehouse records, using computers to enter, access, search, and retrieve data. Post or attach information to claim file. Pay small claims. Transmit claims for payment or further investigation. Contact insured or other involved persons to obtain missing information. Calculate amount of claim. Apply insurance rating systems.

Personality Type: Conventional. These occupations frequently involve following set procedures and routines and can include working with data and details more than with ideas. Usually there is a clear line of authority to follow.

GOE—Interest Area/Cluster: 06. Finance and Insurance. **Work Group:** 06.03. Finance/Insurance Records Processing. **Other Jobs in This Work Group:** Credit Authorizers; Credit Authorizers, Checkers, and Clerks; Credit Checkers; Insurance Claims and Policy Processing Clerks; Insurance Policy Processing Clerks; Proofreaders and Copy Markers.

Skill: Service Orientation: Actively looking for ways to help people.

Education and Training Program: General Office Occupations and Clerical Services. **Related Knowledge/ Courses—Clerical Studies:** Administrative and clerical procedures and systems such as word-processing systems, filing and records management systems, stenography and transcription, forms, design principles, and other office procedures and terminology. **Customer and Personal Service:** Principles and processes for providing customer and personal services, including needs assessment techniques, quality service standards, alternative delivery systems, and customer satisfaction evaluation techniques. **Computers and Electronics:** Electric circuit boards, processors, chips, and computer hardware and software, including applications and programming. **Economics and Accounting:** Economic and accounting principles and practices, the financial markets, banking, and the analysis and reporting of financial data.

Work Environment: Indoors; sitting; repetitive motions.

Insurance Policy Processing Clerks

- Education/Training Required: Moderate-term on-the-job training
- Annual Earnings: $32,040
- Beginning Wage: $21,950
- Earnings Growth Potential: Low
- Growth: –1.3%
- Annual Job Openings: 42,246
- Self-Employed: 0.4%
- Part-Time: 9.7%

The job openings listed here are shared with Insurance Claims Clerks.

Process applications for, changes to, reinstatement of, and cancellation of insurance policies. Duties include reviewing insurance applications to ensure that all questions have been answered, compiling data on insurance policy changes, changing policy records to conform to insured party's specifications, compiling data on lapsed insurance policies to determine automatic reinstatement according to company policies, canceling insurance policies as requested by agents, and verifying the accuracy of insurance company records. Modify, update, and process existing policies and claims to reflect any change in beneficiary, amount of coverage, or type of insurance. Process and record new insurance policies and claims. Review and verify data, such as age, name, address, and principal sum and value of property, on insurance applications and policies. Organize and work with detailed office or warehouse records, maintaining files for each policyholder, including policies that are to be reinstated or cancelled. Examine letters from policyholders or agents, original insurance applications, and other company documents to determine whether changes are needed and effects of changes. Correspond with insured or agent to obtain information or inform them of account status or changes. Transcribe data to worksheets and enter data into computer for use in preparing documents and adjusting accounts. Notify insurance agent and accounting department of policy cancellation. Interview clients and take their calls to provide customer service and obtain information on claims. Compare information from application to criteria for policy reinstatement and approve reinstatement when criteria are met. Process, prepare, and submit business or government forms, such as submitting applications for coverage to insurance carriers. Collect initial premiums and issue receipts. Calculate premiums, refunds, commissions, adjustments, and new reserve requirements, using insurance rate standards. Obtain computer printout of policy cancellations or retrieve cancellation cards from file. Compose business correspondence for supervisors, managers, and professionals. Check computations of interest accrued, premiums due, and settlement surrender on loan values.

Personality Type: Conventional. These occupations frequently involve following set procedures and routines and can include working with data and details more than with ideas. Usually there is a clear line of authority to follow.

GOE—Interest Area/Cluster: 06. Finance and Insurance. **Work Group:** 06.03. Finance/Insurance Records Processing. **Other Jobs in This Work Group:** Credit Authorizers; Credit Authorizers, Checkers, and Clerks; Credit Checkers; Insurance Claims and Policy Processing Clerks; Insurance Claims Clerks; Proofreaders and Copy Markers.

Skill: Critical Thinking: Using logic and analysis to identify the strengths and weaknesses of different approaches.

Education and Training Program: General Office Occupations and Clerical Services. **Related Knowledge/Courses—Clerical Studies:** Administrative and clerical procedures and systems such as word-processing systems, filing and records management systems, stenography and transcription, forms, design principles, and other office procedures and terminology. **Customer and Personal Service:** Principles and processes for providing customer and personal services, including needs assessment techniques, quality service standards, alternative delivery systems, and customer satisfaction evaluation techniques. **Computers and Electronics:** Electric circuit boards, processors, chips, and computer hardware and software, including applications and programming. **Economics and Accounting:** Economic and accounting principles and practices, the financial markets, banking, and the analysis and reporting of financial data. **Sales and Marketing:** Principles and methods involved in showing, promoting, and selling products or services. This includes marketing strategies and tactics, product demonstration and sales techniques, and sales control systems. **Production and Processing:** Inputs, outputs, raw materials, waste, quality control, costs, and techniques for maximizing the manufacture and distribution of goods.

Work Environment: Sitting; repetitive motions.

Interior Designers

- ❋ Education/Training Required: Associate degree
- ❋ Annual Earnings: $43,970
- ❋ Beginning Wage: $25,920
- ❋ Earnings Growth Potential: High
- ❋ Growth: 19.5%
- ❋ Annual Job Openings: 8,434
- ❋ Self-Employed: 26.3%
- ❋ Part-Time: 16.7%

Plan, design, and furnish interiors of residential, commercial, or industrial buildings. Formulate design that is practical, aesthetic, and conducive to intended purposes, such as raising productivity, selling merchandise, or improving lifestyle. May specialize in a particular field, style, or phase of interior design. Estimate material requirements and costs and present design to client for approval. Confer with client to determine factors affecting planning interior environments, such as budget, architectural preferences, and purpose and function. Advise client on interior design factors such as space planning, layout, and utilization of furnishings or equipment and color coordination. Select or design and purchase furnishings, artwork, and accessories. Formulate environmental plan to be practical, esthetic, and conducive to intended purposes such as raising productivity or selling merchandise. Subcontract fabrication, installation, and arrangement of carpeting, fixtures, accessories, draperies, paint and wall coverings, artwork, furniture, and related items. Render design ideas in form of paste-ups or drawings. Plan and design interior environments for boats, planes, buses, trains, and other enclosed spaces.

Personality Type: Artistic. These occupations frequently involve working with forms, designs, and patterns. They often require self-expression, and the work can be done without following a clear set of rules.

GOE—**Interest Area/Cluster:** 03. Arts and Communication. **Work Group:** 03.05. Design. **Other Jobs in This Work Group:** Commercial and Industrial Designers; Fashion Designers; Floral Designers; Graphic Designers; Merchandise Displayers and Window Trimmers; Set and Exhibit Designers.

Skills—Installation: Installing equipment, machines, wiring, or programs to meet specifications. **Management of Financial Resources:** Determining how money will be spent to get the work done and accounting for these expenditures. **Persuasion:** Persuading others to approach things differently. **Operations Analysis:** Analyzing needs and product requirements to create a design. **Negotiation:** Bringing others together and trying to reconcile differences. **Active Learning:** Working with new material or information to grasp its implications. **Mathematics:** Using mathematics to solve problems. **Speaking:** Talking to others to effectively convey information.

Education and Training Programs: Facilities Planning and Management; Interior Architecture; Interior Design; Textile Science. **Related Knowledge/Courses—Design:** Design techniques, principles, tools, and instruments involved in the production and use of precision technical plans, blueprints, drawings, and models. **Sales and Marketing:** Principles and methods involved in showing, promoting, and selling products or services. This includes marketing strategies and tactics, product demonstration and sales techniques, and sales control systems. **Building and Construction:** Materials, methods, and the appropriate tools to construct objects, structures, and buildings. **Clerical Studies:** Administrative and clerical procedures and systems such as word-processing systems, filing and records management systems, stenography and transcription, forms, design principles, and other office procedures and terminology. **Fine Arts:** Theory and techniques required to produce, compose, and perform works of music, dance, visual arts, drama, and sculpture. **Administration and Management:** Principles and processes involved in business and organizational planning, coordination, and execution. This includes strategic planning, resource allocation, manpower modeling, leadership techniques, and production methods.

Work Environment: Indoors; sitting.

Interpreters and Translators

- Education/Training Required: Long-term on-the-job training
- Annual Earnings: $37,490
- Beginning Wage: $21,500
- Earnings Growth Potential: High
- Growth: 23.6%
- Annual Job Openings: 6,630
- Self-Employed: 21.6%
- Part-Time: 28.5%

Translate or interpret written, oral, or sign language text into another language for others. Follow ethical codes that protect the confidentiality of information. Identify and resolve conflicts related to the meanings of words, concepts, practices, or behaviors. Proofread, edit, and revise translated materials. Translate messages simultaneously or consecutively into specified languages orally or by using hand signs, maintaining message content, context, and style as much as possible. Check translations of technical terms and terminology to ensure that they are accurate and remain consistent throughout translation revisions. Read written materials such as legal documents, scientific works, or news reports and rewrite material into specified languages. Refer to reference materials such as dictionaries, lexicons, encyclopedias, and computerized terminology banks as needed to ensure translation accuracy. Compile terminology and information to be used in translations, including technical terms such as those for legal or medical material. Adapt translations to students' cognitive and grade levels, collaborating with educational team members as necessary. Listen to speakers' statements to determine meanings and to prepare translations, using electronic listening systems as necessary. Check original texts or confer with authors to ensure that translations retain the content, meaning, and feeling of the original material. Compile information about the content and context of information to be translated, as well as details of the groups for whom translation or interpretation is being performed. Discuss translation requirements with clients and determine any fees to be charged for services provided. Adapt software and accompanying technical documents to another language and culture. Educate students, parents, staff, and teachers about the roles and functions of educational interpreters. Train and supervise other translators/interpreters.

Travel with or guide tourists who speak another language.

Personality Type: Artistic. These occupations frequently involve working with forms, designs, and patterns. They often require self-expression, and the work can be done without following a clear set of rules.

GOE—Interest Area/Cluster: 03. Arts and Communication. **Work Group:** 03.03. News, Broadcasting, and Public Relations. **Other Jobs in This Work Group:** Broadcast News Analysts; Public Relations Specialists; Reporters and Correspondents.

Skills—Social Perceptiveness: Being aware of others' reactions and understanding why they react the way they do. **Speaking:** Talking to others to effectively convey information. **Active Listening:** Listening to what other people are saying and asking questions as appropriate. **Writing:** Communicating effectively with others in writing as indicated by the needs of the audience. **Reading Comprehension:** Understanding written sentences and paragraphs in work-related documents.

Education and Training Programs: American Sign Language (ASL); Chinese Language and Literature; Classics; Education/Teaching of Individuals with Hearing Impairments; Foreign Languages, Literatures, and Linguistics, others; French Language and Literature; German Language and Literature; Italian Language and Literature; Japanese Language and Literature; Language Interpretation and Translation; Linguistics; Russian Language and Literature; Spanish Language and Literature. **Related Knowledge/Courses—Foreign Language:** The structure and content of a foreign (non-English) language, including the meaning and spelling of words, rules of composition and grammar, and pronunciation. **English Language:** The structure and content of the English language, including the meaning and spelling of words, rules of composition, and grammar. **Geography:** Various methods for describing the location and distribution of land, sea, and air masses, including their physical locations, relationships, and characteristics. **Sociology and Anthropology:** Group behavior and dynamics; societal trends and influences; and cultures and their history, migrations, ethnicity, and origins. **Computers and Electronics:** Electric circuit boards, processors, chips, and computer hardware and software, including applications and programming. **Communications and Media:** Media production, communication, and dissemination techniques and methods, including alternative ways to inform and entertain via written, oral, and visual media.

Work Environment: Indoors; sitting; repetitive motions.

Interviewers, Except Eligibility and Loan

* Education/Training Required: Short-term on-the-job training
* Annual Earnings: $27,320
* Beginning Wage: $17,960
* Earnings Growth Potential: Low
* Growth: 9.5%
* Annual Job Openings: 54,060
* Self-Employed: 0.8%
* Part-Time: 23.4%

Interview persons by telephone, by mail, in person, or by other means for the purpose of completing forms, applications, or questionnaires. Ask specific questions, record answers, and assist persons with completing form. May sort, classify, and file forms. Ask questions in accordance with instructions to obtain various specified information such as person's name, address, age, religious preference, and state of residency. Identify and resolve inconsistencies in interviewees' responses by means of appropriate questioning or explanation. Compile, record, and code results and data from interview or survey, using computer or specified form. Review data obtained from interview for completeness and accuracy. Contact individuals to be interviewed at home, place of business, or field location by telephone, by mail, or in person. Assist individuals in filling out applications or questionnaires. Ensure payment for services by verifying benefits with the person's insurance provider or working out financing options. Identify and report problems in obtaining valid data. Explain survey objectives and procedures to interviewees and interpret survey questions to help interviewees' comprehension. Perform patient services, such as answering the telephone and assisting patients with financial and medical questions. Prepare reports to provide answers in response to specific problems. Locate and list addresses and households. Perform other office duties as needed, such as telemarketing and customer service inquiries, billing patients, and receiving payments. Meet with supervisor daily to submit completed assignments and discuss progress. Collect and analyze data, such as studying old records; tallying the number of outpatients entering each day or week; or participating in federal, state, or local population surveys as a census enumerator.

Personality Type: Conventional. These occupations frequently involve following set procedures and routines and can include working with data and details more than with ideas. Usually there is a clear line of authority to follow.

GOE—Interest Area/Cluster: 10. Human Service. **Work Group:** 10.04. Client Interviewing. **Other Jobs in This Work Group:** Eligibility Interviewers, Government Programs.

Skills—Service Orientation: Actively looking for ways to help people. **Speaking:** Talking to others to effectively convey information.

Education and Training Program: Receptionist Training. **Related Knowledge/Courses—Therapy and Counseling:** Information and techniques needed to rehabilitate physical and mental ailments and to provide career guidance, including alternative treatments, rehabilitation equipment and its proper use, and methods to evaluate treatment effects. **Sales and Marketing:** Principles and methods involved in showing, promoting, and selling products or services. This includes marketing strategies and tactics, product demonstration and sales techniques, and sales control systems. **Customer and Personal Service:** Principles and processes for providing customer and personal services, including needs assessment techniques, quality service standards, alternative delivery systems, and customer satisfaction evaluation techniques. **Psychology:** Human behavior and performance, mental processes, psychological research methods, and the assessment and treatment of behavioral and affective disorders. **Medicine and Dentistry:** The information and techniques needed to diagnose and treat injuries, diseases, and deformities. This includes symptoms, treatment alternatives, drug properties and interactions, and preventive health-care measures. **Education and Training:** Instructional methods and training techniques, including curriculum design principles, learning theory, group and individual teaching techniques, design of individual development plans, and test design principles.

Work Environment: Indoors; sitting; using hands on objects, tools, or controls; repetitive motions.

Laborers and Freight, Stock, and Material Movers, Hand

* Education/Training Required: Short-term on-the-job training
* Annual Earnings: $21,900
* Beginning Wage: $15,420
* Earnings Growth Potential: Low
* Growth: 2.1%
* Annual Job Openings: 630,487
* Self-Employed: 1.1%
* Part-Time: 20.8%

Manually move freight, stock, or other materials or perform other unskilled general labor. Includes all unskilled manual laborers not elsewhere classified. Attach identifying tags to containers or mark them with identifying information. Read work orders or receive oral instructions to determine work assignments and material and equipment needs. Record numbers of units handled and moved, using daily production sheets or work tickets. Move freight, stock, and other materials to and from storage and production areas, loading docks, delivery vehicles, ships, and containers by hand or using trucks, tractors, and other equipment. Sort cargo before loading and unloading. Assemble product containers and crates, using hand tools and precut lumber. Load and unload ship cargo, using winches and other hoisting devices. Connect hoses and operate equipment to move liquid materials into and out of storage tanks on vessels. Pack containers and re-pack damaged containers. Carry needed tools and supplies from storage or trucks and return them after use. Install protective devices, such as bracing, padding, or strapping, to prevent shifting or damage to items being transported. Maintain equipment storage areas to ensure that inventory is protected. Attach slings, hooks, and other devices to lift cargo and guide loads. Carry out general yard duties such as performing shunting on railway lines. Adjust controls to guide, position, and move equipment such as cranes, booms, and cameras. Guide loads being lifted to prevent swinging. Adjust or replace equipment parts such as rollers, belts, plugs, and caps, using hand tools. Stack cargo in locations such as transit sheds or in holds of ships as directed, using pallets or cargo boards. Connect electrical equipment to power sources so that it can be tested before use. Set up the equipment needed to produce special lighting and sound effects during performances. Bundle and band material such as fodder and tobacco leaves, using banding machines. Rig and dismantle props and equipment such as frames, scaffolding, platforms, or backdrops, using hand tools. Check out, rent, or requisition all equipment needed for productions or for set construction. Direct spouts and position receptacles such as bins, carts, and containers so they can be loaded.

Personality Type: Realistic. These occupations frequently involve work activities that include practical, hands-on problems and solutions. They often deal with plants; animals; and real-world materials such as wood, tools, and machinery. Many of the occupations require working outside and don't involve a lot of paperwork or working closely with others.

GOE—Interest Area/Cluster: 16. Transportation, Distribution, and Logistics. **Work Group:** 16.07. Transportation Support Work. **Other Jobs in This Work Group:** Bridge and Lock Tenders; Cargo and Freight Agents; Cleaners of Vehicles and Equipment; Railroad Brake, Signal, and Switch Operators; Traffic Technicians.

Skills: None met the criteria.

Education and Training Programs: No related CIP programs; this job is learned through informal short-term on-the-job training. **Related Knowledge/Courses— Transportation:** Principles and methods for moving people or goods by air, rail, sea, or road, including their relative costs, advantages, and limitations. **Public Safety and Security:** Weaponry; public safety; security operations, rules, regulations, precautions, and prevention; and the protection of people, data, and property. **Production and Processing:** Inputs, outputs, raw materials, waste, quality control, costs, and techniques for maximizing the manufacture and distribution of goods.

Work Environment: Outdoors; noisy; very hot or cold; contaminants; standing; using hands on objects, tools, or controls.

Landscaping and Groundskeeping Workers

* Education/Training Required: Short-term on-the-job training
* Annual Earnings: $22,240
* Beginning Wage: $15,970
* Earnings Growth Potential: Low
* Growth: 18.1%
* Annual Job Openings: 307,138
* Self-Employed: 20.5%
* Part-Time: 14.6%

Landscape or maintain grounds of property, using hand or power tools or equipment. Workers typically perform a variety of tasks, which may include any combination of the following: sod laying, mowing, trimming, planting, watering, fertilizing, digging, raking, sprinkler installation, and installation of mortarless segmental concrete masonry wall units. Operate powered equipment such as mowers, tractors, twin-axle vehicles, snowblowers, chain saws, electric clippers, sod cutters, and pruning saws. Mow and edge lawns, using power mowers and edgers. Shovel snow from walks, driveways, and parking lots and spread salt in those areas. Care for established lawns by mulching; aerating; weeding; grubbing and removing thatch; and trimming and edging around flower beds, walks, and walls. Use hand tools such as shovels, rakes, pruning saws, saws, hedge and brush trimmers, and axes. Prune and trim trees, shrubs, and hedges, using shears, pruners, or chain saws. Maintain and repair tools; equipment; and structures such as buildings, greenhouses, fences, and benches, using hand and power tools. Gather and remove litter. Mix and spray or spread fertilizers, herbicides, or insecticides onto grass, shrubs, and trees, using hand or automatic sprayers or spreaders. Provide proper upkeep of sidewalks, driveways, parking lots, fountains, planters, burial sites, and other grounds features. Water lawns, trees, and plants, using portable sprinkler systems, hoses, or watering cans. Trim and pick flowers and clean flowerbeds. Rake, mulch, and compost leaves. Plant seeds, bulbs, foliage, flowering plants, grass, ground covers, trees, and shrubs and apply mulch for protection, using gardening tools. Follow planned landscaping designs to determine where to lay sod, sow grass, or plant flowers and foliage. Decorate gardens with stones and plants.

Maintain irrigation systems, including winterizing the systems and starting them up in spring. Care for natural turf fields, making sure the underlying soil has the required composition to allow proper drainage and to support the grasses used on the fields. Use irrigation methods to adjust the amount of water consumption and to prevent waste. Haul or spread topsoil and spread straw over seeded soil to hold soil in place. Advise customers on plant selection and care. Care for artificial turf fields, periodically removing the turf and replacing cushioning pads and vacuuming and disinfecting the turf after use to prevent the growth of harmful bacteria.

Personality Type: Realistic. These occupations frequently involve work activities that include practical, hands-on problems and solutions. They often deal with plants; animals; and real-world materials such as wood, tools, and machinery. Many of the occupations require working outside and don't involve a lot of paperwork or working closely with others.

GOE—Interest Area/Cluster: 01. Agriculture and Natural Resources. **Work Group:** 01.05. Nursery, Groundskeeping, and Pest Control. **Other Jobs in This Work Group:** Nursery Workers; Pest Control Workers; Pesticide Handlers, Sprayers, and Applicators, Vegetation; Tree Trimmers and Pruners.

Skills—Equipment Maintenance: Performing routine maintenance and determining when and what kind of maintenance is needed. **Repairing:** Repairing machines or systems, using the needed tools. **Operation Monitoring:** Watching gauges, dials, or other indicators to make sure a machine is working properly. **Installation:** Installing equipment, machines, wiring, or programs to meet specifications. **Equipment Selection:** Determining the kind of tools and equipment needed to do a job.

Education and Training Programs: Landscaping and Groundskeeping; Turf and Turfgrass Management. **Related Knowledge/Course: Mechanical Devices:** Machines and tools, including their designs, uses, benefits, repair, and maintenance.

Work Environment: Outdoors; noisy; very hot or cold; contaminants; standing; using hands on objects, tools, or controls.

Legal Secretaries

* Education/Training Required: Associate degree
* Annual Earnings: $38,810
* Beginning Wage: $24,380
* Earnings Growth Potential: Medium
* Growth: 11.7%
* Annual Job Openings: 38,682
* Self-Employed: 1.4%
* Part-Time: 18.9%

Perform secretarial duties, utilizing legal terminology, procedures, and documents. Prepare legal papers and correspondence, such as summonses, complaints, motions, and subpoenas. May also assist with legal research. Prepare and process legal documents and papers, such as summonses, subpoenas, complaints, appeals, motions, and pretrial agreements. Mail, fax, or arrange for delivery of legal correspondence to clients, witnesses, and court officials. Receive and place telephone calls. Schedule and make appointments. Make photocopies of correspondence, documents, and other printed matter. Organize and maintain law libraries, documents, and case files. Assist attorneys in collecting information such as employment, medical, and other records. Attend legal meetings, such as client interviews, hearings, or depositions, and take notes. Draft and type office memos. Review legal publications and perform database searches to identify laws and court decisions relevant to pending cases. Submit articles and information from searches to attorneys for review and approval for use. Complete various forms such as accident reports, trial and courtroom requests, and applications for clients.

Personality Type: Conventional. These occupations frequently involve following set procedures and routines and can include working with data and details more than with ideas. Usually there is a clear line of authority to follow.

GOE—Interest Area/Cluster: 04. Business and Administration. **Work Group:** 04.04. Secretarial Support. **Other Jobs in This Work Group:** Executive Secretaries and Administrative Assistants; Medical Secretaries; Secretaries, Except Legal, Medical, and Executive.

Skills—Writing: Communicating effectively with others in writing as indicated by the needs of the audience. **Reading Comprehension:** Understanding written sentences and paragraphs in work-related documents. **Time Management:** Managing one's own time and the time of others. **Social Perceptiveness:** Being aware of others' reactions and understanding why they react the way they do. **Judgment and Decision Making:** Weighing the relative costs and benefits of a potential action. **Operation and Control:** Controlling operations of equipment or systems. **Active Listening:** Listening to what other people are saying and asking questions as appropriate. **Speaking:** Talking to others to effectively convey information.

Education and Training Program: Legal Administrative Assistant/Secretary Training. **Related Knowledge/Courses—Clerical Studies:** Administrative and clerical procedures and systems such as word-processing systems, filing and records management systems, stenography and transcription, forms, design principles, and other office procedures and terminology. **Law and Government:** Laws, legal codes, court procedures, precedents, government regulations, executive orders, agency rules, and the democratic political process. **Economics and Accounting:** Economic and accounting principles and practices, the financial markets, banking, and the analysis and reporting of financial data. **Computers and Electronics:** Electric circuit boards, processors, chips, and computer hardware and software, including applications and programming. **Customer and Personal Service:** Principles and processes for providing customer and personal services, including needs assessment techniques, quality service standards, alternative delivery systems, and customer satisfaction evaluation techniques.

Work Environment: Indoors; sitting; repetitive motions.

Library Technicians

* Education/Training Required: Postsecondary vocational training
* Annual Earnings: $27,680
* Beginning Wage: $16,430
* Earnings Growth Potential: High
* Growth: 8.5%
* Annual Job Openings: 29,075
* Self-Employed: 0.0%
* Part-Time: 65.0%

Assist librarians by helping readers in the use of library catalogs, databases, and indexes to locate books and other materials and by answering questions that require only brief consultation of standard reference. Compile records; sort and shelve books; remove or repair damaged books; register patrons; check materials in and out of the circulation process. Replace materials in shelving area (stacks) or files. Includes bookmobile drivers who operate bookmobiles or light trucks that pull trailers to specific locations on a predetermined schedule and assist with providing services in mobile libraries. Reserve, circulate, renew, and discharge books and other materials. Enter and update patrons' records on computers. Provide assistance to teachers and students by locating materials and helping to complete special projects. Guide patrons in finding and using library resources, including reference materials, audiovisual equipment, computers, and electronic resources. Answer routine reference inquiries and refer patrons needing further assistance to librarians. Train other staff, volunteers, or student assistants, and schedule and supervise their work. Sort books, publications, and other items according to procedure and return them to shelves, files, or other designated storage areas. Conduct reference searches, using printed materials and in-house and online databases. Deliver and retrieve items throughout the library by hand or using pushcart. Take actions to halt disruption of library activities by problem patrons. Process interlibrary loans for patrons. Process print and non-print library materials to prepare them for inclusion in library collections. Retrieve information from central databases for storage in a library's computer. Organize and maintain periodicals and reference materials. Compile and maintain records relating to circulation, materials, and equipment. Collect fines and respond to complaints about fines. Issue identification cards to borrowers. Verify bibliographical data for materials, including author, title, publisher, publication date, and edition. Review subject matter of materials to be classified and select classification numbers and headings according to classification systems. Send out notices about lost or overdue books. Prepare order slips for materials to be acquired, checking prices and figuring costs. Design, customize, and maintain databases, Web pages, and local area networks. Operate and maintain audiovisual equipment such as projectors, tape recorders, and videocassette recorders. File catalog cards according to system used. Prepare volumes for binding. Conduct children's programs and other specialized programs such as library tours. Compose explanatory summaries of contents of books and other reference materials.

Personality Type: Conventional. These occupations frequently involve following set procedures and routines and can include working with data and details more than with ideas. Usually there is a clear line of authority to follow.

GOE—Interest Area/Cluster: 05. Education and Training. **Work Group:** 05.04. Library Services. **Other Jobs in This Work Group:** Librarians; Library Assistants, Clerical.

Skills—Service Orientation: Actively looking for ways to help people. **Reading Comprehension:** Understanding written sentences and paragraphs in work-related documents. **Writing:** Communicating effectively with others in writing as indicated by the needs of the audience.

Education and Training Program: Library Assistant/Technician Training. **Related Knowledge/Courses—Clerical Studies:** Administrative and clerical procedures and systems such as word-processing systems, filing and records management systems, stenography and transcription, forms, design principles, and other office procedures and terminology. **Computers and Electronics:** Electric circuit boards, processors, chips, and computer hardware and software, including applications and programming. **Customer and Personal Service:** Principles and processes for providing customer and personal services, including needs assessment techniques, quality service standards, alternative delivery systems, and customer satisfaction evaluation techniques. **English Language:** The structure and content of the English language, including the meaning and spelling of words, rules of composition, and grammar. **Education and Training:** Instructional methods and training techniques, including curriculum design principles, learning theory, group and individual teaching techniques, design of individual development plans, and test design principles. **Administration and Management:** Principles and processes involved in business and organizational planning, coordination, and execution. This includes strategic planning, resource allocation, manpower modeling, leadership techniques, and production methods.

Work Environment: Indoors; sitting; using hands on objects, tools, or controls; repetitive motions.

License Clerks

- ❋ Education/Training Required: Short-term on-the-job training
- ❋ Annual Earnings: $32,330
- ❋ Beginning Wage: $21,050
- ❋ Earnings Growth Potential: Low
- ❋ Growth: 8.8%
- ❋ Annual Job Openings: 16,163
- ❋ Self-Employed: 2.7%
- ❋ Part-Time: 9.6%

The job openings listed here are shared with Court Clerks and with Municipal Clerks.

Issue licenses or permits to qualified applicants. Obtain necessary information, record data, advise applicants on requirements, collect fees, and issue licenses. May conduct oral, written, visual, or performance testing. Collect prescribed fees for licenses. Code information on license applications for entry into computers. Evaluate information on applications to verify completeness and accuracy and to determine whether applicants are qualified to obtain desired licenses. Answer questions and provide advice to the public regarding licensing policies, procedures, and regulations. Maintain records of applications made and licensing fees collected. Question applicants to obtain required information, such as name, address, and age, and record data on prescribed forms. Update operational records and licensing information, using computer terminals. Inform customers by mail or telephone of additional steps they need to take to obtain licenses. Perform routine data entry and other office support activities, including creating, sorting, photocopying, distributing, and filing documents. Stock counters with adequate supplies of forms, film, licenses, and other required materials. Enforce canine licensing regulations, contacting non-compliant owners in person or by mail to inform them of the required regulations and potential enforcement actions. Assemble photographs with printed license information to produce completed documents. Prepare bank deposits and take them to banks. Operate specialized photographic equipment to obtain photographs for drivers' licenses and photo identification cards. Instruct customers in the completion of drivers' license application forms and other forms such as voter registration cards and organ donor forms. Conduct and score oral, visual, written, or performance tests to determine applicant qualifications and notify applicants of their scores. Send by mail drivers' licenses to out-of-county or out-of-state applicants. Perform record checks on past and current licensees as required by investigations. Respond to correspondence from insurance companies regarding the licensure of agents, brokers, and adjusters. Prepare lists of overdue accounts and license suspensions and issuances. Train other workers and coordinate their work as necessary.

Personality Type: Conventional. These occupations frequently involve following set procedures and routines and can include working with data and details more than with ideas. Usually there is a clear line of authority to follow.

GOE—Interest Area/Cluster: 07. Government and Public Administration. **Work Group:** 07.04. Public Administration Clerical Support. **Other Jobs in This Work Group:** Court Clerks; Court Reporters; Court, Municipal, and License Clerks; Municipal Clerks.

Skills—Reading Comprehension: Understanding written sentences and paragraphs in work-related documents. **Service Orientation:** Actively looking for ways to help people. **Instructing:** Teaching others how to do something. **Active Listening:** Listening to what other people are saying and asking questions as appropriate.

Education and Training Program: General Office Occupations and Clerical Services. **Related Knowledge/Courses—Clerical Studies:** Administrative and clerical procedures and systems such as word-processing systems, filing and records management systems, stenography and transcription, forms, design principles, and other office procedures and terminology. **Customer and Personal Service:** Principles and processes for providing customer and personal services, including needs assessment techniques, quality service standards, alternative delivery systems, and customer satisfaction evaluation techniques. **Law and Government:** Laws, legal codes, court procedures, precedents, government regulations, executive orders, agency rules, and the democratic political process. **Computers and Electronics:** Electric circuit boards, processors, chips, and computer hardware and software, including applications and programming.

Work Environment: Indoors; noisy; sitting; using hands on objects, tools, or controls; repetitive motions.

Licensed Practical and Licensed Vocational Nurses

- ❋ Education/Training Required: Postsecondary vocational training
- ❋ Annual Earnings: $37,940
- ❋ Beginning Wage: $27,370
- ❋ Earnings Growth Potential: Low
- ❋ Growth: 14.0%
- ❋ Annual Job Openings: 70,610
- ❋ Self-Employed: 1.5%
- ❋ Part-Time: 18.3%

Care for ill, injured, convalescent, or disabled persons in hospitals, nursing homes, clinics, private homes, group homes, and similar institutions. May work under the supervision of a registered nurse. Licensing required. Administer prescribed medications or start intravenous fluids, recording times and amounts on patients' charts. Observe patients, charting and reporting changes in patients' conditions, such as adverse reactions to medication or treatment, and taking any necessary actions. Provide basic patient care and treatments such as taking temperatures or blood pressures, dressing wounds, treating bedsores, giving enemas or douches, rubbing with alcohol, massaging, or performing catheterizations. Sterilize equipment and supplies, using germicides, sterilizer, or autoclave. Answer patients' calls and determine how to assist them. Work as part of a health-care team to assess patient needs, plan and modify care, and implement interventions. Measure and record patients' vital signs such as height, weight, temperature, blood pressure, pulse, and respiration. Collect samples such as blood, urine, and sputum from patients, and perform routine laboratory tests on samples. Prepare patients for examinations, tests, or treatments, and explain procedures. Assemble and use equipment such as catheters, tracheotomy tubes, and oxygen suppliers. Evaluate nursing intervention outcomes, conferring with other health care team members as necessary. Record food and fluid intake and output. Help patients with bathing, dressing, maintaining personal hygiene, moving in bed, or standing and walking. Apply compresses, ice bags, and hot water bottles. Inventory and requisition supplies and instruments. Clean rooms and make beds. Supervise nurses' aides and assistants. Make appointments, keep records, and perform other clerical duties in doctors' offices and clinics. Provide medical treatment and personal care to patients in private home settings such as cooking, keeping rooms orderly, seeing that patients are comfortable and in good spirits, and instructing family members in simple nursing tasks. Set up equipment and prepare medical treatment rooms. Prepare food trays and examine them for conformance to prescribed diet. Wash and dress bodies of deceased persons. Assist in delivery, care, and feeding of infants.

Personality Type: Social. These occupations frequently involve working with, communicating with, and teaching people and often involve helping or providing service to others.

GOE—Interest Area/Cluster: 08. Health Science. **Work Group:** 08.08. Patient Care and Assistance. **Other Jobs in This Work Group:** Home Health Aides; Nursing Aides, Orderlies, and Attendants; Psychiatric Aides; Psychiatric Technicians.

Skills—Service Orientation: Actively looking for ways to help people. **Systems Analysis:** Determining how a system should work and how changes will affect outcomes. **Management of Personnel Resources:** Motivating, developing, and directing people as they work; identifying the best people for the job. **Social Perceptiveness:** Being aware of others' reactions and understanding why they react the way they do. **Systems Evaluation:** Looking at many indicators of system performance and taking into account their accuracy.

Education and Training Program: Licensed Practical/Vocational Nurse Training (LPN, LVN, Cert, Dipl, AAS). **Related Knowledge/Courses—Psychology:** Human behavior and performance, mental processes, psychological research methods, and the assessment and treatment of behavioral and affective disorders. **Medicine and Dentistry:** The information and techniques needed to diagnose and treat injuries, diseases, and deformities. This includes symptoms, treatment alternatives, drug properties and interactions, and preventive health-care measures. **Therapy and Counseling:** Information and techniques needed to rehabilitate physical and mental ailments and to provide career guidance, including alternative treatments, rehabilitation equipment and its proper use, and methods to evaluate treatment effects. **Biology:** Plant and animal living tissue, cells, organisms, and entities, including their functions, interdependencies, and interactions with each other and the environment. **Philosophy and Theology:**

Different philosophical systems and religions, including their basic principles, values, ethics, ways of thinking, customs, and practices and their impact on human culture. **Customer and Personal Service:** Principles and processes for providing customer and personal services, including needs assessment techniques, quality service standards, alternative delivery systems, and customer satisfaction evaluation techniques.

Work Environment: Indoors; contaminants; disease or infections; standing; walking and running; using hands on objects, tools, or controls.

Licensing Examiners and Inspectors

* Education/Training Required: Long-term on-the-job training
* Annual Earnings: $48,400
* Beginning Wage: $28,980
* Earnings Growth Potential: High
* Growth: 4.9%
* Annual Job Openings: 15,841
* Self-Employed: 0.4%
* Part-Time: 5.0%

The job openings listed here are shared with Coroners; with Environmental Compliance Inspectors; with Equal Opportunity Representatives and Officers; and with Government Property Inspectors and Investigators.

Examine, evaluate, and investigate eligibility for, conformity with, or liability under licenses or permits. Issue licenses to individuals meeting standards. Evaluate applications, records, and documents in order to gather information about eligibility or liability issues. Administer oral, written, road, or flight tests to license applicants. Score tests and observe equipment operation and control in order to rate ability of applicants. Advise licensees and other individuals or groups concerning licensing, permit, or passport regulations. Warn violators of infractions or penalties. Prepare reports of activities, evaluations, recommendations, and decisions. Prepare correspondence to inform concerned parties of licensing decisions and of appeals processes. Confer with and interview officials, technical or professional specialists, and applicants, in order to obtain information or to clarify facts relevant to licensing decisions. Report law or regulation violations to appropriate boards and agencies. Visit establishments to verify that valid licenses and permits are displayed, and that licensing standards are being upheld.

Personality Type: Conventional. These occupations frequently involve following set procedures and routines and can include working with data and details more than with ideas. Usually there is a clear line of authority to follow.

GOE—Interest Area/Cluster: 07. Government and Public Administration. **Work Group:** 07.03. Regulations Enforcement. **Other Jobs in This Work Group:** Agricultural Inspectors; Aviation Inspectors; Compliance Officers, Except Agriculture, Construction, Health and Safety, and **Transportation:** Principles and methods for moving people or goods by air, rail, sea, or road, including their relative costs, advantages, and limitations. Construction and Building Inspectors; Environmental Compliance Inspectors; Equal Opportunity Representatives and Officers; Financial Examiners; Fire Inspectors; Fish and Game Wardens; Forest Fire Inspectors and Prevention Specialists; Freight and Cargo Inspectors; Government Property Inspectors and Investigators; Immigration and Customs Inspectors; Nuclear Monitoring Technicians; Occupational Health and Safety Specialists; Occupational Health and Safety Technicians; Tax Examiners, Collectors, and Revenue Agents; Transportation Vehicle, Equipment, and Systems Inspectors, Except Aviation.

Skills—Speaking: Talking to others to effectively convey information. **Service Orientation:** Actively looking for ways to help people. **Judgment and Decision Making:** Weighing the relative costs and benefits of a potential action. **Active Listening:** Listening to what other people are saying and asking questions as appropriate. **Reading Comprehension:** Understanding written sentences and paragraphs in work-related documents.

Education and Training Program: Public Administration and Social Service Professions, Other. **Related Knowledge/Courses—Clerical Studies:** Administrative and clerical procedures and systems such as word-processing systems, filing and records management systems, stenography and transcription, forms, design principles, and other office procedures and terminology. **Customer and Personal Service:** Principles and processes for providing customer and personal services, including needs assessment techniques, quality service standards, alternative delivery systems, and customer satisfaction evaluation techniques. **Law and Government:** Laws, legal codes, court procedures, precedents, government regulations, executive orders, agency rules, and the democratic political process. **Foreign Language:** The structure and content of a foreign (non-English) language, including the meaning and spelling of words, rules of composition and grammar, and pronunciation. **Psychology:** Human behavior and performance, mental processes, psychological research methods, and the assessment and treatment of behavioral and affective disorders. **Public Safety and Security:** Weaponry; public safety; security operations, rules, regulations, precautions, and prevention; and the protection of people, data, and property.

Work Environment: More often indoors than outdoors; contaminants; sitting; using hands on objects, tools, or controls; repetitive motions.

Loan Interviewers and Clerks

* Education/Training Required: Short-term on-the-job training
* Annual Earnings: $31,680
* Beginning Wage: $21,070
* Earnings Growth Potential: Low
* Growth: –0.9%
* Annual Job Openings: 40,217
* Self-Employed: 2.5%
* Part-Time: 6.3%

Interview loan applicants to elicit information, investigate applicants' backgrounds and verify references, prepare loan request papers, and forward findings, reports, and documents to appraisal department. Review loan papers to ensure completeness and complete transactions between loan establishment, borrowers, and sellers upon approval of loan. Verify and examine information and accuracy of loan application and closing documents. Interview loan applicants in order to obtain personal and financial data, and to assist in completing applications. Assemble and compile documents for loan closings, such as title abstracts, insurance forms, loan forms, and tax receipts. Answer questions and advise customers regarding loans and transactions. Contact customers by mail, telephone, or in person concerning acceptance or rejection of applications. Record applications for loan and credit, loan information, and disbursements of funds, using computers. Prepare and type loan applications, closing documents, legal documents, letters, forms, government notices, and checks, using computers. Present loan and repayment schedules to customers. Calculate, review, and correct errors on interest, principal, payment, and closing costs, using computers or calculators. Check value of customer collateral to be held as loan security. Contact credit bureaus, employers, and other sources in order to check applicants' credit and personal references. File and maintain loan records. Schedule and conduct closings of mortgage transactions. Accept payment on accounts. Submit loan applications with recommendation for underwriting approval. Order property insurance or mortgage insurance policies in order to ensure protection against loss on mortgaged property. Review customer accounts in order to determine whether payments are made on time and that other loan terms are being followed. Establish credit limits and grant extensions of credit on overdue accounts.

Personality Type: Conventional. These occupations frequently involve following set procedures and routines and can include working with data and details more than with ideas. Usually there is a clear line of authority to follow.

GOE—Interest Area/Cluster: 06. Finance and Insurance. **Work Group:** 06.04. Finance/Insurance Customer Service. **Other Jobs in This Work Group:** Bill and Account Collectors; New Accounts Clerks; Tellers.

Skills—Service Orientation: Actively looking for ways to help people. **Learning Strategies:** Using multiple approaches when learning or teaching new things. **Mathematics:** Using mathematics to solve problems. **Time Management:** Managing one's own time and the time of others. **Speaking:** Talking to others to effectively convey information. **Writing:** Communicating effectively with others in writing as indicated by the needs of the audience. **Persuasion:** Persuading others to approach things differently. **Operations Analysis:** Analyzing needs and product requirements to create a design.

Education and Training Program: Banking and Financial Support Services. **Related Knowledge/Courses— Economics and Accounting:** Economic and accounting principles and practices, the financial markets, banking,

and the analysis and reporting of financial data. **Clerical Studies:** Administrative and clerical procedures and systems such as word-processing systems, filing and records management systems, stenography and transcription, forms, design principles, and other office procedures and terminology. **Mathematics:** Numbers and their operations and interrelationships, including arithmetic, algebra, geometry, calculus, and statistics and their applications. **Customer and Personal Service:** Principles and processes for providing customer and personal services, including needs assessment techniques, quality service standards, alternative delivery systems, and customer satisfaction evaluation techniques. **Law and Government:** Laws, legal codes, court procedures, precedents, government regulations, executive orders, agency rules, and the democratic political process.

Work Environment: Indoors; sitting.

Locksmiths and Safe Repairers

- ❋ Education/Training Required: Moderate-term on-the-job training
- ❋ Annual Earnings: $33,230
- ❋ Beginning Wage: $18,580
- ❋ Earnings Growth Potential: High
- ❋ Growth: 22.1%
- ❋ Annual Job Openings: 3,545
- ❋ Self-Employed: 28.3%
- ❋ Part-Time: 10.6%

Repair and open locks, make keys, change locks and safe combinations, and install and repair safes. Cut new or duplicate keys, using keycutting machines. Keep records of company locks and keys. Insert new or repaired tumblers into locks to change combinations. Move picklocks in cylinders to open door locks without keys. Disassemble mechanical or electrical locking devices and repair or replace worn tumblers, springs, and other parts, using hand tools. Repair and adjust safes, vault doors, and vault components, using hand tools, lathes, drill presses, and welding and acetylene cutting apparatus. Install safes, vault doors, and deposit boxes according to blueprints, using equipment such as powered drills, taps, dies, truck cranes, and dollies. Open safe locks by drilling. Remove interior and exterior finishes on safes and vaults and spray on new finishes.

Personality Type: Realistic. These occupations frequently involve work activities that include practical, hands-on problems and solutions. They often deal with plants; animals; and real-world materials such as wood, tools, and machinery. Many of the occupations require working outside and don't involve a lot of paperwork or working closely with others.

GOE—Interest Area/Cluster: 13. Manufacturing. **Work Group:** 13.13. Machinery Repair. **Other Jobs in This Work Group:** Bicycle Repairers; Control and Valve Installers and Repairers, Except Mechanical Door; Home Appliance Repairers; Industrial Machinery Mechanics; Maintenance Workers, Machinery; Mechanical Door Repairers; Millwrights; Signal and Track Switch Repairers.

Skills—Installation: Installing equipment, machines, wiring, or programs to meet specifications. **Repairing:** Repairing machines or systems, using the needed tools. **Equipment Maintenance:** Performing routine maintenance and determining when and what kind of maintenance is needed. **Troubleshooting:** Determining what is causing an operating error and deciding what to do about it. **Equipment Selection:** Determining the kind of tools and equipment needed to do a job. **Service Orientation:** Actively looking for ways to help people. **Technology Design:** Generating or adapting equipment and technology to serve user needs. **Management of Material Resources:** Obtaining and seeing to the appropriate use of equipment, facilities, and materials needed to do certain work.

Education and Training Program: Locksmithing and Safe Repair. **Related Knowledge/Courses—Sales and Marketing:** Principles and methods involved in showing, promoting, and selling products or services. This includes marketing strategies and tactics, product demonstration and sales techniques, and sales control systems. **Clerical Studies:** Administrative and clerical procedures and systems such as word-processing systems, filing and records management systems, stenography and transcription, forms, design principles, and other office procedures and terminology. **Customer and Personal Service:** Principles and processes for providing customer and personal services, including needs assessment techniques, quality service standards, alternative delivery systems, and customer satisfaction evaluation techniques. **Administration and Management:** Principles and processes involved in business and organizational planning, coordination, and execution. This includes strategic planning, resource allocation, manpower

modeling, leadership techniques, and production methods. **Mechanical Devices:** Machines and tools, including their designs, uses, benefits, repair, and maintenance. **Public Safety and Security:** Weaponry; public safety; security operations, rules, regulations, precautions, and prevention; and the protection of people, data, and property.

Work Environment: More often outdoors than indoors; noisy; very bright or dim lighting; standing; using hands on objects, tools, or controls.

Locomotive Engineers

- ✸ Education/Training Required: Moderate-term on-the-job training
- ✸ Annual Earnings: $57,520
- ✸ Beginning Wage: $36,730
- ✸ Earnings Growth Potential: Medium
- ✸ Growth: 2.9%
- ✸ Annual Job Openings: 3,548
- ✸ Self-Employed: 0.0%
- ✸ Part-Time: 1.7%

The job openings listed here are shared with Locomotive Firers and with Rail Yard Engineers, Dinkey Operators, and Hostlers.

Drive electric, diesel-electric, steam, or gas-turbine-electric locomotives to transport passengers or freight. Interpret train orders, electronic or manual signals, and railroad rules and regulations. Monitor gauges and meters that measure speed, amperage, battery charge, and air pressure in brake lines and in main reservoirs. Interpret train orders, signals, and railroad rules and regulations that govern the operation of locomotives. Observe tracks to detect obstructions. Receive starting signals from conductors; then move controls such as throttles and air brakes to drive electric, diesel-electric, steam, or gas-turbine-electric locomotives. Confer with conductors or traffic control center personnel via radiophones to issue or receive information concerning stops, delays, or oncoming trains. Operate locomotives to transport freight or passengers between stations and to assemble and disassemble trains within rail yards. Respond to emergency conditions or breakdowns, following applicable safety procedures and rules. Check to ensure that brake examination tests are conducted at shunting stations. Call out train signals to assistants in order to verify meanings. Inspect locomotives to verify adequate fuel, sand, water, and other supplies before each run and to check for mechanical problems. Prepare reports regarding any problems encountered, such as accidents, signaling problems, unscheduled stops, or delays. Check to ensure that documentation, including procedure manuals and logbooks, is in the driver's cab and available for staff use. Inspect locomotives after runs to detect damaged or defective equipment. Drive diesel-electric rail-detector cars to transport rail-flaw-detecting machines over tracks. Monitor train loading procedures to ensure that freight and rolling stock are loaded or unloaded without damage.

Personality Type: Realistic. These occupations frequently involve work activities that include practical, hands-on problems and solutions. They often deal with plants; animals; and real-world materials such as wood, tools, and machinery. Many of the occupations require working outside and don't involve a lot of paperwork or working closely with others.

GOE—Interest Area/Cluster: 16. Transportation, Distribution, and Logistics. **Work Group:** 16.04. Rail Vehicle Operation. **Other Jobs in This Work Group:** Locomotive Firers; Rail Yard Engineers, Dinkey Operators, and Hostlers; Subway and Streetcar Operators.

Skills—Operation Monitoring: Watching gauges, dials, or other indicators to make sure a machine is working properly. **Operation and Control:** Controlling operations of equipment or systems. **Troubleshooting:** Determining what is causing an operating error and deciding what to do about it. **Instructing:** Teaching others how to do something. **Active Listening:** Listening to what other people are saying and asking questions as appropriate. **Equipment Maintenance:** Performing routine maintenance and determining when and what kind of maintenance is needed. **Service Orientation:** Actively looking for ways to help people. **Quality Control Analysis:** Evaluating the quality or performance of products, services, or processes.

Education and Training Program: Transportation and Materials Moving, Other. **Related Knowledge/Courses—Transportation:** Principles and methods for moving people or goods by air, rail, sea, or road, including their relative costs, advantages, and limitations. **Mechanical Devices:** Machines and tools, including their designs, uses, benefits, repair, and maintenance. **Public Safety and Security:** Weaponry; public safety; security operations, rules,

regulations, precautions, and prevention; and the protection of people, data, and property.

Work Environment: Outdoors; noisy; contaminants; hazardous equipment; using hands on objects, tools, or controls; repetitive motions.

Locomotive Firers

- ❋ Education/Training Required: Moderate-term on-the-job training
- ❋ Annual Earnings: $45,310
- ❋ Beginning Wage: $32,440
- ❋ Earnings Growth Potential: Low
- ❋ Growth: 2.9%
- ❋ Annual Job Openings: 3,548
- ❋ Self-Employed: 0.0%
- ❋ Part-Time: 1.7%

The job openings listed here are shared with Locomotive Engineers and with Rail Yard Engineers, Dinkey Operators, and Hostlers.

Monitor locomotive instruments and watch for dragging equipment, obstacles on rights-of-way, and train signals during run. Watch for and relay traffic signals from yard workers to yard engineer in railroad yard. Signal other workers to set brakes and to throw track switches when switching cars from trains to way stations. Monitor oil, temperature, and pressure gauges on dashboards to determine if engines are operating safely and efficiently. Check to see that trains are equipped with supplies such as fuel, water, and sand. Inspect locomotives to detect damaged or worn parts. Operate locomotives in emergency situations. Receive signals from workers in rear of train and relay that information to engineers. Start diesel engines to warm engines before runs. Observe train signals along routes and verify their meanings for engineers. Observe tracks from left sides of locomotives to detect obstructions on tracks. Monitor trains as they go around curves to detect dragging equipment and smoking journal boxes.

Personality Type: Realistic. These occupations frequently involve work activities that include practical, hands-on problems and solutions. They often deal with plants; animals; and real-world materials such as wood, tools, and machinery. Many of the occupations require working

outside and don't involve a lot of paperwork or working closely with others.

GOE—Interest Area/Cluster: 16. Transportation, Distribution, and Logistics. **Work Group:** 16.04. Rail Vehicle Operation. **Other Jobs in This Work Group:** Locomotive Engineers; Rail Yard Engineers, Dinkey Operators, and Hostlers; Subway and Streetcar Operators.

Skills—Operation Monitoring: Watching gauges, dials, or other indicators to make sure a machine is working properly. **Operation and Control:** Controlling operations of equipment or systems.

Education and Training Program: Transportation and Materials Moving, Other. **Related Knowledge/Courses—Transportation:** Principles and methods for moving people or goods by air, rail, sea, or road, including their relative costs, advantages, and limitations. **Geography:** Various methods for describing the location and distribution of land, sea, and air masses, including their physical locations, relationships, and characteristics. **Mechanical Devices:** Machines and tools, including their designs, uses, benefits, repair, and maintenance. **Engineering and Technology:** Equipment, tools, and mechanical devices and their uses to produce motion, light, power, technology, and other applications.

Work Environment: Outdoors; noisy; very hot or cold; contaminants; hazardous equipment; standing.

Lodging Managers

- ❉ Education/Training Required: Work experience in a related occupation
- ❉ Annual Earnings: $44,240
- ❉ Beginning Wage: $26,880
- ❉ Earnings Growth Potential: Medium
- ❉ Growth: 12.2%
- ❉ Annual Job Openings: 5,529
- ❉ Self-Employed: 53.0%
- ❉ Part-Time: 8.5%

Plan, direct, or coordinate activities of an organization or department that provides lodging and other accommodations. Greet and register guests. Answer inquiries pertaining to hotel policies and services and resolve occupants' complaints. Assign duties to workers and schedule shifts. Coordinate front-office activities of hotels or motels and resolve problems. Participate in financial activities such as the setting of room rates, the establishment of budgets, and the allocation of funds to departments. Confer and cooperate with other managers to ensure coordination of hotel activities. Collect payments and record data pertaining to funds and expenditures. Manage and maintain temporary or permanent lodging facilities. Observe and monitor staff performance to ensure efficient operations and adherence to facility's policies and procedures. Train staff members. Show, rent, or assign accommodations. Develop and implement policies and procedures for the operation of a department or establishment. Inspect guest rooms, public areas, and grounds for cleanliness and appearance. Prepare required paperwork pertaining to departmental functions. Interview and hire applicants. Purchase supplies and arrange for outside services such as deliveries, laundry, maintenance and repair, and trash collection. Arrange telephone answering services, deliver mail and packages, or answer questions regarding locations for eating and entertainment. Organize and coordinate the work of staff and convention personnel for meetings to be held at a particular facility. Perform marketing and public relations activities. Receive and process advance registration payments, mail letters of confirmation, or return checks when registrations cannot be accepted. Meet with clients to schedule and plan details of conventions, banquets, receptions, and other functions. Provide assistance to staff members by inspecting rooms, setting tables, or doing laundry. Book tickets for guests for local tours and attractions.

Personality Type: Enterprising. These occupations frequently involve starting up and carrying out projects and can involve leading people and making many decisions. They sometimes require risk taking and often deal with business.

GOE—Interest Area/Cluster: 09. Hospitality, Tourism, and Recreation. **Work Group:** 09.01. Managerial Work in Hospitality and Tourism. **Other Jobs in This Work Group:** First-Line Supervisors/Managers of Food Preparation and Serving Workers; First-Line Supervisors/Managers of Personal Service Workers; Food Service Managers; Gaming Managers; Gaming Supervisors.

Skills—Management of Financial Resources: Determining how money will be spent to get the work done and accounting for these expenditures. **Management of Material Resources:** Obtaining and seeing to the appropriate use of equipment, facilities, and materials needed to do certain work. **Negotiation:** Bringing others together and trying to reconcile differences. **Social Perceptiveness:** Being aware of others' reactions and understanding why they react the way they do. **Monitoring:** Assessing how well one is doing when learning or doing something. **Management of Personnel Resources:** Motivating, developing, and directing people as they work; identifying the best people for the job. **Persuasion:** Persuading others to approach things differently. **Active Listening:** Listening to what other people are saying and asking questions as appropriate.

Education and Training Programs: Hospitality Administration/Management, General; Hospitality and Recreation Marketing Operations; Hotel/Motel Administration/Management; Resort Management; Selling Skills and Sales Operations. **Related Knowledge/Courses—Sales and Marketing:** Principles and methods involved in showing, promoting, and selling products or services. This includes marketing strategies and tactics, product demonstration and sales techniques, and sales control systems. **Clerical Studies:** Administrative and clerical procedures and systems such as word-processing systems, filing and records management systems, stenography and transcription, forms, design principles, and other office procedures and terminology. **Personnel and Human Resources:** Principles and procedures for personnel recruitment; selection; training; compensation and benefits; labor relations and negotiation; and personnel information systems. **Economics and Accounting:** Economic and accounting principles and practices, the financial markets, banking, and the analysis and reporting of financial data. **Psychology:** Human behavior and performance, mental processes, psychological research methods, and the assessment and treatment of behavioral and affective disorders. **Customer and Personal Service:** Principles and processes for providing customer and personal services, including needs assessment techniques, quality service standards, alternative delivery systems, and customer satisfaction evaluation techniques.

Work Environment: Indoors; sitting.

Machinists

- ❋ Education/Training Required: Long-term on-the-job training
- ❋ Annual Earnings: $35,230
- ❋ Beginning Wage: $21,670
- ❋ Earnings Growth Potential: Medium
- ❋ Growth: –3.1%
- ❋ Annual Job Openings: 39,505
- ❋ Self-Employed: 1.7%
- ❋ Part-Time: 1.7%

Set up and operate a variety of machine tools to produce precision parts and instruments. Includes precision instrument makers who fabricate, modify, or repair mechanical instruments. May also fabricate and modify parts to make or repair machine tools or maintain industrial machines, applying knowledge of mechanics, shop mathematics, metal properties, layout, and machining procedures. Calculate dimensions and tolerances using knowledge of mathematics and instruments such as micrometers and vernier calipers. Align and secure holding fixtures, cutting tools, attachments, accessories, and materials onto machines. Select the appropriate tools, machines, and materials to be used in preparation of machinery work. Monitor the feed and speed of machines during the machining process. Machine parts to specifications using machine tools such as lathes, milling machines, shapers, or grinders. Set up, adjust, and operate all of the basic machine tools and many specialized or advanced variation tools to perform precision machining operations. Measure, examine, and test completed units to detect defects and ensure conformance to specifications, using precision instruments such as micrometers. Set controls to regulate machining, or enter commands to retrieve, input, or edit computerized machine control media. Position and fasten work pieces. Maintain industrial machines, applying knowledge of mechanics, shop mathematics, metal properties, layout, and machining procedures. Observe and listen to operating machines or equipment to diagnose machine malfunctions and to determine need for adjustments or repairs. Check work pieces to ensure that they are properly lubricated and cooled. Lay out, measure, and mark metal stock to display placement of cuts. Study sample parts, blueprints, drawings, and engineering information to determine methods and sequences of operations needed to fabricate products, and determine product dimensions and tolerances. Confer with engineering, supervisory, and manufacturing personnel to exchange technical information. Program computers and electronic instruments such as numerically controlled machine tools. Operate equipment to verify operational efficiency. Clean and lubricate machines, tools, and equipment to remove grease, rust, stains, and foreign matter. Design fixtures, tooling, and experimental parts to meet special engineering needs. Evaluate experimental procedures, and recommend changes or modifications for improved efficiency and adaptability to setup and production.

Personality Type: Realistic. These occupations frequently involve work activities that include practical, hands-on problems and solutions. They often deal with plants; animals; and real-world materials such as wood, tools, and machinery. Many of the occupations require working outside and don't involve a lot of paperwork or working closely with others.

GOE—Interest Area/Cluster: 13. Manufacturing. **Work Group:** 13.05. Production Machining Technology. **Other Jobs in This Work Group:** Computer-Controlled Machine Tool Operators, Metal and Plastic; Foundry Mold and Coremakers; Lay-Out Workers, Metal and Plastic; Model Makers, Metal and Plastic; Numerical Tool and Process Control Programmers; Patternmakers, Metal and Plastic; Tool and Die Makers; Tool Grinders, Filers, and Sharpeners.

Skills—Operation Monitoring: Watching gauges, dials, or other indicators to make sure a machine is working properly. **Repairing:** Repairing machines or systems, using the needed tools. **Operation and Control:** Controlling operations of equipment or systems. **Quality Control Analysis:** Evaluating the quality or performance of products, services, or processes. **Equipment Maintenance:** Performing routine maintenance and determining when and what kind of maintenance is needed. **Troubleshooting:** Determining what is causing an operating error and deciding what to do about it.

Education and Training Programs: Machine Shop Technology/Assistant Training; Machine Tool Technology/Machinist Training. **Related Knowledge/Courses— Mechanical Devices:** Machines and tools, including their designs, uses, benefits, repair, and maintenance. **Design:** Design techniques, principles, tools, and instruments involved in the production and use of precision technical plans, blueprints, drawings, and models. **Engineering and Technology:** Equipment, tools, and mechanical devices and their uses to produce motion, light, power, technology, and other applications. **Production and Processing:** Inputs, outputs, raw materials, waste, quality control, costs, and techniques for maximizing the manufacture and distribution of goods. **Mathematics:** Numbers and their operations and interrelationships, including arithmetic, algebra, geometry, calculus, and statistics and their applications.

Work Environment: Noisy; contaminants; hazardous equipment; minor burns, cuts, bites, or stings; standing; using hands on objects, tools, or controls.

Maintenance and Repair Workers, General

- ❋ Education/Training Required: Moderate-term on-the-job training
- ❋ Annual Earnings: $32,570
- ❋ Beginning Wage: $19,590
- ❋ Earnings Growth Potential: Medium
- ❋ Growth: 10.1%
- ❋ Annual Job Openings: 165,502
- ❋ Self-Employed: 1.5%
- ❋ Part-Time: 5.2%

Perform work involving the skills of two or more maintenance or craft occupations to keep machines, mechanical equipment, or the structure of an establishment in repair. Duties may involve pipe fitting; boiler making; insulating; welding; machining; carpentry; repairing electrical or mechanical equipment; installing, aligning, and balancing new equipment; and repairing buildings, floors, or stairs. Repair or replace defective equipment parts, using hand tools and power tools, and reassemble equipment. Perform routine preventive maintenance to ensure that machines continue to run smoothly, building systems operate efficiently, and the physical condition of buildings does not deteriorate. Inspect drives, motors, and belts; check fluid levels; replace filters; and perform other maintenance actions, following checklists. Use tools ranging from common hand and power tools, such as hammers, hoists, saws, drills, and wrenches, to precision measuring instruments and electrical and electronic testing devices. Assemble, install, or repair wiring, electrical and electronic components, pipe systems and plumbing, machinery, and equipment. Diagnose mechanical problems and determine how to correct them, checking blueprints, repair manuals, and parts catalogs as necessary. Inspect, operate, and test machinery and equipment to diagnose machine malfunctions. Record maintenance and repair work performed and the costs of the work. Clean and lubricate shafts, bearings, gears, and other parts of machinery. Dismantle devices to gain access to and remove defective parts, using hoists, cranes, hand tools, and power tools. Plan and lay out repair work, using diagrams, drawings, blueprints, maintenance manuals, and schematic diagrams. Adjust functional parts of devices and control instruments, using hand tools, levels, plumb bobs, and straightedges. Order parts, supplies, and equipment from catalogs and suppliers or obtain them from storerooms. Paint and repair roofs, windows, doors, floors, woodwork, plaster, drywall, and other parts of building structures. Operate cutting torches or welding equipment to cut or join metal parts. Align and balance new equipment after installation. Inspect used parts to determine changes in dimensional requirements, using rules, calipers, micrometers, and other measuring instruments. Set up and operate machine tools to repair or fabricate machine parts, jigs and fixtures, and tools. Maintain and repair specialized equipment and machinery found in cafeterias, laundries, hospitals, stores, offices, and factories.

Personality Type: Realistic. These occupations frequently involve work activities that include practical, hands-on problems and solutions. They often deal with plants; animals; and real-world materials such as wood, tools, and machinery. Many of the occupations require working outside and don't involve a lot of paperwork or working closely with others.

GOE—Interest Area/Cluster: 02. Architecture and Construction. **Work Group:** 02.05. Systems and Equipment Installation, Maintenance, and Repair. **Other Jobs in This Work Group:** Electrical and Electronics Repairers, Powerhouse, Substation, and Relay; Electrical Power-Line Installers and Repairers; Elevator Installers and Repairers; Heating and Air Conditioning Mechanics and Installers; Refrigeration Mechanics and Installers; Telecommunications Equipment Installers and Repairers, Except Line Installers; Telecommunications Line Installers and Repairers.

Skills—Equipment Maintenance: Performing routine maintenance and determining when and what kind of maintenance is needed. **Installation:** Installing equipment, machines, wiring, or programs to meet specifications. **Repairing:** Repairing machines or systems, using the needed tools. **Troubleshooting:** Determining what is causing an operating error and deciding what to do about it. **Operation Monitoring:** Watching gauges, dials, or other indicators to make sure a machine is working properly. **Operation and Control:** Controlling operations of equipment or systems. **Equipment Selection:** Determining the kind of tools and equipment needed to do a job. **Technology Design:** Generating or adapting equipment and technology to serve user needs.

Education and Training Program: Building/Construction Site Management/Manager Training. **Related Knowledge/Courses—Building and Construction:** Materials, methods, and the appropriate tools to construct objects, structures, and buildings. **Mechanical Devices:** Machines and tools, including their designs, uses, benefits, repair, and maintenance. **Design:** Design techniques, principles, tools, and instruments involved in the production and use of precision technical plans, blueprints, drawings, and models. **Physics:** Physical principles, laws, and applications, including air, water, material dynamics, light, atomic principles, heat, electric theory, earth formations, and meteorological and related natural phenomena. **Engineering and Technology:** Equipment, tools, and mechanical devices and their uses to produce motion, light, power, technology, and other applications. **Public Safety and Security:** Weaponry; public safety; security operations, rules, regulations, precautions, and prevention; and the protection of people, data, and property.

Work Environment: Indoors; noisy; minor burns, cuts, bites, or stings; standing; walking and running; using hands on objects, tools, or controls.

Maintenance Workers, Machinery

* Education/Training Required: Moderate-term on-the-job training
* Annual Earnings: $35,590
* Beginning Wage: $21,890
* Earnings Growth Potential: Medium
* Growth: –1.1%
* Annual Job Openings: 15,055
* Self-Employed: 0.0%
* Part-Time: 4.0%

Lubricate machinery, change parts, or perform other routine machinery maintenance. Reassemble machines after the completion of repair or maintenance work. Start machines and observe mechanical operation to determine efficiency and to detect problems. Inspect or test damaged machine parts, and mark defective areas or advise supervisors of repair needs. Lubricate or apply adhesives or other materials to machines, machine parts, or other equipment, according to specified procedures. Install, replace, or change machine parts and attachments, according to production specifications. Dismantle machines and remove parts for repair, using hand tools, chain falls, jacks, cranes, or hoists. Record production, repair, and machine maintenance information. Read work orders and specifications to determine machines and equipment requiring repair or maintenance. Set up and operate machines, and adjust controls to regulate operations. Collaborate with other workers to repair or move machines, machine parts, or equipment. Inventory and requisition machine parts, equipment, and other supplies so that stock can be maintained and replenished. Transport machine parts, tools, equipment, and other material between work areas and storage, using cranes, hoists, or dollies. Clean machines and machine parts, using cleaning solvents, cloths, air guns, hoses, vacuums, or other equipment. Collect and discard worn machine parts and other refuse in order to maintain machinery and work areas. Replace or repair metal, wood, leather, glass, or other lining in machines or in equipment compartments or containers. Remove hardened material from machines or machine parts, using abrasives, power and hand tools, jackhammers, sledgehammers, or other equipment. Measure, mix, prepare, and test chemical solutions used to clean or repair machinery and equipment. Replace, empty, or replenish machine and equipment containers such as gas tanks or boxes.

Personality Type: Realistic. These occupations frequently involve work activities that include practical, hands-on problems and solutions. They often deal with plants; animals; and real-world materials such as wood, tools, and machinery. Many of the occupations require working outside and don't involve a lot of paperwork or working closely with others.

GOE—Interest Area/Cluster: 13. Manufacturing. **Work Group:** 13.13. Machinery Repair. **Other Jobs in This Work Group:** Bicycle Repairers; Control and Valve Installers and Repairers, Except Mechanical Door; Home Appliance Repairers; Industrial Machinery Mechanics; Locksmiths and Safe Repairers; Mechanical Door Repairers; Millwrights; Signal and Track Switch Repairers.

Skills—Installation: Installing equipment, machines, wiring, or programs to meet specifications. **Repairing:** Repairing machines or systems, using the needed tools. **Equipment Maintenance:** Performing routine maintenance and determining when and what kind of maintenance is needed. **Troubleshooting:** Determining what is causing an operating error and deciding what to do about it. **Operation Monitoring:** Watching gauges, dials, or other indicators to make sure a machine is working properly. **Operation and Control:** Controlling operations of equipment or systems. **Technology Design:** Generating or adapting equipment and technology to serve user needs. **Equipment Selection:** Determining the kind of tools and equipment needed to do a job.

Education and Training Programs: Heavy/Industrial Equipment Maintenance Technologies, Other; Industrial Mechanics and Maintenance Technology. **Related Knowledge/Courses—Mechanical Devices:** Machines and tools, including their designs, uses, benefits, repair, and maintenance. **Building and Construction:** Materials, methods, and the appropriate tools to construct objects, structures, and buildings. **Engineering and Technology:** Equipment, tools, and mechanical devices and their uses to produce motion, light, power, technology, and other applications. **Physics:** Physical principles, laws, and applications, including air, water, material dynamics, light, atomic principles, heat, electric theory, earth formations, and meteorological and related natural phenomena. **Chemistry:** The composition, structure, and properties of substances and of the chemical processes and transformations that they undergo. This includes uses of chemicals and their interactions, danger signs, production techniques, and disposal methods. **Design:** Design techniques, principles, tools, and instruments involved in the production and use of precision technical plans, blueprints, drawings, and models.

Work Environment: Noisy; very hot or cold; contaminants; hazardous equipment; standing; using hands on objects, tools, or controls.

Makeup Artists, Theatrical and Performance

- ✳ Education/Training Required: Postsecondary vocational training
- ✳ Annual Earnings: $35,250
- ✳ Beginning Wage: $15,920
- ✳ Earnings Growth Potential: Very high
- ✳ Growth: 39.8%
- ✳ Annual Job Openings: 392
- ✳ Self-Employed: 39.7%
- ✳ Part-Time: 26.3%

Apply makeup to performers to reflect period, setting, and situation of their role. Confer with stage or motion picture officials and performers in order to determine desired effects. Duplicate work precisely in order to replicate characters' appearances on a daily basis. Establish budgets, and work within budgetary limits. Apply makeup to enhance and/or alter the appearance of people appearing in productions such as movies. Alter or maintain makeup during productions as necessary to compensate for lighting changes or to achieve continuity of effect. Select desired makeup shades from stock, or mix oil, grease, and coloring in order to achieve specific color effects. Cleanse and tone the skin in order to prepare it for makeup application. Assess performers' skin-type in order to ensure that makeup will not cause break-outs or skin irritations. Analyze a script, noting events that affect each character's appearance, so that plans can be made for each scene. Requisition or acquire needed materials for special effects, including wigs, beards, and special cosmetics. Write makeup sheets and take photos in order to document specific looks and the products that were used to achieve the looks. Examine sketches, photographs, and plaster models in order to obtain desired character image depiction. Attach prostheses to performers and apply makeup in order to create special features or effects such as scars, aging, or illness. Evaluate environmental characteristics such as venue size and lighting plans in order to determine makeup requirements. Design rubber or plastic prostheses that can be used to change performers' appearances. Create character drawings or models, based upon independent research, in order to augment period production files. Advise hairdressers on the hairstyles required for character parts. Study production information such as character descriptions, period settings, and situations in order to determine makeup requirements. Provide performers with makeup removal assistance after performances have been completed. Wash and reset wigs. Demonstrate products to clients, and provide instruction in makeup application.

Personality Type: Artistic. These occupations frequently involve working with forms, designs, and patterns. They often require self-expression, and the work can be done without following a clear set of rules.

GOE—Interest Area/Cluster: 03. Arts and Communication. **Work Group:** 03.06. Drama. **Other Jobs in This Work Group:** Actors; Costume Attendants; Directors—Stage, Motion Pictures, Television, and Radio; Public Address System and Other Announcers; Radio and Television Announcers.

Skills—Management of Financial Resources: Determining how money will be spent to get the work done and accounting for these expenditures. **Equipment Selection:** Determining the kind of tools and equipment needed to do a job. **Time Management:** Managing one's own time and the time of others. **Operations Analysis:** Analyzing needs and product requirements to create a design. **Management of Material Resources:** Obtaining and seeing to the appropriate use of equipment, facilities, and materials needed to do certain work. **Management of Personnel Resources:** Motivating, developing, and directing people as they work; identifying the best people for the job. **Negotiation:** Bringing others together and trying to reconcile differences. **Coordination:** Adjusting actions in relation to others' actions.

Education and Training Programs: Cosmetology/CosmetologistTraining, General; Make-Up Artist/Specialist Training; Permanent Cosmetics/Makeup and Tattooing. **Related Knowledge/Courses—Fine Arts:** Theory and techniques required to produce, compose, and perform works of music, dance, visual arts, drama, and sculpture. **Chemistry:** The composition, structure, and properties of substances and of the chemical processes and transformations that they undergo. This includes uses of chemicals and their interactions, danger signs, production techniques, and disposal methods. **Design:** Design techniques, principles, tools, and instruments involved in the production and use of precision technical plans, blueprints, drawings, and models. **Sales and Marketing:** Principles and methods involved in showing, promoting, and selling products or services. This includes marketing strategies and tactics, product demonstration and sales techniques, and sales control systems. **Personnel and Human Resources:** Principles and procedures for personnel recruitment; selection; training; compensation and benefits; labor relations and negotiation; and personnel information systems. **Psychology:** Human behavior and performance, mental processes, psychological research methods, and the assessment and treatment of behavioral and affective disorders.

Work Environment: More often indoors than outdoors; very bright or dim lighting; standing; using hands on objects, tools, or controls; repetitive motions.

Mapping Technicians

- ❈ Education/Training Required: Moderate-term on-the-job training
- ❈ Annual Earnings: $33,640
- ❈ Beginning Wage: $20,670
- ❈ Earnings Growth Potential: Medium
- ❈ Growth: 19.4%
- ❈ Annual Job Openings: 8,299
- ❈ Self-Employed: 4.2%
- ❈ Part-Time: 4.5%

The job openings listed here are shared with Surveying Technicians.

Calculate mapmaking information from field notes and draw and verify accuracy of topographical maps. Check all layers of maps to ensure accuracy, identifying and marking errors and making corrections. Determine scales, line sizes, and colors to be used for hard copies of computerized maps, using plotters. Monitor mapping work and the updating of maps to ensure accuracy, the inclusion of new and/or changed information, and compliance with rules and regulations. Identify and compile database information to create maps in response to requests. Produce and update overlay maps to show information boundaries, water locations, and topographic features on various base maps and at different scales. Trace contours and topographic details to generate maps that denote specific land and property locations and geographic attributes. Lay out and match aerial photographs in sequences in which they were taken and identify any areas missing from photographs. Compare topographical features and contour lines with images from aerial photographs, old maps, and other reference materials to verify the accuracy of their identification. Compute and measure scaled distances between reference points to establish relative positions of adjoining prints and enable the creation of photographic mosaics. Research resources such as survey maps and legal descriptions to verify property lines and to obtain information needed for mapping. Form three-dimensional images of aerial photographs taken from different locations, using mathematical techniques and plotting instruments. Enter GPS data, legal deeds, field notes, and land survey reports into GIS workstations so that information can be transformed into graphic land descriptions such as maps and drawings. Analyze aerial photographs to detect and interpret significant military, industrial, resource, or topographical data. Redraw and correct maps, such as revising parcel maps to reflect tax code area changes, using information from official records and surveys. Train staff members in duties such as tax mapping, the use of computerized mapping equipment, and the interpretation of source documents.

Personality Type: Conventional. These occupations frequently involve following set procedures and routines and can include working with data and details more than with ideas. Usually there is a clear line of authority to follow.

GOE—Interest Area/Cluster: 15. Scientific Research, Engineering, and Mathematics. **Work Group:** 15.09. Engineering Technology. **Other Jobs in This Work Group:** Aerospace Engineering and Operations Technicians; Cartographers and Photogrammetrists; Civil Engineering Technicians; Electrical and Electronic Engineering Technicians; Electrical and Electronics Drafters; Electrical Drafters; Electrical Engineering Technicians; Electro-Mechanical Technicians; Electronic Drafters; Electronics Engineering Technicians; Environmental Engineering Technicians; Mechanical Drafters; Mechanical Engineering Technicians; Surveying and Mapping Technicians; Surveying Technicians.

Skills—**Technology Design:** Generating or adapting equipment and technology to serve user needs. **Operations Analysis:** Analyzing needs and product requirements to create a design. **Programming:** Writing computer programs for various purposes. **Quality Control Analysis:** Evaluating the quality or performance of products, services, or processes. **Science:** Using scientific methods to solve problems. **Troubleshooting:** Determining what is causing an operating error and deciding what to do about it. **Mathematics:** Using mathematics to solve problems. **Complex Problem Solving:** Identifying complex problems, reviewing the options, and implementing solutions.

Education and Training Programs: Cartography; Surveying Technology/Surveying. **Related Knowledge/ Courses—Geography:** Various methods for describing the location and distribution of land, sea, and air masses, including their physical locations, relationships, and characteristics. **Design:** Design techniques, principles, tools, and instruments involved in the production and use of precision technical plans, blueprints, drawings, and models. **Computers and Electronics:** Electric circuit boards, processors, chips, and computer hardware and software, including applications and programming. **Engineering and Technology:** Equipment, tools, and mechanical devices and their uses to produce motion, light, power, technology, and other applications. **Mathematics:** Numbers and their operations and interrelationships, including arithmetic, algebra, geometry, calculus, and statistics and their applications. **Clerical Studies:** Administrative and clerical procedures and systems such as word-processing systems, filing and records management systems, stenography and transcription, forms, design principles, and other office procedures and terminology.

Work Environment: Indoors; sitting; using hands on objects, tools, or controls; repetitive motions.

Massage Therapists

* Education/Training Required: Postsecondary vocational training
* Annual Earnings: $34,870
* Beginning Wage: $16,000
* Earnings Growth Potential: Very high
* Growth: 20.3%
* Annual Job Openings: 9,193
* Self-Employed: 64.0%
* Part-Time: 42.9%

Massage customers for hygienic or remedial purposes. Confer with clients about their medical histories and any problems with stress or pain to determine whether massage would be helpful. Apply finger and hand pressure to specific points of the body. Massage and knead the muscles and soft tissues of the human body to provide courses of treatment for medical conditions and injuries or wellness maintenance. Maintain treatment records. Provide clients with guidance and information about techniques for postural improvement and stretching, strengthening, relaxation, and rehabilitative exercises. Assess clients' soft tissue condition, joint quality and function, muscle strength, and range of motion. Develop and propose client treatment plans that specify which types of massage are to be used. Refer clients to other types of therapists when necessary. Use complementary aids, such as infrared lamps, wet compresses, ice, and whirlpool baths, to promote clients' recovery, relaxation, and well-being. Treat clients in own offices or travel to clients' offices and homes. Consult with other health-care professionals such as physiotherapists, chiropractors, physicians, and psychologists to develop treatment plans for clients. Prepare and blend oils and apply the blends to clients' skin.

Personality Type: Social. These occupations frequently involve working with, communicating with, and teaching people and often involve helping or providing service to others.

GOE—Interest Area/Cluster: 08. Health Science. **Work Group:** 08.07. Medical Therapy. **Other Jobs in This Work Group:** Audiologists; Occupational Therapist Aides; Occupational Therapist Assistants; Occupational Therapists; Physical Therapist Aides; Physical Therapist Assistants; Physical Therapists; Radiation Therapists; Recreational

Therapists; Respiratory Therapists; Respiratory Therapy Technicians; Speech-Language Pathologists.

Skills—Service Orientation: Actively looking for ways to help people. **Active Listening:** Listening to what other people are saying and asking questions as appropriate.

Education and Training Programs: Asian Bodywork Therapy; Massage Therapy/Therapeutic Massage; Somatic Bodywork; Somatic Bodywork and Related Therapeutic Services, Other. **Related Knowledge/Courses—Therapy and Counseling:** Information and techniques needed to rehabilitate physical and mental ailments and to provide career guidance, including alternative treatments, rehabilitation equipment and its proper use, and methods to evaluate treatment effects. **Psychology:** Human behavior and performance, mental processes, psychological research methods, and the assessment and treatment of behavioral and affective disorders. **Sales and Marketing:** Principles and methods involved in showing, promoting, and selling products or services. This includes marketing strategies and tactics, product demonstration and sales techniques, and sales control systems. **Medicine and Dentistry:** The information and techniques needed to diagnose and treat injuries, diseases, and deformities. This includes symptoms, treatment alternatives, drug properties and interactions, and preventive health-care measures. **Chemistry:** The composition, structure, and properties of substances and of the chemical processes and transformations that they undergo. This includes uses of chemicals and their interactions, danger signs, production techniques, and disposal methods. **English Language:** The structure and content of the English language, including the meaning and spelling of words, rules of composition, and grammar.

Work Environment: Indoors; standing; using hands on objects, tools, or controls; repetitive motions.

Mates—Ship, Boat, and Barge

* Education/Training Required: Work experience in a related occupation
* Annual Earnings: $57,210
* Beginning Wage: $29,530
* Earnings Growth Potential: High
* Growth: 17.9%
* Annual Job Openings: 2,665
* Self-Employed: 6.8%
* Part-Time: 4.8%

The job openings listed here are shared with Pilots, Ship, and with Ship and Boat Captains.

Supervise and coordinate activities of crew aboard ships, boats, barges, or dredges. Determine geographical positions of ships, using lorans, azimuths of celestial bodies, or computers, and use this information to determine the course and speed of a ship. Supervise crews in cleaning and maintaining decks, superstructures, and bridges. Supervise crew members in the repair or replacement of defective gear and equipment. Steer vessels, using navigational devices such as compasses and sextons and navigational aids such as lighthouses and buoys. Observe water from ships' mastheads in order to advise on navigational direction. Inspect equipment such as cargo-handling gear, lifesaving equipment, visual-signaling equipment, and fishing, towing, or dredging gear, in order to detect problems. Arrange for ships to be stocked, fueled, and repaired. Assume command of vessels in the event that ships' masters become incapacitated. Participate in activities related to maintenance of vessel security. Stand watches on vessels during specified periods while vessels are under way. Observe loading and unloading of cargo and equipment to ensure that handling and storage are performed according to specifications.

Personality Type: Enterprising. These occupations frequently involve starting up and carrying out projects and can involve leading people and making many decisions. They sometimes require risk taking and often deal with business.

GOE—Interest Area/Cluster: 16. Transportation, Distribution, and Logistics. **Work Group:** 16.05. Water Vehicle Operation. **Other Jobs in This Work Group:** Captains,

Mates, and Pilots of Water Vessels; Dredge Operators; Motorboat Operators; Pilots, Ship; Sailors and Marine Oilers; Ship and Boat Captains.

Skills—Equipment Maintenance: Performing routine maintenance and determining when and what kind of maintenance is needed. **Repairing:** Repairing machines or systems, using the needed tools. **Operation and Control:** Controlling operations of equipment or systems. **Operation Monitoring:** Watching gauges, dials, or other indicators to make sure a machine is working properly. **Troubleshooting:** Determining what is causing an operating error and deciding what to do about it. **Installation:** Installing equipment, machines, wiring, or programs to meet specifications. **Equipment Selection:** Determining the kind of tools and equipment needed to do a job. **Judgment and Decision Making:** Weighing the relative costs and benefits of a potential action.

Education and Training Programs: Commercial Fishing; Marine Science/Merchant Marine Officer Training; Marine Transportation, Other. **Related Knowledge/Courses—Geography:** Various methods for describing the location and distribution of land, sea, and air masses, including their physical locations, relationships, and characteristics. **Transportation:** Principles and methods for moving people or goods by air, rail, sea, or road, including their relative costs, advantages, and limitations. **Public Safety and Security:** Weaponry; public safety; security operations, rules, regulations, precautions, and prevention; and the protection of people, data, and property. **Telecommunications:** Transmission, broadcasting, switching, control, and operation of telecommunications systems. **Personnel and Human Resources:** Principles and procedures for personnel recruitment; selection; training; compensation and benefits; labor relations and negotiation; and personnel information systems. **Mechanical Devices:** Machines and tools, including their designs, uses, benefits, repair, and maintenance.

Work Environment: Outdoors; noisy; very hot or cold; very bright or dim lighting; contaminants; hazardous equipment.

Meat, Poultry, and Fish Cutters and Trimmers

- Education/Training Required: Short-term on-the-job training
- Annual Earnings: $21,050
- Beginning Wage: $15,780
- Earnings Growth Potential: Low
- Growth: 10.9%
- Annual Job Openings: 17,920
- Self-Employed: 1.1%
- Part-Time: 8.3%

Use hand tools to perform routine cutting and trimming of meat, poultry, and fish. Use knives, cleavers, meat saws, band saws, or other equipment to perform meat cutting and trimming. Clean, trim, slice, and section carcasses for future processing. Cut and trim meat to prepare for packing. Remove parts, such as skin, feathers, scales, or bones, from carcass. Inspect meat products for defects, bruises, or blemishes and remove them along with any excess fat. Produce hamburger meat and meat trimmings. Process primal parts into cuts that are ready for retail use. Obtain and distribute specified meat or carcass. Separate meats and byproducts into specified containers and seal containers. Weigh meats and tag containers for weight and contents. Clean and salt hides. Prepare sausages, luncheon meats, hot dogs, and other fabricated meat products, using meat trimmings and hamburger meat. Prepare ready-to-heat foods by filleting meat or fish or cutting it into bite-sized pieces, preparing and adding vegetables or applying sauces or breading.

Personality Type: Realistic. These occupations frequently involve work activities that include practical, hands-on problems and solutions. They often deal with plants; animals; and real-world materials such as wood, tools, and machinery. Many of the occupations require working outside and don't involve a lot of paperwork or working closely with others.

GOE—Interest Area/Cluster: 13. Manufacturing. **Work Group:** 13.03. Production Work, Assorted Materials Processing. **Other Jobs in This Work Group:** Bakers; Cementing and Gluing Machine Operators and Tenders; Chemical Equipment Operators and Tenders; Cleaning, Washing, and Metal Pickling Equipment Operators and

Tenders; Coating, Painting, and Spraying Machine Setters, Operators, and Tenders; Cooling and Freezing Equipment Operators and Tenders; Cutting and Slicing Machine Setters, Operators, and Tenders; Extruding and Forming Machine Setters, Operators, and Tenders, Synthetic and Glass Fibers; Extruding, Forming, Pressing, and Compacting Machine Setters, Operators, and Tenders; Food and Tobacco Roasting, Baking, and Drying Machine Operators and Tenders; Food Batchmakers; Food Cooking Machine Operators and Tenders; Furnace, Kiln, Oven, Drier, and Kettle Operators and Tenders; Heat Treating Equipment Setters, Operators, and Tenders, Metal and Plastic; Helpers—Production Workers; Metal-Refining Furnace Operators and Tenders; Mixing and Blending Machine Setters, Operators, and Tenders; Packaging and Filling Machine Operators and Tenders; Plating and Coating Machine Setters, Operators, and Tenders, Metal and Plastic; Pourers and Casters, Metal; Sawing Machine Setters, Operators, and Tenders, Wood; Separating, Filtering, Clarifying, Precipitating, and Still Machine Setters, Operators, and Tenders; Sewing Machine Operators; Shoe Machine Operators and Tenders; Slaughterers and Meat Packers; Team Assemblers; Textile Bleaching and Dyeing Machine Operators and Tenders; Tire Builders; Woodworking Machine Setters, Operators, and Tenders, Except Sawing.

Skills: None met the criteria.

Education and Training Program: Meat Cutting/Meat Cutter Training. **Related Knowledge/Courses—Food Production:** Techniques and equipment for planting, growing, and harvesting of food for consumption, including crop-rotation methods, animal husbandry, and food storage/handling techniques. **Production and Processing:** Inputs, outputs, raw materials, waste, quality control, costs, and techniques for maximizing the manufacture and distribution of goods. **Mechanical Devices:** Machines and tools, including their designs, uses, benefits, repair, and maintenance.

Work Environment: Indoors; very hot or cold; hazardous equipment; standing; using hands on objects, tools, or controls; repetitive motions.

Mechanical Door Repairers

- ❋ Education/Training Required: Moderate-term on-the-job training
- ❋ Annual Earnings: $31,880
- ❋ Beginning Wage: $21,350
- ❋ Earnings Growth Potential: Low
- ❋ Growth: 14.9%
- ❋ Annual Job Openings: 1,706
- ❋ Self-Employed: 0.3%
- ❋ Part-Time: 0.5%

Install, service, or repair opening and closing mechanisms of automatic doors and hydraulic door closers. Includes garage door mechanics. Adjust doors to open or close with the correct amount of effort and make simple adjustments to electric openers. Wind large springs with upward motion of arm. Inspect job sites, assessing headroom, side room, and other conditions to determine appropriateness of door for a given location. Collect payment upon job completion. Complete required paperwork, such as work orders, according to services performed or required. Fasten angle iron back-hangers to ceilings and tracks, using fasteners or welding equipment. Repair or replace worn or broken door parts, using hand tools. Carry springs to tops of doors, using ladders or scaffolding, and attach springs to tracks in order to install spring systems. Set doors into place or stack hardware sections into openings after rail or track installation. Remove or disassemble defective automatic mechanical door closers, using hand tools. Install door frames, rails, steel rolling curtains, electronic-eye mechanisms, and electric door openers and closers, using power tools, hand tools, and electronic test equipment. Apply hardware to door sections, such as drilling holes to install locks. Assemble and fasten tracks to structures or bucks, using impact wrenches or welding equipment. Run low-voltage wiring on ceiling surfaces, using insulated staples. Cut door stops and angle irons to fit openings. Study blueprints and schematic diagrams to determine appropriate methods of installing and repairing automated door openers. Operate lifts, winches, or chain falls to move heavy curtain doors. Order replacement springs, sections, and slats. Bore and cut holes in flooring as required for installation, using hand tools and power tools. Set in and secure floor treadles for door-activating mechanisms; then connect power packs and electrical panelboards to treadles. Lubricate door closer oil chambers and pack spindles with leather washers. Install dock seals, bumpers, and shelters. Fabricate replacements for worn or broken parts, using welders, lathes, drill presses, and shaping and milling machines. Clean door closer parts, using caustic soda, rotary brushes, and grinding wheels.

Personality Type: Realistic. These occupations frequently involve work activities that include practical, hands-on problems and solutions. They often deal with plants; animals; and real-world materials such as wood, tools, and machinery. Many of the occupations require working outside and don't involve a lot of paperwork or working closely with others.

GOE—Interest Area/Cluster: 13. Manufacturing. **Work Group:** 13.13. Machinery Repair. **Other Jobs in This Work Group:** Bicycle Repairers; Control and Valve Installers and Repairers, Except Mechanical Door; Home Appliance Repairers; Industrial Machinery Mechanics; Locksmiths and Safe Repairers; Maintenance Workers, Machinery; Millwrights; Signal and Track Switch Repairers.

Skills—Installation: Installing equipment, machines, wiring, or programs to meet specifications. **Repairing:** Repairing machines or systems, using the needed tools. **Troubleshooting:** Determining what is causing an operating error and deciding what to do about it. **Equipment Maintenance:** Performing routine maintenance and determining when and what kind of maintenance is needed. **Equipment Selection:** Determining the kind of tools and equipment needed to do a job. **Time Management:** Managing one's own time and the time of others. **Systems Evaluation:** Looking at many indicators of system performance and taking into account their accuracy. **Mathematics:** Using mathematics to solve problems.

Education and Training Program: Industrial Mechanics and Maintenance Technology. **Related Knowledge/Courses—Building and Construction:** Materials, methods, and the appropriate tools to construct objects, structures, and buildings. **Mechanical Devices:** Machines and tools, including their designs, uses, benefits, repair, and maintenance. **Engineering and Technology:** Equipment, tools, and mechanical devices and their uses to produce motion, light, power, technology, and other applications. **Sales and Marketing:** Principles and methods involved in showing, promoting, and selling products or services. This includes marketing strategies and tactics, product demonstration and sales techniques, and sales control systems. **Design:** Design techniques, principles, tools, and instruments involved in the production and use of precision technical plans, blueprints, drawings, and models.

Work Environment: Outdoors; very hot or cold; hazardous equipment; standing; climbing ladders, scaffolds, or poles; using hands on objects, tools, or controls.

Mechanical Drafters

- ❋ Education/Training Required: Postsecondary vocational training
- ❋ Annual Earnings: $44,740
- ❋ Beginning Wage: $28,540
- ❋ Earnings Growth Potential: Medium
- ❋ Growth: 5.2%
- ❋ Annual Job Openings: 10,902
- ❋ Self-Employed: 5.5%
- ❋ Part-Time: 5.9%

Prepare detailed working diagrams of machinery and mechanical devices, including dimensions, fastening methods, and other engineering information. Develop detailed design drawings and specifications for mechanical equipment, dies, tools, and controls, using computer-assisted drafting (CAD) equipment. Coordinate with and consult other workers to design, lay out, or detail components and systems and to resolve design or other problems. Review and analyze specifications, sketches, drawings, ideas, and related data to assess factors affecting component designs and the procedures and instructions to be followed. Position instructions and comments onto drawings. Compute mathematical formulas to develop and design detailed specifications for components or machinery, using computer-assisted equipment. Modify and revise designs to correct operating deficiencies or to reduce production problems. Design scale or full-size blueprints of specialty items such as furniture and automobile body or chassis components. Check dimensions of materials to be used and assign numbers to the materials. Lay out and draw schematic, orthographic, or angle views to depict functional relationships of components, assemblies, systems, and machines. Confer with customer representatives to review schematics and answer questions pertaining to installation of systems. Draw freehand sketches of designs, trace finished drawings onto designated paper for the reproduction of blueprints, and reproduce working drawings on copy machines. Supervise and train other drafters, technologists, and technicians. Lay out, draw, and reproduce illustrations for reference manuals and technical publications to describe operation and maintenance of mechanical systems. Shade or color drawings to clarify and emphasize details and dimensions or eliminate background, using ink, crayon, airbrush, and overlays.

Personality Type: Realistic. These occupations frequently involve work activities that include practical, hands-on problems and solutions. They often deal with plants; animals; and real-world materials such as wood, tools, and machinery. Many of the occupations require working outside and don't involve a lot of paperwork or working closely with others.

GOE—Interest Area/Cluster: 15. Scientific Research, Engineering, and Mathematics. **Work Group:** 15.09. Engineering Technology. **Other Jobs in This Work Group:** Aerospace Engineering and Operations Technicians; Cartographers and Photogrammetrists; Civil Engineering Technicians; Electrical and Electronic Engineering Technicians; Electrical and Electronics Drafters; Electrical Drafters; Electrical Engineering Technicians; Electro-Mechanical Technicians; Electronic Drafters; Electronics Engineering Technicians; Environmental Engineering Technicians; Mapping Technicians; Mechanical Engineering Technicians; Surveying and Mapping Technicians; Surveying Technicians.

Skills—Technology Design: Generating or adapting equipment and technology to serve user needs. **Installation:** Installing equipment, machines, wiring, or programs to meet specifications. **Equipment Selection:** Determining the kind of tools and equipment needed to do a job. **Operations Analysis:** Analyzing needs and product requirements to create a design. **Quality Control Analysis:** Evaluating the quality or performance of products, services, or processes. **Mathematics:** Using mathematics to solve problems. **Repairing:** Repairing machines or systems, using the needed tools. **Science:** Using scientific methods to solve problems.

Education and Training Program: Mechanical Drafting and Mechanical Drafting CAD/CADD. **Related Knowledge/Courses—Design:** Design techniques, principles, tools, and instruments involved in the production and use of precision technical plans, blueprints, drawings, and models. **Engineering and Technology:** Equipment, tools, and mechanical devices and their uses to produce motion, light, power, technology, and other applications. **Building and Construction:** Materials, methods, and the appropriate tools to construct objects, structures, and buildings. **Physics:** Physical principles, laws, and applications, including air, water, material dynamics, light, atomic principles, heat, electric theory, earth formations, and meteorological and related natural phenomena. **Mathematics:** Numbers and their operations and interrelationships, including arithmetic, algebra, geometry, calculus, and statistics and their applications. **English Language:** The structure and content of the English language, including the meaning and spelling of words, rules of composition, and grammar.

Work Environment: Indoors; noisy; sitting; using hands on objects, tools, or controls; repetitive motions.

Mechanical Engineering Technicians

* Education/Training Required: Associate degree
* Annual Earnings: $47,280
* Beginning Wage: $30,960
* Earnings Growth Potential: Low
* Growth: 6.4%
* Annual Job Openings: 3,710
* Self-Employed: 0.8%
* Part-Time: 5.9%

Apply theory and principles of mechanical engineering to modify, develop, and test machinery and equipment under direction of engineering staff or physical scientists. Prepare parts sketches and write work orders and purchase requests to be furnished by outside contractors. Draft detail drawing or sketch for drafting room completion or to request parts fabrication by machine, sheet, or wood shops. Review project instructions and blueprints to ascertain test specifications, procedures, and objectives and test nature of technical problems such as redesign. Review project instructions and specifications to identify, modify, and plan requirements fabrication, assembly, and testing. Devise, fabricate, and assemble new or modified mechanical components for products such as industrial machinery or equipment and measuring instruments. Discuss changes in design, method of manufacture and assembly, and drafting techniques and procedures with staff and coordinate corrections. Set up and conduct tests of complete units and components under operational conditions to investigate proposals for improving equipment performance. Inspect lines and figures for clarity and return erroneous drawings to designer for correction. Analyze test results in relation to design or rated specifications and test objectives and modify or adjust equipment to meet specifications. Evaluate tool drawing designs by measuring drawing dimensions and comparing with original specifications for form and function, using engineering skills. Confer with technicians and submit reports of test results to engineering department and recommend design or material changes. Calculate required capacities for equipment of proposed system to obtain specified performance and submit data to engineering personnel for approval. Record test procedures and results, numerical and graphical data, and recommendations for changes in product or test methods. Read dials and meters to determine amperage, voltage, and electrical output and input at specific operating temperature to analyze parts performance. Estimate cost factors, including labor and material, for purchased and fabricated parts and costs for assembly, testing, or installing. Set up prototype and test apparatus and operate test-controlling equipment to observe and record prototype test results.

Personality Type: Realistic. These occupations frequently involve work activities that include practical, hands-on problems and solutions. They often deal with plants; animals; and real-world materials such as wood, tools, and machinery. Many of the occupations require working outside and don't involve a lot of paperwork or working closely with others.

GOE—Interest Area/Cluster: 15. Scientific Research, Engineering, and Mathematics. **Work Group:** 15.09. Engineering Technology. **Other Jobs in This Work Group:** Aerospace Engineering and Operations Technicians; Cartographers and Photogrammetrists; Civil Engineering Technicians; Electrical and Electronic Engineering Technicians; Electrical and Electronics Drafters; Electrical Drafters; Electrical Engineering Technicians; Electro-Mechanical Technicians; Electronic Drafters; Electronics Engineering Technicians; Environmental Engineering Technicians; Mapping Technicians; Mechanical Drafters; Surveying and Mapping Technicians; Surveying Technicians.

Skills—Installation: Installing equipment, machines, wiring, or programs to meet specifications. **Troubleshooting:** Determining what is causing an operating error and deciding what to do about it. **Technology Design:** Generating or adapting equipment and technology to serve user needs. **Operations Analysis:** Analyzing needs and product requirements to create a design. **Equipment Selection:** Determining the kind of tools and equipment needed to do a job. **Science:** Using scientific methods to solve problems. **Mathematics:** Using mathematics to solve problems. **Systems Evaluation:** Looking at many indicators of system performance and taking into account their accuracy.

Education and Training Programs: Mechanical Engineering Related Technologies/Technician Training, Other; Mechanical Engineering/Mechanical Technology/Technician Training. **Related Knowledge/Courses—Engineering and Technology:** Equipment, tools, and mechanical devices and their uses to produce motion, light, power, technology, and other applications. **Design:** Design techniques, principles, tools, and instruments involved in the production and use of precision technical plans, blueprints, drawings, and models. **Mechanical Devices:** Machines and tools, including their designs, uses, benefits, repair, and maintenance. **Physics:** Physical principles, laws, and applications, including air, water, material dynamics, light, atomic principles, heat, electric theory, earth formations, and meteorological and related natural phenomena. **Chemistry:** The composition, structure, and properties of substances and of the chemical processes and transformations that they undergo. This includes uses of chemicals and their interactions, danger signs, production techniques, and disposal methods. **Production and Processing:** Inputs, outputs, raw materials, waste, quality control, costs, and techniques for maximizing the manufacture and distribution of goods.

Work Environment: Indoors; noisy; contaminants; hazardous equipment; sitting.

Medical and Clinical Laboratory Technicians

* Education/Training Required: Associate degree
* Annual Earnings: $34,270
* Beginning Wage: $22,670
* Earnings Growth Potential: Low
* Growth: 15.0%
* Annual Job Openings: 10,866
* Self-Employed: 0.7%
* Part-Time: 14.3%

Perform routine medical laboratory tests for the diagnosis, treatment, and prevention of disease. May work under the supervision of a medical technologist. Conduct chemical analyses of bodily fluids, such as blood and urine, using microscope or automatic analyzer to detect abnormalities or diseases, and enter findings into computer. Set up, adjust, maintain, and clean medical laboratory equipment. Analyze the results of tests and experiments to ensure conformity to specifications, using special mechanical and electrical devices. Analyze and record test data to issue reports that use charts, graphs and narratives. Conduct blood tests for transfusion purposes and perform blood counts. Perform medical research to further control and cure disease. Obtain specimens, cultivating, isolating, and identifying microorganisms for analysis. Examine cells stained with dye to locate abnormalities. Collect blood or tissue samples from patients, observing principles of asepsis to obtain blood sample. Consult with a pathologist to determine a final diagnosis when abnormal cells are found. Inoculate fertilized eggs, broths, or other bacteriological media with organisms. Cut, stain, and mount tissue samples for examination by pathologists. Supervise and instruct other technicians and laboratory assistants. Prepare standard volumetric solutions and reagents to be combined with samples, following standardized formulas or experimental procedures. Prepare vaccines and serums by standard laboratory methods, testing for virus inactivity and sterility. Test raw materials, processes, and finished products to determine quality and quantity of materials or characteristics of a substance.

Personality Type: Realistic. These occupations frequently involve work activities that include practical, hands-on problems and solutions. They often deal with plants; animals; and real-world materials such as wood, tools, and machinery. Many of the occupations require working outside and don't involve a lot of paperwork or working closely with others.

GOE—Interest Area/Cluster: 08. Health Science. **Work Group:** 08.06. Medical Technology. **Other Jobs in This Work Group:** Biological Technicians; Cardiovascular Technologists and Technicians; Diagnostic Medical Sonographers; Medical and Clinical Laboratory Technologists; Medical Equipment Preparers; Medical Records and Health Information Technicians; Nuclear Medicine Technologists; Opticians, Dispensing; Orthotists and Prosthetists; Radiologic Technicians; Radiologic Technologists; Radiologic Technologists and Technicians.

Skills—Science: Using scientific methods to solve problems. **Equipment Maintenance:** Performing routine maintenance and determining when and what kind of maintenance is needed. **Troubleshooting:** Determining what is causing an operating error and deciding what to do about it. **Quality Control Analysis:** Evaluating the quality or performance of products, services, or processes. **Operation Monitoring:** Watching gauges, dials, or other indicators to make sure a machine is working properly. **Operation and Control:** Controlling operations of equipment or systems. **Monitoring:** Assessing how well one is doing when learning or doing something. **Installation:** Installing equipment, machines, wiring, or programs to meet specifications.

Education and Training Programs: Blood Bank Technology Specialist Training; Clinical/Medical Laboratory Assistant Training; Clinical/Medical Laboratory Technician Training; Hematology Technology/Technician Training; Histologic Technician Training. **Related Knowledge/Courses—Medicine and Dentistry:** The information and techniques needed to diagnose and treat injuries, diseases, and deformities. This includes symptoms, treatment alternatives, drug properties and interactions, and preventive health-care measures. **Therapy and Counseling:** Information and techniques needed to rehabilitate physical and mental ailments and to provide career guidance, including alternative treatments, rehabilitation equipment and its proper use, and methods to evaluate treatment effects. **Biology:** Plant and animal living tissue, cells, organisms, and entities, including their functions, interdependencies, and interactions with each other and the environment.

M

Clerical Studies: Administrative and clerical procedures and systems such as word-processing systems, filing and records management systems, stenography and transcription, forms, design principles, and other office procedures and terminology.

Work Environment: Indoors; disease or infections; standing; walking and running; using hands on objects, tools, or controls.

Medical Assistants

- ✳ Education/Training Required: Moderate-term on-the-job training
- ✳ Annual Earnings: $27,430
- ✳ Beginning Wage: $19,850
- ✳ Earnings Growth Potential: Low
- ✳ Growth: 35.4%
- ✳ Annual Job Openings: 92,977
- ✳ Self-Employed: 0.0%
- ✳ Part-Time: 23.2%

Perform administrative and certain clinical duties under the direction of physicians. Administrative duties may include scheduling appointments, maintaining medical records, billing, and coding for insurance purposes. Clinical duties may include taking and recording vital signs and medical histories, preparing patients for examination, drawing blood, and administering medications as directed by physician. Record patients' medical history, vital statistics, and information such as test results in medical records. Prepare treatment rooms for patient examinations, keeping the rooms neat and clean. Interview patients to obtain medical information and measure their vital signs, weights, and heights. Authorize drug refills and provide prescription information to pharmacies. Clean and sterilize instruments and dispose of contaminated supplies. Prepare and administer medications as directed by a physician. Show patients to examination rooms and prepare them for the physician. Explain treatment procedures, medications, diets, and physicians' instructions to patients. Help physicians examine and treat patients, handing them instruments and materials or performing such tasks as giving injections or removing sutures. Collect blood, tissue, or other laboratory specimens, log the specimens, and prepare them for testing. Perform routine

laboratory tests and sample analyses. Contact medical facilities or departments to schedule patients for tests or admission. Operate x-ray, electrocardiogram (EKG), and other equipment to administer routine diagnostic tests. Change dressings on wounds. Set up medical laboratory equipment. Perform general office duties such as answering telephones, taking dictation, or completing insurance forms. Greet and log in patients arriving at office or clinic. Schedule appointments for patients. Inventory and order medical, lab, or office supplies and equipment. Keep financial records and perform other bookkeeping duties such as handling credit and collections and mailing monthly statements to patients.

Personality Type: Social. These occupations frequently involve working with, communicating with, and teaching people and often involve helping or providing service to others.

GOE—Interest Area/Cluster: 08. Health Science. **Work Group:** 08.02. Medicine and Surgery. **Other Jobs in This Work Group:** Anesthesiologists; Family and General Practitioners; Internists, General; Medical Transcriptionists; Obstetricians and Gynecologists; Pediatricians, General; Pharmacists; Pharmacy Aides; Pharmacy Technicians; Physician Assistants; Psychiatrists; Registered Nurses; Surgeons; Surgical Technologists.

Skill: Systems Analysis: Determining how a system should work and how changes will affect outcomes.

Education and Training Programs: Allied Health and Medical Assisting Services, Other; Anesthesiologist Assistant Training; Chiropractic Assistant/Technician Training; Medical Administrative/Executive Assistant and Medical Secretary Training; Medical Insurance Coding Specialist/Coder Training; Medical Office Assistant/Specialist Training; Medical Office Management/Administration; Medical Reception/Receptionist Training; Medical/Clinical Assistant Training; Opthalmic Technician/Technologist Training; Optomeric Technician/Assistant Training; Orthoptics/Orthoptist Training. **Related Knowledge/Courses—Medicine and Dentistry:** The information and techniques needed to diagnose and treat injuries, diseases, and deformities. This includes symptoms, treatment alternatives, drug properties and interactions, and preventive health-care measures. **Clerical Studies:** Administrative and clerical procedures and systems such as word-processing systems, filing and records management systems, stenography and transcription, forms, design principles, and other office procedures and terminology. **Psychology:** Human behavior and performance, mental processes, psychological research methods, and the assessment and treatment of behavioral and affective disorders. **Therapy and Counseling:** Information and techniques needed to rehabilitate physical and mental ailments and to provide career guidance, including alternative treatments, rehabilitation equipment and its proper use, and methods to evaluate treatment effects. **Customer and Personal Service:** Principles and processes for providing customer and personal services, including needs assessment techniques, quality service standards, alternative delivery systems, and customer satisfaction evaluation techniques. **Public Safety and Security:** Weaponry; public safety; security operations, rules, regulations, precautions, and prevention; and the protection of people, data, and property.

Work Environment: Indoors; disease or infections; standing; walking and running; using hands on objects, tools, or controls; repetitive motions.

Medical Equipment Preparers

- ❋ Education/Training Required: Short-term on-the-job training
- ❋ Annual Earnings: $27,040
- ❋ Beginning Wage: $19,490
- ❋ Earnings Growth Potential: Low
- ❋ Growth: 14.2%
- ❋ Annual Job Openings: 8,363
- ❋ Self-Employed: 2.8%
- ❋ Part-Time: 23.2%

Prepare, sterilize, install, or clean laboratory or health-care equipment. May perform routine laboratory tasks and operate or inspect equipment. Organize and assemble routine and specialty surgical instrument trays and other sterilized supplies, filling special requests as needed. Clean instruments to prepare them for sterilization. Operate and maintain steam autoclaves, keeping records of loads completed, items in loads, and maintenance procedures performed. Record sterilizer test results. Disinfect and sterilize equipment such as respirators, hospital beds, and oxygen and dialysis equipment, using sterilizers, aerators, and washers. Start equipment and observe gauges

and equipment operation to detect malfunctions and to ensure equipment is operating to prescribed standards. Examine equipment to detect leaks, worn or loose parts, or other indications of disrepair. Report defective equipment to appropriate supervisors or staff. Check sterile supplies to ensure that they are not outdated. Maintain records of inventory and equipment usage. Attend hospital in-service programs related to areas of work specialization. Purge wastes from equipment by connecting equipment to water sources and flushing water through systems. Deliver equipment to specified hospital locations or to patients' residences. Assist hospital staff with patient care duties such as providing transportation or setting up traction. Install and set up medical equipment, using hand tools.

Personality Type: Realistic. These occupations frequently involve work activities that include practical, hands-on problems and solutions. They often deal with plants; animals; and real-world materials such as wood, tools, and machinery. Many of the occupations require working outside and don't involve a lot of paperwork or working closely with others.

GOE—Interest Area/Cluster: 08. Health Science. **Work Group:** 08.06. Medical Technology. **Other Jobs in This Work Group:** Biological Technicians; Cardiovascular Technologists and Technicians; Diagnostic Medical Sonographers; Medical and Clinical Laboratory Technicians; Medical and Clinical Laboratory Technologists; Medical Records and Health Information Technicians; Nuclear Medicine Technologists; Opticians, Dispensing; Orthotists and Prosthetists; Radiologic Technicians; Radiologic Technologists; Radiologic Technologists and Technicians.

Skills—Operation Monitoring: Watching gauges, dials, or other indicators to make sure a machine is working properly. **Equipment Maintenance:** Performing routine maintenance and determining when and what kind of maintenance is needed. **Management of Material Resources:** Obtaining and seeing to the appropriate use of equipment, facilities, and materials needed to do certain work. **Quality Control Analysis:** Evaluating the quality or performance of products, services, or processes. **Operation and Control:** Controlling operations of equipment or systems. **Service Orientation:** Actively looking for ways to help people. **Monitoring:** Assessing how well one is doing when learning or doing something. **Science:** Using scientific methods to solve problems.

Education and Training Programs: Allied Health and Medical Assisting Services, Other; Medical/Clinical Assistant Training. **Related Knowledge/Courses— Chemistry:** The composition, structure, and properties of substances and of the chemical processes and transformations that they undergo. This includes uses of chemicals and their interactions, danger signs, production techniques, and disposal methods. **Biology:** Plant and animal living tissue, cells, organisms, and entities, including their functions, interdependencies, and interactions with each other and the environment. **Medicine and Dentistry:** The information and techniques needed to diagnose and treat injuries, diseases, and deformities. This includes symptoms, treatment alternatives, drug properties and interactions, and preventive health-care measures. **Production and Processing:** Inputs, outputs, raw materials, waste, quality control, costs, and techniques for maximizing the manufacture and distribution of goods. **Education and Training:** Instructional methods and training techniques, including curriculum design principles, learning theory, group and individual teaching techniques, design of individual development plans, and test design principles. **Customer and Personal Service:** Principles and processes for providing customer and personal services, including needs assessment techniques, quality service standards, alternative delivery systems, and customer satisfaction evaluation techniques.

Work Environment: Indoors; contaminants; disease or infections; standing; using hands on objects, tools, or controls; repetitive motions.

Medical Equipment Repairers

- ❋ Education/Training Required: Associate degree
- ❋ Annual Earnings: $40,320
- ❋ Beginning Wage: $24,680
- ❋ Earnings Growth Potential: Medium
- ❋ Growth: 21.7%
- ❋ Annual Job Openings: 2,351
- ❋ Self-Employed: 14.0%
- ❋ Part-Time: 10.1%

Test, adjust, or repair biomedical or electromedical equipment. Inspect and test malfunctioning medical and related equipment following manufacturers' specifications, using test and analysis instruments. Examine medical equipment and facility's structural environment and check for proper use of equipment to protect patients and staff from electrical or mechanical hazards and to ensure compliance with safety regulations. Disassemble malfunctioning equipment and remove, repair, and replace defective parts such as motors, clutches, or transformers. Keep records of maintenance, repair, and required updates of equipment. Perform preventive maintenance or service such as cleaning, lubricating, and adjusting equipment. Test and calibrate components and equipment, following manufacturers' manuals and troubleshooting techniques and using hand tools, power tools, and measuring devices. Explain and demonstrate correct operation and preventive maintenance of medical equipment to personnel. Study technical manuals and attend training sessions provided by equipment manufacturers to maintain current knowledge. Plan and carry out work assignments, using blueprints, schematic drawings, technical manuals, wiring diagrams, and liquid and air flow sheets, following prescribed regulations, directives, and other instructions as required. Solder loose connections, using soldering iron. Test, evaluate, and classify excess or in-use medical equipment and determine serviceability, condition, and disposition in accordance with regulations. Research catalogs and repair part lists to locate sources for repair parts, requisitioning parts and recording their receipt. Evaluate technical specifications to identify equipment and systems best suited for intended use and possible purchase based on specifications, user needs, and technical requirements. Contribute expertise to develop medical maintenance standard operating procedures. Compute power and space requirements for installing medical, dental, or related equipment and install units to manufacturers' specifications. Supervise and advise subordinate personnel. Repair shop equipment, metal furniture, and hospital equipment, including welding broken parts and replacing missing parts, or bring item into local shop for major repairs.

Personality Type: Realistic. These occupations frequently involve work activities that include practical, hands-on problems and solutions. They often deal with plants; animals; and real-world materials such as wood, tools, and machinery. Many of the occupations require working outside and don't involve a lot of paperwork or working closely with others.

GOE—Interest Area/Cluster: 13. Manufacturing. **Work Group:** 13.15. Medical and Technical Equipment Repair. **Other Jobs in This Work Group:** Camera and Photographic Equipment Repairers; Watch Repairers.

Skills—Repairing: Repairing machines or systems, using the needed tools. **Installation:** Installing equipment, machines, wiring, or programs to meet specifications. **Equipment Maintenance:** Performing routine maintenance and determining when and what kind of maintenance is needed. **Troubleshooting:** Determining what is causing an operating error and deciding what to do about it. **Science:** Using scientific methods to solve problems. **Operation Monitoring:** Watching gauges, dials, or other indicators to make sure a machine is working properly. **Systems Analysis:** Determining how a system should work and how changes will affect outcomes. **Quality Control Analysis:** Evaluating the quality or performance of products, services, or processes.

Education and Training Program: Biomedical Technology/Technician Training. **Related Knowledge/Courses— Mechanical Devices:** Machines and tools, including their designs, uses, benefits, repair, and maintenance. **Computers and Electronics:** Electric circuit boards, processors, chips, and computer hardware and software, including applications and programming. **Engineering and Technology:** Equipment, tools, and mechanical devices and their uses to produce motion, light, power, technology, and other applications. **Physics:** Physical principles, laws, and applications, including air, water, material dynamics, light, atomic principles, heat, electric theory, earth formations, and meteorological and related natural phenomena. **Telecommunications:** Transmission, broadcasting, switching, control, and operation of telecommunications systems. **Medicine and Dentistry:** The information and techniques needed to diagnose and treat injuries, diseases, and deformities. This includes symptoms, treatment alternatives, drug properties and interactions, and preventive health-care measures.

Work Environment: Indoors; contaminants; disease or infections; standing; using hands on objects, tools, or controls.

Medical Records and Health Information Technicians

* Education/Training Required: Associate degree
* Annual Earnings: $29,290
* Beginning Wage: $19,690
* Earnings Growth Potential: Low
* Growth: 17.8%
* Annual Job Openings: 39,048
* Self-Employed: 0.2%
* Part-Time: 12.5%

Compile, process, and maintain medical records of hospital and clinic patients in a manner consistent with medical, administrative, ethical, legal, and regulatory requirements of the health care system. Process, maintain, compile, and report patient information for health requirements and standards. Protect the security of medical records to ensure that confidentiality is maintained. Review records for completeness, accuracy, and compliance with regulations. Retrieve patient medical records for physicians, technicians, or other medical personnel. Release information to persons and agencies according to regulations. Plan, develop, maintain, and operate a variety of health record indexes and storage and retrieval systems to collect, classify, store, and analyze information. Enter data such as demographic characteristics, history and extent of disease, diagnostic procedures, and treatment into computer. Process and prepare business and government forms. Compile and maintain patients' medical records to document condition and treatment and to provide data for research or cost control and care improvement efforts. Process patient admission and discharge documents. Assign the patient to diagnosis-related groups (DRGs), using appropriate computer software. Transcribe medical reports. Identify, compile, abstract, and code patient data, using standard classification systems. Resolve or clarify codes and diagnoses with conflicting, missing, or unclear information by consulting with doctors or others or by participating in the coding team's regular meetings. Compile medical care and census data for statistical reports on diseases treated, surgeries performed, or use of hospital beds. Post medical insurance billings. Train medical records staff. Prepare statistical reports, narrative reports, and graphic presentations of information such as tumor registry data for use by hospital staff, researchers, or other users. Manage the department and supervise clerical workers, directing and controlling activities of personnel in the medical records department. Develop in-service educational materials. Consult classification manuals to locate information about disease processes.

Personality Type: Conventional. These occupations frequently involve following set procedures and routines and can include working with data and details more than with ideas. Usually there is a clear line of authority to follow.

GOE—Interest Area/Cluster: 08. Health Science. **Work Group:** 08.06. Medical Technology. **Other Jobs in This Work Group:** Biological Technicians; Cardiovascular Technologists and Technicians; Diagnostic Medical Sonographers; Medical and Clinical Laboratory Technicians; Medical and Clinical Laboratory Technologists; Medical Equipment Preparers; Nuclear Medicine Technologists; Opticians, Dispensing; Orthotists and Prosthetists; Radiologic Technicians; Radiologic Technologists; Radiologic Technologists and Technicians.

Skill: Systems Analysis: Determining how a system should work and how changes will affect outcomes.

Education and Training Programs: Health Information/Medical Records Technology/Technician Training; Medical Insurance Coding Specialist/Coder Training. **Related Knowledge/Courses—Clerical Studies:** Administrative and clerical procedures and systems such as word-processing systems, filing and records management systems, stenography and transcription, forms, design principles, and other office procedures and terminology. **Law and Government:** Laws, legal codes, court procedures, precedents, government regulations, executive orders, agency rules, and the democratic political process. **Customer and Personal Service:** Principles and processes for providing customer and personal services, including needs assessment techniques, quality service standards, alternative delivery systems, and customer satisfaction evaluation techniques.

Work Environment: Indoors; disease or infections; sitting; using hands on objects, tools, or controls; repetitive motions.

Medical Secretaries

* Education/Training Required: Moderate-term on-the-job training
* Annual Earnings: $28,950
* Beginning Wage: $20,260
* Earnings Growth Potential: Low
* Growth: 16.7%
* Annual Job Openings: 60,659
* Self-Employed: 1.3%
* Part-Time: 18.9%

Perform secretarial duties, using specific knowledge of medical terminology and hospital, clinical, or laboratory procedures. Duties include scheduling appointments, billing patients, and compiling and recording medical charts, reports, and correspondence. Answer telephones, and direct calls to appropriate staff. Schedule and confirm patient diagnostic appointments, surgeries, and medical consultations. Greet visitors, ascertain purpose of visit, and direct them to appropriate staff. Operate office equipment such as voice mail messaging systems, and use word processing, spreadsheet, and other software applications to prepare reports, invoices, financial statements, letters, case histories, and medical records. Complete insurance and other claim forms. Interview patients to complete documents, case histories, and forms such as intake and insurance forms. Receive and route messages and documents such as laboratory results to appropriate staff. Compile and record medical charts, reports, and correspondence, using typewriter or personal computer. Transmit correspondence and medical records by mail, e-mail, or fax. Maintain medical records, technical library documents, and correspondence files. Perform various clerical and administrative functions such as ordering and maintaining an inventory of supplies. Perform bookkeeping duties such as credits and collections, preparing and sending financial statements and bills, and keeping financial records. Transcribe recorded messages and practitioners' diagnoses and recommendations into patients' medical records. Arrange hospital admissions for patients. Prepare correspondence and assist physicians or medical scientists with preparation of reports, speeches, articles, and conference proceedings.

Personality Type: Conventional. These occupations frequently involve following set procedures and routines and can include working with data and details more than with ideas. Usually there is a clear line of authority to follow.

GOE—Interest Area/Cluster: 04. Business and Administration. **Work Group:** 04.04. Secretarial Support. **Other Jobs in This Work Group:** Executive Secretaries and Administrative Assistants; Legal Secretaries; Secretaries, Except Legal, Medical, and Executive.

Skills: None met the criteria.

Education and Training Programs: Medical Administrative/Executive Assistant and Medical Secretary Training; Medical Insurance Specialist/Medical Biller Training; Medical Office Assistant/Specialist Training. **Related Knowledge/Courses—Clerical Studies:** Administrative and clerical procedures and systems such as word-processing systems, filing and records management systems, stenography and transcription, forms, design principles, and other office procedures and terminology. **Medicine and Dentistry:** The information and techniques needed to diagnose and treat injuries, diseases, and deformities. This includes symptoms, treatment alternatives, drug properties and interactions, and preventive health-care measures. **Customer and Personal Service:** Principles and processes for providing customer and personal services, including needs assessment techniques, quality service standards, alternative delivery systems, and customer satisfaction evaluation techniques. **Computers and Electronics:** Electric circuit boards, processors, chips, and computer hardware and software, including applications and programming. **Economics and Accounting:** Economic and accounting principles and practices, the financial markets, banking, and the analysis and reporting of financial data.

Work Environment: Indoors; disease or infections; sitting; repetitive motions.

Medical Transcriptionists

* Education/Training Required: Postsecondary vocational training
* Annual Earnings: $31,250
* Beginning Wage: $22,160
* Earnings Growth Potential: Low
* Growth: 13.5%
* Annual Job Openings: 18,080
* Self-Employed: 9.7%
* Part-Time: 23.2%

Use transcribing machines with headset and foot pedal to listen to recordings by physicians and other health-care professionals dictating a variety of medical reports, such as emergency room visits, diagnostic imaging studies, operations, chart reviews, and final summaries. Transcribe dictated reports and translate medical jargon and abbreviations into their expanded forms. Edit as necessary and return reports in either printed or electronic form to the dictator for review and signature or correction. Transcribe dictation for a variety of medical reports such as patient histories, physical examinations, emergency room visits, operations, chart reviews, consultation, or discharge summaries. Review and edit transcribed reports or dictated material for spelling, grammar, clarity, consistency, and proper medical terminology. Distinguish between homonyms and recognize inconsistencies and mistakes in medical terms, referring to dictionaries; drug references; and other sources on anatomy, physiology, and medicine. Return dictated reports in printed or electronic form for physicians' review, signature, and corrections and for inclusion in patients' medical records. Translate medical jargon and abbreviations into their expanded forms to ensure the accuracy of patient and health-care facility records. Take dictation, using either shorthand or a stenotype machine or using headsets and transcribing machines; then convert dictated materials or rough notes to written form. Identify mistakes in reports and check with doctors to obtain the correct information. Perform data entry and data retrieval services, providing data for inclusion in medical records and for transmission to physicians. Produce medical reports, correspondence, records, patient-care information, statistics, medical research, and administrative material. Answer inquiries concerning the progress of medical cases within the limits of confidentiality laws. Set up and maintain medical files and databases, including records such as X-ray, lab, and procedure reports; medical histories; diagnostic workups; admission and discharge summaries; and clinical resumes. Perform a variety of clerical and office tasks, such as handling incoming and outgoing mail, completing and submitting insurance claims, typing, filing, and operating office machines. Decide which information should be included or excluded in reports. Receive patients, schedule appointments, and maintain patient records. Receive and screen telephone calls and visitors.

Personality Type: Conventional. These occupations frequently involve following set procedures and routines and can include working with data and details more than with ideas. Usually there is a clear line of authority to follow.

GOE—Interest Area/Cluster: 08. Health Science. **Work Group:** 08.02. Medicine and Surgery. **Other Jobs in This Work Group:** Anesthesiologists; Family and General Practitioners; Internists, General; Medical Assistants; Obstetricians and Gynecologists; Pediatricians, General; Pharmacists; Pharmacy Aides; Pharmacy Technicians; Physician Assistants; Psychiatrists; Registered Nurses; Surgeons; Surgical Technologists.

Skills—Active Listening: Listening to what other people are saying and asking questions as appropriate. **Reading Comprehension:** Understanding written sentences and paragraphs in work-related documents. **Time Management:** Managing one's own time and the time of others.

Education and Training Program: Medical Transcription/Transcriptionist Training. **Related Knowledge/Courses—Clerical Studies:** Administrative and clerical procedures and systems such as word-processing systems, filing and records management systems, stenography and transcription, forms, design principles, and other office procedures and terminology. **English Language:** The structure and content of the English language, including the meaning and spelling of words, rules of composition, and grammar. **Medicine and Dentistry:** The information and techniques needed to diagnose and treat injuries, diseases, and deformities. This includes symptoms, treatment alternatives, drug properties and interactions, and

preventive health-care measures. **Computers and Electronics:** Electric circuit boards, processors, chips, and computer hardware and software, including applications and programming.

Work Environment: Indoors; sitting; using hands on objects, tools, or controls; repetitive motions.

Merchandise Displayers and Window Trimmers

- ❋ Education/Training Required: Moderate-term on-the-job training
- ❋ Annual Earnings: $24,830
- ❋ Beginning Wage: $16,300
- ❋ Earnings Growth Potential: Low
- ❋ Growth: 10.7%
- ❋ Annual Job Openings: 9,103
- ❋ Self-Employed: 28.6%
- ❋ Part-Time: 16.7%

Plan and erect commercial displays, such as those in windows and interiors of retail stores and at trade exhibitions. Take photographs of displays and signage. Plan and erect commercial displays to entice and appeal to customers. Place prices and descriptive signs on backdrops, fixtures, merchandise, or floor. Change or rotate window displays, interior display areas, and signage to reflect changes in inventory or promotion. Obtain plans from display designers or display managers and discuss their implementation with clients or supervisors. Develop ideas or plans for merchandise displays or window decorations. Consult with advertising and sales staff to determine type of merchandise to be featured and time and place for each display. Arrange properties, furniture, merchandise, backdrops, and other accessories as shown in prepared sketches. Construct or assemble displays and display components from fabric, glass, paper, and plastic according to specifications, using hand tools and woodworking power tools. Collaborate with others to obtain products and other display items. Use computers to produce signage. Dress mannequins for displays. Maintain props and mannequins, inspecting them for imperfections and applying preservative coatings as necessary. Select themes, lighting, colors, and props to be used. Attend training sessions and corporate planning meetings to obtain new ideas for product launches. Instruct sales staff in color-coordination of clothing racks and counter displays. Store, pack, and maintain records of props and display items. Prepare sketches, floor plans, or models of proposed displays. Cut out designs on cardboard, hardboard, and plywood according to motif of event. Install booths, exhibits, displays, carpets, and drapes as guided by floor plan of building and specifications. Install decorations such as flags, banners, festive lights, and bunting on or in building, street, exhibit hall, or booth. Create and enhance mannequin faces by mixing and applying paint and attaching measured eyelash strips, using artist's brush, airbrush, pins, ruler, and scissors.

Personality Type: Artistic. These occupations frequently involve working with forms, designs, and patterns. They often require self-expression, and the work can be done without following a clear set of rules.

GOE—Interest Area/Cluster: 03. Arts and Communication. **Work Group:** 03.05. Design. **Other Jobs in This Work Group:** Commercial and Industrial Designers; Fashion Designers; Floral Designers; Graphic Designers; Interior Designers; Set and Exhibit Designers.

Skills—Persuasion: Persuading others to approach things differently. **Negotiation:** Bringing others together and trying to reconcile differences. **Management of Personnel Resources:** Motivating, developing, and directing people as they work; identifying the best people for the job.

Education and Training Program: Commercial and Advertising Art. **Related Knowledge/Courses—Sales and Marketing:** Principles and methods involved in showing, promoting, and selling products or services. This includes marketing strategies and tactics, product demonstration and sales techniques, and sales control systems. **Design:** Design techniques, principles, tools, and instruments involved in the production and use of precision technical plans, blueprints, drawings, and models. **Administration and Management:** Principles and processes involved in business and organizational planning, coordination, and execution. This includes strategic planning, resource allocation, manpower modeling, leadership techniques, and production methods. **Computers and Electronics:** Electric circuit boards, processors, chips, and computer hardware and software, including applications and programming.

Work Environment: Indoors; contaminants; walking and running; using hands on objects, tools, or controls; bending or twisting the body; repetitive motions.

Millwrights

- ❈ Education/Training Required: Long-term on-the-job training
- ❈ Annual Earnings: $46,090
- ❈ Beginning Wage: $28,940
- ❈ Earnings Growth Potential: Medium
- ❈ Growth: 5.8%
- ❈ Annual Job Openings: 4,758
- ❈ Self-Employed: 3.2%
- ❈ Part-Time: 1.5%

Install, dismantle, or move machinery and heavy equipment according to layout plans, blueprints, or other drawings. Replace defective parts of machine or adjust clearances and alignment of moving parts. Align machines and equipment, using hoists, jacks, hand tools, squares, rules, micrometers, and plumb bobs. Connect power unit to machines or steam piping to equipment and test unit to evaluate its mechanical operation. Repair and lubricate machines and equipment. Assemble and install equipment, using hand tools and power tools. Position steel beams to support bedplates of machines and equipment, using blueprints and schematic drawings to determine work procedures. Signal crane operator to lower basic assembly units to bedplate and align unit to centerline. Insert shims, adjust tension on nuts and bolts, or position parts, using hand tools and measuring instruments to set specified clearances between moving and stationary parts. Move machinery and equipment, using hoists, dollies, rollers, and trucks. Attach moving parts and subassemblies to basic assembly unit, using hand tools and power tools. Assemble machines and bolt, weld, rivet, or otherwise fasten them to foundation or other structures, using hand tools and power tools. Lay out mounting holes, using measuring instruments, and drill holes with power drill. Bolt parts, such as side and deck plates, jaw plates, and journals, to basic assembly unit. Dismantle machines, using hammers, wrenches, crowbars, and other hand tools. Level bedplate and establish centerline, using straightedge, levels, and transit. Shrink-fit bushings, sleeves, rings, liners, gears, and wheels to specified items, using portable gas heating equipment. Dismantle machinery and equipment for shipment to installation site, usually performing installation and maintenance work as part of team. Construct foundation for machines, using hand tools and building materials such as wood, cement, and steel. Install robot and modify its program, using teach pendant. Operate engine lathe to grind, file, and turn machine parts to dimensional specifications.

Personality Type: Realistic. These occupations frequently involve work activities that include practical, hands-on problems and solutions. They often deal with plants; animals; and real-world materials such as wood, tools, and machinery. Many of the occupations require working outside and don't involve a lot of paperwork or working closely with others.

GOE—Interest Area/Cluster: 13. Manufacturing. **Work Group:** 13.13. Machinery Repair. **Other Jobs in This Work Group:** Bicycle Repairers; Control and Valve Installers and Repairers, Except Mechanical Door; Home Appliance Repairers; Industrial Machinery Mechanics; Locksmiths and Safe Repairers; Maintenance Workers, Machinery; Mechanical Door Repairers; Signal and Track Switch Repairers.

Skills—Installation: Installing equipment, machines, wiring, or programs to meet specifications. **Repairing:** Repairing machines or systems, using the needed tools. **Troubleshooting:** Determining what is causing an operating error and deciding what to do about it. **Equipment Maintenance:** Performing routine maintenance and determining when and what kind of maintenance is needed. **Equipment Selection:** Determining the kind of tools and equipment needed to do a job. **Mathematics:** Using mathematics to solve problems. **Technology Design:** Generating or adapting equipment and technology to serve user needs. **Operation Monitoring:** Watching gauges, dials, or other indicators to make sure a machine is working properly.

Education and Training Programs: Heavy/Industrial Equipment Maintenance Technologies, Other; Industrial Mechanics and Maintenance Technology. **Related Knowledge/Courses—Mechanical Devices:** Machines and tools, including their designs, uses, benefits, repair, and maintenance. **Building and Construction:** Materials, methods, and the appropriate tools to construct objects, structures, and buildings. **Physics:** Physical principles, laws, and applications, including air, water, material dynamics, light, atomic principles, heat, electric theory,

earth formations, and meteorological and related natural phenomena. **Engineering and Technology:** Equipment, tools, and mechanical devices and their uses to produce motion, light, power, technology, and other applications. **Design:** Design techniques, principles, tools, and instruments involved in the production and use of precision technical plans, blueprints, drawings, and models. **Public Safety and Security:** Weaponry; public safety; security operations, rules, regulations, precautions, and prevention; and the protection of people, data, and property.

Work Environment: Noisy; very hot or cold; very bright or dim lighting; contaminants; hazardous equipment; using hands on objects, tools, or controls.

Mobile Heavy Equipment Mechanics, Except Engines

* Education/Training Required: Long-term on-the-job training
* Annual Earnings: $41,450
* Beginning Wage: $27,200
* Earnings Growth Potential: Low
* Growth: 12.3%
* Annual Job Openings: 11,037
* Self-Employed: 5.0%
* Part-Time: 2.3%

Diagnose, adjust, repair, or overhaul mobile mechanical, hydraulic, and pneumatic equipment, such as cranes, bulldozers, graders, and conveyors, used in construction, logging, and surface mining. Test mechanical products and equipment after repair or assembly to ensure proper performance and compliance with manufacturers' specifications. Repair and replace damaged or worn parts. Diagnose faults or malfunctions to determine required repairs, using engine diagnostic equipment such as computerized test equipment and calibration devices. Operate and inspect machines or heavy equipment to diagnose defects. Dismantle and reassemble heavy equipment, using hoists and hand tools. Clean, lubricate, and perform other routine maintenance work on equipment and vehicles. Examine parts for damage or excessive wear, using micrometers and gauges. Read and understand operating manuals, blueprints, and technical drawings. Schedule maintenance for industrial machines and equipment and keep equipment service records. Overhaul and test machines or equipment to ensure operating efficiency. Assemble gear systems and align frames and gears. Fit bearings to adjust, repair, or overhaul mobile mechanical, hydraulic, and pneumatic equipment. Weld or solder broken parts and structural members, using electric or gas welders and soldering tools. Clean parts by spraying them with grease solvent or immersing them in tanks of solvent. Adjust, maintain, and repair or replace subassemblies, such as transmissions and crawler heads, using hand tools, jacks, and cranes. Adjust and maintain industrial machinery, using control and regulating devices. Fabricate needed parts or items from sheet metal. Direct workers who are assembling or disassembling equipment or cleaning parts.

Personality Type: Realistic. These occupations frequently involve work activities that include practical, hands-on problems and solutions. They often deal with plants; animals; and real-world materials such as wood, tools, and machinery. Many of the occupations require working outside and don't involve a lot of paperwork or working closely with others.

GOE—Interest Area/Cluster: 13. Manufacturing. **Work Group:** 13.14. Vehicle and Facility Mechanical Work. **Other Jobs in This Work Group:** Aircraft Mechanics and Service Technicians; Aircraft Structure, Surfaces, Rigging, and Systems Assemblers; Automotive Body and Related Repairers; Automotive Glass Installers and Repairers; Automotive Master Mechanics; Automotive Service Technicians and Mechanics; Automotive Specialty Technicians; Bus and Truck Mechanics and Diesel Engine Specialists; Farm Equipment Mechanics; Fiberglass Laminators and Fabricators; Motorboat Mechanics; Motorcycle Mechanics; Outdoor Power Equipment and Other Small Engine Mechanics; Rail Car Repairers; Recreational Vehicle Service Technicians; Tire Repairers and Changers.

Skills—Installation: Installing equipment, machines, wiring, or programs to meet specifications. **Repairing:** Repairing machines or systems, using the needed tools. **Equipment Maintenance:** Performing routine maintenance and determining when and what kind of maintenance is needed. **Operation Monitoring:** Watching gauges, dials, or other indicators to make sure a machine is working properly. **Troubleshooting:** Determining what is causing an operating error and deciding what to do about it. **Operation and Control:** Controlling operations of equipment or systems. **Equipment Selection:** Determining the

kind of tools and equipment needed to do a job. **Technology Design:** Generating or adapting equipment and technology to serve user needs.

Education and Training Programs: Agricultural Mechanics and Equipment/Machine Technology; Heavy Equipment Maintenance Technology/Technician Training. **Related Knowledge/Courses—Mechanical Devices:** Machines and tools, including their designs, uses, benefits, repair, and maintenance. **Engineering and Technology:** Equipment, tools, and mechanical devices and their uses to produce motion, light, power, technology, and other applications. **Physics:** Physical principles, laws, and applications, including air, water, material dynamics, light, atomic principles, heat, electric theory, earth formations, and meteorological and related natural phenomena.

Work Environment: Noisy; contaminants; hazardous equipment; minor burns, cuts, bites, or stings; standing; using hands on objects, tools, or controls.

Motorboat Mechanics

- ✻ Education/Training Required: Long-term on-the-job training
- ✻ Annual Earnings: $34,210
- ✻ Beginning Wage: $21,430
- ✻ Earnings Growth Potential: Medium
- ✻ Growth: 19.0%
- ✻ Annual Job Openings: 4,326
- ✻ Self-Employed: 22.6%
- ✻ Part-Time: 11.4%

Repairs and adjusts electrical and mechanical equipment of gasoline or diesel-powered inboard or inboard-outboard boat engines. Disassemble and inspect motors to locate defective parts, using mechanic's hand tools and gauges. Adjust generators and replace faulty wiring, using hand tools and soldering irons. Start motors, and monitor performance for signs of malfunctioning such as smoke, excessive vibration, and misfiring. Adjust carburetor mixtures, electrical point settings, and timing while motors are running in water-filled test tanks. Idle motors and observe thermometers to determine the effectiveness of cooling systems. Inspect and repair or adjust propellers and propeller shafts. Mount motors to boats and operate boats at various speeds on waterways to conduct operational tests. Replace parts such as gears, magneto points, piston rings, and spark plugs, and reassemble engines. Repair or rework parts, using machine tools such as lathes, mills, drills, and grinders. Repair engine mechanical equipment such as power-tilts, bilge pumps, or power take-offs. Set starter locks, and align and repair steering or throttle controls, using gauges, screwdrivers, and wrenches. Document inspection and test results, and work performed or to be performed.

Personality Type: Realistic. These occupations frequently involve work activities that include practical, hands-on problems and solutions. They often deal with plants; animals; and real-world materials such as wood, tools, and machinery. Many of the occupations require working outside and don't involve a lot of paperwork or working closely with others.

GOE—Interest Area/Cluster: 13. Manufacturing. **Work Group:** 13.14. Vehicle and Facility Mechanical Work. **Other Jobs in This Work Group:** Aircraft Mechanics and Service Technicians; Aircraft Structure, Surfaces, Rigging, and Systems Assemblers; Automotive Body and Related Repairers; Automotive Glass Installers and Repairers; Automotive Master Mechanics; Automotive Service Technicians and Mechanics; Automotive Specialty Technicians; Bus and Truck Mechanics and Diesel Engine Specialists; Farm Equipment Mechanics; Fiberglass Laminators and Fabricators; Mobile Heavy Equipment Mechanics, Except Engines; Motorcycle Mechanics; Outdoor Power Equipment and Other Small Engine Mechanics; Rail Car Repairers; Recreational Vehicle Service Technicians; Tire Repairers and Changers.

Skills—Repairing: Repairing machines or systems, using the needed tools. **Installation:** Installing equipment, machines, wiring, or programs to meet specifications. **Equipment Maintenance:** Performing routine maintenance and determining when and what kind of maintenance is needed. **Troubleshooting:** Determining what is causing an operating error and deciding what to do about it. **Technology Design:** Generating or adapting equipment and technology to serve user needs. **Operation Monitoring:** Watching gauges, dials, or other indicators to make sure a machine is working properly. **Operation and Control:** Controlling operations of equipment or systems. **Equipment Selection:** Determining the kind of tools and equipment needed to do a job.

Education and Training Programs: Marine Maintenance/Fitter and Ship Repair Technology/Technician Training; Small Engine Mechanics and Repair Technology/Technician Training. **Related Knowledge/Courses— Mechanical Devices:** Machines and tools, including their designs, uses, benefits, repair, and maintenance. **Engineering and Technology:** Equipment, tools, and mechanical devices and their uses to produce motion, light, power, technology, and other applications. **Design:** Design techniques, principles, tools, and instruments involved in the production and use of precision technical plans, blueprints, drawings, and models. **Physics:** Physical principles, laws, and applications, including air, water, material dynamics, light, atomic principles, heat, electric theory, earth formations, and meteorological and related natural phenomena. **Chemistry:** The composition, structure, and properties of substances and of the chemical processes and transformations that they undergo. This includes uses of chemicals and their interactions, danger signs, production techniques, and disposal methods. **Transportation:** Principles and methods for moving people or goods by air, rail, sea, or road, including their relative costs, advantages, and limitations.

Work Environment: Outdoors; noisy; contaminants; cramped work space, awkward positions; standing; using hands on objects, tools, or controls.

Motorcycle Mechanics

- Education/Training Required: Long-term on-the-job training
- Annual Earnings: $30,300
- Beginning Wage: $19,070
- Earnings Growth Potential: Medium
- Growth: 12.5%
- Annual Job Openings: 3,564
- Self-Employed: 21.9%
- Part-Time: 11.4%

Diagnose, adjust, repair, or overhaul motorcycles, scooters, mopeds, dirt bikes, or similar motorized vehicles. Repair and adjust motorcycle subassemblies such as forks, transmissions, brakes, and drive chains according to specifications. Replace defective parts, using hand tools, arbor presses, flexible power presses, or power tools. Connect test panels to engines and measure generator output, ignition timing, and other engine performance indicators. Listen to engines, examine vehicle frames, and confer with customers to determine nature and extent of malfunction or damage. Reassemble and test subassembly units. Dismantle engines and repair or replace defective parts, such as magnetos, carburetors, and generators. Remove cylinder heads; grind valves; scrape off carbon; and replace defective valves, pistons, cylinders, and rings, using hand tools and power tools. Repair or replace other parts, such as headlights, horns, handlebar controls, gasoline and oil tanks, starters, and mufflers. Disassemble subassembly units and examine condition, movement, or alignment of parts visually or by using gauges. Hammer out dents and bends in frames, weld tears and breaks, and reassemble frames and reinstall engines.

Personality Type: Realistic. These occupations frequently involve work activities that include practical, hands-on problems and solutions. They often deal with plants; animals; and real-world materials such as wood, tools, and machinery. Many of the occupations require working outside and don't involve a lot of paperwork or working closely with others.

GOE—Interest Area/Cluster: 13. Manufacturing. **Work Group:** 13.14. Vehicle and Facility Mechanical Work. **Other Jobs in This Work Group:** Aircraft Mechanics and Service Technicians; Aircraft Structure, Surfaces, Rigging, and Systems Assemblers; Automotive Body and Related Repairers; Automotive Glass Installers and Repairers; Automotive Master Mechanics; Automotive Service Technicians and Mechanics; Automotive Specialty Technicians; Bus and Truck Mechanics and Diesel Engine Specialists; Farm Equipment Mechanics; Fiberglass Laminators and Fabricators; Mobile Heavy Equipment Mechanics, Except Engines; Motorboat Mechanics; Outdoor Power Equipment and Other Small Engine Mechanics; Rail Car Repairers; Recreational Vehicle Service Technicians; Tire Repairers and Changers.

Skills—Repairing: Repairing machines or systems, using the needed tools. **Installation:** Installing equipment, machines, wiring, or programs to meet specifications. **Troubleshooting:** Determining what is causing an operating error and deciding what to do about it. **Equipment Maintenance:** Performing routine maintenance and determining when and what kind of maintenance is needed. **Science:** Using scientific methods to solve problems.

Technology Design: Generating or adapting equipment and technology to serve user needs. **Mathematics:** Using mathematics to solve problems. **Equipment Selection:** Determining the kind of tools and equipment needed to do a job.

Education and Training Program: Motorcycle Maintenance and Repair Technology/Technician Training. **Related Knowledge/Courses—Mechanical Devices:** Machines and tools, including their designs, uses, benefits, repair, and maintenance. **Design:** Design techniques, principles, tools, and instruments involved in the production and use of precision technical plans, blueprints, drawings, and models. **Engineering and Technology:** Equipment, tools, and mechanical devices and their uses to produce motion, light, power, technology, and other applications. **Physics:** Physical principles, laws, and applications, including air, water, material dynamics, light, atomic principles, heat, electric theory, earth formations, and meteorological and related natural phenomena. **Transportation:** Principles and methods for moving people or goods by air, rail, sea, or road, including their relative costs, advantages, and limitations. **Chemistry:** The composition, structure, and properties of substances and of the chemical processes and transformations that they undergo. This includes uses of chemicals and their interactions, danger signs, production techniques, and disposal methods.

Work Environment: Indoors; noisy; contaminants; standing; using hands on objects, tools, or controls; bending or twisting the body.

Multiple Machine Tool Setters, Operators, and Tenders, Metal and Plastic

* Education/Training Required: Moderate-term on-the-job training
* Annual Earnings: $30,390
* Beginning Wage: $19,550
* Earnings Growth Potential: Medium
* Growth: 0.3%
* Annual Job Openings: 15,709
* Self-Employed: 0.0%
* Part-Time: 2.3%

Set up, operate, or tend more than one type of cutting or forming machine tool or robot. Inspect workpieces for defects and measure workpieces to determine accuracy of machine operation, using rules, templates, or other measuring instruments. Observe machine operation to detect workpiece defects or machine malfunctions; adjust machines as necessary. Read blueprints or job orders to determine product specifications and tooling instructions and to plan operational sequences. Set up and operate machines such as lathes, cutters, shears, borers, millers, grinders, presses, drills, and auxiliary machines to make metallic and plastic workpieces. Position, adjust, and secure stock material or workpieces against stops; on arbors; or in chucks, fixtures, or automatic feeding mechanisms manually or by using hoists. Select, install, and adjust alignment of drills, cutters, dies, guides, and holding devices, using templates, measuring instruments, and hand tools. Change worn machine accessories such as cutting tools and brushes, using hand tools. Make minor electrical and mechanical repairs and adjustments to machines and notify supervisors when major service is required. Start machines and turn handwheels or valves to engage feeding, cooling, and lubricating mechanisms. Perform minor machine maintenance, such as oiling or cleaning machines, dies, or workpieces or adding coolant to machine reservoirs. Select the proper coolants and lubricants and start their flow. Remove burrs, sharp edges, rust, or scale from workpieces, using files, hand grinders, wire brushes, or power tools. Instruct other workers in machine setup and operation. Record operational data such as pressure readings, lengths of strokes, feed rates, and speeds. Extract or lift jammed pieces from machines, using fingers, wire hooks, or lift bars. Set machine stops or guides to specified lengths as indicated by scales, rules, or templates. Move controls or mount gears, cams, or templates in machines to set feed rates and cutting speeds, depths, and angles. Compute data such as gear dimensions and machine settings, applying knowledge of shop mathematics. Align layout marks with dies or blades. Measure and mark reference points and cutting lines on workpieces, using traced templates, compasses, and rules.

Personality Type: Realistic. These occupations frequently involve work activities that include practical, hands-on problems and solutions. They often deal with plants; animals; and real-world materials such as wood, tools, and machinery. Many of the occupations require working outside and don't involve a lot of paperwork or working closely with others.

GOE—Interest Area/Cluster: 13. Manufacturing. **Work Group:** 13.02. Machine Setup and Operation. **Other Jobs in This Work Group:** Crushing, Grinding, and Polishing Machine Setters, Operators, and Tenders; Cutting, Punching, and Press Machine Setters, Operators, and Tenders, Metal and Plastic; Drilling and Boring Machine Tool Setters, Operators, and Tenders, Metal and Plastic; Extruding and Drawing Machine Setters, Operators, and Tenders, Metal and Plastic; Forging Machine Setters, Operators, and Tenders, Metal and Plastic; Grinding, Lapping, Polishing, and Buffing Machine Tool Setters, Operators, and Tenders, Metal and Plastic; Lathe and Turning Machine Tool Setters, Operators, and Tenders, Metal and Plastic; Milling and Planing Machine Setters, Operators, and Tenders, Metal and Plastic; Paper Goods Machine Setters, Operators, and Tenders; Rolling Machine Setters, Operators, and Tenders, Metal and Plastic; Textile Cutting Machine Setters, Operators, and Tenders; Textile Knitting and Weaving Machine Setters, Operators, and Tenders; Textile Winding, Twisting, and Drawing Out Machine Setters, Operators, and Tenders.

Skills—Operation Monitoring: Watching gauges, dials, or other indicators to make sure a machine is working properly. **Repairing:** Repairing machines or systems, using the needed tools. **Equipment Maintenance:** Performing routine maintenance and determining when and what kind of maintenance is needed. **Quality Control Analysis:** Evaluating the quality or performance of products, services, or processes. **Operation and Control:** Controlling operations of equipment or systems. **Troubleshooting:** Determining what is causing an operating error and deciding what to do about it. **Installation:** Installing equipment, machines, wiring, or programs to meet specifications. **Learning Strategies:** Using multiple approaches when learning or teaching new things.

Education and Training Programs: Machine Shop Technology/Assistant; Machine Tool Technology/Machinist. **Related Knowledge/Courses—Mechanical Devices:** Machines and tools, including their designs, uses, benefits, repair, and maintenance. **Production and Processing:** Inputs, outputs, raw materials, waste, quality control, costs, and techniques for maximizing the manufacture and distribution of goods. **Design:** Design techniques, principles, tools, and instruments involved in the production and use of precision technical plans, blueprints, drawings, and models. **Engineering and Technology:** Equipment, tools, and mechanical devices and their uses to produce motion, light, power, technology, and other applications.

Work Environment: Noisy; contaminants; hazardous equipment; minor burns, cuts, bites, or stings; standing; using hands on objects, tools, or controls.

Municipal Clerks

- ❋ Education/Training Required: Short-term on-the-job training
- ❋ Annual Earnings: $32,330
- ❋ Beginning Wage: $21,050
- ❋ Earnings Growth Potential: Low
- ❋ Growth: 8.8%
- ❋ Annual Job Openings: 16,163
- ❋ Self-Employed: 2.7%
- ❋ Part-Time: 9.6%

The job openings listed here are shared with Court Clerks and with License Clerks.

Draft agendas and bylaws for town or city council, record minutes of council meetings, answer official correspondence, keep fiscal records and accounts, and prepare reports on civic needs. Participate in the administration of municipal elections, including preparation and distribution of ballots, appointment and training of election officers, and tabulation and certification of results. Record and edit the minutes of meetings; then distribute them to appropriate officials and staff members. Plan and direct the maintenance, filing, safekeeping, and computerization of all municipal documents. Issue public notification of all official activities and meetings. Maintain and update documents such as municipal codes and city charters. Prepare meeting agendas and packets of related information. Prepare ordinances, resolutions, and proclamations so that they can be executed, recorded, archived, and distributed. Respond to requests for information from the public, other municipalities, state officials, and state and federal legislative offices. Maintain fiscal records and accounts. Perform budgeting duties, including assisting in budget preparation, expenditure review, and budget administration. Perform general office duties such as

taking and transcribing dictation, typing and proofreading correspondence, distributing and filing official forms, and scheduling appointments. Coordinate and maintain office-tracking systems for correspondence and follow-up actions. Research information in the municipal archives upon request of public officials and private citizens. Perform contract administration duties, assisting with bid openings and the awarding of contracts. Collaborate with other staff to assist in the development and implementation of goals, objectives, policies, and priorities. Represent municipalities at community events and serve as liaisons on community committees. Serve as a notary of the public. Issue various permits and licenses, including marriage, fishing, hunting, and dog licenses, and collect appropriate fees. Provide assistance to persons with disabilities in reaching less-accessible areas of municipal facilities. Process claims against the municipality, maintaining files and log of claims, and coordinate claim response and handling with municipal claims administrators.

Personality Type: Conventional. These occupations frequently involve following set procedures and routines and can include working with data and details more than with ideas. Usually there is a clear line of authority to follow.

GOE—Interest Area/Cluster: 07. Government and Public Administration. **Work Group:** 07.04. Public Administration Clerical Support. **Other Jobs in This Work Group:** Court Clerks; Court Reporters; Court, Municipal, and License Clerks; License Clerks.

Skills—Service Orientation: Actively looking for ways to help people. **Management of Financial Resources:** Determining how money will be spent to get the work done and accounting for these expenditures. **Writing:** Communicating effectively with others in writing as indicated by the needs of the audience. **Social Perceptiveness:** Being aware of others' reactions and understanding why they react the way they do. **Active Listening:** Listening to what other people are saying and asking questions as appropriate. **Operations Analysis:** Analyzing needs and product requirements to create a design. **Persuasion:** Persuading others to approach things differently. **Management of Personnel Resources:** Motivating, developing, and directing people as they work; identifying the best people for the job.

Education and Training Program: General Office Occupations and Clerical Services. **Related Knowledge/**

Courses—Clerical Studies: Administrative and clerical procedures and systems such as word-processing systems, filing and records management systems, stenography and transcription, forms, design principles, and other office procedures and terminology. **Law and Government:** Laws, legal codes, court procedures, precedents, government regulations, executive orders, agency rules, and the democratic political process. **Economics and Accounting:** Economic and accounting principles and practices, the financial markets, banking, and the analysis and reporting of financial data. **English Language:** The structure and content of the English language, including the meaning and spelling of words, rules of composition, and grammar. **Personnel and Human Resources:** Principles and procedures for personnel recruitment; selection; training; compensation and benefits; labor relations and negotiation; and personnel information systems. **Administration and Management:** Principles and processes involved in business and organizational planning, coordination, and execution. This includes strategic planning, resource allocation, manpower modeling, leadership techniques, and production methods.

Work Environment: Indoors; sitting.

Municipal Fire Fighters

- ❈ Education/Training Required: Long-term on-the-job training
- ❈ Annual Earnings: $43,170
- ❈ Beginning Wage: $21,530
- ❈ Earnings Growth Potential: Very high
- ❈ Growth: 12.1%
- ❈ Annual Job Openings: 18,887
- ❈ Self-Employed: 0.0%
- ❈ Part-Time: 1.3%

The job openings listed here are shared with Forest Fire Fighters.

Control and extinguish municipal fires, protect life and property, and conduct rescue efforts. Administer first aid and cardiopulmonary resuscitation to injured persons. Rescue victims from burning buildings and accident sites. Search burning buildings to locate fire victims. Drive and operate fire fighting vehicles and equipment. Move toward the source of a fire, using knowledge of types of fires, construction design, building materials, and physical layout of properties. Dress with equipment such as fire-resistant clothing and breathing apparatus. Position and climb ladders to gain access to upper levels of buildings or to rescue individuals from burning structures. Take action to contain hazardous chemicals that might catch fire, leak, or spill. Assess fires and situations and report conditions to superiors to receive instructions, using two-way radios. Respond to fire alarms and other calls for assistance, such as automobile and industrial accidents. Operate pumps connected to high-pressure hoses. Select and attach hose nozzles, depending on fire type, and direct streams of water or chemicals onto fires. Create openings in buildings for ventilation or entrance, using axes, chisels, crowbars, electric saws, or core cutters. Inspect fire sites after flames have been extinguished to ensure that there is no further danger. Lay hose lines and connect them to water supplies. Protect property from water and smoke, using waterproof salvage covers, smoke ejectors, and deodorants. Participate in physical training activities to maintain a high level of physical fitness. Salvage property by removing broken glass, pumping out water, and ventilating buildings to remove smoke. Participate in fire drills and demonstrations of fire fighting techniques. Clean and maintain fire stations and fire fighting equipment and apparatus. Collaborate with police to respond to accidents, disasters, and arson investigation calls. Establish firelines to prevent unauthorized persons from entering areas near fires. Inform and educate the public on fire prevention. Inspect buildings for fire hazards and compliance with fire prevention ordinances, testing and checking smoke alarms and fire suppression equipment as necessary.

Personality Type: Realistic. These occupations frequently involve work activities that include practical, hands-on problems and solutions. They often deal with plants; animals; and real-world materials such as wood, tools, and machinery. Many of the occupations require working outside and don't involve a lot of paperwork or working closely with others.

GOE—Interest Area/Cluster: 12. Law and Public Safety. **Work Group:** 12.06. Emergency Responding. **Other Jobs in This Work Group:** Emergency Medical Technicians and Paramedics; Fire Fighters; Forest Fire Fighters.

Skills—Equipment Maintenance: Performing routine maintenance and determining when and what kind of maintenance is needed. **Equipment Selection:** Determining the kind of tools and equipment needed to do a job. **Service Orientation:** Actively looking for ways to help people. **Operation Monitoring:** Watching gauges, dials, or other indicators to make sure a machine is working properly. **Science:** Using scientific methods to solve problems. **Social Perceptiveness:** Being aware of others' reactions and understanding why they react the way they do. **Coordination:** Adjusting actions in relation to others' actions. **Complex Problem Solving:** Identifying complex problems, reviewing the options, and implementing solutions.

Education and Training Programs: Fire Protection, Other; Fire Science/Firefighting. **Related Knowledge/Courses—Medicine and Dentistry:** The information and techniques needed to diagnose and treat injuries, diseases, and deformities. This includes symptoms, treatment alternatives, drug properties and interactions, and preventive health-care measures. **Physics:** Physical principles, laws, and applications, including air, water, material dynamics, light, atomic principles, heat, electric theory, earth formations, and meteorological and related natural phenomena. **Customer and Personal Service:** Principles and processes for providing customer and personal services, including needs assessment techniques, quality service standards, alternative delivery systems, and customer satisfaction evaluation techniques. **Building and Construction:** Materials, methods, and the appropriate tools to construct objects, structures, and buildings. **Chemistry:** The composition, structure, and properties of substances and of the chemical processes and transformations that they undergo. This includes uses of chemicals and their interactions, danger signs, production techniques, and disposal methods. **Public Safety and Security:** Weaponry; public safety; security operations, rules, regulations, precautions, and prevention; and the protection of people, data, and property.

Work Environment: More often outdoors than indoors; noisy; contaminants; disease or infections; hazardous equipment.

Municipal Fire Fighting and Prevention Supervisors

* Education/Training Required: Work experience in a related occupation
* Annual Earnings: $65,040
* Beginning Wage: $37,930
* Earnings Growth Potential: High
* Growth: 11.5%
* Annual Job Openings: 3,771
* Self-Employed: 0.0%
* Part-Time: 0.4%

The job openings listed here are shared with Forest Fire Fighting and Prevention Supervisors.

Supervise fire fighters who control and extinguish municipal fires, protect life and property, and conduct rescue efforts. Assign firefighters to jobs at strategic locations to facilitate rescue of persons and maximize application of extinguishing agents. Provide emergency medical services as required and perform light to heavy rescue functions at emergencies. Assess nature and extent of fire, condition of building, danger to adjacent buildings, and water supply status to determine crew or company requirements. Instruct and drill fire department personnel in assigned duties, including firefighting, medical care, hazardous materials response, fire prevention, and related subjects. Evaluate the performance of assigned firefighting personnel. Direct the training of firefighters, assigning of instructors to training classes, and providing of supervisors with reports on training progress and status. Prepare activity reports listing fire call locations, actions taken, fire types and probable causes, damage estimates, and situation dispositions. Maintain required maps and records. Attend in-service training classes to remain current in knowledge of codes, laws, ordinances, and regulations. Evaluate fire station procedures to ensure efficiency and enforcement of departmental regulations. Direct firefighters in station maintenance duties and participate in these duties. Compile and maintain equipment and personnel records, including accident reports. Direct investigation of cases of suspected arson, hazards, and false alarms and submit reports outlining findings. Recommend personnel actions related to disciplinary procedures, performance, leaves of absence, and grievances. Supervise and participate in the inspection of properties to ensure that they are in compliance with applicable fire codes, ordinances, laws, regulations, and standards. Write and submit proposals for repair, modification, or replacement of firefighting equipment. Coordinate the distribution of fire prevention promotional materials. Identify corrective actions needed to bring properties into compliance with applicable fire codes and ordinances and conduct follow-up inspections to see if corrective actions have been taken. Participate in creating fire safety guidelines and evacuation schemes for non-residential buildings.

Personality Type: Enterprising. These occupations frequently involve starting up and carrying out projects and can involve leading people and making many decisions. They sometimes require risk taking and often deal with business.

GOE—Interest Area/Cluster: 12. Law and Public Safety. **Work Group:** 12.01. Managerial Work in Law and Public Safety. **Other Jobs in This Work Group:** Emergency Management Specialists; First-Line Supervisors/Managers of Correctional Officers; First-Line Supervisors/Managers of Fire Fighting and Prevention Workers; First-Line Supervisors/Managers of Police and Detectives; Forest Fire Fighting and Prevention Supervisors.

Skills—Equipment Maintenance: Performing routine maintenance and determining when and what kind of maintenance is needed. **Management of Personnel Resources:** Motivating, developing, and directing people as they work; identifying the best people for the job. **Service Orientation:** Actively looking for ways to help people. **Operation Monitoring:** Watching gauges, dials, or other indicators to make sure a machine is working properly. **Management of Material Resources:** Obtaining and seeing to the appropriate use of equipment, facilities, and materials needed to do certain work. **Coordination:** Adjusting actions in relation to others' actions. **Operation and Control:** Controlling operations of equipment or systems. **Equipment Selection:** Determining the kind of tools and equipment needed to do a job.

Education and Training Programs: Fire Protection and Safety Technology/Technician Training; Fire Services Administration. **Related Knowledge/Courses—Public Safety and Security:** Weaponry; public safety; security operations, rules, regulations, precautions, and prevention; and the protection of people, data, and property. **Building**

and Construction: Materials, methods, and the appropriate tools to construct objects, structures, and buildings. **Medicine and Dentistry:** The information and techniques needed to diagnose and treat injuries, diseases, and deformities. This includes symptoms, treatment alternatives, drug properties and interactions, and preventive healthcare measures. **Education and Training:** Instructional methods and training techniques, including curriculum design principles, learning theory, group and individual teaching techniques, design of individual development plans, and test design principles. **Mechanical Devices:** Machines and tools, including their designs, uses, benefits, repair, and maintenance. **Therapy and Counseling:** Information and techniques needed to rehabilitate physical and mental ailments and to provide career guidance, including alternative treatments, rehabilitation equipment and its proper use, and methods to evaluate treatment effects.

Work Environment: More often outdoors than indoors; noisy; contaminants; hazardous equipment; using hands on objects, tools, or controls.

Nuclear Equipment Operation Technicians

* Education/Training Required: Associate degree
* Annual Earnings: $66,140
* Beginning Wage: $40,520
* Earnings Growth Potential: Medium
* Growth: 6.7%
* Annual Job Openings: 1,021
* Self-Employed: 0.0%
* Part-Time: 3.9%

The job openings listed here are shared with Nuclear Monitoring Technicians.

Operate equipment used for the release, control, and utilization of nuclear energy to assist scientists in laboratory and production activities. Follow policies and procedures for radiation workers to ensure personnel safety. Modify, devise, and maintain equipment used in operations. Set control panel switches, according to standard procedures, to route electric power from sources and direct particle beams through injector units. Submit computations to supervisors for review. Calculate equipment operating factors, such as radiation times, dosages, temperatures, gamma intensities, and pressures, using standard formulas and conversion tables. Perform testing, maintenance, repair, and upgrading of accelerator systems. Warn maintenance workers of radiation hazards and direct workers to vacate hazardous areas. Monitor instruments, gauges, and recording devices in control rooms during operation of equipment under direction of nuclear experimenters. Write summaries of activities and record experimental data, such as accelerator performance, systems status, particle beam specification, and beam conditions obtained.

Personality Type: Realistic. These occupations frequently involve work activities that include practical, hands-on problems and solutions. They often deal with plants; animals; and real-world materials such as wood, tools, and machinery. Many of the occupations require working outside and don't involve a lot of paperwork or working closely with others.

GOE—Interest Area/Cluster: 15. Scientific Research, Engineering, and Mathematics. **Work Group:** 15.05. Physical Science Laboratory Technology. **Other Jobs in This Work Group:** Chemical Technicians; Nuclear Technicians.

Skills—Operation Monitoring: Watching gauges, dials, or other indicators to make sure a machine is working properly. **Operation and Control:** Controlling operations of equipment or systems. **Science:** Using scientific methods to solve problems. **Mathematics:** Using mathematics to solve problems. **Equipment Maintenance:** Performing routine maintenance and determining when and what kind of maintenance is needed. **Quality Control Analysis:** Evaluating the quality or performance of products, services, or processes. **Troubleshooting:** Determining what is causing an operating error and deciding what to do about it. **Reading Comprehension:** Understanding written sentences and paragraphs in work-related documents.

Education and Training Programs: Industrial Radiologic Technology/Technician Training; Nuclear and Industrial Radiologic Technologies/Technician Training, Other; Nuclear Engineering Technology/Technician Training; Nuclear/Nuclear Power Technology/Technician Training; Radiation Protection/Health Physics Technician Training. **Related Knowledge/Courses—Physics:** Physical principles, laws, and applications, including air, water, material

dynamics, light, atomic principles, heat, electric theory, earth formations, and meteorological and related natural phenomena. **Chemistry:** The composition, structure, and properties of substances and of the chemical processes and transformations that they undergo. This includes uses of chemicals and their interactions, danger signs, production techniques, and disposal methods. **Engineering and Technology:** Equipment, tools, and mechanical devices and their uses to produce motion, light, power, technology, and other applications. **Public Safety and Security:** Weaponry; public safety; security operations, rules, regulations, precautions, and prevention; and the protection of people, data, and property. **Mechanical Devices:** Machines and tools, including their designs, uses, benefits, repair, and maintenance. **Telecommunications:** Transmission, broadcasting, switching, control, and operation of telecommunications systems.

Work Environment: Indoors; noisy; very hot or cold; radiation; hazardous conditions; hazardous equipment.

Nuclear Medicine Technologists

❋ Education/Training Required: Associate degree

❋ Annual Earnings: $64,670

❋ Beginning Wage: $47,370

❋ Earnings Growth Potential: Low

❋ Growth: 14.8%

❋ Annual Job Openings: 1,290

❋ Self-Employed: 1.0%

❋ Part-Time: 17.3%

Prepare, administer, and measure radioactive isotopes in therapeutic, diagnostic, and tracer studies, using a variety of radioisotope equipment. Prepare stock solutions of radioactive materials and calculate doses to be administered by radiologists. Subject patients to radiation. Execute blood volume, red cell survival, and fat absorption studies, following standard laboratory techniques. Detect and map radiopharmaceuticals in patients' bodies, using a camera to produce photographic or computer images. Administer radiopharmaceuticals or radiation intravenously to detect or treat diseases, using radioisotope equipment, under direction of a physician. Produce computer-generated or film images for interpretation by physicians. Calculate, measure, and record radiation dosages or radiopharmaceuticals received, used, and disposed, using computers and following physicians' prescriptions. Perform quality control checks on laboratory equipment and cameras. Maintain and calibrate radioisotope and laboratory equipment. Dispose of radioactive materials and store radiopharmaceuticals, following radiation safety procedures. Process cardiac function studies, using computers. Prepare stock radiopharmaceuticals, adhering to safety standards that minimize radiation exposure to workers and patients. Record and process results of procedures. Explain test procedures and safety precautions to patients and provide them with assistance during test procedures. Gather information on patients' illnesses and medical histories to guide choices of diagnostic procedures for therapies. Measure glandular activity, blood volume, red cell survival, and radioactivity of patient, using scanners, Geiger counters, scintillation counters, and other laboratory equipment. Train and supervise student or subordinate nuclear medicine technologists. Position radiation fields, radiation beams, and patients to allow for most effective treatment of patients' diseases, using computers. Add radioactive substances to biological specimens such as blood, urine, and feces to determine therapeutic drug or hormone levels. Develop treatment procedures for nuclear medicine treatment programs.

Personality Type: Investigative. These occupations frequently involve working with ideas and require an extensive amount of thinking. They can involve searching for facts and figuring out problems mentally.

GOE—Interest Area/Cluster: 08. Health Science. **Work Group:** 08.06. Medical Technology. **Other Jobs in This Work Group:** Biological Technicians; Cardiovascular Technologists and Technicians; Diagnostic Medical Sonographers; Medical and Clinical Laboratory Technicians; Medical and Clinical Laboratory Technologists; Medical Equipment Preparers; Medical Records and Health Information Technicians; Opticians, Dispensing; Orthotists and Prosthetists; Radiologic Technicians; Radiologic Technologists; Radiologic Technologists and Technicians.

Skills—Operation Monitoring: Watching gauges, dials, or other indicators to make sure a machine is working properly. **Equipment Maintenance:** Performing routine maintenance and determining when and what kind of maintenance is needed. **Quality Control Analysis:** Evaluating the quality or performance of products, services, or

processes. **Systems Analysis:** Determining how a system should work and how changes will affect outcomes. **Operation and Control:** Controlling operations of equipment or systems. **Systems Evaluation:** Looking at many indicators of system performance and taking into account their accuracy.

Education and Training Programs: Nuclear Medical Technology/Technologist Training; Radiation Protection/Health Physics Technician Training. **Related Knowledge/Courses—Medicine and Dentistry:** The information and techniques needed to diagnose and treat injuries, diseases, and deformities. This includes symptoms, treatment alternatives, drug properties and interactions, and preventive health-care measures. **Biology:** Plant and animal living tissue, cells, organisms, and entities, including their functions, interdependencies, and interactions with each other and the environment. **Chemistry:** The composition, structure, and properties of substances and of the chemical processes and transformations that they undergo. This includes uses of chemicals and their interactions, danger signs, production techniques, and disposal methods. **Physics:** Physical principles, laws, and applications, including air, water, material dynamics, light, atomic principles, heat, electric theory, earth formations, and meteorological and related natural phenomena. **Customer and Personal Service:** Principles and processes for providing customer and personal services, including needs assessment techniques, quality service standards, alternative delivery systems, and customer satisfaction evaluation techniques. **Therapy and Counseling:** Information and techniques needed to rehabilitate physical and mental ailments and to provide career guidance, including alternative treatments, rehabilitation equipment and its proper use, and methods to evaluate treatment effects.

Work Environment: Indoors; contaminants; radiation; disease or infections; standing; using hands on objects, tools, or controls.

Nuclear Monitoring Technicians

- ❈ Education/Training Required: Associate degree
- ❈ Annual Earnings: $66,140
- ❈ Beginning Wage: $40,520
- ❈ Earnings Growth Potential: Medium
- ❈ Growth: 6.7%
- ❈ Annual Job Openings: 1,021
- ❈ Self-Employed: 0.0%
- ❈ Part-Time: 3.9%

The job openings listed here are shared with Nuclear Equipment Operation Technicians.

Collect and test samples to monitor results of nuclear experiments and contamination of humans, facilities, and environment. Calculate safe radiation exposure times for personnel, using plant contamination readings and prescribed safe levels of radiation. Provide initial response to abnormal events and to alarms from radiation monitoring equipment. Monitor personnel in order to determine the amounts and intensities of radiation exposure. Inform supervisors when individual exposures or area radiation levels approach maximum permissible limits. Instruct personnel in radiation safety procedures and demonstrate use of protective clothing and equipment. Determine intensities and types of radiation in work areas, equipment, and materials, using radiation detectors and other instruments. Collect samples of air, water, gases, and solids to determine radioactivity levels of contamination. Set up equipment that automatically detects area radiation deviations and test detection equipment to ensure its accuracy. Determine or recommend radioactive decontamination procedures according to the size and nature of equipment and the degree of contamination. Decontaminate objects by cleaning with soap or solvents or by abrading with wire brushes, buffing wheels, or sandblasting machines. Place radioactive waste, such as sweepings and broken sample bottles, into containers for disposal. Calibrate and maintain chemical instrumentation sensing elements and sampling system equipment, using calibration instruments and hand tools. Place irradiated nuclear fuel materials in environmental chambers for testing and observe reactions through cell windows. Enter data into computers in order to record characteristics of nuclear events and locating coordinates of particles. Operate manipulators from outside cells to move specimens into and out of shielded containers, to remove specimens from cells, or to place specimens on benches or equipment workstations. Prepare reports describing contamination tests, material and equipment decontaminated, and methods used in decontamination processes. Confer with scientists directing projects to determine significant events to monitor during tests. Immerse samples in chemical compounds to prepare them for testing.

Personality Type: Realistic. These occupations frequently involve work activities that include practical, hands-on problems and solutions. They often deal with plants; animals; and real-world materials such as wood, tools, and machinery. Many of the occupations require working outside and don't involve a lot of paperwork or working closely with others.

GOE—Interest Area/Cluster: 07. Government and Public Administration. **Work Group:** 07.03. Regulations Enforcement. **Other Jobs in This Work Group:** Agricultural Inspectors; Aviation Inspectors; Compliance Officers, Except Agriculture, Construction, Health and Safety, and Transportation; Construction and Building Inspectors; Environmental Compliance Inspectors; Equal Opportunity Representatives and Officers; Financial Examiners; Fire Inspectors; Fish and Game Wardens; Forest Fire Inspectors and Prevention Specialists; Freight and Cargo Inspectors; Government Property Inspectors and Investigators; Immigration and Customs Inspectors; Licensing Examiners and Inspectors; Occupational Health and Safety Specialists; Occupational Health and Safety Technicians; Tax Examiners, Collectors, and Revenue Agents; Transportation Vehicle, Equipment, and Systems Inspectors, Except Aviation.

Skills—Science: Using scientific methods to solve problems. **Operation Monitoring:** Watching gauges, dials, or other indicators to make sure a machine is working properly. **Equipment Maintenance:** Performing routine maintenance and determining when and what kind of maintenance is needed. **Mathematics:** Using mathematics to solve problems. **Operation and Control:** Controlling operations of equipment or systems. **Equipment Selection:** Determining the kind of tools and equipment needed to do a job. **Technology Design:** Generating or adapting equipment and technology to serve user needs. **Systems Analysis:** Determining how a system should work and how changes will affect outcomes.

Education and Training Programs: Industrial Radiologic Technology/Technician Training; Nuclear and Industrial Radiologic Technologies/Technician Training, Other; Nuclear Engineering Technology/Technician Training; Nuclear/Nuclear Power Technology/Technician Training; Radiation Protection/Health Physics Technician Training. **Related Knowledge/Courses—Physics:** Physical principles, laws, and applications, including air, water, material dynamics, light, atomic principles, heat, electric theory, earth formations, and meteorological and related natural phenomena. **Chemistry:** The composition, structure, and properties of substances and of the chemical processes and transformations that they undergo. This includes uses of chemicals and their interactions, danger signs, production techniques, and disposal methods. **Public Safety and Security:** Weaponry; public safety; security operations, rules, regulations, precautions, and prevention; and the protection of people, data, and property. **Engineering and Technology:** Equipment, tools, and mechanical devices and their uses to produce motion, light, power, technology, and other applications. **Biology:** Plant and animal living tissue, cells, organisms, and entities, including their functions, interdependencies, and interactions with each other and the environment. **Design:** Design techniques, principles, tools, and instruments involved in the production and use of precision technical plans, blueprints, drawings, and models.

Work Environment: Indoors; noisy; very hot or cold; contaminants; radiation; hazardous conditions.

Nuclear Power Reactor Operators

- ❋ Education/Training Required: Long-term on-the-job training
- ❋ Annual Earnings: $70,410
- ❋ Beginning Wage: $53,730
- ❋ Earnings Growth Potential: Very low
- ❋ Growth: 10.6%
- ❋ Annual Job Openings: 233
- ❋ Self-Employed: 0.0%
- ❋ Part-Time: 0.6%

Control nuclear reactors. Adjust controls to position rod and to regulate flux level, reactor period, coolant temperature, and rate of power flow, following standard procedures. Respond to system or unit abnormalities, diagnosing the cause and recommending or taking corrective action. Monitor all systems for normal running conditions, performing activities such as checking gauges to assess output or assess the effects of generator loading on other equipment. Implement operational procedures such as those controlling startup and shutdown activities. Note malfunctions of equipment, instruments, or controls and report these conditions to supervisors. Monitor and operate boilers, turbines, wells, and auxiliary power plant equipment. Dispatch orders and instructions to personnel through radiotelephone or intercommunication systems to coordinate auxiliary equipment operation. Record operating data such as the results of surveillance tests. Participate in nuclear fuel element handling activities such as preparation, transfer, loading, and unloading. Conduct inspections and operations outside of control rooms as necessary. Direct reactor operators in emergency situations in accordance with emergency operating procedures. Authorize maintenance activities on units and changes in equipment and system operational status.

Personality Type: Realistic. These occupations frequently involve work activities that include practical, hands-on problems and solutions. They often deal with plants; animals; and real-world materials such as wood, tools, and machinery. Many of the occupations require working outside and don't involve a lot of paperwork or working closely with others.

GOE—Interest Area/Cluster: 13. Manufacturing. **Work Group:** 13.16. Utility Operation and Energy Distribution. **Other Jobs in This Work Group:** Chemical Plant and System Operators; Gas Compressor and Gas Pumping Station Operators; Gas Plant Operators; Petroleum Pump System Operators, Refinery Operators, and Gaugers; Power Distributors and Dispatchers; Power Plant Operators; Ship Engineers; Stationary Engineers and Boiler Operators; Water and Liquid Waste Treatment Plant and System Operators.

Skills—Operation Monitoring: Watching gauges, dials, or other indicators to make sure a machine is working properly. **Operation and Control:** Controlling operations of equipment or systems. **Science:** Using scientific methods to solve problems. **Systems Analysis:** Determining how a system should work and how changes will affect outcomes. **Troubleshooting:** Determining what is causing an operating error and deciding what to do about it. **Equipment Maintenance:** Performing routine maintenance and determining when and what kind of maintenance is needed. **Quality Control Analysis:** Evaluating the quality or performance of products, services, or processes. **Reading Comprehension:** Understanding written sentences and paragraphs in work-related documents.

Education and Training Program: Nuclear/Nuclear Power Technology/Technician Training. **Related Knowledge/Courses—Physics:** Physical principles, laws, and applications, including air, water, material dynamics, light, atomic principles, heat, electric theory, earth formations, and meteorological and related natural phenomena. **Engineering and Technology:** Equipment, tools, and mechanical devices and their uses to produce motion, light, power, technology, and other applications. **Chemistry:** The composition, structure, and properties of substances and of the chemical processes and transformations that they undergo. This includes uses of chemicals and their interactions, danger signs, production techniques, and disposal methods. **Mechanical Devices:** Machines and tools, including their designs, uses, benefits, repair, and maintenance. **Public Safety and Security:** Weaponry; public safety; security operations, rules, regulations, precautions, and prevention; and the protection of people, data, and property. **Design:** Design techniques, principles, tools, and instruments involved in the production and use of precision technical plans, blueprints, drawings, and models.

Work Environment: Indoors; noisy; radiation; hazardous conditions; hazardous equipment; using hands on objects, tools, or controls.

Nursing Aides, Orderlies, and Attendants

- ❀ Education/Training Required: Postsecondary vocational training
- ❀ Annual Earnings: $23,160
- ❀ Beginning Wage: $16,850
- ❀ Earnings Growth Potential: Low
- ❀ Growth: 18.2%
- ❀ Annual Job Openings: 321,036
- ❀ Self-Employed: 2.4%
- ❀ Part-Time: 24.0%

Provide basic patient care under direction of nursing staffs. Perform duties such as feeding, bathing, dressing, grooming, or moving patients or changing linens. Answer patients' call signals. Turn and reposition bedridden patients, alone or with assistance, to prevent bedsores. Observe patients' conditions, measuring and recording food and liquid intake and output and vital signs, and report changes to professionals. Feed patients who are unable to feed themselves. Provide patients with help walking, exercising, and moving in and out of bed. Provide patient care by supplying and emptying bed pans, applying dressings and supervising exercise routines. Bathe, groom, shave, dress, or drape patients to prepare them for surgery, treatment, or examination. Transport patients to treatment units, using a wheelchair or stretcher. Clean rooms and change linens. Collect specimens such as urine, feces, or sputum. Prepare, serve, and collect food trays. Deliver messages, documents, and specimens. Answer phones and direct visitors. Restrain patients if necessary. Set up equipment such as oxygen tents, portable x-ray machines, and overhead irrigation bottles. Explain medical instructions to patients and family members. Work as part of a medical team that examines and treats clinic outpatients. Maintain inventories by storing, preparing, sterilizing, and issuing supplies such as dressing packs and treatment trays. Administer medications and treatments such as catheterizations, suppositories, irrigations, enemas, massages, and douches as directed by a physician or nurse. Perform clerical duties such as processing documents and scheduling appointments.

Personality Type: Social. These occupations frequently involve working with, communicating with, and teaching people and often involve helping or providing service to others.

GOE—Interest Area/Cluster: 08. Health Science. **Work Group:** 08.08. Patient Care and Assistance. **Other Jobs in This Work Group:** Home Health Aides; Licensed Practical and Licensed Vocational Nurses; Psychiatric Aides; Psychiatric Technicians.

Skills: None met the criteria.

Education and Training Programs: Health Aide Training; Nurse/Nursing Assistant/Aide and Patient Care Assistant Training. **Related Knowledge/Courses—Medicine and Dentistry:** The information and techniques needed to diagnose and treat injuries, diseases, and deformities. This includes symptoms, treatment alternatives, drug properties and interactions, and preventive health-care measures. **Psychology:** Human behavior and performance, mental processes, psychological research methods, and the assessment and treatment of behavioral and affective disorders. **Therapy and Counseling:** Information and techniques needed to rehabilitate physical and mental ailments and to provide career guidance, including alternative treatments, rehabilitation equipment and its proper use, and methods to evaluate treatment effects. **Customer and Personal Service:** Principles and processes for providing customer and personal services, including needs assessment techniques, quality service standards, alternative delivery systems, and customer satisfaction evaluation techniques.

Work Environment: Disease or infections; standing; walking and running; using hands on objects, tools, or controls; bending or twisting the body; repetitive motions.

Occupational Therapist Assistants

* Education/Training Required: Associate degree
* Annual Earnings: $45,050
* Beginning Wage: $27,870
* Earnings Growth Potential: Medium
* Growth: 25.4%
* Annual Job Openings: 2,634
* Self-Employed: 3.5%
* Part-Time: 17.8%

Assist occupational therapists in providing occupational therapy treatments and procedures. May, in accordance with state laws, assist in development of treatment plans, carry out routine functions, direct activity programs, and document the progress of treatments. Generally requires formal training. Observe and record patients' progress, attitudes, and behavior and maintain this information in client records. Maintain and promote a positive attitude toward clients and their treatment programs. Monitor patients' performance in therapy activities, providing encouragement. Select therapy activities to fit patients' needs and capabilities. Instruct, or assist in instructing, patients and families in home programs, basic living skills, and the care and use of adaptive equipment. Evaluate the daily living skills and capacities of physically, developmentally, or emotionally disabled clients. Aid patients in dressing and grooming themselves. Implement, or assist occupational therapists with implementing, treatment plans designed to help clients function

independently. Report to supervisors, verbally or in writing, on patients' progress, attitudes, and behavior. Alter treatment programs to obtain better results if treatment is not having the intended effect. Work under the direction of occupational therapists to plan, implement, and administer educational, vocational, and recreational programs that restore and enhance performance in individuals with functional impairments. Design, fabricate, and repair assistive devices and make adaptive changes to equipment and environments. Assemble, clean, and maintain equipment and materials for patient use. Teach patients how to deal constructively with their emotions. Perform clerical duties such as scheduling appointments, collecting data, and documenting health insurance billings. Transport patients to and from the occupational therapy work area. Demonstrate therapy techniques such as manual and creative arts or games. Order any needed educational or treatment supplies. Assist educational specialists or clinical psychologists in administering situational or diagnostic tests to measure client's abilities or progress.

Personality Type: Social. These occupations frequently involve working with, communicating with, and teaching people and often involve helping or providing service to others.

GOE—Interest Area/Cluster: 08. Health Science. **Work Group:** 08.07. Medical Therapy. **Other Jobs in This Work Group:** Audiologists; Massage Therapists; Occupational Therapist Aides; Occupational Therapists; Physical Therapist Aides; Physical Therapist Assistants; Physical Therapists; Radiation Therapists; Recreational Therapists; Respiratory Therapists; Respiratory Therapy Technicians; Speech-Language Pathologists.

Skills—Social Perceptiveness: Being aware of others' reactions and understanding why they react the way they do. **Operations Analysis:** Analyzing needs and product requirements to create a design. **Equipment Selection:** Determining the kind of tools and equipment needed to do a job. **Service Orientation:** Actively looking for ways to help people. **Writing:** Communicating effectively with others in writing as indicated by the needs of the audience. **Persuasion:** Persuading others to approach things differently. **Monitoring:** Assessing how well one is doing when learning or doing something. **Time Management:** Managing one's own time and the time of others.

Education and Training Program: Occupational Therapist Assistant Training. **Related Knowledge/**

Courses—Therapy and Counseling: Information and techniques needed to rehabilitate physical and mental ailments and to provide career guidance, including alternative treatments, rehabilitation equipment and its proper use, and methods to evaluate treatment effects. **Psychology:** Human behavior and performance, mental processes, psychological research methods, and the assessment and treatment of behavioral and affective disorders. **Sociology and Anthropology:** Group behavior and dynamics; societal trends and influences; and cultures and their history, migrations, ethnicity, and origins. **Philosophy and Theology:** Different philosophical systems and religions, including their basic principles, values, ethics, ways of thinking, customs, and practices and their impact on human culture. **Medicine and Dentistry:** The information and techniques needed to diagnose and treat injuries, diseases, and deformities. This includes symptoms, treatment alternatives, drug properties and interactions, and preventive healthcare measures. **Biology:** Plant and animal living tissue, cells, organisms, and entities, including their functions, interdependencies, and interactions with each other and the environment.

Work Environment: Indoors; disease or infections; standing; walking and running; using hands on objects, tools, or controls; bending or twisting the body.

Office Clerks, General

- ❋ Education/Training Required: Short-term on-the-job training
- ❋ Annual Earnings: $24,460
- ❋ Beginning Wage: $15,490
- ❋ Earnings Growth Potential: Medium
- ❋ Growth: 12.6%
- ❋ Annual Job Openings: 765,803
- ❋ Self-Employed: 0.7%
- ❋ Part-Time: 26.0%

Perform duties too varied and diverse to be classified in any specific office clerical occupation requiring limited knowledge of office management systems and procedures. Clerical duties may be assigned in accordance with the office procedures of individual establishments and may include a combination of answering telephones, bookkeeping, typing or word processing, stenography, office machine operation, and filing. Collect, count, and disburse money; do basic bookkeeping; and complete banking transactions. Communicate with customers, employees, and other individuals to answer questions, disseminate or explain information, take orders, and address complaints. Answer telephones, direct calls, and take messages. Compile, copy, sort, and file records of office activities, business transactions, and other activities. Complete and mail bills, contracts, policies, invoices, or checks. Operate office machines such as photocopiers and scanners, facsimile machines, voice mail systems, and personal computers. Compute, record, and proofread data and other information, such as records or reports. Maintain and update filing, inventory, mailing, and database systems, either manually or using a computer. Open, sort, and route incoming mail; answer correspondence; and prepare outgoing mail. Review files, records, and other documents to obtain information to respond to requests. Deliver messages and run errands. Inventory and order materials, supplies, and services. Complete work schedules, manage calendars, and arrange appointments. Process and prepare documents such as business or government forms and expense reports. Monitor and direct the work of lower-level clerks. Type, format, proofread, and edit correspondence and other documents from notes or dictating machines, using computers or typewriters. Count, weigh, measure, or organize materials. Train other staff members to perform work activities, such as using computer applications. Prepare meeting agendas, attend meetings, and record and transcribe minutes. Troubleshoot problems involving office equipment, such as computer hardware and software. Make travel arrangements for office personnel.

Personality Type: Conventional. These occupations frequently involve following set procedures and routines and can include working with data and details more than with ideas. Usually there is a clear line of authority to follow.

GOE—Interest Area/Cluster: 04. Business and Administration. **Work Group:** 04.07. Records and Materials Processing. **Other Jobs in This Work Group:** Correspondence Clerks; File Clerks; Human Resources Assistants, Except Payroll and Timekeeping; Marking Clerks; Meter Readers, Utilities; Order Fillers, Wholesale and Retail Sales; Postal Service Clerks; Postal Service Mail Sorters, Processors, and Processing Machine Operators; Procurement Clerks; Production, Planning, and Expediting Clerks; Shipping, Receiving, and Traffic Clerks; Stock Clerks and Order Fillers; Stock Clerks, Sales Floor; Stock Clerks—Stockroom,

Warehouse, or Storage Yard; Weighers, Measurers, Checkers, and Samplers, Recordkeeping.

Skills: None met the criteria.

Education and Training Program: General Office Occupations and Clerical Services. **Related Knowledge/ Courses—Clerical Studies:** Administrative and clerical procedures and systems such as word-processing systems, filing and records management systems, stenography and transcription, forms, design principles, and other office procedures and terminology. **Economics and Accounting:** Economic and accounting principles and practices, the financial markets, banking, and the analysis and reporting of financial data. **Customer and Personal Service:** Principles and processes for providing customer and personal services, including needs assessment techniques, quality service standards, alternative delivery systems, and customer satisfaction evaluation techniques. **Personnel and Human Resources:** Principles and procedures for personnel recruitment; selection; training; compensation and benefits; labor relations and negotiation; and personnel information systems. **Mathematics:** Numbers and their operations and interrelationships, including arithmetic, algebra, geometry, calculus, and statistics and their applications. **Computers and Electronics:** Electric circuit boards, processors, chips, and computer hardware and software, including applications and programming.

Work Environment: Indoors; sitting; using hands on objects, tools, or controls.

Operating Engineers and Other Construction Equipment Operators

- ❋ Education/Training Required: Moderate-term on-the-job training
- ❋ Annual Earnings: $38,130
- ❋ Beginning Wage: $24,840
- ❋ Earnings Growth Potential: Low
- ❋ Growth: 8.4%
- ❋ Annual Job Openings: 55,468
- ❋ Self-Employed: 5.7%
- ❋ Part-Time: 2.1%

Operate one or several types of power construction equipment, such as motor graders, bulldozers, scrapers, compressors, pumps, derricks, shovels, tractors, or front-end loaders, to excavate, move, and grade earth; erect structures; or pour concrete or other hard-surface pavement. May repair and maintain equipment in addition to other duties. Learn and follow safety regulations. Take actions to avoid potential hazards and obstructions such as utility lines, other equipment, other workers, and falling objects. Adjust handwheels and depress pedals to control attachments such as blades, buckets, scrapers, and swing booms. Start engines; move throttles, switches, and levers; and depress pedals to operate machines such as bulldozers, trench excavators, road graders, and backhoes. Locate underground services, such as pipes and wires, prior to beginning work. Monitor operations to ensure that health and safety standards are met. Align machines, cutterheads, or depth gauge makers with reference stakes and guidelines or ground or position equipment by following hand signals of other workers. Load and move dirt, rocks, equipment, and materials, using trucks, crawler tractors, power cranes, shovels, graders, and related equipment. Drive and maneuver equipment equipped with blades in successive passes over working areas to remove topsoil, vegetation, and rocks and to distribute and level earth or terrain. Coordinate machine actions with other activities, positioning or moving loads in response to hand or audio signals from crew members. Operate tractors and bulldozers to perform such tasks as clearing land, mixing sludge, trimming backfills, and building roadways and parking lots. Repair and maintain equipment, making emergency adjustments or assisting with major repairs as necessary. Check fuel supplies at sites to ensure adequate availability. Connect hydraulic hoses, belts, mechanical linkages, or power takeoff shafts to tractors. Operate loaders to pull out stumps, rip asphalt or concrete, rough-grade properties, bury refuse, or perform general cleanup. Select and fasten bulldozer blades or other attachments to tractors, using hitches. Test atmosphere for adequate oxygen and explosive conditions when working in confined spaces. Operate compactors, scrapers, and rollers to level, compact, and cover refuse at disposal grounds. Talk to clients and study instructions, plans, and diagrams to establish work requirements.

Personality Type: Realistic. These occupations frequently involve work activities that include practical, hands-on problems and solutions. They often deal with plants; animals; and real-world materials such as wood, tools, and machinery. Many of the occupations require working outside and don't involve a lot of paperwork or working closely with others.

GOE—Interest Area/Cluster: 02. Architecture and Construction. **Work Group:** 02.04. Construction Crafts. **Other Jobs in This Work Group:** Boilermakers; Brickmasons and Blockmasons; Carpet Installers; Cement Masons and Concrete Finishers; Commercial Divers; Construction Carpenters; Crane and Tower Operators; Drywall and Ceiling Tile Installers; Electricians; Fence Erectors; Floor Layers, Except Carpet, Wood, and Hard Tiles; Floor Sanders and Finishers; Glaziers; Hazardous Materials Removal Workers; Insulation Workers, Floor, Ceiling, and Wall; Insulation Workers, Mechanical; Manufactured Building and Mobile Home Installers; Painters, Construction and Maintenance; Paperhangers; Paving, Surfacing, and Tamping Equipment Operators; Pile-Driver Operators; Pipe Fitters and Steamfitters; Pipelayers; Plasterers and Stucco Masons; Plumbers; Plumbers, Pipefitters, and Steamfitters; Rail-Track Laying and Maintenance Equipment Operators; Refractory Materials Repairers, Except Brickmasons; Reinforcing Iron and Rebar Workers; Riggers; Roofers; Rough Carpenters; Security and Fire Alarm Systems Installers; Segmental Pavers; Sheet Metal Workers; Stone Cutters and Carvers, Manufacturing; Stonemasons; Structural Iron and Steel Workers; Tapers; Terrazzo Workers and Finishers; Tile and Marble Setters.

Skills—Equipment Maintenance: Performing routine maintenance and determining when and what kind of maintenance is needed. **Installation:** Installing equipment, machines, wiring, or programs to meet specifications. **Operation and Control:** Controlling operations of equipment or systems. **Operation Monitoring:** Watching gauges, dials, or other indicators to make sure a machine is working properly. **Repairing:** Repairing machines or systems, using the needed tools. **Equipment Selection:** Determining the kind of tools and equipment needed to do a job. **Management of Financial Resources:** Determining how money will be spent to get the work done and accounting for these expenditures. **Management of Material Resources:** Obtaining and seeing to the appropriate use of equipment, facilities, and materials needed to do certain work.

Education and Training Program: Mobile Crane Operation/Operator Training. **Related Knowledge/Courses— Building and Construction:** Materials, methods, and the appropriate tools to construct objects, structures, and buildings. **Mechanical Devices:** Machines and tools, including their designs, uses, benefits, repair, and maintenance.

Engineering and Technology: Equipment, tools, and mechanical devices and their uses to produce motion, light, power, technology, and other applications. **Design:** Design techniques, principles, tools, and instruments involved in the production and use of precision technical plans, blueprints, drawings, and models. **Production and Processing:** Inputs, outputs, raw materials, waste, quality control, costs, and techniques for maximizing the manufacture and distribution of goods. **Public Safety and Security:** Weaponry; public safety; security operations, rules, regulations, precautions, and prevention; and the protection of people, data, and property.

Work Environment: Outdoors; noisy; very hot or cold; contaminants; whole-body vibration; using hands on objects, tools, or controls.

Painters, Construction and Maintenance

- Education/Training Required: Moderate-term on-the-job training
- Annual Earnings: $32,080
- Beginning Wage: $21,720
- Earnings Growth Potential: Low
- Growth: 11.8%
- Annual Job Openings: 101,140
- Self-Employed: 42.2%
- Part-Time: 9.8%

Paint walls, equipment, buildings, bridges, and other structural surfaces with brushes, rollers, and spray guns. May remove old paint to prepare surfaces before painting. May mix colors or oils to obtain desired color or consistencies. Cover surfaces with dropcloths or masking tape and paper to protect surfaces during painting. Fill cracks, holes, and joints with caulk, putty, plaster, or other fillers, using caulking guns or putty knives. Apply primers or sealers to prepare new surfaces such as bare wood or metal for finish coats. Apply paint, stain, varnish, enamel, and other finishes to equipment, buildings, bridges, and/or other structures, using brushes, spray guns, or rollers. Calculate amounts of required materials and estimate costs, based on surface measurements and/or work orders. Read work orders or receive instructions from supervisors or homeowners in order to determine work requirements.

Erect scaffolding and swing gates, or set up ladders, to work above ground level. Remove fixtures such as pictures, door knobs, lamps, and electric switch covers prior to painting. Wash and treat surfaces with oil, turpentine, mildew remover, or other preparations, and sand rough spots to ensure that finishes will adhere properly. Mix and match colors of paint, stain, or varnish with oil and thinning and drying additives in order to obtain desired colors and consistencies. Remove old finishes by stripping, sanding, wire brushing, burning, or using water and/or abrasive blasting. Select and purchase tools and finishes for surfaces to be covered, considering durability, ease of handling, methods of application, and customers' wishes. Smooth surfaces, using sandpaper, scrapers, brushes, steel wool, and/or sanding machines. Polish final coats to specified finishes. Use special finishing techniques such as sponging, ragging, layering, or faux finishing. Waterproof buildings, using waterproofers and caulking. Cut stencils, and brush and spray lettering and decorations on surfaces. Spray or brush hot plastics or pitch onto surfaces. Bake finishes on painted and enameled articles, using baking ovens.

Personality Type: Realistic. These occupations frequently involve work activities that include practical, hands-on problems and solutions. They often deal with plants; animals; and real-world materials such as wood, tools, and machinery. Many of the occupations require working outside and don't involve a lot of paperwork or working closely with others.

GOE—Interest Area/Cluster: 02. Architecture and Construction. **Work Group:** 02.04. Construction Crafts. **Other Jobs in This Work Group:** Boilermakers; Brickmasons and Blockmasons; Carpet Installers; Cement Masons and Concrete Finishers; Commercial Divers; Construction Carpenters; Crane and Tower Operators; Drywall and Ceiling Tile Installers; Electricians; Fence Erectors; Floor Layers, Except Carpet, Wood, and Hard Tiles; Floor Sanders and Finishers; Glaziers; Hazardous Materials Removal Workers; Insulation Workers, Floor, Ceiling, and Wall; Insulation Workers, Mechanical; Manufactured Building and Mobile Home Installers; Operating Engineers and Other Construction Equipment Operators; Paperhangers; Paving, Surfacing, and Tamping Equipment Operators; Pile-Driver Operators; Pipe Fitters and Steamfitters; Pipelayers; Plasterers and Stucco Masons; Plumbers; Plumbers, Pipefitters, and Steamfitters; Rail-Track Laying and Maintenance Equipment Operators; Refractory Materials Repairers, Except Brickmasons; Reinforcing Iron and Rebar Workers; Riggers; Roofers; Rough Carpenters; Security and Fire Alarm Systems Installers; Segmental Pavers; Sheet Metal Workers; Stone Cutters and Carvers, Manufacturing; Stonemasons; Structural Iron and Steel Workers; Tapers; Terrazzo Workers and Finishers; Tile and Marble Setters.

Skills—Equipment Maintenance: Performing routine maintenance and determining when and what kind of maintenance is needed. **Management of Material Resources:** Obtaining and seeing to the appropriate use of equipment, facilities, and materials needed to do certain work. **Equipment Selection:** Determining the kind of tools and equipment needed to do a job. **Repairing:** Repairing machines or systems, using the needed tools. **Management of Personnel Resources:** Motivating, developing, and directing people as they work; identifying the best people for the job. **Monitoring:** Assessing how well one is doing when learning or doing something. **Coordination:** Adjusting actions in relation to others' actions.

Education and Training Program: Painting/Painter and Wall Coverer Training. **Related Knowledge/Courses— Building and Construction:** Materials, methods, and the appropriate tools to construct objects, structures, and buildings. **Design:** Design techniques, principles, tools, and instruments involved in the production and use of precision technical plans, blueprints, drawings, and models. **Transportation:** Principles and methods for moving people or goods by air, rail, sea, or road, including their relative costs, advantages, and limitations. **Customer and Personal Service:** Principles and processes for providing customer and personal services, including needs assessment techniques, quality service standards, alternative delivery systems, and customer satisfaction evaluation techniques. **Production and Processing:** Inputs, outputs, raw materials, waste, quality control, costs, and techniques for maximizing the manufacture and distribution of goods. **Administration and Management:** Principles and processes involved in business and organizational planning, coordination, and execution. This includes strategic planning, resource allocation, manpower modeling, leadership techniques, and production methods.

Work Environment: Contaminants; standing; climbing ladders, scaffolds, or poles; using hands on objects, tools, or controls; bending or twisting the body; repetitive motions.

Painters, Transportation Equipment

* Education/Training Required: Moderate-term on-the-job training
* Annual Earnings: $36,000
* Beginning Wage: $22,560
* Earnings Growth Potential: Medium
* Growth: 8.4%
* Annual Job Openings: 3,268
* Self-Employed: 3.8%
* Part-Time: 3.7%

Operate or tend painting machines to paint surfaces of transportation equipment, such as automobiles, buses, trucks, trains, boats, and airplanes. Dispose of hazardous waste in an appropriate manner. Select paint according to company requirements and match colors of paint following specified color charts. Mix paints to match color specifications or vehicles' original colors; then stir and thin the paints, using spatulas or power mixing equipment. Remove grease, dirt, paint, and rust from vehicle surfaces in preparation for paint application, using abrasives, solvents, brushes, blowtorches, washing tanks, or sandblasters. Pour paint into spray guns and adjust nozzles and paint mixes to get the proper paint flow and coating thickness. Monitor painting operations to identify flaws such as blisters and streaks so that their causes can be corrected. Sand vehicle surfaces between coats of paint or primer to remove flaws and enhance adhesion for subsequent coats. Disassemble, clean, and reassemble sprayers and power equipment, using solvents, wire brushes, and cloths for cleaning duties. Remove accessories from vehicles, such as chrome or mirrors, and mask other surfaces with tape or paper to protect them from paint. Spray prepared surfaces with specified amounts of primers and decorative or finish coatings. Allow the sprayed product to dry and then touch up any spots that may have been missed. Apply rust-resistant undercoats and caulk and seal seams. Select the correct spray gun system for the material being applied. Apply primer over any repairs made to vehicle surfaces. Adjust controls on infrared ovens, heat lamps, portable ventilators, and exhaust units to speed the drying of vehicles between coats. Fill small dents and scratches with body fillers and smooth surfaces to prepare vehicles for painting. Apply designs, lettering, or other identifying or decorative items to finished products, using paint brushes or paint sprayers.

Paint by hand areas that cannot be reached with a spray gun or those that need retouching, using brushes. Sand the final finish and apply sealer once a vehicle has dried properly. Buff and wax the finished paintwork. Lay out logos, symbols, or designs on painted surfaces according to blueprint specifications, using measuring instruments, stencils, and patterns.

Personality Type: Realistic. These occupations frequently involve work activities that include practical, hands-on problems and solutions. They often deal with plants; animals; and real-world materials such as wood, tools, and machinery. Many of the occupations require working outside and don't involve a lot of paperwork or working closely with others.

GOE—Interest Area/Cluster: 13. Manufacturing. **Work Group:** 13.09. Hands-On Work, Assorted Materials. **Other Jobs in This Work Group:** Coil Winders, Tapers, and Finishers; Cutters and Trimmers, Hand; Fabric and Apparel Patternmakers; Glass Blowers, Molders, Benders, and Finishers; Grinding and Polishing Workers, Hand; Molding and Casting Workers; Painting, Coating, and Decorating Workers; Sewers, Hand.

Skills—Repairing: Repairing machines or systems, using the needed tools. **Equipment Maintenance:** Performing routine maintenance and determining when and what kind of maintenance is needed. **Monitoring:** Assessing how well one is doing when learning or doing something. **Operation and Control:** Controlling operations of equipment or systems. **Technology Design:** Generating or adapting equipment and technology to serve user needs. **Science:** Using scientific methods to solve problems. **Equipment Selection:** Determining the kind of tools and equipment needed to do a job. **Quality Control Analysis:** Evaluating the quality or performance of products, services, or processes.

Education and Training Program: Autobody/Collision and Repair Technology/Technician Training. **Related Knowledge/Courses—Chemistry:** The composition, structure, and properties of substances and of the chemical processes and transformations that they undergo. This includes uses of chemicals and their interactions, danger signs, production techniques, and disposal methods. **Production and Processing:** Inputs, outputs, raw materials, waste, quality control, costs, and techniques for maximizing the manufacture and distribution of goods. **Mechanical**

Devices: Machines and tools, including their designs, uses, benefits, repair, and maintenance.

Work Environment: Noisy; contaminants; hazardous conditions; standing; using hands on objects, tools, or controls; repetitive motions.

Paralegals and Legal Assistants

* Education/Training Required: Associate degree
* Annual Earnings: $44,990
* Beginning Wage: $28,360
* Earnings Growth Potential: Medium
* Growth: 22.2%
* Annual Job Openings: 22,756
* Self-Employed: 2.2%
* Part-Time: 11.0%

Assist lawyers by researching legal precedent, investigating facts, or preparing legal documents. Conduct research to support a legal proceeding, to formulate a defense, or to initiate legal action. Prepare legal documents, including briefs, pleadings, appeals, wills, contracts, and real estate closing statements. Prepare affidavits or other documents, maintain document file, and file pleadings with court clerk. Gather and analyze research data, such as statutes; decisions; and legal articles, codes, and documents. Investigate facts and law of cases to determine causes of action and to prepare cases. Call upon witnesses to testify at hearing. Direct and coordinate law office activity, including delivery of subpoenas. Arbitrate disputes between parties and assist in real estate closing process. Keep and monitor legal volumes to ensure that law library is up to date. Appraise and inventory real and personal property for estate planning.

Personality Type: Conventional. These occupations frequently involve following set procedures and routines and can include working with data and details more than with ideas. Usually there is a clear line of authority to follow.

GOE—Interest Area/Cluster: 12. Law and Public Safety. **Work Group:** 12.03. Legal Support. **Other Jobs in This Work Group:** Law Clerks; Title Examiners, Abstractors, and Searchers.

Skills—Writing: Communicating effectively with others in writing as indicated by the needs of the audience. **Active Listening:** Listening to what other people are saying and asking questions as appropriate. **Speaking:** Talking to others to effectively convey information. **Time Management:** Managing one's own time and the time of others. **Reading Comprehension:** Understanding written sentences and paragraphs in work-related documents. **Monitoring:** Assessing how well one is doing when learning or doing something.

Education and Training Program: Legal Assistant/Paralegal Training. **Related Knowledge/Courses—Clerical Studies:** Administrative and clerical procedures and systems such as word-processing systems, filing and records management systems, stenography and transcription, forms, design principles, and other office procedures and terminology. **Law and Government:** Laws, legal codes, court procedures, precedents, government regulations, executive orders, agency rules, and the democratic political process. **Computers and Electronics:** Electric circuit boards, processors, chips, and computer hardware and software, including applications and programming. **Personnel and Human Resources:** Principles and procedures for personnel recruitment; selection; training; compensation and benefits; labor relations and negotiation; and personnel information systems. **English Language:** The structure and content of the English language, including the meaning and spelling of words, rules of composition, and grammar. **Customer and Personal Service:** Principles and processes for providing customer and personal services, including needs assessment techniques, quality service standards, alternative delivery systems, and customer satisfaction evaluation techniques.

Work Environment: Indoors; sitting; repetitive motions.

P

Parts Salespersons

* Education/Training Required: Moderate-term on-the-job training
* Annual Earnings: $28,130
* Beginning Wage: $17,310
* Earnings Growth Potential: Medium
* Growth: –2.2%
* Annual Job Openings: 52,414
* Self-Employed: 1.6%
* Part-Time: 8.3%

Sell spare and replacement parts and equipment in repair shop or parts store. Read catalogs, microfiche viewers, or computer displays to determine replacement part stock numbers and prices. Determine replacement parts required according to inspections of old parts, customer requests, or customers' descriptions of malfunctions. Receive and fill telephone orders for parts. Fill customer orders from stock. Prepare sales slips or sales contracts. Receive payment or obtain credit authorization. Take inventory of stock. Advise customers on substitution or modification of parts when identical replacements are not available. Examine returned parts for defects and exchange defective parts or refund money. Mark and store parts in stockrooms according to prearranged systems. Discuss use and features of various parts, based on knowledge of machines or equipment. Demonstrate equipment to customers and explain functioning of equipment. Place new merchandise on display. Measure parts, using precision measuring instruments, to determine whether similar parts may be machined to required sizes. Repair parts or equipment.

Personality Type: Enterprising. These occupations frequently involve starting up and carrying out projects and can involve leading people and making many decisions. They sometimes require risk taking and often deal with business.

GOE—Interest Area/Cluster: 14. Retail and Wholesale Sales and Service. **Work Group:** 14.03. General Sales. **Other Jobs in This Work Group:** Real Estate Brokers; Real Estate Sales Agents; Retail Salespersons; Sales Representatives, Wholesale and Manufacturing, Except Technical and Scientific Products; Service Station Attendants.

Skills—Service Orientation: Actively looking for ways to help people. **Management of Personnel Resources:** Motivating, developing, and directing people as they work; identifying the best people for the job. **Negotiation:** Bringing others together and trying to reconcile differences. **Equipment Selection:** Determining the kind of tools and equipment needed to do a job. **Operations Analysis:** Analyzing needs and product requirements to create a design. **Management of Financial Resources:** Determining how money will be spent to get the work done and accounting for these expenditures. **Social Perceptiveness:** Being aware of others' reactions and understanding why they react the way they do. **Persuasion:** Persuading others to approach things differently.

Education and Training Program: Vehicle and Vehicle Parts and Accessories Marketing Operations. **Related Knowledge/Courses—Sales and Marketing:** Principles and methods involved in showing, promoting, and selling products or services. This includes marketing strategies and tactics, product demonstration and sales techniques, and sales control systems. **Customer and Personal Service:** Principles and processes for providing customer and personal services, including needs assessment techniques, quality service standards, alternative delivery systems, and customer satisfaction evaluation techniques. **Mechanical Devices:** Machines and tools, including their designs, uses, benefits, repair, and maintenance. **Computers and Electronics:** Electric circuit boards, processors, chips, and computer hardware and software, including applications and programming. **Production and Processing:** Inputs, outputs, raw materials, waste, quality control, costs, and techniques for maximizing the manufacture and distribution of goods. **Mathematics:** Numbers and their operations and interrelationships, including arithmetic, algebra, geometry, calculus, and statistics and their applications.

Work Environment: Indoors; noisy; contaminants; standing; repetitive motions.

Payroll and Timekeeping Clerks

* Education/Training Required: Moderate-term on-the-job training
* Annual Earnings: $33,810
* Beginning Wage: $22,450
* Earnings Growth Potential: Low
* Growth: 3.1%
* Annual Job Openings: 18,544
* Self-Employed: 1.2%
* Part-Time: 15.9%

Compile and post employee time and payroll data. May compute employees' time worked, production, and commission. May compute and post wages and deductions. May prepare paychecks. Process and issue employee paychecks and statements of earnings and deductions. Compute wages and deductions and enter data into computers. Compile employee time, production, and payroll data from time sheets and other records. Review time sheets, work charts, wage computation, and other information to detect and reconcile payroll discrepancies. Verify attendance, hours worked, and pay adjustments and post information onto designated records. Record employee information, such as exemptions, transfers, and resignations, to maintain and update payroll records. Keep informed about changes in tax and deduction laws that apply to the payroll process. Issue and record adjustments to pay related to previous errors or retroactive increases. Provide information to employees and managers on payroll matters, tax issues, benefit plans, and collective agreement provisions. Complete time sheets showing employees' arrival and departure times. Post relevant work hours to client files to bill clients properly. Distribute and collect timecards each pay period. Complete, verify, and process forms and documentation for administration of benefits such as pension plans and unemployment and medical insurance. Prepare and balance period-end reports and reconcile issued payrolls to bank statements. Compile statistical reports, statements, and summaries related to pay and benefits accounts and submit them to appropriate departments. Coordinate special programs, such as United Way campaigns, that involve payroll deductions.

Personality Type: Conventional. These occupations frequently involve following set procedures and routines and can include working with data and details more than with ideas. Usually there is a clear line of authority to follow.

GOE—Interest Area/Cluster: 04. Business and Administration. **Work Group:** 04.06. Mathematical Clerical Support. **Other Jobs in This Work Group:** Billing and Posting Clerks and Machine Operators; Billing, Cost, and Rate Clerks; Bookkeeping, Accounting, and Auditing Clerks; Brokerage Clerks; Statement Clerks; Tax Preparers.

Skills—Mathematics: Using mathematics to solve problems. **Time Management:** Managing one's own time and the time of others. **Writing:** Communicating effectively with others in writing as indicated by the needs of the audience. **Active Listening:** Listening to what other people are saying and asking questions as appropriate. **Judgment and Decision Making:** Weighing the relative costs and benefits of a potential action. **Speaking:** Talking to others to effectively convey information. **Learning Strategies:** Using multiple approaches when learning or teaching new things. **Reading Comprehension:** Understanding written sentences and paragraphs in work-related documents.

Education and Training Program: Accounting Technology/Technician and Bookkeeping. **Related Knowledge/Courses—Clerical Studies:** Administrative and clerical procedures and systems such as word-processing systems, filing and records management systems, stenography and transcription, forms, design principles, and other office procedures and terminology. **Economics and Accounting:** Economic and accounting principles and practices, the financial markets, banking, and the analysis and reporting of financial data. **Mathematics:** Numbers and their operations and interrelationships, including arithmetic, algebra, geometry, calculus, and statistics and their applications. **Administration and Management:** Principles and processes involved in business and organizational planning, coordination, and execution. This includes strategic planning, resource allocation, manpower modeling, leadership techniques, and production methods. **Personnel and Human Resources:** Principles and procedures for personnel recruitment; selection; training; compensation and benefits; labor relations and negotiation; and personnel information systems. **Computers and Electronics:** Electric circuit boards, processors, chips, and computer hardware and software, including applications and programming.

Work Environment: Indoors; noisy; sitting; repetitive motions.

Pest Control Workers

- ✸ Education/Training Required: Moderate-term on-the-job training
- ✸ Annual Earnings: $29,030
- ✸ Beginning Wage: $18,970
- ✸ Earnings Growth Potential: Low
- ✸ Growth: 15.5%
- ✸ Annual Job Openings: 6,006
- ✸ Self-Employed: 8.7%
- ✸ Part-Time: 4.4%

Spray or release chemical solutions or toxic gases and set traps to kill pests and vermin, such as mice, termites, and roaches, that infest buildings and surrounding areas. Record work activities performed. Inspect premises to identify infestation source and extent of damage to property, wall and roof porosity, and access to infested locations. Spray or dust chemical solutions, powders, or gases into rooms; onto clothing, furnishings, or wood; and over marshlands, ditches, and catch-basins. Clean work site after completion of job. Direct or assist other workers in treatment and extermination processes to eliminate and control rodents, insects, and weeds. Drive truck equipped with power spraying equipment. Measure area dimensions requiring treatment, using rule; calculate fumigant requirements; and estimate cost for service. Post warning signs and lock building doors to secure area to be fumigated. Cut or bore openings in building or surrounding concrete, access infested areas, insert nozzle, and inject pesticide to impregnate ground. Study preliminary reports and diagrams of infested area and determine treatment type required to eliminate and prevent recurrence of infestation. Dig up and burn or spray weeds with herbicides. Set mechanical traps and place poisonous paste or bait in sewers, burrows, and ditches. Clean and remove blockages from infested areas to facilitate spraying procedure and provide drainage, using broom, mop, shovel, and rake. Position and fasten edges of tarpaulins over building and tape vents to ensure airtight environment and check for leaks.

Personality Type: Realistic. These occupations frequently involve work activities that include practical, hands-on problems and solutions. They often deal with plants; animals; and real-world materials such as wood, tools, and machinery. Many of the occupations require working outside and don't involve a lot of paperwork or working closely with others.

GOE—Interest Area/Cluster: 01. Agriculture and Natural Resources. **Work Group:** 01.05. Nursery, Groundskeeping, and Pest Control. **Other Jobs in This Work Group:** Landscaping and Groundskeeping Workers; Nursery Workers; Pesticide Handlers, Sprayers, and Applicators, Vegetation; Tree Trimmers and Pruners.

Skills—Equipment Selection: Determining the kind of tools and equipment needed to do a job. **Persuasion:** Persuading others to approach things differently. **Service Orientation:** Actively looking for ways to help people. **Social Perceptiveness:** Being aware of others' reactions and understanding why they react the way they do. **Management of Material Resources:** Obtaining and seeing to the appropriate use of equipment, facilities, and materials needed to do certain work. **Active Learning:** Working with new material or information to grasp its implications. **Equipment Maintenance:** Performing routine maintenance and determining when and what kind of maintenance is needed. **Coordination:** Adjusting actions in relation to others' actions.

Education and Training Program: Agricultural/Farm Supplies Retailing and Wholesaling. **Related Knowledge/Courses—Sales and Marketing:** Principles and methods involved in showing, promoting, and selling products or services. This includes marketing strategies and tactics, product demonstration and sales techniques, and sales control systems. **Biology:** Plant and animal living tissue, cells, organisms, and entities, including their functions, interdependencies, and interactions with each other and the environment. **Chemistry:** The composition, structure, and properties of substances and of the chemical processes and transformations that they undergo. This includes uses of chemicals and their interactions, danger signs, production techniques, and disposal methods. **Customer and Personal Service:** Principles and processes for providing customer and personal services, including needs assessment techniques, quality service standards, alternative delivery systems, and customer satisfaction evaluation techniques. **Building and Construction:** Materials, methods, and the appropriate tools to construct objects, structures, and buildings. **Law and Government:** Laws, legal codes, court procedures, precedents, government regulations, executive orders, agency rules, and the democratic political process.

Work Environment: More often outdoors than indoors; very hot or cold; contaminants; hazardous conditions; using hands on objects, tools, or controls.

Pesticide Handlers, Sprayers, and Applicators, Vegetation

- ❀ Education/Training Required: Moderate-term on-the-job training
- ❀ Annual Earnings: $28,560
- ❀ Beginning Wage: $18,780
- ❀ Earnings Growth Potential: Low
- ❀ Growth: 14.0%
- ❀ Annual Job Openings: 7,443
- ❀ Self-Employed: 20.5%
- ❀ Part-Time: 14.6%

Mix or apply pesticides, herbicides, fungicides, or insecticides through sprays, dusts, vapors, soil incorporation, or chemical application on trees, shrubs, lawns, or botanical crops. Usually requires specific training and state or federal certification. Fill sprayer tanks with water and chemicals, according to formulas. Mix pesticides, herbicides, and fungicides for application to trees, shrubs, lawns, or botanical crops. Cover areas to specified depths with pesticides, applying knowledge of weather conditions, droplet sizes, elevation-to-distance ratios, and obstructions. Lift, push, and swing nozzles, hoses, and tubes in order to direct spray over designated areas. Start motors and engage machinery such as sprayer agitators and pumps or portable spray equipment. Connect hoses and nozzles selected according to terrain, distribution pattern requirements, types of infestations, and velocities. Clean and service machinery to ensure operating efficiency, using water, gasoline, lubricants, and/or hand tools. Provide driving instructions to truck drivers to ensure complete coverage of designated areas, using hand and horn signals. Plant grass with seed spreaders, and operate straw blowers to cover seeded areas with mixtures of asphalt and straw.

Personality Type: Realistic. These occupations frequently involve work activities that include practical, hands-on problems and solutions. They often deal with plants; animals; and real-world materials such as wood, tools, and machinery. Many of the occupations require working

outside and don't involve a lot of paperwork or working closely with others.

GOE—Interest Area/Cluster: 01. Agriculture and Natural Resources. **Work Group:** 01.05. Nursery, Groundskeeping, and Pest Control. **Other Jobs in This Work Group:** Landscaping and Groundskeeping Workers; Nursery Workers; Pest Control Workers; Tree Trimmers and Pruners.

Skills—Repairing: Repairing machines or systems, using the needed tools. **Equipment Maintenance:** Performing routine maintenance and determining when and what kind of maintenance is needed. **Operation Monitoring:** Watching gauges, dials, or other indicators to make sure a machine is working properly. **Management of Material Resources:** Obtaining and seeing to the appropriate use of equipment, facilities, and materials needed to do certain work. **Installation:** Installing equipment, machines, wiring, or programs to meet specifications. **Operation and Control:** Controlling operations of equipment or systems. **Quality Control Analysis:** Evaluating the quality or performance of products, services, or processes. **Science:** Using scientific methods to solve problems.

Education and Training Programs: Landscaping and Groundskeeping; Plant Nursery Operations and Management; Turf and Turfgrass Management. **Related Knowledge/Courses—Biology:** Plant and animal living tissue, cells, organisms, and entities, including their functions, interdependencies, and interactions with each other and the environment. **Chemistry:** The composition, structure, and properties of substances and of the chemical processes and transformations that they undergo. This includes uses of chemicals and their interactions, danger signs, production techniques, and disposal methods. **Mechanical Devices:** Machines and tools, including their designs, uses, benefits, repair, and maintenance. **Transportation:** Principles and methods for moving people or goods by air, rail, sea, or road, including their relative costs, advantages, and limitations. **Customer and Personal Service:** Principles and processes for providing customer and personal services, including needs assessment techniques, quality service standards, alternative delivery systems, and customer satisfaction evaluation techniques. **Public Safety and Security:** Weaponry; public safety; security operations, rules, regulations, precautions, and prevention; and the protection of people, data, and property.

Work Environment: Outdoors; noisy; contaminants; hazardous conditions; using hands on objects, tools, or controls; repetitive motions.

Petroleum Pump System Operators, Refinery Operators, and Gaugers

- ❋ Education/Training Required: Long-term on-the-job training
- ❋ Annual Earnings: $53,010
- ❋ Beginning Wage: $32,600
- ❋ Earnings Growth Potential: Medium
- ❋ Growth: –13.4%
- ❋ Annual Job Openings: 4,477
- ❋ Self-Employed: 0.1%
- ❋ Part-Time: 0.6%

Control the operation of petroleum-refining or -processing units. May specialize in controlling manifold and pumping systems, gauging or testing oil in storage tanks, or regulating the flow of oil into pipelines. Monitor process indicators, instruments, gauges, and meters in order to detect and report any possible problems. Control or operate manifold and pumping systems to circulate liquids through a petroleum refinery. Operate control panels to coordinate and regulate process variables such as temperature and pressure and to direct product flow rate according to process schedules. Lower thermometers into tanks to obtain temperature readings. Perform tests to check the qualities and grades of products, such as assessing levels of bottom sediment, water, and foreign materials in oil samples, using centrifugal testers. Inspect pipelines, tightening connections and lubricating valves as necessary. Calculate test result values, using standard formulas. Coordinate shutdowns and major projects. Conduct general housekeeping of units, including wiping up oil spills and performing general cleaning duties. Clean interiors of processing units by circulating chemicals and solvents within units. Clamp seals around valves to secure tanks. Verify that incoming and outgoing products are moving through the correct meters and that meters are working properly. Synchronize activities with other pumphouses to ensure a continuous flow of products and a minimum of contamination between products. Start pumps and open valves or use automated equipment to regulate the flow of oil in pipelines and into and out of tanks.

Maintain and repair equipment or report malfunctioning equipment to supervisors so that repairs can be scheduled. Plan movement of products through lines to processing, storage, and shipping units, utilizing knowledge of system interconnections and capacities. Read and analyze specifications, schedules, logs, test results, and laboratory recommendations to determine how to set equipment controls to produce the required qualities and quantities of products. Read automatic gauges at specified intervals to determine the flow rate of oil into or from tanks and the amount of oil in tanks. Record and compile operating data, instrument readings, documentation, and results of laboratory analyses. Signal other workers by telephone or radio to operate pumps, open and close valves, and check temperatures.

Personality Type: Realistic. These occupations frequently involve work activities that include practical, hands-on problems and solutions. They often deal with plants; animals; and real-world materials such as wood, tools, and machinery. Many of the occupations require working outside and don't involve a lot of paperwork or working closely with others.

GOE—Interest Area/Cluster: 13. Manufacturing. **Work Group:** 13.16. Utility Operation and Energy Distribution. **Other Jobs in This Work Group:** Chemical Plant and System Operators; Gas Compressor and Gas Pumping Station Operators; Gas Plant Operators; Nuclear Power Reactor Operators; Power Distributors and Dispatchers; Power Plant Operators; Ship Engineers; Stationary Engineers and Boiler Operators; Water and Liquid Waste Treatment Plant and System Operators.

Skills—Operation Monitoring: Watching gauges, dials, or other indicators to make sure a machine is working properly. **Operation and Control:** Controlling operations of equipment or systems. **Science:** Using scientific methods to solve problems. **Troubleshooting:** Determining what is causing an operating error and deciding what to do about it. **Repairing:** Repairing machines or systems, using the needed tools. **Equipment Maintenance:** Performing routine maintenance and determining when and what kind of maintenance is needed. **Quality Control Analysis:** Evaluating the quality or performance of products, services, or processes. **Installation:** Installing equipment, machines, wiring, or programs to meet specifications.

Education and Training Program: Mechanic and Repair Technologies/Technician Training, Other. **Related**

Knowledge/Courses—Mechanical Devices: Machines and tools, including their designs, uses, benefits, repair, and maintenance. **Chemistry:** The composition, structure, and properties of substances and of the chemical processes and transformations that they undergo. This includes uses of chemicals and their interactions, danger signs, production techniques, and disposal methods. **Engineering and Technology:** Equipment, tools, and mechanical devices and their uses to produce motion, light, power, technology, and other applications. **Public Safety and Security:** Weaponry; public safety; security operations, rules, regulations, precautions, and prevention; and the protection of people, data, and property. **Production and Processing:** Inputs, outputs, raw materials, waste, quality control, costs, and techniques for maximizing the manufacture and distribution of goods. **Education and Training:** Instructional methods and training techniques, including curriculum design principles, learning theory, group and individual teaching techniques, design of individual development plans, and test design principles.

Work Environment: More often outdoors than indoors; noisy; very hot or cold; contaminants; hazardous conditions.

Pharmacy Technicians

- ❋ Education/Training Required: Moderate-term on-the-job training
- ❋ Annual Earnings: $26,720
- ❋ Beginning Wage: $18,520
- ❋ Earnings Growth Potential: Low
- ❋ Growth: 32.0%
- ❋ Annual Job Openings: 54,453
- ❋ Self-Employed: 0.2%
- ❋ Part-Time: 20.8%

Prepare medications under the direction of a pharmacist. May measure, mix, count out, label, and record amounts and dosages of medications. Receive written prescription or refill requests and verify that information is complete and accurate. Maintain proper storage and security conditions for drugs. Answer telephones, responding to questions or requests. Fill bottles with prescribed medications and type and affix labels. Assist customers by answering simple questions, locating items, or referring them to the pharmacist for medication information. Price and file prescriptions that have been filled. Clean and help maintain equipment and work areas and sterilize glassware according to prescribed methods. Establish and maintain patient profiles, including lists of medications taken by individual patients. Order, label, and count stock of medications, chemicals, and supplies and enter inventory data into computer. Receive and store incoming supplies, verify quantities against invoices, and inform supervisors of stock needs and shortages. Transfer medication from vials to the appropriate number of sterile disposable syringes, using aseptic techniques. Under pharmacist supervision, add measured drugs or nutrients to intravenous solutions under sterile conditions to prepare intravenous (IV) packs. Supply and monitor robotic machines that dispense medicine into containers and label the containers. Prepare and process medical insurance claim forms and records. Mix pharmaceutical preparations according to written prescriptions. Operate cash registers to accept payment from customers. Compute charges for medication and equipment dispensed to hospital patients and enter data in computer. Deliver medications and pharmaceutical supplies to patients, nursing stations, or surgery. Price stock and mark items for sale. Maintain and merchandise home health-care products and services.

Personality Type: Conventional. These occupations frequently involve following set procedures and routines and can include working with data and details more than with ideas. Usually there is a clear line of authority to follow.

GOE—Interest Area/Cluster: 08. Health Science. **Work Group:** 08.02. Medicine and Surgery. **Other Jobs in This Work Group:** Anesthesiologists; Family and General Practitioners; Internists, General; Medical Assistants; Medical Transcriptionists; Obstetricians and Gynecologists; Pediatricians, General; Pharmacists; Pharmacy Aides; Physician Assistants; Psychiatrists; Registered Nurses; Surgeons; Surgical Technologists.

Skills—Service Orientation: Actively looking for ways to help people. **Active Listening:** Listening to what other people are saying and asking questions as appropriate. **Instructing:** Teaching others how to do something. **Mathematics:** Using mathematics to solve problems. **Speaking:** Talking to others to effectively convey information. **Active Learning:** Working with new material or information to grasp its implications. **Troubleshooting:** Determining what is causing an operating error and deciding what to do about it. **Writing:** Communicating effectively with others in writing as indicated by the needs of the audience.

Education and Training Program: Pharmacy Technician/Assistant Training. **Related Knowledge/Courses—Medicine and Dentistry:** The information and techniques needed to diagnose and treat injuries, diseases, and deformities. This includes symptoms, treatment alternatives, drug properties and interactions, and preventive health-care measures. **Chemistry:** The composition, structure, and properties of substances and of the chemical processes and transformations that they undergo. This includes uses of chemicals and their interactions, danger signs, production techniques, and disposal methods. **Customer and Personal Service:** Principles and processes for providing customer and personal services, including needs assessment techniques, quality service standards, alternative delivery systems, and customer satisfaction evaluation techniques. **Mathematics:** Using mathematics to solve problems. **Clerical Studies:** Administrative and clerical procedures and systems such as word-processing systems, filing and records management systems, stenography and transcription, forms, design principles, and other office procedures and terminology.

Work Environment: Indoors; standing; using hands on objects, tools, or controls; repetitive motions.

Photographers

- ❋ Education/Training Required: Long-term on-the-job training
- ❋ Annual Earnings: $27,720
- ❋ Beginning Wage: $16,170
- ❋ Earnings Growth Potential: High
- ❋ Growth: 10.3%
- ❋ Annual Job Openings: 16,100
- ❋ Self-Employed: 54.3%
- ❋ Part-Time: 22.1%

Photograph persons, subjects, merchandise, or other commercial products. May develop negatives and produce finished prints. Take pictures of individuals, families, and small groups, either in studio or on location. Adjust apertures, shutter speeds, and camera focus based on a combination of factors such as lighting, field depth, subject motion, film type, and film speed. Use traditional

or digital cameras, along with a variety of equipment such as tripods, filters, and flash attachments. Create artificial light, using flashes and reflectors. Determine desired images and picture composition; select and adjust subjects, equipment, and lighting to achieve desired effects. Scan photographs into computers for editing, storage, and electronic transmission. Test equipment prior to use to ensure that it is in good working order. Review sets of photographs to select the best work. Estimate or measure light levels, distances, and numbers of exposures needed, using measuring devices and formulas. Manipulate and enhance scanned or digital images to create desired effects, using computers and specialized software. Perform maintenance tasks necessary to keep equipment working properly. Perform general office duties such as scheduling appointments, keeping books, and ordering supplies. Consult with clients or advertising staff and study assignments to determine project goals, locations, and equipment needs. Select and assemble equipment and required background properties according to subjects, materials, and conditions. Enhance, retouch, and resize photographs and negatives, using airbrushing and other techniques. Set up, mount, or install photographic equipment and cameras. Produce computer-readable digital images from film, using flatbed scanners and photofinishing laboratories. Develop and print exposed film, using chemicals, touchup tools, and developing and printing equipment, or send film to photofinishing laboratories for processing. Direct activities of workers who are setting up photographic equipment. Employ a variety of specialized photographic materials and techniques, including infrared and ultraviolet films, macro-photography, photogrammetry, and sensitometry. Engage in research to develop new photographic procedures and materials.

Personality Type: Artistic. These occupations frequently involve working with forms, designs, and patterns. They often require self-expression, and the work can be done without following a clear set of rules.

GOE—Interest Area/Cluster: 03. Arts and Communication. **Work Group:** 03.09. Media Technology. **Other Jobs in This Work Group:** Audio and Video Equipment Technicians; Broadcast Technicians; Camera Operators, Television, Video, and Motion Picture; Film and Video Editors; Multi-Media Artists and Animators; Radio Operators; Sound Engineering Technicians.

Skills—Persuasion: Persuading others to approach things differently. **Equipment Maintenance:** Performing routine maintenance and determining when and what kind of maintenance is needed. **Management of Financial Resources:** Determining how money will be spent to get the work done and accounting for these expenditures. **Operation Monitoring:** Watching gauges, dials, or other indicators to make sure a machine is working properly. **Service Orientation:** Actively looking for ways to help people. **Equipment Selection:** Determining the kind of tools and equipment needed to do a job. **Technology Design:** Generating or adapting equipment and technology to serve user needs. **Operations Analysis:** Analyzing needs and product requirements to create a design.

Education and Training Programs: Art/Art Studies, General; Commercial Photography; Film/Video and Photographic Arts, Other; Photography; Photojournalism; Visual and Performing Arts, General. **Related Knowledge/Courses—Sales and Marketing:** Principles and methods involved in showing, promoting, and selling products or services. This includes marketing strategies and tactics, product demonstration and sales techniques, and sales control systems. **Fine Arts:** Theory and techniques required to produce, compose, and perform works of music, dance, visual arts, drama, and sculpture. **Clerical Studies:** Administrative and clerical procedures and systems such as word-processing systems, filing and records management systems, stenography and transcription, forms, design principles, and other office procedures and terminology. **Customer and Personal Service:** Principles and processes for providing customer and personal services, including needs assessment techniques, quality service standards, alternative delivery systems, and customer satisfaction evaluation techniques. **Communications and Media:** Media production, communication, and dissemination techniques and methods, including alternative ways to inform and entertain via written, oral, and visual media. **Production and Processing:** Inputs, outputs, raw materials, waste, quality control, costs, and techniques for maximizing the manufacture and distribution of goods.

Work Environment: More often indoors than outdoors; sitting; using hands on objects, tools, or controls.

Physical Therapist Aides

- ❋ Education/Training Required: Short-term on-the-job training
- ❋ Annual Earnings: $22,990
- ❋ Beginning Wage: $16,740
- ❋ Earnings Growth Potential: Low
- ❋ Growth: 24.4%
- ❋ Annual Job Openings: 4,092
- ❋ Self-Employed: 0.2%
- ❋ Part-Time: 27.1%

Under close supervision of physical therapists or physical therapy assistants, perform delegated, selected, or routine tasks in specific situations. These duties include preparing patients and treatment areas. Clean and organize work areas and disinfect equipment after treatment. Administer active and passive manual therapeutic exercises, therapeutic massages, and heat, light, sound, water, or electrical modality treatments such as ultrasound. Instruct, motivate, safeguard, and assist patients practicing exercises and functional activities, under direction of medical staff. Record treatment given and equipment used. Confer with physical therapy staff or others to discuss and evaluate patient information for planning, modifying, and coordinating treatment. Observe patients during treatment to compile and evaluate data on patients' responses and progress, and report to physical therapists. Secure patients into or onto therapy equipment. Change linens such as bed sheets and pillow cases. Transport patients to and from treatment areas, using wheelchairs or providing standing support. Arrange treatment supplies to keep them in order. Maintain equipment and furniture to keep it in good working condition, including performing the assembly and disassembly of equipment and accessories. Assist patients to dress, undress, and put on and remove supportive devices such as braces, splints, and slings. Perform clerical duties such as taking inventory, ordering supplies, answering telephones, taking messages, and filling out forms. Administer traction to relieve neck and back pain, using intermittent and static traction equipment. Schedule patient appointments with physical therapists and coordinate therapists' schedules. Train patients to use orthopedic braces, prostheses, or supportive devices. Measure patient's range-of-joint motion, body parts, and vital signs to determine effects of treatments or for patient evaluations. Participate in patient

P

care tasks such as assisting with passing food trays, feeding residents, or bathing residents on bed rest. Fit patients for orthopedic braces, prostheses, or supportive devices, adjusting fit as needed.

Personality Type: Social. These occupations frequently involve working with, communicating with, and teaching people and often involve helping or providing service to others.

GOE—Interest Area/Cluster: 08. Health Science. **Work Group:** 08.07. Medical Therapy. **Other Jobs in This Work Group:** Audiologists; Massage Therapists; Occupational Therapist Aides; Occupational Therapist Assistants; Occupational Therapists; Physical Therapist Assistants; Physical Therapists; Radiation Therapists; Recreational Therapists; Respiratory Therapists; Respiratory Therapy Technicians; Speech-Language Pathologists.

Skills: None met the criteria.

Education and Training Program: Physical Therapist Assistant Training. **Related Knowledge/Courses—Medicine and Dentistry:** The information and techniques needed to diagnose and treat injuries, diseases, and deformities. This includes symptoms, treatment alternatives, drug properties and interactions, and preventive healthcare measures. **Therapy and Counseling:** Information and techniques needed to rehabilitate physical and mental ailments and to provide career guidance, including alternative treatments, rehabilitation equipment and its proper use, and methods to evaluate treatment effects. **Customer and Personal Service:** Principles and processes for providing customer and personal services, including needs assessment techniques, quality service standards, alternative delivery systems, and customer satisfaction evaluation techniques. **Psychology:** Human behavior and performance, mental processes, psychological research methods, and the assessment and treatment of behavioral and affective disorders. **Public Safety and Security:** Weaponry; public safety; security operations, rules, regulations, precautions, and prevention; and the protection of people, data, and property.

Work Environment: Indoors; disease or infections; standing; walking and running; using hands on objects, tools, or controls; bending or twisting the body.

Physical Therapist Assistants

- ❋ Education/Training Required: Associate degree
- ❋ Annual Earnings: $44,130
- ❋ Beginning Wage: $27,800
- ❋ Earnings Growth Potential: Medium
- ❋ Growth: 32.4%
- ❋ Annual Job Openings: 5,957
- ❋ Self-Employed: 0.2%
- ❋ Part-Time: 27.1%

Assist physical therapists in providing physical therapy treatments and procedures. May, in accordance with state laws, assist in the development of treatment plans, carry out routine functions, document the progress of treatment, and modify specific treatments in accordance with patient status and within the scope of treatment plans established by physical therapists. Generally requires formal training. Instruct, motivate, safeguard, and assist patients as they practice exercises and functional activities. Observe patients during treatments to compile and evaluate data on their responses and progress, and provide results to physical therapists in person or through progress notes. Confer with physical therapy staffs or others to discuss and evaluate patient information for planning, modifying, and coordinating treatment. Transport patients to and from treatment areas, lifting and transferring them according to positioning requirements. Secure patients into or onto therapy equipment. Administer active and passive manual therapeutic exercises, therapeutic massages, aquatic physical therapy, and heat, light, sound, and electrical modality treatments such as ultrasound. Communicate with or instruct caregivers and family members on patient therapeutic activities and treatment plans. Measure patients' ranges-of-joint motion, body parts, and vital signs to determine effects of treatments or for patient evaluations. Monitor operation of equipment and record use of equipment and administration of treatment. Fit patients for orthopedic braces, prostheses, and supportive devices such as crutches. Train patients in the use of orthopedic braces, prostheses, or supportive devices. Clean work areas and check and store equipment after treatments. Assist patients to dress, undress, or put on and remove supportive devices such as braces, splints, and slings. Attend or conduct continuing education courses, seminars, or in-service activities. Perform clerical duties such as taking inventory, ordering supplies, answering telephones, taking messages, and filling out forms. Prepare treatment areas and electrotherapy equipment for use by physiotherapists. Administer traction to relieve neck and back pain, using intermittent and static traction equipment. Perform postural drainage, percussions and vibrations, and teach deep breathing exercises to treat respiratory conditions.

Personality Type: Social. These occupations frequently involve working with, communicating with, and teaching people and often involve helping or providing service to others.

GOE—Interest Area/Cluster: 08. Health Science. **Work Group:** 08.07. Medical Therapy. **Other Jobs in This Work Group:** Audiologists; Massage Therapists; Occupational Therapist Aides; Occupational Therapist Assistants; Occupational Therapists; Physical Therapist Aides; Physical Therapists; Radiation Therapists; Recreational Therapists; Respiratory Therapists; Respiratory Therapy Technicians; Speech-Language Pathologists.

Skill: Service Orientation: Actively looking for ways to help people.

Education and Training Program: Physical Therapist Assistant Training. **Related Knowledge/Courses—Therapy and Counseling:** Information and techniques needed to rehabilitate physical and mental ailments and to provide career guidance, including alternative treatments, rehabilitation equipment and its proper use, and methods to evaluate treatment effects. **Medicine and Dentistry:** The information and techniques needed to diagnose and treat injuries, diseases, and deformities. This includes symptoms, treatment alternatives, drug properties and interactions, and preventive health-care measures. **Psychology:** Human behavior and performance, mental processes, psychological research methods, and the assessment and treatment of behavioral and affective disorders. **Biology:** Plant and animal living tissue, cells, organisms, and entities, including their functions, interdependencies, and interactions with each other and the environment. **Customer and Personal Service:** Principles and processes for providing customer and personal services, including needs assessment techniques, quality service standards, alternative delivery systems, and customer satisfaction evaluation techniques. **Education and Training:** Instructional methods and training techniques, including curriculum design

principles, learning theory, group and individual teaching techniques, design of individual development plans, and test design principles.

Work Environment: Indoors; disease or infections; standing; walking and running.

Pile-Driver Operators

- Education/Training Required: Moderate-term on-the-job training
- Annual Earnings: $47,550
- Beginning Wage: $28,430
- Earnings Growth Potential: High
- Growth: 8.3%
- Annual Job Openings: 701
- Self-Employed: 5.0%
- Part-Time: 4.6%

Operate pile drivers mounted on skids, barges, crawler treads, or locomotive cranes to drive pilings for retaining walls, bulkheads, and foundations of structures such as buildings, bridges, and piers. Move hand and foot levers of hoisting equipment to position piling leads, hoist piling into leads, and position hammers over pilings. Conduct pre-operational checks on equipment to ensure proper functioning. Drive pilings to provide support for buildings or other structures, using heavy equipment with a pile driver head. Move levers and turn valves to activate power hammers or to raise and lower drophammers that drive piles to required depths. Clean, lubricate, and refill equipment.

Personality Type: Realistic. These occupations frequently involve work activities that include practical, hands-on problems and solutions. They often deal with plants; animals; and real-world materials such as wood, tools, and machinery. Many of the occupations require working outside and don't involve a lot of paperwork or working closely with others.

GOE—Interest Area/Cluster: 02. Architecture and Construction. **Work Group:** 02.04. Construction Crafts. **Other Jobs in This Work Group:** Boilermakers; Brickmasons and Blockmasons; Carpet Installers; Cement Masons and Concrete Finishers; Commercial Divers; Construction Carpenters; Crane and Tower Operators; Drywall and

Ceiling Tile Installers; Electricians; Fence Erectors; Floor Layers, Except Carpet, Wood, and Hard Tiles; Floor Sanders and Finishers; Glaziers; Hazardous Materials Removal Workers; Insulation Workers, Floor, Ceiling, and Wall; Insulation Workers, Mechanical; Manufactured Building and Mobile Home Installers; Operating Engineers and Other Construction Equipment Operators; Painters, Construction and Maintenance; Paperhangers; Paving, Surfacing, and Tamping Equipment Operators; Pipe Fitters and Steamfitters; Pipelayers; Plasterers and Stucco Masons; Plumbers; Plumbers, Pipefitters, and Steamfitters; Rail-Track Laying and Maintenance Equipment Operators; Refractory Materials Repairers, Except Brickmasons; Reinforcing Iron and Rebar Workers; Riggers; Roofers; Rough Carpenters; Security and Fire Alarm Systems Installers; Segmental Pavers; Sheet Metal Workers; Stone Cutters and Carvers, Manufacturing; Stonemasons; Structural Iron and Steel Workers; Tapers; Terrazzo Workers and Finishers; Tile and Marble Setters.

Skills—Repairing: Repairing machines or systems, using the needed tools. **Operation and Control:** Controlling operations of equipment or systems. **Equipment Maintenance:** Performing routine maintenance and determining when and what kind of maintenance is needed. **Operation Monitoring:** Watching gauges, dials, or other indicators to make sure a machine is working properly. **Equipment Selection:** Determining the kind of tools and equipment needed to do a job. **Coordination:** Adjusting actions in relation to others' actions. **Systems Analysis:** Determining how a system should work and how changes will affect outcomes. **Installation:** Installing equipment, machines, wiring, or programs to meet specifications.

Education and Training Program: Construction/Heavy Equipment/Earthmoving Equipment Operation. **Related Knowledge/Courses—Building and Construction:** Materials, methods, and the appropriate tools to construct objects, structures, and buildings. **Mechanical Devices:** Machines and tools, including their designs, uses, benefits, repair, and maintenance. **Transportation:** Principles and methods for moving people or goods by air, rail, sea, or road, including their relative costs, advantages, and limitations. **Physics:** Physical principles, laws, and applications, including air, water, material dynamics, light, atomic principles, heat, electric theory, earth formations, and meteorological and related natural phenomena. **Design:** Design techniques, principles, tools, and instruments involved in

the production and use of precision technical plans, blueprints, drawings, and models. **Engineering and Technology:** Equipment, tools, and mechanical devices and their uses to produce motion, light, power, technology, and other applications.

Work Environment: Outdoors; noisy; very hot or cold; contaminants; whole-body vibration; hazardous equipment.

Pilots, Ship

- Education/Training Required: Work experience in a related occupation
- Annual Earnings: $57,210
- Beginning Wage: $29,530
- Earnings Growth Potential: High
- Growth: 17.9%
- Annual Job Openings: 2,665
- Self-Employed: 6.8%
- Part-Time: 4.8%

The job openings listed here are shared with Mates—Ship, Boat, and Barge, and with Ship and Boat Captains.

Command ships to steer them into and out of harbors, estuaries, straits, and sounds and on rivers, lakes, and bays. Must be licensed by U.S. Coast Guard with limitations indicating class and tonnage of vessels for which licenses are valid and routes and waters that may be piloted. Maintain and repair boats and equipment. Give directions to crew members who are steering ships. Make nautical maps. Set ships' courses to avoid reefs, outlying shoals, and other hazards, using navigational aids such as lighthouses and buoys. Report to appropriate authorities any violations of federal or state pilotage laws. Relieve crew members on tugs and launches. Provide assistance to vessels approaching or leaving seacoasts, navigating harbors, and docking and undocking. Provide assistance in maritime rescue operations. Prevent ships under their navigational control from engaging in unsafe operations. Operate amphibious craft during troop landings. Maintain ships' logs. Learn to operate new technology systems and procedures, through the use of instruction, simulators, and models. Advise ships' masters on harbor rules and customs procedures. Steer ships into and out of berths or signal tugboat captains to berth and unberth ships. Serve as vessels' docking masters upon arrival at a port and when at a berth.

Operate ship-to-shore radios to exchange information needed for ship operations. Consult maps, charts, weather reports, and navigation equipment to determine and direct ship movements. Direct courses and speeds of ships, based on specialized knowledge of local winds, weather, water depths, tides, currents, and hazards. Oversee cargo storage on or below decks.

Personality Type: Realistic. These occupations frequently involve work activities that include practical, hands-on problems and solutions. They often deal with plants; animals; and real-world materials such as wood, tools, and machinery. Many of the occupations require working outside and don't involve a lot of paperwork or working closely with others.

GOE—Interest Area/Cluster: 16. Transportation, Distribution, and Logistics. **Work Group:** 16.05. Water Vehicle Operation. **Other Jobs in This Work Group:** Captains, Mates, and Pilots of Water Vessels; Dredge Operators; Mates—Ship, Boat, and Barge; Motorboat Operators; Sailors and Marine Oilers; Ship and Boat Captains.

Skills—Operation and Control: Controlling operations of equipment or systems. **Operation Monitoring:** Watching gauges, dials, or other indicators to make sure a machine is working properly. **Judgment and Decision Making:** Weighing the relative costs and benefits of a potential action. **Management of Personnel Resources:** Motivating, developing, and directing people as they work; identifying the best people for the job. **Troubleshooting:** Determining what is causing an operating error and deciding what to do about it. **Equipment Maintenance:** Performing routine maintenance and determining when and what kind of maintenance is needed. **Negotiation:** Bringing others together and trying to reconcile differences. **Coordination:** Adjusting actions in relation to others' actions.

Education and Training Programs: Commercial Fishing; Marine Science/Merchant Marine Officer Training; Marine Transportation, Other. **Related Knowledge/Courses—Transportation:** Principles and methods for moving people or goods by air, rail, sea, or road, including their relative costs, advantages, and limitations. **Geography:** Various methods for describing the location and distribution of land, sea, and air masses, including their physical locations, relationships, and characteristics. **Public Safety and Security:** Weaponry; public safety; security

operations, rules, regulations, precautions, and prevention; and the protection of people, data, and property. **Telecommunications:** Transmission, broadcasting, switching, control, and operation of telecommunications systems. **Mechanical Devices:** Machines and tools, including their designs, uses, benefits, repair, and maintenance. **Law and Government:** Laws, legal codes, court procedures, precedents, government regulations, executive orders, agency rules, and the democratic political process.

Work Environment: Outdoors; noisy; very hot or cold; very bright or dim lighting; contaminants; using hands on objects, tools, or controls.

Pipe Fitters and Steamfitters

- ⁂ Education/Training Required: Long-term on-the-job training
- ⁂ Annual Earnings: $44,090
- ⁂ Beginning Wage: $26,550
- ⁂ Earnings Growth Potential: Medium
- ⁂ Growth: 10.6%
- ⁂ Annual Job Openings: 68,643
- ⁂ Self-Employed: 12.3%
- ⁂ Part-Time: 3.4%

The job openings listed here are shared with Plumbers.

Lay out, assemble, install, and maintain pipe systems, pipe supports, and related hydraulic and pneumatic equipment for steam, hot water, heating, cooling, lubricating, sprinkling, and industrial production and processing systems. Cut, thread, and hammer pipe to specifications, using tools such as saws, cutting torches, and pipe threaders and benders. Assemble and secure pipes, tubes, fittings, and related equipment according to specifications by welding, brazing, cementing, soldering, and threading joints. Attach pipes to walls, structures, and fixtures, such as radiators or tanks, using brackets, clamps, tools, or welding equipment. Inspect, examine, and test installed systems and pipelines, using pressure gauge, hydrostatic testing, observation, or other methods. Measure and mark pipes for cutting and threading. Lay out full scale drawings of pipe systems, supports, and related equipment, following blueprints. Plan pipe system layout, installation, or repair according to specifications. Select pipe sizes and types and related materials, such as supports, hangers, and hydraulic cylinders, according to specifications. Cut and bore holes in structures such as bulkheads, decks, walls, and mains prior to pipe installation, using hand and power tools. Modify, clean, and maintain pipe systems, units, fittings, and related machines and equipment, following specifications and using hand and power tools. Install automatic controls used to regulate pipe systems. Turn valves to shut off steam, water, or other gases or liquids from pipe sections, using valve keys or wrenches. Remove and replace worn components. Prepare cost estimates for clients. Inspect work sites for obstructions and to ensure that holes will not cause structural weakness. Operate motorized pumps to remove water from flooded manholes, basements, or facility floors. Dip nonferrous piping materials in a mixture of molten tin and lead to obtain a coating that prevents erosion or galvanic and electrolytic action.

Personality Type: Realistic. These occupations frequently involve work activities that include practical, hands-on problems and solutions. They often deal with plants; animals; and real-world materials such as wood, tools, and machinery. Many of the occupations require working outside and don't involve a lot of paperwork or working closely with others.

GOE—Interest Area/Cluster: 02. Architecture and Construction. **Work Group:** 02.04. Construction Crafts. **Other Jobs in This Work Group:** Boilermakers; Brickmasons and Blockmasons; Carpet Installers; Cement Masons and Concrete Finishers; Commercial Divers; Construction Carpenters; Crane and Tower Operators; Drywall and Ceiling Tile Installers; Electricians; Fence Erectors; Floor Layers, Except Carpet, Wood, and Hard Tiles; Floor Sanders and Finishers; Glaziers; Hazardous Materials Removal Workers; Insulation Workers, Floor, Ceiling, and Wall; Insulation Workers, Mechanical; Manufactured Building and Mobile Home Installers; Operating Engineers and Other Construction Equipment Operators; Painters, Construction and Maintenance; Paperhangers; Paving, Surfacing, and Tamping Equipment Operators; Pile-Driver Operators; Pipelayers; Plasterers and Stucco Masons; Plumbers; Plumbers, Pipefitters, and Steamfitters; Rail-Track Laying and Maintenance Equipment Operators; Refractory Materials Repairers, Except Brickmasons; Reinforcing Iron and Rebar Workers; Riggers; Roofers; Rough Carpenters; Security and Fire Alarm Systems Installers; Segmental Pavers;

Sheet Metal Workers; Stone Cutters and Carvers, Manufacturing; Stonemasons; Structural Iron and Steel Workers; Tapers; Terrazzo Workers and Finishers; Tile and Marble Setters.

Skills—Installation: Installing equipment, machines, wiring, or programs to meet specifications. **Repairing:** Repairing machines or systems, using the needed tools. **Systems Analysis:** Determining how a system should work and how changes will affect outcomes. **Management of Personnel Resources:** Motivating, developing, and directing people as they work; identifying the best people for the job. **Equipment Maintenance:** Performing routine maintenance and determining when and what kind of maintenance is needed. **Operation Monitoring:** Watching gauges, dials, or other indicators to make sure a machine is working properly. **Operation and Control:** Controlling operations of equipment or systems. **Technology Design:** Generating or adapting equipment and technology to serve user needs.

Education and Training Program: Pipefitting/Pipefitter and Sprinkler Fitter Training. **Related Knowledge/Courses—Building and Construction:** Materials, methods, and the appropriate tools to construct objects, structures, and buildings. **Design:** Design techniques, principles, tools, and instruments involved in the production and use of precision technical plans, blueprints, drawings, and models. **Mechanical Devices:** Machines and tools, including their designs, uses, benefits, repair, and maintenance. **Engineering and Technology:** Equipment, tools, and mechanical devices and their uses to produce motion, light, power, technology, and other applications. **Economics and Accounting:** Economic and accounting principles and practices, the financial markets, banking, and the analysis and reporting of financial data. **Transportation:** Principles and methods for moving people or goods by air, rail, sea, or road, including their relative costs, advantages, and limitations.

Work Environment: Outdoors; hazardous equipment; minor burns, cuts, bites, or stings; standing; using hands on objects, tools, or controls; repetitive motions.

Pipelayers

- Education/Training Required: Moderate-term on-the-job training
- Annual Earnings: $31,280
- Beginning Wage: $21,270
- Earnings Growth Potential: Low
- Growth: 8.7%
- Annual Job Openings: 8,902
- Self-Employed: 11.6%
- Part-Time: 3.4%

Lay pipe for storm or sanitation sewers, drains, and water mains. Perform any combination of these tasks: grade trenches or culverts, position pipe, or seal joints. Check slopes for conformance to requirements, using levels or lasers. Cover pipes with earth or other materials. Cut pipes to required lengths. Connect pipe pieces and seal joints, using welding equipment, cement, or glue. Install and repair sanitary and stormwater sewer structures and pipe systems. Install and use instruments such as lasers, grade rods, and transit levels. Grade and level trench bases, using tamping machines and hand tools. Lay out pipe routes, following written instructions or blueprints, and coordinating layouts with supervisors. Align and position pipes to prepare them for welding or sealing. Dig trenches to desired or required depths, by hand or using trenching tools. Operate mechanized equipment such as pickup trucks, rollers, tandem dump trucks, front-end loaders, and backhoes. Train others in pipe-laying, and provide supervision. Tap and drill holes into pipes to introduce auxiliary lines or devices. Locate existing pipes needing repair or replacement, using magnetic or radio indicators.

Personality Type: Realistic. These occupations frequently involve work activities that include practical, hands-on problems and solutions. They often deal with plants; animals; and real-world materials such as wood, tools, and machinery. Many of the occupations require working outside and don't involve a lot of paperwork or working closely with others.

GOE—Interest Area/Cluster: 02. Architecture and Construction. **Work Group:** 02.04. Construction Crafts. **Other Jobs in This Work Group:** Boilermakers; Brickmasons and Blockmasons; Carpet Installers; Cement Masons and Concrete Finishers; Commercial Divers; Construction Carpenters; Crane and Tower Operators; Drywall and Ceiling Tile Installers; Electricians; Fence Erectors; Floor Layers, Except Carpet, Wood, and Hard Tiles; Floor Sanders and Finishers; Glaziers; Hazardous Materials Removal Workers; Insulation Workers, Floor, Ceiling, and Wall; Insulation Workers, Mechanical; Manufactured Building and Mobile Home Installers; Operating Engineers and Other Construction Equipment Operators; Painters, Construction and Maintenance; Paperhangers; Paving, Surfacing, and Tamping Equipment Operators; Pile-Driver Operators; Pipe Fitters and Steamfitters; Plasterers and Stucco Masons; Plumbers; Plumbers, Pipefitters, and Steamfitters; Rail-Track Laying and Maintenance Equipment Operators; Refractory Materials Repairers, Except Brickmasons; Reinforcing Iron and Rebar Workers; Riggers; Roofers; Rough Carpenters; Security and Fire Alarm Systems Installers; Segmental Pavers; Sheet Metal Workers; Stone Cutters and Carvers, Manufacturing; Stonemasons; Structural Iron and Steel Workers; Tapers; Terrazzo Workers and Finishers; Tile and Marble Setters.

Skills—Installation: Installing equipment, machines, wiring, or programs to meet specifications. **Quality Control Analysis:** Evaluating the quality or performance of products, services, or processes. **Operation and Control:** Controlling operations of equipment or systems. **Operation Monitoring:** Watching gauges, dials, or other indicators to make sure a machine is working properly. **Equipment Maintenance:** Performing routine maintenance and determining when and what kind of maintenance is needed. **Equipment Selection:** Determining the kind of tools and equipment needed to do a job. **Repairing:** Repairing machines or systems, using the needed tools. **Technology Design:** Generating or adapting equipment and technology to serve user needs.

Education and Training Program: Plumbing Technology/Plumber Training. **Related Knowledge/Courses— Building and Construction:** Materials, methods, and the appropriate tools to construct objects, structures, and buildings. **Mechanical Devices:** Machines and tools, including their designs, uses, benefits, repair, and maintenance.

Work Environment: Outdoors; noisy; hazardous equipment; standing; using hands on objects, tools, or controls; repetitive motions.

Plasterers and Stucco Masons

* Education/Training Required: Long-term on-the-job training
* Annual Earnings: $36,430
* Beginning Wage: $23,670
* Earnings Growth Potential: Medium
* Growth: 8.1%
* Annual Job Openings: 4,509
* Self-Employed: 15.7%
* Part-Time: 4.3%

Apply interior or exterior plaster, cement, stucco, or similar materials. May also set ornamental plaster. Apply coats of plaster or stucco to walls, ceilings, or partitions of buildings, using trowels, brushes, or spray guns. Mix mortar and plaster to desired consistency or direct workers who perform mixing. Create decorative textures in finish coat, using brushes or trowels, sand, pebbles, or stones. Apply insulation to building exteriors by installing prefabricated insulation systems over existing walls or by covering the outer wall with insulation board, reinforcing mesh, and a base coat. Cure freshly plastered surfaces. Clean and prepare surfaces for applications of plaster, cement, stucco, or similar materials, such as by drywall taping. Rough the undercoat surface with a scratcher so the finish coat will adhere. Apply weatherproof decorative coverings to exterior surfaces of buildings, such as troweling or spraying on coats of stucco. Install guide wires on exterior surfaces of buildings to indicate thickness of plaster or stucco and nail wire mesh, lath, or similar materials to the outside surface to hold stucco in place. Spray acoustic materials or texture finish over walls and ceilings. Mold and install ornamental plaster pieces, panels, and trim.

Personality Type: Realistic. These occupations frequently involve work activities that include practical, hands-on problems and solutions. They often deal with plants; animals; and real-world materials such as wood, tools, and machinery. Many of the occupations require working outside and don't involve a lot of paperwork or working closely with others.

GOE—Interest Area/Cluster: 02. Architecture and Construction. **Work Group:** 02.04. Construction Crafts. **Other Jobs in This Work Group:** Boilermakers; Brickmasons and Blockmasons; Carpet Installers; Cement Masons and Concrete Finishers; Commercial Divers; Construction Carpenters; Crane and Tower Operators; Drywall and Ceiling Tile Installers; Electricians; Fence Erectors; Floor Layers, Except Carpet, Wood, and Hard Tiles; Floor Sanders and Finishers; Glaziers; Hazardous Materials Removal Workers; Insulation Workers, Floor, Ceiling, and Wall; Insulation Workers, Mechanical; Manufactured Building and Mobile Home Installers; Operating Engineers and Other Construction Equipment Operators; Painters, Construction and Maintenance; Paperhangers; Paving, Surfacing, and Tamping Equipment Operators; Pile-Driver Operators; Pipe Fitters and Steamfitters; Pipelayers; Plumbers; Plumbers, Pipefitters, and Steamfitters; Rail-Track Laying and Maintenance Equipment Operators; Refractory Materials Repairers, Except Brickmasons; Reinforcing Iron and Rebar Workers; Riggers; Roofers; Rough Carpenters; Security and Fire Alarm Systems Installers; Segmental Pavers; Sheet Metal Workers; Stone Cutters and Carvers, Manufacturing; Stonemasons; Structural Iron and Steel Workers; Tapers; Terrazzo Workers and Finishers; Tile and Marble Setters.

Skills—Management of Material Resources: Obtaining and seeing to the appropriate use of equipment, facilities, and materials needed to do certain work. **Repairing:** Repairing machines or systems, using the needed tools. **Installation:** Installing equipment, machines, wiring, or programs to meet specifications. **Technology Design:** Generating or adapting equipment and technology to serve user needs. **Equipment Maintenance:** Performing routine maintenance and determining when and what kind of maintenance is needed. **Management of Financial Resources:** Determining how money will be spent to get the work done and accounting for these expenditures. **Equipment Selection:** Determining the kind of tools and equipment needed to do a job. **Operations Analysis:** Analyzing needs and product requirements to create a design.

Education and Training Program: Construction Trades, Other. **Related Knowledge/Courses—Building and Construction:** Materials, methods, and the appropriate tools to construct objects, structures, and buildings. **Public Safety and Security:** Weaponry; public safety; security operations, rules, regulations, precautions, and prevention; and the protection of people, data, and property.

Work Environment: High places; standing; walking and running; using hands on objects, tools, or controls; bending or twisting the body; repetitive motions.

Plumbers

- ❋ Education/Training Required: Long-term on-the-job training
- ❋ Annual Earnings: $44,090
- ❋ Beginning Wage: $26,550
- ❋ Earnings Growth Potential: Medium
- ❋ Growth: 10.6%
- ❋ Annual Job Openings: 68,643
- ❋ Self-Employed: 12.3%
- ❋ Part-Time: 3.4%

The job openings listed here are shared with Pipe Fitters and Steamfitters.

Assemble, install, and repair pipes, fittings, and fixtures of heating, water, and drainage systems according to specifications and plumbing codes. Measure, cut, thread, and bend pipe to required angles, using hand and power tools or machines such as pipe cutters, pipe-threading machines, and pipe-bending machines. Study building plans and inspect structures to assess material and equipment needs in order to establish the sequence of pipe installations, and to plan installation around obstructions such as electrical wiring. Locate and mark the position of pipe installations, connections, passage holes, and fixtures in structures, using measuring instruments such as rulers and levels. Assemble pipe sections, tubing, and fittings, using couplings, clamps, screws, bolts, cement, plastic solvent, caulking, or soldering, brazing, and welding equipment. Fill pipes or plumbing fixtures with water or air and observe pressure gauges to detect and locate leaks. Install pipe assemblies, fittings, valves, appliances such as dishwashers and water heaters, and fixtures such as sinks and toilets, using hand and power tools. Direct workers engaged in pipe cutting and preassembly and installation of plumbing systems and components. Cut openings in structures to accommodate pipes and pipe fittings, using hand and power tools. Review blueprints and building codes and specifications to determine work details and procedures. Install underground storm, sanitary, and water piping systems and extend piping to connect fixtures and plumbing to these systems. Repair and maintain plumbing, replacing defective washers, replacing or mending broken pipes, and opening clogged drains. Keep records of assignments and produce detailed work reports. Hang steel supports from ceiling joists to hold pipes in place. Perform complex calculations and planning for special or very large jobs. Clear away debris in renovations. Install oxygen and medical gas in hospitals. Prepare written work cost estimates and negotiate contracts. Use specialized techniques, equipment, or materials, such as performing computer-assisted welding of small pipes or working with the special piping used in microchip fabrication.

Personality Type: Realistic. These occupations frequently involve work activities that include practical, hands-on problems and solutions. They often deal with plants; animals; and real-world materials such as wood, tools, and machinery. Many of the occupations require working outside and don't involve a lot of paperwork or working closely with others.

GOE—Interest Area/Cluster: 02. Architecture and Construction. **Work Group:** 02.04. Construction Crafts. **Other Jobs in This Work Group:** Boilermakers; Brickmasons and Blockmasons; Carpet Installers; Cement Masons and Concrete Finishers; Commercial Divers; Construction Carpenters; Crane and Tower Operators; Drywall and Ceiling Tile Installers; Electricians; Fence Erectors; Floor Layers, Except Carpet, Wood, and Hard Tiles; Floor Sanders and Finishers; Glaziers; Hazardous Materials Removal Workers; Insulation Workers, Floor, Ceiling, and Wall; Insulation Workers, Mechanical; Manufactured Building and Mobile Home Installers; Operating Engineers and Other Construction Equipment Operators; Painters, Construction and Maintenance; Paperhangers; Paving, Surfacing, and Tamping Equipment Operators; Pile-Driver Operators; Pipe Fitters and Steamfitters; Pipelayers; Plasterers and Stucco Masons; Plumbers, Pipefitters, and Steamfitters; Rail-Track Laying and Maintenance Equipment Operators; Refractory Materials Repairers, Except Brickmasons; Reinforcing Iron and Rebar Workers; Riggers; Roofers; Rough Carpenters; Security and Fire Alarm Systems Installers; Segmental Pavers; Sheet Metal Workers; Stone Cutters and Carvers, Manufacturing; Stonemasons; Structural Iron and Steel Workers; Tapers; Terrazzo Workers and Finishers; Tile and Marble Setters.

Skills—Installation: Installing equipment, machines, wiring, or programs to meet specifications. **Quality Control Analysis:** Evaluating the quality or performance of products, services, or processes. **Repairing:** Repairing machines or systems, using the needed tools. **Operation and Control:** Controlling operations of equipment or systems. **Operation Monitoring:** Watching gauges, dials, or other indicators to make sure a machine is working properly. **Mathematics:** Numbers and their operations and interrelationships, including arithmetic, algebra, geometry, calculus, and statistics and their applications. **Systems Analysis:** Determining how a system should work and how changes will affect outcomes.

Education and Training Programs: Plumbing and Related Water Supply Services, Other; Plumbing Technology/Plumber Training. **Related Knowledge/Courses— Building and Construction:** Materials, methods, and the appropriate tools to construct objects, structures, and buildings. **Physics:** Physical principles, laws, and applications, including air, water, material dynamics, light, atomic principles, heat, electric theory, earth formations, and meteorological and related natural phenomena. **Mechanical Devices:** Machines and tools, including their designs, uses, benefits, repair, and maintenance. **Design:** Design techniques, principles, tools, and instruments involved in the production and use of precision technical plans, blueprints, drawings, and models. **Engineering and Technology:** Equipment, tools, and mechanical devices and their uses to produce motion, light, power, technology, and other applications. **Customer and Personal Service:** Principles and processes for providing customer and personal services, including needs assessment techniques, quality service standards, alternative delivery systems, and customer satisfaction evaluation techniques.

Work Environment: Outdoors; noisy; very hot or cold; hazardous equipment; standing; using hands on objects, tools, or controls.

Police Detectives

* Education/Training Required: Work experience in a related occupation
* Annual Earnings: $59,930
* Beginning Wage: $35,600
* Earnings Growth Potential: High
* Growth: 17.3%
* Annual Job Openings: 14,746
* Self-Employed: 0.3%
* Part-Time: 2.2%

The job openings listed here are shared with Criminal Investigators and Special Agents, with Immigration and Customs Inspectors, and with Police Identification and Records Officers.

Conduct investigations to prevent crimes or solve criminal cases. Provide testimony as witnesses in court. Secure deceased bodies and obtain evidence from them, preventing bystanders from tampering with bodies prior to medical examiners' arrival. Examine crime scenes to obtain clues and evidence such as loose hairs, fibers, clothing, or weapons. Obtain evidence from suspects. Record progress of investigations, maintain informational files on suspects, and submit reports to commanding officers or magistrates to authorize warrants. Check victims for signs of life such as breathing and pulse. Prepare charges or responses to charges, or information for court cases, according to formalized procedures. Obtain facts or statements from complainants, witnesses, and accused persons and record interviews, using recording devices. Prepare and serve search and arrest warrants. Note, mark, and photograph locations of objects found such as footprints, tire tracks, bullets, and bloodstains, and take measurements of each scene. Question individuals or observe persons and establishments to confirm information given to patrol officers. Preserve, process, and analyze items of evidence obtained from crime scenes and suspects, placing them in proper containers and destroying evidence no longer needed. Secure persons at scenes, keeping witnesses from conversing or leaving scenes before investigators arrive. Take photographs from all angles of relevant parts of crime scenes, including entrance and exit routes and streets and intersections. Analyze completed police reports to determine what additional information and investigative work is needed. Obtain summary of incidents from officers in charge at crime scenes, taking care to avoid disturbing evidence. Provide information to lab personnel concerning the source of each item of evidence and tests to be performed. Examine records and governmental agency files to find identifying data about suspects. Block or rope off scenes and check perimeters to ensure that scenes are completely secured. Summon medical help for injured individuals and alert medical personnel to take statements from them. Observe and photograph narcotic purchase transactions to compile evidence and protect undercover investigators.

Personality Type: Enterprising. These occupations frequently involve starting up and carrying out projects and can involve leading people and making many decisions. They sometimes require risk taking and often deal with business.

GOE—Interest Area/Cluster: 12. Law and Public Safety. **Work Group:** 12.04. Law Enforcement and Public Safety. **Other Jobs in This Work Group:** Bailiffs; Correctional Officers and Jailers; Criminal Investigators and Special Agents; Detectives and Criminal Investigators; Fire Investigators; Forensic Science Technicians; Parking Enforcement Workers; Police and Sheriff's Patrol Officers; Police Identification and Records Officers; Police Patrol Officers; Sheriffs and Deputy Sheriffs; Transit and Railroad Police.

Skills—Persuasion: Persuading others to approach things differently. **Systems Analysis:** Determining how a system should work and how changes will affect outcomes. **Social Perceptiveness:** Being aware of others' reactions and understanding why they react the way they do. **Systems Evaluation:** Looking at many indicators of system performance and taking into account their accuracy. **Complex Problem Solving:** Identifying complex problems, reviewing the options, and implementing solutions. **Critical Thinking:** Using logic and analysis to identify the strengths and weaknesses of different approaches. **Negotiation:** Bringing others together and trying to reconcile differences. **Active Listening:** Listening to what other people are saying and asking questions as appropriate.

Education and Training Programs: Criminal Justice/Police Science; Criminalistics and Criminal Science. **Related Knowledge/Courses—Public Safety and Security:** Weaponry; public safety; security operations, rules, regulations, precautions, and prevention; and the protection of people, data, and property. **Law and Government:** Laws, legal codes, court procedures, precedents, government regulations, executive orders, agency rules, and the democratic political process. **Psychology:** Human behavior and performance, mental processes, psychological research methods, and the assessment and treatment of behavioral and affective disorders. **Therapy and Counseling:** Information and techniques needed to rehabilitate physical and mental ailments and to provide career guidance, including alternative treatments, rehabilitation equipment and its proper use, and methods to evaluate treatment effects. **Customer and Personal Service:** Principles and processes for providing customer and personal services, including needs assessment techniques, quality service standards, alternative delivery systems, and customer satisfaction

evaluation techniques. **Philosophy and Theology:** Different philosophical systems and religions, including their basic principles, values, ethics, ways of thinking, customs, and practices and their impact on human culture.

Work Environment: More often outdoors than indoors; noisy; very hot or cold; contaminants; sitting.

Police Identification and Records Officers

- ❋ Education/Training Required: Work experience in a related occupation
- ❋ Annual Earnings: $59,930
- ❋ Beginning Wage: $35,600
- ❋ Earnings Growth Potential: High
- ❋ Growth: 17.3%
- ❋ Annual Job Openings: 14,746
- ❋ Self-Employed: 0.3%
- ❋ Part-Time: 2.2%

The job openings listed here are shared with Criminal Investigators and Special Agents, with Immigration and Customs Inspectors, and with Police Detectives.

Collect evidence at crime scene, classify and identify fingerprints, and photograph evidence for use in criminal and civil cases. Photograph crime or accident scenes for evidence records. Analyze and process evidence at crime scenes and in the laboratory, wearing protective equipment and using powders and chemicals. Look for trace evidence, such as fingerprints, hairs, fibers, or shoe impressions, using alternative light sources when necessary. Dust selected areas of crime scene and lift latent fingerprints, adhering to proper preservation procedures. Testify in court and present evidence. Package, store, and retrieve evidence. Serve as technical advisor and coordinate with other law enforcement workers to exchange information on crime scene collection activities. Perform emergency work during off-hours. Submit evidence to supervisors. Process film and prints from crime or accident scenes. Identify, classify, and file fingerprints, using systems such as the Henry Classification system.

Personality Type: Conventional. These occupations frequently involve following set procedures and routines and can include working with data and details more than with ideas. Usually there is a clear line of authority to follow.

GOE—Interest Area/Cluster: 12. Law and Public Safety. **Work Group:** 12.04. Law Enforcement and Public Safety. **Other Jobs in This Work Group:** Bailiffs; Correctional Officers and Jailers; Criminal Investigators and Special Agents; Detectives and Criminal Investigators; Fire Investigators; Forensic Science Technicians; Parking Enforcement Workers; Police and Sheriff's Patrol Officers; Police Detectives; Police Patrol Officers; Sheriffs and Deputy Sheriffs; Transit and Railroad Police.

Skills—Persuasion: Persuading others to approach things differently. **Judgment and Decision Making:** Weighing the relative costs and benefits of a potential action. **Negotiation:** Bringing others together and trying to reconcile differences. **Service Orientation:** Actively looking for ways to help people. **Social Perceptiveness:** Being aware of others' reactions and understanding why they react the way they do. **Critical Thinking:** Using logic and analysis to identify the strengths and weaknesses of different approaches. **Speaking:** Talking to others to effectively convey information. **Science:** Using scientific methods to solve problems.

Education and Training Programs: Criminal Justice/ Police Science; Criminalistics and Criminal Science. **Related Knowledge/Courses—Law and Government:** Laws, legal codes, court procedures, precedents, government regulations, executive orders, agency rules, and the democratic political process. **Public Safety and Security:** Weaponry; public safety; security operations, rules, regulations, precautions, and prevention; and the protection of people, data, and property. **Telecommunications:** Transmission, broadcasting, switching, control, and operation of telecommunications systems. **Customer and Personal Service:** Principles and processes for providing customer and personal services, including needs assessment techniques, quality service standards, alternative delivery systems, and customer satisfaction evaluation techniques. **Psychology:** Human behavior and performance, mental processes, psychological research methods, and the assessment and treatment of behavioral and affective disorders. **Computers and Electronics:** Electric circuit boards, processors, chips, and computer hardware and software, including applications and programming.

Work Environment: More often outdoors than indoors; noisy; very hot or cold; contaminants; using hands on objects, tools, or controls.

Police Patrol Officers

- ❇ Education/Training Required: Long-term on-the-job training
- ❇ Annual Earnings: $49,630
- ❇ Beginning Wage: $28,820
- ❇ Earnings Growth Potential: High
- ❇ Growth: 10.8%
- ❇ Annual Job Openings: 37,842
- ❇ Self-Employed: 0.0%
- ❇ Part-Time: 1.1%

The job openings listed here are shared with Sheriffs and Deputy Sheriffs.

Patrol assigned areas to enforce laws and ordinances, regulate traffic, control crowds, prevent crime, and arrest violators. Provide for public safety by maintaining order, responding to emergencies, protecting people and property, enforcing motor vehicle and criminal laws, and promoting good community relations. Monitor, note, report, and investigate suspicious persons and situations, safety hazards, and unusual or illegal activity in patrol area. Record facts to prepare reports that document incidents and activities. Identify, pursue, and arrest suspects and perpetrators of criminal acts. Patrol specific areas on foot, horseback, or motorized conveyance, responding promptly to calls for assistance. Review facts of incidents to determine if criminal acts or statute violations were involved. Investigate traffic accidents and other accidents to determine causes and to determine if crimes have been committed. Render aid to accident victims and other persons requiring first aid for physical injuries. Testify in court to present evidence or act as witness in traffic and criminal cases. Photograph or draw diagrams of crime or accident scenes and interview principals and eyewitnesses. Relay complaint and emergency-request information to appropriate agency dispatchers. Evaluate complaint and emergency-request information to determine response requirements. Process prisoners, and prepare and maintain records of prisoner bookings and prisoner statuses during booking and pre-trial processes. Monitor traffic to ensure motorists observe traffic regulations and exhibit safe driving procedures. Issue citations or warnings to violators of motor vehicle ordinances. Direct traffic flow and reroute traffic in case of emergencies. Inform citizens of community services and recommend options to facilitate longer-term problem resolution. Provide road information to assist motorists. Inspect public establishments to ensure compliance with rules and regulations. Act as official escorts at times such as when leading funeral processions or firefighters.

Personality Type: Realistic. These occupations frequently involve work activities that include practical, hands-on problems and solutions. They often deal with plants; animals; and real-world materials such as wood, tools, and machinery. Many of the occupations require working outside and don't involve a lot of paperwork or working closely with others.

GOE—Interest Area/Cluster: 12. Law and Public Safety. **Work Group:** 12.04. Law Enforcement and Public Safety. **Other Jobs in This Work Group:** Bailiffs; Correctional Officers and Jailers; Criminal Investigators and Special Agents; Detectives and Criminal Investigators; Fire Investigators; Forensic Science Technicians; Parking Enforcement Workers; Police and Sheriff's Patrol Officers; Police Detectives; Police Identification and Records Officers; Sheriffs and Deputy Sheriffs; Transit and Railroad Police.

Skills—Negotiation: Bringing others together and trying to reconcile differences. **Service Orientation:** Actively looking for ways to help people. **Management of Personnel Resources:** Motivating, developing, and directing people as they work; identifying the best people for the job. **Systems Analysis:** Determining how a system should work and how changes will affect outcomes. **Systems Evaluation:** Looking at many indicators of system performance and taking into account their accuracy.

Education and Training Programs: Criminal Justice/Police Science; Criminalistics and Criminal Science. **Related Knowledge/Courses—Psychology:** Human behavior and performance, mental processes, psychological research methods, and the assessment and treatment of behavioral and affective disorders. **Public Safety and Security:** Weaponry; public safety; security operations, rules, regulations, precautions, and prevention; and the protection of people, data, and property. **Law and Government:** Laws, legal codes, court procedures, precedents, government regulations, executive orders, agency rules, and the democratic political process. **Customer and Personal Service:** Principles and processes for providing customer and personal services, including needs assessment techniques, quality service standards, alternative delivery

systems, and customer satisfaction evaluation techniques. **Therapy and Counseling:** Information and techniques needed to rehabilitate physical and mental ailments and to provide career guidance, including alternative treatments, rehabilitation equipment and its proper use, and methods to evaluate treatment effects. **Sociology and Anthropology:** Group behavior and dynamics; societal trends and influences; and cultures and their history, migrations, ethnicity, and origins.

Work Environment: More often outdoors than indoors; noisy; very hot or cold; hazardous equipment; sitting.

Police, Fire, and Ambulance Dispatchers

- ❀ Education/Training Required: Moderate-term on-the-job training
- ❀ Annual Earnings: $32,660
- ❀ Beginning Wage: $20,910
- ❀ Earnings Growth Potential: Medium
- ❀ Growth: 13.6%
- ❀ Annual Job Openings: 17,628
- ❀ Self-Employed: 1.2%
- ❀ Part-Time: 6.3%

Receive complaints from public concerning crimes and police emergencies. Broadcast orders to police patrol units in vicinity of complaint to investigate. Operate radio, telephone, or computer equipment to receive reports of fires and medical emergencies and relay information or orders to proper officials. Question callers to determine their locations, and the nature of their problems to determine types of response needed. Receive incoming telephone or alarm system calls regarding emergency and non-emergency police and fire service, emergency ambulance service, information, and after hours calls for departments within a city. Determine response requirements and relative priorities of situations, and dispatch units in accordance with established procedures. Record details of calls, dispatches, and messages. Enter, update, and retrieve information from teletype networks and computerized data systems regarding such things as wanted persons, stolen property, vehicle registration, and stolen vehicles. Maintain access to, and security of, highly sensitive materials. Relay information and messages to and from emergency sites, to law enforcement agencies, and to all other individuals or groups requiring notification. Scan status charts and computer screens, and contact emergency response field units to determine emergency units available for dispatch. Observe alarm registers and scan maps to determine whether a specific emergency is in the dispatch service area. Maintain files of information relating to emergency calls such as personnel rosters, and emergency call-out and pager files. Monitor various radio frequencies such as those used by public works departments, school security, and civil defense to keep apprised of developing situations. Learn material and pass required tests for certification. Read and effectively interpret small-scale maps and information from a computer screen to determine locations and provide directions. Answer routine inquiries, and refer calls not requiring dispatches to appropriate departments and agencies. Test and adjust communication and alarm systems, and report malfunctions to maintenance units. Provide emergency medical instructions to callers. Monitor alarm systems to detect emergencies such as fires and illegal entry into establishments. Operate and maintain mobile dispatch vehicles and equipment.

Personality Type: Conventional. These occupations frequently involve following set procedures and routines and can include working with data and details more than with ideas. Usually there is a clear line of authority to follow.

GOE—Interest Area/Cluster: 03. Arts and Communication. **Work Group:** 03.10. Communications Technology. **Other Jobs in This Work Group:** Air Traffic Controllers; Airfield Operations Specialists; Dispatchers, Except Police, Fire, and Ambulance; Telephone Operators.

Skills—Negotiation: Bringing others together and trying to reconcile differences. **Operation Monitoring:** Watching gauges, dials, or other indicators to make sure a machine is working properly.

Education and Training Programs: No related CIP programs; this job is learned through moderate-term on-the-job training. **Related Knowledge/Courses—Telecommunications:** Transmission, broadcasting, switching, control, and operation of telecommunications systems. **Customer and Personal Service:** Principles and processes for providing customer and personal services, including needs assessment techniques, quality service standards, alternative delivery systems, and customer satisfaction evaluation techniques. **Clerical Studies:** Administrative

and clerical procedures and systems such as word-processing systems, filing and records management systems, stenography and transcription, forms, design principles, and other office procedures and terminology. **Law and Government:** Laws, legal codes, court procedures, precedents, government regulations, executive orders, agency rules, and the democratic political process. **Psychology:** Human behavior and performance, mental processes, psychological research methods, and the assessment and treatment of behavioral and affective disorders. **Public Safety and Security:** Weaponry; public safety; security operations, rules, regulations, precautions, and prevention; and the protection of people, data, and property.

Work Environment: Indoors; noisy; contaminants; sitting; using hands on objects, tools, or controls; repetitive motions.

Postal Service Clerks

- ❋ Education/Training Required: Short-term on-the-job training
- ❋ Annual Earnings: $45,050
- ❋ Beginning Wage: $40,300
- ❋ Earnings Growth Potential: Very low
- ❋ Growth: 1.2%
- ❋ Annual Job Openings: 3,703
- ❋ Self-Employed: 0.0%
- ❋ Part-Time: 4.2%

Perform any combination of tasks in a post office, such as receiving letters and parcels; selling postage and revenue stamps, postal cards, and stamped envelopes; filling out and selling money orders; placing mail in pigeonholes of mail rack or in bags according to state, address, or other scheme; and examining mail for correct postage. Keep money drawers in order and record and balance daily transactions. Weigh letters and parcels; compute mailing costs based on type, weight, and destination; and affix correct postage. Obtain signatures from recipients of registered or special delivery mail. Register, certify, and insure letters and parcels. Sell and collect payment for products such as stamps, prepaid mail envelopes, and money orders. Check mail to ensure correct postage and ensure that packages and letters are in proper condition for mailing. Answer questions regarding mail regulations and procedures, postage rates, and post office boxes. Complete forms regarding changes of address, theft or loss of mail, or special services such as registered or priority mail. Provide assistance to the public in complying with federal regulations of Postal Service and other federal agencies. Sort incoming and outgoing mail according to type and destination by hand or by operating electronic mail-sorting and scanning devices. Cash money orders. Rent post office boxes to customers. Put undelivered parcels away, retrieve them when customers come to claim them, and complete any related documentation. Provide customers with assistance in filing claims for mail theft or lost or damaged mail. Respond to complaints regarding mail theft, delivery problems, and lost or damaged mail, filling out forms and making appropriate referrals for investigation. Receive letters and parcels and place mail into bags. Feed mail into postage-canceling devices or hand-stamp mail to cancel postage. Transport mail from one work station to another. Set postage meters and calibrate them to ensure correct operation. Post announcements or government information on public bulletin boards.

Personality Type: Conventional. These occupations frequently involve following set procedures and routines and can include working with data and details more than with ideas. Usually there is a clear line of authority to follow.

GOE—Interest Area/Cluster: 04. Business and Administration. **Work Group:** 04.07. Records and Materials Processing. **Other Jobs in This Work Group:** Correspondence Clerks; File Clerks; Human Resources Assistants, Except Payroll and Timekeeping; Marking Clerks; Meter Readers, Utilities; Office Clerks, General; Order Fillers, Wholesale and Retail Sales; Postal Service Mail Sorters, Processors, and Processing Machine Operators; Procurement Clerks; Production, Planning, and Expediting Clerks; Shipping, Receiving, and Traffic Clerks; Stock Clerks and Order Fillers; Stock Clerks, Sales Floor; Stock Clerks—Stockroom, Warehouse, or Storage Yard; Weighers, Measurers, Checkers, and Samplers, Recordkeeping.

Skills: None met the criteria.

Education and Training Program: General Office Occupations and Clerical Services. **Related Knowledge/Courses—Sales and Marketing:** Principles and methods involved in showing, promoting, and selling products or services. This includes marketing strategies and tactics, product demonstration and sales techniques, and sales control systems. **Transportation:** Principles and methods for moving people or goods by air, rail, sea, or road, including their relative costs, advantages, and limitations. **Clerical Studies:** Administrative and clerical procedures and systems such as word-processing systems, filing and records management systems, stenography and transcription, forms, design principles, and other office procedures and terminology. **Public Safety and Security:** Weaponry; public safety; security operations, rules, regulations, precautions, and prevention; and the protection of people, data, and property.

Work Environment: Indoors; noisy; contaminants; standing; bending or twisting the body; repetitive motions.

Postal Service Mail Carriers

- ❀ Education/Training Required: Short-term on-the-job training
- ❀ Annual Earnings: $44,500
- ❀ Beginning Wage: $34,990
- ❀ Earnings Growth Potential: Very low
- ❀ Growth: 1.0%
- ❀ Annual Job Openings: 16,710
- ❀ Self-Employed: 0.0%
- ❀ Part-Time: 7.1%

Sort mail for delivery. Deliver mail on established routes by vehicle or on foot. Obtain signed receipts for registered, certified, and insured mail; collect associated charges; and complete any necessary paperwork. Sort mail for delivery, arranging it in delivery sequence. Deliver mail to residences and business establishments along specified routes by walking and/or driving, using a combination of satchels, carts, cars, and small trucks. Return to the post office with mail collected from homes, businesses, and public mailboxes. Turn in money and receipts collected along mail routes. Sign for cash-on-delivery and registered mail before leaving post offices. Record address changes and redirect mail for those addresses. Hold mail for customers who are away from delivery locations. Bundle mail in preparation for delivery or transportation to relay boxes. Leave notices telling patrons where to collect mail that could not be delivered. Meet schedules for the collection and return of mail. Return incorrectly addressed mail to senders. Maintain accurate records of deliveries. Answer customers' questions about postal services and regulations. Provide customers with change of address cards and other forms. Report any unusual circumstances concerning mail delivery, including the condition of street letter boxes. Register, certify, and insure parcels and letters. Travel to post offices to pick up the mail for routes and/or pick up mail from postal relay boxes. Enter change of address orders into computers that process forwarding address stickers. Complete forms that notify publishers of address changes. Sell stamps and money orders.

Personality Type: Conventional. These occupations frequently involve following set procedures and routines and can include working with data and details more than with ideas. Usually there is a clear line of authority to follow.

GOE—Interest Area/Cluster: 16. Transportation, Distribution, and Logistics. **Work Group:** 16.06. Other Services Requiring Driving. **Other Jobs in This Work Group:** Ambulance Drivers and Attendants, Except Emergency Medical Technicians; Bus Drivers, School; Bus Drivers, Transit and Intercity; Couriers and Messengers; Driver/Sales Workers; Parking Lot Attendants; Taxi Drivers and Chauffeurs.

Skills: None met the criteria.

Education and Training Program: General Office Occupations and Clerical Services. **Related Knowledge/Courses—Transportation:** Principles and methods for moving people or goods by air, rail, sea, or road, including their relative costs, advantages, and limitations. **Public Safety and Security:** Weaponry; public safety; security operations, rules, regulations, precautions, and prevention; and the protection of people, data, and property.

Work Environment: Outdoors; very hot or cold; contaminants; standing; using hands on objects, tools, or controls; repetitive motions.

Postal Service Mail Sorters, Processors, and Processing Machine Operators

- ❋ Education/Training Required: Short-term on-the-job training
- ❋ Annual Earnings: $43,700
- ❋ Beginning Wage: $26,100
- ❋ Earnings Growth Potential: High
- ❋ Growth: –8.4%
- ❋ Annual Job Openings: 6,855
- ❋ Self-Employed: 0.0%
- ❋ Part-Time: 3.8%

Prepare incoming and outgoing mail for distribution. Examine, sort, and route mail by state, type of mail, or other scheme. Load, operate, and occasionally adjust and repair mail-processing, -sorting, and -canceling machinery. Keep records of shipments, pouches, and sacks and perform other duties related to mail handling within the postal service. Must complete a competitive exam. Direct items according to established routing schemes, using computer-controlled keyboards or voice recognition equipment. Bundle, label, and route sorted mail to designated areas depending on destinations and according to established procedures and deadlines. Serve the public at counters or windows, such as by selling stamps and weighing parcels. Supervise other mail sorters. Train new workers. Distribute incoming mail into the correct boxes or pigeonholes. Operate various types of equipment, such as computer scanning equipment, addressographs, mimeographs, optical character readers, and bar-code sorters. Search directories to find correct addresses for redirected mail. Clear jams in sorting equipment. Open and label mail containers. Check items to ensure that addresses are legible and correct, that sufficient postage has been paid or the appropriate documentation is attached, and that items are in a suitable condition for processing. Rewrap soiled or broken parcels. Weigh articles to determine required postage. Move containers of mail, using equipment such as forklifts and automated "trains." Sort odd-sized mail by hand, sort mail that other workers have been unable to sort, and segregate items requiring special handling. Accept and check containers of mail from large-volume mailers, couriers, and contractors. Load and unload mail trucks, sometimes lifting containers of mail onto equipment that transports items to sorting stations. Cancel letter or parcel post stamps by hand. Dump sacks of mail onto conveyors for culling and sorting.

Personality Type: Conventional. These occupations frequently involve following set procedures and routines and can include working with data and details more than with ideas. Usually there is a clear line of authority to follow.

GOE—Interest Area/Cluster: 04. Business and Administration. **Work Group:** 04.07. Records and Materials Processing. **Other Jobs in This Work Group:** Correspondence Clerks; File Clerks; Human Resources Assistants, Except Payroll and Timekeeping; Marking Clerks; Meter Readers, Utilities; Office Clerks, General; Order Fillers, Wholesale and Retail Sales; Postal Service Clerks; Procurement Clerks; Production, Planning, and Expediting Clerks; Shipping, Receiving, and Traffic Clerks; Stock Clerks and Order Fillers; Stock Clerks, Sales Floor; Stock Clerks—Stockroom, Warehouse, or Storage Yard; Weighers, Measurers, Checkers, and Samplers, Recordkeeping.

Skills: None met the criteria.

Education and Training Program: General Office Occupations and Clerical Services. **Related Knowledge/Courses—Geography:** Various methods for describing the location and distribution of land, sea, and air masses, including their physical locations, relationships, and characteristics. **Public Safety and Security:** Weaponry; public safety; security operations, rules, regulations, precautions, and prevention; and the protection of people, data, and property.

Work Environment: Indoors; noisy; contaminants; standing; using hands on objects, tools, or controls; repetitive motions.

Postmasters and Mail Superintendents

* Education/Training Required: Work experience in a related occupation
* Annual Earnings: $57,900
* Beginning Wage: $38,540
* Earnings Growth Potential: Low
* Growth: –0.8%
* Annual Job Openings: 1,627
* Self-Employed: 0.0%
* Part-Time: 3.2%

Direct and coordinate operational, administrative, management, and supportive services of a U.S. post office or coordinate activities of workers engaged in postal and related work in assigned post office. Organize and supervise activities such as the processing of incoming and outgoing mail. Direct and coordinate operational, management, and supportive services of one or a number of postal facilities. Resolve customer complaints. Hire and train employees and evaluate their performance. Prepare employee work schedules. Negotiate labor disputes. Prepare and submit detailed and summary reports of post office activities to designated supervisors. Collect rents for post office boxes. Issue and cash money orders. Inform the public of available services and of postal laws and regulations. Select and train postmasters and managers of associate postal units. Confer with suppliers to obtain bids for proposed purchases and to requisition supplies; disburse funds according to federal regulations.

Personality Type: Enterprising. These occupations frequently involve starting up and carrying out projects and can involve leading people and making many decisions. They sometimes require risk taking and often deal with business.

GOE—Interest Area/Cluster: 16. Transportation, Distribution, and Logistics. **Work Group:** 16.01. Managerial Work in Transportation. **Other Jobs in This Work Group:** Aircraft Cargo Handling Supervisors; First-Line Supervisors/Managers of Transportation and Material-Moving Machine and Vehicle Operators; Railroad Conductors and Yardmasters; Storage and Distribution Managers; Transportation Managers; Transportation, Storage, and Distribution Managers.

P

Skills—Negotiation: Bringing others together and trying to reconcile differences. **Persuasion:** Persuading others to approach things differently. **Monitoring:** Assessing how well one is doing when learning or doing something. **Service Orientation:** Actively looking for ways to help people. **Management of Financial Resources:** Determining how money will be spent to get the work done and accounting for these expenditures. **Management of Personnel Resources:** Motivating, developing, and directing people as they work; identifying the best people for the job. **Active Listening:** Listening to what other people are saying and asking questions as appropriate. **Coordination:** Adjusting actions in relation to others' actions.

Education and Training Program: Public Administration. **Related Knowledge/Courses—Production and Processing:** Inputs, outputs, raw materials, waste, quality control, costs, and techniques for maximizing the manufacture and distribution of goods. **Personnel and Human Resources:** Principles and procedures for personnel recruitment; selection; training; compensation and benefits; labor relations and negotiation; and personnel information systems. **Public Safety and Security:** Weaponry; public safety; security operations, rules, regulations, precautions, and prevention; and the protection of people, data, and property. **Clerical Studies:** Administrative and clerical procedures and systems such as word-processing systems, filing and records management systems, stenography and transcription, forms, design principles, and other office procedures and terminology. **Economics and Accounting:** Economic and accounting principles and practices, the financial markets, banking, and the analysis and reporting of financial data. **Psychology:** Human behavior and performance, mental processes, psychological research methods, and the assessment and treatment of behavioral and affective disorders.

Work Environment: Indoors; contaminants; standing.

Power Plant Operators

- Education/Training Required: Long-term on-the-job training
- Annual Earnings: $56,640
- Beginning Wage: $37,040
- Earnings Growth Potential: Low
- Growth: 2.7%
- Annual Job Openings: 1,796
- Self-Employed: 0.0%
- Part-Time: 0.6%

Control, operate, or maintain machinery to generate electric power. Includes auxiliary equipment operators. Operate or control power-generating equipment, including boilers, turbines, generators, and reactors, using control boards or semi-automatic equipment. Monitor and inspect power plant equipment and indicators to detect evidence of operating problems. Adjust controls to generate specified electrical power or to regulate the flow of power between generating stations and substations. Regulate equipment operations and conditions such as water levels based on data from recording and indicating instruments or from computers. Take readings from charts, meters, and gauges at established intervals and take corrective steps as necessary. Inspect records and logbook entries and communicate with other plant personnel to assess equipment operating status. Start or stop generators, auxiliary pumping equipment, turbines, and other power plant equipment and connect or disconnect equipment from circuits. Control and maintain auxiliary equipment, such as pumps, fans, compressors, condensers, feedwater heaters, filters, and chlorinators, to supply water, fuel, lubricants, air, and auxiliary power. Clean, lubricate, and maintain equipment such as generators, turbines, pumps, and compressors in order to prevent equipment failure or deterioration. Communicate with systems operators to regulate and coordinate transmission loads and frequencies and line voltages. Record and compile operational data, completing and maintaining forms, logs, and reports. Open and close valves and switches in sequence upon signals from other workers in order to start or shut down auxiliary units. Collect oil, water, and electrolyte samples for laboratory analysis. Make adjustments or minor repairs, such as tightening leaking gland and pipe joints; report any needs for major repairs. Control generator output to match the phase, frequency, and voltage of electricity supplied to panels. Place standby emergency electrical generators on line in emergencies and monitor the temperature, output, and lubrication of the system. Receive outage calls and call in necessary personnel during power outages and emergencies.

Personality Type: Realistic. These occupations frequently involve work activities that include practical, hands-on problems and solutions. They often deal with plants; animals; and real-world materials such as wood, tools, and machinery. Many of the occupations require working outside and don't involve a lot of paperwork or working closely with others.

GOE—Interest Area/Cluster: 13. Manufacturing. **Work Group:** 13.16. Utility Operation and Energy Distribution. **Other Jobs in This Work Group:** Chemical Plant and System Operators; Gas Compressor and Gas Pumping Station Operators; Gas Plant Operators; Nuclear Power Reactor Operators; Petroleum Pump System Operators, Refinery Operators, and Gaugers; Power Distributors and Dispatchers; Ship Engineers; Stationary Engineers and Boiler Operators; Water and Liquid Waste Treatment Plant and System Operators.

Skills—Operation Monitoring: Watching gauges, dials, or other indicators to make sure a machine is working properly. **Equipment Maintenance:** Performing routine maintenance and determining when and what kind of maintenance is needed. **Operation and Control:** Controlling operations of equipment or systems. **Technology Design:** Generating or adapting equipment and technology to serve user needs. **Systems Evaluation:** Looking at many indicators of system performance and taking into account their accuracy. **Science:** Using scientific methods to solve problems. **Equipment Selection:** Determining the kind of tools and equipment needed to do a job. **Coordination:** Adjusting actions in relation to others' actions.

Education and Training Programs: No related CIP programs; this job is learned through long-term on-the-job training. **Related Knowledge/Courses—Physics:** Physical principles, laws, and applications, including air, water, material dynamics, light, atomic principles, heat, electric theory, earth formations, and meteorological and related natural phenomena. **Mechanical Devices:** Machines and tools, including their designs, uses, benefits, repair, and maintenance. **Chemistry:** The composition, structure, and properties of substances and of the chemical processes

and transformations that they undergo. This includes uses of chemicals and their interactions, danger signs, production techniques, and disposal methods. **Engineering and Technology:** Equipment, tools, and mechanical devices and their uses to produce motion, light, power, technology, and other applications. **Public Safety and Security:** Weaponry; public safety; security operations, rules, regulations, precautions, and prevention; and the protection of people, data, and property. **Computers and Electronics:** Electric circuit boards, processors, chips, and computer hardware and software, including applications and programming.

Work Environment: Indoors; noisy; very hot or cold; contaminants; high places; hazardous conditions.

Preschool Teachers, Except Special Education

- ❋ Education/Training Required: Postsecondary vocational training
- ❋ Annual Earnings: $23,130
- ❋ Beginning Wage: $15,380
- ❋ Earnings Growth Potential: Low
- ❋ Growth: 26.3%
- ❋ Annual Job Openings: 78,172
- ❋ Self-Employed: 1.1%
- ❋ Part-Time: 25.1%

Instruct children (normally up to 5 years of age) in activities designed to promote social, physical, and intellectual growth needed for primary school in preschool, day care center, or other child development facility. May be required to hold state certification. Provide a variety of materials and resources for children to explore, manipulate, and use, both in learning activities and in imaginative play. Attend to children's basic needs by feeding them, dressing them, and changing their diapers. Establish and enforce rules for behavior and procedures for maintaining order. Read books to entire classes or to small groups. Teach basic skills such as color, shape, number, and letter recognition; personal hygiene; and social skills. Organize and lead activities designed to promote physical, mental, and social development, such as games, arts and crafts, music, storytelling, and field trips. Observe and evaluate children's performance, behavior, social development, and physical health. Meet with parents and guardians to discuss their children's progress and needs, determine their priorities for their children, and suggest ways that they can promote learning and development. Identify children showing signs of emotional, developmental, or health-related problems and discuss them with supervisors, parents or guardians, and child development specialists. Enforce all administration policies and rules governing students. Prepare materials and classrooms for class activities. Serve meals and snacks in accordance with nutritional guidelines. Teach proper eating habits and personal hygiene. Assimilate arriving children to the school environment by greeting them, helping them remove outerwear, and selecting activities of interest to them. Adapt teaching methods and instructional materials to meet students' varying needs and interests. Establish clear objectives for all lessons, units, and projects and communicate those objectives to children. Demonstrate activities to children. Arrange indoor and outdoor space to facilitate creative play, motor-skill activities, and safety. Plan and conduct activities for a balanced program of instruction, demonstration, and work time that provides students with opportunities to observe, question, and investigate. Maintain accurate and complete student records as required by laws, district policies, and administrative regulations.

Personality Type: Social. These occupations frequently involve working with, communicating with, and teaching people and often involve helping or providing service to others.

GOE—Interest Area/Cluster: 05. Education and Training. **Work Group:** 05.02. Preschool, Elementary, and Secondary Teaching and Instructing. **Other Jobs in This Work Group:** Elementary School Teachers, Except Special Education; Kindergarten Teachers, Except Special Education; Middle School Teachers, Except Special and Vocational Education; Secondary School Teachers, Except Special and Vocational Education; Special Education Teachers, Middle School; Special Education Teachers, Preschool, Kindergarten, and Elementary School; Special Education Teachers, Secondary School; Teacher Assistants; Vocational Education Teachers, Middle School; Vocational Education Teachers, Secondary School.

Skills—Learning Strategies: Using multiple approaches when learning or teaching new things. **Social Perceptiveness:** Being aware of others' reactions and understanding why they react the way they do. **Writing:** Communicating effectively with others in writing as indicated by the needs of the audience. **Negotiation:** Bringing others together and trying to reconcile differences.

Education and Training Programs: Child Care and Support Services Management; Early Childhood Education and Teaching; Montessori Teacher Education. **Related Knowledge/Courses—Philosophy and Theology:** Different philosophical systems and religions, including their basic principles, values, ethics, ways of thinking, customs, and practices and their impact on human culture. **Sociology and Anthropology:** Group behavior and dynamics; societal trends and influences; and cultures and their history, migrations, ethnicity, and origins. **Psychology:** Human behavior and performance, mental processes, psychological research methods, and the assessment and treatment of behavioral and affective disorders. **Customer and Personal Service:** Principles and processes for providing customer and personal services, including needs assessment techniques, quality service standards, alternative delivery systems, and customer satisfaction evaluation techniques. **Education and Training:** Instructional methods and training techniques, including curriculum design principles, learning theory, group and individual teaching techniques, design of individual development plans, and test design principles.

Work Environment: Indoors; standing; walking and running; bending or twisting the body.

Private Detectives and Investigators

- ❋ Education/Training Required: Work experience in a related occupation
- ❋ Annual Earnings: $37,640
- ❋ Beginning Wage: $20,990
- ❋ Earnings Growth Potential: High
- ❋ Growth: 18.2%
- ❋ Annual Job Openings: 7,329
- ❋ Self-Employed: 29.7%
- ❋ Part-Time: 11.1%

Detect occurrences of unlawful acts or infractions of rules in private establishments or seek, examine, and compile information for clients. Question persons to obtain evidence for cases of divorce, child custody, or missing persons or information about an individual's character or financial status. Conduct private investigations on a paid basis. Confer with establishment officials, security departments, police, or postal officials to identify problems, provide information, and receive instructions. Observe and document activities of individuals to detect unlawful acts or to obtain evidence for cases, using binoculars and still or video cameras. Investigate companies' financial standings or locate funds stolen by embezzlers, using accounting skills. Monitor industrial or commercial properties to enforce conformance to establishment rules and to protect people or property. Search computer databases, credit reports, public records, tax and legal filings, and other resources to locate persons or to compile information for investigations. Write reports and case summaries to document investigations. Count cash and review transactions, sales checks, and register tapes to verify amounts and to identify shortages. Perform undercover operations such as evaluating employee performance and honesty by posing as customers or employees. Expose fraudulent insurance claims or stolen funds. Alert appropriate personnel to suspects' locations. Conduct background investigations of individuals, such as pre-employment checks, to obtain information about each individual's character, financial status, or personal history. Testify at hearings and court trials to present evidence. Warn troublemakers causing problems on establishment premises and eject them from premises when necessary. Obtain and analyze information on suspects, crimes, and disturbances to solve cases, identify criminal activity, and gather information for court cases. Apprehend suspects and release them to law-enforcement authorities or security personnel.

Personality Type: Enterprising. These occupations frequently involve starting up and carrying out projects and can involve leading people and making many decisions. They sometimes require risk taking and often deal with business.

GOE—Interest Area/Cluster: 12. Law and Public Safety. **Work Group:** 12.05. Safety and Security. **Other Jobs in This Work Group:** Animal Control Workers; Crossing Guards; Gaming Surveillance Officers and Gaming Investigators; Lifeguards, Ski Patrol, and Other Recreational Protective Service Workers; Security Guards; Transportation Security Screeners.

Skills—Management of Financial Resources: Determining how money will be spent to get the work done and accounting for these expenditures. **Persuasion:** Persuading others to approach things differently. **Time Management:** Managing one's own time and the time of others. **Writing:** Communicating effectively with others in writing as indicated by the needs of the audience. **Service Orientation:** Actively looking for ways to help people. **Technology Design:** Generating or adapting equipment and technology to serve user needs. **Speaking:** Talking to others to effectively convey information. **Judgment and Decision Making:** Weighing the relative costs and benefits of a potential action.

Education and Training Program: Criminal Justice/Police Science. **Related Knowledge/Courses—Clerical Studies:** Administrative and clerical procedures and systems such as word-processing systems, filing and records management systems, stenography and transcription, forms, design principles, and other office procedures and terminology. **Law and Government:** Laws, legal codes, court procedures, precedents, government regulations, executive orders, agency rules, and the democratic political process. **Customer and Personal Service:** Principles and processes for providing customer and personal services, including needs assessment techniques, quality service standards, alternative delivery systems, and customer satisfaction evaluation techniques. **Computers and Electronics:** Electric circuit boards, processors, chips, and computer hardware and software, including applications and programming. **Sales and Marketing:** Principles and methods involved in showing, promoting, and selling products or services. This includes marketing strategies and tactics, product demonstration and sales techniques, and sales control systems. **Mathematics:** Numbers and their operations and interrelationships, including arithmetic, algebra, geometry, calculus, and statistics and their applications.

Work Environment: Outdoors; noisy; very hot or cold; very bright or dim lighting; sitting; using hands on objects, tools, or controls.

Production, Planning, and Expediting Clerks

* Education/Training Required: Moderate-term on-the-job training
* Annual Earnings: $39,690
* Beginning Wage: $24,520
* Earnings Growth Potential: Medium
* Growth: 4.2%
* Annual Job Openings: 52,735
* Self-Employed: 1.4%
* Part-Time: 6.7%

Coordinate and expedite the flow of work and materials within or between departments of an establishment according to production schedules. Duties include reviewing and distributing production, work, and shipment schedules; conferring with department supervisors to determine progress of work and completion dates; and compiling reports on progress of work, inventory levels, costs, and production problems. Examine documents, materials, and products, and monitor work processes in order to assess completeness, accuracy, and conformance to standards and specifications. Review documents such as production schedules, work orders, and staffing tables to determine personnel and materials requirements, and material priorities. Revise production schedules when required due to design changes, labor or material shortages, backlogs, or other interruptions, collaborating with management, marketing, sales, production, and engineering. Confer with department supervisors and other personnel to assess progress and discuss needed changes. Confer with establishment personnel, vendors, and customers to coordinate production and shipping activities, and to resolve complaints or eliminate delays. Record production data, including volume produced, consumption of raw materials, and quality control measures. Requisition and maintain inventories of materials and supplies necessary to meet production demands. Calculate figures such as required amounts of labor and materials, manufacturing costs, and wages, using pricing schedules, adding machines, calculators, or computers. Distribute production schedules and work orders to departments. Compile information such as production rates and progress, materials inventories, materials used, and customer information, so that status reports can be completed. Arrange for delivery, assembly, and distribution of supplies and parts in order to expedite flow of materials and meet production schedules. Contact suppliers to verify shipment details. Maintain files such as maintenance records, bills of lading, and cost reports. Plan production commitments and timetables for business units, specific programs, and/or jobs, using sales forecasts. Establish and prepare product construction directions and locations; information on required tools, materials, and equipment; numbers of workers needed; and cost projections. Compile and prepare documentation related to production sequences, transportation, personnel schedules, and purchase, maintenance, and repair orders. Provide documentation and information to account for delays, difficulties, and changes to cost estimates.

Personality Type: Conventional. These occupations frequently involve following set procedures and routines and can include working with data and details more than with ideas. Usually there is a clear line of authority to follow.

GOE—Interest Area/Cluster: 04. Business and Administration. **Work Group:** 04.07. Records and Materials Processing. **Other Jobs in This Work Group:** Correspondence Clerks; File Clerks; Human Resources Assistants, Except Payroll and Timekeeping; Marking Clerks; Meter Readers, Utilities; Office Clerks, General; Order Fillers, Wholesale and Retail Sales; Postal Service Clerks; Postal Service Mail Sorters, Processors, and Processing Machine Operators; Procurement Clerks; Shipping, Receiving, and Traffic Clerks; Stock Clerks and Order Fillers; Stock Clerks, Sales Floor; Stock Clerks—Stockroom, Warehouse, or Storage Yard; Weighers, Measurers, Checkers, and Samplers, Recordkeeping.

Skills—Management of Material Resources: Obtaining and seeing to the appropriate use of equipment, facilities, and materials needed to do certain work. **Operations Analysis:** Analyzing needs and product requirements to create a design. **Management of Financial Resources:** Determining how money will be spent to get the work done and accounting for these expenditures. **Systems Evaluation:** Looking at many indicators of system performance and taking into account their accuracy. **Negotiation:** Bringing others together and trying to reconcile differences. **Mathematics:** Using mathematics to solve problems. **Coordination:** Adjusting actions in relation to others' actions. **Persuasion:** Persuading others to approach things differently.

Education and Training Program: Parts, Warehousing, and Inventory Management Operations. **Related Knowledge/Courses—Production and Processing:** Inputs, outputs, raw materials, waste, quality control, costs, and techniques for maximizing the manufacture and distribution of goods. **Clerical Studies:** Administrative and clerical procedures and systems such as word-processing systems, filing and records management systems, stenography and transcription, forms, design principles, and other office procedures and terminology. **Computers and Electronics:** Electric circuit boards, processors, chips, and computer hardware and software, including applications and programming. **Administration and Management:** Principles and processes involved in business and organizational planning, coordination, and execution. This includes strategic planning, resource allocation, manpower modeling, leadership techniques, and production methods. **Mathematics:** Numbers and their operations and interrelationships, including arithmetic, algebra, geometry, calculus, and statistics and their applications. **Customer and Personal Service:** Principles and processes for providing customer and personal services, including needs assessment techniques, quality service standards, alternative delivery systems, and customer satisfaction evaluation techniques.

Work Environment: Indoors; noisy; contaminants; sitting.

Purchasing Agents, Except Wholesale, Retail, and Farm Products

⚹ Education/Training Required: Long-term on-the-job training
⚹ Annual Earnings: $52,460
⚹ Beginning Wage: $32,580
⚹ Earnings Growth Potential: Medium
⚹ Growth: 0.1%
⚹ Annual Job Openings: 22,349
⚹ Self-Employed: 1.6%
⚹ Part-Time: 3.8%

Purchase machinery, equipment, tools, parts, supplies, or services necessary for the operation of an establishment. Purchase raw or semi-finished materials for manufacturing. Purchase the highest-quality merchandise at the lowest possible price and in correct amounts. Prepare purchase orders, solicit bid proposals, and review requisitions for goods and services. Research and evaluate suppliers based on price, quality, selection, service, support, availability, reliability, production and distribution capabilities, and the supplier's reputation and history. Analyze price proposals, financial reports, and other data and information to determine reasonable prices. Monitor and follow applicable laws and regulations. Negotiate, or renegotiate, and administer contracts with suppliers, vendors, and other representatives. Monitor shipments to ensure that goods come in on time and trace shipments and follow up undelivered goods in the event of problems. Confer with staff, users, and vendors to discuss defective or unacceptable goods or services and determine corrective action. Evaluate and monitor contract performance to ensure compliance with contractual obligations and to determine need for changes. Maintain and review computerized or manual records of items purchased, costs, delivery, product performance, and inventories. Review catalogs, industry periodicals, directories, trade journals, and Internet sites and consult with other department personnel to locate necessary goods and services. Study sales records and inventory levels of current stock to develop strategic purchasing programs that facilitate employee access to supplies. Interview vendors and visit suppliers' plants and distribution centers to examine and learn about products, services, and prices. Arrange the payment of duty and freight charges. Hire, train, and/or supervise purchasing clerks, buyers, and expediters. Write and review product specifications, maintaining a working technical knowledge of the goods or services to be purchased. Monitor changes affecting supply and demand, tracking market conditions, price trends, or futures markets. Formulate policies and procedures for bid proposals and procurement of goods and services. Attend meetings, trade shows, conferences, conventions, and seminars to network with people in other purchasing departments.

Personality Type: Conventional. These occupations frequently involve following set procedures and routines and can include working with data and details more than with ideas. Usually there is a clear line of authority to follow.

GOE—Interest Area/Cluster: 14. Retail and Wholesale Sales and Service. **Work Group:** 14.05. Purchasing. **Other Jobs in This Work Group:** Wholesale and Retail Buyers, Except Farm Products.

Skills—Operations Analysis: Analyzing needs and product requirements to create a design. **Management of Financial Resources:** Determining how money will be spent to get the work done and accounting for these expenditures. **Management of Material Resources:** Obtaining and seeing to the appropriate use of equipment, facilities, and materials needed to do certain work. **Mathematics:** Using mathematics to solve problems. **Writing:** Communicating effectively with others in writing as indicated by the needs of the audience. **Management of Personnel Resources:** Motivating, developing, and directing people as they work; identifying the best people for the job. **Speaking:** Talking to others to effectively convey information. **Judgment and Decision Making:** Weighing the relative costs and benefits of a potential action.

Education and Training Programs: Merchandising and Buying Operations; Sales, Distribution, and Marketing Operations, General. **Related Knowledge/Courses—Clerical Studies:** Administrative and clerical procedures and systems such as word-processing systems, filing and records management systems, stenography and transcription, forms, design principles, and other office procedures and terminology. **Economics and Accounting:** Economic and accounting principles and practices, the financial markets, banking, and the analysis and reporting of financial data. **Production and Processing:** Inputs, outputs, raw materials, waste, quality control, costs, and techniques for maximizing the manufacture and distribution of goods. **Administration and Management:** Principles and processes involved in business and organizational planning, coordination, and execution. This includes strategic planning, resource allocation, manpower modeling, leadership techniques, and production methods. **Computers and Electronics:** Electric circuit boards, processors, chips, and computer hardware and software, including applications and programming. **Communications and Media:** Media production, communication, and dissemination techniques and methods, including alternative ways to inform and entertain via written, oral, and visual media.

Work Environment: Indoors; sitting; using hands on objects, tools, or controls; repetitive motions.

Radiation Therapists

- ❋ Education/Training Required: Associate degree
- ❋ Annual Earnings: $70,010
- ❋ Beginning Wage: $46,580
- ❋ Earnings Growth Potential: Low
- ❋ Growth: 24.8%
- ❋ Annual Job Openings: 1,461
- ❋ Self-Employed: 0.0%
- ❋ Part-Time: 10.3%

Provide radiation therapy to patients as prescribed by radiologists according to established practices and standards. Duties may include reviewing prescriptions and diagnoses; acting as liaisons with physicians and supportive care personnel; preparing equipment such as immobilization, treatment, and protection devices; and maintaining records, reports, and files. May assist in dosimetry procedures and tumor localization. Position patients for treatment with accuracy according to prescription. Administer prescribed doses of radiation to specific body parts, using radiation therapy equipment according to established practices and standards. Check radiation therapy equipment to ensure proper operation. Review prescriptions, diagnoses, patient charts, and identification. Follow principles of radiation protection for patients, radiation therapists, and others. Maintain records, reports, and files as required, including such information as radiation dosages, equipment settings, and patients' reactions. Conduct most treatment sessions independently, in accordance with long-term treatment plans and under general direction of patients' physicians. Enter data into computers and set controls to operate and adjust equipment and regulate dosages. Observe and reassure patients during treatments and report unusual reactions to physicians or turn equipment off if unexpected adverse reactions occur. Calculate actual treatment dosages delivered during each session. Check for side effects such as skin irritation, nausea, and hair loss to assess patients' reaction to treatment. Prepare and construct equipment such as immobilization, treatment, and protection devices. Educate, prepare, and reassure patients and their families by answering questions, providing physical assistance, and reinforcing physicians' advice regarding treatment reactions and post-treatment care. Provide assistance to other health care personnel during dosimetry procedures and tumor localization. Help physicians, radiation oncologists, and clinical physicists to prepare physical and technical aspects of radiation treatment plans, using information about patient conditions and anatomies. Photograph treated areas of patients and process film. Act as liaisons with medical physicists and supportive care personnel. Train and supervise student or subordinate radiotherapy technologists. Implement appropriate follow-up care plans. Assist in the preparation of sealed radioactive materials such as cobalt, radium, cesium, and isotopes for use in radiation treatments. Store, sterilize, or prepare the special applicators containing the radioactive substances implanted by physicians.

Personality Type: Social. These occupations frequently involve working with, communicating with, and teaching people and often involve helping or providing service to others.

GOE—Interest Area/Cluster: 08. Health Science. **Work Group:** 08.07. Medical Therapy. **Other Jobs in This Work Group:** Audiologists; Massage Therapists; Occupational Therapist Aides; Occupational Therapist Assistants; Occupational Therapists; Physical Therapist Aides; Physical Therapist Assistants; Physical Therapists; Recreational Therapists; Respiratory Therapists; Respiratory Therapy Technicians; Speech-Language Pathologists.

Skills—Operation Monitoring: Watching gauges, dials, or other indicators to make sure a machine is working properly. **Operation and Control:** Controlling operations of equipment or systems. **Quality Control Analysis:** Evaluating the quality or performance of products, services, or processes.

Education and Training Program: Medical Radiologic Technology/Science—Radiation Therapist Training. **Related Knowledge/Courses—Medicine and Dentistry:** The information and techniques needed to diagnose and treat injuries, diseases, and deformities. This includes symptoms, treatment alternatives, drug properties and interactions, and preventive health-care measures. **Biology:** Plant and animal living tissue, cells, organisms, and entities, including their functions, interdependencies, and interactions with each other and the environment. **Physics:** Physical principles, laws, and applications, including air, water, material dynamics, light, atomic principles, heat, electric theory, earth formations, and meteorological and related natural phenomena. **Psychology:** Human behavior

and performance, mental processes, psychological research methods, and the assessment and treatment of behavioral and affective disorders. **Philosophy and Theology:** Different philosophical systems and religions, including their basic principles, values, ethics, ways of thinking, customs, and practices and their impact on human culture. **Therapy and Counseling:** Information and techniques needed to rehabilitate physical and mental ailments and to provide career guidance, including alternative treatments, rehabilitation equipment and its proper use, and methods to evaluate treatment effects.

Work Environment: Indoors; radiation; disease or infections; standing; walking and running; using hands on objects, tools, or controls.

Radiologic Technicians

- ❋ Education/Training Required: Associate degree
- ❋ Annual Earnings: $50,260
- ❋ Beginning Wage: $33,910
- ❋ Earnings Growth Potential: Low
- ❋ Growth: 15.1%
- ❋ Annual Job Openings: 12,836
- ❋ Self-Employed: 1.1%
- ❋ Part-Time: 17.3%

The job openings listed here are shared with Radiologic Technologists.

Maintain and use equipment and supplies necessary to demonstrate portions of the human body on X-ray film or fluoroscopic screen for diagnostic purposes. Use beam-restrictive devices and patient-shielding techniques to minimize radiation exposure to patient and staff. Position X-ray equipment and adjust controls to set exposure factors, such as time and distance. Position patient on examining table and set up and adjust equipment to obtain optimum view of specific body area as requested by physician. Determine patients' X-ray needs by reading requests or instructions from physicians. Make exposures necessary for the requested procedures, rejecting and repeating work that does not meet established standards. Process exposed radiographs, using film processors or computer-generated methods. Explain procedures to patients to reduce anxieties and obtain cooperation. Perform procedures such as

R

linear tomography; mammography; sonograms; joint and cyst aspirations; routine contrast studies; routine fluoroscopy; and examinations of the head, trunk, and extremities under supervision of physician. Prepare and set up X-ray room for patient. Assure that sterile supplies, contrast materials, catheters, and other required equipment are present and in working order, requisitioning materials as necessary. Maintain records of patients examined, examinations performed, views taken, and technical factors used. Provide assistance to physicians or other technologists in the performance of more complex procedures. Monitor equipment operation and report malfunctioning equipment to supervisor. Provide students and other technologists with suggestions of additional views, alternate positioning, or improved techniques to ensure the images produced are of the highest quality. Coordinate work of other technicians or technologists when procedures require more than one person. Assist with on-the-job training of new employees and students and provide input to supervisors regarding training performance. Maintain a current file of examination protocols. Operate mobile X-ray equipment in operating room, in emergency room, or at patient's bedside. Provide assistance in radiopharmaceutical administration, monitoring patients' vital signs and notifying the radiologist of any relevant changes.

Personality Type: Realistic. These occupations frequently involve work activities that include practical, hands-on problems and solutions. They often deal with plants; animals; and real-world materials such as wood, tools, and machinery. Many of the occupations require working outside and don't involve a lot of paperwork or working closely with others.

GOE—Interest Area/Cluster: 08. Health Science. **Work Group:** 08.06. Medical Technology. **Other Jobs in This Work Group:** Biological Technicians; Cardiovascular Technologists and Technicians; Diagnostic Medical Sonographers; Medical and Clinical Laboratory Technicians; Medical and Clinical Laboratory Technologists; Medical Equipment Preparers; Medical Records and Health Information Technicians; Nuclear Medicine Technologists; Opticians, Dispensing; Orthotists and Prosthetists; Radiologic Technologists; Radiologic Technologists and Technicians.

Skills—Science: Using scientific methods to solve problems. **Operation Monitoring:** Watching gauges, dials, or other indicators to make sure a machine is working

properly. **Equipment Selection:** Determining the kind of tools and equipment needed to do a job. **Operation and Control:** Controlling operations of equipment or systems. **Service Orientation:** Actively looking for ways to help people. **Active Listening:** Listening to what other people are saying and asking questions as appropriate. **Negotiation:** Bringing others together and trying to reconcile differences. **Writing:** Communicating effectively with others in writing as indicated by the needs of the audience.

Education and Training Programs: Allied Health Diagnostic, Intervention, and Treatment Professions, Other; Medical Radiologic Technology/Science—Radiation Therapist Training; Radiologic Technology/Science—Radiographer Training. **Related Knowledge/Courses—Medicine and Dentistry:** The information and techniques needed to diagnose and treat injuries, diseases, and deformities. This includes symptoms, treatment alternatives, drug properties and interactions, and preventive health-care measures. **Clerical Studies:** Administrative and clerical procedures and systems such as word-processing systems, filing and records management systems, stenography and transcription, forms, design principles, and other office procedures and terminology. **Psychology:** Human behavior and performance, mental processes, psychological research methods, and the assessment and treatment of behavioral and affective disorders. **Physics:** Physical principles, laws, and applications, including air, water, material dynamics, light, atomic principles, heat, electric theory, earth formations, and meteorological and related natural phenomena. **Biology:** Plant and animal living tissue, cells, organisms, and entities, including their functions, interdependencies, and interactions with each other and the environment. **Chemistry:** The composition, structure, and properties of substances and of the chemical processes and transformations that they undergo. This includes uses of chemicals and their interactions, danger signs, production techniques, and disposal methods.

Work Environment: Indoors; radiation; disease or infections; standing; walking and running; using hands on objects, tools, or controls.

Radiologic Technologists

* Education/Training Required: Associate degree
* Annual Earnings: $50,260
* Beginning Wage: $33,910
* Earnings Growth Potential: Low
* Growth: 15.1%
* Annual Job Openings: 12,836
* Self-Employed: 1.1%
* Part-Time: 17.3%

The job openings listed here are shared with Radiologic Technicians.

Take X rays and Computerized Axial Tomography (CAT or CT) scans or administer nonradioactive materials into patient's bloodstream for diagnostic purposes. Includes technologists who specialize in other modalities such as computed tomography, ultrasound, and magnetic resonance. Use radiation safety measures and protection devices to comply with government regulations and to ensure safety of patients and staff. Review and evaluate developed X rays, video tape, or computer generated information to determine if images are satisfactory for diagnostic purposes. Position imaging equipment and adjust controls to set exposure times and distances, according to specification of examinations. Explain procedures and observe patients to ensure safety and comfort during scans. Key commands and data into computers to document and specify scan sequences, adjust transmitters and receivers, or photograph certain images. Operate or oversee operation of radiologic and magnetic imaging equipment to produce images of the body for diagnostic purposes. Position and immobilize patients on examining tables. Record, process, and maintain patient data and treatment records, and prepare reports. Take thorough and accurate patient medical histories. Remove and process film. Set up examination rooms, ensuring that all necessary equipment is ready. Monitor patients' conditions and reactions, reporting abnormal signs to physicians. Coordinate work with clerical personnel or other technologists. Provide assistance in dressing or changing seriously ill, injured, or disabled patients. Demonstrate new equipment, procedures, and techniques to staff, and provide technical assistance. Collaborate with other medical team members such as physicians and nurses to conduct angiography or special vascular procedures. Prepare and administer oral or injected contrast media to patients. Monitor video displays of areas being scanned and adjust density or contrast to improve picture quality. Operate fluoroscope to aid physicians to view and guide wires or catheters through blood vessels to areas of interest. Assign duties to radiologic staffs to maintain patient flows and achieve production goals. Perform scheduled maintenance and minor emergency repairs on radiographic equipment. Perform administrative duties such as developing departmental operating budgets, coordinating purchases of supplies and equipment, and preparing work schedules.

Personality Type: Realistic. These occupations frequently involve work activities that include practical, hands-on problems and solutions. They often deal with plants; animals; and real-world materials such as wood, tools, and machinery. Many of the occupations require working outside and don't involve a lot of paperwork or working closely with others.

GOE—Interest Area/Cluster: 08. Health Science. **Work Group:** 08.06. Medical Technology. **Other Jobs in This Work Group:** Biological Technicians; Cardiovascular Technologists and Technicians; Diagnostic Medical Sonographers; Medical and Clinical Laboratory Technicians; Medical and Clinical Laboratory Technologists; Medical Equipment Preparers; Medical Records and Health Information Technicians; Nuclear Medicine Technologists; Opticians, Dispensing; Orthotists and Prosthetists; Radiologic Technicians; Radiologic Technologists and Technicians.

Skills—Operation Monitoring: Watching gauges, dials, or other indicators to make sure a machine is working properly. **Operation and Control:** Controlling operations of equipment or systems.

Education and Training Programs: Allied Health Diagnostic, Intervention, and Treatment Professions, Other; Medical Radiologic Technology/Science—Radiation Therapist Training; Radiologic Technology/Science—Radiographer Training. **Related Knowledge/Courses—Medicine and Dentistry:** The information and techniques needed to diagnose and treat injuries, diseases, and deformities. This includes symptoms, treatment alternatives, drug properties and interactions, and preventive healthcare measures. **Physics:** Physical principles, laws, and applications, including air, water, material dynamics, light, atomic principles, heat, electric theory, earth formations, and meteorological and related natural phenomena. **Customer and Personal Service:** Principles and processes for providing customer and personal services, including needs assessment techniques, quality service standards, alternative delivery systems, and customer satisfaction evaluation techniques. **Biology:** Plant and animal living tissue, cells, organisms, and entities, including their functions, interdependencies, and interactions with each other and the environment. **Psychology:** Human behavior and performance, mental processes, psychological research methods, and the assessment and treatment of behavioral and affective disorders. **Chemistry:** The composition, structure, and properties of substances and of the chemical processes and transformations that they undergo. This includes uses of chemicals and their interactions, danger signs, production techniques, and disposal methods.

Work Environment: Indoors; radiation; disease or infections; standing; using hands on objects, tools, or controls; repetitive motions.

Rail Car Repairers

- ❋ Education/Training Required: Long-term on-the-job training
- ❋ Annual Earnings: $44,970
- ❋ Beginning Wage: $28,220
- ❋ Earnings Growth Potential: Medium
- ❋ Growth: 5.1%
- ❋ Annual Job Openings: 1,989
- ❋ Self-Employed: 4.0%
- ❋ Part-Time: 2.3%

Diagnose, adjust, repair, or overhaul railroad rolling stock, mine cars, or mass-transit rail cars. Repair or replace defective or worn parts such as bearings, pistons, and gears, using hand tools, torque wrenches, power tools, and welding equipment. Test units for operability before and after repairs. Remove locomotives, car mechanical units, or other components, using pneumatic hoists and jacks, pinch bars, hand tools, and cutting torches. Record conditions of cars and repair and maintenance work performed or to be performed. Inspect components such as bearings, seals, gaskets, wheels, and coupler assemblies to determine if repairs are needed. Inspect the interior and exterior of rail cars coming into rail yards to identify defects and to determine the extent of wear and damage. Adjust repaired or replaced units as needed to ensure proper operation. Perform scheduled maintenance and clean units and components. Repair and maintain electrical and electronic controls for propulsion and braking systems. Repair, fabricate, and install steel or wood fittings, using blueprints, shop sketches, and instruction manuals. Disassemble units such as water pumps, control valves, and compressors so that repairs can be made. Align car sides for installation of car ends and crossties, using width gauges, turnbuckles, and wrenches. Measure diameters of axle wheel seats, using micrometers, and mark dimensions on axles so that wheels can be bored to specified dimensions. Replace defective wiring and insulation and tighten electrical connections, using hand tools. Test electrical systems of cars by operating systems and using testing equipment such as ammeters. Install and repair interior flooring, fixtures, walls, plumbing, steps, and platforms. Examine car roofs for wear and damage and repair defective sections, using roofing material, cement, nails, and waterproof paint. Paint car exteriors, interiors, and fixtures. Repair car upholstery. Repair window sash frames, attach weather stripping and channels to frames, and replace window glass, using hand tools.

Personality Type: Realistic. These occupations frequently involve work activities that include practical, hands-on problems and solutions. They often deal with plants; animals; and real-world materials such as wood, tools, and machinery. Many of the occupations require working outside and don't involve a lot of paperwork or working closely with others.

GOE—Interest Area/Cluster: 13. Manufacturing. **Work Group:** 13.14. Vehicle and Facility Mechanical Work. **Other Jobs in This Work Group:** Aircraft Mechanics and Service Technicians; Aircraft Structure, Surfaces, Rigging, and Systems Assemblers; Automotive Body and Related Repairers; Automotive Glass Installers and Repairers; Automotive Master Mechanics; Automotive Service Technicians and Mechanics; Automotive Specialty Technicians; Bus and Truck Mechanics and Diesel Engine Specialists; Farm Equipment Mechanics; Fiberglass Laminators and Fabricators; Mobile Heavy Equipment Mechanics, Except Engines; Motorboat Mechanics; Motorcycle Mechanics; Outdoor Power Equipment and Other Small Engine Mechanics; Recreational Vehicle Service Technicians; Tire Repairers and Changers.

Skills—Repairing: Repairing machines or systems, using the needed tools. **Installation:** Installing equipment, machines, wiring, or programs to meet specifications. **Equipment Maintenance:** Performing routine maintenance and determining when and what kind of maintenance is needed. **Troubleshooting:** Determining what is causing an operating error and deciding what to do about it. **Operation Monitoring:** Watching gauges, dials, or other indicators to make sure a machine is working properly. **Technology Design:** Generating or adapting equipment and technology to serve user needs. **Operation and Control:** Controlling operations of equipment or systems. **Systems Analysis:** Determining how a system should work and how changes will affect outcomes.

Education and Training Program: Heavy Equipment Maintenance Technology/Technician. **Related Knowledge/Courses—Mechanical Devices:** Machines and tools, including their designs, uses, benefits, repair, and maintenance. **Public Safety and Security:** Weaponry; public safety; security operations, rules, regulations, precautions, and prevention; and the protection of people, data, and property. **Production and Processing:** Inputs, outputs, raw materials, waste, quality control, costs, and techniques for maximizing the manufacture and distribution of goods.

Work Environment: Outdoors; noisy; very hot or cold; contaminants; standing; using hands on objects, tools, or controls.

Rail Yard Engineers, Dinkey Operators, and Hostlers

- ❋ Education/Training Required: Moderate-term on-the-job training
- ❋ Annual Earnings: $39,020
- ❋ Beginning Wage: $24,020
- ❋ Earnings Growth Potential: Medium
- ❋ Growth: 2.9%
- ❋ Annual Job Openings: 3,548
- ❋ Self-Employed: 0.0%
- ❋ Part-Time: 1.7%

The job openings listed here are shared with Locomotive Engineers and with Locomotive Firers.

Drive switching or other locomotive or dinkey engines within railroad yard, industrial plant, quarry, construction project, or similar location. Confer with conductors and other workers via radio-telephones or computers to exchange switching information. Signal crew members for movement of engines or trains, using lanterns, hand signals, radios, or telephones. Observe and respond to wayside and cab signals, including colored light signals, position signals, torpedoes, flags, and hot box detectors. Drive engines within railroad yards or other establishments to couple, uncouple, or switch railroad cars. Inspect engines before and after use to ensure proper operation. Apply and release hand brakes. Read switching instructions and daily car schedules to determine work to be performed or receive orders from yard conductors. Inspect the condition of stationary trains, rolling stock, and equipment. Observe water levels and oil, air, and steam pressure gauges to ensure proper operation of equipment. Spot cars for loading and unloading at customer locations. Inspect track for defects such as broken rails and switch malfunctions. Ride on moving cars by holding onto grab irons and standing on ladder steps. Operate track switches, derails, automatic switches, and retarders to change routing of train or cars. Receive, relay, and act upon instructions and inquiries from train operations and customer service center personnel. Couple and uncouple air hoses and electrical connections between cars. Report arrival and departure times, train delays, work order completion, and time on duty. Pull knuckles to open them for coupling. Provide assistance in aligning drawbars, using available equipment to lift, pull, or push on the drawbars. Drive locomotives to and from various stations in roundhouses to have locomotives cleaned, serviced, repaired, or supplied. Record numbers of cars available, numbers of cars sent to repair stations, and types of service needed. Perform routine repair and maintenance duties. Operate and control dinkey engines to transport and shunt cars at industrial or mine sites. Operate flatcars equipped with derricks or railcars to transport personnel or equipment. Provide assistance in the installation or repair of rails and ties.

Personality Type: Realistic. These occupations frequently involve work activities that include practical, hands-on problems and solutions. They often deal with plants; animals; and real-world materials such as wood, tools, and machinery. Many of the occupations require working outside and don't involve a lot of paperwork or working closely with others.

R

GOE—Interest Area/Cluster: 16. Transportation, Distribution, and Logistics. **Work Group:** 16.04. Rail Vehicle Operation. **Other Jobs in This Work Group:** Locomotive Engineers; Locomotive Firers; Subway and Streetcar Operators.

Skills—Operation and Control: Controlling operations of equipment or systems. **Operation Monitoring:** Watching gauges, dials, or other indicators to make sure a machine is working properly. **Equipment Maintenance:** Performing routine maintenance and determining when and what kind of maintenance is needed. **Troubleshooting:** Determining what is causing an operating error and deciding what to do about it. **Repairing:** Repairing machines or systems, using the needed tools. **Instructing:** Teaching others how to do something. **Coordination:** Adjusting actions in relation to others' actions. **Active Listening:** Listening to what other people are saying and asking questions as appropriate.

Education and Training Program: Truck and Bus Driver Training/Commercial Vehicle Operation. **Related Knowledge/Courses—Transportation:** Principles and methods for moving people or goods by air, rail, sea, or road, including their relative costs, advantages, and limitations. **Telecommunications:** Transmission, broadcasting, switching, control, and operation of telecommunications systems. **Public Safety and Security:** Weaponry; public safety; security operations, rules, regulations, precautions, and prevention; and the protection of people, data, and property. **Law and Government:** Laws, legal codes, court procedures, precedents, government regulations, executive orders, agency rules, and the democratic political process. **Personnel and Human Resources:** Principles and procedures for personnel recruitment; selection; training; compensation and benefits; labor relations and negotiation; and personnel information systems. **Mechanical Devices:** Machines and tools, including their designs, uses, benefits, repair, and maintenance.

Work Environment: Outdoors; noisy; very hot or cold; contaminants; sitting; using hands on objects, tools, or controls.

Railroad Conductors and Yardmasters

- ❋ Education/Training Required: Moderate-term on-the-job training
- ❋ Annual Earnings: $58,650
- ❋ Beginning Wage: $37,490
- ❋ Earnings Growth Potential: Medium
- ❋ Growth: 9.1%
- ❋ Annual Job Openings: 3,235
- ❋ Self-Employed: 0.0%
- ❋ Part-Time: 0.3%

Conductors coordinate activities of train crew on passenger or freight train. Coordinate activities of switch-engine crew within yard of railroad, industrial plant, or similar location. Yardmasters coordinate activities of workers engaged in railroad traffic operations, such as the makeup or breakup of trains; yard switching; and review train schedules and switching orders. Signal engineers to begin train runs, stop trains, or change speed, using telecommunications equipment or hand signals. Receive information regarding train or rail problems from dispatchers or from electronic monitoring devices. Direct and instruct workers engaged in yard activities, such as switching tracks, coupling and uncoupling cars, and routing inbound and outbound traffic. Keep records of the contents and destination of each train car and make sure that cars are added or removed at proper points on routes. Operate controls to activate track switches and traffic signals. Instruct workers to set warning signals in front and at rear of trains during emergency stops. Direct engineers to move cars to fit planned train configurations, combining or separating cars to make up or break up trains. Receive instructions from dispatchers regarding trains' routes, timetables, and cargoes. Review schedules, switching orders, way bills, and shipping records to obtain cargo loading and unloading information and to plan work. Confer with engineers regarding train routes, timetables, and cargoes and to discuss alternative routes when there are rail defects or obstructions. Arrange for the removal of defective cars from trains at stations or stops. Inspect each car periodically during runs. Observe yard traffic to determine tracks available to accommodate inbound and outbound traffic. Document and prepare reports of accidents, unscheduled stops, or delays. Confirm routes and destination information for freight cars. Supervise and coordinate crew activities to transport freight and passengers and to provide boarding, porter, maid, and meal services to passengers. Supervise workers in the inspection and maintenance of mechanical equipment to ensure efficient and safe train operation. Record departure and arrival times, messages, tickets and revenue collected, and passenger accommodations and destinations. Inspect freight cars for compliance with sealing procedures and record car numbers and seal numbers. Collect tickets, fares, or passes from passengers. Verify accuracy of timekeeping instruments with engineers to ensure that trains depart on time.

Personality Type: Enterprising. These occupations frequently involve starting up and carrying out projects and can involve leading people and making many decisions. They sometimes require risk taking and often deal with business.

GOE—Interest Area/Cluster: 16. Transportation, Distribution, and Logistics. **Work Group:** 16.01. Managerial Work in Transportation. **Other Jobs in This Work Group:** Aircraft Cargo Handling Supervisors; First-Line Supervisors/Managers of Transportation and Material-Moving Machine and Vehicle Operators; Postmasters and Mail Superintendents; Storage and Distribution Managers; Transportation Managers; Transportation, Storage, and Distribution Managers.

Skills—Operation and Control: Controlling operations of equipment or systems. **Operation Monitoring:** Watching gauges, dials, or other indicators to make sure a machine is working properly. **Coordination:** Adjusting actions in relation to others' actions. **Equipment Maintenance:** Performing routine maintenance and determining when and what kind of maintenance is needed. **Troubleshooting:** Determining what is causing an operating error and deciding what to do about it. **Instructing:** Teaching others how to do something.

Education and Training Program: Truck and Bus Driver Training/Commercial Vehicle Operation. **Related Knowledge/Courses—Transportation:** Principles and methods for moving people or goods by air, rail, sea, or road, including their relative costs, advantages, and limitations. **Public Safety and Security:** Weaponry; public safety; security operations, rules, regulations, precautions, and prevention; and the protection of people, data, and property. **Mechanical Devices:** Machines and tools, including their designs, uses, benefits, repair, and maintenance.

Work Environment: Outdoors; noisy; very hot or cold; very bright or dim lighting; contaminants; hazardous equipment.

Real Estate Brokers

- ❋ Education/Training Required: Work experience in a related occupation
- ❋ Annual Earnings: $58,860
- ❋ Beginning Wage: $25,990
- ❋ Earnings Growth Potential: Very high
- ❋ Growth: 11.1%
- ❋ Annual Job Openings: 18,689
- ❋ Self-Employed: 63.5%
- ❋ Part-Time: 15.5%

Operate real estate office or work for commercial real estate firm, overseeing real estate transactions. Other duties usually include selling real estate or renting properties and arranging loans. Sell, for a fee, real estate owned by others. Obtain agreements from property owners to place properties for sale with real estate firms. Monitor fulfillment of purchase contract terms to ensure that they are handled in a timely manner. Compare a property with similar properties that have recently sold to determine its competitive market price. Act as an intermediary in negotiations between buyers and sellers over property prices and settlement details and during the closing of sales. Generate lists of properties for sale, their locations and descriptions, and available financing options, using computers. Maintain knowledge of real estate law; local economies; fair housing laws; and types of available mortgages, financing options, and government programs. Check work completed by loan officers, attorneys, and other professionals to ensure that it is performed properly. Arrange for financing of property purchases. Appraise property values, assessing income potential when relevant. Maintain awareness of current income tax regulations, local zoning, building and tax laws, and growth possibilities of the area where a property is located. Manage and operate real estate offices, handling associated business details. Supervise agents who handle real estate transactions. Rent properties or manage rental properties. Arrange for title searches of properties being sold. Give buyers virtual tours of properties in which they are interested, using computers. Review property details to ensure that environmental regulations are

R

met. Develop, sell, or lease property used for industry or manufacturing. Maintain working knowledge of various factors that determine a farm's capacity to produce, including agricultural variables and proximity to market centers and transportation facilities.

Personality Type: Enterprising. These occupations frequently involve starting up and carrying out projects and can involve leading people and making many decisions. They sometimes require risk taking and often deal with business.

GOE—Interest Area/Cluster: 14. Retail and Wholesale Sales and Service. **Work Group:** 14.03. General Sales. **Other Jobs in This Work Group:** Parts Salespersons; Real Estate Sales Agents; Retail Salespersons; Sales Representatives, Wholesale and Manufacturing, Except Technical and Scientific Products; Service Station Attendants.

Skills—Management of Financial Resources: Determining how money will be spent to get the work done and accounting for these expenditures. **Negotiation:** Bringing others together and trying to reconcile differences. **Mathematics:** Using mathematics to solve problems. **Judgment and Decision Making:** Weighing the relative costs and benefits of a potential action. **Active Listening:** Listening to what other people are saying and asking questions as appropriate. **Persuasion:** Persuading others to approach things differently. **Service Orientation:** Actively looking for ways to help people. **Complex Problem Solving:** Identifying complex problems, reviewing the options, and implementing solutions.

Education and Training Program: Real Estate. **Related Knowledge/Courses—Sales and Marketing:** Principles and methods involved in showing, promoting, and selling products or services. This includes marketing strategies and tactics, product demonstration and sales techniques, and sales control systems. **Law and Government:** Laws, legal codes, court procedures, precedents, government regulations, executive orders, agency rules, and the democratic political process. **Building and Construction:** Materials, methods, and the appropriate tools to construct objects, structures, and buildings. **Customer and Personal Service:** Principles and processes for providing customer and personal services, including needs assessment techniques, quality service standards, alternative delivery systems, and customer satisfaction evaluation techniques. **Personnel and Human Resources:** Principles and procedures for

personnel recruitment; selection; training; compensation and benefits; labor relations and negotiation; and personnel information systems. **Economics and Accounting:** Economic and accounting principles and practices, the financial markets, banking, and the analysis and reporting of financial data.

Work Environment: More often indoors than outdoors; sitting.

Real Estate Sales Agents

- ✳ Education/Training Required: Postsecondary vocational training
- ✳ Annual Earnings: $40,600
- ✳ Beginning Wage: $20,930
- ✳ Earnings Growth Potential: High
- ✳ Growth: 10.6%
- ✳ Annual Job Openings: 61,232
- ✳ Self-Employed: 60.2%
- ✳ Part-Time: 15.5%

Rent, buy, or sell property for clients. Perform duties such as studying property listings, interviewing prospective clients, accompanying clients to property site, discussing conditions of sale, and drawing up real estate contracts. Includes agents who represent buyer. Present purchase offers to sellers for consideration. Confer with escrow companies, lenders, home inspectors, and pest control operators to ensure that terms and conditions of purchase agreements are met before closing dates. Interview clients to determine what kinds of properties they are seeking. Prepare documents such as representation contracts, purchase agreements, closing statements, deeds, and leases. Coordinate property closings, overseeing signing of documents and disbursement of funds. Act as an intermediary in negotiations between buyers and sellers, generally representing one or the other. Promote sales of properties through advertisements, open houses, and participation in multiple listing services. Compare a property with similar properties that have recently sold to determine its competitive market price. Coordinate appointments to show homes to prospective buyers. Generate lists of properties that are compatible with buyers' needs and financial resources. Display commercial, industrial, agricultural, and residential properties to clients and explain their features. Arrange for title searches to determine whether clients have clear property titles. Review plans for new construction with clients, enumerating and recommending available options and features. Answer clients' questions regarding construction work, financing, maintenance, repairs, and appraisals. Accompany buyers during visits to and inspections of property, advising them on the suitability and value of the homes they are visiting. Inspect condition of premises and arrange for necessary maintenance or notify owners of maintenance needs. Advise sellers on how to make homes more appealing to potential buyers. Arrange meetings between buyers and sellers when details of transactions need to be negotiated. Advise clients on market conditions, prices, mortgages, legal requirements, and related matters. Evaluate mortgage options to help clients obtain financing at the best prevailing rates and terms. Review property listings, trade journals, and relevant literature and attend conventions, seminars, and staff and association meetings to remain knowledgeable about real estate markets.

Personality Type: Enterprising. These occupations frequently involve starting up and carrying out projects and can involve leading people and making many decisions. They sometimes require risk taking and often deal with business.

GOE—Interest Area/Cluster: 14. Retail and Wholesale Sales and Service. **Work Group:** 14.03. General Sales. **Other Jobs in This Work Group:** Parts Salespersons; Real Estate Brokers; Retail Salespersons; Sales Representatives, Wholesale and Manufacturing, Except Technical and Scientific Products; Service Station Attendants.

Skills—Negotiation: Bringing others together and trying to reconcile differences. **Service Orientation:** Actively looking for ways to help people. **Coordination:** Adjusting actions in relation to others' actions. **Speaking:** Talking to others to effectively convey information. **Management of Financial Resources:** Determining how money will be spent to get the work done and accounting for these expenditures. **Writing:** Communicating effectively with others in writing as indicated by the needs of the audience. **Time Management:** Managing one's own time and the time of others. **Mathematics:** Using mathematics to solve problems.

Education and Training Program: Real Estate. **Related Knowledge/Courses—Sales and Marketing:** Principles and methods involved in showing, promoting, and selling products or services. This includes marketing strategies and tactics, product demonstration and sales techniques, and sales control systems. **Clerical Studies:** Administrative and clerical procedures and systems such as word-processing systems, filing and records management systems, stenography and transcription, forms, design principles, and other office procedures and terminology. **Law and Government:** Laws, legal codes, court procedures, precedents, government regulations, executive orders, agency rules, and the democratic political process. **Customer and Personal Service:** Principles and processes for providing customer and personal services, including needs assessment techniques, quality service standards, alternative delivery systems, and customer satisfaction evaluation techniques. **Economics and Accounting:** Economic and accounting principles and practices, the financial markets, banking, and the analysis and reporting of financial data. **Building and Construction:** Materials, methods, and the appropriate tools to construct objects, structures, and buildings.

Work Environment: More often indoors than outdoors; sitting.

Receptionists and Information Clerks

- ❋ Education/Training Required: Short-term on-the-job training
- ❋ Annual Earnings: $23,710
- ❋ Beginning Wage: $16,290
- ❋ Earnings Growth Potential: Low
- ❋ Growth: 17.2%
- ❋ Annual Job Openings: 334,124
- ❋ Self-Employed: 1.4%
- ❋ Part-Time: 31.7%

Answer inquiries and obtain information for general public, customers, visitors, and other interested parties. Provide information regarding activities conducted at establishment and location of departments, offices, and employees within organization. Operate telephone switchboard to answer, screen, and forward calls, providing information, taking messages, and scheduling appointments. Receive payment and record receipts for services. Perform administrative support tasks such as proofreading, transcribing handwritten information, and operating calculators or computers to work with pay records, invoices, balance sheets, and other documents. Greet persons entering establishment, determine nature and purpose of visit, and direct or escort them to specific destinations. Hear and resolve complaints from customers and public. File and maintain records. Transmit information or documents to customers, using computer, mail, or facsimile machine. Schedule appointments and maintain and update appointment calendars. Analyze data to determine answers to questions from customers or members of the public. Provide information about establishment such as location of departments or offices, employees within the organization, or services provided. Keep a current record of staff members' whereabouts and availability. Collect, sort, distribute, and prepare mail, messages, and courier deliveries. Calculate and quote rates for tours, stocks, insurance policies, or other products and services. Take orders for merchandise or materials and send them to the proper departments to be filled. Process and prepare memos, correspondence, travel vouchers, or other documents. Schedule space and equipment for special programs and prepare lists of participants. Enroll individuals to participate in programs and notify them of their acceptance. Conduct tours or deliver talks describing features of public facility such as a historic site or national park. Perform duties such as taking care of plants and straightening magazines to maintain lobby or reception area.

Personality Type: Conventional. These occupations frequently involve following set procedures and routines and can include working with data and details more than with ideas. Usually there is a clear line of authority to follow.

GOE—Interest Area/Cluster: 14. Retail and Wholesale Sales and Service. **Work Group:** 14.06. Customer Service. **Other Jobs in This Work Group:** Cashiers; Counter and Rental Clerks; Customer Service Representatives; Gaming Cage Workers; Gaming Change Persons and Booth Cashiers; Order Clerks.

Skills—Active Listening: Listening to what other people are saying and asking questions as appropriate. **Service Orientation:** Actively looking for ways to help people. **Writing:** Communicating effectively with others in writing as indicated by the needs of the audience. **Social Perceptiveness:** Being aware of others' reactions and understanding why they react the way they do. **Reading Comprehension:** Understanding written sentences and paragraphs in work-related documents.

Education and Training Programs: Health Unit Coordinator/Ward Clerk Training; Medical Reception/

Receptionist Training; Receptionist Training. **Related Knowledge/Courses—Clerical Studies:** Administrative and clerical procedures and systems such as word-processing systems, filing and records management systems, stenography and transcription, forms, design principles, and other office procedures and terminology. **Customer and Personal Service:** Principles and processes for providing customer and personal services, including needs assessment techniques, quality service standards, alternative delivery systems, and customer satisfaction evaluation techniques. **Computers and Electronics:** Electric circuit boards, processors, chips, and computer hardware and software, including applications and programming.

Work Environment: Indoors; sitting; repetitive motions.

Recreational Vehicle Service Technicians

- ❋ Education/Training Required: Long-term on-the-job training
- ❋ Annual Earnings: $31,760
- ❋ Beginning Wage: $20,460
- ❋ Earnings Growth Potential: Medium
- ❋ Growth: 18.2%
- ❋ Annual Job Openings: 2,442
- ❋ Self-Employed: 3.5%
- ❋ Part-Time: 14.6%

Diagnose, inspect, adjust, repair, or overhaul recreational vehicles, including travel trailers. May specialize in maintaining gas, electrical, hydraulic, plumbing, or chassis/towing systems as well as repairing generators, appliances, and interior components. Examine or test operation of parts or systems that have been repaired to ensure completeness of repairs. Repair plumbing and propane gas lines, using caulking compounds and plastic or copper pipe. Inspect recreational vehicles to diagnose problems; then perform necessary adjustment, repair, or overhaul. Locate and repair frayed wiring, broken connections, or incorrect wiring, using ohmmeters, soldering irons, tape, and hand tools. Confer with customers, read work orders, and examine vehicles needing repair to determine the nature and extent of damage. List parts needed, estimate costs, and plan work procedures, using parts lists, technical manuals, and diagrams. Connect electrical systems to outside power sources and activate switches to test the operation of appliances and light fixtures. Connect water hoses to inlet pipes of plumbing systems and test operation of toilets and sinks. Remove damaged exterior panels and repair and replace structural frame members. Open and close doors, windows, and drawers to test their operation, trimming edges to fit as necessary. Repair leaks with caulking compound or replace pipes, using pipe wrenches. Refinish wood surfaces on cabinets, doors, moldings, and floors, using power sanders, putty, spray equipment, brushes, paints, or varnishes. Reset hardware, using chisels, mallets, and screwdrivers. Seal open sides of modular units to prepare them for shipment, using polyethylene sheets, nails, and hammers.

Personality Type: Realistic. These occupations frequently involve work activities that include practical, hands-on problems and solutions. They often deal with plants; animals; and real-world materials such as wood, tools, and machinery. Many of the occupations require working outside and don't involve a lot of paperwork or working closely with others.

GOE—Interest Area/Cluster: 13. Manufacturing. **Work Group:** 13.14. Vehicle and Facility Mechanical Work. **Other Jobs in This Work Group:** Aircraft Mechanics and Service Technicians; Aircraft Structure, Surfaces, Rigging, and Systems Assemblers; Automotive Body and Related Repairers; Automotive Glass Installers and Repairers; Automotive Master Mechanics; Automotive Service Technicians and Mechanics; Automotive Specialty Technicians; Bus and Truck Mechanics and Diesel Engine Specialists; Farm Equipment Mechanics; Fiberglass Laminators and Fabricators; Mobile Heavy Equipment Mechanics, Except Engines; Motorboat Mechanics; Motorcycle Mechanics; Outdoor Power Equipment and Other Small Engine Mechanics; Rail Car Repairers; Tire Repairers and Changers.

Skills—Repairing: Repairing machines or systems, using the needed tools. **Installation:** Installing equipment, machines, wiring, or programs to meet specifications. **Troubleshooting:** Determining what is causing an operating error and deciding what to do about it. **Equipment Maintenance:** Performing routine maintenance and determining when and what kind of maintenance is needed. **Technology Design:** Generating or adapting equipment and technology to serve user needs. **Operation Monitoring:** Watching gauges, dials, or other indicators to make

sure a machine is working properly. **Equipment Selection:** Determining the kind of tools and equipment needed to do a job. **Systems Evaluation:** Looking at many indicators of system performance and taking into account their accuracy.

Education and Training Program: Vehicle Maintenance and Repair Technologies, Other. **Related Knowledge/Courses—Mechanical Devices:** Machines and tools, including their designs, uses, benefits, repair, and maintenance. **Building and Construction:** Materials, methods, and the appropriate tools to construct objects, structures, and buildings. **Chemistry:** The composition, structure, and properties of substances and of the chemical processes and transformations that they undergo. This includes uses of chemicals and their interactions, danger signs, production techniques, and disposal methods. **Physics:** Physical principles, laws, and applications, including air, water, material dynamics, light, atomic principles, heat, electric theory, earth formations, and meteorological and related natural phenomena. **Engineering and Technology:** Equipment, tools, and mechanical devices and their uses to produce motion, light, power, technology, and other applications. **Design:** Design techniques, principles, tools, and instruments involved in the production and use of precision technical plans, blueprints, drawings, and models.

Work Environment: Noisy; contaminants; cramped work space, awkward positions; hazardous equipment; standing; using hands on objects, tools, or controls.

Refrigeration Mechanics and Installers

* Education/Training Required: Long-term on-the-job training
* Annual Earnings: $38,360
* Beginning Wage: $24,240
* Earnings Growth Potential: Medium
* Growth: 8.7%
* Annual Job Openings: 29,719
* Self-Employed: 12.7%
* Part-Time: 3.6%

The job openings listed here are shared with Heating and Air Conditioning Mechanics and Installers.

Install and repair industrial and commercial refrigerating systems. Braze or solder parts to repair defective joints and leaks. Observe and test system operation, using gauges and instruments. Test lines, components, and connections for leaks. Dismantle malfunctioning systems and test components, using electrical, mechanical, and pneumatic testing equipment. Adjust or replace worn or defective mechanisms and parts and reassemble repaired systems. Read blueprints to determine location, size, capacity, and type of components needed to build refrigeration system. Supervise and instruct assistants. Perform mechanical overhauls and refrigerant reclaiming. Install wiring to connect components to an electric power source. Cut, bend, thread, and connect pipe to functional components and water, power, or refrigeration system. Adjust valves according to specifications and charge system with proper type of refrigerant by pumping the specified gas or fluid into the system. Estimate, order, pick up, deliver, and install materials and supplies needed to maintain equipment in good working condition. Install expansion and control valves, using acetylene torches and wrenches. Mount compressor, condenser, and other components in specified locations on frames, using hand tools and acetylene welding equipment. Keep records of repairs and replacements made and causes of malfunctions. Schedule work with customers and initiate work orders, house requisitions, and orders from stock. Lay out reference points for installation of structural and functional components, using measuring instruments. Fabricate and assemble structural and functional components of refrigeration system, using hand tools, power tools, and welding equipment. Lift and align components into position, using hoist or block and tackle. Drill holes and install mounting brackets and hangers into floor and walls of building. Insulate shells and cabinets of systems.

Personality Type: Realistic. These occupations frequently involve work activities that include practical, hands-on problems and solutions. They often deal with plants; animals; and real-world materials such as wood, tools, and machinery. Many of the occupations require working outside and don't involve a lot of paperwork or working closely with others.

GOE—Interest Area/Cluster: 02. Architecture and Construction. **Work Group:** 02.05. Systems and Equipment Installation, Maintenance, and Repair. **Other Jobs in This Work Group:** Electrical and Electronics Repairers, Powerhouse, Substation, and Relay; Electrical Power-Line Installers and Repairers; Elevator Installers and Repairers; Heating and Air Conditioning Mechanics and Installers; Maintenance and Repair Workers, General; Telecommunications Equipment Installers and Repairers, Except Line Installers; Telecommunications Line Installers and Repairers.

Skills—Installation: Installing equipment, machines, wiring, or programs to meet specifications. **Repairing:** Repairing machines or systems, using the needed tools. **Equipment Maintenance:** Performing routine maintenance and determining when and what kind of maintenance is needed. **Operation Monitoring:** Watching gauges, dials, or other indicators to make sure a machine is working properly. **Science:** Using scientific methods to solve problems. **Systems Evaluation:** Looking at many indicators of system performance and taking into account their accuracy. **Systems Analysis:** Determining how a system should work and how changes will affect outcomes. **Troubleshooting:** Determining what is causing an operating error and deciding what to do about it.

Education and Training Programs: Heating, Air Conditioning, and Refrigeration Technology/Technician Training (ACH/ACR/ACHR/HRAC/HVAC); Heating, Air Conditioning, Ventilation, and Refrigeration Maintenance Technology/Technician Training; Solar Energy Technology/Technician Training. **Related Knowledge/Courses—Building and Construction:** Materials, methods, and the appropriate tools to construct objects, structures, and buildings. **Mechanical Devices:** Machines and tools, including their designs, uses, benefits, repair, and maintenance. **Engineering and Technology:** Equipment, tools, and mechanical devices and their uses to produce motion, light, power, technology, and other applications. **Physics:** Physical principles, laws, and applications, including air, water, material dynamics, light, atomic principles, heat, electric theory, earth formations, and meteorological and related natural phenomena. **Chemistry:** The composition, structure, and properties of substances and of the chemical processes and transformations that they undergo. This includes uses of chemicals and their interactions, danger signs, production techniques, and disposal methods. **Design:** Design techniques, principles, tools, and instruments involved in the production and use of precision technical plans, blueprints, drawings, and models.

Work Environment: Outdoors; very hot or cold; cramped work space, awkward positions; minor burns, cuts, bites, or stings; standing; using hands on objects, tools, or controls.

Refuse and Recyclable Material Collectors

- ❋ Education/Training Required: Short-term on-the-job training
- ❋ Annual Earnings: $29,420
- ❋ Beginning Wage: $17,070
- ❋ Earnings Growth Potential: High
- ❋ Growth: 7.4%
- ❋ Annual Job Openings: 37,785
- ❋ Self-Employed: 6.1%
- ❋ Part-Time: 13.4%

Collect and dump refuse or recyclable materials from containers into truck. May drive truck. Inspect trucks prior to beginning routes to ensure safe operating condition. Refuel trucks and add other necessary fluids, such as oil. Fill out any needed reports for defective equipment. Drive to disposal sites to empty trucks that have been filled. Drive trucks along established routes through residential streets and alleys or through business and industrial areas. Operate equipment that compresses the collected refuse. Operate automated or semi-automated hoisting devices that raise refuse bins and dump contents into openings in truck bodies. Dismount garbage trucks to collect garbage and remount trucks to ride to the next collection point. Communicate with dispatchers concerning delays, unsafe sites, accidents, equipment breakdowns, and other maintenance problems. Keep informed of road and weather conditions to determine how routes will be affected. Tag garbage or recycling containers to inform customers of problems such as excess garbage or inclusion of items that are not permitted. Clean trucks and compactor bodies after routes have been completed. Sort items set out for recycling and throw materials into designated truck compartments. Organize schedules for refuse collection. Provide quotes for refuse collection contracts.

Personality Type: Realistic. These occupations frequently involve work activities that include practical, hands-on problems and solutions. They often deal with plants; animals; and real-world materials such as wood, tools, and machinery. Many of the occupations require working outside and don't involve a lot of paperwork or working closely with others.

GOE—Interest Area/Cluster: 13. Manufacturing. **Work Group:** 13.17. Loading, Moving, Hoisting, and Conveying. **Other Jobs in This Work Group:** Conveyor Operators and Tenders; Hoist and Winch Operators; Industrial Truck and Tractor Operators; Machine Feeders and Off-bearers; Packers and Packagers, Hand; Pump Operators, Except Wellhead Pumpers; Tank Car, Truck, and Ship Loaders.

Skills—Equipment Maintenance: Performing routine maintenance and determining when and what kind of maintenance is needed. **Operation and Control:** Controlling operations of equipment or systems. **Operation Monitoring:** Watching gauges, dials, or other indicators to make sure a machine is working properly. **Repairing:** Repairing machines or systems, using the needed tools.

Education and Training Programs: No related CIP programs; this job is learned through informal short-term on-the-job training. **Related Knowledge/Courses—Transportation:** Principles and methods for moving people or goods by air, rail, sea, or road, including their relative costs, advantages, and limitations. **Customer and Personal Service:** Principles and processes for providing customer and personal services, including needs assessment techniques, quality service standards, alternative delivery systems, and customer satisfaction evaluation techniques.

Work Environment: Outdoors; noisy; contaminants; using hands on objects, tools, or controls; bending or twisting the body; repetitive motions.

Registered Nurses

- ❋ Education/Training Required: Associate degree
- ❋ Annual Earnings: $60,010
- ❋ Beginning Wage: $42,020
- ❋ Earnings Growth Potential: Low
- ❋ Growth: 23.5%
- ❋ Annual Job Openings: 233,499
- ❋ Self-Employed: 0.8%
- ❋ Part-Time: 21.8%

Assess patient health problems and needs, develop and implement nursing care plans, and maintain medical records. Administer nursing care to ill, injured,

convalescent, or disabled patients. **May advise patients on health maintenance and disease prevention or provide case management. Licensing or registration required. Includes advance practice nurses such as nurse practitioners, clinical nurse specialists, certified nurse midwives, and certified registered nurse anesthetists. Advanced practice nursing is practiced by RNs who have specialized formal, post-basic education and who function in highly autonomous and specialized roles.** Monitor, record, and report symptoms and changes in patients' conditions. Maintain accurate, detailed reports and records. Record patients' medical information and vital signs. Order, interpret, and evaluate diagnostic tests to identify and assess patients' conditions. Modify patient treatment plans as indicated by patients' responses and conditions. Direct and supervise less skilled nursing or health care personnel or supervise particular units. Consult and coordinate with health-care team members to assess, plan, implement and evaluate patient care plans. Monitor all aspects of patient care, including diet and physical activity. Instruct individuals, families, and other groups on topics such as health education, disease prevention, and childbirth, and develop health improvement programs. Prepare patients for, and assist with, examinations and treatments. Assess the needs of individuals, families, or communities, including assessment of individuals' home or work environments to identify potential health or safety problems. Provide health care, first aid, immunizations, and assistance in convalescence and rehabilitation in locations such as schools, hospitals, and industry. Prepare rooms, sterile instruments, equipment, and supplies, and ensure that stock of supplies is maintained. Inform physicians of patients' conditions during anesthesia. Administer local, inhalation, intravenous, and other anesthetics. Perform physical examinations, make tentative diagnoses, and treat patients en route to hospitals or at disaster site triage centers. Observe nurses and visit patients to ensure proper nursing care. Conduct specified laboratory tests. Direct and coordinate infection control programs, advising and consulting with specified personnel about necessary precautions. Prescribe or recommend drugs, medical devices, or other forms of treatment such as physical therapy, inhalation therapy, or related therapeutic procedures. Perform administrative and managerial functions such as taking responsibility for a unit's staff, budget, planning, and long-range goals. Hand items to surgeons during operations.

Personality Type: Social. These occupations frequently involve working with, communicating with, and teaching people and often involve helping or providing service to others.

GOE—Interest Area/Cluster: 08. Health Science. **Work Group:** 08.02. Medicine and Surgery. **Other Jobs in This Work Group:** Anesthesiologists; Family and General Practitioners; Internists, General; Medical Assistants; Medical Transcriptionists; Obstetricians and Gynecologists; Pediatricians, General; Pharmacists; Pharmacy Aides; Pharmacy Technicians; Physician Assistants; Psychiatrists; Surgeons; Surgical Technologists.

Skills—Negotiation: Bringing others together and trying to reconcile differences. **Systems Analysis:** Determining how a system should work and how changes will affect outcomes. **Operation Monitoring:** Watching gauges, dials, or other indicators to make sure a machine is working properly. **Service Orientation:** Actively looking for ways to help people. **Systems Evaluation:** Looking at many indicators of system performance and taking into account their accuracy.

Education and Training Programs: Adult Health Nurse Training/Nursing; Clinical Nurse Specialist Training; Critical Care Nursing; Maternal/Child Health and Neonatal Nursing; Nurse Anesthetist Training; Nurse Practitioner Training; Nursing Midwifery; Nursing Science (MS, PhD); Nursing/Registered Nurse Training (RN, ASN, BSN, MSN); Occupational and Environmental Health Nursing; Pediatric Nursing; Perioperative/Operating Room and Surgical Nurse Training/Nursing; Psychiatric/Mental Health Nurse Training/Nursing; Public Health/Community Nurse Training/Nursing; others. **Related Knowledge/Courses—Medicine and Dentistry:** The information and techniques needed to diagnose and treat injuries, diseases, and deformities. This includes symptoms, treatment alternatives, drug properties and interactions, and preventive health-care measures. **Psychology:** Human behavior and performance, mental processes, psychological research methods, and the assessment and treatment of behavioral and affective disorders. **Therapy and Counseling:** Information and techniques needed to rehabilitate physical and mental ailments and to provide career guidance, including alternative treatments, rehabilitation equipment and its proper use, and methods to evaluate treatment effects. **Biology:** Plant and animal living tissue, cells, organisms, and entities, including their functions, interdependencies, and interactions with each other and the environment. **Philosophy and Theology:** Different philosophical systems and religions, including their basic principles, values, ethics, ways of thinking, customs, and practices and their impact on human culture. **Sociology and Anthropology:** Group behavior and dynamics; societal trends and influences; and cultures and their history, migrations, ethnicity, and origins.

Work Environment: Indoors; disease or infections; standing; walking and running; using hands on objects, tools, or controls.

Reinforcing Iron and Rebar Workers

- ⊛ Education/Training Required: Long-term on-the-job training
- ⊛ Annual Earnings: $37,890
- ⊛ Beginning Wage: $23,010
- ⊛ Earnings Growth Potential: Medium
- ⊛ Growth: 11.5%
- ⊛ Annual Job Openings: 4,502
- ⊛ Self-Employed: 0.0%
- ⊛ Part-Time: 5.8%

Position and secure steel bars or mesh in concrete forms to reinforce concrete. Use a variety of fasteners, rod-bending machines, blowtorches, and hand tools. Cut rods to required lengths, using metal shears, hacksaws, bar cutters, or acetylene torches. Determine quantities, sizes, shapes, and locations of reinforcing rods from blueprints, sketches, or oral instructions. Space and fasten together rods in forms according to blueprints, using wire and pliers. Place blocks under rebar to hold the bars off the deck when reinforcing floors. Bend steel rods with hand tools and rod-bending machines, and weld them with arc-welding equipment. Cut and fit wire mesh or fabric, using hooked rods, and position fabric or mesh in concrete to reinforce concrete. Position and secure steel bars, rods, cables, or mesh in concrete forms, using fasteners, rod-bending machines, blowtorches, and hand tools.

Personality Type: Realistic. These occupations frequently involve work activities that include practical, hands-on problems and solutions. They often deal with plants; animals; and real-world materials such as wood, tools, and machinery. Many of the occupations require working outside and don't involve a lot of paperwork or working closely with others.

GOE—Interest Area/Cluster: 02. Architecture and Construction. **Work Group:** 02.04. Construction Crafts. **Other Jobs in This Work Group:** Boilermakers; Brickmasons and Blockmasons; Carpet Installers; Cement Masons and Concrete Finishers; Commercial Divers; Construction Carpenters; Crane and Tower Operators; Drywall and Ceiling Tile Installers; Electricians; Fence Erectors; Floor Layers, Except Carpet, Wood, and Hard Tiles; Floor Sanders and Finishers; Glaziers; Hazardous Materials Removal Workers; Insulation Workers, Floor, Ceiling, and Wall; Insulation Workers, Mechanical; Manufactured Building and Mobile Home Installers; Operating Engineers and Other Construction Equipment Operators; Painters, Construction and Maintenance; Paperhangers; Paving, Surfacing, and Tamping Equipment Operators; Pile-Driver Operators; Pipe Fitters and Steamfitters; Pipelayers; Plasterers and Stucco Masons; Plumbers; Plumbers, Pipefitters, and Steamfitters; Rail-Track Laying and Maintenance Equipment Operators; Refractory Materials Repairers, Except Brickmasons; Riggers; Roofers; Rough Carpenters; Security and Fire Alarm Systems Installers; Segmental Pavers; Sheet Metal Workers; Stone Cutters and Carvers, Manufacturing; Stonemasons; Structural Iron and Steel Workers; Tapers; Terrazzo Workers and Finishers; Tile and Marble Setters.

Skills—Installation: Installing equipment, machines, wiring, or programs to meet specifications. **Equipment Selection:** Determining the kind of tools and equipment needed to do a job. **Coordination:** Adjusting actions in relation to others' actions. **Management of Material Resources:** Obtaining and seeing to the appropriate use of equipment, facilities, and materials needed to do certain work. **Mathematics:** Using mathematics to solve problems. **Operation and Control:** Controlling operations of equipment or systems. **Monitoring:** Assessing how well one is doing when learning or doing something. **Management of Personnel Resources:** Motivating, developing, and directing people as they work; identifying the best people for the job.

Education and Training Program: Construction Trades, Other. **Related Knowledge/Courses—Building and Construction:** Materials, methods, and the appropriate tools to construct objects, structures, and buildings. **Mechanical Devices:** Machines and tools, including their designs, uses, benefits, repair, and maintenance. **Public**

Safety and Security: Weaponry; public safety; security operations, rules, regulations, precautions, and prevention; and the protection of people, data, and property. **Transportation:** Principles and methods for moving people or goods by air, rail, sea, or road, including their relative costs, advantages, and limitations.

Work Environment: Outdoors; contaminants; standing; walking and running; using hands on objects, tools, or controls; repetitive motions.

Reservation and Transportation Ticket Agents and Travel Clerks

* Education/Training Required: Short-term on-the-job training
* Annual Earnings: $29,820
* Beginning Wage: $18,290
* Earnings Growth Potential: Medium
* Growth: 1.1%
* Annual Job Openings: 30,754
* Self-Employed: 3.7%
* Part-Time: 15.9%

Make and confirm reservations and sell tickets to passengers and for large hotel or motel chains. May check baggage and direct passengers to designated concourse, pier, or track; make reservations; deliver tickets; arrange for visas; contact individuals and groups to inform them of package tours; or provide tourists with travel information, such as points of interest, restaurants, rates, and emergency service. Plan routes, itineraries, and accommodation details and compute fares and fees, using schedules, rate books, and computers. Make and confirm reservations for transportation and accommodations, using telephones, faxes, mail, and computers. Prepare customer invoices and accept payment. Answer inquiries regarding such information as schedules, accommodations, procedures, and policies. Assemble and issue required documentation such as tickets, travel insurance policies, and itineraries. Determine whether space is available on travel dates requested by customers and assign requested spaces when available. Inform clients of essential travel information such as travel times, transportation connections, and medical and visa requirements. Maintain computerized inventories of available passenger space and provide information on space reserved or available. Confer with customers to determine their service requirements and travel preferences. Examine passenger documentation to determine destinations and to assign boarding passes. Provide boarding or disembarking assistance to passengers needing special assistance. Check baggage and cargo and direct passengers to designated locations for loading. Announce arrival and departure information, using public-address systems. Trace lost, delayed, or misdirected baggage for customers. Promote particular destinations, tour packages, and other travel services. Provide clients with assistance in preparing required travel documents and forms. Open and close information facilities and keep them clean during operation. Provide customers with travel suggestions and information such as guides, directories, brochures, and maps. Contact customers or travel agents to advise them of travel conveyance changes or to confirm reservations. Contact motel, hotel, resort, and travel operators to obtain current advertising literature.

Personality Type: Conventional. These occupations frequently involve following set procedures and routines and can include working with data and details more than with ideas. Usually there is a clear line of authority to follow.

GOE—Interest Area/Cluster: 09. Hospitality, Tourism, and Recreation. **Work Group:** 09.03. Hospitality and Travel Services. **Other Jobs in This Work Group:** Baggage Porters and Bellhops; Concierges; Flight Attendants; Hotel, Motel, and Resort Desk Clerks; Janitors and Cleaners, Except Maids and Housekeeping Cleaners; Maids and Housekeeping Cleaners; Tour Guides and Escorts; Transportation Attendants, Except Flight Attendants and Baggage Porters; Travel Agents; Travel Guides.

Skills—Service Orientation: Actively looking for ways to help people. **Operation and Control:** Controlling operations of equipment or systems. **Instructing:** Teaching others how to do something. **Operations Analysis:** Analyzing needs and product requirements to create a design. **Operation Monitoring:** Watching gauges, dials, or other indicators to make sure a machine is working properly. **Active Listening:** Listening to what other people are saying and asking questions as appropriate. **Speaking:** Talking to others to effectively convey information.

Education and Training Programs: Hospitality/Travel Services Sales Operations; Selling Skills and Sales Operations; Tourism and Travel Services Marketing Operations;

Tourism Promotion Operations. **Related Knowledge/Courses—Customer and Personal Service:** Principles and processes for providing customer and personal services, including needs assessment techniques, quality service standards, alternative delivery systems, and customer satisfaction evaluation techniques. **Transportation:** Principles and methods for moving people or goods by air, rail, sea, or road, including their relative costs, advantages, and limitations. **Sales and Marketing:** Principles and methods involved in showing, promoting, and selling products or services. This includes marketing strategies and tactics, product demonstration and sales techniques, and sales control systems. **Clerical Studies:** Administrative and clerical procedures and systems such as word-processing systems, filing and records management systems, stenography and transcription, forms, design principles, and other office procedures and terminology.

Work Environment: Indoors; noisy; sitting; using hands on objects, tools, or controls; repetitive motions.

Residential Advisors

- ⊛ Education/Training Required: Short-term on-the-job training
- ⊛ Annual Earnings: $23,050
- ⊛ Beginning Wage: $15,560
- ⊛ Earnings Growth Potential: Low
- ⊛ Growth: 18.5%
- ⊛ Annual Job Openings: 8,053
- ⊛ Self-Employed: 4.9%
- ⊛ Part-Time: 21.3%

Coordinate activities for residents of boarding schools, college fraternities or sororities, college dormitories, or similar establishments. Order supplies and determine need for maintenance, repairs, and furnishings. May maintain household records and assign rooms. May refer residents to counseling resources if needed. Enforce rules and regulations to ensure the smooth and orderly operation of dormitory programs. Provide emergency first aid and summon medical assistance when necessary. Mediate interpersonal problems between residents. Administer, coordinate, or recommend disciplinary and corrective actions. Communicate with other staff to resolve problems with individual students. Counsel students in the handling of issues such as family, financial, and educational problems. Make regular rounds to ensure that residents and areas are safe and secure. Observe students to detect and report unusual behavior. Determine the need for facility maintenance and repair and notify appropriate personnel. Collaborate with counselors to develop counseling programs that address the needs of individual students. Develop program plans for individuals or assist in plan development. Hold regular meetings with each assigned unit. Direct and participate in on- and off-campus recreational activities for residents of institutions, boarding schools, fraternities or sororities, children's homes, or similar establishments. Assign rooms to students. Provide requested information on students' progress and the development of case plans. Confer with medical personnel to better understand the backgrounds and needs of individual residents. Answer telephones and route calls or deliver messages. Supervise participants in work-study programs. Process contract cancellations for students who are unable to follow residence hall policies and procedures. Sort and distribute mail. Supervise the activities of housekeeping personnel. Order supplies for facilities. Supervise students' housekeeping work to ensure that it is done properly. Chaperone group-sponsored trips and social functions. Compile information such as residents' daily activities and the quantities of supplies used to prepare required reports. Accompany and supervise students during meals. Provide transportation or escort for expeditions such as shopping trips or visits to doctors or dentists. Inventory, pack, and remove items left behind by former residents.

Personality Type: Social. These occupations frequently involve working with, communicating with, and teaching people and often involve helping or providing service to others.

GOE—Interest Area/Cluster: 10. Human Service. **Work Group:** 10.01. Counseling and Social Work. **Other Jobs in This Work Group:** Child, Family, and School Social Workers; Clinical Psychologists; Clinical, Counseling, and School Psychologists; Counseling Psychologists; Marriage and Family Therapists; Medical and Public Health Social Workers; Mental Health and Substance Abuse Social Workers; Mental Health Counselors; Probation Officers and Correctional Treatment Specialists; Rehabilitation Counselors; Social and Human Service Assistants; Substance Abuse and Behavioral Disorder Counselors.

Skills—Social Perceptiveness: Being aware of others' reactions and understanding why they react the way

R

they do. **Monitoring:** Assessing how well one is doing when learning or doing something. **Management of Personnel Resources:** Motivating, developing, and directing people as they work; identifying the best people for the job. **Time Management:** Managing one's own time and the time of others. **Persuasion:** Persuading others to approach things differently. **Service Orientation:** Actively looking for ways to help people. **Management of Financial Resources:** Determining how money will be spent to get the work done and accounting for these expenditures. **Negotiation:** Bringing others together and trying to reconcile differences.

Education and Training Program: Hotel/Motel Administration/Management. **Related Knowledge/Courses— Therapy and Counseling:** Information and techniques needed to rehabilitate physical and mental ailments and to provide career guidance, including alternative treatments, rehabilitation equipment and its proper use, and methods to evaluate treatment effects. **Philosophy and Theology:** Different philosophical systems and religions, including their basic principles, values, ethics, ways of thinking, customs, and practices and their impact on human culture. **Sociology and Anthropology:** Group behavior and dynamics; societal trends and influences; and cultures and their history, migrations, ethnicity, and origins. **Psychology:** Human behavior and performance, mental processes, psychological research methods, and the assessment and treatment of behavioral and affective disorders. **Personnel and Human Resources:** Principles and procedures for personnel recruitment; selection; training; compensation and benefits; labor relations and negotiation; and personnel information systems. **Public Safety and Security:** Weaponry; public safety; security operations, rules, regulations, precautions, and prevention; and the protection of people, data, and property.

Work Environment: Indoors; noisy; sitting.

Respiratory Therapists

* Education/Training Required: Associate degree
* Annual Earnings: $50,070
* Beginning Wage: $36,650
* Earnings Growth Potential: Low
* Growth: 22.6%
* Annual Job Openings: 5,563
* Self-Employed: 1.1%
* Part-Time: 15.0%

Assess, treat, and care for patients with breathing disorders. Assume primary responsibility for all respiratory care modalities, including the supervision of respiratory therapy technicians. Initiate and conduct therapeutic procedures; maintain patient records; and select, assemble, check, and operate equipment. Set up and operate devices such as mechanical ventilators, therapeutic gas administration apparatus, environmental control systems, and aerosol generators, following specified parameters of treatment. Provide emergency care, including artificial respiration, external cardiac massage, and assistance with cardiopulmonary resuscitation. Determine requirements for treatment, such as type, method, and duration of therapy; precautions to be taken; and medication and dosages, compatible with physicians' orders. Monitor patient's physiological responses to therapy, such as vital signs, arterial blood gases, and blood chemistry changes, and consult with physician if adverse reactions occur. Read prescription, measure arterial blood gases, and review patient information to assess patient condition. Work as part of a team of physicians, nurses, and other health-care professionals to manage patient care. Enforce safety rules and ensure careful adherence to physicians' orders. Maintain charts that contain patients' pertinent identification and therapy information. Inspect, clean, test, and maintain respiratory therapy equipment to ensure equipment is functioning safely and efficiently, ordering repairs when necessary. Educate patients and their families about their conditions and teach appropriate disease management techniques, such as breathing exercises and the use of medications and respiratory equipment. Explain treatment procedures to patients to gain cooperation and allay fears. Relay blood analysis results to a physician. Perform pulmonary function and adjust equipment to obtain optimum results in therapy.

Perform bronchopulmonary drainage and assist or instruct patients in performance of breathing exercises. Demonstrate respiratory care procedures to trainees and other health-care personnel. Teach, train, supervise, and utilize the assistance of students, respiratory therapy technicians, and assistants. Make emergency visits to resolve equipment problems. Use a variety of testing techniques to assist doctors in cardiac and pulmonary research and to diagnose disorders. Conduct tests, such as electrocardiograms (EKGs), stress testing, and lung capacity tests, to evaluate patients' cardiopulmonary functions.

Personality Type: Social. These occupations frequently involve working with, communicating with, and teaching people and often involve helping or providing service to others.

GOE—Interest Area/Cluster: 08. Health Science. **Work Group:** 08.07. Medical Therapy. **Other Jobs in This Work Group:** Audiologists; Massage Therapists; Occupational Therapist Aides; Occupational Therapist Assistants; Occupational Therapists; Physical Therapist Aides; Physical Therapist Assistants; Physical Therapists; Radiation Therapists; Recreational Therapists; Respiratory Therapy Technicians; Speech-Language Pathologists.

Skills—Science: Using scientific methods to solve problems. **Mathematics:** Using mathematics to solve problems. **Operation Monitoring:** Watching gauges, dials, or other indicators to make sure a machine is working properly. **Reading Comprehension:** Understanding written sentences and paragraphs in work-related documents. **Active Learning:** Working with new material or information to grasp its implications. **Troubleshooting:** Determining what is causing an operating error and deciding what to do about it. **Instructing:** Teaching others how to do something. **Service Orientation:** Actively looking for ways to help people.

Education and Training Program: Respiratory Care Therapy/Therapist Training. **Related Knowledge/Courses—Medicine and Dentistry:** The information and techniques needed to diagnose and treat injuries, diseases, and deformities. This includes symptoms, treatment alternatives, drug properties and interactions, and preventive health-care measures. **Biology:** Plant and animal living tissue, cells, organisms, and entities, including their functions, interdependencies, and interactions with each other and the environment. **Psychology:** Human behavior

and performance, mental processes, psychological research methods, and the assessment and treatment of behavioral and affective disorders. **Customer and Personal Service:** Principles and processes for providing customer and personal services, including needs assessment techniques, quality service standards, alternative delivery systems, and customer satisfaction evaluation techniques. **Therapy and Counseling:** Information and techniques needed to rehabilitate physical and mental ailments and to provide career guidance, including alternative treatments, rehabilitation equipment and its proper use, and methods to evaluate treatment effects. **Chemistry:** The composition, structure, and properties of substances and of the chemical processes and transformations that they undergo. This includes uses of chemicals and their interactions, danger signs, production techniques, and disposal methods.

Work Environment: Indoors; disease or infections; standing.

Roofers

* Education/Training Required: Moderate-term on-the-job training
* Annual Earnings: $33,240
* Beginning Wage: $21,290
* Earnings Growth Potential: Medium
* Growth: 14.3%
* Annual Job Openings: 38,398
* Self-Employed: 20.1%
* Part-Time: 7.6%

Cover roofs of structures with shingles, slate, asphalt, aluminum, wood, and related materials. May spray roofs, sidings, and walls with material to bind, seal, insulate, or soundproof sections of structures. Install, repair, or replace single-ply roofing systems, using waterproof sheet materials such as modified plastics, elastomeric, or other asphaltic compositions. Apply alternate layers of hot asphalt or tar and roofing paper to roofs, according to specification. Apply gravel or pebbles over top layers of roofs, using rakes or stiff-bristled brooms. Cement or nail flashing-strips of metal or shingle over joints to make them watertight. Punch holes in slate, tile, terra cotta, or wooden shingles, using punches and hammers. Hammer and chisel away rough spots or remove them with rubbing bricks to prepare surfaces for waterproofing. Align roofing materials with edges of roofs. Mop or pour hot asphalt or tar onto roof bases. Apply plastic coatings and membranes, fiberglass, or felt over sloped roofs before applying shingles. Install vapor barriers and/or layers of insulation on the roof decks of flat roofs, and seal the seams. Install partially overlapping layers of material over roof insulation surfaces, determining distance of roofing material overlap using chalk lines, gauges on shingling hatchets, or lines on shingles. Inspect problem roofs to determine the best procedures for repairing them. Glaze top layers to make a smooth finish, or embed gravel in the bitumen for rough surfaces. Cut roofing paper to size using knives; and nail or staple roofing paper to roofs in overlapping strips to form bases for other materials. Cut felt, shingles, and strips of flashing; and fit them into angles formed by walls, vents, and intersecting roof surfaces. Cover roofs and exterior walls of structures with slate, asphalt, aluminum, wood, gravel, gypsum, and/or related materials, using brushes, knives, punches, hammers, and other tools. Clean and maintain equipment. Cover exposed nailheads with roofing cement or caulking to prevent water leakage and rust. Waterproof and damp-proof walls, floors, roofs, foundations, and basements by painting or spraying surfaces with waterproof coatings, or by attaching waterproofing membranes to surfaces. Spray roofs, sidings, and walls with material to bind, seal, insulate, or soundproof sections of structures, using spray guns, air compressors, and heaters.

Personality Type: Realistic. These occupations frequently involve work activities that include practical, hands-on problems and solutions. They often deal with plants; animals; and real-world materials such as wood, tools, and machinery. Many of the occupations require working outside and don't involve a lot of paperwork or working closely with others.

GOE—Interest Area/Cluster: 02. Architecture and Construction. **Work Group:** 02.04. Construction Crafts. **Other Jobs in This Work Group:** Boilermakers; Brickmasons and Blockmasons; Carpet Installers; Cement Masons and Concrete Finishers; Commercial Divers; Construction Carpenters; Crane and Tower Operators; Drywall and Ceiling Tile Installers; Electricians; Fence Erectors; Floor Layers, Except Carpet, Wood, and Hard Tiles; Floor Sanders and Finishers; Glaziers; Hazardous Materials Removal Workers; Insulation Workers, Floor, Ceiling, and Wall; Insulation Workers, Mechanical; Manufactured Building and Mobile Home Installers; Operating Engineers and Other Construction Equipment Operators; Painters, Construction and Maintenance; Paperhangers; Paving, Surfacing, and Tamping Equipment Operators; Pile-Driver Operators; Pipe Fitters and Steamfitters; Pipelayers; Plasterers and Stucco Masons; Plumbers; Plumbers, Pipefitters, and Steamfitters; Rail-Track Laying and Maintenance Equipment Operators; Refractory Materials Repairers, Except Brickmasons; Reinforcing Iron and Rebar Workers; Riggers; Rough Carpenters; Security and Fire Alarm Systems Installers; Segmental Pavers; Sheet Metal Workers; Stone Cutters and Carvers, Manufacturing; Stonemasons; Structural Iron and Steel Workers; Tapers; Terrazzo Workers and Finishers; Tile and Marble Setters.

Skills—Repairing: Repairing machines or systems, using the needed tools. **Installation:** Installing equipment, machines, wiring, or programs to meet specifications. **Equipment Maintenance:** Performing routine maintenance and determining when and what kind of maintenance is needed. **Operations Analysis:** Analyzing needs and product requirements to create a design. **Technology Design:** Generating or adapting equipment and technology to serve user needs. **Mathematics:** Using mathematics to solve problems. **Management of Personnel Resources:** Motivating, developing, and directing people as they work; identifying the best people for the job. **Coordination:** Adjusting actions in relation to others' actions.

Education and Training Program: Roofer Training. **Related Knowledge/Courses—Building and Construction:** Materials, methods, and the appropriate tools to construct objects, structures, and buildings. **Design:** Design techniques, principles, tools, and instruments involved in the production and use of precision technical plans, blueprints, drawings, and models. **Engineering and Technology:** Equipment, tools, and mechanical devices and their uses to produce motion, light, power, technology, and other applications. **Transportation:** Principles and methods for moving people or goods by air, rail, sea, or road, including their relative costs, advantages, and limitations.

Work Environment: Outdoors; very hot or cold; high places; standing; walking and running; using hands on objects, tools, or controls.

Rough Carpenters

- ❋ Education/Training Required: Long-term on-the-job training
- ❋ Annual Earnings: $37,660
- ❋ Beginning Wage: $23,370
- ❋ Earnings Growth Potential: Medium
- ❋ Growth: 10.3%
- ❋ Annual Job Openings: 223,225
- ❋ Self-Employed: 31.8%
- ❋ Part-Time: 6.1%

The job openings listed here are shared with Construction Carpenters.

Build rough wooden structures, such as concrete forms, scaffolds, tunnel, bridge, or sewer supports, billboard signs, and temporary frame shelters, according to sketches, blueprints, or oral instructions. Study blueprints and diagrams to determine dimensions of structure or form to be constructed. Measure materials or distances, using square, measuring tape, or rule to lay out work. Cut or saw boards, timbers, or plywood to required size, using handsaw, power saw, or woodworking machine. Assemble and fasten material together to construct wood or metal framework of structure, using bolts, nails, or screws. Anchor and brace forms and other structures in place, using nails, bolts, anchor rods, steel cables, planks, wedges, and timbers. Mark cutting lines on materials, using pencil and scriber. Erect forms, framework, scaffolds, hoists, roof supports, or chutes, using hand tools, plumb rule, and level. Install rough door and window frames, subflooring, fixtures, or temporary supports in structures undergoing construction or repair. Examine structural timbers and supports to detect decay and replace timbers as required, using hand tools, nuts, and bolts. Bore boltholes in timber, masonry, or concrete walls, using power drill. Fabricate parts, using woodworking and metalworking machines. Dig or direct digging of post holes and set poles to support structures. Build sleds from logs and timbers for use in hauling camp buildings and machinery through wooded areas. Build chutes for pouring concrete.

Personality Type: Realistic. These occupations frequently involve work activities that include practical, hands-on problems and solutions. They often deal with plants; animals; and real-world materials such as wood, tools, and machinery. Many of the occupations require working outside and don't involve a lot of paperwork or working closely with others.

GOE—Interest Area/Cluster: 02. Architecture and Construction. **Work Group:** 02.04. Construction Crafts. **Other Jobs in This Work Group:** Boilermakers; Brickmasons and Blockmasons; Carpet Installers; Cement Masons and Concrete Finishers; Commercial Divers; Construction Carpenters; Crane and Tower Operators; Drywall and Ceiling Tile Installers; Electricians; Fence Erectors; Floor Layers, Except Carpet, Wood, and Hard Tiles; Floor Sanders and Finishers; Glaziers; Hazardous Materials Removal Workers; Insulation Workers, Floor, Ceiling, and Wall; Insulation Workers, Mechanical; Manufactured Building and Mobile Home Installers; Operating Engineers and Other Construction Equipment Operators; Painters, Construction and Maintenance; Paperhangers; Paving, Surfacing, and Tamping Equipment Operators; Pile-Driver Operators; Pipe Fitters and Steamfitters; Pipelayers; Plasterers and Stucco Masons; Plumbers; Plumbers, Pipefitters, and Steamfitters; Rail-Track Laying and Maintenance Equipment Operators; Refractory Materials Repairers, Except Brickmasons; Reinforcing Iron and Rebar Workers; Riggers; Roofers; Security and Fire Alarm Systems Installers; Segmental Pavers; Sheet Metal Workers; Stone Cutters and Carvers, Manufacturing; Stonemasons; Structural Iron and Steel Workers; Tapers; Terrazzo Workers and Finishers; Tile and Marble Setters.

Skills—Repairing: Repairing machines or systems, using the needed tools. **Installation:** Installing equipment, machines, wiring, or programs to meet specifications. **Management of Personnel Resources:** Motivating, developing, and directing people as they work; identifying the best people for the job. **Equipment Selection:** Determining the kind of tools and equipment needed to do a job. **Mathematics:** Using mathematics to solve problems. **Technology Design:** Generating or adapting equipment and technology to serve user needs. **Equipment Maintenance:** Performing routine maintenance and determining when and what kind of maintenance is needed. **Coordination:** Adjusting actions in relation to others' actions.

Education and Training Program: Carpentry/Carpenter Training. **Related Knowledge/Courses—Building and Construction:** Materials, methods, and the appropriate tools to construct objects, structures, and buildings. **Design:** Design techniques, principles, tools, and instruments involved in the production and use of precision technical plans, blueprints, drawings, and models. **Engineering and Technology:** Equipment, tools, and mechanical devices and their uses to produce motion, light, power, technology, and other applications. **Mechanical Devices:** Machines and tools, including their designs, uses, benefits, repair, and maintenance. **Production and Processing:** Inputs, outputs, raw materials, waste, quality control, costs, and techniques for maximizing the manufacture and distribution of goods. **Physics:** Physical principles, laws, and applications, including air, water, material dynamics, light, atomic principles, heat, electric theory, earth formations, and meteorological and related natural phenomena.

Work Environment: Outdoors; noisy; very hot or cold; contaminants; standing; using hands on objects, tools, or controls.

Sailors and Marine Oilers

- ❋ Education/Training Required: Short-term on-the-job training
- ❋ Annual Earnings: $32,570
- ❋ Beginning Wage: $19,500
- ❋ Earnings Growth Potential: High
- ❋ Growth: 15.7%
- ❋ Annual Job Openings: 8,600
- ❋ Self-Employed: 0.1%
- ❋ Part-Time: 5.7%

Stand watch to look for obstructions in path of vessels; measure water depths; turn wheels on bridges; or use emergency equipment as directed by captains, mates, or pilots. Break out, rig, overhaul, and store cargo-handling gear, stationary rigging, and running gear. Perform a variety of maintenance tasks to preserve the painted surface of ships and to maintain line and ship equipment. Must hold government-issued certification and tankerman certification when working aboard liquid-carrying vessels. Provide engineers with assistance in repairing and adjusting machinery. Attach hoses and operate pumps in order to transfer substances to and from liquid cargo tanks. Give directions to crew members engaged in cleaning wheelhouses and quarterdecks. Load or unload materials from vessels. Lower and man lifeboats when emergencies occur. Participate in shore patrols. Read pressure and temperature gauges or displays, and record data in engineering logs. Record in ships' logs data such as weather conditions and distances traveled. Stand by wheels when ships are on automatic pilot, and verify accuracy of courses, using magnetic compasses. Steer ships under the direction of commanders or navigating officers, or direct helmsmen to steer, following designated courses. Chip and clean rust spots on decks, superstructures, and sides of ships, using wire brushes and hand or air chipping machines. Relay specified signals to other ships, using visual signaling devices such as blinker lights and semaphores. Splice and repair ropes, wire cables, and cordage, using marlinespikes, wirecutters, twine, and hand tools. Paint or varnish decks, superstructures, lifeboats, or sides of ships. Overhaul lifeboats and lifeboat gear, and lower or raise lifeboats with winches or falls. Operate, maintain, and repair ship equipment such as winches, cranes, derricks, and weapons systems. Measure depths of water in shallow or unfamiliar waters, using leadlines, and telephone or shout depth information to vessel bridges. Maintain ships' engines under direction of ships' engineering officers. Lubricate machinery, equipment, and engine parts such as gears, shafts, and bearings. Handle lines to moor vessels to wharfs, to tie up vessels to other vessels, or to rig towing lines. Examine machinery to verify specified pressures and lubricant flows. Clean and polish wood trim, brass, and other metal parts. Break out, rig, and stow cargo-handling gear, stationary rigging, and running gear. Stand gangway watches to prevent unauthorized persons from boarding ships while they are in port. Tie barges together into tow units for tugboats to handle, inspecting barges periodically during voyages and disconnecting them when destinations are reached.

Personality Type: Realistic. These occupations frequently involve work activities that include practical, hands-on problems and solutions. They often deal with plants; animals; and real-world materials such as wood, tools, and machinery. Many of the occupations require working outside and don't involve a lot of paperwork or working closely with others.

GOE—Interest Area/Cluster: 16. Transportation, Distribution, and Logistics. **Work Group:** 16.05. Water Vehicle Operation. **Other Jobs in This Work Group:** Captains, Mates, and Pilots of Water Vessels; Dredge Operators; Mates—Ship, Boat, and Barge; Motorboat Operators; Pilots, Ship; Ship and Boat Captains.

Skills—Repairing: Repairing machines or systems, using the needed tools. **Equipment Maintenance:** Performing routine maintenance and determining when and what kind of maintenance is needed.

Education and Training Program: Marine Transportation Services, Other. **Related Knowledge/Courses— Mechanical Devices:** Machines and tools, including their designs, uses, benefits, repair, and maintenance. **Transportation:** Principles and methods for moving people or goods by air, rail, sea, or road, including their relative costs, advantages, and limitations. **Engineering and Technology:** Equipment, tools, and mechanical devices and their uses to produce motion, light, power, technology, and other applications. **Public Safety and Security:** Weaponry; public safety; security operations, rules, regulations, precautions, and prevention; and the protection of people, data, and property. **Geography:** Various methods for describing the location and distribution of land, sea, and air masses, including their physical locations, relationships, and characteristics. **Production and Processing:** Inputs, outputs, raw materials, waste, quality control, costs, and techniques for maximizing the manufacture and distribution of goods.

Work Environment: More often outdoors than indoors; noisy; very hot or cold; contaminants; standing.

Sales Representatives, Wholesale and Manufacturing, Except Technical and Scientific Products

- ❋ Education/Training Required: Work experience in a related occupation
- ❋ Annual Earnings: $50,750
- ❋ Beginning Wage: $26,490
- ❋ Earnings Growth Potential: High
- ❋ Growth: 8.4%
- ❋ Annual Job Openings: 156,215
- ❋ Self-Employed: 4.0%
- ❋ Part-Time: 6.7%

Sell goods for wholesalers or manufacturers to businesses or groups of individuals. Work requires substantial knowledge of items sold. Answer customers' questions about products, prices, availability, product uses, and credit terms. Recommend products to customers based on customers' needs and interests. Contact regular and prospective customers to demonstrate products, explain product features, and solicit orders. Estimate or quote prices, credit or contract terms, warranties, and delivery dates. Consult with clients after sales or contract signings to resolve problems and to provide ongoing support. Prepare drawings, estimates, and bids that meet specific customer needs. Provide customers with product samples and catalogs. Identify prospective customers by using business directories, following leads from existing clients, participating in organizations and clubs, and attending trade shows and conferences. Arrange and direct delivery and installation of products and equipment. Monitor market conditions; product innovations; and competitors' products, prices, and sales. Negotiate details of contracts and payments and prepare sales contracts and order forms. Perform administrative duties, such as preparing sales budgets and reports, keeping sales records, and filing expense account reports. Obtain credit information about prospective customers. Forward orders to manufacturers. Check stock levels and reorder merchandise as necessary. Plan, assemble, and stock product displays in retail stores or make recommendations to retailers regarding product displays, promotional programs, and advertising. Negotiate with retail merchants to improve product exposure such as shelf positioning and advertising. Train customers' employees to operate and maintain new equipment. Buy products from manufacturers or brokerage firms and distribute them to wholesale and retail clients.

Personality Type: Conventional. These occupations frequently involve following set procedures and routines and can include working with data and details more than with ideas. Usually there is a clear line of authority to follow.

GOE—Interest Area/Cluster: 14. Retail and Wholesale Sales and Service. **Work Group:** 14.03. General Sales. **Other Jobs in This Work Group:** Parts Salespersons; Real Estate Brokers; Real Estate Sales Agents; Retail Salespersons; Service Station Attendants.

Skills—Negotiation: Bringing others together and trying to reconcile differences. **Persuasion:** Persuading others to approach things differently. **Service Orientation:** Actively looking for ways to help people. **Management of Financial Resources:** Determining how money will be spent to get the work done and accounting for these expenditures. **Operations Analysis:** Analyzing needs and product requirements to create a design. **Time Management:** Managing one's own time and the time of others. **Speaking:**

Talking to others to effectively convey information. **Installation:** Installing equipment, machines, wiring, or programs to meet specifications.

Education and Training Programs: Apparel and Accessories Marketing Operations; Business, Management, Marketing, and Related Support Services, Other; Fashion Merchandising; General Merchandising, Sales, and Related Marketing Operations, Other; Insurance; Sales, Distribution, and Marketing Operations, General; Special Products Marketing Operations; Specialized Merchandising, Sales, and Related Marketing Operations, Other. **Related Knowledge/Courses—Sales and Marketing:** Principles and methods involved in showing, promoting, and selling products or services. This includes marketing strategies and tactics, product demonstration and sales techniques, and sales control systems. **Economics and Accounting:** Economic and accounting principles and practices, the financial markets, banking, and the analysis and reporting of financial data. **Customer and Personal Service:** Principles and processes for providing customer and personal services, including needs assessment techniques, quality service standards, alternative delivery systems, and customer satisfaction evaluation techniques. **Transportation:** Principles and methods for moving people or goods by air, rail, sea, or road, including their relative costs, advantages, and limitations. **Mathematics:** Numbers and their operations and interrelationships, including arithmetic, algebra, geometry, calculus, and statistics and their applications. **Administration and Management:** Principles and processes involved in business and organizational planning, coordination, and execution. This includes strategic planning, resource allocation, manpower modeling, leadership techniques, and production methods.

Work Environment: Outdoors; noisy; contaminants; more often standing than sitting; walking and running.

Sales Representatives, Wholesale and Manufacturing, Technical and Scientific Products

* Education/Training Required: Work experience in a related occupation
* Annual Earnings: $68,270
* Beginning Wage: $35,090
* Earnings Growth Potential: High
* Growth: 12.4%
* Annual Job Openings: 43,469
* Self-Employed: 4.2%
* Part-Time: 6.7%

Sell goods for wholesalers or manufacturers where technical or scientific knowledge is required in such areas as biology, engineering, chemistry, and electronics, normally obtained from at least 2 years of postsecondary education. Contact new and existing customers to discuss their needs, and to explain how these needs could be met by specific products and services. Answer customers' questions about products, prices, availability, product uses, and credit terms. Quote prices, credit terms, and other bid specifications. Emphasize product features based on analyses of customers' needs, and on technical knowledge of product capabilities and limitations. Negotiate prices and terms of sales and service agreements. Maintain customer records, using automated systems. Identify prospective customers by using business directories, following leads from existing clients, participating in organizations and clubs, and attending trade shows and conferences. Prepare sales contracts for orders obtained, and submit orders for processing. Select the correct products or assist customers in making product selections, based on customers' needs, product specifications, and applicable regulations. Collaborate with colleagues to exchange information such as selling strategies and marketing information. Prepare sales presentations and proposals that explain product specifications and applications. Provide customers with ongoing technical support. Demonstrate and explain the operation and use of products. Inform customers of estimated delivery schedules, service contracts, warranties, or other information pertaining to purchased products. Attend sales and trade meetings, and read related publications in order to obtain information about market conditions, business trends, and industry developments. Visit establishments to evaluate needs and to promote product or service sales. Complete expense reports, sales reports, and other paperwork. Initiate sales campaigns and follow marketing plan guidelines in order to meet sales and production expectations. Recommend ways for customers to alter product usage in order to improve production. Complete product and development training as required. Provide feedback to companys' product design teams so that products can be tailored to clients' needs. Arrange for installation and test-operation of machinery.

Personality Type: Enterprising. These occupations frequently involve starting up and carrying out projects and can involve leading people and making many decisions. They sometimes require risk taking and often deal with business.

GOE—Interest Area/Cluster: 14. Retail and Wholesale Sales and Service. **Work Group:** 14.02. Technical Sales. **Other Jobs in This Work Group:** Sales Engineers.

Skills—Persuasion: Persuading others to approach things differently. **Negotiation:** Bringing others together and trying to reconcile differences. **Science:** Using scientific methods to solve problems. **Management of Financial Resources:** Determining how money will be spent to get the work done and accounting for these expenditures. **Service Orientation:** Actively looking for ways to help people. **Coordination:** Adjusting actions in relation to others' actions. **Operations Analysis:** Analyzing needs and product requirements to create a design. **Social Perceptiveness:** Being aware of others' reactions and understanding why they react the way they do.

Education and Training Programs: Business, Management, Marketing, and Related Support Services; Selling Skills and Sales Operations. **Related Knowledge/Courses—Sales and Marketing:** Principles and methods involved in showing, promoting, and selling products or services. This includes marketing strategies and tactics, product demonstration and sales techniques, and sales control systems. **Customer and Personal Service:** Principles and processes for providing customer and personal services, including needs assessment techniques, quality service standards, alternative delivery systems, and customer satisfaction evaluation techniques. **Production and Processing:** Inputs, outputs, raw materials, waste, quality control, costs, and techniques for maximizing the manufacture

and distribution of goods. **Administration and Management:** Principles and processes involved in business and organizational planning, coordination, and execution. This includes strategic planning, resource allocation, manpower modeling, leadership techniques, and production methods. **Computers and Electronics:** Electric circuit boards, processors, chips, and computer hardware and software, including applications and programming. **Transportation:** Principles and methods for moving people or goods by air, rail, sea, or road, including their relative costs, advantages, and limitations.

Work Environment: Indoors; sitting.

Secretaries, Except Legal, Medical, and Executive

- ❋ Education/Training Required: Moderate-term on-the-job training
- ❋ Annual Earnings: $28,220
- ❋ Beginning Wage: $17,920
- ❋ Earnings Growth Potential: Medium
- ❋ Growth: 1.2%
- ❋ Annual Job Openings: 239,630
- ❋ Self-Employed: 1.4%
- ❋ Part-Time: 18.9%

Perform routine clerical and administrative functions such as drafting correspondence, scheduling appointments, organizing and maintaining paper and electronic files, or providing information to callers. Operate office equipment such as fax machines, copiers, and phone systems and use computers for spreadsheet, word-processing, database management, and other applications. Answer telephones and give information to callers, take messages, or transfer calls to appropriate individuals. Greet visitors and callers, handle their inquiries, and direct them to the appropriate persons according to their needs. Set up and maintain paper and electronic filing systems for records, correspondence, and other material. Locate and attach appropriate files to incoming correspondence requiring replies. Open, read, route, and distribute incoming mail and other material and prepare answers to routine letters. Complete forms in accordance with company procedures. Make copies of correspondence and other printed material. Review work done by others to check for correct spelling and grammar, ensure that company format policies are followed, and recommend revisions. Compose, type, and distribute meeting notes, routine correspondence, and reports. Learn to operate new office technologies as they are developed and implemented. Maintain scheduling and event calendars. Schedule and confirm appointments for clients, customers, or supervisors. Manage projects and contribute to committee and team work. Mail newsletters, promotional material, and other information. Order and dispense supplies. Conduct searches to find needed information, using such sources as the Internet. Provide services to customers, such as order placement and account information. Collect and disburse funds from cash accounts and keep records of collections and disbursements. Prepare and mail checks. Establish work procedures and schedules and keep track of the daily work of clerical staff. Coordinate conferences and meetings. Take dictation in shorthand or by machine and transcribe information. Arrange conferences, meetings, and travel reservations for office personnel. Operate electronic mail systems and coordinate the flow of information both internally and with other organizations. Supervise other clerical staff and provide training and orientation to new staff.

Personality Type: Conventional. These occupations frequently involve following set procedures and routines and can include working with data and details more than with ideas. Usually there is a clear line of authority to follow.

GOE—Interest Area/Cluster: 04. Business and Administration. **Work Group:** 04.04. Secretarial Support. **Other Jobs in This Work Group:** Executive Secretaries and Administrative Assistants; Legal Secretaries; Medical Secretaries.

Skill: Writing: Communicating effectively with others in writing as indicated by the needs of the audience.

Education and Training Programs: Administrative Assistant and Secretarial Science, General; Executive Assistant/Executive Secretary Training. **Related Knowledge/ Courses—Clerical Studies:** Administrative and clerical procedures and systems such as word-processing systems, filing and records management systems, stenography and transcription, forms, design principles, and other office procedures and terminology. **Customer and Personal Service:** Principles and processes for providing customer and personal services, including needs assessment techniques, quality service standards, alternative delivery systems, and

customer satisfaction evaluation techniques. **Computers and Electronics:** Electric circuit boards, processors, chips, and computer hardware and software, including applications and programming. **Economics and Accounting:** Economic and accounting principles and practices, the financial markets, banking, and the analysis and reporting of financial data. **English Language:** The structure and content of the English language, including the meaning and spelling of words, rules of composition, and grammar. **Personnel and Human Resources:** Principles and procedures for personnel recruitment; selection; training; compensation and benefits; labor relations and negotiation; and personnel information systems.

Work Environment: Indoors; sitting; repetitive motions.

Security and Fire Alarm Systems Installers

- ✻ Education/Training Required: Postsecondary vocational training
- ✻ Annual Earnings: $35,390
- ✻ Beginning Wage: $22,800
- ✻ Earnings Growth Potential: Medium
- ✻ Growth: 20.2%
- ✻ Annual Job Openings: 5,729
- ✻ Self-Employed: 7.2%
- ✻ Part-Time: 2.7%

Install, program, maintain, and repair security and fire alarm wiring and equipment. Ensure that work is in accordance with relevant codes. Examine systems to locate problems such as loose connections or broken insulation. Test backup batteries, keypad programming, sirens, and all security features in order to ensure proper functioning, and to diagnose malfunctions. Mount and fasten control panels, door and window contacts, sensors, and video cameras, and attach electrical and telephone wiring in order to connect components. Install, maintain, or repair security systems, alarm devices, and related equipment, following blueprints of electrical layouts and building plans. Inspect installation sites and study work orders, building plans, and installation manuals in order to determine materials requirements and installation procedures. Feed cables through access holes, roof spaces, and cavity walls to reach fixture outlets; then position and terminate cables, wires and strapping. Adjust sensitivity of units based on room structures and manufacturers' recommendations, using programming keypads. Test and repair circuits and sensors, following wiring and system specifications. Drill holes for wiring in wall studs, joists, ceilings, and floors. Demonstrate systems for customers, and explain details such as the causes and consequences of false alarms. Consult with clients to assess risks and to determine security requirements. Keep informed of new products and developments. Mount raceways and conduits, and fasten wires to wood framing, using staplers. Prepare documents such as invoices and warranties. Provide customers with cost estimates for equipment installation. Order replacement parts.

Personality Type: Realistic. These occupations frequently involve work activities that include practical, hands-on problems and solutions. They often deal with plants; animals; and real-world materials such as wood, tools, and machinery. Many of the occupations require working outside and don't involve a lot of paperwork or working closely with others.

GOE—Interest Area/Cluster: 02. Architecture and Construction. **Work Group:** 02.04. Construction Crafts. **Other Jobs in This Work Group:** Boilermakers; Brickmasons and Blockmasons; Carpet Installers; Cement Masons and Concrete Finishers; Commercial Divers; Construction Carpenters; Crane and Tower Operators; Drywall and Ceiling Tile Installers; Electricians; Fence Erectors; Floor Layers, Except Carpet, Wood, and Hard Tiles; Floor Sanders and Finishers; Glaziers; Hazardous Materials Removal Workers; Insulation Workers, Floor, Ceiling, and Wall; Insulation Workers, Mechanical; Manufactured Building and Mobile Home Installers; Operating Engineers and Other Construction Equipment Operators; Painters, Construction and Maintenance; Paperhangers; Paving, Surfacing, and Tamping Equipment Operators; Pile-Driver Operators; Pipe Fitters and Steamfitters; Pipelayers; Plasterers and Stucco Masons; Plumbers; Plumbers, Pipefitters, and Steamfitters; Rail-Track Laying and Maintenance Equipment Operators; Refractory Materials Repairers, Except Brickmasons; Reinforcing Iron and Rebar Workers; Riggers; Roofers; Rough Carpenters; Segmental Pavers; Sheet Metal Workers; Stone Cutters and Carvers, Manufacturing; Stonemasons; Structural Iron and Steel Workers; Tapers; Terrazzo Workers and Finishers; Tile and Marble Setters.

Skills—Installation: Installing equipment, machines, wiring, or programs to meet specifications. **Repairing:** Repairing machines or systems, using the needed tools. **Troubleshooting:** Determining what is causing an operating error and deciding what to do about it. **Equipment Maintenance:** Performing routine maintenance and determining when and what kind of maintenance is needed. **Systems Evaluation:** Looking at many indicators of system performance and taking into account their accuracy. **Technology Design:** Generating or adapting equipment and technology to serve user needs. **Operations Analysis:** Analyzing needs and product requirements to create a design. **Programming:** Writing computer programs for various purposes.

Education and Training Programs: Electrician Training; Security System Installation, Repair, and Inspection Technology/Technician Training. **Related Knowledge/Courses—Telecommunications:** Transmission, broadcasting, switching, control, and operation of telecommunications systems. **Building and Construction:** Materials, methods, and the appropriate tools to construct objects, structures, and buildings. **Mechanical Devices:** Machines and tools, including their designs, uses, benefits, repair, and maintenance. **Computers and Electronics:** Electric circuit boards, processors, chips, and computer hardware and software, including applications and programming. **Public Safety and Security:** Weaponry; public safety; security operations, rules, regulations, precautions, and prevention; and the protection of people, data, and property. **Design:** Design techniques, principles, tools, and instruments involved in the production and use of precision technical plans, blueprints, drawings, and models.

Work Environment: More often indoors than outdoors; noisy; very hot or cold; standing; using hands on objects, tools, or controls.

Security Guards

- ✹ Education/Training Required: Short-term on-the-job training
- ✹ Annual Earnings: $22,570
- ✹ Beginning Wage: $15,880
- ✹ Earnings Growth Potential: Low
- ✹ Growth: 16.9%
- ✹ Annual Job Openings: 222,085
- ✹ Self-Employed: 0.7%
- ✹ Part-Time: 15.5%

Guard, patrol, or monitor premises to prevent theft, violence, or infractions of rules. Monitor and authorize entrance and departure of employees, visitors, and other persons to guard against theft and maintain security of premises. Write reports of daily activities and irregularities such as equipment or property damage, theft, presence of unauthorized persons, or unusual occurrences. Call police or fire departments in cases of emergency such as fire or presence of unauthorized persons. Answer alarms and investigate disturbances. Circulate among visitors, patrons, or employees to preserve order and protect property. Patrol industrial or commercial premises to prevent and detect signs of intrusion and ensure security of doors, windows, and gates. Escort or drive motor vehicle to transport individuals to specified locations or to provide personal protection. Operate detecting devices to screen individuals and prevent passage of prohibited articles into restricted areas. Answer telephone calls to take messages, answer questions, and provide information during non-business hours or when switchboard is closed. Warn persons of rule infractions or violations, and apprehend or evict violators from premises, using force when necessary. Inspect and adjust security systems, equipment, or machinery to ensure operational use and to detect evidence of tampering. Monitor and adjust controls that regulate building systems, such as air conditioning, furnace, or boiler.

Personality Type: Realistic. These occupations frequently involve work activities that include practical, hands-on problems and solutions. They often deal with plants; animals; and real-world materials such as wood, tools, and machinery. Many of the occupations require working outside and don't involve a lot of paperwork or working closely with others.

GOE—Interest Area/Cluster: 12. Law and Public Safety. **Work Group:** 12.05. Safety and Security. **Other Jobs in This Work Group:** Animal Control Workers; Crossing Guards; Gaming Surveillance Officers and Gaming Investigators; Lifeguards, Ski Patrol, and Other Recreational Protective Service Workers; Private Detectives and Investigators; Transportation Security Screeners.

Skills: None met the criteria.

Education and Training Programs: Securities Services Administration/Management; Security and Loss Prevention Services. **Related Knowledge/Course: Public Safety and Security:** Weaponry; public safety; security operations, rules, regulations, precautions, and prevention; and the protection of people, data, and property.

Work Environment: More often indoors than outdoors; noisy; standing; walking and running; using hands on objects, tools, or controls.

Self-Enrichment Education Teachers

- ✹ Education/Training Required: Work experience in a related occupation
- ✹ Annual Earnings: $34,580
- ✹ Beginning Wage: $18,530
- ✹ Earnings Growth Potential: High
- ✹ Growth: 23.1%
- ✹ Annual Job Openings: 64,449
- ✹ Self-Employed: 21.5%
- ✹ Part-Time: 41.3%

Teach or instruct courses other than those that normally lead to an occupational objective or degree. Courses may include self-improvement, nonvocational, and non-academic subjects. Teaching may or may not take place in a traditional educational institution. Adapt teaching methods and instructional materials to meet students' varying needs and interests. Conduct classes, workshops, and demonstrations and provide individual instruction to teach topics and skills such as cooking, dancing, writing, physical fitness, photography, personal finance, and flying. Monitor students' performance to make suggestions for improvement and to ensure that they satisfy course standards, training requirements, and objectives. Observe students to determine qualifications, limitations, abilities, interests, and other individual characteristics. Instruct students individually and in groups, using various teaching methods such as lectures, discussions, and demonstrations. Establish clear objectives for all lessons, units, and projects and communicate those objectives to students. Instruct and monitor students in use and care of equipment and materials to prevent injury and damage. Prepare students for further development by encouraging them to explore learning opportunities and to persevere with challenging tasks. Prepare materials and classrooms for class activities. Enforce policies and rules governing students. Plan and conduct activities for a balanced program of instruction, demonstration, and work time that provides students with opportunities to observe, question, and investigate. Prepare instructional program objectives, outlines, and lesson plans. Maintain accurate and complete student records as required by administrative policy. Participate in publicity planning and student recruitment. Plan and supervise class projects, field trips, visits by guest speakers, contests, or other experiential activities and guide students in learning from those activities. Attend professional meetings, conferences, and workshops in order to maintain and improve professional competence. Meet with other instructors to discuss individual students and their progress. Confer with other teachers and professionals to plan and schedule lessons promoting learning and development. Attend staff meetings and serve on committees as required. Prepare and administer written, oral, and performance tests and issue grades in accordance with performance.

Personality Type: Social. These occupations frequently involve working with, communicating with, and teaching people and often involve helping or providing service to others.

GOE—Interest Area/Cluster: 05. Education and Training. **Work Group:** 05.03. Postsecondary and Adult Teaching and Instructing. **Other Jobs in This Work Group:** Adult Literacy, Remedial Education, and GED Teachers and Instructors; Agricultural Sciences Teachers, Postsecondary; Anthropology and Archeology Teachers, Postsecondary; Architecture Teachers, Postsecondary; Area, Ethnic, and Cultural Studies Teachers, Postsecondary; Art, Drama, and Music Teachers, Postsecondary; Atmospheric, Earth, Marine, and Space Sciences Teachers, Postsecondary; Biological Science Teachers, Postsecondary; Business Teachers, Postsecondary; Chemistry Teachers,

Postsecondary; Communications Teachers, Postsecondary; Computer Science Teachers, Postsecondary; Criminal Justice and Law Enforcement Teachers, Postsecondary; Economics Teachers, Postsecondary; Education Teachers, Postsecondary; Engineering Teachers, Postsecondary; English Language and Literature Teachers, Postsecondary; Environmental Science Teachers, Postsecondary; Farm and Home Management Advisors; Foreign Language and Literature Teachers, Postsecondary; Forestry and Conservation Science Teachers, Postsecondary; Geography Teachers, Postsecondary; Graduate Teaching Assistants; Health Specialties Teachers, Postsecondary; History Teachers, Postsecondary; Home Economics Teachers, Postsecondary; Law Teachers, Postsecondary; Library Science Teachers, Postsecondary; Mathematical Science Teachers, Postsecondary; Nursing Instructors and Teachers, Postsecondary; Philosophy and Religion Teachers, Postsecondary; Physics Teachers, Postsecondary; Political Science Teachers, Postsecondary; Psychology Teachers, Postsecondary; Recreation and Fitness Studies Teachers, Postsecondary; Social Work Teachers, Postsecondary; Sociology Teachers, Postsecondary; Vocational Education Teachers, Postsecondary.

Skills—Instructing: Teaching others how to do something. **Learning Strategies:** Using multiple approaches when learning or teaching new things. **Social Perceptiveness:** Being aware of others' reactions and understanding why they react the way they do. **Service Orientation:** Actively looking for ways to help people. **Monitoring:** Assessing how well one is doing when learning or doing something. **Speaking:** Talking to others to effectively convey information. **Persuasion:** Persuading others to approach things differently. **Time Management:** Managing one's own time and the time of others.

Education and Training Program: Adult and Continuing Education and Teaching. **Related Knowledge/Courses— Fine Arts:** Theory and techniques required to produce, compose, and perform works of music, dance, visual arts, drama, and sculpture. **Education and Training:** Instructional methods and training techniques, including curriculum design principles, learning theory, group and individual teaching techniques, design of individual development plans, and test design principles. **Psychology:** Human behavior and performance, mental processes, psychological research methods, and the assessment and treatment of behavioral and affective disorders. **Customer and Personal Service:** Principles and processes for providing customer and personal services, including needs assessment techniques, quality service standards, alternative delivery systems, and customer satisfaction evaluation techniques. **Sales and Marketing:** Principles and methods involved in showing, promoting, and selling products or services. This includes marketing strategies and tactics, product demonstration and sales techniques, and sales control systems. **Administration and Management:** Principles and processes involved in business and organizational planning, coordination, and execution. This includes strategic planning, resource allocation, manpower modeling, leadership techniques, and production methods.

Work Environment: Indoors; standing.

Septic Tank Servicers and Sewer Pipe Cleaners

* Education/Training Required: Moderate-term on-the-job training
* Annual Earnings: $32,740
* Beginning Wage: $20,060
* Earnings Growth Potential: Medium
* Growth: 10.2%
* Annual Job Openings: 3,156
* Self-Employed: 6.4%
* Part-Time: 9.9%

Clean and repair septic tanks, sewer lines, or drains. May patch walls and partitions of tank, replace damaged drain tile, or repair breaks in underground piping. Drive trucks to transport crews, materials, and equipment. Communicate with supervisors and other workers, using equipment such as wireless phones, pagers, or radio telephones. Prepare and keep records of actions taken, including maintenance and repair work. Operate sewer cleaning equipment, including power rodders, high velocity water jets, sewer flushers, bucket machines, wayne balls, and vac-alls. Ensure that repaired sewer line joints are tightly sealed before backfilling begins. Withdraw cables from pipes and examine them for evidence of mud, roots, grease, and other deposits indicating broken or clogged sewer lines. Install rotary knives on flexible cables mounted on machine reels according to the diameters of pipes to be cleaned. Measure excavation sites, using plumbers' snakes, tapelines, or lengths of cutting heads within sewers, and mark areas for

digging. Locate problems, using specially designed equipment, and mark where digging must occur to reach damaged tanks or pipes. Start machines to feed revolving cables or rods into openings, stopping machines and changing knives to conform to pipe sizes. Clean and repair septic tanks; sewer lines; or related structures such as manholes, culverts, and catch basins. Service, adjust, and make minor repairs to equipment, machines, and attachments. Inspect manholes to locate sewer line stoppages. Cut damaged sections of pipe with cutters; remove broken sections from ditches; and replace pipe sections, using pipe sleeves. Dig out sewer lines manually, using shovels. Break asphalt and other pavement so that pipes can be accessed, using airhammers, picks, and shovels. Cover repaired pipes with dirt and pack backfilled excavations, using air and gasoline tampers. Requisition or order tools and equipment. Rotate cleaning rods manually, using turning pins. Clean and disinfect domestic basements and other areas flooded by sewer stoppages. Tap mainline sewers to install sewer saddles. Update sewer maps and manhole charts.

Personality Type: Realistic. These occupations frequently involve work activities that include practical, hands-on problems and solutions. They often deal with plants; animals; and real-world materials such as wood, tools, and machinery. Many of the occupations require working outside and don't involve a lot of paperwork or working closely with others.

GOE—Interest Area/Cluster: 02. Architecture and Construction. **Work Group:** 02.06. Construction Support/Labor. **Other Jobs in This Work Group:** Construction Laborers; Helpers—Brickmasons, Blockmasons, Stonemasons, and Tile and Marble Setters; Helpers—Carpenters; Helpers—Electricians; Helpers—Installation, Maintenance, and Repair Workers; Helpers—Painters, Paperhangers, Plasterers, and Stucco Masons; Helpers—Pipelayers, Plumbers, Pipefitters, and Steamfitters; Helpers—Roofers; Highway Maintenance Workers.

Skills—Equipment Maintenance: Performing routine maintenance and determining when and what kind of maintenance is needed. **Repairing:** Repairing machines or systems, using the needed tools. **Installation:** Installing equipment, machines, wiring, or programs to meet specifications. **Operation Monitoring:** Watching gauges, dials, or other indicators to make sure a machine is working properly. **Operation and Control:** Controlling operations of equipment or systems. **Troubleshooting:** Determining what is causing an operating error and deciding what to do about it. **Systems Analysis:** Determining how a system should work and how changes will affect outcomes. **Management of Material Resources:** Obtaining and seeing to the appropriate use of equipment, facilities, and materials needed to do certain work.

Education and Training Program: Plumbing Technology/Plumber Training. **Related Knowledge/Courses—Building and Construction:** Materials, methods, and the appropriate tools to construct objects, structures, and buildings. **Mechanical Devices:** Machines and tools, including their designs, uses, benefits, repair, and maintenance. **Sales and Marketing:** Principles and methods involved in showing, promoting, and selling products or services. This includes marketing strategies and tactics, product demonstration and sales techniques, and sales control systems. **Transportation:** Principles and methods for moving people or goods by air, rail, sea, or road, including their relative costs, advantages, and limitations. **Production and Processing:** Inputs, outputs, raw materials, waste, quality control, costs, and techniques for maximizing the manufacture and distribution of goods. **Customer and Personal Service:** Principles and processes for providing customer and personal services, including needs assessment techniques, quality service standards, alternative delivery systems, and customer satisfaction evaluation techniques.

Work Environment: Outdoors; noisy; very hot or cold; contaminants; hazardous equipment; using hands on objects, tools, or controls.

Sheet Metal Workers

- ❋ Education/Training Required: Long-term on-the-job training
- ❋ Annual Earnings: $39,210
- ❋ Beginning Wage: $22,820
- ❋ Earnings Growth Potential: High
- ❋ Growth: 6.7%
- ❋ Annual Job Openings: 31,677
- ❋ Self-Employed: 4.7%
- ❋ Part-Time: 4.2%

Fabricate, assemble, install, and repair sheet metal products and equipment, such as ducts, control boxes, drainpipes, and furnace casings. Work may involve any of the following: setting up and operating fabricating machines to cut, bend, and straighten sheet metal; shaping metal over anvils, blocks, or forms, using hammer; operating soldering and welding equipment to join sheet metal parts; and inspecting, assembling, and smoothing seams and joints of burred surfaces. Determine project requirements, including scope, assembly sequences, and required methods and materials, according to blueprints, drawings, and written or verbal instructions. Lay out, measure, and mark dimensions and reference lines on material such as roofing panels according to drawings or templates, using calculators, scribes, dividers, squares, and rulers. Maneuver completed units into position for installation and anchor the units. Convert blueprints into shop drawings to be followed in the construction and assembly of sheet metal products. Install assemblies such as flashing, pipes, tubes, heating and air conditioning ducts, furnace casings, rain gutters, and downspouts in supportive frameworks. Select gauges and types of sheet metal or non-metallic material according to product specifications. Drill and punch holes in metal for screws, bolts, and rivets. Fasten seams and joints together with welds, bolts, cement, rivets, solder, caulks, metal drive clips, and bonds to assemble components into products or to repair sheet metal items. Fabricate or alter parts at construction sites, using shears, hammers, punches, and drills. Finish parts, using hacksaws and hand, rotary, or squaring shears. Trim, file, grind, deburr, buff, and smooth surfaces, seams, and joints of assembled parts, using hand tools and portable power tools. Maintain equipment, making repairs and modifications when necessary. Shape metal material over anvils, blocks, or other forms, using hand tools. Transport prefabricated parts to construction sites for assembly and installation. Develop and lay out patterns that use materials most efficiently, using computerized metalworking equipment to experiment with different layouts. Inspect individual parts, assemblies, and installations for conformance to specifications and building codes, using measuring instruments such as calipers, scales, and micrometers. Secure metal roof panels in place and interlock and fasten grooved panel edges. Fasten roof panel edges and machine-made molding to structures, nailing or welding pieces into place.

Personality Type: Realistic. These occupations frequently involve work activities that include practical, hands-on problems and solutions. They often deal with plants; animals; and real-world materials such as wood, tools, and machinery. Many of the occupations require working

outside and don't involve a lot of paperwork or working closely with others.

GOE—Interest Area/Cluster: 02. Architecture and Construction. **Work Group:** 02.04. Construction Crafts. **Other Jobs in This Work Group:** Boilermakers; Brickmasons and Blockmasons; Carpet Installers; Cement Masons and Concrete Finishers; Commercial Divers; Construction Carpenters; Crane and Tower Operators; Drywall and Ceiling Tile Installers; Electricians; Fence Erectors; Floor Layers, Except Carpet, Wood, and Hard Tiles; Floor Sanders and Finishers; Glaziers; Hazardous Materials Removal Workers; Insulation Workers, Floor, Ceiling, and Wall; Insulation Workers, Mechanical; Manufactured Building and Mobile Home Installers; Operating Engineers and Other Construction Equipment Operators; Painters, Construction and Maintenance; Paperhangers; Paving, Surfacing, and Tamping Equipment Operators; Pile-Driver Operators; Pipe Fitters and Steamfitters; Pipelayers; Plasterers and Stucco Masons; Plumbers; Plumbers, Pipefitters, and Steamfitters; Rail-Track Laying and Maintenance Equipment Operators; Refractory Materials Repairers, Except Brickmasons; Reinforcing Iron and Rebar Workers; Riggers; Roofers; Rough Carpenters; Security and Fire Alarm Systems Installers; Segmental Pavers; Stone Cutters and Carvers, Manufacturing; Stonemasons; Structural Iron and Steel Workers; Tapers; Terrazzo Workers and Finishers; Tile and Marble Setters.

Skills—Installation: Installing equipment, machines, wiring, or programs to meet specifications. **Repairing:** Repairing machines or systems, using the needed tools. **Equipment Maintenance:** Performing routine maintenance and determining when and what kind of maintenance is needed. **Mathematics:** Using mathematics to solve problems. **Technology Design:** Generating or adapting equipment and technology to serve user needs. **Equipment Selection:** Determining the kind of tools and equipment needed to do a job. **Troubleshooting:** Determining what is causing an operating error and deciding what to do about it. **Coordination:** Adjusting actions in relation to others' actions.

Education and Training Program: Sheet Metal Technology/Sheetworking. **Related Knowledge/Courses—Building and Construction:** Materials, methods, and the appropriate tools to construct objects, structures, and buildings. **Mechanical Devices:** Machines and tools, including their designs, uses, benefits, repair, and maintenance.

Physics: Physical principles, laws, and applications, including air, water, material dynamics, light, atomic principles, heat, electric theory, earth formations, and meteorological and related natural phenomena. **Design:** Design techniques, principles, tools, and instruments involved in the production and use of precision technical plans, blueprints, drawings, and models. **Production and Processing:** Inputs, outputs, raw materials, waste, quality control, costs, and techniques for maximizing the manufacture and distribution of goods. **Mathematics:** Numbers and their operations and interrelationships, including arithmetic, algebra, geometry, calculus, and statistics and their applications.

Work Environment: Noisy; contaminants; hazardous equipment; minor burns, cuts, bites, or stings; standing; using hands on objects, tools, or controls.

Sheriffs and Deputy Sheriffs

- ❊ Education/Training Required: Long-term on-the-job training
- ❊ Annual Earnings: $49,630
- ❊ Beginning Wage: $28,820
- ❊ Earnings Growth Potential: High
- ❊ Growth: 10.8%
- ❊ Annual Job Openings: 37,842
- ❊ Self-Employed: 0.0%
- ❊ Part-Time: 1.1%

The job openings listed here are shared with Police Patrol Officers.

Enforce law and order in rural or unincorporated districts or serve legal processes of courts. May patrol courthouse, guard court or grand jury, or escort defendants. Drive vehicles or patrol specific areas to detect law violators, issue citations, and make arrests. Investigate illegal or suspicious activities. Verify that the proper legal charges have been made against law offenders. Execute arrest warrants, locating and taking persons into custody. Record daily activities and submit logs and other related reports and paperwork to appropriate authorities. Patrol and guard courthouses, grand jury rooms, or assigned areas to provide security, enforce laws, maintain order, and arrest violators. Notify patrol units to take violators into custody or to provide needed assistance or medical aid. Place people in protective custody. Serve statements of claims, subpoenas, summonses, jury summonses, orders to pay alimony, and other court orders. Take control of accident scenes to maintain traffic flow, to assist accident victims, and to investigate causes. Question individuals entering secured areas to determine their business, directing and rerouting individuals as necessary. Transport or escort prisoners and defendants en route to courtrooms, prisons or jails, attorneys' offices, or medical facilities. Locate and confiscate real or personal property, as directed by court order. Manage jail operations and tend to jail inmates.

Personality Type: Enterprising. These occupations frequently involve starting up and carrying out projects and can involve leading people and making many decisions. They sometimes require risk taking and often deal with business.

GOE—Interest Area/Cluster: 12. Law and Public Safety. **Work Group:** 12.04. Law Enforcement and Public Safety. **Other Jobs in This Work Group:** Bailiffs; Correctional Officers and Jailers; Criminal Investigators and Special Agents; Detectives and Criminal Investigators; Fire Investigators; Forensic Science Technicians; Parking Enforcement Workers; Police and Sheriff's Patrol Officers; Police Detectives; Police Identification and Records Officers; Police Patrol Officers; Transit and Railroad Police.

Skills—Negotiation: Bringing others together and trying to reconcile differences. **Persuasion:** Persuading others to approach things differently. **Social Perceptiveness:** Being aware of others' reactions and understanding why they react the way they do. **Service Orientation:** Actively looking for ways to help people. **Equipment Selection:** Determining the kind of tools and equipment needed to do a job. **Complex Problem Solving:** Identifying complex problems, reviewing the options, and implementing solutions. **Judgment and Decision Making:** Weighing the relative costs and benefits of a potential action. **Coordination:** Adjusting actions in relation to others' actions.

Education and Training Programs: Criminal Justice/Police Science; Criminalistics and Criminal Science. **Related Knowledge/Courses—Public Safety and Security:** Weaponry; public safety; security operations, rules, regulations, precautions, and prevention; and the protection of people, data, and property. **Law and Government:** Laws, legal codes, court procedures, precedents, government regulations, executive orders, agency rules, and

the democratic political process. **Telecommunications:** Transmission, broadcasting, switching, control, and operation of telecommunications systems. **Psychology:** Human behavior and performance, mental processes, psychological research methods, and the assessment and treatment of behavioral and affective disorders. **Therapy and Counseling:** Information and techniques needed to rehabilitate physical and mental ailments and to provide career guidance, including alternative treatments, rehabilitation equipment and its proper use, and methods to evaluate treatment effects. **Philosophy and Theology:** Different philosophical systems and religions, including their basic principles, values, ethics, ways of thinking, customs, and practices and their impact on human culture.

Work Environment: More often outdoors than indoors; very hot or cold; contaminants; disease or infections; sitting.

Ship and Boat Captains

- ❋ Education/Training Required: Work experience in a related occupation
- ❋ Annual Earnings: $57,210
- ❋ Beginning Wage: $29,530
- ❋ Earnings Growth Potential: High
- ❋ Growth: 17.9%
- ❋ Annual Job Openings: 2,665
- ❋ Self-Employed: 6.8%
- ❋ Part-Time: 4.8%

The job openings listed here are shared with Mates—Ship, Boat, and Barge and with Pilots, Ship.

Command vessels in oceans, bays, lakes, rivers, and coastal waters. Assign watches and living quarters to crew members. Sort logs, form log booms, and salvage lost logs. Perform various marine duties such as checking for oil spills or other pollutants around ports and harbors, and patrolling beaches. Contact buyers to sell cargo such as fish. Tow and maneuver barges, or signal for tugboats to tow barges to destinations. Signal passing vessels, using whistles, flashing lights, flags, and radios. Resolve questions or problems with customs officials. Read gauges to verify sufficient levels of hydraulic fluid, air pressure, and oxygen. Purchase supplies and equipment. Measure depths of water, using depth-measuring equipment. Maintain boats and equipment on board, such as engines, winches, navigational systems, fire extinguishers, and life preservers. Collect fares from customers, or signal ferryboat helpers to collect fares. Arrange for ships to be fueled, restocked with supplies, and/or repaired. Signal crew members or deck-hands to rig tow lines, open or close gates and ramps, and pull guard chains across entries. Maintain records of daily activities, personnel reports, ship positions and movements, ports of call, weather and sea conditions, pollution control efforts, and/or cargo and passenger statuses. Inspect vessels to ensure efficient and safe operation of vessels and equipment, and conformance to regulations. Direct and coordinate crew members or workers performing activities such as loading and unloading cargo, steering vessels, operating engines, and operating, maintaining, and repairing ship equipment. Compute positions, set courses, and determine speeds by using charts, area plotting sheets, compasses, sextants, and knowledge of local conditions. Calculate sightings of land, using electronic sounding devices, and following contour lines on charts. Monitor the loading and discharging of cargo or passengers. Interview and hire crew members. Steer and operate vessels, using radios, depth finders, radars, lights, buoys, and lighthouses.

Personality Type: Enterprising. These occupations frequently involve starting up and carrying out projects and can involve leading people and making many decisions. They sometimes require risk taking and often deal with business.

GOE—Interest Area/Cluster: 16. Transportation, Distribution, and Logistics. **Work Group:** 16.05. Water Vehicle Operation. **Other Jobs in This Work Group:** Captains, Mates, and Pilots of Water Vessels; Dredge Operators; Mates—Ship, Boat, and Barge; Motorboat Operators; Pilots, Ship; Sailors and Marine Oilers.

Skills—Operation and Control: Controlling operations of equipment or systems. **Operation Monitoring:** Watching gauges, dials, or other indicators to make sure a machine is working properly. **Equipment Maintenance:** Performing routine maintenance and determining when and what kind of maintenance is needed. **Judgment and Decision Making:** Weighing the relative costs and benefits of a potential action. **Troubleshooting:** Determining what is causing an operating error and deciding what to do about it. **Management of Personnel Resources:** Motivating, developing, and directing people as they work; identifying the best people for the job. **Repairing:** Repairing

machines or systems, using the needed tools. **Management of Material Resources:** Obtaining and seeing to the appropriate use of equipment, facilities, and materials needed to do certain work.

Education and Training Programs: Commercial Fishing; Marine Science/Merchant Marine Officer Training; Marine Transportation, Other. **Related Knowledge/Courses—Transportation:** Principles and methods for moving people or goods by air, rail, sea, or road, including their relative costs, advantages, and limitations. **Geography:** Various methods for describing the location and distribution of land, sea, and air masses, including their physical locations, relationships, and characteristics. **Public Safety and Security:** Weaponry; public safety; security operations, rules, regulations, precautions, and prevention; and the protection of people, data, and property. **Telecommunications:** Transmission, broadcasting, switching, control, and operation of telecommunications systems. **Psychology:** Human behavior and performance, mental processes, psychological research methods, and the assessment and treatment of behavioral and affective disorders. **Mechanical Devices:** Machines and tools, including their designs, uses, benefits, repair, and maintenance.

Work Environment: More often outdoors than indoors; noisy; very bright or dim lighting; contaminants; using hands on objects, tools, or controls.

Ship Engineers

* Education/Training Required: Work experience in a related occupation
* Annual Earnings: $56,090
* Beginning Wage: $34,450
* Earnings Growth Potential: Medium
* Growth: 14.1%
* Annual Job Openings: 1,102
* Self-Employed: 0.0%
* Part-Time: 5.7%

Supervise and coordinate activities of crew engaged in operating and maintaining engines; boilers; deck machinery; and electrical, sanitary, and refrigeration equipment aboard ship. Record orders for changes in ship speed and direction, and note gauge readings and test data, such as revolutions per minute and voltage output, in engineering logs and bellbooks. Install engine controls, propeller shafts, and propellers. Perform and participate in emergency drills as required. Fabricate engine replacement parts such as valves, stay rods, and bolts, using metalworking machinery. Operate and maintain off-loading liquid pumps and valves. Maintain and repair engines, electric motors, pumps, winches and other mechanical and electrical equipment, or assist other crew members with maintenance and repair duties. Maintain electrical power, heating, ventilation, refrigeration, water, and sewerage. Monitor and test operations of engines and other equipment so that malfunctions and their causes can be identified. Monitor engine, machinery, and equipment indicators when vessels are underway, and report abnormalities to appropriate shipboard staff. Start engines to propel ships, and regulate engines and power transmissions to control speeds of ships, according to directions from captains or bridge computers. Order and receive engine rooms' stores such as oil and spare parts; maintain inventories and record usage of supplies. Act as liaisons between ships' captains and shore personnel to ensure that schedules and budgets are maintained and that ships are operated safely and efficiently. Clean engine parts, and keep engine rooms clean. Supervise the activities of marine engine technicians engaged in the maintenance and repair of mechanical and electrical marine vessels, and inspect their work to ensure that it is performed properly. Maintain complete records of engineering department activities, including machine operations. Perform general marine vessel maintenance and repair work such as repairing leaks, finishing interiors, refueling, and maintaining decks. Monitor the availability, use, and condition of life-saving equipment and pollution preventatives, in order to ensure that international regulations are followed.

Personality Type: Realistic. These occupations frequently involve work activities that include practical, hands-on problems and solutions. They often deal with plants; animals; and real-world materials such as wood, tools, and machinery. Many of the occupations require working outside and don't involve a lot of paperwork or working closely with others.

GOE—Interest Area/Cluster: 13. Manufacturing. **Work Group:** 13.16. Utility Operation and Energy Distribution. **Other Jobs in This Work Group:** Chemical Plant and System Operators; Gas Compressor and Gas Pumping Station Operators; Gas Plant Operators; Nuclear Power Reactor Operators; Petroleum Pump System Operators,

Refinery Operators, and Gaugers; Power Distributors and Dispatchers; Power Plant Operators; Stationary Engineers and Boiler Operators; Water and Liquid Waste Treatment Plant and System Operators.

Skills—Repairing: Repairing machines or systems, using the needed tools. **Installation:** Installing equipment, machines, wiring, or programs to meet specifications. **Equipment Maintenance:** Performing routine maintenance and determining when and what kind of maintenance is needed. **Operation Monitoring:** Watching gauges, dials, or other indicators to make sure a machine is working properly. **Operation and Control:** Controlling operations of equipment or systems. **Troubleshooting:** Determining what is causing an operating error and deciding what to do about it. **Systems Analysis:** Determining how a system should work and how changes will affect outcomes. **Science:** Using scientific methods to solve problems.

Education and Training Program: Marine Maintenance/Fitter and Ship Repair Technology/Technician Training. **Related Knowledge/Courses—Mechanical Devices:** Machines and tools, including their designs, uses, benefits, repair, and maintenance. **Engineering and Technology:** Equipment, tools, and mechanical devices and their uses to produce motion, light, power, technology, and other applications. **Building and Construction:** Materials, methods, and the appropriate tools to construct objects, structures, and buildings. **Transportation:** Principles and methods for moving people or goods by air, rail, sea, or road, including their relative costs, advantages, and limitations. **Chemistry:** The composition, structure, and properties of substances and of the chemical processes and transformations that they undergo. This includes uses of chemicals and their interactions, danger signs, production techniques, and disposal methods. **Public Safety and Security:** Weaponry; public safety; security operations, rules, regulations, precautions, and prevention; and the protection of people, data, and property.

Work Environment: Outdoors; noisy; very hot or cold; contaminants; hazardous equipment; using hands on objects, tools, or controls.

Shipping, Receiving, and Traffic Clerks

* Education/Training Required: Short-term on-the-job training
* Annual Earnings: $26,990
* Beginning Wage: $17,390
* Earnings Growth Potential: Medium
* Growth: 3.7%
* Annual Job Openings: 138,967
* Self-Employed: 0.2%
* Part-Time: 8.9%

Verify and keep records on incoming and outgoing shipments. Prepare items for shipment. Duties include assembling, addressing, stamping, and shipping merchandise or material; receiving, unpacking, verifying, and recording incoming merchandise or material; and arranging for the transportation of products. Examine contents and compare with records such as manifests, invoices, or orders to verify accuracy of incoming or outgoing shipment. Prepare documents such as work orders, bills of lading, and shipping orders to route materials. Determine shipping method for materials, using knowledge of shipping procedures, routes, and rates. Record shipment data such as weight, charges, space availability, and damages and discrepancies for reporting, accounting, and recordkeeping purposes. Contact carrier representative to make arrangements and to issue instructions for shipping and delivery of materials. Confer and correspond with establishment representatives to rectify problems such as damages, shortages, and nonconformance to specifications. Requisition and store shipping materials and supplies to maintain inventory of stock. Deliver or route materials to departments, using work devices such as handtruck, conveyor, or sorting bins. Compute amounts such as space available and shipping, storage, and demurrage charges, using calculator or price list. Pack, seal, label, and affix postage to prepare materials for shipping, using work devices such as hand tools, power tools, and postage meter.

Personality Type: Conventional. These occupations frequently involve following set procedures and routines and can include working with data and details more than with ideas. Usually there is a clear line of authority to follow.

GOE—Interest Area/Cluster: 04. Business and Administration. **Work Group:** 04.07. Records and Materials Processing. **Other Jobs in This Work Group:** Correspondence Clerks; File Clerks; Human Resources Assistants, Except Payroll and Timekeeping; Marking Clerks; Meter Readers, Utilities; Office Clerks, General; Order Fillers, Wholesale and Retail Sales; Postal Service Clerks; Postal Service Mail Sorters, Processors, and Processing Machine Operators; Procurement Clerks; Production, Planning, and Expediting Clerks; Stock Clerks and Order Fillers; Stock Clerks, Sales Floor; Stock Clerks—Stockroom, Warehouse, or Storage Yard; Weighers, Measurers, Checkers, and Samplers, Recordkeeping.

Skills—Mathematics: Using mathematics to solve problems. **Learning Strategies:** Using multiple approaches when learning or teaching new things. **Management of Financial Resources:** Determining how money will be spent to get the work done and accounting for these expenditures. **Writing:** Communicating effectively with others in writing as indicated by the needs of the audience. **Speaking:** Talking to others to effectively convey information. **Negotiation:** Bringing others together and trying to reconcile differences. **Social Perceptiveness:** Being aware of others' reactions and understanding why they react the way they do. **Time Management:** Managing one's own time and the time of others.

Education and Training Programs: General Office Occupations and Clerical Services; Traffic, Customs, and Transportation Clerk/Technician Training. **Related Knowledge/Courses—Clerical Studies:** Administrative and clerical procedures and systems such as word-processing systems, filing and records management systems, stenography and transcription, forms, design principles, and other office procedures and terminology. **Production and Processing:** Inputs, outputs, raw materials, waste, quality control, costs, and techniques for maximizing the manufacture and distribution of goods. **Transportation:** Principles and methods for moving people or goods by air, rail, sea, or road, including their relative costs, advantages, and limitations. **Computers and Electronics:** Electric circuit boards, processors, chips, and computer hardware and software, including applications and programming. **Education and Training:** Instructional methods and training techniques, including curriculum design principles, learning theory, group and individual teaching techniques, design of individual development plans, and test design principles. **Public Safety and Security:** Weaponry; public safety; security operations, rules, regulations, precautions, and prevention; and the protection of people, data, and property.

Work Environment: Indoors; noisy; contaminants; sitting; walking and running; using hands on objects, tools, or controls.

Skin Care Specialists

- ❋ Education/Training Required: Postsecondary vocational training
- ❋ Annual Earnings: $27,190
- ❋ Beginning Wage: $15,230
- ❋ Earnings Growth Potential: High
- ❋ Growth: 34.3%
- ❋ Annual Job Openings: 6,643
- ❋ Self-Employed: 38.9%
- ❋ Part-Time: 26.3%

Provide skin care treatments to face and body to enhance an individual's appearance. Sterilize equipment and clean work areas. Keep records of client needs and preferences and the services provided. Demonstrate how to clean and care for skin properly and recommend skin-care regimens. Examine clients' skin, using magnifying lamps or visors when necessary, to evaluate skin condition and appearance. Select and apply cosmetic products such as creams, lotions, and tonics. Cleanse clients' skin with water, creams, or lotions. Treat the facial skin to maintain and improve its appearance, using specialized techniques and products such as peels and masks. Refer clients to medical personnel for treatment of serious skin problems. Determine which products or colors will improve clients' skin quality and appearance. Perform simple extractions to remove blackheads. Provide facial and body massages. Remove body and facial hair by applying wax. Apply chemical peels in order to reduce fine lines and age spots. Advise clients about colors and types of makeup and instruct them in makeup application techniques. Sell makeup to clients. Collaborate with plastic surgeons and dermatologists to provide patients with preoperative and postoperative skin care. Give manicures and pedicures and apply artificial nails. Tint eyelashes and eyebrows.

Personality Type: Enterprising. These occupations frequently involve starting up and carrying out projects and can involve leading people and making many decisions. They sometimes require risk taking and often deal with business.

GOE—Interest Area/Cluster: 09. Hospitality, Tourism, and Recreation. **Work Group:** 09.07. Barber and Beauty Services. **Other Jobs in This Work Group:** Barbers; Hairdressers, Hairstylists, and Cosmetologists; Manicurists and Pedicurists; Shampooers.

Skills—Equipment Selection: Determining the kind of tools and equipment needed to do a job. **Service Orientation:** Actively looking for ways to help people. **Science:** Using scientific methods to solve problems. **Equipment Maintenance:** Performing routine maintenance and determining when and what kind of maintenance is needed. **Time Management:** Managing one's own time and the time of others. **Social Perceptiveness:** Being aware of others' reactions and understanding why they react the way they do. **Technology Design:** Generating or adapting equipment and technology to serve user needs. **Active Learning:** Working with new material or information to grasp its implications.

Education and Training Programs: Aesthetician/Esthetician and Skin Care Specialist Training; Cosmetology/Cosmetologist Training, General; Facial Treatment Specialist/Facialist Training. **Related Knowledge/Courses—Sales and Marketing:** Principles and methods involved in showing, promoting, and selling products or services. This includes marketing strategies and tactics, product demonstration and sales techniques, and sales control systems. **Chemistry:** The composition, structure, and properties of substances and of the chemical processes and transformations that they undergo. This includes uses of chemicals and their interactions, danger signs, production techniques, and disposal methods. **Customer and Personal Service:** Principles and processes for providing customer and personal services, including needs assessment techniques, quality service standards, alternative delivery systems, and customer satisfaction evaluation techniques.

Work Environment: Indoors; standing; using hands on objects, tools, or controls; bending or twisting the body; repetitive motions.

Slaughterers and Meat Packers

* Education/Training Required: Moderate-term on-the-job training
* Annual Earnings: $22,500
* Beginning Wage: $16,510
* Earnings Growth Potential: Low
* Growth: 12.7%
* Annual Job Openings: 15,511
* Self-Employed: 1.2%
* Part-Time: 8.3%

Work in slaughtering, meat packing, or wholesale establishments performing precision functions involving the preparation of meat. Work may include specialized slaughtering tasks, cutting standard or premium cuts of meat for marketing, making sausage, or wrapping meat. Skin sections of animals or whole animals. Trim, clean, and/or cure animal hides. Cut, trim, skin, sort, and wash viscera of slaughtered animals to separate edible portions from offal. Shackle hind legs of animals to raise them for slaughtering or skinning. Slaughter animals in accordance with religious laws, and determine that carcasses meet specified religious standards. Wrap dressed carcasses and/or meat cuts. Trim head meat, and sever or remove parts of animals' heads or skulls. Stun animals prior to slaughtering. Slit open, eviscerate, and trim carcasses of slaughtered animals. Shave or singe and defeather carcasses, and wash them in preparation for further processing or packaging. Sever jugular veins to drain blood and facilitate slaughtering. Saw, split, or scribe carcasses into smaller portions to facilitate handling. Remove bones, and cut meat into standard cuts in preparation for marketing. Grind meat into hamburger, and into trimmings used to prepare sausages, luncheon meats, and other meat products. Tend assembly lines, performing a few of the many cuts needed to process carcasses.

Personality Type: Realistic. These occupations frequently involve work activities that include practical, hands-on problems and solutions. They often deal with plants; animals; and real-world materials such as wood, tools, and machinery. Many of the occupations require working outside and don't involve a lot of paperwork or working closely with others.

GOE—Interest Area/Cluster: 13. Manufacturing. **Work Group:** 13.03. Production Work, Assorted Materials Processing. **Other Jobs in This Work Group:** Bakers; Cementing and Gluing Machine Operators and Tenders; Chemical Equipment Operators and Tenders; Cleaning, Washing, and Metal Pickling Equipment Operators and Tenders; Coating, Painting, and Spraying Machine Setters, Operators, and Tenders; Cooling and Freezing Equipment Operators and Tenders; Cutting and Slicing Machine Setters, Operators, and Tenders; Extruding and Forming Machine Setters, Operators, and Tenders, Synthetic and Glass Fibers; Extruding, Forming, Pressing, and Compacting Machine Setters, Operators, and Tenders; Food and Tobacco Roasting, Baking, and Drying Machine Operators and Tenders; Food Batchmakers; Food Cooking Machine Operators and Tenders; Furnace, Kiln, Oven, Drier, and Kettle Operators and Tenders; Heat Treating Equipment Setters, Operators, and Tenders, Metal and Plastic; Helpers—Production Workers; Meat, Poultry, and Fish Cutters and Trimmers; Metal-Refining Furnace Operators and Tenders; Mixing and Blending Machine Setters, Operators, and Tenders; Packaging and Filling Machine Operators and Tenders; Plating and Coating Machine Setters, Operators, and Tenders, Metal and Plastic; Pourers and Casters, Metal; Sawing Machine Setters, Operators, and Tenders, Wood; Separating, Filtering, Clarifying, Precipitating, and Still Machine Setters, Operators, and Tenders; Sewing Machine Operators; Shoe Machine Operators and Tenders; Team Assemblers; Textile Bleaching and Dyeing Machine Operators and Tenders; Tire Builders; Woodworking Machine Setters, Operators, and Tenders, Except Sawing.

Skills—Operation and Control: Controlling operations of equipment or systems. **Operation Monitoring:** Watching gauges, dials, or other indicators to make sure a machine is working properly. **Equipment Maintenance:** Performing routine maintenance and determining when and what kind of maintenance is needed. **Quality Control Analysis:** Evaluating the quality or performance of products, services, or processes. **Repairing:** Repairing machines or systems, using the needed tools. **Service Orientation:** Actively looking for ways to help people. **Monitoring:** Assessing how well one is doing when learning or doing something. **Management of Material Resources:** Obtaining and seeing to the appropriate use of equipment, facilities, and materials needed to do certain work.

Education and Training Program: Meat Cutting/Meat Cutter Training. **Related Knowledge/Courses—Food Production:** Techniques and equipment for planting, growing, and harvesting of food for consumption, including crop-rotation methods, animal husbandry, and food storage/handling techniques. **Chemistry:** The composition, structure, and properties of substances and of the chemical processes and transformations that they undergo. This includes uses of chemicals and their interactions, danger signs, production techniques, and disposal methods. **Mechanical Devices:** Machines and tools, including their designs, uses, benefits, repair, and maintenance. **Production and Processing:** Inputs, outputs, raw materials, waste, quality control, costs, and techniques for maximizing the manufacture and distribution of goods.

Work Environment: Noisy; very hot or cold; minor burns, cuts, bites, or stings; standing; using hands on objects, tools, or controls; repetitive motions.

Social and Human Service Assistants

- ❈ Education/Training Required: Moderate-term on-the-job training
- ❈ Annual Earnings: $26,630
- ❈ Beginning Wage: $17,350
- ❈ Earnings Growth Potential: Low
- ❈ Growth: 33.6%
- ❈ Annual Job Openings: 80,142
- ❈ Self-Employed: 0.1%
- ❈ Part-Time: 12.0%

Assist professionals from a wide variety of fields such as psychology, rehabilitation, or social work to provide client services, as well as support for families. May assist clients in identifying available benefits and social and community services and help clients obtain them. May assist social workers with developing, organizing, and conducting programs to prevent and resolve problems relevant to substance abuse, human relationships, rehabilitation, or adult daycare. Keep records and prepare reports for owner or management concerning visits with clients. Submit reports and review reports or problems with superior. Interview individuals and family members to compile information on social, educational, criminal, institutional, or drug histories. Provide information and refer individuals to public or private agencies or community services for assistance. Consult with supervisors concerning programs for individual families. Advise clients regarding food stamps, child care, food, money management, sanitation, or housekeeping. Oversee day-to-day group activities of residents in institution. Visit individuals in homes or attend group meetings to provide information on agency services, requirements, and procedures. Monitor free, supplementary meal program to ensure cleanliness of facility and that eligibility guidelines are met for persons receiving meals. Meet with youth groups to acquaint them with consequences of delinquent acts. Assist in planning of food budgets, using charts and sample budgets. Transport and accompany clients to shopping areas or to appointments, using automobiles. Assist in locating housing for displaced individuals. Observe and discuss meal preparation and suggest alternate methods of food preparation. Observe clients' food selections and recommend alternate economical and nutritional food choices. Explain rules established by owner or management, such as sanitation and maintenance requirements, and parking regulations. Care for children in clients' homes during clients' appointments. Inform tenants of facilities such as laundries and playgrounds. Assist clients with preparation of forms such as tax or rent forms. Demonstrate use and care of equipment for tenant use.

Personality Type: Conventional. These occupations frequently involve following set procedures and routines and can include working with data and details more than with ideas. Usually there is a clear line of authority to follow.

GOE—Interest Area/Cluster: 10. Human Service. **Work Group:** 10.01. Counseling and Social Work. **Other Jobs in This Work Group:** Child, Family, and School Social Workers; Clinical Psychologists; Clinical, Counseling, and School Psychologists; Counseling Psychologists; Marriage and Family Therapists; Medical and Public Health Social Workers; Mental Health and Substance Abuse Social Workers; Mental Health Counselors; Probation Officers and Correctional Treatment Specialists; Rehabilitation Counselors; Residential Advisors; Substance Abuse and Behavioral Disorder Counselors.

Skill: Negotiation: Bringing others together and trying to reconcile differences.

Education and Training Program: Mental and Social Health Services and Allied Professions, Other. **Related Knowledge/Courses—Therapy and Counseling:** Information and techniques needed to rehabilitate physical and mental ailments and to provide career guidance, including alternative treatments, rehabilitation equipment and its proper use, and methods to evaluate treatment effects. **Philosophy and Theology:** Different philosophical systems and religions, including their basic principles, values, ethics, ways of thinking, customs, and practices and their impact on human culture. **Psychology:** Human behavior and performance, mental processes, psychological research methods, and the assessment and treatment of behavioral and affective disorders. **Customer and Personal Service:** Principles and processes for providing customer and personal services, including needs assessment techniques, quality service standards, alternative delivery systems, and customer satisfaction evaluation techniques. **Sociology and Anthropology:** Group behavior and dynamics; societal trends and influences; and cultures and their history, migrations, ethnicity, and origins. **Clerical Studies:** Administrative and clerical procedures and systems such as word-processing systems, filing and records management systems, stenography and transcription, forms, design principles, and other office procedures and terminology.

Work Environment: Indoors; sitting.

Social Science Research Assistants

- Education/Training Required: Associate degree
- Annual Earnings: $35,870
- Beginning Wage: $21,940
- Earnings Growth Potential: Medium
- Growth: 12.4%
- Annual Job Openings: 3,571
- Self-Employed: 1.7%
- Part-Time: 19.4%

The job openings listed here are shared with City and Regional Planning Aides.

Assist social scientists in laboratory, survey, and other social research. May perform publication activities, laboratory analysis, quality control, or data management. Normally these individuals work under the direct supervision of social scientists and assist in those activities that are more routine. Code data in preparation for computer entry. Provide assistance in the design of survey instruments such as questionnaires. Prepare, manipulate, and manage extensive databases. Prepare tables, graphs, fact sheets, and written reports summarizing research results. Obtain informed consent of research subjects and/or their guardians. Edit and submit protocols and other required research documentation. Screen potential subjects in order to determine their suitability as study participants. Conduct Internet-based and library research. Supervise the work of survey interviewers. Perform descriptive and multivariate statistical analyses of data, using computer software. Recruit and schedule research participants. Develop and implement research quality control procedures. Track research participants, and perform any necessary follow-up tasks. Verify the accuracy and validity of data entered in databases; correct any errors. Track laboratory supplies and expenses such as participant reimbursement. Provide assistance with the preparation of project-related reports, manuscripts, and presentations. Present research findings to groups of people. Perform needs assessments and/or consult with clients in order to determine the types of research and information that are required. Allocate and manage laboratory space and resources. Design and create special programs for tasks such as statistical analysis and data entry and cleaning. Perform data entry and other clerical work as required for project completion. Administer standardized tests to research subjects, and/or interview them in order to collect research data. Collect specimens such as blood samples, as required by research projects.

Personality Type: Conventional. These occupations frequently involve following set procedures and routines and can include working with data and details more than with ideas. Usually there is a clear line of authority to follow.

GOE—Interest Area/Cluster: 15. Scientific Research, Engineering, and Mathematics. **Work Group:** 15.06. Mathematics and Data Analysis. **Other Jobs in This Work Group:** Actuaries; Mathematical Technicians; Mathematicians; Statistical Assistants; Statisticians.

Skills—Programming: Writing computer programs for various purposes. **Science:** Using scientific methods to solve problems. **Writing:** Communicating effectively with others in writing as indicated by the needs of the audience.

Mathematics: Using mathematics to solve problems. **Active Learning:** Working with new material or information to grasp its implications. **Learning Strategies:** Using multiple approaches when learning or teaching new things. **Operations Analysis:** Analyzing needs and product requirements to create a design. **Time Management:** Managing one's own time and the time of others.

Education and Training Program: Social Sciences, General. **Related Knowledge/Courses—Psychology:** Human behavior and performance, mental processes, psychological research methods, and the assessment and treatment of behavioral and affective disorders. **Sociology and Anthropology:** Group behavior and dynamics; societal trends and influences; and cultures and their history, migrations, ethnicity, and origins. **Clerical Studies:** Administrative and clerical procedures and systems such as word-processing systems, filing and records management systems, stenography and transcription, forms, design principles, and other office procedures and terminology. **Computers and Electronics:** Electric circuit boards, processors, chips, and computer hardware and software, including applications and programming. **English Language:** The structure and content of the English language, including the meaning and spelling of words, rules of composition, and grammar. **Communications and Media:** Media production, communication, and dissemination techniques and methods, including alternative ways to inform and entertain via written, oral, and visual media.

Work Environment: Indoors; sitting.

Solderers and Brazers

- ❋ Education/Training Required: Postsecondary vocational training
- ❋ Annual Earnings: $32,270
- ❋ Beginning Wage: $21,680
- ❋ Earnings Growth Potential: Low
- ❋ Growth: 5.1%
- ❋ Annual Job Openings: 61,125
- ❋ Self-Employed: 6.3%
- ❋ Part-Time: 1.9%

The job openings listed here are shared with Welders, Cutters, and Welder Fitters.

Braze or solder together components to assemble fabricated metal parts with soldering iron, torch, or welding machine and flux. Melt and apply solder along adjoining edges of workpieces to solder joints, using soldering irons, gas torches, or ultrasonic equipment. Heat soldering irons or workpieces to specified temperatures for soldering, using gas flames or electrical current. Examine seams for defects, and rework defective joints or broken parts. Melt and separate brazed or soldered joints to remove and straighten damaged or misaligned components, using hand torches, irons, or furnaces. Melt and apply solder to fill holes, indentations, and seams of fabricated metal products, using soldering equipment. Clean workpieces to remove dirt and excess acid, using chemical solutions, files, wire brushes, or grinders. Guide torches and rods along joints of workpieces to heat them to brazing temperature, melt braze alloys, and bond workpieces together. Adjust electrical current and timing cycles of resistance welding machines to heat metals to bonding temperature. Clean equipment parts such as tips of soldering irons, using chemical solutions or cleaning compounds. Turn valves to start flow of gases, and light flames and adjust valves to obtain desired colors and sizes of flames. Brush flux onto joints of workpieces or dip braze rods into flux to prevent oxidation of metal. Remove workpieces from fixtures, using tongs, and cool workpieces, using air or water. Align and clamp workpieces together, using rules, squares, or hand tools, or position items in fixtures, jigs, or vises. Sweat together workpieces coated with solder. Smooth soldered areas with alternate strokes of paddles and torches, leaving soldered sections slightly higher than surrounding areas for later filing. Remove workpieces from molten solder and hold parts together until color indicates that solder has set. Select torch tips, flux, and brazing alloys from data charts or work orders. Turn dials to set intensity and duration of ultrasonic impulses, according to work order specifications. Dip workpieces into molten solder, or place solder strips between seams and heat seams with irons, to bond items together. Clean joints of workpieces with wire brushes or by dipping them into cleaning solutions.

Personality Type: Realistic. These occupations frequently involve work activities that include practical, hands-on problems and solutions. They often deal with plants; animals; and real-world materials such as wood, tools, and machinery. Many of the occupations require working outside and don't involve a lot of paperwork or working closely with others.

GOE—Interest Area/Cluster: 13. Manufacturing. **Work Group:** 13.04. Welding, Brazing, and Soldering. **Other Jobs in This Work Group:** Structural Metal Fabricators and Fitters; Welders, Cutters, and Welder Fitters; Welders, Cutters, Solderers, and Brazers; Welding, Soldering, and Brazing Machine Setters, Operators, and Tenders.

Skills—Quality Control Analysis: Evaluating the quality or performance of products, services, or processes. **Installation:** Installing equipment, machines, wiring, or programs to meet specifications. **Operation and Control:** Controlling operations of equipment or systems. **Equipment Selection:** Determining the kind of tools and equipment needed to do a job. **Troubleshooting:** Determining what is causing an operating error and deciding what to do about it. **Repairing:** Repairing machines or systems, using the needed tools. **Equipment Maintenance:** Performing routine maintenance and determining when and what kind of maintenance is needed. **Technology Design:** Generating or adapting equipment and technology to serve user needs.

Education and Training Program: Welding Technology/Welder Training. **Related Knowledge/Courses—Production and Processing:** Inputs, outputs, raw materials, waste, quality control, costs, and techniques for maximizing the manufacture and distribution of goods. **Mechanical Devices:** Machines and tools, including their designs, uses, benefits, repair, and maintenance. **Engineering and Technology:** Equipment, tools, and mechanical devices and their uses to produce motion, light, power, technology, and other applications.

Work Environment: Indoors; noisy; contaminants; minor burns, cuts, bites, or stings; using hands on objects, tools, or controls; repetitive motions.

Sound Engineering Technicians

* Education/Training Required: Postsecondary vocational training
* Annual Earnings: $46,550
* Beginning Wage: $23,370
* Earnings Growth Potential: High
* Growth: 9.1%
* Annual Job Openings: 1,194
* Self-Employed: 11.3%
* Part-Time: 12.9%

Operate machines and equipment to record, synchronize, mix, or reproduce music, voices, or sound effects in sporting arenas, theater productions, recording studios, or movie and video productions. Confer with producers, performers, and others in order to determine and achieve the desired sound for a production such as a musical recording or a film. Set up, test, and adjust recording equipment for recording sessions and live performances; tear down equipment after event completion. Regulate volume level and sound quality during recording sessions, using control consoles. Prepare for recording sessions by performing activities such as selecting and setting up microphones. Report equipment problems and ensure that required repairs are made. Mix and edit voices, music, and taped sound effects for live performances and for prerecorded events, using sound mixing boards. Synchronize and equalize prerecorded dialogue, music, and sound effects with visual action of motion pictures or television productions, using control consoles. Record speech, music, and other sounds on recording media, using recording equipment. Reproduce and duplicate sound recordings from original recording media, using sound editing and duplication equipment. Separate instruments, vocals, and other sounds; then combine sounds later during the mixing or post-production stage. Keep logs of recordings. Create musical instrument digital interface programs for music projects, commercials, or film post-production.

Personality Type: Realistic. These occupations frequently involve work activities that include practical, hands-on problems and solutions. They often deal with plants; animals; and real-world materials such as wood, tools, and machinery. Many of the occupations require working outside and don't involve a lot of paperwork or working closely with others.

GOE—Interest Area/Cluster: 03. Arts and Communication. Work Group: 03.09. Media Technology. Other Jobs in This Work Group: Audio and Video Equipment Technicians; Broadcast Technicians; Camera Operators, Television, Video, and Motion Picture; Film and Video Editors; Multi-Media Artists and Animators; Photographers; Radio Operators.

Skills—Technology Design: Generating or adapting equipment and technology to serve user needs. Operation and Control: Controlling operations of equipment or systems. Operation Monitoring: Watching gauges, dials, or other indicators to make sure a machine is working properly. Installation: Installing equipment, machines, wiring, or programs to meet specifications. Equipment Maintenance: Performing routine maintenance and determining when and what kind of maintenance is needed. Troubleshooting: Determining what is causing an operating error and deciding what to do about it. Management of Material Resources: Obtaining and seeing to the appropriate use of equipment, facilities, and materials needed to do certain work. Social Perceptiveness: Being aware of others' reactions and understanding why they react the way they do.

Education and Training Programs: Communications Technology/Technician Training; Recording Arts Technology/Technician Training. Related Knowledge/Courses—Fine Arts: Theory and techniques required to produce, compose, and perform works of music, dance, visual arts, drama, and sculpture. Communications and Media: Media production, communication, and dissemination techniques and methods, including alternative ways to inform and entertain via written, oral, and visual media. Telecommunications: Transmission, broadcasting, switching, control, and operation of telecommunications systems. Computers and Electronics: Electric circuit boards, processors, chips, and computer hardware and software, including applications and programming. Customer and Personal Service: Principles and processes for providing customer and personal services, including needs assessment techniques, quality service standards, alternative delivery systems, and customer satisfaction evaluation techniques. Production and Processing: Inputs, outputs, raw materials, waste, quality control, costs, and techniques for maximizing the manufacture and distribution of goods.

Work Environment: Indoors; noisy; sitting; using hands on objects, tools, or controls; repetitive motions.

Statement Clerks

* Education/Training Required: Moderate-term on-the-job training
* Annual Earnings: $29,970
* Beginning Wage: $20,930
* Earnings Growth Potential: Low
* Growth: 4.4%
* Annual Job Openings: 81,885
* Self-Employed: 1.6%
* Part-Time: 14.3%

The job openings listed here are shared with Billing, Cost, and Rate Clerks and with Billing, Posting, and Calculating Machine Operators.

Prepare and distribute bank statements to customers, answer inquiries, and reconcile discrepancies in records and accounts. Encode and cancel checks, using bank machines. Take orders for imprinted checks. Compare previously prepared bank statements with canceled checks and reconcile discrepancies. Verify signatures and required information on checks. Post stop-payment notices to prevent payment of protested checks. Maintain files of canceled checks and customers' signatures. Match statements with batches of canceled checks by account numbers. Weigh envelopes containing statements to determine correct postage and affix postage, using stamps or metering equipment. Load machines with statements, cancelled checks, and envelopes to prepare statements for distribution to customers or stuff envelopes by hand. Retrieve checks returned to customers in error, adjusting customer accounts and answering inquiries about errors as necessary. Route statements for mailing or over-the-counter delivery to customers. Monitor equipment to ensure proper operation. Fix minor problems, such as equipment jams, and notify repair personnel of major equipment problems.

Personality Type: Conventional. These occupations frequently involve following set procedures and routines and can include working with data and details more than with ideas. Usually there is a clear line of authority to follow.

GOE—Interest Area/Cluster: 04. Business and Administration. Work Group: 04.06. Mathematical Clerical Support. Other Jobs in This Work Group: Billing and Posting Clerks and Machine Operators; Billing, Cost, and Rate Clerks; Bookkeeping, Accounting, and Auditing Clerks; Brokerage Clerks; Payroll and Timekeeping Clerks; Tax Preparers.

Skills: None met the criteria.

Education and Training Program: Accounting Technology/Technician Training and Bookkeeping. **Related Knowledge/Courses—Economics and Accounting:** Economic and accounting principles and practices, the financial markets, banking, and the analysis and reporting of financial data. **Clerical Studies:** Administrative and clerical procedures and systems such as word-processing systems, filing and records management systems, stenography and transcription, forms, design principles, and other office procedures and terminology. **Administration and Management:** Principles and processes involved in business and organizational planning, coordination, and execution. This includes strategic planning, resource allocation, manpower modeling, leadership techniques, and production methods.

Work Environment: Indoors; sitting; repetitive motions.

Stationary Engineers and Boiler Operators

- ❋ Education/Training Required: Long-term on-the-job training
- ❋ Annual Earnings: $47,640
- ❋ Beginning Wage: $29,480
- ❋ Earnings Growth Potential: Medium
- ❋ Growth: 3.4%
- ❋ Annual Job Openings: 1,892
- ❋ Self-Employed: 0.0%
- ❋ Part-Time: 2.6%

Operate or maintain stationary engines, boilers, or other mechanical equipment to provide utilities for buildings or industrial processes. Operate equipment such as steam engines, generators, motors, turbines, and steam boilers. Operate or tend stationary engines; boilers; and auxiliary equipment such as pumps, compressors and air-conditioning equipment to supply and maintain steam or heat for buildings, marine vessels, or pneumatic tools. Observe and interpret readings on gauges, meters, and charts registering various aspects of boiler operation

to ensure that boilers are operating properly. Test boiler water quality or arrange for testing and take any necessary corrective action, such as adding chemicals to prevent corrosion and harmful deposits. Activate valves to maintain required amounts of water in boilers, to adjust supplies of combustion air, and to control the flow of fuel into burners. Monitor boiler water, chemical, and fuel levels and make adjustments to maintain required levels. Fire coal furnaces by hand or with stokers and gas- or oil-fed boilers, using automatic gas feeds or oil pumps. Monitor and inspect equipment, computer terminals, switches, valves, gauges, alarms, safety devices, and meters to detect leaks or malfunctions and to ensure that equipment is operating efficiently and safely. Analyze problems and take appropriate action to ensure continuous and reliable operation of equipment and systems. Maintain daily logs of operation, maintenance, and safety activities, including test results, instrument readings, and details of equipment malfunctions and maintenance work. Adjust controls or valves on equipment to provide power and to regulate and set operations of system or industrial processes. Switch from automatic controls to manual controls and isolate equipment mechanically and electrically to allow for safe inspection and repair work. Clean and lubricate boilers and auxiliary equipment and make minor adjustments as needed, using hand tools. Check the air quality of ventilation systems and make adjustments to ensure compliance with mandated safety codes. Perform or arrange for repairs, such as complete overhauls; replacement of defective valves, gaskets, or bearings; or fabrication of new parts. Weigh, measure, and record fuel used.

Personality Type: Realistic. These occupations frequently involve work activities that include practical, hands-on problems and solutions. They often deal with plants; animals; and real-world materials such as wood, tools, and machinery. Many of the occupations require working outside and don't involve a lot of paperwork or working closely with others.

GOE—Interest Area/Cluster: 13. Manufacturing. **Work Group:** 13.16. Utility Operation and Energy Distribution. **Other Jobs in This Work Group:** Chemical Plant and System Operators; Gas Compressor and Gas Pumping Station Operators; Gas Plant Operators; Nuclear Power Reactor Operators; Petroleum Pump System Operators, Refinery Operators, and Gaugers; Power Distributors and

Dispatchers; Power Plant Operators; Ship Engineers; Water and Liquid Waste Treatment Plant and System Operators.

Skills—Repairing: Repairing machines or systems, using the needed tools. **Equipment Maintenance:** Performing routine maintenance and determining when and what kind of maintenance is needed. **Operation Monitoring:** Watching gauges, dials, or other indicators to make sure a machine is working properly. **Installation:** Installing equipment, machines, wiring, or programs to meet specifications. **Operation and Control:** Controlling operations of equipment or systems. **Systems Analysis:** Determining how a system should work and how changes will affect outcomes. **Operations Analysis:** Analyzing needs and product requirements to create a design. **Troubleshooting:** Determining what is causing an operating error and deciding what to do about it.

Education and Training Program: Building/Property Maintenance and Management. **Related Knowledge/ Courses—Mechanical Devices:** Machines and tools, including their designs, uses, benefits, repair, and maintenance. **Building and Construction:** Materials, methods, and the appropriate tools to construct objects, structures, and buildings. **Chemistry:** The composition, structure, and properties of substances and of the chemical processes and transformations that they undergo. This includes uses of chemicals and their interactions, danger signs, production techniques, and disposal methods. **Physics:** Physical principles, laws, and applications, including air, water, material dynamics, light, atomic principles, heat, electric theory, earth formations, and meteorological and related natural phenomena. **Engineering and Technology:** Equipment, tools, and mechanical devices and their uses to produce motion, light, power, technology, and other applications. **Design:** Design techniques, principles, tools, and instruments involved in the production and use of precision technical plans, blueprints, drawings, and models.

Work Environment: Noisy; very hot or cold; very bright or dim lighting; contaminants; hazardous conditions; hazardous equipment.

Statistical Assistants

- ❀ Education/Training Required: Moderate-term on-the-job training
- ❀ Annual Earnings: $32,540
- ❀ Beginning Wage: $20,440
- ❀ Earnings Growth Potential: Medium
- ❀ Growth: 7.6%
- ❀ Annual Job Openings: 4,836
- ❀ Self-Employed: 6.6%
- ❀ Part-Time: 10.1%

Compile and compute data according to statistical formulas for use in statistical studies. May perform actuarial computations and compile charts and graphs for use by actuaries. Includes actuarial clerks. Compute and analyze data, using statistical formulas and computers or calculators. Enter data into computers for use in analyses and reports. Compile statistics from source materials, such as production and sales records, quality-control and test records, time sheets, and survey sheets. Compile reports, charts, and graphs that describe and interpret findings of analyses. Check source data to verify its completeness and accuracy. Participate in the publication of data and information. Discuss data presentation requirements with clients. File data and related information and maintain and update databases. Select statistical tests for analyzing data. Organize paperwork such as survey forms and reports for distribution and for analysis. Code data as necessary prior to computer entry, using lists of codes. Check survey responses for errors such as the use of pens instead of pencils and set aside response forms that cannot be used. Interview people and keep track of their responses. Send out surveys.

Personality Type: Conventional. These occupations frequently involve following set procedures and routines and can include working with data and details more than with ideas. Usually there is a clear line of authority to follow.

GOE—Interest Area/Cluster: 15. Scientific Research, Engineering, and Mathematics. **Work Group:** 15.06. Mathematics and Data Analysis. **Other Jobs in This Work Group:** Actuaries; Mathematical Technicians; Mathematicians; Social Science Research Assistants; Statisticians.

Skills—Mathematics: Using mathematics to solve problems. **Operations Analysis:** Analyzing needs and product requirements to create a design. **Quality Control Analysis:** Evaluating the quality or performance of products, services, or processes. **Complex Problem Solving:** Identifying complex problems, reviewing the options, and implementing solutions. **Programming:** Writing computer programs for various purposes. **Monitoring:** Assessing how well one is doing when learning or doing something. **Writing:** Communicating effectively with others in writing as indicated by the needs of the audience. **Active Learning:** Working with new material or information to grasp its implications.

Education and Training Program: Accounting Technology/Technician Training and Bookkeeping. **Related Knowledge/Courses—Mathematics:** Numbers and their operations and interrelationships, including arithmetic, algebra, geometry, calculus, and statistics and their applications. **Clerical Studies:** Administrative and clerical procedures and systems such as word-processing systems, filing and records management systems, stenography and transcription, forms, design principles, and other office procedures and terminology. **Computers and Electronics:** Electric circuit boards, processors, chips, and computer hardware and software, including applications and programming. **Communications and Media:** Media production, communication, and dissemination techniques and methods, including alternative ways to inform and entertain via written, oral, and visual media. **Administration and Management:** Principles and processes involved in business and organizational planning, coordination, and execution. This includes strategic planning, resource allocation, manpower modeling, leadership techniques, and production methods. **Customer and Personal Service:** Principles and processes for providing customer and personal services, including needs assessment techniques, quality service standards, alternative delivery systems, and customer satisfaction evaluation techniques.

Work Environment: Indoors; sitting.

Stonemasons

* Education/Training Required: Long-term on-the-job training
* Annual Earnings: $36,950
* Beginning Wage: $22,630
* Earnings Growth Potential: Medium
* Growth: 10.0%
* Annual Job Openings: 2,657
* Self-Employed: 22.8%
* Part-Time: 7.9%

Build stone structures, such as piers, walls, and abutments. Lay walks; curbstones; or special types of masonry for vats, tanks, and floors. Lay out wall patterns or foundations, using straight edge, rule, or staked lines. Shape, trim, face, and cut marble or stone preparatory to setting, using power saws, cutting equipment, and hand tools. Set vertical and horizontal alignment of structures, using plumb bob, gauge line, and level. Mix mortar or grout and pour or spread mortar or grout on marble slabs, stone, or foundation. Remove wedges; fill joints between stones; finish joints between stones, using a trowel; and smooth the mortar to an attractive finish, using a tuck-pointer. Clean excess mortar or grout from surface of marble, stone, or monument, using sponge, brush, water, or acid. Set stone or marble in place according to layout or pattern. Lay brick to build shells of chimneys and smokestacks or to line or reline industrial furnaces, kilns, boilers, and similar installations. Replace broken or missing masonry units in walls or floors. Smooth, polish, and bevel surfaces, using hand tools and power tools. Drill holes in marble or ornamental stone and anchor brackets in holes. Repair cracked or chipped areas of stone or marble, using blowtorch and mastic, and remove rough or defective spots from concrete, using power grinder or chisel and hammer. Remove sections of monument from truck bed and guide stone onto foundation, using skids, hoist, or truck crane. Construct and install prefabricated masonry units. Dig trench for foundation of monument, using pick and shovel. Position mold along guidelines of wall, press mold in place, and remove mold and paper from wall. Line interiors of molds with treated paper and fill molds with composition-stone mixture.

Personality Type: Realistic. These occupations frequently involve work activities that include practical, hands-on problems and solutions. They often deal with plants; animals; and real-world materials such as wood, tools, and machinery. Many of the occupations require working outside and don't involve a lot of paperwork or working closely with others.

GOE—Interest Area/Cluster: 02. Architecture and Construction. **Work Group:** 02.04. Construction Crafts. **Other Jobs in This Work Group:** Boilermakers; Brickmasons and Blockmasons; Carpet Installers; Cement Masons and Concrete Finishers; Commercial Divers; Construction Carpenters; Crane and Tower Operators; Drywall and Ceiling Tile Installers; Electricians; Fence Erectors; Floor Layers, Except Carpet, Wood, and Hard Tiles; Floor Sanders and Finishers; Glaziers; Hazardous Materials Removal Workers; Insulation Workers, Floor, Ceiling, and Wall; Insulation Workers, Mechanical; Manufactured Building and Mobile Home Installers; Operating Engineers and Other Construction Equipment Operators; Painters, Construction and Maintenance; Paperhangers; Paving, Surfacing, and Tamping Equipment Operators; Pile-Driver Operators; Pipe Fitters and Steamfitters; Pipelayers; Plasterers and Stucco Masons; Plumbers; Plumbers, Pipefitters, and Steamfitters; Rail-Track Laying and Maintenance Equipment Operators; Refractory Materials Repairers, Except Brickmasons; Reinforcing Iron and Rebar Workers; Riggers; Roofers; Rough Carpenters; Security and Fire Alarm Systems Installers; Segmental Pavers; Sheet Metal Workers; Stone Cutters and Carvers, Manufacturing; Structural Iron and Steel Workers; Tapers; Terrazzo Workers and Finishers; Tile and Marble Setters.

Skills—Installation: Installing equipment, machines, wiring, or programs to meet specifications. **Management of Personnel Resources:** Motivating, developing, and directing people as they work; identifying the best people for the job. **Equipment Selection:** Determining the kind of tools and equipment needed to do a job. **Repairing:** Repairing machines or systems, using the needed tools. **Equipment Maintenance:** Performing routine maintenance and determining when and what kind of maintenance is needed. **Mathematics:** Using mathematics to solve problems. **Management of Material Resources:** Obtaining and seeing to the appropriate use of equipment, facilities, and materials needed to do certain work. **Technology Design:** Generating or adapting equipment and technology to serve user needs.

Education and Training Program: Mason Training/ Masonry. **Related Knowledge/Courses—Building and Construction:** Materials, methods, and the appropriate tools to construct objects, structures, and buildings. **Mechanical Devices:** Machines and tools, including their designs, uses, benefits, repair, and maintenance. **Design:** Design techniques, principles, tools, and instruments involved in the production and use of precision technical plans, blueprints, drawings, and models. **Mathematics:** Numbers and their operations and interrelationships, including arithmetic, algebra, geometry, calculus, and statistics and their applications. **Public Safety and Security:** Weaponry; public safety; security operations, rules, regulations, precautions, and prevention; and the protection of people, data, and property. **Education and Training:** Instructional methods and training techniques, including curriculum design principles, learning theory, group and individual teaching techniques, design of individual development plans, and test design principles.

Work Environment: Outdoors; noisy; standing; kneeling; crouching, stooping, or crawling; using hands on objects, tools, or controls; bending or twisting the body.

Storage and Distribution Managers

- ❋ Education/Training Required: Work experience in a related occupation
- ❋ Annual Earnings: $76,310
- ❋ Beginning Wage: $44,900
- ❋ Earnings Growth Potential: High
- ❋ Growth: 8.3%
- ❋ Annual Job Openings: 6,994
- ❋ Self-Employed: 2.6%
- ❋ Part-Time: 2.3%

The job openings listed here are shared with Transportation Managers.

Plan, direct, and coordinate the storage and distribution operations within organizations or the activities of organizations that are engaged in storing and distributing materials and products. Prepare and manage departmental budgets. Supervise the activities of workers engaged in receiving, storing, testing, and shipping products or materials. Interview, select, and train warehouse and supervisory personnel. Plan, develop, and implement warehouse safety and security programs and activities. Prepare or direct preparation of correspondence, reports, and operations, maintenance, and safety manuals. Issue shipping instructions and provide routing information to ensure that delivery times and locations are coordinated. Review invoices, work orders, consumption reports, and demand forecasts to estimate peak delivery periods and to issue work assignments. Confer with department heads to coordinate warehouse activities such as production, sales, records control, and purchasing. Inspect physical conditions of warehouses, vehicle fleets and equipment, and order testing, maintenance, repair, or replacement as necessary. Schedule and monitor air or surface pickup, delivery, or distribution of products or materials. Respond to customers' or shippers' questions and complaints regarding storage and distribution services. Develop and document standard and emergency operating procedures for receiving, handling, storing, shipping, or salvaging products or materials. Develop and implement plans for facility modification or expansion such as equipment purchase or changes in space allocation or structural design. Track and trace goods while they are en route to their destinations, expediting orders when necessary. Negotiate with carriers, warehouse operators, and insurance company representatives for services and preferential rates. Arrange for necessary shipping documentation, and contact customs officials to effect release of shipments. Evaluate freight costs and the inventory costs associated with transit times to ensure that costs are appropriate. Advise sales and billing departments of transportation charges for customers' accounts. Examine invoices and shipping manifests for conformity to tariff and customs regulations. Evaluate locations for new warehouses and distribution networks to determine their potential usefulness.

Personality Type: Enterprising. These occupations frequently involve starting up and carrying out projects and can involve leading people and making many decisions. They sometimes require risk taking and often deal with business.

GOE—Interest Area/Cluster: 16. Transportation, Distribution, and Logistics. **Work Group:** 16.01. Managerial Work in Transportation. **Other Jobs in This Work Group:** Aircraft Cargo Handling Supervisors; First-Line Supervisors/Managers of Transportation and Material-Moving Machine and Vehicle Operators; Postmasters and Mail Superintendents; Railroad Conductors and Yardmasters; Transportation Managers; Transportation, Storage, and Distribution Managers.

Skills—Management of Financial Resources: Determining how money will be spent to get the work done and accounting for these expenditures. **Systems Analysis:** Determining how a system should work and how changes will affect outcomes. **Management of Personnel Resources:** Motivating, developing, and directing people as they work; identifying the best people for the job. **Management of Material Resources:** Obtaining and seeing to the appropriate use of equipment, facilities, and materials needed to do certain work. **Systems Evaluation:** Looking at many indicators of system performance and taking into account their accuracy. **Negotiation:** Bringing others together and trying to reconcile differences. **Persuasion:** Persuading others to approach things differently.

Education and Training Programs: Aeronautics/Aviation/Aerospace Science and Technology, General; Aviation/Airway Management and Operations; Business Administration and Management, General; Logistics and Materials Management; Public Administration; Transportation/Transportation Management. **Related Knowledge/Courses—Transportation:** Principles and methods for moving people or goods by air, rail, sea, or road, including their relative costs, advantages, and limitations. **Personnel and Human Resources:** Principles and procedures for personnel recruitment; selection; training; compensation and benefits; labor relations and negotiation; and personnel information systems. **Production and Processing:** Inputs, outputs, raw materials, waste, quality control, costs, and techniques for maximizing the manufacture and distribution of goods. **Administration and Management:** Principles and processes involved in business and organizational planning, coordination, and execution. This includes strategic planning, resource allocation, manpower modeling, leadership techniques, and production methods. **Economics and Accounting:** Economic and accounting principles and practices, the financial markets, banking, and the analysis and reporting of financial data. **Psychology:** Human behavior and performance, mental processes, psychological research methods, and the assessment and treatment of behavioral and affective disorders.

Work Environment: Indoors; standing.

Structural Iron and Steel Workers

- ❋ Education/Training Required: Long-term on-the-job training
- ❋ Annual Earnings: $42,130
- ❋ Beginning Wage: $24,180
- ❋ Earnings Growth Potential: High
- ❋ Growth: 6.0%
- ❋ Annual Job Openings: 6,969
- ❋ Self-Employed: 5.3%
- ❋ Part-Time: 5.8%

Raise, place, and unite iron or steel girders, columns, and other structural members to form completed structures or structural frameworks. May erect metal storage tanks and assemble prefabricated metal buildings. Read specifications and blueprints to determine the locations, quantities, and sizes of materials required. Verify vertical and horizontal alignment of structural-steel members, using plumb bobs, laser equipment, transits, and/or levels. Connect columns, beams, and girders with bolts, following blueprints and instructions from supervisors. Hoist steel beams, girders, and columns into place, using cranes, or signal hoisting equipment operators to lift and position structural-steel members. Bolt aligned structural-steel members in position for permanent riveting, bolting, or welding into place. Ride on girders or other structural-steel members to position them, or use rope to guide them into position. Fabricate metal parts such as steel frames, columns, beams, and girders, according to blueprints or instructions from supervisors. Pull, push, or pry structural-steel members into approximate positions for bolting into place. Cut, bend, and weld steel pieces, using metal shears, torches, and welding equipment. Fasten structural-steel members to hoist cables, using chains, cables, or rope. Assemble hoisting equipment and rigging such as cables, pulleys, and hooks to move heavy equipment and materials. Force structural-steel members into final positions, using turnbuckles, crowbars, jacks, and hand tools. Erect metal and precast concrete components for structures such as buildings, bridges, dams, towers, storage tanks, fences, and highway guard rails. Unload and position prefabricated steel units for hoisting as needed. Drive drift pins through rivet holes in order to align rivet holes in structural-steel members with corresponding holes in previously placed members. Dismantle structures and equipment. Insert sealing strips, wiring, insulating material, ladders, flanges, gauges, and valves, depending on types of structures being assembled. Catch hot rivets in buckets and insert rivets in holes, using tongs. Place blocks under reinforcing bars used to reinforce floors. Hold rivets while riveters use air-hammers to form heads on rivets.

Personality Type: Realistic. These occupations frequently involve work activities that include practical, hands-on problems and solutions. They often deal with plants; animals; and real-world materials such as wood, tools, and machinery. Many of the occupations require working outside and don't involve a lot of paperwork or working closely with others.

GOE—Interest Area/Cluster: 02. Architecture and Construction. **Work Group:** 02.04. Construction Crafts. **Other Jobs in This Work Group:** Boilermakers; Brickmasons and Blockmasons; Carpet Installers; Cement Masons and Concrete Finishers; Commercial Divers; Construction Carpenters; Crane and Tower Operators; Drywall and Ceiling Tile Installers; Electricians; Fence Erectors; Floor Layers, Except Carpet, Wood, and Hard Tiles; Floor Sanders and Finishers; Glaziers; Hazardous Materials Removal Workers; Insulation Workers, Floor, Ceiling, and Wall; Insulation Workers, Mechanical; Manufactured Building and Mobile Home Installers; Operating Engineers and Other Construction Equipment Operators; Painters, Construction and Maintenance; Paperhangers; Paving, Surfacing, and Tamping Equipment Operators; Pile-Driver Operators; Pipe Fitters and Steamfitters; Pipelayers; Plasterers and Stucco Masons; Plumbers; Plumbers, Pipefitters, and Steamfitters; Rail-Track Laying and Maintenance Equipment Operators; Refractory Materials Repairers, Except Brickmasons; Reinforcing Iron and Rebar Workers; Riggers; Roofers; Rough Carpenters; Security and Fire Alarm Systems Installers; Segmental Pavers; Sheet Metal Workers; Stone Cutters and Carvers, Manufacturing; Stonemasons; Tapers; Terrazzo Workers and Finishers; Tile and Marble Setters.

Skills—Equipment Maintenance: Performing routine maintenance and determining when and what kind of maintenance is needed. **Installation:** Installing equipment, machines, wiring, or programs to meet specifications. **Troubleshooting:** Determining what is causing an operating error and deciding what to do about it. **Equipment Selection:** Determining the kind of tools and equipment needed to do a job. **Coordination:** Adjusting actions in relation to others' actions. **Technology Design:** Generating or adapting equipment and technology to serve user needs. **Operation Monitoring:** Watching gauges, dials, or other indicators to make sure a machine is working properly. **Repairing:** Repairing machines or systems, using the needed tools.

Education and Training Programs: Construction Trades, Other; Metal Building Assembly/Assembler Training. **Related Knowledge/Courses—Building and Construction:** Materials, methods, and the appropriate tools to construct objects, structures, and buildings. **Engineering and Technology:** Equipment, tools, and mechanical devices and their uses to produce motion, light, power, technology, and other applications. **Mechanical Devices:** Machines and tools, including their designs, uses, benefits, repair, and maintenance. **Production and Processing:** Inputs, outputs, raw materials, waste, quality control, costs, and techniques for maximizing the manufacture and distribution of goods. **Design:** Design techniques, principles, tools, and instruments involved in the production and use of precision technical plans, blueprints, drawings, and models. **Physics:** Physical principles, laws, and applications, including air, water, material dynamics, light, atomic principles, heat, electric theory, earth formations, and meteorological and related natural phenomena.

Work Environment: Outdoors; noisy; very hot or cold; high places; hazardous equipment; using hands on objects, tools, or controls.

Structural Metal Fabricators and Fitters

- ❋ Education/Training Required: Moderate-term on-the-job training
- ❋ Annual Earnings: $31,030
- ❋ Beginning Wage: $20,310
- ❋ Earnings Growth Potential: Low
- ❋ Growth: –0.2%
- ❋ Annual Job Openings: 20,746
- ❋ Self-Employed: 2.0%
- ❋ Part-Time: 2.4%

Fabricate, lay out, position, align, and fit parts of structural metal products. Position, align, fit, and weld parts to form complete units or subunits, following blueprints and layout specifications and using jigs, welding torches, and hand tools. Verify conformance of workpieces to specifications, using squares, rulers, and measuring tapes. Tack-weld fitted parts together. Lay out and examine metal stock or workpieces to be processed to ensure that specifications are met. Align and fit parts according to specifications, using jacks, turnbuckles, wedges, drift pins, pry bars, and hammers. Locate and mark workpiece bending and cutting lines, allowing for stock thickness, machine and welding shrinkage, and other component specifications. Position or tighten braces, jacks, clamps, ropes, or bolt straps or bolt parts in position for welding or riveting. Study engineering drawings and blueprints to determine materials requirements and task sequences. Move parts into position manually or by using hoists or cranes. Set up and operate fabricating machines such as brakes, rolls, shears, flame cutters, grinders, and drill presses to bend, cut, form, punch, drill, or otherwise form and assemble metal components. Hammer, chip, and grind workpieces to cut, bend, and straighten metal. Smooth workpiece edges and fix taps, tubes, and valves. Design and construct templates and fixtures, using hand tools. Straighten warped or bent parts, using sledges, hand torches, straightening presses, or bulldozers. Mark reference points onto floors or face blocks and transpose them to workpieces, using measuring devices, squares, chalk, and soapstone. Set up face blocks, jigs, and fixtures. Remove high spots and cut bevels, using hand files, portable grinders, and cutting torches. Direct welders to build up low spots or short pieces with weld. Lift or move materials and finished products, using large cranes. Heat-treat parts, using acetylene torches. Preheat workpieces to make them malleable, using hand torches or furnaces. Install boilers, containers, and other structures. Erect ladders and scaffolding to fit together large assemblies.

Personality Type: Realistic. These occupations frequently involve work activities that include practical, hands-on problems and solutions. They often deal with plants; animals; and real-world materials such as wood, tools, and machinery. Many of the occupations require working outside and don't involve a lot of paperwork or working closely with others.

GOE—Interest Area/Cluster: 13. Manufacturing. **Work Group:** 13.04. Welding, Brazing, and Soldering. **Other Jobs in This Work Group:** Solderers and Brazers; Welders, Cutters, and Welder Fitters; Welders, Cutters, Solderers, and Brazers; Welding, Soldering, and Brazing Machine Setters, Operators, and Tenders.

Skills—**Quality Control Analysis:** Evaluating the quality or performance of products, services, or processes. **Operation Monitoring:** Watching gauges, dials, or other indicators to make sure a machine is working properly. **Equipment Maintenance:** Performing routine maintenance and determining when and what kind of maintenance is needed. **Installation:** Installing equipment, machines, wiring, or programs to meet specifications. **Repairing:** Repairing machines or systems, using the needed tools. **Operation and Control:** Controlling operations of equipment or systems. **Technology Design:** Generating or adapting equipment and technology to serve user needs. **Equipment Selection:** Determining the kind of tools and equipment needed to do a job.

Education and Training Program: Machine Shop Technology/Assistant Training. **Related Knowledge/Courses—Design:** Design techniques, principles, tools, and instruments involved in the production and use of precision technical plans, blueprints, drawings, and models. **Building and Construction:** Materials, methods, and the appropriate tools to construct objects, structures, and buildings. **Mechanical Devices:** Machines and tools, including their designs, uses, benefits, repair, and maintenance. **Production and Processing:** Inputs, outputs, raw materials, waste, quality control, costs, and techniques for maximizing the manufacture and distribution of goods.

Work Environment: Noisy; contaminants; hazardous equipment; minor burns, cuts, bites, or stings; standing; using hands on objects, tools, or controls.

Subway and Streetcar Operators

- ❀ Education/Training Required: Moderate-term on-the-job training
- ❀ Annual Earnings: $50,520
- ❀ Beginning Wage: $32,830
- ❀ Earnings Growth Potential: Medium
- ❀ Growth: 12.1%
- ❀ Annual Job Openings: 587
- ❀ Self-Employed: 0.0%
- ❀ Part-Time: 0.9%

Operate subway or elevated suburban train with no separate locomotive or electric-powered streetcar to transport passengers. May handle fares. Operate controls to open and close transit vehicle doors. Drive and control rail-guided public transportation such as subways; elevated trains; and electric-powered streetcars, trams, or trolleys in order to transport passengers. Monitor lights indicating obstructions or other trains ahead and watch for car and truck traffic at crossings to stay alert to potential hazards. Direct emergency evacuation procedures. Regulate vehicle speed and the time spent at each stop, in order to maintain schedules. Report delays, mechanical problems, and emergencies to supervisors or dispatchers, using radios. Make announcements to passengers, such as notifications of upcoming stops or schedule delays. Complete reports, including shift summaries and incident or accident reports. Greet passengers, provide information, and answer questions concerning fares, schedules, transfers, and routings. Attend meetings on driver and passenger safety in order to learn ways in which job performance might be affected. Collect fares from passengers, and issue change and transfers. Record transactions and coin receptor readings in order to verify the amount of money collected.

Personality Type: Realistic. These occupations frequently involve work activities that include practical, hands-on problems and solutions. They often deal with plants; animals; and real-world materials such as wood, tools, and machinery. Many of the occupations require working outside and don't involve a lot of paperwork or working closely with others.

GOE—Interest Area/Cluster: 16. Transportation, Distribution, and Logistics. **Work Group:** 16.04. Rail Vehicle Operation. **Other Jobs in This Work Group:** Locomotive Engineers; Locomotive Firers; Rail Yard Engineers, Dinkey Operators, and Hostlers.

Skills—Operation and Control: Controlling operations of equipment or systems. **Operation Monitoring:** Watching gauges, dials, or other indicators to make sure a machine is working properly. **Troubleshooting:** Determining what is causing an operating error and deciding what to do about it. **Active Listening:** Listening to what other people are saying and asking questions as appropriate. **Service Orientation:** Actively looking for ways to help people.

Education and Training Program: Truck and Bus Driver Training/Commercial Vehicle Operation. **Related Knowledge/Courses—Transportation:** Principles and methods for moving people or goods by air, rail, sea, or road, including their relative costs, advantages, and limitations. **Public**

Safety and Security: Weaponry; public safety; security operations, rules, regulations, precautions, and prevention; and the protection of people, data, and property. **Customer and Personal Service:** Principles and processes for providing customer and personal services, including needs assessment techniques, quality service standards, alternative delivery systems, and customer satisfaction evaluation techniques. **Telecommunications:** Transmission, broadcasting, switching, control, and operation of telecommunications systems. **Mechanical Devices:** Machines and tools, including their designs, uses, benefits, repair, and maintenance. **Communications and Media:** Media production, communication, and dissemination techniques and methods, including alternative ways to inform and entertain via written, oral, and visual media.

Work Environment: Outdoors; noisy; contaminants; sitting; using hands on objects, tools, or controls; repetitive motions.

Surgical Technologists

- ✷ Education/Training Required: Postsecondary vocational training
- ✷ Annual Earnings: $37,540
- ✷ Beginning Wage: $26,650
- ✷ Earnings Growth Potential: Low
- ✷ Growth: 24.5%
- ✷ Annual Job Openings: 15,365
- ✷ Self-Employed: 0.2%
- ✷ Part-Time: 20.8%

Assist in operations under the supervision of surgeons, registered nurses, or other surgical personnel. May help set up operating rooms; prepare and transport patients for surgery; adjust lights and equipment; pass instruments and other supplies to surgeons and surgeons' assistants; hold retractors; cut sutures; and help count sponges, needles, supplies, and instruments. Count sponges, needles, and instruments before and after operations. Maintain a proper sterile field during surgical procedures. Hand instruments and supplies to surgeons and surgeons' assistants, hold retractors and cut sutures, and perform other tasks as directed by surgeons during operations. Prepare patients for surgery, including positioning patients on operating tables and covering them with sterile

surgical drapes to prevent exposure. Scrub arms and hands, and assist surgical teams to scrub and put on gloves, masks, and surgical clothing. Wash and sterilize equipment, using germicides and sterilizers. Monitor and continually assess operating room conditions, including patient and surgical team needs. Prepare dressings or bandages and apply or assist with their application following surgeries. Clean and restock operating rooms, gathering and placing equipment and supplies and arranging instruments according to instructions such as those found on a preference card. Operate, assemble, adjust, or monitor sterilizers, lights, suction machines, and diagnostic equipment to ensure proper operation. Prepare, care for, and dispose of tissue specimens taken for laboratory analysis. Provide technical assistance to surgeons, surgical nurses, and anesthesiologists. Maintain supply of fluids such as plasma, saline, blood, and glucose, for use during operations. Maintain files and records of surgical procedures. Observe patients' vital signs to assess physical condition. Order surgical supplies.

Personality Type: Realistic. These occupations frequently involve work activities that include practical, hands-on problems and solutions. They often deal with plants; animals; and real-world materials such as wood, tools, and machinery. Many of the occupations require working outside and don't involve a lot of paperwork or working closely with others.

GOE—Interest Area/Cluster: 08. Health Science. **Work Group:** 08.02. Medicine and Surgery. **Other Jobs in This Work Group:** Anesthesiologists; Family and General Practitioners; Internists, General; Medical Assistants; Medical Transcriptionists; Obstetricians and Gynecologists; Pediatricians, General; Pharmacists; Pharmacy Aides; Pharmacy Technicians; Physician Assistants; Psychiatrists; Registered Nurses; Surgeons.

Skills—Operation Monitoring: Watching gauges, dials, or other indicators to make sure a machine is working properly. **Quality Control Analysis:** Evaluating the quality or performance of products, services, or processes.

Education and Training Programs: Pathology/Pathologist Assistant Training; Surgical Technology/Technologist Training. **Related Knowledge/Courses—Medicine and Dentistry:** The information and techniques needed to diagnose and treat injuries, diseases, and deformities. This includes symptoms, treatment alternatives, drug properties and interactions, and preventive health-care measures.

Biology: Plant and animal living tissue, cells, organisms, and entities, including their functions, interdependencies, and interactions with each other and the environment. **Psychology:** Human behavior and performance, mental processes, psychological research methods, and the assessment and treatment of behavioral and affective disorders. **Chemistry:** The composition, structure, and properties of substances and of the chemical processes and transformations that they undergo. This includes uses of chemicals and their interactions, danger signs, production techniques, and disposal methods. **Therapy and Counseling:** Information and techniques needed to rehabilitate physical and mental ailments and to provide career guidance, including alternative treatments, rehabilitation equipment and its proper use, and methods to evaluate treatment effects. **Customer and Personal Service:** Principles and processes for providing customer and personal services, including needs assessment techniques, quality service standards, alternative delivery systems, and customer satisfaction evaluation techniques.

Work Environment: Indoors; contaminants; radiation; disease or infections; standing; using hands on objects, tools, or controls.

Surveying Technicians

- ❋ Education/Training Required: Moderate-term on-the-job training
- ❋ Annual Earnings: $33,640
- ❋ Beginning Wage: $20,670
- ❋ Earnings Growth Potential: Medium
- ❋ Growth: 19.4%
- ❋ Annual Job Openings: 8,299
- ❋ Self-Employed: 4.2%
- ❋ Part-Time: 4.5%

The job openings listed here are shared with Mapping Technicians.

Adjust and operate surveying instruments such as theodolite and electronic distance-measuring equipment, and compile notes, make sketches, and enter data into computers. Perform calculations to determine earth curvature corrections, atmospheric impacts on measurements, traverse closures and adjustments, azimuths, level runs, and placement of markers. Record survey measurements and descriptive data using notes, drawings, sketches, and inked tracings. Search for section corners, property irons, and survey points. Position and hold the vertical rods, or targets, that theodolite operators use for sighting to measure angles, distances, and elevations. Lay out grids, and determine horizontal and vertical controls. Compare survey computations with applicable standards to determine adequacy of data. Set out and recover stakes, marks, and other monumentation. Conduct surveys to ascertain the locations of natural features and man-made structures on the Earth's surface, underground, and underwater using electronic distance-measuring equipment and other surveying instruments. Direct and supervise work of subordinate members of surveying parties. Compile information necessary to stake projects for construction, using engineering plans. Prepare topographic and contour maps of land surveyed, including site features and other relevant information such as charts, drawings, and survey notes. Place and hold measuring tapes when electronic distance-measuring equipment is not used. Collect information needed to carry out new surveys using source maps, previous survey data, photographs, computer records, and other relevant information. Operate and manage land-information computer systems, performing tasks such as storing data, making inquiries, and producing plots and reports. Run rods for benches and cross-section elevations. Perform manual labor, such as cutting brush for lines, carrying stakes, rebar, and other heavy items, and stacking rods. Maintain equipment and vehicles used by surveying crews. Provide assistance in the development of methods and procedures for conducting field surveys.

Personality Type: Realistic. These occupations frequently involve work activities that include practical, hands-on problems and solutions. They often deal with plants; animals; and real-world materials such as wood, tools, and machinery. Many of the occupations require working outside and don't involve a lot of paperwork or working closely with others.

GOE—Interest Area/Cluster: 15. Scientific Research, Engineering, and Mathematics. **Work Group:** 15.09. Engineering Technology. **Other Jobs in This Work Group:** Aerospace Engineering and Operations Technicians; Cartographers and Photogrammetrists; Civil Engineering Technicians; Electrical and Electronic Engineering Technicians; Electrical and Electronics Drafters; Electrical Drafters; Electrical Engineering Technicians;

Electro-Mechanical Technicians; Electronic Drafters; Electronics Engineering Technicians; Environmental Engineering Technicians; Mapping Technicians; Mechanical Drafters; Mechanical Engineering Technicians; Surveying and Mapping Technicians.

Skills—Mathematics: Using mathematics to solve problems. **Operation and Control:** Controlling operations of equipment or systems. **Management of Personnel Resources:** Motivating, developing, and directing people as they work; identifying the best people for the job. **Operation Monitoring:** Watching gauges, dials, or other indicators to make sure a machine is working properly. **Systems Analysis:** Determining how a system should work and how changes will affect outcomes.

Education and Training Programs: Cartography; Surveying Technology/Surveying. **Related Knowledge/ Courses—Geography:** Various methods for describing the location and distribution of land, sea, and air masses, including their physical locations, relationships, and characteristics. **Design:** Design techniques, principles, tools, and instruments involved in the production and use of precision technical plans, blueprints, drawings, and models. **Building and Construction:** Materials, methods, and the appropriate tools to construct objects, structures, and buildings. **Mathematics:** Numbers and their operations and interrelationships, including arithmetic, algebra, geometry, calculus, and statistics and their applications. **Law and Government:** Laws, legal codes, court procedures, precedents, government regulations, executive orders, agency rules, and the democratic political process. **Engineering and Technology:** Equipment, tools, and mechanical devices and their uses to produce motion, light, power, technology, and other applications.

Work Environment: Outdoors; hazardous equipment; minor burns, cuts, bites, or stings; standing; walking and running; using hands on objects, tools, or controls.

Talent Directors

- Education/Training Required: Long-term on-the-job training
- Annual Earnings: $61,090
- Beginning Wage: $28,980
- Earnings Growth Potential: Very high
- Growth: 11.1%
- Annual Job Openings: 8,992
- Self-Employed: 29.5%
- Part-Time: 9.0%

The job openings listed here are shared with Directors—Stage, Motion Pictures, Television, and Radio, with Producers, with Program Directors, and with Technical Directors/Managers.

Audition and interview performers to select most appropriate talent for parts in stage, television, radio, or motion picture productions. Review performer information such as photos, resumes, voice tapes, videos, and union membership, in order to decide whom to audition for parts. Read scripts and confer with producers in order to determine the types and numbers of performers required for a given production. Select performers for roles or submit lists of suitable performers to producers or directors for final selection. Audition and interview performers in order to match their attributes to specific roles or to increase the pool of available acting talent. Maintain talent files that include information such as performers' specialties, past performances, and availability. Prepare actors for auditions by providing scripts and information about roles and casting requirements. Serve as liaisons between directors, actors, and agents. Attend or view productions in order to maintain knowledge of available actors. Negotiate contract agreements with performers, with agents, or between performers and agents or production companies. Contact agents and actors in order to provide notification of audition and performance opportunities and to set up audition times. Hire and supervise workers who help locate people with specified attributes and talents. Arrange for and/or design screen tests or auditions for prospective performers. Locate performers or extras for crowd and background scenes, and stand-ins or photo doubles for actors, by direct contact or through agents.

Personality Type: Enterprising. These occupations frequently involve starting up and carrying out projects and can involve leading people and making many decisions. They sometimes require risk taking and often deal with business.

GOE—Interest Area/Cluster: 03. Arts and Communication. **Work Group:** 03.07. Music. **Other Jobs in This Work Group:** Music Composers and Arrangers; Music Directors; Music Directors and Composers; Musicians and Singers; Musicians, Instrumental; Singers.

Skills—Management of Financial Resources: Determining how money will be spent to get the work done and accounting for these expenditures. **Management of Personnel Resources:** Motivating, developing, and directing people as they work; identifying the best people for the job. **Persuasion:** Persuading others to approach things differently. **Social Perceptiveness:** Being aware of others' reactions and understanding why they react the way they do. **Negotiation:** Bringing others together and trying to reconcile differences. **Judgment and Decision Making:** Weighing the relative costs and benefits of a potential action. **Time Management:** Managing one's own time and the time of others. **Management of Material Resources:** Obtaining and seeing to the appropriate use of equipment, facilities, and materials needed to do certain work.

Education and Training Programs: Cinematography and Film/Video Production; Directing and Theatrical Production; Drama and Dramatics/Theatre Arts, General; Dramatic/Theatre Arts and Stagecraft, Other; Film/Cinema Studies; Radio and Television; Theatre/Theatre Arts Management. **Related Knowledge/Courses—Fine Arts:** Theory and techniques required to produce, compose, and perform works of music, dance, visual arts, drama, and sculpture. **Communications and Media:** Media production, communication, and dissemination techniques and methods, including alternative ways to inform and entertain via written, oral, and visual media. **Clerical Studies:** Administrative and clerical procedures and systems such as word-processing systems, filing and records management systems, stenography and transcription, forms, design principles, and other office procedures and terminology. **Computers and Electronics:** Electric circuit boards, processors, chips, and computer hardware and software, including applications and programming. **Sales and Marketing:** Principles and methods involved in showing, promoting, and selling products or services. This includes marketing strategies and tactics, product demonstration and sales techniques, and sales control systems. **Telecommunications:**

Transmission, broadcasting, switching, control, and operation of telecommunications systems.

Work Environment: Indoors; noisy; sitting.

Tank Car, Truck, and Ship Loaders

* Education/Training Required: Moderate-term on-the-job training
* Annual Earnings: $33,140
* Beginning Wage: $19,570
* Earnings Growth Potential: High
* Growth: 9.2%
* Annual Job Openings: 4,519
* Self-Employed: 0.0%
* Part-Time: 2.7%

Load and unload chemicals and bulk solids such as coal, sand, and grain into or from tank cars, trucks, or ships by using material moving equipment. May perform various other tasks relating to shipment of products. May gauge or sample shipping tanks and test them for leaks. Verify tank car, barge, or truck load numbers to ensure car placement accuracy based on written or verbal instructions. Observe positions of cars passing loading spouts and swing spouts into the correct positions at the appropriate times. Operate ship loading and unloading equipment, conveyors, hoists, and other specialized material handling equipment such as railroad tank car unloading equipment. Monitor product movement to and from storage tanks, coordinating activities with other workers to ensure constant product flow. Record operating data such as products and quantities pumped, gauge readings, and operating times manually or by using computers. Check conditions and weights of vessels to ensure cleanliness and compliance with loading procedures. Operate industrial trucks, tractors, loaders, and other equipment to transport materials to and from transportation vehicles and loading docks and to store and retrieve materials in warehouses. Connect ground cables to carry off static electricity when unloading tanker cars. Seal outlet valves on tank cars, barges, and trucks. Test samples for specific gravity, using hydrometers, or send samples to laboratories for testing. Remove and replace tank car dome caps or direct other workers in their removal and replacement. Lower gauge rods into tanks or read meters in order to verify contents, temperatures, and volumes of liquid loads. Clean interiors of tank cars or tank trucks, using mechanical spray nozzles. Operate conveyors and equipment to transfer grain or other materials from transportation vehicles. Test vessels for leaks, damage, and defects and repair or replace defective parts as necessary. Unload cars containing liquids by connecting hoses to outlet plugs and pumping compressed air into cars to force liquids into storage tanks. Copy and attach load specifications to loaded tanks. Start pumps and adjust valves or cables in order to regulate the flow of products to vessels, utilizing knowledge of loading procedures.

Personality Type: Realistic. These occupations frequently involve work activities that include practical, hands-on problems and solutions. They often deal with plants; animals; and real-world materials such as wood, tools, and machinery. Many of the occupations require working outside and don't involve a lot of paperwork or working closely with others.

GOE—Interest Area/Cluster: 13. Manufacturing. **Work Group:** 13.17. Loading, Moving, Hoisting, and Conveying. **Other Jobs in This Work Group:** Conveyor Operators and Tenders; Hoist and Winch Operators; Industrial Truck and Tractor Operators; Machine Feeders and Offbearers; Packers and Packagers, Hand; Pump Operators, Except Wellhead Pumpers; Refuse and Recyclable Material Collectors.

Skills—Operation Monitoring: Watching gauges, dials, or other indicators to make sure a machine is working properly. **Operation and Control:** Controlling operations of equipment or systems. **Troubleshooting:** Determining what is causing an operating error and deciding what to do about it. **Repairing:** Repairing machines or systems, using the needed tools. **Equipment Maintenance:** Performing routine maintenance and determining when and what kind of maintenance is needed.

Education and Training Program: Ground Transportation, Other. **Related Knowledge/Courses—Production and Processing:** Inputs, outputs, raw materials, waste, quality control, costs, and techniques for maximizing the manufacture and distribution of goods. **Transportation:** Principles and methods for moving people or goods by air, rail, sea, or road, including their relative costs, advantages, and limitations. **Mechanical Devices:** Machines and tools, including their designs, uses, benefits, repair, and maintenance. **Public Safety and Security:** Weaponry; public safety; security operations, rules, regulations,

precautions, and prevention; and the protection of people, data, and property. **Building and Construction:** Materials, methods, and the appropriate tools to construct objects, structures, and buildings. **Chemistry:** The composition, structure, and properties of substances and of the chemical processes and transformations that they undergo. This includes uses of chemicals and their interactions, danger signs, production techniques, and disposal methods.

Work Environment: Outdoors; noisy; very hot or cold; contaminants; high places; hazardous equipment.

Tapers

- ✸ Education/Training Required: Moderate-term on-the-job training
- ✸ Annual Earnings: $42,050
- ✸ Beginning Wage: $25,310
- ✸ Earnings Growth Potential: Medium
- ✸ Growth: 7.1%
- ✸ Annual Job Openings: 9,026
- ✸ Self-Employed: 24.9%
- ✸ Part-Time: 6.1%

Seal joints between plasterboard or other wallboard to prepare wall surfaces for painting or papering. Sand rough spots of dried cement between applications of compounds. Remove extra compound after surfaces have been covered sufficiently. Press paper tape over joints to embed tape into sealing compound and to seal joints. Mix sealing compounds by hand or with portable electric mixers. Install metal molding at wall corners to secure wallboards. Seal joints between plasterboard or other wallboard in order to prepare wall surfaces for painting or papering. Check adhesives to ensure that they will work and will remain durable. Apply texturizing compounds and primers to walls and ceilings before final finishing, using trowels, brushes, rollers, or spray guns. Sand or patch nicks or cracks in plasterboard or wallboard. Apply additional coats to fill in holes and make surfaces smooth. Use mechanical applicators that spread compounds and embed tape in one operation. Spread sealing compound between boards or panels and over cracks, holes, and nail and screw heads, using trowels, broadknives, or spatulas. Spread and smooth cementing material over tape, using trowels or floating machines to blend joints with wall surfaces. Select the correct sealing compound or tape. Countersink nails or screws below surfaces of walls before applying sealing compounds, using hammers or screwdrivers.

Personality Type: Realistic. These occupations frequently involve work activities that include practical, hands-on problems and solutions. They often deal with plants; animals; and real-world materials such as wood, tools, and machinery. Many of the occupations require working outside and don't involve a lot of paperwork or working closely with others.

GOE—Interest Area/Cluster: 02. Architecture and Construction. **Work Group:** 02.04. Construction Crafts. **Other Jobs in This Work Group:** Boilermakers; Brickmasons and Blockmasons; Carpet Installers; Cement Masons and Concrete Finishers; Commercial Divers; Construction Carpenters; Crane and Tower Operators; Drywall and Ceiling Tile Installers; Electricians; Fence Erectors; Floor Layers, Except Carpet, Wood, and Hard Tiles; Floor Sanders and Finishers; Glaziers; Hazardous Materials Removal Workers; Insulation Workers, Floor, Ceiling, and Wall; Insulation Workers, Mechanical; Manufactured Building and Mobile Home Installers; Operating Engineers and Other Construction Equipment Operators; Painters, Construction and Maintenance; Paperhangers; Paving, Surfacing, and Tamping Equipment Operators; Pile-Driver Operators; Pipe Fitters and Steamfitters; Pipelayers; Plasterers and Stucco Masons; Plumbers; Plumbers, Pipefitters, and Steamfitters; Rail-Track Laying and Maintenance Equipment Operators; Refractory Materials Repairers, Except Brickmasons; Reinforcing Iron and Rebar Workers; Riggers; Roofers; Rough Carpenters; Security and Fire Alarm Systems Installers; Segmental Pavers; Sheet Metal Workers; Stone Cutters and Carvers, Manufacturing; Stonemasons; Structural Iron and Steel Workers; Terrazzo Workers and Finishers; Tile and Marble Setters.

Skills—Installation: Installing equipment, machines, wiring, or programs to meet specifications. **Management of Personnel Resources:** Motivating, developing, and directing people as they work; identifying the best people for the job. **Management of Material Resources:** Obtaining and seeing to the appropriate use of equipment, facilities, and materials needed to do certain work. **Repairing:** Repairing machines or systems, using the needed tools. **Equipment Selection:** Determining the kind of tools and equipment needed to do a job. **Equipment Maintenance:** Performing routine maintenance and determining when and what kind of maintenance is needed.

Education and Training Program: Construction Trades, Other. **Related Knowledge/Courses—Building and Construction:** Materials, methods, and the appropriate tools to construct objects, structures, and buildings. **Design:** Design techniques, principles, tools, and instruments involved in the production and use of precision technical plans, blueprints, drawings, and models. **Public Safety and Security:** Weaponry; public safety; security operations, rules, regulations, precautions, and prevention; and the protection of people, data, and property.

Work Environment: Contaminants; standing; walking and running; using hands on objects, tools, or controls; bending or twisting the body; repetitive motions.

Teacher Assistants

- ❋ Education/Training Required: Short-term on-the-job training
- ❋ Annual Earnings: $21,580
- ❋ Beginning Wage: $14,650
- ❋ Earnings Growth Potential: Low
- ❋ Growth: 10.4%
- ❋ Annual Job Openings: 193,986
- ❋ Self-Employed: 0.2%
- ❋ Part-Time: 38.0%

Perform duties that are instructional in nature or deliver direct services to students or parents. Serve in a position for which a teacher or another professional has ultimate responsibility for the design and implementation of educational programs and services. Provide extra assistance to students with special needs, such as non-English-speaking students or those with physical and mental disabilities. Tutor and assist children individually or in small groups to help them master assignments and to reinforce learning concepts presented by teachers. Supervise students in classrooms, halls, cafeterias, school yards, and gymnasiums or on field trips. Enforce administration policies and rules governing students. Observe students' performance and record relevant data to assess progress. Discuss assigned duties with classroom teachers to coordinate instructional efforts. Instruct and monitor students in the use and care of equipment and materials to prevent injuries and damage. Present subject matter to students under the direction and guidance of teachers, using lectures, discussions, or supervised role-playing methods. Organize and label materials and display students' work in a manner appropriate for their eye levels and perceptual skills. Distribute tests and homework assignments and collect them when they are completed. Type, file, and duplicate materials. Distribute teaching materials such as textbooks, workbooks, papers, and pencils to students. Use computers, audiovisual aids, and other equipment and materials to supplement presentations. Attend staff meetings and serve on committees as required. Prepare lesson materials, bulletin board displays, exhibits, equipment, and demonstrations. Carry out therapeutic regimens such as behavior modification and personal development programs under the supervision of special education instructors, psychologists, or speech-language pathologists. Provide disabled students with assistive devices, supportive technology, and assistance accessing facilities such as restrooms. Assist in bus loading and unloading. Take class attendance and maintain attendance records. Grade homework and tests, and compute and record results, using answer sheets or electronic marking devices. Organize and supervise games and other recreational activities to promote physical, mental, and social development.

Personality Type: Social. These occupations frequently involve working with, communicating with, and teaching people and often involve helping or providing service to others.

GOE—Interest Area/Cluster: 05. Education and Training. **Work Group:** 05.02. Preschool, Elementary, and Secondary Teaching and Instructing. **Other Jobs in This Work Group:** Elementary School Teachers, Except Special Education; Kindergarten Teachers, Except Special Education; Middle School Teachers, Except Special and Vocational Education; Preschool Teachers, Except Special Education; Secondary School Teachers, Except Special and Vocational Education; Special Education Teachers, Middle School; Special Education Teachers, Preschool, Kindergarten, and Elementary School; Special Education Teachers, Secondary School; Vocational Education Teachers, Middle School; Vocational Education Teachers, Secondary School.

Skills—Social Perceptiveness: Being aware of others' reactions and understanding why they react the way they do. **Learning Strategies:** Using multiple approaches when learning or teaching new things. **Instructing:** Teaching others how to do something. **Active Listening:** Listening

to what other people are saying and asking questions as appropriate. **Persuasion:** Persuading others to approach things differently. **Negotiation:** Bringing others together and trying to reconcile differences. **Service Orientation:** Actively looking for ways to help people. **Writing:** Communicating effectively with others in writing as indicated by the needs of the audience.

Education and Training Programs: Teacher Assistant/Aide Training; Teaching Assistants/Aide Training, Other. **Related Knowledge/Courses—Geography:** Various methods for describing the location and distribution of land, sea, and air masses, including their physical locations, relationships, and characteristics. **History and Archeology:** Historical events and their causes, indicators, and impact on particular civilizations and cultures. **Psychology:** Human behavior and performance, mental processes, psychological research methods, and the assessment and treatment of behavioral and affective disorders. **Therapy and Counseling:** Information and techniques needed to rehabilitate physical and mental ailments and to provide career guidance, including alternative treatments, rehabilitation equipment and its proper use, and methods to evaluate treatment effects. **Sociology and Anthropology:** Group behavior and dynamics; societal trends and influences; and cultures and their history, migrations, ethnicity, and origins. **English Language:** The structure and content of the English language, including the meaning and spelling of words, rules of composition, and grammar.

Work Environment: Indoors; noisy; standing.

Team Assemblers

- ❈ Education/Training Required: Moderate-term on-the-job training
- ❈ Annual Earnings: $24,630
- ❈ Beginning Wage: $16,450
- ❈ Earnings Growth Potential: Low
- ❈ Growth: 0.1%
- ❈ Annual Job Openings: 264,135
- ❈ Self-Employed: 1.7%
- ❈ Part-Time: 6.2%

Work as part of a team having responsibility for assembling an entire product or component of a product. Team assemblers can perform all tasks conducted by

the team in the assembly process and rotate through all or most of them rather than being assigned to a specific task on a permanent basis. **May participate in making management decisions affecting the work. Team leaders who work as part of the team should be included.** Rotate through all the tasks required in a particular production process. Determine work assignments and procedures. Shovel and sweep work areas. Operate heavy equipment such as forklifts. Provide assistance in the production of wiring assemblies.

Personality Type: Realistic. These occupations frequently involve work activities that include practical, hands-on problems and solutions. They often deal with plants; animals; and real-world materials such as wood, tools, and machinery. Many of the occupations require working outside and don't involve a lot of paperwork or working closely with others.

GOE—Interest Area/Cluster: 13. Manufacturing. **Work Group:** 13.03. Production Work, Assorted Materials Processing. **Other Jobs in This Work Group:** Bakers; Cementing and Gluing Machine Operators and Tenders; Chemical Equipment Operators and Tenders; Cleaning, Washing, and Metal Pickling Equipment Operators and Tenders; Coating, Painting, and Spraying Machine Setters, Operators, and Tenders; Cooling and Freezing Equipment Operators and Tenders; Cutting and Slicing Machine Setters, Operators, and Tenders; Extruding and Forming Machine Setters, Operators, and Tenders, Synthetic and Glass Fibers; Extruding, Forming, Pressing, and Compacting Machine Setters, Operators, and Tenders; Food and Tobacco Roasting, Baking, and Drying Machine Operators and Tenders; Food Batchmakers; Food Cooking Machine Operators and Tenders; Furnace, Kiln, Oven, Drier, and Kettle Operators and Tenders; Heat Treating Equipment Setters, Operators, and Tenders, Metal and Plastic; Helpers—Production Workers; Meat, Poultry, and Fish Cutters and Trimmers; Metal-Refining Furnace Operators and Tenders; Mixing and Blending Machine Setters, Operators, and Tenders; Packaging and Filling Machine Operators and Tenders; Plating and Coating Machine Setters, Operators, and Tenders, Metal and Plastic; Pourers and Casters, Metal; Sawing Machine Setters, Operators, and Tenders, Wood; Separating, Filtering, Clarifying, Precipitating, and Still Machine Setters, Operators, and Tenders; Sewing Machine Operators; Shoe Machine Operators and Tenders; Slaughterers and Meat Packers; Textile Bleaching and Dyeing Machine Operators and Tenders; Tire

Builders; Woodworking Machine Setters, Operators, and Tenders, Except Sawing.

Skills—Operation Monitoring: Watching gauges, dials, or other indicators to make sure a machine is working properly. **Installation:** Installing equipment, machines, wiring, or programs to meet specifications. **Quality Control Analysis:** Evaluating the quality or performance of products, services, or processes. **Equipment Maintenance:** Performing routine maintenance and determining when and what kind of maintenance is needed. **Technology Design:** Generating or adapting equipment and technology to serve user needs. **Equipment Selection:** Determining the kind of tools and equipment needed to do a job. **Repairing:** Repairing machines or systems, using the needed tools. **Operation and Control:** Controlling operations of equipment or systems.

Education and Training Program: Precision Production, Other. **Related Knowledge/Courses—Production and Processing:** Inputs, outputs, raw materials, waste, quality control, costs, and techniques for maximizing the manufacture and distribution of goods. **Mechanical Devices:** Machines and tools, including their designs, uses, benefits, repair, and maintenance.

Work Environment: Indoors; noisy; contaminants; standing; using hands on objects, tools, or controls; repetitive motions.

Technical Directors/Managers

- ❋ Education/Training Required: Long-term on-the-job training
- ❋ Annual Earnings: $61,090
- ❋ Beginning Wage: $28,980
- ❋ Earnings Growth Potential: Very high
- ❋ Growth: 11.1%
- ❋ Annual Job Openings: 8,992
- ❋ Self-Employed: 29.5%
- ❋ Part-Time: 9.0%

The job openings listed here are shared with Directors—Stage, Motion Pictures, Television, and Radio, with Producers, with Program Directors, and with Talent Directors.

Coordinate activities of technical departments, such as taping, editing, engineering, and maintenance, to

produce radio or television programs. Direct technical aspects of newscasts and other productions, checking and switching between video sources and taking responsibility for the on-air product, including camera shots and graphics. Test equipment to ensure proper operation. Monitor broadcasts to ensure that programs conform to station or network policies and regulations. Observe pictures through monitors and direct camera and video staff concerning shading and composition. Act as liaisons between engineering and production departments. Supervise and assign duties to workers engaged in technical control and production of radio and television programs. Schedule use of studio and editing facilities for producers and engineering and maintenance staff. Confer with operations directors to formulate and maintain fair and attainable technical policies for programs. Operate equipment to produce programs or broadcast live programs from remote locations. Train workers in use of equipment such as switchers, cameras, monitors, microphones, and lights. Switch between video sources in a studio or on multi-camera remotes, using equipment such as switchers, video slide projectors, and video effects generators. Set up and execute video transitions and special effects such as fades, dissolves, cuts, keys, and supers, using computers to manipulate pictures as necessary. Collaborate with promotions directors to produce on-air station promotions. Discuss filter options, lens choices, and the visual effects of objects being filmed with photography directors and video operators. Follow instructions from production managers and directors during productions, such as commands for camera cuts, effects, graphics, and takes.

Personality Type: Enterprising. These occupations frequently involve starting up and carrying out projects and can involve leading people and making many decisions. They sometimes require risk taking and often deal with business.

GOE—Interest Area/Cluster: 03. Arts and Communication. **Work Group:** 03.01. Managerial Work in Arts and Communication. **Other Jobs in This Work Group:** Agents and Business Managers of Artists, Performers, and Athletes; Art Directors; Producers; Producers and Directors; Program Directors; Public Relations Managers.

Skills—Operation and Control: Controlling operations of equipment or systems. **Operation Monitoring:** Watching gauges, dials, or other indicators to make sure a machine is working properly. **Monitoring:** Assessing how well one is doing when learning or doing something.

Systems Analysis: Determining how a system should work and how changes will affect outcomes. **Equipment Selection:** Determining the kind of tools and equipment needed to do a job. **Troubleshooting:** Determining what is causing an operating error and deciding what to do about it. **Installation:** Installing equipment, machines, wiring, or programs to meet specifications. **Time Management:** Managing one's own time and the time of others.

Education and Training Programs: Cinematography and Film/Video Production; Directing and Theatrical Production; Drama and Dramatics/Theatre Arts, General; Dramatic/Theatre Arts and Stagecraft, Other; Film/Cinema Studies; Radio and Television; Theatre/Theatre Arts Management. **Related Knowledge/Courses—Communications and Media:** Media production, communication, and dissemination techniques and methods, including alternative ways to inform and entertain via written, oral, and visual media. **Telecommunications:** Transmission, broadcasting, switching, control, and operation of telecommunications systems. **Computers and Electronics:** Electric circuit boards, processors, chips, and computer hardware and software, including applications and programming. **Philosophy and Theology:** Different philosophical systems and religions, including their basic principles, values, ethics, ways of thinking, customs, and practices and their impact on human culture. **Engineering and Technology:** Equipment, tools, and mechanical devices and their uses to produce motion, light, power, technology, and other applications. **Sales and Marketing:** Principles and methods involved in showing, promoting, and selling products or services. This includes marketing strategies and tactics, product demonstration and sales techniques, and sales control systems.

Work Environment: Indoors; noisy; sitting; using hands on objects, tools, or controls.

Telecommunications Equipment Installers and Repairers, Except Line Installers

- ❋ Education/Training Required: Postsecondary vocational training
- ❋ Annual Earnings: $54,070
- ❋ Beginning Wage: $31,520
- ❋ Earnings Growth Potential: High
- ❋ Growth: 2.5%
- ❋ Annual Job Openings: 13,541
- ❋ Self-Employed: 4.1%
- ❋ Part-Time: 3.1%

Set up, rearrange, or remove switching and dialing equipment used in central offices. Service or repair telephones and other communication equipment on customers' properties. May install equipment in new locations or install wiring and telephone jacks in buildings under construction. Note differences in wire and cable colors so that work can be performed correctly. Test circuits and components of malfunctioning telecommunications equipment to isolate sources of malfunctions, using test meters, circuit diagrams, polarity probes, and other hand tools. Test repaired, newly installed, or updated equipment to ensure that it functions properly and conforms to specifications, using test equipment and observation. Drive crew trucks to and from work areas. Inspect equipment on a regular basis in order to ensure proper functioning. Repair or replace faulty equipment such as defective and damaged telephones, wires, switching system components, and associated equipment. Remove and remake connections in order to change circuit layouts, following work orders or diagrams. Demonstrate equipment to customers and explain how it is to be used, and respond to any inquiries or complaints. Analyze test readings, computer printouts, and trouble reports to determine equipment repair needs and required repair methods. Adjust or modify equipment to enhance equipment performance or to respond to customer requests. Remove loose wires and other debris after work is completed. Request support from technical service centers when on-site procedures fail to solve installation or maintenance problems. Communicate with bases, using telephones or two-way radios, to receive instructions or technical advice, or to

report equipment status. Assemble and install communication equipment such as data and telephone communication lines, wiring, switching equipment, wiring frames, power apparatus, computer systems, and networks. Collaborate with other workers in order to locate and correct malfunctions. Review manufacturers' instructions, manuals, technical specifications, building permits, and ordinances in order to determine communication equipment requirements and procedures. Test connections to ensure that power supplies are adequate and that communications links function. Refer to manufacturers' manuals to obtain maintenance instructions pertaining to specific malfunctions. Climb poles and ladders, use truck-mounted booms, and enter areas such as manholes and cable vaults, in order to install, maintain, or inspect equipment.

Personality Type: Realistic. These occupations frequently involve work activities that include practical, hands-on problems and solutions. They often deal with plants; animals; and real-world materials such as wood, tools, and machinery. Many of the occupations require working outside and don't involve a lot of paperwork or working closely with others.

GOE—Interest Area/Cluster: 02. Architecture and Construction. **Work Group:** 02.05. Systems and Equipment Installation, Maintenance, and Repair. **Other Jobs in This Work Group:** Electrical and Electronics Repairers, Powerhouse, Substation, and Relay; Electrical Power-Line Installers and Repairers; Elevator Installers and Repairers; Heating and Air Conditioning Mechanics and Installers; Maintenance and Repair Workers, General; Refrigeration Mechanics and Installers; Telecommunications Line Installers and Repairers.

Skills—Installation: Installing equipment, machines, wiring, or programs to meet specifications. **Repairing:** Repairing machines or systems, using the needed tools. **Troubleshooting:** Determining what is causing an operating error and deciding what to do about it. **Technology Design:** Generating or adapting equipment and technology to serve user needs. **Equipment Selection:** Determining the kind of tools and equipment needed to do a job. **Systems Analysis:** Determining how a system should work and how changes will affect outcomes. **Quality Control Analysis:** Evaluating the quality or performance of products, services, or processes. **Equipment Maintenance:** Performing routine maintenance and determining when and what kind of maintenance is needed.

Education and Training Program: Communications Systems Installation and Repair Technology. **Related Knowledge/Courses—Telecommunications:** Transmission, broadcasting, switching, control, and operation of telecommunications systems. **Mechanical Devices:** Machines and tools, including their designs, uses, benefits, repair, and maintenance. **Computers and Electronics:** Electric circuit boards, processors, chips, and computer hardware and software, including applications and programming. **Engineering and Technology:** Equipment, tools, and mechanical devices and their uses to produce motion, light, power, technology, and other applications. **Design:** Design techniques, principles, tools, and instruments involved in the production and use of precision technical plans, blueprints, drawings, and models. **Public Safety and Security:** Weaponry; public safety; security operations, rules, regulations, precautions, and prevention; and the protection of people, data, and property.

Work Environment: Outdoors; noisy; very hot or cold; contaminants; cramped work space, awkward positions; using hands on objects, tools, or controls.

Telecommunications Line Installers and Repairers

- ❈ Education/Training Required: Long-term on-the-job training
- ❈ Annual Earnings: $47,220
- ❈ Beginning Wage: $25,140
- ❈ Earnings Growth Potential: High
- ❈ Growth: 4.6%
- ❈ Annual Job Openings: 14,719
- ❈ Self-Employed: 3.3%
- ❈ Part-Time: 1.9%

String and repair telephone and television cable, including fiber optics and other equipment for transmitting messages or television programming. Travel to customers' premises to install, maintain, and repair audio and visual electronic reception equipment and accessories. Inspect and test lines and cables, recording and analyzing test results, to assess transmission characteristics and locate faults and malfunctions. Splice cables, using hand tools, epoxy, or mechanical equipment. Measure signal strength at utility poles, using electronic test equipment. Set up service for customers, installing, connecting, testing, and adjusting equipment. Place insulation over conductors, and seal splices with moisture-proof covering. Access specific areas to string lines and install terminal boxes, auxiliary equipment, and appliances, using bucket trucks, or by climbing poles and ladders or entering tunnels, trenches, or crawl spaces. String cables between structures and lines from poles, towers, or trenches and pull lines to proper tension. Install equipment such as amplifiers and repeaters in order to maintain the strength of communications transmissions. Lay underground cable directly in trenches, or string it through conduits running through trenches. Pull up cable by hand from large reels mounted on trucks; then pull lines through ducts by hand or with winches. Clean and maintain tools and test equipment. Explain cable service to subscribers after installation, and collect any installation fees that are due. Compute impedance of wires from poles to houses in order to determine additional resistance needed for reducing signals to desired levels. Use a variety of construction equipment to complete installations, including digger derricks, trenchers, and cable plows. Dig trenches for underground wires and cables. Dig holes for power poles, using power augers or shovels, set poles in place with cranes, and hoist poles upright, using winches. Fill and tamp holes, using cement, earth, and tamping devices. Participate in the construction and removal of telecommunication towers and associated support structures.

Personality Type: Realistic. These occupations frequently involve work activities that include practical, hands-on problems and solutions. They often deal with plants; animals; and real-world materials such as wood, tools, and machinery. Many of the occupations require working outside and don't involve a lot of paperwork or working closely with others.

GOE—Interest Area/Cluster: 02. Architecture and Construction. **Work Group:** 02.05. Systems and Equipment Installation, Maintenance, and Repair. **Other Jobs in This Work Group:** Electrical and Electronics Repairers, Powerhouse, Substation, and Relay; Electrical Power-Line Installers and Repairers; Elevator Installers and Repairers; Heating and Air Conditioning Mechanics and Installers; Maintenance and Repair Workers, General; Refrigeration Mechanics and Installers; Telecommunications Equipment Installers and Repairers, Except Line Installers.

Skills—Installation: Installing equipment, machines, wiring, or programs to meet specifications. **Troubleshooting:**

Determining what is causing an operating error and deciding what to do about it. **Repairing:** Repairing machines or systems, using the needed tools. **Equipment Maintenance:** Performing routine maintenance and determining when and what kind of maintenance is needed. **Programming:** Writing computer programs for various purposes. **Technology Design:** Generating or adapting equipment and technology to serve user needs. **Quality Control Analysis:** Evaluating the quality or performance of products, services, or processes. **Equipment Selection:** Determining the kind of tools and equipment needed to do a job.

Education and Training Program: Communications Systems Installation and Repair Technology. **Related Knowledge/Courses—Telecommunications:** Transmission, broadcasting, switching, control, and operation of telecommunications systems. **Engineering and Technology:** Equipment, tools, and mechanical devices and their uses to produce motion, light, power, technology, and other applications. **Building and Construction:** Materials, methods, and the appropriate tools to construct objects, structures, and buildings. **Customer and Personal Service:** Principles and processes for providing customer and personal services, including needs assessment techniques, quality service standards, alternative delivery systems, and customer satisfaction evaluation techniques. **Design:** Design techniques, principles, tools, and instruments involved in the production and use of precision technical plans, blueprints, drawings, and models. **Mechanical Devices:** Machines and tools, including their designs, uses, benefits, repair, and maintenance.

Work Environment: Outdoors; very hot or cold; contaminants; cramped work space, awkward positions; hazardous equipment; using hands on objects, tools, or controls.

Tellers

- ❋ Education/Training Required: Short-term on-the-job training
- ❋ Annual Earnings: $22,920
- ❋ Beginning Wage: $17,360
- ❋ Earnings Growth Potential: Very low
- ❋ Growth: 13.5%
- ❋ Annual Job Openings: 146,077
- ❋ Self-Employed: 0.0%
- ❋ Part-Time: 27.1%

Receive and pay out money. Keep records of money and negotiable instruments involved in a financial institution's various transactions. Balance currency, coin, and checks in cash drawers at ends of shifts and calculate daily transactions, using computers, calculators, or adding machines. Cash checks and pay out money after verifying that signatures are correct, that written and numerical amounts agree, and that accounts have sufficient funds. Receive checks and cash for deposit, verify amounts, and check accuracy of deposit slips. Examine checks for endorsements and to verify other information such as dates, bank names, identification of the persons receiving payments, and the legality of the documents. Enter customers' transactions into computers to record transactions and issue computer-generated receipts. Count currency, coins, and checks received, by hand or using currency-counting machine, to prepare them for deposit or shipment to branch banks or the Federal Reserve Bank. Identify transaction mistakes when debits and credits do not balance. Prepare and verify cashier's checks. Arrange monies received in cash boxes and coin dispensers according to denomination. Process transactions such as term deposits, retirement savings plan contributions, automated teller transactions, night deposits, and mail deposits. Receive mortgage, loan, or public utility bill payments, verifying payment dates and amounts due. Resolve problems or discrepancies concerning customers' accounts. Explain, promote, or sell products or services such as travelers' checks, savings bonds, money orders, and cashier's checks, using computerized information about customers to tailor recommendations. Perform clerical tasks such as typing, filing, and microfilm photography. Monitor bank vaults to ensure cash balances are correct. Order a supply of cash to meet daily needs. Sort and file deposit slips and checks. Receive and count daily inventories of cash, drafts, and travelers' checks. Process and maintain records of customer loans. Count, verify, and post armored car deposits. Carry out special services for customers, such as ordering bank cards and checks. Compute financial fees, interest, and service charges. Obtain and process information required for the provision of services, such as opening accounts, savings plans, and purchasing bonds.

Personality Type: Conventional. These occupations frequently involve following set procedures and routines and can include working with data and details more than with ideas. Usually there is a clear line of authority to follow.

GOE—Interest Area/Cluster: 06. Finance and Insurance. **Work Group:** 06.04. Finance/Insurance Customer Service. **Other Jobs in This Work Group:** Bill and Account Collectors; Loan Interviewers and Clerks; New Accounts Clerks.

Skills—Service Orientation: Actively looking for ways to help people. **Mathematics:** Using mathematics to solve problems.

Education and Training Program: Banking and Financial Support Services. **Related Knowledge/Courses—Customer and Personal Service:** Principles and processes for providing customer and personal services, including needs assessment techniques, quality service standards, alternative delivery systems, and customer satisfaction evaluation techniques. **Sales and Marketing:** Principles and methods involved in showing, promoting, and selling products or services. This includes marketing strategies and tactics, product demonstration and sales techniques, and sales control systems. **English Language:** The structure and content of the English language, including the meaning and spelling of words, rules of composition, and grammar. **Clerical Studies:** Administrative and clerical procedures and systems such as word-processing systems, filing and records management systems, stenography and transcription, forms, design principles, and other office procedures and terminology.

Work Environment: Indoors; more often standing than sitting; using hands on objects, tools, or controls; repetitive motions.

Tile and Marble Setters

* Education/Training Required: Long-term on-the-job training
* Annual Earnings: $38,720
* Beginning Wage: $21,890
* Earnings Growth Potential: High
* Growth: 15.4%
* Annual Job Openings: 9,066
* Self-Employed: 33.8%
* Part-Time: 7.2%

Apply hard tile, marble, and wood tile to walls, floors, ceilings, and roof decks. Align and straighten tile, using levels, squares, and straightedges. Determine and implement the best layout to achieve a desired pattern. Cut and shape tile to fit around obstacles and into odd spaces and corners, using hand- and power-cutting tools. Finish and dress the joints and wipe excess grout from between tiles, using damp sponge. Apply mortar to tile back, position the tile, and press or tap with trowel handle to affix tile to base. Mix, apply, and spread plaster, concrete, mortar, cement, mastic, glue, or other adhesives to form a bed for the tiles, using brush, trowel, and screed. Prepare cost and labor estimates based on calculations of time and materials needed for project. Measure and mark surfaces to be tiled, following blueprints. Level concrete and allow to dry. Build underbeds and install anchor bolts, wires, and brackets. Prepare surfaces for tiling by attaching lath or waterproof paper or by applying a cement mortar coat onto a metal screen. Study blueprints and examine surface to be covered to determine amount of material needed. Cut, surface, polish, and install marble and granite or install pre-cast terrazzo, granite, or marble units. Install and anchor fixtures in designated positions, using hand tools. Cut tile backing to required size, using shears. Remove any old tile, grout, and adhesive, using chisels and scrapers, and clean the surface carefully. Lay and set mosaic tiles to create decorative wall, mural, and floor designs. Assist customers in selection of tile and grout. Remove and replace cracked or damaged tile. Measure and cut metal lath to size for walls and ceilings, using tin snips. Select and order tile and other items to be installed, such as bathroom accessories, walls, panels, and cabinets, according to specifications. Mix and apply mortar or cement to edges and ends of drain tiles to seal halves and joints. Spread mastic or other adhesive base on roof deck to form base for promenade tile, using serrated spreader. Apply a sealer to make grout stain- and water-resistant. Brush glue onto manila paper on which design has been drawn and position tiles, finished side down, onto paper.

Personality Type: Realistic. These occupations frequently involve work activities that include practical, hands-on problems and solutions. They often deal with plants; animals; and real-world materials such as wood, tools, and machinery. Many of the occupations require working outside and don't involve a lot of paperwork or working closely with others.

GOE—Interest Area/Cluster: 02. Architecture and Construction. **Work Group:** 02.04. Construction Crafts. **Other Jobs in This Work Group:** Boilermakers; Brickmasons and

Blockmasons; Carpet Installers; Cement Masons and Concrete Finishers; Commercial Divers; Construction Carpenters; Crane and Tower Operators; Drywall and Ceiling Tile Installers; Electricians; Fence Erectors; Floor Layers, Except Carpet, Wood, and Hard Tiles; Floor Sanders and Finishers; Glaziers; Hazardous Materials Removal Workers; Insulation Workers, Floor, Ceiling, and Wall; Insulation Workers, Mechanical; Manufactured Building and Mobile Home Installers; Operating Engineers and Other Construction Equipment Operators; Painters, Construction and Maintenance; Paperhangers; Paving, Surfacing, and Tamping Equipment Operators; Pile-Driver Operators; Pipe Fitters and Steamfitters; Pipelayers; Plasterers and Stucco Masons; Plumbers; Plumbers, Pipefitters, and Steamfitters; Rail-Track Laying and Maintenance Equipment Operators; Refractory Materials Repairers, Except Brickmasons; Reinforcing Iron and Rebar Workers; Riggers; Roofers; Rough Carpenters; Security and Fire Alarm Systems Installers; Segmental Pavers; Sheet Metal Workers; Stone Cutters and Carvers, Manufacturing; Stonemasons; Structural Iron and Steel Workers; Tapers; Terrazzo Workers and Finishers.

Skills—Installation: Installing equipment, machines, wiring, or programs to meet specifications. **Management of Financial Resources:** Determining how money will be spent to get the work done and accounting for these expenditures. **Mathematics:** Using mathematics to solve problems. **Equipment Selection:** Determining the kind of tools and equipment needed to do a job. **Technology Design:** Generating or adapting equipment and technology to serve user needs. **Management of Material Resources:** Obtaining and seeing to the appropriate use of equipment, facilities, and materials needed to do certain work. **Social Perceptiveness:** Being aware of others' reactions and understanding why they react the way they do. **Equipment Maintenance:** Performing routine maintenance and determining when and what kind of maintenance is needed.

Education and Training Program: Mason Training/Masonry. **Related Knowledge/Courses—Building and Construction:** Materials, methods, and the appropriate tools to construct objects, structures, and buildings. **Design:** Design techniques, principles, tools, and instruments involved in the production and use of precision technical plans, blueprints, drawings, and models. **Production and Processing:** Inputs, outputs, raw materials, waste,

quality control, costs, and techniques for maximizing the manufacture and distribution of goods. **Economics and Accounting:** Economic and accounting principles and practices, the financial markets, banking, and the analysis and reporting of financial data. **Administration and Management:** Principles and processes involved in business and organizational planning, coordination, and execution. This includes strategic planning, resource allocation, manpower modeling, leadership techniques, and production methods. **Transportation:** Principles and methods for moving people or goods by air, rail, sea, or road, including their relative costs, advantages, and limitations.

Work Environment: Noisy; contaminants; cramped work space, awkward positions; standing; using hands on objects, tools, or controls; bending or twisting the body.

Tire Repairers and Changers

- ❋ Education/Training Required: Short-term on-the-job training
- ❋ Annual Earnings: $21,880
- ❋ Beginning Wage: $15,890
- ❋ Earnings Growth Potential: Low
- ❋ Growth: 20.2%
- ❋ Annual Job Openings: 18,829
- ❋ Self-Employed: 3.3%
- ❋ Part-Time: 14.6%

Repair and replace tires. Identify and inflate tires correctly for the size and ply. Place wheels on balancing machines to determine counterweights required to balance wheels. Raise vehicles, using hydraulic jacks. Remount wheels onto vehicles. Locate punctures in tubeless tires by visual inspection or by immersing inflated tires in water baths and observing air bubbles. Unbolt wheels from vehicles and remove them, using lug wrenches and other hand and power tools. Reassemble tires onto wheels. Replace valve stems and remove puncturing objects. Hammer required counterweights onto rims of wheels. Rotate tires to different positions on vehicles, using hand tools. Inspect tire casings for defects, such as holes and tears. Seal punctures in tubeless tires by inserting adhesive material and expanding rubber plugs into punctures, using hand tools. Glue boots (tire patches) over ruptures in tire casings, using rubber cement. Assist mechanics and perform other duties as directed. Separate tubed tires from wheels, using rubber mallets and metal bars or mechanical tire changers. Patch tubes with adhesive rubber patches or seal rubber patches to tubes by using hot vulcanizing plates. Inflate innertubes and immerse them in water to locate leaks. Clean sides of whitewall tires. Apply rubber cement to buffed tire casings prior to vulcanization process. Drive automobile or service trucks to industrial sites to provide services and respond to emergency calls. Prepare rims and wheel drums for reassembly by scraping, grinding, or sandblasting. Order replacements for tires and tubes. Roll new rubber treads, known as camelbacks, over tire casings and mold the semi-raw rubber treads onto the buffed casings. Buff defective areas of innertubes, using scrapers. Place casing-camelback assemblies in tire molds for the vulcanization process and exert pressure on the camelbacks to ensure good adhesion.

Personality Type: Realistic. These occupations frequently involve work activities that include practical, hands-on problems and solutions. They often deal with plants; animals; and real-world materials such as wood, tools, and machinery. Many of the occupations require working outside and don't involve a lot of paperwork or working closely with others.

GOE—Interest Area/Cluster: 13. Manufacturing. **Work Group:** 13.14. Vehicle and Facility Mechanical Work. **Other Jobs in This Work Group:** Aircraft Mechanics and Service Technicians; Aircraft Structure, Surfaces, Rigging, and Systems Assemblers; Automotive Body and Related Repairers; Automotive Glass Installers and Repairers; Automotive Master Mechanics; Automotive Service Technicians and Mechanics; Automotive Specialty Technicians; Bus and Truck Mechanics and Diesel Engine Specialists; Farm Equipment Mechanics; Fiberglass Laminators and Fabricators; Mobile Heavy Equipment Mechanics, Except Engines; Motorboat Mechanics; Motorcycle Mechanics; Outdoor Power Equipment and Other Small Engine Mechanics; Rail Car Repairers; Recreational Vehicle Service Technicians.

Skills—Repairing: Repairing machines or systems, using the needed tools. **Installation:** Installing equipment, machines, wiring, or programs to meet specifications. **Equipment Maintenance:** Performing routine maintenance and determining when and what kind of maintenance is needed. **Troubleshooting:** Determining what is causing an operating error and deciding what to do about it. **Management of Material Resources:** Obtaining and

seeing to the appropriate use of equipment, facilities, and materials needed to do certain work. **Operation and Control:** Controlling operations of equipment or systems.

Education and Training Programs: No related CIP programs; this job is learned through informal short-term on-the-job training. **Related Knowledge/Courses—Mechanical Devices:** Machines and tools, including their designs, uses, benefits, repair, and maintenance. **Transportation:** Principles and methods for moving people or goods by air, rail, sea, or road, including their relative costs, advantages, and limitations. **Engineering and Technology:** Equipment, tools, and mechanical devices and their uses to produce motion, light, power, technology, and other applications. **Sales and Marketing:** Principles and methods involved in showing, promoting, and selling products or services. This includes marketing strategies and tactics, product demonstration and sales techniques, and sales control systems.

Work Environment: Noisy; contaminants; standing; walking and running; using hands on objects, tools, or controls; repetitive motions.

Title Examiners, Abstractors, and Searchers

- ✳ Education/Training Required: Moderate-term on-the-job training
- ✳ Annual Earnings: $37,200
- ✳ Beginning Wage: $22,840
- ✳ Earnings Growth Potential: Medium
- ✳ Growth: –1.2%
- ✳ Annual Job Openings: 6,880
- ✳ Self-Employed: 7.4%
- ✳ Part-Time: 13.6%

Search real estate records, examine titles, or summarize pertinent legal or insurance details for a variety of purposes. May compile lists of mortgages, contracts, and other instruments pertaining to titles by searching public and private records for law firms, real estate agencies, or title insurance companies. Prepare lists of all legal instruments applying to a specific piece of land and the buildings on it. Read search requests in order to ascertain types of title evidence required and to obtain descriptions of properties and names of involved parties. Examine documentation such as mortgages, liens, judgments, easements, plat books, maps, contracts, and agreements in order to verify factors such as properties' legal descriptions, ownership, or restrictions. Copy or summarize recorded documents, such as mortgages, trust deeds, and contracts, that affect property titles. Examine individual titles to determine if restrictions, such as delinquent taxes, will affect titles and limit property use. Prepare reports describing any title encumbrances encountered during searching activities and outlining actions needed to clear titles. Verify accuracy and completeness of land-related documents accepted for registration; prepare rejection notices when documents are not acceptable. Confer with real estate agents, lending institution personnel, buyers, sellers, contractors, surveyors, and courthouse personnel to exchange title-related information or to resolve problems. Enter into recordkeeping systems appropriate data needed to create new title records or update existing ones. Direct activities of workers who search records and examine titles, assigning, scheduling, and evaluating work and providing technical guidance as necessary. Obtain maps or drawings delineating properties from company title plants, county surveyors, and/or assessors' offices. Prepare and issue title commitments and title insurance policies based on information compiled from title searches. Summarize pertinent legal or insurance details or sections of statutes or case law from reference books so that they can be used in examinations or as proofs or ready reference. Retrieve and examine real estate closing files for accuracy and to ensure that information included is recorded and executed according to regulations. Prepare real estate closing statements, utilizing knowledge and expertise in real estate procedures.

Personality Type: Conventional. These occupations frequently involve following set procedures and routines and can include working with data and details more than with ideas. Usually there is a clear line of authority to follow.

GOE—Interest Area/Cluster: 12. Law and Public Safety. **Work Group:** 12.03. Legal Support. **Other Jobs in This Work Group:** Law Clerks; Paralegals and Legal Assistants.

Skills—Writing: Communicating effectively with others in writing as indicated by the needs of the audience. **Critical Thinking:** Using logic and analysis to identify the strengths and weaknesses of different approaches. **Management of Financial Resources:** Determining how money will be spent to get the work done and accounting for these expenditures. **Reading Comprehension:** Understanding written sentences and paragraphs in work-related documents. **Operations Analysis:** Analyzing needs and product requirements to create a design. **Technology Design:** Generating or adapting equipment and technology to serve user needs. **Management of Material Resources:** Obtaining and seeing to the appropriate use of equipment, facilities, and materials needed to do certain work. **Speaking:** Talking to others to effectively convey information.

Education and Training Program: Legal Assistant/Paralegal Training. **Related Knowledge/Courses—Clerical Studies:** Administrative and clerical procedures and systems such as word-processing systems, filing and records management systems, stenography and transcription, forms, design principles, and other office procedures and terminology. **Law and Government:** Laws, legal codes, court procedures, precedents, government regulations, executive orders, agency rules, and the democratic political process. **Geography:** Various methods for describing the location and distribution of land, sea, and air masses, including their physical locations, relationships, and characteristics. **Customer and Personal Service:** Principles and processes for providing customer and personal services, including needs assessment techniques, quality service standards, alternative delivery systems, and customer satisfaction evaluation techniques. **English Language:** The structure and content of the English language, including the meaning and spelling of words, rules of composition, and grammar. **Computers and Electronics:** Electric circuit boards, processors, chips, and computer hardware and software, including applications and programming.

Work Environment: Indoors; sitting; repetitive motions.

Tour Guides and Escorts

- ❋ Education/Training Required: Moderate-term on-the-job training
- ❋ Annual Earnings: $22,110
- ❋ Beginning Wage: $14,820
- ❋ Earnings Growth Potential: Low
- ❋ Growth: 21.2%
- ❋ Annual Job Openings: 15,027
- ❋ Self-Employed: 20.1%
- ❋ Part-Time: 29.0%

Escort individuals or groups on sightseeing tours or through places of interest such as industrial establishments, public buildings, and art galleries. Conduct educational activities for schoolchildren. Escort individuals or groups on cruises; on sightseeing tours; or through places of interest such as industrial establishments, public buildings, and art galleries. Describe tour points of interest to group members and respond to questions. Monitor visitors' activities to ensure compliance with establishment or tour regulations and safety practices. Greet and register visitors and issue any required identification badges or safety devices. Distribute brochures, show audiovisual presentations, and explain establishment processes and operations at tour sites. Provide directions and other pertinent information to visitors. Provide for physical safety of groups, performing such activities as providing first aid and directing emergency evacuations. Research environmental conditions and clients' skill and ability levels to plan expeditions, instruction, and commentary that are appropriate. Provide information about wildlife varieties and habitats, as well as any relevant regulations, such as those pertaining to hunting and fishing. Collect fees and tickets from group members. Teach skills, such as proper climbing methods, and demonstrate and advise on the use of equipment. Select travel routes and sites to be visited based on knowledge of specific areas. Solicit tour patronage and sell souvenirs. Speak foreign languages to communicate with foreign visitors. Assemble and check the required supplies and equipment prior to departure. Perform clerical duties such as filing, typing, operating switchboards, and routing mail and messages. Drive motor vehicles to transport visitors to establishments and tour site locations.

Personality Type: Social. These occupations frequently involve working with, communicating with, and teaching people and often involve helping or providing service to others.

GOE—Interest Area/Cluster: 09. Hospitality, Tourism, and Recreation. **Work Group:** 09.03. Hospitality and Travel Services. **Other Jobs in This Work Group:** Baggage Porters and Bellhops; Concierges; Flight Attendants; Hotel, Motel, and Resort Desk Clerks; Janitors and Cleaners, Except Maids and Housekeeping Cleaners; Maids and Housekeeping Cleaners; Reservation and Transportation Ticket Agents and Travel Clerks; Transportation Attendants, Except Flight Attendants and Baggage Porters; Travel Agents; Travel Guides.

Skills—Reading Comprehension: Understanding written sentences and paragraphs in work-related documents. **Speaking:** Talking to others to effectively convey information.

Education and Training Program: Tourism and Travel Services Management. **Related Knowledge/Courses—History and Archeology:** Historical events and their causes, indicators, and impact on particular civilizations and cultures. **Fine Arts:** Theory and techniques required to produce, compose, and perform works of music, dance, visual arts, drama, and sculpture. **Philosophy and Theology:** Different philosophical systems and religions, including their basic principles, values, ethics, ways of thinking, customs, and practices and their impact on human culture. **Sociology and Anthropology:** Group behavior and dynamics; societal trends and influences; and cultures and their history, migrations, ethnicity, and origins. **Customer and Personal Service:** Principles and processes for providing customer and personal services, including needs assessment techniques, quality service standards, alternative delivery systems, and customer satisfaction evaluation techniques. **Communications and Media:** Media production, communication, and dissemination techniques and methods, including alternative ways to inform and entertain via written, oral, and visual media.

Work Environment: Standing.

Transportation Managers

* Education/Training Required: Work experience in a related occupation
* Annual Earnings: $76,310
* Beginning Wage: $44,900
* Earnings Growth Potential: High
* Growth: 8.3%
* Annual Job Openings: 6,994
* Self-Employed: 2.6%
* Part-Time: 2.3%

The job openings listed here are shared with Storage and Distribution Managers.

Plan, direct, and coordinate the transportation operations within an organization or the activities of organizations that provide transportation services. Direct activities related to dispatching, routing, and tracking transportation vehicles such as aircraft and railroad cars. Plan, organize, and manage the work of subordinate staff to ensure that the work is accomplished in a manner consistent with organizational requirements. Direct investigations to verify and resolve customer or shipper complaints. Serve as contact persons for all workers within assigned territories. Implement schedule and policy changes. Collaborate with other managers and staff members to formulate and implement policies, procedures, goals, and objectives. Monitor operations to ensure that staff members comply with administrative policies and procedures, safety rules, union contracts, and government regulations. Promote safe work activities by conducting safety audits, attending company safety meetings, and meeting with individual staff members. Develop criteria, application instructions, procedural manuals, and contracts for federal and state public transportation programs. Monitor spending to ensure that expenses are consistent with approved budgets. Direct and coordinate, through subordinates, activities of operations department to obtain use of equipment, facilities, and human resources. Direct activities of staff performing repairs and maintenance to equipment, vehicles, and facilities. Conduct investigations in cooperation with government agencies to determine causes of transportation accidents and to improve safety procedures. Analyze expenditures and other financial information to develop plans, policies, and budgets for increasing profits and improving services. Negotiate and authorize contracts with equipment and materials suppliers and monitor contract fulfillment. Supervise workers assigning tariff classifications and preparing billing. Set operations policies and standards, including determination of safety procedures for the handling of dangerous goods. Recommend or authorize capital expenditures for acquisition of new equipment or property to increase efficiency and services of operations department. Prepare management recommendations, such as proposed fee and tariff increases or schedule changes.

Personality Type: Enterprising. These occupations frequently involve starting up and carrying out projects and can involve leading people and making many decisions. They sometimes require risk taking and often deal with business.

GOE—Interest Area/Cluster: 16. Transportation, Distribution, and Logistics. **Work Group:** 16.01. Managerial Work in Transportation. **Other Jobs in This Work**

Group: Aircraft Cargo Handling Supervisors; First-Line Supervisors/Managers of Transportation and Material-Moving Machine and Vehicle Operators; Postmasters and Mail Superintendents; Railroad Conductors and Yardmasters; Storage and Distribution Managers; Transportation, Storage, and Distribution Managers.

Skills—Negotiation: Bringing others together and trying to reconcile differences. **Time Management:** Managing one's own time and the time of others. **Coordination:** Adjusting actions in relation to others' actions. **Management of Financial Resources:** Determining how money will be spent to get the work done and accounting for these expenditures. **Mathematics:** Using mathematics to solve problems. **Monitoring:** Assessing how well one is doing when learning or doing something. **Management of Material Resources:** Obtaining and seeing to the appropriate use of equipment, facilities, and materials needed to do certain work. **Writing:** Communicating effectively with others in writing as indicated by the needs of the audience.

Education and Training Programs: Aeronautics/Aviation/Aerospace Science and Technology, General; Aviation/Airway Management and Operations; Business Administration and Management, General; Logistics and Materials Management; Public Administration; Transportation/Transportation Management. **Related Knowledge/Courses—Transportation:** Principles and methods for moving people or goods by air, rail, sea, or road, including their relative costs, advantages, and limitations. **Clerical Studies:** Administrative and clerical procedures and systems such as word-processing systems, filing and records management systems, stenography and transcription, forms, design principles, and other office procedures and terminology. **Customer and Personal Service:** Principles and processes for providing customer and personal services, including needs assessment techniques, quality service standards, alternative delivery systems, and customer satisfaction evaluation techniques. **Sales and Marketing:** Principles and methods involved in showing, promoting, and selling products or services. This includes marketing strategies and tactics, product demonstration and sales techniques, and sales control systems. **Production and Processing:** Inputs, outputs, raw materials, waste, quality control, costs, and techniques for maximizing the manufacture and distribution of goods. **Psychology:** Human behavior and performance, mental processes, psychological research methods, and the assessment and treatment of behavioral and affective disorders.

Work Environment: Indoors; noisy; sitting.

Transportation Vehicle, Equipment and Systems Inspectors, Except Aviation

* Education/Training Required: Work experience in a related occupation
* Annual Earnings: $51,440
* Beginning Wage: $27,340
* Earnings Growth Potential: High
* Growth: 16.4%
* Annual Job Openings: 2,122
* Self-Employed: 5.9%
* Part-Time: 3.7%

The job openings listed here are shared with Aviation Inspectors and with Freight and Cargo Inspectors.

Inspect and monitor transportation equipment, vehicles, or systems to ensure compliance with regulations and safety standards. Conduct vehicle or transportation equipment tests, using diagnostic equipment. Investigate and make recommendations on carrier requests for waiver of federal standards. Prepare reports on investigations or inspections, and actions taken. Issue notices and recommend corrective actions when infractions or problems are found. Investigate incidents or violations such as delays, accidents, and equipment failures. Investigate complaints regarding safety violations. Inspect repairs to transportation vehicles and equipment to ensure that repair work was performed properly. Examine transportation vehicles, equipment, or systems to detect damage, wear, or malfunction. Inspect vehicles and other equipment for evidence of abuse, damage, or mechanical malfunction. Examine carrier operating rules, employee qualification guidelines, and carrier training and testing programs for compliance with regulations or safety standards. Inspect vehicles or equipment to ensure compliance with rules, standards, or regulations.

Personality Type: Realistic. These occupations frequently involve work activities that include practical, hands-on

problems and solutions. They often deal with plants; animals; and real-world materials such as wood, tools, and machinery. Many of the occupations require working outside and don't involve a lot of paperwork or working closely with others.

GOE—Interest Area/Cluster: 07. Government and Public Administration. **Work Group:** 07.03. Regulations Enforcement. **Other Jobs in This Work Group:** Agricultural Inspectors; Aviation Inspectors; Compliance Officers, Except Agriculture, Construction, Health and Safety, and Transportation; Construction and Building Inspectors; Environmental Compliance Inspectors; Equal Opportunity Representatives and Officers; Financial Examiners; Fire Inspectors; Fish and Game Wardens; Forest Fire Inspectors and Prevention Specialists; Freight and Cargo Inspectors; Government Property Inspectors and Investigators; Immigration and Customs Inspectors; Licensing Examiners and Inspectors; Nuclear Monitoring Technicians; Occupational Health and Safety Specialists; Occupational Health and Safety Technicians; Tax Examiners, Collectors, and Revenue Agents.

Skills—Repairing: Repairing machines or systems, using the needed tools. **Equipment Maintenance:** Performing routine maintenance and determining when and what kind of maintenance is needed. **Troubleshooting:** Determining what is causing an operating error and deciding what to do about it. **Installation:** Installing equipment, machines, wiring, or programs to meet specifications. **Quality Control Analysis:** Evaluating the quality or performance of products, services, or processes. **Operation Monitoring:** Watching gauges, dials, or other indicators to make sure a machine is working properly. **Systems Analysis:** Determining how a system should work and how changes will affect outcomes. **Systems Evaluation:** Looking at many indicators of system performance and taking into account their accuracy.

Education and Training Programs: No related CIP programs; this job is learned through work experience in a related occupation. **Related Knowledge/Courses— Mechanical Devices:** Machines and tools, including their designs, uses, benefits, repair, and maintenance. **Transportation:** Principles and methods for moving people or goods by air, rail, sea, or road, including their relative costs, advantages, and limitations. **Public Safety and Security:** Weaponry; public safety; security operations, rules, regulations, precautions, and prevention; and the protection of people, data, and property. **Engineering and Technology:** Equipment, tools, and mechanical devices and their uses to produce motion, light, power, technology, and other applications. **Administration and Management:** Principles and processes involved in business and organizational planning, coordination, and execution. This includes strategic planning, resource allocation, manpower modeling, leadership techniques, and production methods. **Physics:** Physical principles, laws, and applications, including air, water, material dynamics, light, atomic principles, heat, electric theory, earth formations, and meteorological and related natural phenomena.

Work Environment: Noisy; very hot or cold; contaminants; cramped work space, awkward positions; hazardous equipment; using hands on objects, tools, or controls.

Tree Trimmers and Pruners

- ❋ Education/Training Required: Short-term on-the-job training
- ❋ Annual Earnings: $29,800
- ❋ Beginning Wage: $19,370
- ❋ Earnings Growth Potential: Medium
- ❋ Growth: 11.1%
- ❋ Annual Job Openings: 9,621
- ❋ Self-Employed: 28.9%
- ❋ Part-Time: 14.6%

Cut away dead or excess branches from trees or shrubs to maintain right-of-way for roads, sidewalks, or utilities or to improve appearance, health, and value of trees. Prune or treat trees or shrubs, using handsaws, pruning hooks, shears, and clippers. May use truck-mounted lifts and power pruners. May fill cavities in trees to promote healing and prevent deterioration. Supervise others engaged in tree trimming work and train lower-level employees. Transplant and remove trees and shrubs, and prepare trees for moving. Operate shredding and chipping equipment, and feed limbs and brush into the machines. Remove broken limbs from wires, using hooked extension poles. Prune, cut down, fertilize, and spray trees as directed by tree surgeons. Spray trees to treat diseased or unhealthy trees, including mixing chemicals and calibrating spray equipment. Clean, sharpen, and lubricate tools and equipment. Clear sites, streets, and grounds of woody and herbaceous materials such as tree stumps and fallen trees and

limbs. Load debris and refuse onto trucks and haul it away for disposal. Inspect trees to determine if they have diseases or pest problems. Cut away dead and excess branches from trees, or clear branches around power lines, using climbing equipment or buckets of extended truck booms, and/or chainsaws, hooks, handsaws, shears, and clippers. Collect debris and refuse from tree trimming and removal operations into piles, using shovels, rakes, or other tools. Operate boom trucks, loaders, stump chippers, brush chippers, tractors, power saws, trucks, sprayers, and other equipment and tools. Apply tar or other protective substances to cut surfaces to seal them and to protect them from fungi and insects. Climb trees, using climbing hooks and belts, or climb ladders to gain access to work areas. Split logs or wooden blocks into bolts, pickets, posts, or stakes, using hand tools such as ax wedges, sledgehammers, and mallets. Cable, brace, tie, bolt, stake, and guy trees and branches to provide support. Trim jagged stumps, using saws or pruning shears. Trim, top, and reshape trees to achieve attractive shapes or to remove low-hanging branches. Water, root-feed, and fertilize trees. Harvest tanbark by cutting rings and slits in bark and stripping bark from trees, using spuds or axes. Install lightning protection on trees. Plan and develop budgets for tree work, and estimate the monetary value of trees. Provide information to the public regarding trees, such as advice on tree care.

Personality Type: Realistic. These occupations frequently involve work activities that include practical, hands-on problems and solutions. They often deal with plants; animals; and real-world materials such as wood, tools, and machinery. Many of the occupations require working outside and don't involve a lot of paperwork or working closely with others.

GOE—Interest Area/Cluster: 01. Agriculture and Natural Resources. **Work Group:** 01.05. Nursery, Groundskeeping, and Pest Control. **Other Jobs in This Work Group:** Landscaping and Groundskeeping Workers; Nursery Workers; Pest Control Workers; Pesticide Handlers, Sprayers, and Applicators, Vegetation.

Skills—Equipment Maintenance: Performing routine maintenance and determining when and what kind of maintenance is needed. **Equipment Selection:** Determining the kind of tools and equipment needed to do a job. **Repairing:** Repairing machines or systems, using the needed tools. **Operation and Control:** Controlling operations of equipment or systems. **Management of Personnel**

Resources: Motivating, developing, and directing people as they work; identifying the best people for the job. **Science:** Using scientific methods to solve problems. **Operation Monitoring:** Watching gauges, dials, or other indicators to make sure a machine is working properly. **Installation:** Installing equipment, machines, wiring, or programs to meet specifications.

Education and Training Program: Applied Horticulture/Horicultural Business Services, Other. **Related Knowledge/Courses—Biology:** Plant and animal living tissue, cells, organisms, and entities, including their functions, interdependencies, and interactions with each other and the environment. **Mechanical Devices:** Machines and tools, including their designs, uses, benefits, repair, and maintenance. **Transportation:** Principles and methods for moving people or goods by air, rail, sea, or road, including their relative costs, advantages, and limitations. **Physics:** Physical principles, laws, and applications, including air, water, material dynamics, light, atomic principles, heat, electric theory, earth formations, and meteorological and related natural phenomena. **Public Safety and Security:** Weaponry; public safety; security operations, rules, regulations, precautions, and prevention; and the protection of people, data, and property. **Sales and Marketing:** Principles and methods involved in showing, promoting, and selling products or services. This includes marketing strategies and tactics, product demonstration and sales techniques, and sales control systems.

Work Environment: Outdoors; noisy; contaminants; hazardous equipment; minor burns, cuts, bites, or stings; using hands on objects, tools, or controls.

Truck Drivers, Heavy and Tractor-Trailer

- ❋ Education/Training Required: Moderate-term on-the-job training
- ❋ Annual Earnings: $36,220
- ❋ Beginning Wage: $23,380
- ❋ Earnings Growth Potential: Medium
- ❋ Growth: 10.4%
- ❋ Annual Job Openings: 279,032
- ❋ Self-Employed: 8.8%
- ❋ Part-Time: 7.2%

Drive a tractor-trailer combination or a truck with a capacity of at least 26,000 GVW to transport and deliver goods, livestock, or materials in liquid, loose, or packaged form. May be required to unload truck. May require use of automated routing equipment. Requires commercial drivers' license. Follow appropriate safety procedures when transporting dangerous goods. Check vehicles before driving them to ensure that mechanical, safety, and emergency equipment is in good working order. Maintain logs of working hours and of vehicle service and repair status, following applicable state and federal regulations. Obtain receipts or signatures when loads are delivered and collect payment for services when required. Check all load-related documentation to ensure that it is complete and accurate. Maneuver trucks into loading or unloading positions, following signals from loading crew as needed; check that vehicle position is correct and any special loading equipment is properly positioned. Drive trucks with capacities greater than 3 tons, including tractor-trailer combinations, to transport and deliver products, livestock, or other materials. Secure cargo for transport, using ropes, blocks, chain, binders, or covers. Read bills of lading to determine assignment details. Report vehicle defects, accidents, traffic violations, or damage to the vehicles. Read and interpret maps to determine vehicle routes. Couple and uncouple trailers by changing trailer jack positions, connecting or disconnecting air and electrical lines, and manipulating fifth-wheel locks. Collect delivery instructions from appropriate sources, verifying instructions and routes. Drive trucks to weigh stations before and after loading and along routes to document weights and to comply with state regulations. Operate equipment such as truck cab computers, CB radios, and telephones to exchange necessary information with bases, supervisors, or other drivers. Check conditions of trailers after contents have been unloaded to ensure that there has been no damage. Crank trailer landing gear up and down to safely secure vehicles. Wrap goods, using pads, packing paper, and containers, and secure loads to trailer walls, using straps. Perform basic vehicle maintenance tasks such as adding oil, fuel, and radiator fluid or performing minor repairs. Load and unload trucks or help others with loading and unloading, operating any special loading-related equipment on vehicles and using other equipment as necessary.

Personality Type: Realistic. These occupations frequently involve work activities that include practical, hands-on problems and solutions. They often deal with plants;

animals; and real-world materials such as wood, tools, and machinery. Many of the occupations require working outside and don't involve a lot of paperwork or working closely with others.

GOE—Interest Area/Cluster: 16. Transportation, Distribution, and Logistics. **Work Group:** 16.03. Truck Driving. **Other Jobs in This Work Group:** Truck Drivers, Light or Delivery Services.

Skills—Equipment Maintenance: Performing routine maintenance and determining when and what kind of maintenance is needed. **Repairing:** Repairing machines or systems, using the needed tools. **Operation Monitoring:** Watching gauges, dials, or other indicators to make sure a machine is working properly. **Troubleshooting:** Determining what is causing an operating error and deciding what to do about it. **Operation and Control:** Controlling operations of equipment or systems.

Education and Training Program: Truck and Bus Driver Training/Commercial Vehicle Operation. **Related Knowledge/Courses—Transportation:** Principles and methods for moving people or goods by air, rail, sea, or road, including their relative costs, advantages, and limitations. **Geography:** Various methods for describing the location and distribution of land, sea, and air masses, including their physical locations, relationships, and characteristics. **Public Safety and Security:** Weaponry; public safety; security operations, rules, regulations, precautions, and prevention; and the protection of people, data, and property. **Law and Government:** Laws, legal codes, court procedures, precedents, government regulations, executive orders, agency rules, and the democratic political process. **Mechanical Devices:** Machines and tools, including their designs, uses, benefits, repair, and maintenance.

Work Environment: Outdoors; very hot or cold; contaminants; sitting; using hands on objects, tools, or controls; repetitive motions.

Truck Drivers, Light or Delivery Services

* Education/Training Required: Short-term on-the-job training
* Annual Earnings: $26,380
* Beginning Wage: $16,180
* Earnings Growth Potential: Medium
* Growth: 8.4%
* Annual Job Openings: 154,330
* Self-Employed: 9.3%
* Part-Time: 7.2%

Drive a truck or van with a capacity of under 26,000 GVW primarily to deliver or pick up merchandise or to deliver packages within a specified area. May require use of automatic routing or location software. May load and unload truck. Obey traffic laws and follow established traffic and transportation procedures. Inspect and maintain vehicle supplies and equipment such as gas, oil, water, tires, lights, and brakes to ensure that vehicles are in proper working condition. Report any mechanical problems encountered with vehicles. Present bills and receipts and collect payments for goods delivered or loaded. Load and unload trucks, vans, or automobiles. Turn in receipts and money received from deliveries. Verify the contents of inventory loads against shipping papers. Maintain records such as vehicle logs, records of cargo, or billing statements in accordance with regulations. Read maps and follow written and verbal geographic directions. Report delays, accidents, or other traffic and transportation situations to bases or other vehicles, using telephones or mobile two-way radios. Sell and keep records of sales for products from truck inventory. Drive vehicles with capacities under three tons to transport materials to and from specified destinations such as railroad stations, plants, residences, and offices or within industrial yards. Drive trucks equipped with public address systems through city streets to broadcast announcements for advertising or publicity purposes. Use and maintain the tools and equipment found on commercial vehicles, such as weighing and measuring devices. Perform emergency repairs such as changing tires or installing light bulbs, fuses, tire chains, and spark plugs.

Personality Type: Realistic. These occupations frequently involve work activities that include practical, hands-on problems and solutions. They often deal with plants; animals; and real-world materials such as wood, tools, and machinery. Many of the occupations require working outside and don't involve a lot of paperwork or working closely with others.

GOE—Interest Area/Cluster: 16. Transportation, Distribution, and Logistics. **Work Group:** 16.03. Truck Driving. **Other Jobs in This Work Group:** Truck Drivers, Heavy and Tractor-Trailer.

Skills—Equipment Maintenance: Performing routine maintenance and determining when and what kind of maintenance is needed. **Operation and Control:** Controlling operations of equipment or systems. **Operation Monitoring:** Watching gauges, dials, or other indicators to make sure a machine is working properly. **Social Perceptiveness:** Being aware of others' reactions and understanding why they react the way they do.

Education and Training Program: Truck and Bus Driver Training/Commercial Vehicle Operation. **Related Knowledge/Course: Transportation:** Principles and methods for moving people or goods by air, rail, sea, or road, including their relative costs, advantages, and limitations.

Work Environment: Outdoors; very hot or cold; contaminants; cramped work space, awkward positions; minor burns, cuts, bites, or stings; using hands on objects, tools, or controls.

Umpires, Referees, and Other Sports Officials

- ❋ Education/Training Required: Long-term on-the-job training
- ❋ Annual Earnings: $24,770
- ❋ Beginning Wage: $14,930
- ❋ Earnings Growth Potential: Medium
- ❋ Growth: 16.0%
- ❋ Annual Job Openings: 4,461
- ❋ Self-Employed: 24.0%
- ❋ Part-Time: 39.1%

Officiate at competitive athletic or sporting events. Detect infractions of rules and decide penalties according to established regulations. Officiate at sporting events, games, or competitions, to maintain standards of play and to ensure that game rules are observed. Judge performances in sporting competitions in order to award points, impose scoring penalties, and determine results. Inspect sporting equipment and/or examine participants in order to ensure compliance with event and safety regulations. Keep track of event times, including race times and elapsed time during game segments, starting or stopping play when necessary. Signal participants or other officials to make them aware of infractions or to otherwise regulate play or competition. Verify scoring calculations before competition winners are announced. Resolve claims of rule infractions or complaints by participants and assess any necessary penalties, according to regulations. Start races and competitions. Teach and explain the rules and regulations governing a specific sport. Confer with other sporting officials, coaches, players, and facility managers in order to provide information, coordinate activities, and discuss problems. Verify credentials of participants in sporting events, and make other qualifying determinations such as starting order or handicap number. Report to regulating organizations regarding sporting activities, complaints made, and actions taken or needed, such as fines or other disciplinary actions. Compile scores and other athletic records. Direct participants to assigned areas such as starting blocks or penalty areas. Research and study players and teams in order to anticipate issues that might arise in future engagements.

Personality Type: Realistic. These occupations frequently involve work activities that include practical, hands-on problems and solutions. They often deal with plants; animals; and real-world materials such as wood, tools, and machinery. Many of the occupations require working outside and don't involve a lot of paperwork or working closely with others.

GOE—Interest Area/Cluster: 09. Hospitality, Tourism, and Recreation. **Work Group:** 09.06. Sports. **Other Jobs in This Work Group:** Athletes and Sports Competitors; Coaches and Scouts.

Skills—Judgment and Decision Making: Weighing the relative costs and benefits of a potential action. **Negotiation:** Bringing others together and trying to reconcile differences. **Persuasion:** Persuading others to approach things differently.

Education and Training Program: Personal and Culinary Services, Other. **Related Knowledge/Course: Psychology:** Human behavior and performance, mental processes, psychological research methods, and the assessment and treatment of behavioral and affective disorders.

Work Environment: Outdoors; noisy; standing; walking and running.

Veterinary Technologists and Technicians

- ❋ Education/Training Required: Associate degree
- ❋ Annual Earnings: $27,970
- ❋ Beginning Wage: $18,840
- ❋ Earnings Growth Potential: Low
- ❋ Growth: 41.0%
- ❋ Annual Job Openings: 14,674
- ❋ Self-Employed: 0.2%
- ❋ Part-Time: 20.8%

Perform medical tests in a laboratory environment for use in the treatment and diagnosis of diseases in animals. Prepare vaccines and serums for prevention of diseases. Prepare tissue samples; take blood samples; and execute laboratory tests, such as urinalysis and blood counts. Clean and sterilize instruments and materials and maintain equipment and machines. Administer anesthesia to animals, under the direction of a veterinarian, and monitor animals' responses to anesthetics so that dosages can be adjusted. Care for and monitor the condition of animals recovering from surgery. Prepare and administer medications, vaccines, serums, and treatments as prescribed by veterinarians. Perform laboratory tests on blood, urine, and feces, such as urinalyses and blood counts, to assist in the diagnosis and treatment of animal health problems. Administer emergency first aid, such as performing emergency resuscitation or other life-saving procedures. Collect, prepare, and label samples for laboratory testing, culture, or microscopic examination. Clean and sterilize instruments, equipment, and materials. Provide veterinarians with the correct equipment and instruments as needed. Fill prescriptions, measuring medications and labeling containers. Prepare animals for surgery, performing such tasks as shaving surgical areas. Take animals into treatment areas and assist with physical examinations by performing such duties as obtaining temperature, pulse, and respiration data. Observe the behavior and condition of animals and monitor their clinical symptoms. Take and develop diagnostic radiographs, using X-ray equipment. Maintain laboratory, research, and treatment records, as well as inventories of pharmaceuticals, equipment, and supplies. Give enemas and perform catheterizations, ear flushes, intravenous feedings, and gavages. Prepare treatment rooms for surgery. Maintain instruments, equipment, and machinery to ensure proper working condition. Perform dental work such as cleaning, polishing, and extracting teeth. Clean kennels, animal holding areas, surgery suites, examination rooms, and animal loading/unloading facilities to control the spread of disease. Provide information and counseling regarding issues such as animal health care, behavior problems, and nutrition. Provide assistance with animal euthanasia and the disposal of remains. Dress and suture wounds and apply splints and other protective devices. Perform a variety of office, clerical, and accounting duties, such as reception, billing, bookkeeping, or selling products.

Personality Type: Realistic. These occupations frequently involve work activities that include practical, hands-on problems and solutions. They often deal with plants; animals; and real-world materials such as wood, tools, and machinery. Many of the occupations require working outside and don't involve a lot of paperwork or working closely with others.

GOE—Interest Area/Cluster: 08. Health Science. **Work Group:** 08.05. Animal Care. **Other Jobs in This Work Group:** Animal Breeders; Animal Trainers; Nonfarm Animal Caretakers; Veterinarians; Veterinary Assistants and Laboratory Animal Caretakers.

Skills—Science: Using scientific methods to solve problems. **Operation Monitoring:** Watching gauges, dials, or other indicators to make sure a machine is working properly. **Instructing:** Teaching others how to do something. **Equipment Maintenance:** Performing routine maintenance and determining when and what kind of maintenance is needed. **Social Perceptiveness:** Being aware of others' reactions and understanding why they react the way they do. **Operation and Control:** Controlling operations of equipment or systems. **Mathematics:** Using mathematics to solve problems. **Reading Comprehension:** Understanding written sentences and paragraphs in work-related documents.

Education and Training Program: Veterinary/Animal Health Technology/Technician and Veterinary Assistant

Training. **Related Knowledge/Courses—Biology:** Plant and animal living tissue, cells, organisms, and entities, including their functions, interdependencies, and interactions with each other and the environment. **Medicine and Dentistry:** The information and techniques needed to diagnose and treat injuries, diseases, and deformities. This includes symptoms, treatment alternatives, drug properties and interactions, and preventive health-care measures. **Chemistry:** The composition, structure, and properties of substances and of the chemical processes and transformations that they undergo. This includes uses of chemicals and their interactions, danger signs, production techniques, and disposal methods. **Sales and Marketing:** Principles and methods involved in showing, promoting, and selling products or services. This includes marketing strategies and tactics, product demonstration and sales techniques, and sales control systems. **Customer and Personal Service:** Principles and processes for providing customer and personal services, including needs assessment techniques, quality service standards, alternative delivery systems, and customer satisfaction evaluation techniques. **Mathematics:** Numbers and their operations and interrelationships, including arithmetic, algebra, geometry, calculus, and statistics and their applications.

Work Environment: Indoors; contaminants; radiation; disease or infections; minor burns, cuts, bites, or stings; standing.

Vocational Education Teachers, Postsecondary

* Education/Training Required: Work experience in a related occupation
* Annual Earnings: $45,850
* Beginning Wage: $26,380
* Earnings Growth Potential: High
* Growth: 22.9%
* Annual Job Openings: 19,313
* Self-Employed: 0.4%
* Part-Time: 27.8%

Teach or instruct vocational or occupational subjects at the postsecondary level (but at less than the baccalaureate) to students who have graduated or left high school.

Includes correspondence school instructors; industrial, commercial, and government training instructors; and adult education teachers and instructors who prepare persons to operate industrial machinery and equipment and transportation and communications equipment. Teaching may take place in public or private schools whose primary business is education or in a school associated with an organization whose primary business is other than education. Supervise and monitor students' use of tools and equipment. Observe and evaluate students' work to determine progress, provide feedback, and make suggestions for improvement. Present lectures and conduct discussions to increase students' knowledge and competence, using visual aids such as graphs, charts, videotapes, and slides. Administer oral, written, or performance tests to measure progress and to evaluate training effectiveness. Prepare reports and maintain records such as student grades, attendance rolls, and training activity details. Supervise independent or group projects, field placements, laboratory work, or other training. Determine training needs of students or workers. Provide individualized instruction and tutorial or remedial instruction. Conduct on-the-job training, classes, or training sessions to teach and demonstrate principles, techniques, procedures, and methods of designated subjects. Develop curricula and plan course content and methods of instruction. Prepare outlines of instructional programs and training schedules and establish course goals. Integrate academic and vocational curricula so that students can obtain a variety of skills. Develop teaching aids such as instructional software, multimedia visual aids, or study materials. Select and assemble books, materials, supplies, and equipment for training, courses, or projects. Advise students on course selection, career decisions, and other academic and vocational concerns. Participate in conferences, seminars, and training sessions to keep abreast of developments in the field and integrate relevant information into training programs. Serve on faculty and school committees concerned with budgeting, curriculum revision, and course and diploma requirements. Review enrollment applications and correspond with applicants to obtain additional information. Arrange for lectures by experts in designated fields.

Personality Type: Social. These occupations frequently involve working with, communicating with, and teaching people and often involve helping or providing service to others.

GOE—Interest Area/Cluster: 05. Education and Training. **Work Group:** 05.03. Postsecondary and Adult Teaching and Instructing. **Other Jobs in This Work Group:** Adult Literacy, Remedial Education, and GED Teachers and Instructors; Agricultural Sciences Teachers, Postsecondary; Anthropology and Archeology Teachers, Postsecondary; Architecture Teachers, Postsecondary; Area, Ethnic, and Cultural Studies Teachers, Postsecondary; Art, Drama, and Music Teachers, Postsecondary; Atmospheric, Earth, Marine, and Space Sciences Teachers, Postsecondary; Biological Science Teachers, Postsecondary; Business Teachers, Postsecondary; Chemistry Teachers, Postsecondary; Communications Teachers, Postsecondary; Computer Science Teachers, Postsecondary; Criminal Justice and Law Enforcement Teachers, Postsecondary; Economics Teachers, Postsecondary; Education Teachers, Postsecondary; Engineering Teachers, Postsecondary; English Language and Literature Teachers, Postsecondary; Environmental Science Teachers, Postsecondary; Farm and Home Management Advisors; Foreign Language and Literature Teachers, Postsecondary; Forestry and Conservation Science Teachers, Postsecondary; Geography Teachers, Postsecondary; Graduate Teaching Assistants; Health Specialties Teachers, Postsecondary; History Teachers, Postsecondary; Home Economics Teachers, Postsecondary; Law Teachers, Postsecondary; Library Science Teachers, Postsecondary; Mathematical Science Teachers, Postsecondary; Nursing Instructors and Teachers, Postsecondary; Philosophy and Religion Teachers, Postsecondary; Physics Teachers, Postsecondary; Political Science Teachers, Postsecondary; Psychology Teachers, Postsecondary; Recreation and Fitness Studies Teachers, Postsecondary; Self-Enrichment Education Teachers; Social Work Teachers, Postsecondary; Sociology Teachers, Postsecondary; Teachers, Postsecondary.

Skills—Instructing: Teaching others how to do something. **Learning Strategies:** Using multiple approaches when learning or teaching new things. **Social Perceptiveness:** Being aware of others' reactions and understanding why they react the way they do. **Service Orientation:** Actively looking for ways to help people. **Speaking:** Talking to others to effectively convey information. **Time Management:** Managing one's own time and the time of others. **Science:** Using scientific methods to solve problems. **Writing:** Communicating effectively with others in writing as indicated by the needs of the audience.

Education and Training Programs: Agricultural Teacher Education; Business Teacher Education; Health Occupations Teacher Education; Sales and Marketing Operations/Marketing and Distribution Teacher Education; Teacher Education and Professional Development, Specific Subject Areas, Other; Technical Teacher Education; Technology Teacher Education/Industrial Arts Teacher Education; Trade and Industrial Teacher Education. **Related Knowledge/Courses—Education and Training:** Instructional methods and training techniques, including curriculum design principles, learning theory, group and individual teaching techniques, design of individual development plans, and test design principles. **Psychology:** Human behavior and performance, mental processes, psychological research methods, and the assessment and treatment of behavioral and affective disorders. **Therapy and Counseling:** Information and techniques needed to rehabilitate physical and mental ailments and to provide career guidance, including alternative treatments, rehabilitation equipment and its proper use, and methods to evaluate treatment effects. **Computers and Electronics:** Electric circuit boards, processors, chips, and computer hardware and software, including applications and programming. **Sales and Marketing:** Principles and methods involved in showing, promoting, and selling products or services. This includes marketing strategies and tactics, product demonstration and sales techniques, and sales control systems. **Design:** Design techniques, principles, tools, and instruments involved in the production and use of precision technical plans, blueprints, drawings, and models.

Work Environment: Indoors; standing; using hands on objects, tools, or controls.

Water and Liquid Waste Treatment Plant and System Operators

- ❈ Education/Training Required: Long-term on-the-job training
- ❈ Annual Earnings: $37,090
- ❈ Beginning Wage: $22,570
- ❈ Earnings Growth Potential: Medium
- ❈ Growth: 13.8%
- ❈ Annual Job Openings: 9,575
- ❈ Self-Employed: 1.3%
- ❈ Part-Time: 3.4%

Operate or control an entire process or system of machines, often through the use of control boards, to transfer or treat water or liquid waste. Add chemicals such as ammonia, chlorine, or lime to disinfect and deodorize water and other liquids. Operate and adjust controls on equipment to purify and clarify water, process or dispose of sewage, and generate power. Inspect equipment or monitor operating conditions, meters, and gauges to determine load requirements and detect malfunctions. Collect and test water and sewage samples, using test equipment and color analysis standards. Record operational data, personnel attendance, or meter and gauge readings on specified forms. Maintain, repair, and lubricate equipment, using hand tools and power tools. Clean and maintain tanks and filter beds, using hand tools and power tools. Direct and coordinate plant workers engaged in routine operations and maintenance activities.

Personality Type: Realistic. These occupations frequently involve work activities that include practical, hands-on problems and solutions. They often deal with plants; animals; and real-world materials such as wood, tools, and machinery. Many of the occupations require working outside and don't involve a lot of paperwork or working closely with others.

GOE—Interest Area/Cluster: 13. Manufacturing. **Work Group:** 13.16. Utility Operation and Energy Distribution. **Other Jobs in This Work Group:** Chemical Plant and System Operators; Gas Compressor and Gas Pumping Station Operators; Gas Plant Operators; Nuclear Power Reactor Operators; Petroleum Pump System Operators, Refinery Operators, and Gaugers; Power Distributors and Dispatchers; Power Plant Operators; Ship Engineers; Stationary Engineers and Boiler Operators.

Skills—Operation Monitoring: Watching gauges, dials, or other indicators to make sure a machine is working properly. **Operation and Control:** Controlling operations of equipment or systems. **Installation:** Installing equipment, machines, wiring, or programs to meet specifications. **Troubleshooting:** Determining what is causing an operating error and deciding what to do about it. **Operations Analysis:** Analyzing needs and product requirements to create a design. **Management of Material Resources:** Obtaining and seeing to the appropriate use of equipment, facilities, and materials needed to do certain work. **Equipment Maintenance:** Performing routine maintenance and determining when and what kind of maintenance is needed.

Science: Using scientific methods to solve problems.

Education and Training Program: Water Quality and Wastewater Treatment Management and Recycling Technology/Technician Training. **Related Knowledge/Courses—Biology:** Plant and animal living tissue, cells, organisms, and entities, including their functions, interdependencies, and interactions with each other and the environment. **Chemistry:** The composition, structure, and properties of substances and of the chemical processes and transformations that they undergo. This includes uses of chemicals and their interactions, danger signs, production techniques, and disposal methods. **Physics:** Physical principles, laws, and applications, including air, water, material dynamics, light, atomic principles, heat, electric theory, earth formations, and meteorological and related natural phenomena. **Public Safety and Security:** Weaponry; public safety; security operations, rules, regulations, precautions, and prevention; and the protection of people, data, and property. **Mechanical Devices:** Machines and tools, including their designs, uses, benefits, repair, and maintenance. **Law and Government:** Laws, legal codes, court procedures, precedents, government regulations, executive orders, agency rules, and the democratic political process.

Work Environment: More often outdoors than indoors; noisy; very hot or cold; contaminants; minor burns, cuts, bites, or stings.

Welders, Cutters, and Welder Fitters

- ❋ Education/Training Required: Postsecondary vocational training
- ❋ Annual Earnings: $32,270
- ❋ Beginning Wage: $21,680
- ❋ Earnings Growth Potential: Low
- ❋ Growth: 5.1%
- ❋ Annual Job Openings: 61,125
- ❋ Self-Employed: 6.3%
- ❋ Part-Time: 1.9%

The job openings listed here are shared with Solderers and Brazers.

Use hand-welding or flame-cutting equipment to weld or join metal components or to fill holes, indentations,

or seams of fabricated metal products. Operate safety equipment and use safe work habits. Weld components in flat, vertical, or overhead positions. Ignite torches or start power supplies and strike arcs by touching electrodes to metals being welded, completing electrical circuits. Clamp, hold, tack-weld, heat-bend, grind, or bolt component parts to obtain required configurations and positions for welding. Detect faulty operation of equipment or defective materials and notify supervisors. Operate manual or semi-automatic welding equipment to fuse metal segments, using processes such as gas tungsten arc, gas metal arc, flux-cored arc, plasma arc, shielded metal arc, resistance welding, and submerged arc welding. Monitor the fitting, burning, and welding processes to avoid overheating of parts or warping, shrinking, distortion, or expansion of material. Examine workpieces for defects and measure workpieces with straightedges or templates to ensure conformance with specifications. Recognize, set up, and operate hand and power tools common to the welding trade, such as shielded metal arc and gas metal arc welding equipment. Lay out, position, align, and secure parts and assemblies prior to assembly, using straightedges, combination squares, calipers, and rulers. Chip or grind off excess weld, slag, or spatter, using hand scrapers or power chippers, portable grinders, or arc-cutting equipment. Analyze engineering drawings, blueprints, specifications, sketches, work orders, and material safety data sheets to plan layout, assembly, and welding operations. Connect and turn regulator valves to activate and adjust gas flow and pressure so that desired flames are obtained. Weld separately or in combination, using aluminum, stainless steel, cast iron, and other alloys. Determine required equipment and welding methods, applying knowledge of metallurgy, geometry, and welding techniques. Mark or tag material with proper job number, piece marks, and other identifying marks as required. Prepare all material surfaces to be welded, ensuring that there is no loose or thick scale, slag, rust, moisture, grease, or other foreign matter.

Personality Type: Realistic. These occupations frequently involve work activities that include practical, hands-on problems and solutions. They often deal with plants; animals; and real-world materials such as wood, tools, and machinery. Many of the occupations require working outside and don't involve a lot of paperwork or working closely with others.

GOE—Interest Area/Cluster: 13. Manufacturing. **Work Group:** 13.04. Welding, Brazing, and Soldering. **Other Jobs in This Work Group:** Solderers and Brazers; Structural Metal Fabricators and Fitters; Welders, Cutters, Solderers, and Brazers; Welding, Soldering, and Brazing Machine Setters, Operators, and Tenders.

Skills—Repairing: Repairing machines or systems, using the needed tools. **Equipment Maintenance:** Performing routine maintenance and determining when and what kind of maintenance is needed. **Installation:** Installing equipment, machines, wiring, or programs to meet specifications. **Equipment Selection:** Determining the kind of tools and equipment needed to do a job. **Operation and Control:** Controlling operations of equipment or systems. **Quality Control Analysis:** Evaluating the quality or performance of products, services, or processes.

Education and Training Program: Welding Technology/Welder Training. **Related Knowledge/Courses—Building and Construction:** Materials, methods, and the appropriate tools to construct objects, structures, and buildings. **Mechanical Devices:** Machines and tools, including their designs, uses, benefits, repair, and maintenance. **Design:** Design techniques, principles, tools, and instruments involved in the production and use of precision technical plans, blueprints, drawings, and models. **Engineering and Technology:** Equipment, tools, and mechanical devices and their uses to produce motion, light, power, technology, and other applications.

Work Environment: Noisy; contaminants; minor burns, cuts, bites, or stings; standing; using hands on objects, tools, or controls; repetitive motions.

Wholesale and Retail Buyers, Except Farm Products

- ✸ Education/Training Required: Long-term on-the-job training
- ✸ Annual Earnings: $46,960
- ✸ Beginning Wage: $27,810
- ✸ Earnings Growth Potential: High
- ✸ Growth: –0.1%
- ✸ Annual Job Openings: 19,847
- ✸ Self-Employed: 12.0%
- ✸ Part-Time: 15.6%

Buy merchandise or commodities, other than farm products, for resale to consumers at the wholesale or retail level, including both durable and nondurable goods. Analyze past buying trends, sales records, price, and quality of merchandise to determine value and yield. Select, order, and authorize payment for merchandise according to contractual agreements. May conduct meetings with sales personnel and introduce new products. Examine, select, order, and purchase at the most favorable price merchandise consistent with quality, quantity, specification requirements, and other factors. Negotiate prices, discount terms, and transportation arrangements for merchandise. Analyze and monitor sales records, trends, and economic conditions to anticipate consumer buying patterns and determine what the company will sell and how much inventory is needed. Interview and work closely with vendors to obtain and develop desired products. Authorize payment of invoices or return of merchandise. Inspect merchandise or products to determine value or yield. Set or recommend markup rates, markdown rates, and selling prices for merchandise. Confer with sales and purchasing personnel to obtain information about customer needs and preferences. Consult with store or merchandise managers about budget and goods to be purchased. Conduct staff meetings with sales personnel to introduce new merchandise. Manage the department for which they buy. Use computers to organize and locate inventory and operate spreadsheet and word processing software. Provide clerks with information to print on price tags, such as price, markups or markdowns, manufacturer number, season code, and style number. Train and supervise sales and clerical staff. Determine which products should be featured in advertising, the advertising medium to be used, and when the ads should be run. Monitor competitors' sales activities by following their advertisements in newspapers and other media.

Personality Type: Enterprising. These occupations frequently involve starting up and carrying out projects and can involve leading people and making many decisions. They sometimes require risk taking and often deal with business.

GOE—Interest Area/Cluster: 14. Retail and Wholesale Sales and Service. **Work Group:** 14.05. Purchasing. **Other Jobs in This Work Group:** Purchasing Agents, Except Wholesale, Retail, and Farm Products.

Skills—Management of Financial Resources: Determining how money will be spent to get the work done and accounting for these expenditures. **Management of Material Resources:** Obtaining and seeing to the appropriate use of equipment, facilities, and materials needed to do certain work. **Operations Analysis:** Analyzing needs and product requirements to create a design. **Quality Control Analysis:** Evaluating the quality or performance of products, services, or processes. **Negotiation:** Bringing others together and trying to reconcile differences. **Service Orientation:** Actively looking for ways to help people. **Equipment Selection:** Determining the kind of tools and equipment needed to do a job. **Management of Personnel Resources:** Motivating, developing, and directing people as they work; identifying the best people for the job.

Education and Training Programs: Apparel and Accessories Marketing Operations; Apparel and Textile Marketing Management; Fashion Merchandising; Merchandising and Buying Operations; Sales, Distribution, and Marketing Operations, General. **Related Knowledge/Courses— Sales and Marketing:** Principles and methods involved in showing, promoting, and selling products or services. This includes marketing strategies and tactics, product demonstration and sales techniques, and sales control systems. **Economics and Accounting:** Economic and accounting principles and practices, the financial markets, banking, and the analysis and reporting of financial data. **Clerical Studies:** Administrative and clerical procedures and systems such as word-processing systems, filing and records management systems, stenography and transcription, forms, design principles, and other office procedures and terminology. **Customer and Personal Service:** Principles and processes for providing customer and personal services, including needs assessment techniques, quality service standards, alternative delivery systems, and customer satisfaction evaluation techniques. **Administration and Management:** Principles and processes involved in business and organizational planning, coordination, and execution. This includes strategic planning, resource allocation, manpower modeling, leadership techniques, and production methods. **Mathematics:** Numbers and their operations and interrelationships, including arithmetic, algebra, geometry, calculus, and statistics and their applications.

Work Environment: Indoors; sitting; repetitive motions.

Index

M

N

O

P–Q